The Palgrave Handbook of Institutional Ethnography

"In the past half-century, institutional ethnography has been arguably the most significant initiative in remaking sociology, and an important tool in remaking our troubled world. With illuminating contributions from seasoned practitioners and from innovative emerging scholars, this handbook will be an indispensable resource for critical sociologists, social-justice protagonists and progressive policy communities."

—William K. Carroll, *Professor of Sociology, University of Victoria, Canada, editor of* Critical Strategies for Social Research *(2004), and author of* The Making of a Transnational Capitalist Class *(2010)*

"Knowledge that makes a difference. Here finally is a comprehensive guide to institutional ethnography (IE), the approach that can help us discover the ruling relations within the very relations of our everyday world. And it covers it all: from theoretical foundations to current research areas, research application and political action. Studies that connect local and global relations of ruling relations but also combine IE with other approaches, concepts and methods. And all of it richly illustrated empirically, illuminating the very knowledge production in practice. Here's something for everybody—researcher, teacher or student. A gift to us all!"

—Karin Widerberg, *Professor of Sociology and Human Geography, University of Oslo, Norway*

"This is a wonderful book—lively, readable and instructive! Readers are drawn into institutional ethnographic efforts to understand today's ordinarily opaque ruling regimes. Some contributors introduce readers to research settings where IE's core concepts, e.g., 'standpoint' and 'ruling relations'— recognized as operative in particular people's lives—become more than theory. Knowing how things actually work provides new ideas for responding. The handbook displays IE's remarkable scope of topics, geographic diffusion, and developing analytic maturity."

—Marie L. Campbell, *Professor Emerita of Human and Social Development, University of Victoria, Canada, and co-author of* Mapping Social Relations *(2002) and* Managing to Nurse *(2006)*

"Attractive, refreshing, readable and challenging. The handbook offers the reader an unparalleled opportunity to discover the width and depth of institutional ethnography that is not evident in any other books. This book is for those who seek ways of doing sociology to make changes."

—Frank T. Y. Wang, *Professor of Social Work, National Chengchi University, Taiwan*

"The publication of this powerful collection signifies the culmination of decades of exciting interdisciplinary research that draws on the brilliant insights of Canadian scholar Dorothy E. Smith. Chapters include one by Smith and many contributions by the innovative scholars she mentored who, years ago, formed an activist-scholar collective dedicated to bringing this form of social inquiry into fields of sociology, health, education, comparative research, social policy, social activism and beyond.

As this extensive volume demonstrates, the influence of institutional ethnography has expanded from a challenge to ontological and epistemological assumptions of theory and methods in social science to a broader effect on transnational and applied approaches to social change and social justice. The authors represent several generations of researchers and scholar activists whose collective contributions in this book now form the basis of a resource for generations to come."

—Nancy Naples, *Distinguished Board of Trustees Professor of Sociology and Women's, Gender and Sexuality Studies, University of Connecticut, USA, author of* Feminism and Method *(2003) and co-editor of* Border Politics: Social Movements, Collective Identities, and Globalization *(2014)*

"The inclusion of theory and methodological concerns within a single text is welcome and will aid novice researchers seeking to understand and utilize IE. I think it is particularly important that the handbook includes contributions from students and neophytes as well as established researchers. Indeed, I believe this to be a strength of the book."

—James Reid, *Senior Lecturer of Education and Community Studies, University of Huddersfield, UK*

Paul C. Luken · Suzanne Vaughan
Editors

The Palgrave Handbook of Institutional Ethnography

palgrave
macmillan

Editors
Paul C. Luken
University of West Georgia
Carrollton, GA, USA

Suzanne Vaughan
Arizona State University
Phoenix, AZ, USA

ISBN 978-3-030-54221-4   ISBN 978-3-030-54222-1 (eBook)
https://doi.org/10.1007/978-3-030-54222-1

© The Editor(s) (if applicable) and The Author(s), under exclusive license to Springer Nature Switzerland AG 2021
This work is subject to copyright. All rights are solely and exclusively licensed by the Publisher, whether the whole or part of the material is concerned, specifically the rights of translation, reprinting, reuse of illustrations, recitation, broadcasting, reproduction on microfilms or in any other physical way, and transmission or information storage and retrieval, electronic adaptation, computer software, or by similar or dissimilar methodology now known or hereafter developed.
The use of general descriptive names, registered names, trademarks, service marks, etc. in this publication does not imply, even in the absence of a specific statement, that such names are exempt from the relevant protective laws and regulations and therefore free for general use.
The publisher, the authors and the editors are safe to assume that the advice and information in this book are believed to be true and accurate at the date of publication. Neither the publisher nor the authors or the editors give a warranty, expressed or implied, with respect to the material contained herein or for any errors or omissions that may have been made. The publisher remains neutral with regard to jurisdictional claims in published maps and institutional affiliations.

Cover illustration: "Walking the Ravines of Toronto," courtesy of Herbert D. Hughes, Architect

This Palgrave Macmillan imprint is published by the registered company Springer Nature Switzerland AG
The registered company address is: Gewerbestrasse 11, 6330 Cham, Switzerland

In memory of
Alison I. Griffith

Acknowledgments

As the saying goes, "It takes a village to raise a child." This is no less the case for a book project about the work people are doing using institutional ethnography as their mode of inquiry investigating the social. We are indebted to many people.

The book emerged out of a dinner during the 2018 World Forum of Sociology, International Sociological Association meetings in Toronto, Canada, attended by current/past officers and members of the Thematic Group on Institutional Ethnography (TG06; now a Working Group). From this beginning they provided invaluable advice about the intellectual joys and hurdles of editing such a large volume. We are grateful for their encouragement and ultimate contributions to this project including recruiting contributors to this handbook.

From the participants in this project we have learned immeasurably: about the potential of institutional ethnography to show us "how things happen as they do," about the diversity of institutional ethnographic work done in various countries, about the struggles we all have faced in maintaining epistemological and ontological commitments as we incorporate other methods or frameworks, about how transnational/global relations organize education, the environment, and indigenous and human rights, about how public sector management regimes across different countries and service arenas organized frontline work, and about activists efforts to bring about change within their communities. Most importantly, the contributors to this volume made us students again by encouraging us to re-read some key texts (*The Everyday World as Problematic* (1987) *Texts, Facts, and Femininity* (1990), *The Conceptual Practices of Power* (1990), *Institutional Ethnography: A Sociology for People* (2005)) and make new discoveries about institutional ethnography. We thank you.

This volume was made possible by the invisible work of many reviewers who participated by reading, commenting on, talking about, and editing enumerable chapters several times over. We extend a special thanks to an international group of scholars and community activists doing institutional ethnography who generously participated in the review process and provided critical eyes on topics with which we were not entirely familiar. Many of the reviewers are part of a network of researchers who meet regularly (except during the 2019–2020 World Pandemic) as part of the Institutional Ethnography Division of Society for the Study of Social Problems and the Working Group on Institutional Ethnography of the International Sociological Association. Thank you to our reviewers and consultants: Dottie Broaddus, Marie Campbell, Kathryn Church, Linda Wright DeAguero, Marjorie DeVault, Timothy Diamond, Tonia Freeman, Colin Hastings, Helen Helwig, Herb Hughes, Liza McCoy, Eric Mykhalovskiy, Janet Rankin, Brian Richardson, and Kevin Walby.

We thank Mary Al-Sayed, Commissioning Editor Palgrave Macmillan, for reaching out to us about the potential for this handbook and swiftly ushering our proposal through the review process. Madison Allums, Assistant Editor, has tirelessly answered our questions weekly as we prepared this volume. We thank them both.

Finally, we raise a glass of wine in toast to Dorothy E. Smith, whose mentorship, intellectual engagement and friendship, has inspired us all. We thank you for helping us change our sociology.

Contents

1 Institutional Ethnography: Sociology for Today   1
    Paul C. Luken

Part I   Exploring Historical and Ontological Foundations

2 Elements of an Expansive Institutional Ethnography:
    A Conceptual History of Its North American Origins   11
    Marjorie L. DeVault

3 Materialist Matters: A Case for Revisiting the Social
    Ontology of Institutional Ethnography   35
    Liza McCoy

4 Teaching Institutional Ethnography as an Alternative
    Sociology   47
    Eric Mykhalovskiy, Colin Hastings, Leigha Comer,
    Julia Gruson-Wood, and Matthew Strang

5 Exploring Institutional Words as People's Practices   65
    Dorothy E. Smith

Part II   Developing Strategies and Exploring Challenges

6 Mapping Ruling Relations: Advancing the Use of Visual
    Methods in Institutional Ethnography   81
    Nicole K. Dalmer

7   Discovering the Social Organization of Perinatal Care
    for Women Living with HIV: Reflections from a Novice
    Institutional Ethnographer   99
    Allyson Ion

8   IE and Visual Research Methods: An Open-Ended
    Discussion   121
    Morena Tartari

9   And Then There Was Copyright   141
    Suzanne Vaughan

10 Invoking Work Knowledge: Exploring the Social
    Organization of Producing Gender Studies   157
    Rebecca W. B. Lund

11 Teaching Institutional Ethnography to Undergraduate
    Students   175
    Kathryn Church

Part III   Explicating Global/Transnational Ruling Relations

12 Using Institutional Ethnography to Investigate
    Intergovernmental Environmental Policy-Making   193
    Lauren E. Eastwood

13 Regulating the Duty to Consult: Exploring the Textually
    Mediated Nature of Indigenous Dispossession in Chile   213
    Magdalena Ugarte

14 Transnational Power Relations in Education: How It
    Works Down South   237
    Nerida Spina and Barbara Comber

15 The Struggle for "Survival" in Contemporary Higher
    Education: The Lived Experiences of Junior Academics
    in Taiwan   259
    Li-Fang Liang and Yu-Hsuan Lin

Part IV Making Change within Communities

16 Building Change On and Off Reserve: Six Nations
of the Grand River Territory — 283
Susan Marie Turner and Julia Bomberry

17 Mapping Institutional Relations for Local Policy Change:
The Case of Lead Poisoning in Syracuse New York — 309
Frank Ridzi

18 The Institutional Analysis: Matching What Institutions
Do with What Works for People — 329
Ellen Pence

Part V Critiquing Public Sector Management Regimes

19 Professional Talk: Unpacking Professional Language — 359
Ann Christin E. Nilsen

20 Frontline Interpretive Work of Activating the Americans
with Disabilities Act — 375
Erik D. Rodriguez

21 Contested Forms of Knowledge in the Criminal-Legal
System: Evidence-Based Practice and Other Ways
of Knowing Among Frontline Workers — 397
Nicole Kaufman and Megan Welsh

22 Public Protection as a Ruling Concept in the Management
of Nurses' Substance Use — 423
Charlotte A. Ross

23 Producing *Functional Equivalency* in Video Relay Service — 447
Jeremy L. Brunson

Part VI Bringing Together Different Approaches and Perspectives

24 Using Composites to Craft Institutional Ethnographic
Accounts — 465
Michael K. Corman

25 Attending to Messy Troubles of the Anthropocene with Institutional Ethnography and Material Semiotics: The Case for Vital Institutional Ethnography 483
Karly Burch

26 Institutional Ethnography for Social Work 505
Gerald de Montigny

27 Institutional Ethnography and Youth Participatory Action Research: A Praxis Approach 527
Naomi Nichols and Jessica Ruglis

Index 551

Notes on Contributors

Julia Bomberry is the Clanmother of the Turtle Clan, Cayuga Nation, mother to a beautiful daughter and grandmother to two wonderful grandsons. Julia has been a staff member for 27 years at Ganohkwasra Family Assault Support Services, whose vision statement reads "with Ganohkwasra (love among us) we bury our weapons of violence to create a safe and caring community for all generations." Julia is the Manager of Therapeutic Services and oversees the Community Counselling Supervisor, Outreach Services Supervisor, and Sexual Violence Healing Centre. She is a graduate of the Child & Youth Program, Mohawk College, and Bachelors and Masters of Social Work Programs, Ryerson University.

Jeremy L. Brunson has research interests in the broad area of the sociology of interpreting. He has published and presented about video relay service, educational interpreting, invisible labor deaf people perform, professionalization of sign language interpreting, and ethics. He was awarded The Irving K. Zola Award for Emerging Scholars in Disability Studies in 2009. He was also named a Fulbright Specialist in 2017 and spent 6 weeks in Ulaanbaatar, Mongolia helping to establish the country's first formal Interpreter Preparation Program.

Dr. Karly Burch is a postdoctoral research fellow at the University of Otago's Centre for Sustainability. Karly's research interests are in the fields of science and technology studies (STS), environmental sociology, and the sociology of agriculture and food. She has a deep passion for collaborative and transdisciplinary research. Through her research, Karly addresses questions of social and environmental justice both present and emerging within socio-technical projects and controversies. She is currently working on the MaaraTech Project, a multi-year transdisciplinary project to collaboratively design artificial intelligence and robotic technologies for use in orchards and vineyards in Aotearoa New Zealand.

Kathryn Church is Associate Professor in the School of Disability Studies at Ryerson University, Toronto, Canada. Her research fuses ethnographic studies of participation, work and learning with arts-informed approaches to creating and communicating knowledge. As an ally of the psychiatric survivor movement, she is participating in the emergence of Mad Studies. Serving two terms as program director left her with a lively interest in managerial ruling.

Barbara Comber is a Research Professor in the School of Education at the University of South Australia. Her research interests include teachers' work, critical literacy, place-conscious pedagogy, and social justice. She has conducted longitudinal ethnographic case studies and collaborative action research with teachers working in high poverty and diverse communities. Her research examines the kinds of teaching that make a difference to young people's literacy learning trajectories and what gets in the way. Her ongoing research explores transdisciplinary curriculum development and pedagogies of reconnection. Books include *Literacy, Place and Pedagogies of Possibility* (Comber, 2016) and *Literacy, Leading and Learning: Beyond Pedagogies of Poverty* (Hayes, Hattam Comber, Kerkham, Lupton & Thomson, 2017).

Leigha Comer is a Ph.D. candidate at York University, Toronto, Canada. Her work focuses on chronic pain, the social organization of opioid use for chronic pain management, and medico-legal responses to the "opioid crisis." Her past research includes an exploration of medical school curricula and how medical students are taught to diagnose, treat, and conceptualize chronic pain. Leigha's doctoral research is being supported by a Vanier Canada Graduate Scholarship.

Dr. Michael K. Corman, Ph.D. is an Assistant Professor of Sociology in the Department of Social, Cultural, and Media Studies at the University of the Fraser Valley in British Columbia, Canada. Dr. Corman's teaching and research interests include a variety of topics that intersect with the sociological study of health, illness, and society. Dr. Corman's research has appeared in *Perspectives on Medical Education, Social Theory & Health, Symbolic Interaction, The Journal of Contemporary Ethnography, Qualitative Health Research*, the *International Journal of Educational Research, Families in Society: The Journal of Contemporary Social Services*, and the *International Journal of Social Sciences* and multiple edited book volumes. He has recently published a book by the University of Toronto Press entitled, *Paramedics on and Off the Streets: Emergency Medical Services in the Age of Technological Governance*.

Nicole K. Dalmer, M.L.I.S., Ph.D. is an Assistant Professor in the Department of Health, Aging and Society at McMaster University (Ontario, Canada). With a background in Library and Information Science, Nicole often works at the intersection of information and care, studying how aging in place contexts, changes in information availability, and evolving family responsibilities shape who is able and who is expected to be informed in care relationships. Other ongoing projects include an international collaboration examining the impact of digital infrastructures on feelings of connectedness in later life as well as an investigation into the role of public libraries in mitigating older adults' experiences of social isolation.

Gerald de Montigny retired after teaching social work for 34 years, 5 years at University of Manitoba in Thompson, MB and 29 years at the School of Social Work at Carleton University. Dorothy Smith was the supervisor for both his M.A. and Ph.D. thesis at OISE in Toronto. Through Smith and IE he was able to bridge sociological study of socially organized practices with social workers' mundane local accomplishment of extra-local institutional orders. Gerald lives in Ottawa, Ontario.

Marjorie L. DeVault is Professor Emerita of Sociology, Syracuse University, and now lives in Brewster, MA. She has written extensively on qualitative and feminist research methodologies, especially institutional ethnography. Her books include *Feeding the Family: The Social Organization of Caring as Gendered Work*; *Liberating Method: Feminism and Social Research*; and an edited volume, *People at Work: Life, Power, and Social Inclusion in the New Economy*.

Lauren E. Eastwood is an Associate Professor of Sociology at the State University of New York, College at Plattsburgh. She teaches a range of courses including environmental sociology, international development, sociological theory, introduction to social justice, and introduction to environmental studies. Dr. Eastwood has conducted extensive research on nongovernmental participation in the negotiation of environmental policy through the UN. In addition, she has been engaging in research related to civic responses to fossil fuel extraction and infrastructure, as well as the increasing criminalization of anti-fossil-fuel activism.

Julia Gruson-Wood has a Ph.D. in Science and Technology Studies from York University and is completing a Postdoctoral Research Fellowship in the area of Gender, Family and Health at the University of Guelph. She is completing her first book, *Remaking Therapy, Reshaping Autism* which will be published by University of British Columbia Press.

Colin Hastings is an SSHRC Postdoctoral Fellow at Concordia University. His research blends the sociology of health, socio-legal studies, and media studies. He is the author of studies about community-based HIV education, media representation of HIV criminal non-disclosure cases, and key trends and patterns in HIV criminalization in Canada. Colin's dissertation project was an institutional ethnographic study of how news stories about HIV criminalization are produced in Canada.

Allyson Ion, M.Sc., Ph.D. is currently a Lecturer in the School of Social Work at McMaster University. Allyson has worked and volunteered in the HIV sector since 2001 contributing to community development, education, and research initiatives including community-based HIV research in the areas of women, peer support and mothering. Allyson's doctoral research used institutional ethnography to investigate the health services that women living with HIV utilize during pregnancy, childbirth and early postpartum.

Nicole Kaufman is Assistant Professor of Sociology at Ohio University. Her research examines citizenship, punishment, the civic sector, and the institutional arrangements that facilitate and limit social inclusion for people with criminal records. In her newest project, "Governing through Collaboration," she is conducting research on the history of Ohio's drug policy particularly as it was shaped through relationships between state agencies and religious organizations. She has published in *Law & Social Inquiry, Punishment & Society*, and *Theoretical Criminology*. She received her Ph.D. in Sociology from the University of Wisconsin-Madison.

Li-Fang Liang is an assistant professor at the Department of Sociology in National Dong-Hwa University, Taiwan. As a feminist sociologist, she is interested in the 'invisible work' mostly done by women. Her current research investigates how Indonesian migrant live-in care workers and their families that are left/stay behind collaborate with each other to exchange care and sustain relationships in a transnational context. In particular, she examines how the use of information and communication technologies changes the form of care as well as the idea of family and distance.

Yu-Hsuan Lin is an associate professor at the Department of Applied Sociology in Nanhua University, Taiwan. Her research interests center on the sociology of gender, institutional ethnography, and the structural transformations of higher education under the influence of new managerialism. Her previous work examined how performance indicators as a new form of managerial technique have been implemented at universities and how they changed academics' working processes/practices. Her present research explores how academic mothers creatively negotiate work demands and family expectations through what she terms "intellectual mothering".

Paul C. Luken is Associate Professor Emeritus in Sociology, University of West Georgia. He is a founder of the Institutional Ethnography Division of the SSSP and the Thematic Group (now Working Group) on Institutional Ethnography of the ISA. With Suzanne Vaughan he published studies of housing in *Social Problems, Social Forces, Sociological Quarterly, Sociology and Social Welfare, and Housing and Society*. They are completing a manuscript on changes in the social institution of housing in the US. He currently resides in Villa Rica, Georgia, USA, where he has begun investigating the social relations shaping the work of voting.

Rebecca W. B. Lund is a researcher at the Centre for Gender Research, University of Oslo. She uses and develops Instutitonal Ethnography for exploring social relations in knowledge production within and beyond the university, with a particular interest in how relations of inequality become manifested in epistemic orientations She is currently the Editor-in-Chief of *NORA: Nordic Journal of Feminist and Gender Research* and recently published the edited book *Institutional Ethnography in the Nordic Region* at Routledge. She publishes in journals such as *Gender, Work and Organization, Gender and Education,* and *Organization: The Critical Journal of Organization, Theory and Society.*

Liza McCoy is Associate Professor of Sociology at the University of Calgary in Canada. She has been learning, teaching and doing institutional ethnography for more than thirty years. Her research interests, past and present, include photographic representation, accounting, health care, immigration, and social dance.

Eric Mykhalovskiy, Ph.D. is a Professor of Sociology at York University, Toronto, Canada. While he has published on a range of topics, a recurring focus of his research is the social organization of the public health response to the HIV epidemic. He is the co-editor of *Thinking Differently about HIV/AIDS: Contributions from Critical Social Science,* UBC Press, 2019) and of *Health Matters: Evidence, Critical Social Science, and Health Care in Canada,* University of Toronto Press (2020). He is a senior editor of the *Canadian Journal of Public Health* and a board member of the Canadian HIV/AIDS Legal Network.

Naomi Nichols engages in research activities and publications that span the areas of youth homelessness; youth justice; alternative education and safe schools; inter-organizational relations in the youth sector; "youth at risk;" and community-academic research collaborations. She is an Associate Professor of Sociology and Canada Research Chair in Community-Partnered Social Justice at Trent University. In 2014, the University of Toronto Press published her first book: *Youth Work: An Institutional Ethnography of Youth Homelessness,* and in 2019. The University of Toronto Press released Nichols' second book: *Youth, School and Community: Participatory Institutional Ethnographies.*

Ann Christin E. Nilsen holds a Ph.D. in sociology and is associate professor at the Department of Sociology and Social Work, University of Agder, Norway. She is currently one of the coordinators of the Nordic network of institutional ethnography. Her research interests include childhood and families, gender, early intervention, professional work, and interdisciplinary collaboration. She is one of the editors of the book *Institutional Ethnography in the Nordic Region,* published by Routledge. Her research appears in a number of international journals, as well as in diverse journals and books in Norwegian.

Ellen Pence, Ph.D. founder and first Executive Director of Praxis International, worked for over 30 years to end gender-based violence before she passed away in 2012. She was the chief author and architect of the Praxis Institutional Analysis and worked extensively to address institutionally-generated inequities in the criminal and civil legal systems, the child welfare system, and supervised visitation. She received numerous awards including the 2008 *Dorothy E. Smith Scholar Activist Award*. She authored two books, five educational curriculums, three manuals and over a dozen scholarly articles on institutional change and advocacy on behalf of battered women and their children.

Frank Ridzi, Ph.D., M.P.A. is Vice President for Community Investment at the Central New York Community Foundation, Associate Professor of Sociology at Le Moyne College and President of the Board of Directors for the Community Indicators Consortium. Frank has helped to launch and lead community initiatives in areas such as increasing community literacy, reducing lead poisoning and addressing poverty and economic inclusion. His writings have appeared in such places as the *Journal of Applied Social Sciences*, the *Journal of Organizational Change Management*, and *Review of Policy Research*.

Erik D. Rodriguez, Ph.D. is the Program Director for Sociology at Gwinnett Technical College, Georgia, USA. He recently completed his Ph.D. at Syracuse University and will soon publish his dissertation, titled, *Time, Schedules, and the College Student with ADHD*.

Dr. Charlotte A. Ross is a registered nurse and registered psychiatric nurse, nurse researcher, and nurse educator. She is a faculty instructor in the Baccalaureate of Sciences in Nursing, Health Sciences Faculty at Douglas College in Coquitlam, British Columbia, Canada. Her clinical background and teaching activities are in mental health and treatment of substance use problems. Her research areas include nurses' health, mental health, and substance use.

Dr. Jessica Ruglis engages in work that centers on participatory, critical race/ethnic, social justice, feminist, and inclusive approaches to research and teaching in the areas of public education, public health, justice, and youth development. Professor Ruglis' research program is organized around three main axes: (1) Contexts and institutions of youth development, (2) Social determinants of health (SDH) and education, (3) Participatory and community engaged approaches to research, policy and professional training (e.g., participatory action research, PAR; youth participatory action research, YPAR; community based participatory research, CBPR; community engaged participatory action research, CEPAR; participatory policymaking).

Dorothy E. Smith is Professor Emerita, Ontario Institute for Studies in Education/University of Toronto and Adjunct Professor in Sociology at the University of Victoria. She has published numerous papers and several books: with Sarah David (Ed.) *Women and Psychiatry: I'm Not Mad, I'm angry* (1975); *The Everyday World as Problematic: A Feminist Sociology* (1987); *Texts, Facts, and Femininity: Exploring the Relations of Ruling* (1990); *The Conceptual Practices of Power: A Feminist Sociology of Knowledge* (1990);*Writing the Social: Critique, Theory and Investigations* (1999); *Institutional Ethnography:*

A Sociology for People (2005); with Alison Griffith, *Mothering for Schooling* (2005): an edited collection of studies, *Institutional Ethnography in Practice* (2006); and with David Livingstone and Warren Smith, *Manufacturing Meltdown: Reshaping Steelwork* (2010). In 2019 she was awarded the Order of Canada for her work in Institutional Ethnography.

Nerida Spina is a lecturer in the Faculty of Education at the Queensland University of Technology in Queensland, Australia. Her research interests centre around the sociology of numbers, education policy, social justice and equity. She has a particular focus on the datafication of education and its effects on teachers, students and communities. Nerida also researches the everyday experiences of precariously-employed academics. She examines the effects of this growing form of employment on people who work in universities, and on the research they undertake.

Matthew Strang (ABD Sociology, York University) is a Research Associate at the Institute for Better Health, Trillium Health Partners. His work combines the sociology of health, illness, and medicine with social justice. He has co-published articles on shame and prejudice in PREP use and using virtual reality as a tool to teach medical professionals about empathy. He is an Adjunct Faculty in Health & Society, and Human Rights & Equity Studies, York University. His dissertation is an institutional ethnography of living organ donation. He is keenly interested in the body and emotional work that living organ donors do to be donors.

Morena Tartari is, currently, a Marie Sklodowska-Curie Research Fellow at the Department of Sociology, University of Antwerp, Belgium. After she worked for several years as a legal psychologist and researcher in the public and private sector, in 2012, she completed her Ph.D. (Sociology) at the University of Padua, Italy. From 2014 to 2019, she was contract lecturer-in-charge of Sociology, Sociology of Communication, Sociology of Cultural Processes, Health and Sociology at the University of Padua.

Susan Marie Turner lives in Guelph, Canada. She studied with Dorothy Smith at the Ontario Institute for Studies in Education, University of Toronto (OISE/UT). Her dissertation developed IE graphical mapping in an investigation of land use planning, winning OISE/UT's 2004 Outstanding Thesis of the Year Award. Her work with numerous community groups won the 2010 Society for the Study of Social Problems Institutional Ethnography Division Dorothy E. Smith Scholar Activist Award. She gives IE mapping training and has given IE workshops with Dorothy at OISE/UT since 2009.

Magdalena Ugarte is an Assistant Professor in Urban and Regional Planning at Ryerson University, where she teaches social planning, planning theory, and policy. Her research examines the role of planning, policy, and law in the dispossession of certain communities, particularly Indigenous peoples and immigrants. She also explores possibilities for intercultural collaboration in contexts marked by structural power imbalances—such as settler colonialism and forced migration. She holds a M.A. (Political Science) from Memorial University and a Ph.D. (Planning) from the University of British Columbia. Magdalena's current work with Mapuche partners in Chile engages with questions of Indigenous planning and law.

Suzanne Vaughan is an Associate Professor Emeritus of Sociology in the School of Social and Behavioral Sciences at Arizona State University, USA, and was co-founder and is secretary/treasurer of the ISA IE Working Group. She and her co author, Paul Luken, have published a number of substantive articles on homeownership, childrearing, retirement housing, independence in old age, and methodological articles about institutional ethnography. They are writing a book based upon the oral housing histories of women which explicates the ways in which ordinary work of people in the housing industry transformed housing in the US over the twentieth century.

Megan Welsh is an Associate Professor in the School of Public Affairs at San Diego State University. Her current research examines the health and sanitation needs of people experiencing homelessness and the criminalization of poverty. Her published work appears in *Feminist Criminology*, the *Journal of Contemporary Ethnography*, and *Qualitative Sociology*. She received her Ph.D. in Criminal Justice from the Graduate Center of the City University of New York.

List of Figures

Fig. 6.1	Alice's information world	87
Fig. 6.2	Marge's information world	88
Fig. 6.3	Sylvia's information world	89
Fig. 8.1	Me at the desk	130
Fig. 8.2	Me at the one-way mirror	130
Fig. 8.3	Me explaining the role of CCTV	131
Fig. 8.4	A CCTV's technical error	131
Fig. 13.1	First page of Supreme Decree 66 (DS66) *Source* Government of Chile [2014])	220
Fig. 13.2	Article 13 of Constitutional Tribunal's ruling (2008) (*Source* Government of Chile [2008])	222
Fig. 13.3	Selective intertextual relations shaping the regulation of the duty to consult in Chile	225
Fig. 13.4	The duty to consult and the social organization of state planning with Indigenous peoples	231
Fig. 16.1	Where a victim reports	294
Fig. 16.2	Policing standards at the scene	296
Fig. 16.3	No fit	298
Fig. 16.4	The Crown's work	299
Fig. 16.5	Mapping, discovery, and working with texts	300
Fig. 16.6	The map used at the final gathering	301
Fig. 17.1	Map of the initial institution that did not prevent lead poisoning	314
Fig. 17.2	Mapping of revised institution evolving to prevent lead poisoning	316
Fig. 17.3	Policy progress	320
Fig. 18.1	Institutions of social management	331
Fig. 18.2	Eight methods institutions use to coordinate worker's actions (*Source* Pence & Sadusky, 2005)	339
Fig. 18.3	Sequential layout of the key points in a criminal court case	348
Fig. 18.4	Detailed map highlighting the sentencing stage of a criminal court case	351

Fig. 18.5	Specific steps of conducting a misdemeanor pre-sentence investigation	352
Fig. 27.1	Youth development as social practice	538
Table 18.1	Identifying problems and solutions in the writing of a pre-sentence investigation	354

CHAPTER 1

Institutional Ethnography: Sociology for Today

Paul C. Luken

Over dinner at a meeting of the Pacific Sociological Association in 1996, Dorothy Smith mentioned that just before coming to the United States she read John Dos Passos' *U.S.A.* I had never read it, but then, a budding institutional ethnographer, I was motivated to get the book. It was first published in 1930, and the preface describes a young man who is walking city streets at night. He is alone but very attentive to the people around him and his "muscles ache for the knowledge of jobs" (Dos Passos, 1960, p. v). At first he seems like an unemployed man who is struggling to survive during the Great Depression, but later we learn that he does not want a job. He wants all jobs and more: "One bed is not enough, one job is not enough, one life is not enough" (p. v), we are told, and we realize that it is the knowledge, not the work itself, that he is seeking, that he is listening for.

I have read this preface many times, in part because Dos Passos is a wonderful writer, but also because the wanderer reminds me of so many people who have come to study and practice institutional ethnography (IE). Many, myself included, were not satisfied with the sociology or women's studies orientations that they learned in graduate school, and Smith's feminist alternative sociology provided us with the direction that we needed. Others were drawn to institutional ethnography's grounding in the everyday world with its commonplace and often hidden struggles. When we found institutional ethnography, we found what we were looking for.

P. C. Luken (✉)
University of West Georgia, Carrollton, GA, USA
e-mail: pluken@westga.edu

I am also attracted to the preface of *U.S.A.* because of its final paragraph in which Dos Passos transitions from the man (small hero/ethnographer?) to a description of the United States:

> U.S.A. is the slice of a continent. U.S.A. is a group of holding companies, some aggregations of trade unions, a set of laws bound in calf, a radio network, a chain of moving picture theaters, a column of stockquotations rubbed out and written in by a Western Union boy on a blackboard, a publiclibrary full of old newspapers and dogeared historybooks with protests scrawled on the margins in pencil. U.S.A. is the world's greatest rivervalley fringed with mountains and hills. U.S.A. is a set of bigmouthed officials with too many bankaccounts. U.S.A. is a lot of men buried in their uniforms in Arlington Cemetery. U.S.A. is the letters at the end of an address when you are away from home. But mostly U.S.A. is the speech of the people. (p. vi)

To borrow a phrase from the title of an old rhythm and blues song (Brown, 1966), "this is a man's world" that Dos Passos sketches, although I am certain women appeared on the screens in the theaters and some may have placed their own annotations in the history books. Matters of interest to men dominated, and how that domination could occur and where it would be evident was in the speech of the people, in varieties of discourse. But what are the connections of speech, of language, to the endeavors that Dos Passos alludes to—business, economics, law, media, education, politics, labor, and war—and what are the consequences of these connections? That is the province of institutional ethnography.

Now, as I write this introduction, there is a new discourse that appears ubiquitous. You recognize the words and phrases—facemask, pandemic, shelter in place, self-quarantine, disinfectant, social distance, confirmed cases, wash your hands for 20 seconds, lockdown, ventilators, stay safe—as part of the vocabulary of the COVID-19 discourse. You altered many of the patterns of your everyday life—the people you see, the work that you do, how you forage for food, what you eat, how much you drink—as you and others are affected by this discourse, as you take it up in your actions. To the best of my knowledge I have not come into contact with the virus that causes COVID-19 (and I hope you have not either), but we have been unable to avoid the COVID-19 discourse. It extends beyond any particular speech acts or texts to all forms of communication. The discourse is not tied to any place or to any particular social institution. The language of COVID-19 is the new vernacular.

Many of the authors of the chapters in this handbook were still finishing their essays when the COVID-19 discourse became dominant in their lives. These authors are largely university faculty or advanced graduate students. Through emails I learned that some were having trouble finding opportunities to write because their children's schools were closed and the kids were at home; they became engrossed in the work of childcare and homeschooling. Many were also changing their university courses from face-to-face to online formats, and for several this was their first foray into distance education.

They were, in some instances, cut off from colleagues and the technology that their workplaces offered. Some, even when they had the time to write, said they found it difficult to concentrate and that frustration compounded the problem. As diverse as their experiences may be, I am confident there is something that they have in common. They know that we will need institutional ethnography to understand the social ramifications of the pandemic.

PURPOSE AND ORGANIZATION

Smith's early books are collections of articles she produced while developing what came to be known as Institutional Ethnography. These articles, along with her instruction, provided the basic ideas that her students had to work with while producing their theses and dissertations at the University of British Columbia and the Ontario Institute for Studies in Education (OISE) of the University of Toronto. The research projects became outstanding pieces of IE that were worked into publications in various forms. Since that time there has been considerable development of IE, and it is impossible to keep up with everything that is being produced. Nonetheless, significant research was undertaken in the 1980s because the core ideas had already been developed. For this reason, I highly recommend that students of IE return to Smith's early collections: *The Everyday World as Problematic: A Feminist Sociology*; *Text, Facts, and Femininity: Exploring the Relations of Ruling*; *The Conceptual Practices of Power: A Feminist Sociology of Knowledge*; and *Writing the Social: Critique, Theory, and Investigations*. They contain all that one needs to engage in institutional ethnography.

As evidence of the value of these early writings, look to some of the books, chapters, and articles written by Smith's students and other institutional ethnographers decades ago. In Campbell and Manicom's 1995 collection *Knowledge, Experience and Ruling Relations: Essays in the Social Organization of Knowledge* you will find excellent institutional ethnography at a time when the link of Smith's work to the field of the sociology of knowledge was clearly evident. Timothy Diamond's landmark book *Making Gray Gold: Narratives of Nursing Home Care* (1992) is an outstanding experience-based account of the regulation of the work done by both nursing assistants and the residents of nursing homes. George Smith's groundbreaking article "Political Activist as Ethnographer" (1990) details how he used institutional ethnography while working as a political activist and how he used confrontation as a technique to discover ruling regimes work.

The chapters in this handbook are all original works and they are intended to extend rather than substitute for the existing institutional ethnography literature produced by Smith, her students, and other scholars over the past thirty years. The handbook serves as a comprehensive guide to the alternative sociology that began in Vancouver, Canada, as a "sociology *for* women" and grew into a "sociology *for* people" with global reach. Institutional ethnography provides the tools to discover the social relations shaping the everyday world in which we live; and it is widely utilized by scholars and social activists beyond sociology, in such fields as education, nursing, social work, linguistics, health and medical care, environmental studies, and other social service-related endeavors. Covering the theoretical and methodological underpinnings of institutional ethnography, along with recent developments, and current areas of research and application, this handbook is suitable for both experienced practitioners of institutional ethnography and those who are exploring this approach for the first time.

This handbook is divided into six parts and, while we hope readers find the arrangement useful, we recognize that the problems inherent in categorization are here as well. First there is the problem of overlap. Many of the chapters could easily fit into multiple sections. Second, nothing in institutional ethnography demands that we organize the materials as we have. We settled on the schema we did because we felt that it covers basic and enduring topics along with those that have arisen more recently. We also felt that this organization would be appropriate for novice as well as experienced institutional ethnographers. We hope that this plan works for you.

Part I: "Exploring Historical and Ontological Foundations." These chapters provide readers with a basis in how institutional ethnography has developed, how its theory (of knowing) contrasts with other theories, and institutional ethnography's use of theory. The chapters by Marj DeVault and Liza McCoy provide a basis for understanding the underlying premises of institutional ethnography and how they guide research, its conceptual development, and possibilities for extension to new areas. Eric Mykhalovskiy and graduate students explore the situation of institutional ethnography as alternative sociology, its relationship to theory and to other research approaches, to politics and to critique. Dorothy Smith's chapter shows the value of the generalizing capacities of institutional language to institutional ethnographers as it is taken up in the process of defining actions as institutional.

Part II: "Developing Strategies and Exploring Challenges" continues the instructive mode elaborated in Smith's *Institutional Ethnography as Practice* (2006) and *Incorporating Texts into Institutional Ethnography* (2014) with chapters describing challenges and opportunities encountered in the process of producing research studies—copyright issues, mapping and visual approaches, reflexivity, institutional capture, among others. Readers can learn about the challenges they might contend with in the course of a research project. The challenges of teaching institutional ethnography to undergraduates are also discussed.

The four chapters in Part III: "Explicating Global/Transnational Ruling Relations" examine issues from standpoints on different continents, yet the problematics connect with discourses established by national and multinational organizations connected through professional and governmental networks. This section illustrates the ways in which ruling operates transnationally. The chapters demonstrate how particular people are caught in extensive, global social relations. This section is valuable in showing institutional ethnography's contribution to making visible how global ruling works and how remote ruling standpoints can be inserted into locally made decisions. The knowledge gained through these investigations can be used to critique aspects of global development.

Part IV: "Making Change within Communities" consists of three chapters that use institutional ethnography differently from one another in order to identify problems in their settings and to develop strategies designed to improve the existing textually-mediated social relations and, ultimately, the lives of people. For activist-oriented institutional ethnographers, they illustrate the value of a sociology that (1) begins in and remains in the everyday world and (2) is flexible enough to allow for innovation and adaptation to specific settings. Susan Turner and Julia Bomberry utilize collaborative mapping with a Haudenosaunee First Nations community in Canada to explore police investigations and services for Indigenous victims of sexual violence. Frank Ridzi develops maps of relations that establish and maintain unsafe housing conditions (lead-based paint). These are then used for advocacy and for philanthropic interventions that make a difference to the subjects in his research. Ellen Pence and Praxis International's institutional analysis approach was designed to improve institutional responses to gender-based violence. The chapter describes how a team of community-based professionals can investigate work practices and policies and make systemic change in these areas.

The chapters in Part V: "Critiquing Public Sector Management Regimes" cover a wide variety of dilemmas faced by workers and clients in contemporary public institutions, a theme previously taken up by Griffith and Smith and associates (2014). In these chapters we learn how students with disabilities in the United States are burdened with additional work because of the institutional policies that are purported to assist them, how forms of knowledge grounded in evidence-based practices are both produced and resisted by workers in the criminal justice system in the United States, how regulatory practices in Canada related to substance use by nurses often caused problems rather than diminished potential dangers, and the documentation of functional equivalency undermines the work of sign language interpreters. The area of public management has attracted a great deal of interest by institutional ethnographers, and this sociology excels at examining how people's work lives are formed to fit the administrative demands of institutions, often at the expense of their clients.

The most controversial section of this handbook might be Part VI: "Bringing Together Different Approaches and Perspectives," since it takes up some challenging issues among institutional ethnographers. Is one still doing institutional ethnography if one supplements it with other sociological theory or other research practices? While the claim is made that institutional ethnography is not an "orthodoxy," can it be combined with other approaches that conflict with its ontological and epistemological commitments? Do those who say that institutional ethnography is insufficient really know all that IE has to offer? Should consistency be important to those social and political activists who see political value in using objectified forms of knowledge? If one's aims are broader than those of institutional ethnography, is it appropriate to shift in and out of IE?

In order to write institutional ethnography that will give readers a clear understanding of work processes and the social relations shaping them, Michael Corman proposes the use of composite accounts built from the data collected rather than the words and actions of any set of particular individuals. Karly Burch proposes vital institutional ethnography, a combination of IE and material semiotics, as a worthy approach to the study of ruling relations in the Anthropocene. This would allow scholars to discover the textually-mediated ruling relations in which their subjects are embedded while also examining other human and more-than-human involvements that contribute to our experiences of the messes we are in. Gerald de Montigny presents transcriptions of talk using conventions of conversation analysis in order to preserve the morphology of talk. This approach, he argues, allows us to see talk as more than words; rather, it remains an embodied social exchange which reveals socially organized practices. Naomi Nichols and Jessica Ruglis, maintaining compatibility with the ontological and epistemological stance of institutional ethnography, undertake techniques of Youth Participatory Action Research in order to engage youth as part of their research team. They argue that this combination can enhance critical analysis. It is doubtful that the chapters in this part will bring institutional ethnographers to consensus, nonetheless, they raise issues and suggestions that are worthy of discussion and debate.

SOCIOLOGY FOR TODAY

While I was collecting signatures on a petition to form a Division on Institutional Ethnography within the Society for the Study of Social Problems, one supporter, someone familiar with institutional ethnography but not a practitioner, commented, "This division will spend the first five years trying to figure out what it is." I understood the remark to be a slight criticism of institutional ethnography, but it did not irritate me. I was happy to hear that he thought the IE Division would last for five years. (That was in 2003 and the division is still going strong.) I also knew that institutional ethnography is not a fixed and finalized set of ideas and practices[1] and so, yes, we would be figuring it out for some time to come. Furthermore, the conditions under which we work change as well and we must adapt to new circumstances.

Two years ago I was investigating political practice from the ground up by taking up the work myself. I was going door-to-door canvassing for a candidate for the US Congress, joining meetings of the county Democratic Party, attending fundraising dinners, and serving as an observer at my county elections office for the local chapter of the League of Women Voters. I was also a poll worker, a clerk working 14-hour days whenever there was an election.

Two days from now, the time I am writing this introduction, there will be an election. I have not canvassed, attended Democratic Party meetings, or observed at the elections office, and I will not be assisting voters who show up on Tuesday to cast their ballots. COVID-19 has disrupted my work, my research. Phonebanking has replaced canvassing, the county Democrats no longer meet, and neither does the board of elections. Voters will not be required to wear masks, the incidence of COVID-19 cases is increasing in this area, I am 70 years old and under a stay-at-home order; therefore, I sadly opted out of poll work. Anyone who was engaged in fieldwork when the pandemic occurred is probably having similar problems. Fortunately, I also have a network of ethnographers with whom I can plot alternative avenues for my investigations. And I am mindful that Dos Passos also had to deal with a pandemic, and he was quarantined in 1918 because of the flu; so I will borrow from him as I close this introduction.

IE is an alternative sociology founded by Dorothy E. Smith. IE is a scientific method with feminist origins that always starts with real people's situations and always keeps the researcher as an active participant in the discoveries. IE is a growing literature describing how ruling operates through texts. IE is a compass used to create maps of social relations. IE is a dedicated network of scholars and activists. But mostly IE is doing the work.

Note

1. "What we all want, and cannot have, is the ideological equivalent of a Forever stamp, the assurance that our version of enlightenment will withstand the passage of years, without requiring ungainly supplementation" (Appiah, 2020, p. 19). When he writes "we," Kwame Anthony Appiah is referring to grand scholars or those who hope to be grand scholars. I think this statement is widely true, yet Dorothy Smith's institutional ethnography must be regarded as an exception. It was always a collective project, what she sometimes calls "the work," influenced by feminist activists, her graduate students, and others who took up "the work" as well.

References

Appiah, K. A. (2020, May). The defender of differences. *The New York Review of Books, 67*(9), 17–19.
Brown, J. (1966). It's a man's man's man's world. On *It's a man's man's man's world.*
Campbell, M., & Manicom, A. (Eds.). (1995). *Knowledge, experience and ruling relations: Essays in the social organization of knowledge.* Toronto: University of Toronto Press.
Diamond, T. (1992). *Making gray gold: Narratives of nursing home care.* Chicago, IL: University of Chicago Press.
Dos Passos, J. (1960). *U.S.A.* Boston, MA: Houghton Mifflin Company.

Griffith, A. I., & Smith, D. E. (Eds.). (2014). *Under new public management: Institutional ethnographies of changing front-line work.* Toronto: University of Toronto Press.

Smith, G. W. (1990). Political activist as ethnographer. *Social Problems, 37*(4), 401–421.

PART I

Exploring Historical and Ontological Foundations

CHAPTER 2

Elements of an Expansive Institutional Ethnography: A Conceptual History of Its North American Origins

Marjorie L. DeVault

When Dorothy Smith began to study sociology in the 1950s, it was unusual for a woman to forge a career as a scholar; she was one of the first woman graduates of the PhD program at the University of California, Berkeley in an age when most of the faculty did not expect those women to follow the path of their male counterparts who would enter academic life. Smith resisted those expectations—and, after her husband left the family, she needed to support her two young sons (Smith, 1994). She also resisted what seemed to her peculiar ideological practices of the sociology she had been taught—a sociology that operated in abstractions, tidying up the messiness of people's complex lives in order to produce concepts that were woven into ruling practices. Steeped in the free-speech and anti-war activism of the times, she considered how political protest came to be defined by authorities as disorderly conduct (1990b, Ch. 5)—and by academics as an object of study (1990b, Ch. 3). Along with a small group of ethnomethodologists, she began to see that concepts and texts are active and consequential in people's doings. Along with other women, she considered how women's unconventional behavior could come to be identified as mental illness, and how such labeling could operate as social control. Smith understood these early investigations as studies in the social organization of knowledge—and although at the time the phrase *sociology of knowledge* was more often used to refer to the cultural contexts of knowledge production (as in the work of Karl Mannheim, for example), she had in mind a more

---

M. L. DeVault (✉)
Syracuse University, Syracuse, NY, USA
e-mail: mdevault@syr.edu

© The Author(s) 2021
P. C. Luken and S. Vaughan (eds.), *The Palgrave Handbook of Institutional Ethnography*,
https://doi.org/10.1007/978-3-030-54222-1_2

fundamental investigation of how objective knowledge comes to be, and what is left behind or concealed as it is produced. From these early explorations, Smith embarked on her career-long search for a sturdier and more useful way to conduct sociological inquiry, a project that continues to the present and that has generated a network of students and colleagues—stretching across disciplinary boundaries and national borders—who have joined her in developing the institutional ethnography approach.

Smith and her comrades began to examine ideological constructions that shaped women's lives, insisting that people's experiences and activities should always be the point of entry to these investigations. They drew from Marx the idea that people's activities are concealed in concepts that then come to have a life of their own—as, in Marx's analyses, the activities of production and market exchange are concealed in the concept of the commodity (Smith, 1977). Two key ideas drove Smith's thinking, and they have characterized all of her work: First, she wanted an "insider's" sociology. Again, her formulation went beyond the ideas of the time (e.g., Robert Merton's discussion of similarity as the basis for knowing-in-common), insisting that all people are located in the social, and thus any knower is connected, in relations with others. In addition, she wanted a sociology that spoke to puzzles in the world at hand and did not only produce the descriptive abstractions of theory-building. Instead she sought to open a greater understanding of extended *social relations* that were not fully visible from the knower's location. These two principles continue to be central to the epistemology of institutional ethnography (IE); I will not unpack them fully here, but I will touch on them as the chapter proceeds. I will say, however, that despite Smith's resolute rejection of starting inquiry in theory and of conducting inquiry with the goal of building or extending theory, she certainly saw the thinking and writing underpinning IE as theoretical practice. I believe she felt some ambivalence about her installation by others as a "major sociological theorist" (Campbell & DeVault, 2011), but what she rejects is the type of peculiar formal theory that was so dominant in the functionalist era when she began, and that lives on in much of contemporary sociology. IE is designed for a different type of theorizing: it does not aim to develop general theory, but to theorize about the organization of people's everyday lives as they are unfolding.

In a recent book related to this chapter, Liz Stanley (2018) notes the remarkable consistency of Smith's work over time, and I agree that at its core, Smith's approach retains its central ideas, such as its critique of abstraction and its grounding in people's activities. But I have been especially interested in how IE strategies for inquiry have developed and changed as Smith and others have pursued questions about how to move beyond that generative critique. My intention in this chapter is to write a conceptual history of those developments—that is, an account of continuity and change in IE's ideas, vocabularies, and research strategies—as I have observed and participated in them. My goals are to situate key developments in IE in their contexts (times and places), and also to call attention to the varied and fruitful lines of investigation it has produced.

My account is not strictly chronological, but is organized around my sense of several periods in the trajectory of institutional ethnography, characterized by different emphases and approaches. It is not a conventional, institutional history—I have not tried to recount all of the events, groups, and organizations that have been part of IE's development. I have certainly not been able to reference all of the North American practitioners who have participated in these developments. But I have foregrounded some of the colleagues and research partners who have worked closely with Smith; I chose to include them because the varied directions she took often seemed tied, at least in part, to these working relationships. That finding, I think, offers an indication of Smith's openness to the new questions people brought to her, and of her commitment to working collaboratively to develop the approach. Finally, I did not set out to write a personal account, but as I proceeded, I found that including some personal stories helped me to explain and provide context for these developments.

I met Dorothy Smith, first in text and then in person, in the early days of academic feminism, around 1980, when there were really no women in the canon of sociological theorists. During that time, some of my teachers and mentors in US sociology were taking up the political work of calling attention to women's scholarship; a group of them joined the almost-entirely-male theory section of the US sociological association and began to organize speaking opportunities for leading feminists—working to place Dorothy Smith and others, organizationally, in the realm of theory. I recall too that my grad-student friends and I were observing our own reading practices—it seemed that we read articles by women, while we studied the entire corpus of works by canonical male theorists—and we resolved to read Dorothy's work in that fuller, more sustained, and more attentive way, taking her seriously as a scholar with a large, complex, and ambitious intellectual agenda. I suppose that this chapter represents yet another iteration of that project—one that has afforded me great insight and great pleasure for many years.

CONCEPTUAL PRACTICES OF POWER

Before institutional ethnography had a name, the *social organization of knowledge* rubric captured Smith's explorations of the ideological practices of authorized knowledge, including sociology's implications in *ruling*, the term she generally used in order to populate and enliven abstractions like *power*. When she took up a teaching position at the University of British Columbia in 1968, she began to teach under that rubric. A women's movement was developing in Vancouver, as in many other places, and Smith and many of the students she attracted found that women's activism fueled their scholarship, and vice versa. Smith herself wrote primarily about mental illness; students in a first generation took up ideological constructs that troubled them, such as *single parent* (Griffith, 1995), *women in Peru* (Mueller, 1995), and *nursing education* (Campbell, 1995). In each case, investigation began with women living lives of purposeful action—women at work. In each case, the question at issue was how the particulars of those purposeful lives and activities were reduced to abstracted conceptualizations and how those abstractions were consequential—that is, how teachers came to treat students as the children of single mothers; how an abstracted way of knowing about women in Peru locked feminist development specialists into particular ways of working with women; how student nurses learn to act in ways that can be documented as good nursing practice. These analysts were implicated in the social relations they examined, and they noticed that events unfolded around them in ways they did not intend and did not fully understand. As Mueller argued, "We thus have the possibility and the responsibility to investigate the ways that our own professional work practices may participate in reproducing other women's marginalization" (1995, p. 106).

The foundations of these investigations lay in close attention to words, concepts, and discourses that contributed to a *documentary reality* (Smith, 1974a). As noted above, Marx provided the materialist ontology: it is human activity that produces fact, objectivity, concept, and documentary reality (McCoy, this volume). But Smith was also interested in exploring how people navigate between their grounding in the actual and the discursive realities their activities produce. She identified two distinct experiences in her own life: she was a mother tending to the embodied lives of young sons, and she was also a member of the intelligentsia, who had learned to enter conversations conducted in and about a discourse of sociology, structured through the organizational forms of the university. She observed and theorized her movement between those two realities.

It is important to locate Smith's work in the broader context of social theory at the time; although she wrote against abstracted theory, she was steeped in social theory and deeply committed to developing a better sociology. Her insights in this period developed alongside the work of those in ethnomethodology and science studies, who were also interested in the activities that constructed scientific (and other) facts (e.g., Latour & Woolgar, 1979; Lynch, 1985; Zimmerman, 1974), and kept the primordial grounding of social order in place, through activities such as ordinary sense-making and the practices of face-to-face interaction and conversation (Garfinkel, 1967). Smith's project was not only to understand the production of the conceptual order, but to preserve as well the embodied experiences that are set aside as people contribute to it. In pursuing that project, she drew on the work of G.H. Mead (1947) and the phenomenologist Alfred Schutz (1962), who offered analyses of different provinces of meaning. Following those ideas, Smith began to explore disjunctures in consciousness, which offered fleeting clues to transitions from one mode of knowing to another.

Key articles from this time are organized to illuminate such transitions. In "K is Mentally Ill" (Smith, 1990b, Chapter 2), the question is how activities such as bathing frequently and sweeping the floor are worked up by roommates into a lay diagnosis of mental illness. In "The Active Text" (1990b, Chapter 5), Smith shows how a mayor's letter to a concerned citizen transforms an encounter that appeared to be an instance of police brutality into a properly warranted arrest. For Smith, these are not functionalist questions of social order—as they would have been seen by most ethnomethodologists—but fundamentally political questions about ruling. Smith chooses the side of embodied experience, and the project of understanding precisely how it is left behind.

These early works were produced as social scientists were just beginning to approach the linguistic turn that would gain such prominence a bit later, in the 1980s. Marxists were making their own turn toward an emphasis on ideology, and Foucault's writing (e.g., 1979) was bringing terms such as *discourse* into the forefront. Smith was keenly attentive to these developments, reading widely in linguistics and literary theory as well as the social sciences. Against those who moved into discourse and remained there, however, her work was always characterized by a commitment to an *actual* as the foundation of the social. Of course, one does not have direct access to the actual; it must be communicated somehow, in words or text. But one can read through those words about *what actually happened* and know that people are there, embodied and active (Smith, 1974a). Later, as the linguistic turn gained steam, Smith would defend that view and her conception of the social, against those who argued that discourse was all, in her compellingly titled theoretical essay, "Telling the Truth After Postmodernism" (1996).

One more building block in these social organization of knowledge studies was the idea that sociology and other fields of academic knowledge are themselves taken up and deployed in the practices of ruling. Social scientists develop concepts such as *family violence* or indicators of *risk*, and their research contributes to the knowledge base of social workers and other professionals, such that they may unwittingly come to see through the eyes of administrators. Smith's approach involved noticing *disjunctures* between everyday knowledge and these ruling concepts, exploring the contours of these gaps and making them touchstones for empirical work. She noted that people are active in making the barely noticed shift from one mode of knowing to another. Thus, Gerald de Montigny's dissertation research on social work practice included moving reflections on how he had learned to bracket his working-class background and look at troubled families in ways that made them into cases (1995); and Alison Griffith's work on educators' views of single parents included reflections on how she had learned to see her own mothering as defective, against an idealized standard (Griffith & Smith, 1987). Maintaining a sense of both embodied and documentary realities was critical to preserving the politics of the approach.

Smith's foundational work on the social organization of knowledge was collected in two volumes, both published in 1990 (1990a, b); students from this period later produced a collection of their research in the social organization of knowledge (Campbell & Manicom, 1995). Smith used a classroom exercise during this time that she called "botanizing ideology" (1990b, pp. 165–167 & p. 242, n25). She conceived it as a kind of study like early botany, in which scientists collected specimens and then examined and reported on them. In her own writing, one can see such an approach in her analyses of mental illness and suicide (1990a), and in the small empirical investigations she includes in *Writing the Social*, e.g., her analysis of the phrase *politically correct* as an "organizer of public discourse" (Smith, 1999, Chapter 9). One can also get a sense of IE practice during this period from the methodological "primer" *Mapping Social Relations*, by Marie Campbell and Frances Gregor (2002). They emphasize that the researcher is always located in, or in relation to, the field of the investigation, and they guide students in reading the literature of their fields as also always located. Since most of the research literature is written within and for the administrative state, one can examine it as a piece of the social relations under investigation. For an example, see Kamini Maraj Grahame's [1998a, 1999] discussion of human capital theory as an element in the organization of the job training programs she studied.

There are several ideas from this period that I've continued to deploy and have found especially useful in my own work with graduate students. For example, we sometimes spoke of *conceptual currencies*, scraps of discourse that fit well into prevailing ideas of a moment. Frank Ridzi (2009) found that construction useful when he studied the reorganization of US welfare assistance in the 1990s. Talking with welfare agency administrators, he saw that they were adopting a vocabulary of *work first* welfare, which geared more easily into broader conversations of the time than would the traditional ways of talking about assistance for vulnerable families. As with monetary currencies, some words and ideas bought more success than others.

Smith also wrote about *ideological codes*, conceptual constellations so powerful that they implant and replicate (these are metaphors, of course) without always making themselves fully visible. The key example was the idea of a *Standard North American Family (SNAF)*, which projected and naturalized an ostensibly self-sufficient, heterosexual couple with children (Smith, 1993). The code comes to be so widely shared, implicitly, that it seems natural for an organization to assume such a reality. Paul Luken and Suzanne Vaughan (2006) found that a related discourse of the *Standard American Home* organized and upheld an early twentieth century industry of home financing and construction that has had profound effects on North American lives. And when I worked with Li-Fang Liang (2010) on her study of migrant care workers in Taiwan, I thought we could see another ideological code at work in Taiwanese media accounts of migrants as unsanitary, diseased, and dangerous. With such a code so widely shared among the public, policy makers did not need to be explicit when they developed ethnically-based exclusions and restrictions in law and regulations.

Finally, I found that work on these discursive aspects of social organization offered us the idea of struggle on the terrain of language. Gillian Walker's analysis of the evolution of family violence policy (1990) provides one early example; activists worked to foreground male dominance, but policy makers and therapists pulled the discourse toward more neutral language and strategies. Similarly, when Lauren Eastwood (2005) worked with environmental activists at UN forest policy meetings, she saw that they had successfully pushed states toward a vocabulary of sustainability in the policy documents. But it was quickly apparent that the victory was fragile, as new struggles were opening around what would count as a sustainable forest (see also Eastwood, 2019).

A Sociology for Women

In 1977, Smith moved from a sociology department at the University of British Columbia to the Department of Sociology in Education at the Ontario Institute for Studies in Education (OISE), a graduate school of education; a core group of students moved with her. The department, which has since remade itself as a Department of Equity Studies, was one in which ethnomethodology had a foothold and feminism was young but firmly established. This environment, in which social theory was in conversation with the concerns of human service professionals, was to prove most congenial for the development of Smith's *sociology for women*, and later, for people.

In a time when academics were not connected electronically, but shared work by handing out papers at conferences or mailing hard copies to colleagues, Smith's feminist essays (e.g., 1974b, 1975a, 1978) had begun to circulate widely among feminist scholars. Alongside writers such as Sandra Harding, Donna Haraway, and others, she was developing a critique of male-centered bias in knowledge and culture, and its consequences for women's consciousness. Developing the idea of disjuncture, she illustrated with a quote from Marxist-feminist Sheila Rowbotham's account of watching the Beatles' *Magical Mystery Tour*. Rowbotham realized that she had learned to watch "through men's eyes." She tells of following the characters to a strip-tease and being asked to "desire myself," so that she suddenly felt "sliced in two ...poised for an instant in two halves" (cited in Smith, 1987, p. 52). Women in many realms of society were noticing and sharing such *lines of fault* in their experiences. Smith's social organization of knowledge approach offered feminist scholars a way of working on the puzzles they were just beginning to express, and the women's movement offered Smith an audience hungry for the ideas she was developing.

I first encountered the name "institutional ethnography" in Smith's essay "A Sociology for Women," published in a 1979 anthology representing the then-new thinking of feminist scholars across the disciplines (1979). That essay later became the foundation of *The Everyday World as Problematic* (1987), Smith's first book-length explication of her sociology for women. I met Dorothy around 1980, when she was developing the chapters that would make up that book; she visited Northwestern University for one term and offered a course titled "Women's Standpoint in the Sociological Organization of Knowledge." For organizational reasons, the course was listed for undergraduates, and a half-dozen students in the new field of women's studies sat at a table in the center of the classroom. Around them were a large number of graduate students—virtually all women—eager to hear Dorothy, and on the edges of the room, feminist faculty who came from various disciplines and from universities throughout the Chicago metropolitan area. There was lively, vigorous, high-level discussion, and occasionally Dorothy would pause and check to make sure the undergraduate students who were actually enrolled in the class had had a chance to ask the questions of interest to them.

Many feminist scholars of that era had begun to see that women's experiences were ignored, obscured, distorted, or mis-named in the knowledge of the time, and there was a widespread commitment to revealing and documenting what women really did and thought. Smith added the idea of researching for rather than about women—that is, the idea that scholars could do more than simply document women's experience; they could also make knowledge useful for women by illuminating how their experiences were put together. The central illustration of this possibility—the first sketch of something called *institutional ethnography*—was an analysis of Smith's own experience of confronting her sons' schooling as a single mother.

The figure that accompanied Smith's discussion of IE (1987, p. 171, Fig. 4.1) was an early *small hero map*, as she later came to call it. The point of entry to the investigation is depicted by a female figure on the ground—a single mother in the everyday world. Her experiences—the work she does to make a living and raise her children—are central. The next level in the analysis is sketched out in a box that represents the work organization of mothering and teaching: presumably, a mother's daily routines, the school schedule, and teachers' work. Around those figures are shapes that depict what Smith calls *extra-local* institutions and ideologies: the "bureaucratic organization of education" (the school board, for example, where authorities allocate staff and classroom sizes); "professional discourse" (e.g., a mothering discourse that holds moms responsible for all that happens to their children); then a box representing the state, and a notation that social class is operative as well. Smith's interpretation of the figure sketches how mothers in two-parent families, with time for tutoring and volunteer work, support the school by taking on teaching work at home; by contrast, single mothers, who may support their children less visibly or struggle simply to get them to school on time, may appear to teachers and administrators uninterested or incapable of proper mothering.

The example—which Smith would continue to develop, with Alison Griffith (Griffith & Smith, 2005)—showed the value of turning the analytic gaze. Rather than writing about single mothers, no matter how sympathetically, this approach to a sociology *for* single mothers begins to explain what they may not easily see: the institutional forces arrayed against them, how their mothering work comes to be judged as defective, and the consequences of that perception for their children at school. One can see that policies on class size, for example, take for granted the work of mothers, and limit the help teachers can provide. Following this model, others in the growing circle of feminist IE researchers could take up the puzzles of women doing other kinds of work, such as the teachers who stood in relation to mothers (Manicom, 1995). A strength of the IE approach was that analysts did not have to choose sides: they could show how both mothers and teachers were caught up in institutional processes and the discourses that organized their work, whether paid or unpaid—the analytic focus was on ruling relations, rather than on individuals. Researchers in predominantly female fields of work were drawn to the approach and started investigations into the puzzles of clerical workers (Reimer, 1995), nurses (Campbell, 1995), adult educators (Jackson, 1995), corporate wives (Ueda, 1995), and so on. None of these starting points was to be taken as the content of *women's experience*; that idea was radically open, always to be filled in as new puzzles were developed.

Tim Diamond was another US scholar who came to know Smith well during her visit to Northwestern University. At the time, he was beginning work on an ethnography of long-term care in the US, which became his landmark book *Making Gray Gold* (1992). He was inspired by Smith's commitment to preserving the activities, knowledge, and daily experiences of those on the front lines of *carework* (and, in the case of residents, the work of survival in the institution), and he wondered how a man could pursue a sociology for women. In order to do so, he adopted the ethnographer's strategy of working alongside the nursing assistants—virtually all women of color—who did hands-on care. He also listened attentively to the residents of the facility, who were mostly women, and mostly impoverished by the demands of US healthcare policy, which depletes individual assets before benefits for long-term care can be accessed. Diamond's chillingly compelling analysis pointed to such policies, and also to an emergent industry of long-term care that offered lucrative investment opportunities, turning the care needs of elderly people into "gray gold."

In this period, institutional ethnography began to take shape as a distinct strategy for inquiry, and ruling was located in extra-local institutions and processes. The idea of a *ruling apparatus* identified interlocking institutional complexes made up of work that was guided by abstracted knowledge. Workers on the front lines, often women (teachers, nurses and healthcare aides, social workers, and secretaries, for example), learned to perceive and work up the "inexhaustibly messy" (Smith, 1987, p. 159) realities of people's daily lives, so that they fit into actionable conceptual boxes. Administrators and policy makers—more removed from people's everyday lives—could then do their work as if those documentary realities told the story.

Later, Smith and others would develop more specific methods for working with texts, using the idea of a *text-reader conversation* to analyze the workings of documents—an important advance in the power of IE. In this period, however, the meanings of *extra-local* were more open, and analyses were equally often built on the governing powers of more diffuse *discourses*. Smith and Griffith continued to develop analyses of a powerful *mothering discourse* (Griffith & Smith, 1987), and Smith wrote on a *discourse of femininity* (1990b) that women took up—mostly from mass media—in order to *do femininity*. In my own work on women's household work of feeding the family (DeVault, 1991), I referenced discourses that organized *the family dinner*, and *healthy eating*; I found, for example, that women who organized their cooking work for convenience spoke guiltily about falling short of some ideal. And when I wrote about families visiting the zoo (DeVault, 2000), I found a discourse of *things to do*, communicated through media pieces about families spending *quality time* together and calendars of community events in parenting publications. Many feminists, including Smith, were interested in Foucault's approach to such discourses. But she noted that Foucault's historical method began and ended in discourse; she wanted instead a method that would preserve people's activities, so that we could see them *gearing into* (McCoy, 2008) and enacting the elements of a discourse.

Tim Diamond's work on nursing home life is a notable exception, given its focus on the nexus between care policy regulations and the private, often for-profit enterprises that dominate the long-term care landscape in the US. Managerial texts appear frequently in his analysis; for example, he emphasizes the work of charting care activities, and all that the patients' charts leave out; he also examines the kinds of institutional technologies that IE scholars would later discuss as *accountability circuits* (Griffith & Smith, 2014). Smith discusses Diamond's method (that is, documenting his own work activities) as *experiential analysis* (2005, pp. 178–179), and his work certainly demonstrates the potential of ethnographic observation for IE (see also Diamond, 2008).

The prominence of discourse in the analytic strategies of this period, as opposed to texts and documents, is perhaps partly the result of a focus on women's positioning as unpaid workers in family households and communities, rather than or in addition to, workers in the administrative state. Paid workers' activities, such as those of the nursing aides Diamond studied, are shaped by job descriptions, workplace policy, government regulations, and so on; work in a household is organized more invisibly, and often idiosyncratically, by broad notions of what should be done in a proper family, and who should do it. Mothering discourse, for example, dictates that mothers are responsible, no matter who else may participate in caring for children; such ideas are powerful, even if they are implicit until they are challenged.

Some of Smith's students in this period also relied on discourse-based analyses to examine racialized aspects of governance, as in Himani Banerji's analysis of the ideological character of colonial historiography (1995), Roxana Ng's investigation of Canadian policies of *multiculturalism* (1995), and Kamini Grahame's account of white feminist activists' misguided understandings of *outreach* to community-based women of color (1998b). The differences of gender and race are sometimes written explicitly into bureaucratic texts that prescribe discriminatory actions, but perhaps more often, they are carried by discourses and "dispersed over a range of sites within the institutions of ruling" (Smith, 1990b, p. 65). These studies point to possibilities for IE that remain relatively underdeveloped and offer possible directions for future work.

The Activist as Ethnographer

By contrast with other feminist theorists, Smith did not specify the content of *women's standpoint* (Smith, 2005, Chapter 1). That open character of IE, and its analytic power, would lead to its growth into a broader *sociology for people*. That development began in many small ways, but gained momentum when two extraordinary activists, George Smith and Ellen Pence, saw its potential for strengthening their efforts. George Smith (no relation to Dorothy—except through their deep friendship) was an intellectual and activist in left gay circles of the 1970s and 80s, first in Vancouver and later in Toronto. He studied with Dorothy Smith and, as a research associate at OISE, worked with her to conduct interviews with steel workers, exploring the everyday knowledge and skill they brought to the job (Smith & Smith, 1990). Talking and working together, they advanced Dorothy's critique of established sociology and thought together about finding an alternative way to work (Smith, 2006).

George Smith was active in a movement to resist the harsh policing of gay men in Toronto, but he also questioned some forms of activism that were prevalent. He saw the typical demands and responses—such as sensitivity training for officers or adding gay officers to the force—as unlikely to bring real change. Instead, he saw the oppression of gay men as rooted in the state and he began to study the law regulating public spaces and how it was applied by police. In a very influential academic article, he tells the story of his analysis, and the moves it suggested for activism (G. Smith, 1990). As the HIV/AIDS epidemic worsened, George worked with others to increase access to newly developed treatments for people living with HIV/AIDS. That project is also chronicled in the 1990 article. Later, Eric Mykhalovskiy and Liza McCoy worked with community activist partners to extend that effort in a project on the broader contours of the health work done by men living with HIV/AIDS (Bresalier et al., 2002; Mykhalovskiy & McCoy, 2010)—and numerous scholars inspired by George Smith continue to develop related work.

George Smith's approach was not like the participatory research of some sociologists and anthropologists, who take up an agenda forged by a community group; George was embedded in community groups and had participated in developing the activist agenda. Given that agenda, he organized some in the groups to pursue what knowledge they could about the institutions they confronted—scientists working on new treatments, drug companies who distributed medication, and provincial health officials who regulated access. He did not set out to collect research data as such; instead, confrontations with these ruling institutions were a resource. By considering their responses, he and his team could learn how things worked and then intervene more effectively. The credibility of their analyses came from the success of their interventions. Activists who worked with him recall that he often spoke of "documents and demonstrations" as two essential elements of political activism: demonstrations to gain attention and press for change, and documents to define changes that will matter and provide the kind of actionable analysis that speaks to policy makers (Documents and Demonstrations, AIDS Activist History Project, n.d.).

Ellen Pence (2001) was another influential figure who developed activist IE in distinctive ways, taking time off from her work as a domestic violence advocate in Duluth, Minnesota, to study with Dorothy Smith in Toronto. Advocates of that era had succeeded in their push for police intervention in cases of abuse, but outcomes for women were still often unsatisfactory, at best. Pence's strategy was to investigate the processing of domestic violence cases, from the initial emergency response through the judicial process, and on to the sentencing of offenders. She examined how cases were processed by workers in disparate sites—the 911 emergency-call dispatcher, responding police officers, prosecutors, pre-sentencing investigators, and so on. She saw that the women involved became "cases" moving through the system; in the process, some information about a woman's situation was passed along and much useful information was lost. Even with well-intentioned workers along the way, those who made decisions were often unable to prioritize the women's safety. Pence used the concept of *processing interchanges* to call attention to the points in case processing when a matter is passed from one worker to another—key points where circumstances are redefined and where the complexity of everyday realities is easily lost.

Given the insights she had gained from her research, Pence devised a way of working collaboratively with community representatives of the various agencies involved in processing incidents of domestic abuse. Small teams of local people observed and discussed the organization of work at various nodes in the system and looked for ways to preserve information that might lead to better outcomes. In one early investigation in Duluth, for example, they developed new guidelines that responding officers could use in recording more of what had happened in an incident; they found that carrying more and different kinds of information forward allowed judges to make decisions more responsive to a woman's circumstances. Pence was a charismatic and extraordinarily effective leader of these investigations, and she and her colleagues disseminated the approach widely; the organization she co-founded continues to provide training in the approach and to extend its scope (Renzetti & Hart, 2010; Praxis International, n.d.).

George Smith and those who followed him referred to his method as *political activist ethnography* (Frampton, Kinsman, Thompson, & Tilleczek, 2006); Ellen Pence first labeled her community approach a *safety audit* method, and later called it *institutional analysis* (2011). Both activists were important translators of Smith's ideas into terms that could be understood and taken up by and with community partners—and they were also important teachers for academics who wished to combine scholarly work and activism, such as Gary Kinsman, in Sudbury, Ontario, and Suzanne Vaughan in Arizona (see Frampton et al., 2006; Vaughan, 2016). Their projects also helped to clarify and strengthen the meaning of research that was for rather than about a standpoint group, as their studies were aimed directly at providing knowledge that sharpened activist agendas. The analyses of ruling institutions produced by their teams offered powerful models of how IE might be useful in community work, and this kind of activist IE remains an important branch of institutional ethnographic work in North America (See, e.g., Nichols, 2014, for work on youth homelessness in Montreal; Bomberry, Turner, & Werner, 2018, for work with First Nations communities in Ontario).

Governance and the New Public Management

IE was taken up in the 1990s by researchers in diverse fields of study, not only sociology but in the various human service professions—teaching, nursing, social work, and others. Across these different sites in the administrative state—and across international borders—IE analysts were noticing points of connection. Front-line professionals were feeling squeezed by budget cuts and increasingly stringent surveillance of their activities. The new regimes they faced were implemented through similar managerial technologies and were discussed and justified by similar managerial vocabularies. Seeking to explore these connections, Alison Griffith organized a 1998 conference at York University, focused on restructuring in public sector organizations. She proposed that attendees might work with the idea of inter-institutional technologies (Griffith & Andre-Bechley, 2008; Griffith & Smith, 2014), that is, managerial ideas, strategies, and document types that were developed at the level of policy making and upper administration, and then adapted to the front-line circumstances of particular fields of work and localities. Looking across their various analyses, IE scholars began to see the local effects of a "New Public Management" (Clarke & Newman, 1997) and other versions of total quality management strategies imported from business. Those at the York University conference discussed an emergent governing discourse that touted a *New Economy*, and those discussions inspired me to organize another conference at Syracuse University, titled "Embodied Workers in a New Economy" (DeVault, 2008). Later, Griffith and Smith convened a working group to meet again at York, where participants collaborated on planning chapters for an edited volume, *Under New Public Management* (Griffith & Smith, 2014).

Those of us attending these conferences were struck by our ability to see connections among our investigations—not just conceptual parallels, but actual ties to the academic, political, and corporate actors who shared philosophies of governance and worked together on tools to implement new modes of administration. Dorothy Smith had always argued that IE studies were meant to connect (2005, pp. 212 ff.), coming together like jigsaw pieces as they mapped different sites in the same broad terrain. In our research on neoliberal governance, we saw and were inspired by that effect; the Griffith and Smith volume even includes chapters that were produced collectively, by authors who came to see that the different local sites they had investigated were subject to the same ruling regimes. In my edited collection *People at Work* (DeVault, 2008), I wrote section and chapter introductions that drew out the connections I could see. I recall listening for those connections at the conference. I took note of common vocabularies that appeared in the diverse presentations—words and phrases that struck me as pieces of a managerial discourse. Some were technical terms such as *performance monitoring*, while others were more casual phrases that carried, for example, a common-sense justification for policies designed to shrink funding and services, as in *more bang for the buck*. Since my early research on women's household work, I had been intrigued by Smith's comment that one could find social organization "in the talk" (1987, pp. 187–189); for example, when women told me they felt guilty about their household work. Now, I could see even more clearly that social organization was also carried and transmitted in the talk of policy makers, public sector administrators, and front-line service workers and their supervisors.

Another landmark in this period was a major work on the restructuring of Canadian health care, by Janet Rankin and Marie Campbell (2006), undertaken from the standpoint of nurses. They showed how it was that nurses were coming to think like administrators, thinking of and working toward efficiencies that could sometimes over-ride their best professional judgment. An idea I found particularly helpful was their discussion of the dual-sidedness of organizational concepts; they illustrate, for example, how nurses might use a term such as *quality of care* in two senses, referring to their hands-on work with patients and also to measures of quality that were being used to assess and direct institutional performance. Important ideas about texts were also developed in the discussions at the Toronto workshop on new public management. Smith had written in the *Sociology for People* book about a hierarchy of ruling texts, such that texts developed at higher levels of institutional activity control the more specific texts that direct front-line work. Speaking about that hierarchy, she had begun to refer to regulatory frames and contexts, carried in *boss texts*, that express more general ideological discourses. Participants at the Toronto workshop also worked with the idea of *accountability circuits*—sequences of text and action that were designed not only to direct the actions of subordinates, but also to represent them back to managers so as to make compliance or non-compliance more visible.

The intensive collaborative work of this period focused researchers on neoliberalism and allowed them to see broad changes in the ideas and tools of governance creeping steadily across different sectors, more clearly than would be possible in any single study. The invention of new systems for managing organizations, and the many new technologies designed to implement them, offered a fertile laboratory in which to put governing texts under the IE microscope. As a result, Smith and others began to develop more clearly specified accounts of just how texts manifested their powers.

WORK KNOWLEDGE AND TEXTUAL COORDINATION

Smith's *Institutional Ethnography: A Sociology for People* (2005) provided an elaboration and specification of the IE approach. The book offered two newly conceived versions of IE's analytic tools. First, Smith focuses more sharply on people's work and, importantly, their *work knowledge*. From the earliest sketch of IE, the *generous concept of work* had been fundamental; people living in the everyday/everynight world are to be seen as at work. The 2005 *Sociology for People* book emphasized what those people know: they know how to do their work, and they know how to *gear into* institutions (McCoy, 2008, p. 110, citing Schutz). Sometimes, their knowing comes from a job description, explicit training and instruction, workplace rules or program regulations; sometimes, from more diffuse sources such as a mothering discourse or a discourse of femininity; sometimes, it may be an implicit knowing gained from working with others, as when a secretary comes to understand what does or doesn't go into meeting minutes. There is also, sometimes, unspoken hands-on knowledge, such as the experiential learning that underlies cooking skill, or the coordination of those doing physical work, who see and feel how to move together. The point is that IE researchers can learn about institutional practices not only from descriptions of the work people do, but also from finding out how they learn and know what to do.

A Sociology for People also specified a metaphor useful for analyzing the coordinative power of texts, the idea of a *text-reader conversation*. In developing this idea, Smith returned to some of her early ethnomethodological studies of texts and their consequences, but here for somewhat different purposes. Institutional ethnography is often used to make visible how things happen in organizations, and much of what happens is coordinated by texts. Finding the how of that coordination requires that one see and analyze *texts in action*, rather than as static documents. In a "conversation" with a text, the reader first activates the text, taking up its framing and searching for its sense. Then the reader responds to the text; the response may be internal or may involve some action, perhaps speaking about the text with others, or adding to it somehow, or passing it on. For example, a reader faced with a text billed as an account of someone becoming mentally ill will look for clues to that process, and will likely go on to draw conclusions; a reader who picks up an application form will look to see what it asks, and will perhaps begin to fill it out—or may stare at it in confusion or dismay, and then set it aside. Smith's analysis of a grade appeal procedure in an academic department (2005, pp. 145–149) offers an example of the interplay among actors in the grade appeal process, the policy statement that holds them accountable, and the texts they engage with or produce in order to move the process forward.

Susan Turner (2008) was an important colleague in Smith's conceptual work on texts. Turner's dissertation research took up the issue of citizen input into a local land-use planning dispute, and—because much that was happening was not visible to the public—led her deep into municipal work organization in the various departments of city government. Mapping that organization was challenging but productive; as she learned more, her maps became larger and more complex, and she developed conventions for mapping that allowed her to portray visually the back-and-forth of text and action. Later, Smith and Turner (2014) produced a collection of studies that illustrate IE analyses focused on diverse types of text. While many IE analyses focused on organizational documents designed to organize front-line work activities, Smith and Turner make clear that texts can take many different forms. A text such as an album of wedding photos can coordinate a conversation among friends (McCoy 1995); a musical score coordinates rehearsal and performance (Warren 2014); a software system organizes hospital discharges, sometimes against the better judgment of nurses (Rankin & Campbell, 2014). One creative approach to studying personal documents is Tim Diamond's idea of conducting a "wallet biopsy": he interviews informants about the various cards they carry in order to follow threads of connection into their entitlements and eligibilities in the confusing welter of US healthcare programs and insurance arrangements, and to make visible the work people must do to access benefits. Within organizations, IE researchers find different kinds of texts that are taken up in different places and find that texts operate in different ways. Researchers often focus on texts that coordinate action quite directly (the grade appeal procedure, an application for benefits, a pre-sentencing report); but they may also look for texts whose coordinative force may work in the background, or at a supervisory level (a mission statement, for example, or a budget report [McCoy, 2014]).

Smith's emphasis on textual coordination arose from her interest in the social organization of knowledge and the construction of a documentary reality that threatens to supersede people's everyday knowledge. She also emphasized that texts and documents are the medium of governance in post-industrial capitalism; her writings on the development of the ruling relations (e.g., 1999, Chapter 5) provide an account of the turn away from face-to-face management of commercial enterprises to the bureaucratic modes of coordination that require impersonal forms of record-keeping. And she has argued that one must analyze how texts work in order to see how it is that organizations exist—a question, she notes, that organizational scholars rarely think to ask (Smith, 2001). Paper documents have been central elements of governance; but IE has developed as corporate bureaucracies seem to be giving way to something different, due in part to more data-based managerial strategies and in part to the capacities of new modes of data processing. IE researchers who are studying emergent modes of governance continue to analyze textual coordination as we can see it in online activity, electronic data processing, and software-based administration and controls. And as in the early days of

Smith's social organization of knowledge studies, there are parallels with work in science studies on the social powers of non-human actors.

Working with students and others, Smith had long been developing a repertoire of strategies for text analysis, observing the various ways that texts, and increasingly, digital technologies, could coordinate people's activities. With the concept of the text-reader conversation, she provided a way to think about how a reader takes up a text or screen, and how the conversation governs a person's activity going forward. Like a face-to-face conversation, the text-reader conversation unfolds in time; the idea helps to "get texts going" (Smith, 2005, p. 120), so that one can see how they coordinate action.

Conclusion

My account has emphasized early work on ideological practices and the changes that led to the consolidation of IE as a full sociology—that is, not only a method of inquiry, but also an ontology and epistemology. The developments I've discussed have brought increasing precision to IE analyses, but sometimes I have felt that heightened precision in the analysis of text-based coordination has narrowed our sense of possibilities. In the title for this chapter, I promised an "expansive" IE. What I mean by that is an IE that is informed by the full range of the approach, and that leaves it open to further development. I envision an IE that is freed from any cookbook-like, codified approach (see also Mykhalovskiy, this volume), but is still true to the core insights and strategies found in the literature of IE. That is surely the goal—and the dilemma of institutionalization—for any sociological approach that has come to the point of having its own handbook. My hope is that I may have spurred IE practitioners to gain insight from studying and re-reading the earlier work that has brought us to the current moment, and that can certainly still be of use.

I've named this account a history of North American origins. That naming was first the kind of apologetic qualification we often feel obliged to offer; I needed to make clear that I wrote as a US sociologist, though one who has read and worked in Canadian IE circles for decades, and that my account would not include developments elsewhere. Writing and thinking more deeply, however, I've wanted to acknowledge—even if I don't fully understand—the located character of the approach. That has become more evident as IE has traveled internationally; there are now centers of IE scholarship on several continents, each with its own history and explorations of distinctive ruling relations. Those who are pursuing IE in varied national and regional contexts might be interested to consult an early Smith comment (1975b) on "what it might mean to do a Canadian sociology"; in that essay, she argues that the peculiar practices of conceptually-based sociology transform local circumstances into resources for a generalized discourse of an intelligentsia. By contrast, taking up the everyday world as problematic offers the possibility of inquiry into "how it happens" in a world where people live—always a local world, even if it is connected to and shaped by activities undertaken elsewhere.

As IE has developed and traveled, some scholars have discussed the possibility and desirability of combining IE with other theoretical approaches. I have constructed my account in part to illustrate how Smith's thinking about IE has been located in the intellectual currents of her times; she has been keenly aware of other approaches and has incorporated and contributed to the work of other scholars investigating the social production and organization of knowledge, the social organization of women's lives, and changes in the management and governance of education and the public sector, among other topics. Although she insists that inquiry should begin in everyday life and not in theory, she has always read widely and has been open to learning from research based in other approaches; she has also been very critical of approaches that display the problems she has written of for decades! IE's ontology—its conception of the social—keeps people and their activities always in view; it is people who put the social together. Thus, when I hear scholars arguing that we need "a theory of x" or a "theory of y" to complement an IE analysis, I often feel that what we need is to look more closely at how people *do* "x" or "y." But there certainly may be ways to learn and borrow from related scholarship; the recent collection of work by IE scholars in the Nordic region (Lund & Nilson, 2019) offers promising examples of a "hybrid" approach, in which different perspectives are brought together, but without forcing a synthesis that introduces ontological or epistemological inconsistency.

Dorothy Smith conceived the "ruling apparatus" (1987, pp. 158–161) or "ruling relations" (1999, Chapter 5) as located in time and place. She wrote early on about changes in the ruling relations of North America, as the face-to-face control of life and labor, in an early industrial period, gave way to the bureaucratic governance associated with larger corporate enterprises (Smith, 1985). She drew on socialist feminist writing and the writings of historians to flesh out a picture of how women were situated in ruling relations, differentiating their circumstances by class. Working-class women often labored for pay and also sustained households through their unpaid work. Middle-class women were educated but excluded from positions of power; they were prepared to reproduce their class through child-rearing, supporting their husbands, and undertaking voluntary work on behalf of their class. These accounts did not attend in detail to the related histories of indigenous peoples or people of color in Canada or the US; but IE scholars would, in my view, find it useful to continue developing views of ruling relations that include those histories. Smith also wrote about the implications of bureaucratic governance, as corporations became complex organizations, with power vested in positions rather than people (1999, Chapter 5). The political compromises of North American industrial capitalism, including its welfare "safety net," held for decades, but as corporate powers expanded and global markets developed, neoliberal ideologies took hold, and those changes drove the research that Smith, Griffith, and others were doing on changes in the public sector (Griffith & Smith, 2014).

As I write now, in 2019, it is clear that profound changes are underway. Global capitalism has produced alarming levels of inequality, both within and across nations. Policy makers increasingly view universities as centers and sources of economic value, training grounds producing a nation's workforce with skills to be measured against those of other countries. Technological developments are rapidly changing modes of governance, seemingly replacing human agency with processes based on electronic monitoring and algorithmic action. Migration for work and safety will only increase as climate change puts increasing pressure on the natural environment that sustains us all. Previously excluded, racialized groups—First Nations people and Native Americans, and people of color who are marginalized based on constructions of race/ethnicity and histories of exploitation—are engaged in new resistance movements. And nationalist political groups have risen in anger and protest in North America and elsewhere.

I am confident that the principles and strategies of institutional ethnography can be fruitfully applied to these emerging problems, and equally confident that the approach will continue to grow and change. I look forward to the expansiveness of IE scholarship developed in new places and in response to new challenges. However, I hope that looking to the origins of IE, as I have done here, will underline the two central principles of the approach: first, that it is always people who "put things together"; and second, that one must look beyond the local everyday world to find the coordination of that putting together. It is people living everyday lives—sometimes ourselves—whose puzzles motivate IE inquiries. And IE analyses look to text, discourse, ruling, and so on, but in ways that recognize and reveal how these are taken up and activated by people, whether in homes and communities, as workers in offices and agencies, or in the higher echelons of administration and policy making. IE is a sociology that keeps people in view, and it is the IE focus on social relations—the ways that people gear into the activities of others—that allows us to connect IE analyses and accumulate knowledge that can reveal how ruling works.

Acknowlegements I am grateful beyond words for the pleasures of learning from Dorothy Smith, and for her friendship. I am also thankful to the editors of this volume for their guidance of the overall project and the opportunity to work through these ideas. Eric Mykhalovskiy urged me to sharpen my account and provided comments that inspired and helped me to do that. And my long-time writing partners, Catherine Riessman and Wendy Luttrell, usefully reminded and helped me, as usual, to explain IE terms and ideas more clearly.

REFERENCES

Banerji, H. (1995). Beyond the ruling category to what actually happens: Notes on James Mills' historiography in *The history of British India*. In M. Campbell & A.

Manicom (Eds.), *Knowledge, experience, and ruling relations: Studies in the social organization of knowledge* (pp. 49–64). Toronto: University of Toronto Press.

Bomberry, J., Turner, S. M., & Werner, A. (2018). *Building change on and off-reserve: Six nations of the grand river territory*. Special Workshop for the Institutional Ethnography Thematic Group of the International Sociological Association, July 19, Ryerson University, Toronto.

Bresalier, M., Gillis, L., McClure, C., McCoy, L., Myhalovskiy, E., Taylor, D., & Webber, M. (2002). *Making care visible: Antiretroviral therapy and the health work of people living with HIV/AIDS*. Research report of the Making Care Visible Working Group. Ottawa: Canadian HIV/AIDS Clearinghouse.

Campbell, M. L. (1995). Teaching accountability: What counts as nursing education? In M. Campbell & A. Manicom (Eds.), *Knowledge, experience, and ruling relations: Studies in the social organization of knowledge* (pp. 221–233). Toronto: University of Toronto Press.

Campbell, M. L., & DeVault, M. L. (2011). Dorothy E. Smith. In G. Ritzer & J. Stepnisky (Eds.), *The Wiley-Blackwell companion to major social theorists: Vol. II: Contemporary theorists* (pp. 268–286). Hoboken, NJ: Wiley-Blackwell.

Campbell, M., & Gregor, F. (2002). *Mapping social relations: A primer in doing institutional ethnography*. Toronto: University of Toronto Press.

Campbell, M., & Manicom, A. (1995). *Knowledge, experience, and ruling relations: Studies in the social organization of knowledge*. Toronto: University of Toronto Press.

Clarke, J., & Newman, J. (1997). *The managerial state: Power, politics and ideology in the remaking of social welfare*. London: Sage.

De Montigny, G. A. J. (1995). *Social working: An ethnography of front-line practice*. Toronto: University of Toronto Press.

DeVault, M. L. (1991). *Feeding the family: The social organization of caring as gendered work*. Chicago, IL: University of Chicago Press.

DeVault, M. L. (2000). Producing family time: Practices of leisure activity beyond the home. *Qualitative Sociology, 23*(4), 485–503.

DeVault, M. L. (Ed.). (2008). *People at work: Life, power, and social inclusion in the new economy*. New York, NY: New York University Press.

Diamond, T. (1992). *Making gray gold: Narratives of nursing home care*. Chicago, IL: University of Chicago Press.

Diamond, T. (2008). Participant observation in institutional ethnography. In D. E. Smith (Ed.), *Institutional ethnography as practice* (pp. 45–63). Lanham, MD: Rowman and Littlefield.

Documents and Demonstrations. (n.d.). *AIDS activist history project*. Retrieved from https://aidsactivisthistory.ca/features/george-w-smith/documents-and-demonstrations/.

Eastwood, L. E. (2005). *The social organization of policy: An institutional ethnography of UN forest deliberations*. New York, NY: Routledge.

Eastwood, L. E. (2019). *Negotiating the environment: Civil society, globalization and the UN*. London: Routledge.

Foucault, M. (1979). *The history of sexuality Volume 1: An introduction*. London: Allen Lane.

Frampton, C., Kinsman, G., Thompson, A. K., & Tilleczek, K. (Eds.). (2006). *Sociology for changing the world: Social movements/social research*. Black Point, Nova Scotia: Fernwood.

Garfinkel, H. (1967). *Studies in ethnomethodology*. Englewood Cliffs, NJ: Prentice-Hall.

Grahame, K. M. (1998a). Asian women, job training, and the social organization of immigrant labor markets. *Qualitative Sociology, 21*(1), 75–90.

Grahame, K. M. (1998b). Feminist organizing and the politics of exclusion. *Human Studies, 21*(4), 377–393.

Grahame, K. M. (1999). *State, community, and Asian immigrant women's work: A study in labor market organization*. (Unpublished doctoral dissertation). Ontario Institute for Studies in Education, University of Toronto.

Griffith, A. I. (1995). Mothering, schooling, and children's development. In M. Campbell & A. Manicom (Eds.), *Knowledge, experience, and ruling relations: Studies in the social organization of knowledge* (pp. 108–121). Toronto: University of Toronto Press.

Griffith, A. I., & Andre-Bechely, L. (2008). Institutional technologies: Coordinating families and schools, bodies and texts. In M. L. DeVault (Ed.), *People at work: Life, power, and social inclusion in the new economy* (pp. 40–56). New York, NY: New York University Press.

Griffith, A. I., & Smith, D. E. (1987). Constructing cultural knowledge: Mothering as discourse. In J. Gaskell. & A. McLaren (Eds.), *Women and education: A Canadian perspective* (pp. 87–103). Calgary, AB: Detselig.

Griffith, A. I., & Smith, D. E. (2005). *Mothering for schooling*. New York, NY: RoutledgeFalmer.

Griffith, A. I., & Smith, D. E. (2014). *Under new public management: Institutional ethnographies of changing front-line work*. Toronto: University of Toronto Press.

Jackson, N. (1995). "These things just happen": Talk, text, and curriculum reform. In M. Campbell & A. Manicom (Eds.), *Knowledge, experience, and ruling relations: Studies in the social organization of knowledge* (pp. 164–180). Toronto: University of Toronto Press.

Latour, B., & Woolgar, S. (1979). *Laboratory life: Social construction of scientific facts*. New York, NY: Sage.

Liang, L. (2010). *Constructing migrant care labor: A study of institutional process and the discourse of migration and work*. (Unpublished doctoral dissertation). Syracuse University.

Luken, P. C., & Vaughan, S. (2006). Standardizing childrearing through housing. *Social Problems, 53*(3), 299–331.

Lund, R. W. B., & Nilson, A. C. E. (2019). *Institutional ethnography in the Nordic region*. London: Routledge.

Lynch, M. (1985). *Art and artifact in laboratory science: A study of shop work and shop talk in a research laboratory*. London: Routledge and Kegan Paul.

Manicom, N. (1995). What's health got to do with it? Class, gender, and teachers' work. In M. Campbell & A. Manicom (Eds.), *Knowledge, experience, and ruling relations: Studies in the social organization of knowledge* (pp. 135–148). Toronto: University of Toronto Press.

McCoy, L. (1995). Activating the photographic text. In M. Campbell & A. Manicom (Eds.), *Knowledge, experience, and ruling relations: Studies in the social organization of knowledge* (pp. 181–192). Toronto: University of Toronto Press.

McCoy, L. (2008). Keeping the institution in view: Working with interview accounts of everyday experience. In D. E. Smith (Ed.), *Institutional ethnography as practice* (pp. 109–125). Lanham, MD: Rowman and Littlefield.

McCoy, L. (2014). Producing "what the deans know": Cost accounting and the restructuring of post-secondary education. In D. E. Smith & S. M. Turner (Eds.), *Incorporating texts into institutional ethnographies* (pp. 93–119). Toronto: University of Toronto Press.

Mead, G. H. (1947). *Mind, self, and society: From the perspective of a social behaviorist*. In C. W. Morris (Ed.). Chicago, IL: University of Chicago Press.

Mueller, A. (1995). Beginning in the standpoint of women: An investigation of the gap between *cholas* and "Women in Peru." In M. Campbell & A. Manicom (Eds.), *Knowledge, experience, and ruling relations: Studies in the social organization of knowledge* (pp. 96–107). Toronto: University of Toronto Press.

Mykhalovskiy, E., & McCoy, L. (2010). Troubling ruling discourses of health: Using institutional ethnography in community-based research. *Critical Public Health*, *12*(1), 17–37.

Ng, R. (1995). Multiculturalism as ideology: A textual analysis. In M. Campbell & A. Manicom (Eds.), *Knowledge, experience, and ruling relations: Studies in the social organization of knowledge* (pp. 35–48). Toronto: University of Toronto Press.

Nichols, N. (2014). *Youth work: An institutional ethnography of youth homelessness*. Toronto: University of Toronto Press.

Pence, E. (2001). Safety for battered women in a textually-mediated legal system. *Studies in Cultures, Organizations, and Societies*, *7*(2), 159–198.

Pence, E., with Smith, D. E. (2011). *The institutional analysis: Matching what institutions do with what works for people*. Duluth, MN: Praxis International.

Praxis International. (n.d.). Retrieved from praxisinternational.org.

Rankin, J. M., & Campbell, M. L. (2006). *Managing to nurse: Inside Canada's health care reform*. Toronto: University of Toronto Press.

Rankin, J. M., & Campbell, M. L. (2014). "Three in a bed": Nurses and technologies of bed utilization in a hospital. In D. E. Smith & S. M. Turner (Eds.), *Incorporating texts into institutional ethnographies* (pp. 147–169). Toronto: University of Toronto Press.

Reimer, M. (1995). Downgrading clerical work in a textually-mediated labour process. In M. Campbell & A. Manicom (Eds.), *Knowledge, experience, and ruling relations: Studies in the social organization of knowledge* (pp. 193–208). Toronto: University of Toronto Press.

Renzetti, C., & Hart, B. J. (Eds.). (2010). Special issue on contributions of Ellen Pence. *Violence Against Women*, *16*(9), 979–1060.

Ridzi, F. (2009). *Selling welfare reform: Work-first and the new common sense of employment*. New York, NY: New York University Press.

Schutz, A. (1962). On multiple realities. In M. Natanson (Ed.), *Collected papers I: The problem of social reality* (pp. 207–259). The Hague: Martinus Nijhoff.

Smith, D. E. (1974a). The social construction of documentary reality. *Sociological Inquiry*, *44*(4), 257–268.

Smith, D. E. (1974b). Women's perspective as a radical critique of sociology. *Sociological Inquiry*, *44*(1), 1–13.

Smith, D. E. (1975a.) An analysis of ideological structures and how women are excluded. *Canadian Review of Sociology and Anthropology*, *12*(4, Part I), 252–267.

Smith, D. E. (1975b). What it might mean to do a Canadian sociology: The everyday world as problematic. *The Canadian Journal of Sociology*, *1*(3), 363–376.

Smith, D. E. (1977). *Feminism and marxism: A place to begin, a way to go*. Vancouver, BC: New Star Books.

Smith, D. E. (1978). A peculiar eclipsing: Women's exclusion from men's culture. *Women's Studies International Quarterly, 1*(4), 281–295.
Smith, D. E. (1979). A sociology for women. In J. A. Sherman & E. T. Beck (Eds.), *The prism of sex: Essays in the sociology of knowledge* (pp. 135–187). Madison, WI: University of Wisconsin Press.
Smith, D. E. (1985). Women, class and family. In D. E. Smith & V. Burstyn (Eds.), *Women, class, family and the state* (with an introduction by R. Ng.), (pp. 1–44). Toronto: Garamond.
Smith, D. E. (1987). *The everyday world as problematic: A feminist sociology*. Boston, MA: Northeastern University Press.
Smith, D. E. (1990a). *Conceptual practices of power: A feminist sociology of knowledge*. Boston, MA: Northeastern University Press.
Smith, D. E. (1990b). *Texts, facts, and femininity: Exploring the relations of ruling*. London: Routledge.
Smith, G. W. (1990c). Political activist as ethnographer. *Social Problems, 37*(4), 629–648.
Smith, D. E. (1993). The standard North American family: SNAF as an ideological code. *Journal of Family Issues, 14*(1), 50–65.
Smith, D. E. (1994). A Berkeley education. In K. P. M. Orlans & R. A. Wallace (Eds.), *Gender and the academic experience: Berkeley women sociologists* (pp. 45–56). Lincoln, NE: University of Nebraska Press.
Smith, D. E. (1996). Telling the truth after postmodernism. *Symbolic Interaction, 19*(3), 171–202.
Smith, D. E. (1999). *Writing the social: Critique, theory, and investigations*. Toronto: University of Toronto Press.
Smith, D. E. (2001). Texts and the ontology of organizations and institutions. *Studies in Cultures, Organizations, and Societies, 7*(2), 159–198.
Smith, D. E. (2005). *Institutional ethnography: A sociology for people*. Lanham, MD: Alta Mira.
Smith, D. E. (2006). George Smith, political activist as ethnographer and sociology for people. Foreword, In C. Frampton, G. Kinsman, A. K. Thompson, & K. Tilleczek (Eds.), *Sociology for changing the world: Social movements/social research* (pp. 18–26). Black Point, Nova Scotia: Fernwood.
Smith, D. E., & Smith, G. W. (1990). The job-skills training nexus: Changing context and managerial practice. In J. Muller (Ed.), *Education for work, education as work: Canada's changing community colleges* (pp. 171–196). Toronto: Garamond.
Smith, D. E., & Turner, S. M. (2014). *Incorporating texts into institutional ethnographies*. Toronto: University of Toronto Press.
Stanley, L. (2018). *Dorothy E. Smith, feminist sociology and institutional ethnography*. Edinburgh: X Press.
Turner, S. M. (2008). Mapping institutions as work and texts. In D. E. Smith (Ed.), *Institutional ethnography as practice* (pp. 139–161). Lanham, MD: Rowman and Littlefield.
Ueda, Y. (1995). Corporate wives: Gendered education of their children. In M. Campbell & A. Manicom (Eds.), *Knowledge, experience, and ruling relations: Studies in the social organization of knowledge* (pp. 122–134). Toronto: University of Toronto Press.

Vaughan, S. (2016). *Making institutional change in small ways: Introducing institutional ethnography to first generation university students*. Paper presented at the Third ISA Forum of Sociology, Vienna.

Walker, G. (1990). *Family violence and the women's movement: The conceptual politics of struggle*. Toronto: University of Toronto Press.

Warren, L. D. (2014). Text in performance: The making of a Haydn concerto". In D. E. Smith & S. M. Turner (Eds.), *Incorporating texts into institutional ethnographies* (pp. 120–146). Toronto: University of Toronto Press.

Zimmerman, D. H. (1974). Fact as a practical accomplishment. In R. Turner (Ed.), *Ethnomethodology: Selected readings* (pp. 128–143). Harmondsworth: Penguin.

CHAPTER 3

Materialist Matters: A Case for Revisiting the Social Ontology of Institutional Ethnography

Liza McCoy

Institutional ethnography has an explicit ontology that focuses researchers' attention on the materiality of people's lives and the socially organized practices of coordination that shape the conditions that people encounter. In this chapter, I discuss the main elements of institutional ethnography's ontology, as I understand it and as it informs my approach to research. I argue that renewed attention to the ontology can serve as a springboard for extending the way institutional ethnographies are done, and I offer suggestions for how a refreshed sense of this ontology might inform new strategies and expose new empirical fields for institutional ethnographic analysis.

SOCIAL ONTOLOGY AND SOCIAL INQUIRY

Ontology is a branch of philosophy concerned with the study of being, that is, systematic reflection on the nature and processes of what can be known to exist. The field of *social* ontology in philosophy focuses attention on the entities and processes of human beings. Over in the social sciences, ontological questions are not the main object of thought, but ontological assumptions do provide a necessary foundation for empirical inquiry. If you are going to investigate some set of affairs you consider part of something social, then it helps to have a clear sense of what this social involves—and to be able to reflect critically on the conceptual language used to name and describe it.

L. McCoy (✉)
Department of Sociology, University of Calgary, Calgary, AB, Canada
e-mail: mccoy@ucalgary.ca

© The Author(s) 2021
P. C. Luken and S. Vaughan (eds.), *The Palgrave Handbook of Institutional Ethnography*,
https://doi.org/10.1007/978-3-030-54222-1_3

It is in this sense that the term social ontology is used in the social sciences to designate any specific framework of ontological assumptions that underlie a given approach to social research.

Social structure, social roles, social relations, norms, values, habitus, field, attitudes, meaning, agency, and assemblage: each of these terms posits a social entity or process and trails with it a set of assumptions about how the social comes about and its characteristics. These assumptions shape what will be brought into view for study and the kinds of analytic claims that can be generated. Much of the time, however, ontological assumptions in social research are implicit and go unexamined, and researchers' sense of social being remains inchoate, provided primarily by the language they have learned for writing authoritatively in their field, which commits them to an underlying ontology they may never have considered as such.

Institutional ethnography is one project of inquiry that does have an explicitly formulated social ontology. Dorothy Smith has discussed ontological matters in all of her books, from her earliest critiques of mainstream sociology through to her development of an alternative sociology she came to call institutional ethnography (e.g., Smith, 1987, 1999, 2005). Her 2005 book devotes an entire chapter to "Designing an ontology for institutional ethnography." She calls this a "modest" social ontology (2005, p. 52) whose purpose is to ground and focus inquiry that can show people how their/our world is put together to happen as it does; that is, it has been developed to orient researchers engaged in the analytic project of institutional ethnography.

The Social Ontology of Institutional Ethnography

> Individuals are there [in time and place]; they are in their bodies; they are active; and what they're doing is coordinated with the doings of others. That is the four-part package that is foundational to the institutional ethnographic project. (Smith, 2005, p. 59)

One sentence, and easy to remember: the social ontology of institutional ethnography in a nutshell. I have added the time and place part, which Smith did not include in this formulation, although she does point out a few pages earlier that social processes go on "in time and place" (p. 52), and this can be taken as specification of what "are there" means. As I will go on to argue, keeping the *thereness* of coordinated activity in view is important for guiding fuller accounts of institutional processes as well as extending the reach of institutional ethnographic research.

This is a decidedly materialist ontology, in the sense of starting with attention to what is materially there, that is, from people and what they do, rather than from ideas about people, or even their ideas about themselves. This is what Marx and Engels mean when they propose a materialist method and outline its first premises in a famous passage (which Smith is obliquely referencing):

> The premises from which we begin are not arbitrary ones, not dogmas, but real premises from which abstraction can only be made in the imagination. They are the real individuals, their activity and the material conditions under which they live, both those which they find already existing and those produced by their activity. (Marx & Engels, 1970, p. 42)

Marx and Engels contrast this materialist approach with an idealist approach, one that begins from a priori abstract concepts or treats people's ideas about the world as the decisive force in their lives. The target of their criticism is the writing of some of their contemporary philosophers, but a sociological version from the same period can be found in the work of Auguste Comte (1893), who posits three universal stages of human societal development defined by the modes of knowing dominant in each stage. Of course, Marx and Engels are very interested in the ways people know their world (as is Smith), but they argue that this is, ontologically, the wrong place to start. Ideas are generated by people who are engaged in doing definite things; they are part of that doing. Therefore, it is necessary to start from real people and their activity, as it arises within particular material conditions, which include the natural and built environments as well as the relations among people through which their lives and doings are organized.

It is important to note that while Smith expresses the four parts of the ontology in a sequence, starting with "individuals [being] there," this must not be understood as positing a temporal process in which individuals precede the social. As George Herbert Mead (1934), another of Smith's sources for this ontology, wrote,

> [Individual] selves must be accounted for in terms of the social process, and in terms of communication; and individuals must be brought into essential relation within that process before communication, or the contact between the minds of different individuals, becomes possible. The body is not a self, as such; it becomes a self only when it has developed a mind within the context of social experience. (pp. 49–50)

Mead's point is that it is an ontological mistake to suggest that individual minds and selves come together in some way to make the social. It is the other way around: we have our individual minds and selves (that is, certain kinds of mental processes and ways of viewing ourselves as the objects of our reflection) because we develop them through our immersion from infancy in social experience with other people, and a key part of this is learning language. Mind for Mead is an "individual importation of a social process" (1934, p. 186) and involves an ongoing internal conversation which, says Mead, we learn to do as children *after* and *because* we start learning to communicate with other people.

Mind and self are relationally developed, as well as being the ongoing capacities that allow us to participate in coordinative relations with other people, to, in Mead's terms, *adjust ourselves* to one another (p. 75). This constant adjustment goes on through communication, which can be both gestural and symbol-based (i.e., language).

The ontology expressed by Smith starts with embodied individuals, but insists we must always see these individuals relationally, not just in terms of what they observably do with other people, but in terms of the socially acquired selves and resources (e.g., language and conceptual frameworks) they bring to this coordinated activity and which are also continually shaped by that activity.

In this ontology, the social happens in the ongoing, coordinated, mutually adjusted activity of people. This is a view that emphasizes the social as a process rather than an entity composed of, but separate from, individuals and their doings. This latter view is well established in sociology by way of conceptualizations in which social structure is contrasted with individual agency. Positing the social as a more-or-less crystallized *something* exterior to individuals has a long history in sociological thought (e.g., Durkheim, 1964). For Smith, the social *is* the ongoing coordinating itself, not a thing-like by-product of it (e.g., society or social structure or social facts). We can see this social-as-coordination and examine it by starting, as the ontology does, with definite people in definite places doing things that are in some discoverable way organized. How do individuals take part in that ongoing coordination—and how does it shape the possibilities for them and their experience? How are they active and how do they come to be positioned within that coordinating of their and other people's activity?

Here it will be useful to pause and consider some of the terms used in Smith's formulation of the ontology. The reference to individuals being active is best understood as pointing to the full range of human doing: not just physically observable activity or interaction with people or other animals, but thinking and feeling and other activities of consciousness, as well as the deliberate withholding of outward action. It also includes the learned, habituated doing that much of the time happens below the level of an individual's awareness. This element of the ontology corresponds to the orienting concept of *work* in institutional ethnographic research, which draws investigative attention to the kinds of physical or mental effort and acquired skill involved in whatever people might be doing, as well as the ways that doing is evoked by and gears into the doings of others.

The notion of what people do being "coordinated with the doings of other people" also requires consideration and elaboration. There are many ways that this coordination happens. There are the often-intricate physical and verbal mutual adjustments of people who are co-present[1] to each other in some way (e.g., walking on crowded city pavements, dancing in a community hall, talking in person or on the phone, fighting outside a bar, conducting a medical examination, working together in a busy restaurant kitchen). This kind of verbal and physical coordination has been studied by Goffman (1971), ethnomethodologists, and conversation analysts, while ethnographic researchers have offered detailed accounts of interaction and practice in local settings, such as workplaces, schools, and neighborhoods. But what people observably do or experience in one local setting is often shaped by and oriented toward what people have done, are doing, or will do in other settings. Language is one of the main ways this occurs because language is integral to consciousness and language in written form (or in oral transmission) can connect up activity in diverse times and places; this also happens with other kinds of symbolic material, such as images and written numerals. The coordination of people's activities, in other words, does not require co-presence (or even technologically facilitated co-presence) because it can be mediated by exteriorized symbolic material and, more broadly, by the built environment and human-made things. People in one setting activate textual and symbolic objects created elsewhere; the buildings they inhabit and the things they use, which bear the traces of the past activity that created them, also coordinatively shape the possibilities for what people can do.

In sociology it is common to refer to the contemporary social world, taken as an object of analysis, as a matter of levels: micro, meso, and macro, like a three-dimensional chess game, with sharp but vaguely defined leaps between one board and the next. The ontology of institutional ethnography, however, avoids the metaphor of levels, recognizing that we are always in our bodies in some locality, but that what happens in that setting is often connected into extended chains of action—social relations—that reach forward and back in time, and extend geographically. Texts, symbolic objects, and the products of human activity mediate these chains of coordinated action, especially so as human social organization and forms of rule based in distinctive and constantly evolving contemporary modes of knowledge (e.g., big data), have become more complex, more dispersed, digitally circulated, and global in reach.

To speak of people coordinating their doings, locally or trans-locally, is most emphatically *not* to posit a state of comfortable collaboration, smooth functioning, or willing participation in purposes everyone fully understands. Collaborative attempts to do things often fail or produce unintended troubles. Violence, domination, and other power relations occur through forms of coordinated human practice. People's ordinary activities contribute to processes of large-scale coordination and rule (e.g., capitalism) that they might not fully understand and that do not operate in their interests. Participation (willing or otherwise) in coordinating/coordinated relations regularly produces difference, whether this is the difference of perspective that necessarily arises because we are never exactly in the same position as another person, physically or biographically, or the kinds of inequality produced through systematic relations of exclusion, domination, racialization, class, gender, and economic exploitation. Investigating concerns arising from such forms of oppression is often a goal in institutional ethnography; the ontology directs us to explore how they come about through the embodied, emplaced, and trans-locally coordinated activities of people. This demands an "ontological shift" (Deveau, 2009; G.W. Smith, 1990) away from explaining specific experiences of discrimination primarily in terms of attitudes, ideas, or abstract concepts; instead, by examining empirically what people are actually doing and how it is trans-locally organized, researchers can contribute practically useful information to activist projects aimed at making effective change.

Summary:

An ontological recognition of the social as occurring through the concerted and symbolically mediated activities of people engaged in locally situated practices is shared by neighboring projects of research, such as ethnomethodology and symbolic interactionism. What is particular to institutional ethnography is the expanded sense of coordinated doing to include—and to highlight for examination—coordination across time and place, with an emphasis on what Smith calls relations of ruling, which can also be understood as extended relations of administrative control or domination. This is foundational to the project of institutional ethnography as a method of inquiry for investigating modes of coordination that operate trans-locally, occurring through chains of action and conceptual practices by means of which what people do in one local setting is represented, known, and coordinated with what people do in others. For many institutional ethnographers, the warrant for this kind of investigation is a politically engaged interest in accurately knowing some distinct set of practices in order to help change them. I argue below that a refreshed consideration of the ontology of institutional ethnography can open more ways to pursue this focus through an expanded sense of how coordination and rule might be occurring; at the same time, it can also support a widened scope of institutional ethnographic research, bringing into view a broader range of socially organized forms of coordination and embodied, emplaced doing. Both of these expansions will contribute to the continuing vigor and innovation of institutional ethnographic research.

THREE IMPLICATIONS OF REVISITING THE ONTOLOGY FOR DOING INSTITUTIONAL ETHNOGRAPHY, WITH RELATED SUGGESTIONS

Investigate with a Broad Awareness of How Coordination Occurs

It is not uncommon to encounter descriptions of institutional ethnography along the lines that IE studies texts or text-mediated relations of rule; I have written such statements myself. This is certainly accurate as a description of what most institutional ethnographic research has done, and it also accurately reflects the emphasis in Smith's own writing and her continuing interest in the characteristic forms of knowledge and text-based conceptual practices associated with administration/rule/domination in contemporary life. But when we go back to the ontology—people in bodies, in time and place, doing things that are coordinated with what other people are doing—we might begin not by asking where are the texts, but by asking, what are people doing and how is all this coordinated? We will most probably find texts in settings shaped by relations of governance, administration, professional knowledge and media discourse, but we may also find things and places that mediate the operative modes of knowledge and figure significantly in the practices we want to explore.

As a teacher and mentor, I am sometimes asked by students conducting institutional ethnographic research if something or other can be called a text. For example, one student doing observation noticed staff orienting to a kind of instrument display panel as they did their work; another student observed that clocks and timepieces were important to the people in her research setting. These things involve symbolic material (lights, numbers), and they are clearly part of trans-locally coordinated work processes. But to subsume them into the category of texts in the context of analytic description would be to cancel some of their distinctive specificity and deflect attention from how they work.

We need to be able to recognize and describe coordination, both local and trans-local, as it actually happens. Institutional ethnographers are skilled at investigating and mapping text-based, conceptual practices of rule, and this remains a central feature of IE analysis, because such forms of coordination are central in the organization of our contemporary world. But trans-local coordination also happens through places and things, many of which are designed precisely in order to evoke, direct, or limit people's activities and modes of consciousness. Think about the way smart phones as physical devices, together with the algorithms substructing their textual contents, organize our attention and produce it as a saleable commodity. Think about the way buildings and the design of public spaces shape our possibilities for action, inviting some uses and discouraging others, particularly for people whose use of public space is seen by those with more power as troublesome or unsightly (e.g., teenagers, homeless people). There is always a lot going on in any setting or set of institutional processes, and what to pay attention to is necessarily a matter of choice in relation to which aspects are of most concern to understand within a project of institutional ethnography. But it is invigorating to approach research with an ontological orientation that opens the possibility of discovering the range of ways that trans-local relations are coordinated, reach into local settings, and leave material traces there.

This point has two implications for doing institutional ethnography. First, in order to discover other-than-textual modes of coordination, or to explore more fully the embodied and emplaced aspects of text-mediated relations, it is helpful to do observational research where possible. A book that many continue to find inspiring is Tim Diamond's (1992) account of front-line care work in a nursing home. Diamond makes the analytic point that the lived experiences of care workers and residents take shape within a particular way of funding and administering nursing home care, and that the mandated documentary procedures (e.g., charting) poorly represent what the work really involves; in fact, they disrupt the doing of care work in ways that do not help either the care workers or the residents. This is a familiar line of institutional ethnographic analysis. But what also stays with the reader are the descriptions of the bodily and emotional work of care, the detailed, vivid accounts of places, things, conversations, events, and practices which Diamond is able to write because, to do this research, he entered nursing homes as an employee, a low-paid health care aide, participating in and subject to the relations he wished to investigate. (This kind of semi-covert observation would, however, probably not be possible in today's world of institutionalized research ethics oversight.) Michael Corman (2017) studied the social organization of emergency medical work by riding along for months with paramedic teams who welcomed his presence as a researcher. He focusses on the bodily and equipment-mediated work of emergency medical care as it intersects with the use of a new electronic patient record accessed through a hand-held device. He describes in detail the configuration of the ambulance as a workspace and the kinds of adjustment required by the introduction of a new type of ambulance unit. To get this kind of ethnographic richness, the researcher first needs to be where things are happening—but also, once on site, to be able to notice, and then describe in field notes, what people (including the researcher) are doing, and where and with what they are doing it. (See Diamond's [2006] argument for doing participant observation in institutional ethnography.)

Second, we can see from these examples that it is not necessary to borrow from actor network studies (Latour, 2005) or theories of a new materialism (Coole & Frost, 2010) in order to obtain the warrant to examine the material places and things that are involved in the coordination of local and trans-local relations. There may not be a ready conceptual language in institutional ethnography or a wealth of examples, but the warrant, I am arguing, is already in IE's materialist ontology (see also the discussion in Corman & Barron, 2018). This does not mean there is no reason to engage with actor network studies or the emerging literature associated with the "material turn" in social research, to learn from researchers working in those areas, and to consider the differences as well as convergences between these projects and institutional ethnography. But I hope to see this done from a strong understanding of what is already in IE's cupboard. I am eager to see the ways that institutional ethnographers can activate that potential in the ontology and bring more bodies, places, and things into our studies of trans-local relations, in ways that are rooted in the ontology and analytic project of institutional ethnography. Doing so from an IE ("old materialism"?) approach could offer something of value to the evolving conversation about "new materialist" modes of investigation.

Broaden the Range of Trans-Local Relations and Modes of Knowledge Identified for Investigation

Returning to the ontology as a ground for the project of institutional ethnography can serve as a springboard for extending inquiry into zones of practice not hitherto examined. To date, institutional ethnography has been most actively taken up by researchers in professional practice disciplines and among those whose research interests are in the areas of health, education, international development, immigration, and social services. Much of my own research has been in these areas. But it seems to me that the rich vein of research in these areas has been accompanied by a narrowing of investigative scope over time. Newcomers to institutional ethnography learn about it from the published studies they encounter, and this plays a role in shaping how they view the world as potentially researchable in an institutional ethnographic way. Those whose interests fall outside the empirical areas often researched in institutional ethnography may come to see it as a project that cannot encompass what they want to explore (see the chapter by Mykhalovskiy and others, this Handbook). But if we go back to the ontology and think about all the things people do that occur within relations of trans-local coordination, we can see how an institutional ethnographic approach might illuminate a broader swath of social practice.

Here are a few examples. In the late 1980s, when I was studying what was then still called the social organization of knowledge (see chapter by Marjorie DeVault, this Handbook), I saw in this project an exciting way to analyze photographic representation (a strong interest of mine) and I went on to study peoples' practices of making and using wedding photographs (McCoy, 1995). Leanne Warren saw the potential for analyzing how the text of a musical score is activated by an ensemble of chamber musicians (Warren, 2014). Warren and I were both students in classes with Dorothy Smith; the possibilities we saw to take this approach in new directions became visible to us in dialogue with her, and she was enthusiastic about what we were doing. Most institutional ethnographic studies are animated by social justice concerns, but as these examples show, it is not necessary that every IE study investigate social relations that cause people problems. From an institutional ethnographic perspective, any ontologically consistent study that contributes to our collective understanding of everyday experience and extended social relations is useful. To my knowledge, however, these are the only published works in the institutional ethnographic corpus focussed on artistic or cultural practices, although such practices certainly occur within trans-local relations of coordination. Some other less-trodden paths explored by institutional ethnographers have included whale watching and the social organization of visual practice (Grahame, 2018), organic farming certification (Warner, 2014), and historical advertisements for homes (Luken & Vaughan, 2005).

Researchers in professional practice disciplines are understandably committed to conducting research relevant to their practice fields, and activist-researchers understandably wish to investigate ruling relations into which they hope to intervene more effectively. Institutional ethnography as a project of inquiry and as an international community is particularly accessible to researchers from these locations. My hope is that we can maintain this strength while also inspiring researchers interested in exploring experience and institutional relations in areas such as media, science, religion, art, commerce, informational technology, and design, to name just a few. I am aware of several current research projects that are taking institutional ethnography into new territory,[2] and I look forward to seeing this work reach publication. Our collective sense of what can be done with institutional ethnography is stretched with every new study that pushes out the boundaries while remaining grounded in the shared ontology and analytic project.

Revisit the Ontology as a Strong Base for Projects of Dialogue and Critique

A refreshed sense of the ontology can also serve to inform both internal critique and engagement with other projects of inquiry. Institutional ethnography is not a closed system; it can and needs to develop as a shared project through critique and the incorporation of new ideas, as well as through the innovations of researchers. Some researchers have contributed critical reflections to the literature of institutional ethnography, considering inconsistencies they have identified (e.g., Walby, 2007), or seeking to expand IE through engagement with concepts or theories from other approaches (e.g., Reid, 2018). A strong grasp of the fundamentals of institutional ethnography, including the ontology, is an important resource for developing and evaluating such projects. With such a grasp, a researcher can assess or adjust the ontological compatibility of concepts drawn from other approaches. For example, Smith makes the point that Marx's theoretical language is always relational (Smith, 2005, p. 60). His analytic concepts, such as *commodity*, point toward relations among people (e.g., in IE terms, coordinated activity, both local and trans-local). Thus, when exploring concepts or research strategies from other approaches, an institutional ethnographer with a strong working knowledge of the ontology might consider whether they are consistent with an ontological emphasis on the social as relational process. How do such concepts contribute to the project of investigating social processes as they occur through the concerted activities of people who are always in bodies, time, and place? I believe that institutional ethnographers engaged in dialogue with other theories and projects should be able to make an ontological case for whichever borrowings or hybrids result from that encounter. In this way, the continuing development of institutional ethnography will spring from and replenish a strong core.

CONCLUSION

In this chapter I have presented my take on the ontology that informs the project of institutional ethnography. I have made three suggestions, which I argue follow from and depend on a strong engagement with the ontology: (1) Recognize the different ways that coordination happens, and do more observational research that can attend to the built environment and material emplacement of embodied human lives; (2) Go off the beaten path and examine coordinative relations in fields of practice not yet explored through institutional ethnography; (3) Ground projects of dialogue and critique in a supple knowledge of the ontology and its relationship to the IE project. One final suggestion still needs to be made: (Re)read Smith's chapter on ontology in her 2005 book and establish (or revisit) your own relationship with this ontology. What possibilities for new directions does it open for you?

Notes

1. In contemporary society, co-presence is increasingly mediated by technology, such as mobile phones, Skype, Zoom, and the like. I am considering as a form of co-presence any way that people can be in a position to engage in real-time, mutual adjustment. It is probably most useful to think of this on a continuum. Texting can function as real-time communication or with delays in reading and responding. Many people make and send photographs to their friends in real time, eliciting real-time comments that then enter into their further doing and photographing. It is quite common nowadays for people to be in situations where they are physically co-present to some people and technologically co-present to others.
2. For example, Hasmik Tovmasyan (personal communication) is studying the way institutionalized commemorative practices and shared narratives of the 1915 Armenian Genocide work coordinatively to organize the international community of diaspora Armenians.

References

Comte, A. (1893). *The positive philosophy of Auguste Comte* (H. Martineau, Trans.). London: Kegan, Paul, Teench, Teubnee and Co.

Coole, D., & Frost, S. (2010). *New materialisms: Ontology, agency, and politics.* Durham, NC: Duke University Perss.

Corman, M. K. (2017). *Paramedics on and off the streets: Emergency medical services in the age of technological governance.* Toronto: University of Toronto Press.

Corman, M. K., & Barron, G. R. S. (2018). Institutional ethnography and actor-network theory: In dialogue. In J. Reid & L. Russell (Eds.), *Perspectives on and from institutional ethnography* (pp. 49–70). Bingley, UK: Emerald Publishing.

Deveau, J. L. (2009). Examining the institutional ethnographer's toolkit. *Socialist Studies/Etudes Socialistes, 4*(2), 1–20. https://doi.org/10.18740/S4F60Z.

Diamond, T. (1992). *Making gray gold: Narratives of nursing home care.* Chicago, IL: University of Chicago Press.

Diamond, T. (2006). "Where did you get that fur coat, Fern?" Participant observation in institutional ethnography. In D. E. Smith (Ed.), *Institutional ethnography as practice* (pp. 45–63). Lanham, MD: Rowman & Littlefield.

Durkheim, E. (1964). *The rules of sociological method* (S. A. Solovay & J. H. Mueller, Trans.). New York: The Free Press.

Goffman, E. (1971). *Relations in public: Microstudies of the public order*. New York, NY: Basic Books.

Grahame, P. (2018). Looking at whales: Narration and the organization of visual experience. *Journal of Contemporary Ethnography, 47*(6), 782–806.

Latour, B. (2005). *Reassembling the social*. Oxford: Oxford University Press.

Luken, P. C., & Vaughan, S. (2005). "… be a genuine homemaker in your own home": Gender and familial relations in state housing practices, 1917–1922. *Social Forces, 83*, 1603–1626.

Marx, K., & Engels, F. (1970). The German ideology. C. J. Arthur (Ed.). New York, NY: International Publishers.

McCoy, L. (1995). Activating the photographic text. In M. Campbell & A. Manicom (Eds.), *Knowledge, experience and ruling relations: Studies in the social organization of knowledge* (pp. 181–192). Toronto: University of Toronto Press.

Mead, G. H. (1934). Mind, self and society from the standpoint of a social behaviorist. C. W. Morris (Ed.). Chicago, IL: University of Chicago Press.

Reid, J. (2018). Standpoint: Using Bourdieu to understand IE and the researcher's relation with knowledge generation. In J. Reid & L. Russell (Eds.), *Perspectives on and from institutional ethnography* (pp. 71–90). Bingley, UK: Emerald Publishing.

Smith, D. E. (1987). *The everyday world as problematic: A feminist sociology*. Toronto: University of Toronto Press.

Smith, D. E. (1999). *Writing the social: Critique, theory, and investigations*. Toronto: University of Toronto Press.

Smith, D. E. (2005). *Institutional ethnography: A sociology for people*. Lanham, MD: AltaMira.

Smith, G. W. (1990). Political activist as ethnographer. *Social Problems, 37*(4), 629–648.

Walby, K. (2007). On the social relations of research: A critical assessment of institutional ethnography. *Qualitative Inquiry, 13*(7), 1008–1030.

Warner, K. (2014). Regulating the alternative: Certifying organic farming on Vancouver Island, British Columbia. In D. E. Smith & S. M. Turner (Eds.), *Incorporating texts into institutional ethnographies* (pp. 41–63). Toronto: University of Toronto Press.

Warren, L. D. (2014). Text in performance: The making of a Haydn concerto. In D. E. Smith & S. M. Turner (Eds.), *Incorporating texts into institutional ethnographies* (pp. 120–146). Toronto: University of Toronto Press.

CHAPTER 4

Teaching Institutional Ethnography as an Alternative Sociology

Eric Mykhalovskiy, Colin Hastings, Leigha Comer, Julia Gruson-Wood, and Matthew Strang

Institutional ethnography (IE) begins from the standpoint of people's everyday experiences. It explores how what people do in given local settings is coordinated with what other people are doing at different times and in different places. While the specific character, empirical sites, and concerns of institutional ethnographic inquiries vary, a recurring focus is the critique of objectifying discourses of knowledge, particularly as they are brought forward

E. Mykhalovskiy (✉) · L. Comer
Department of Sociology, York University, Toronto, Canada
e-mail: ericm@yorku.ca

L. Comer
e-mail: leigha1@yorku.ca

C. Hastings
Department of Sociology and Anthropology, Concordia University, Montreal, Canada
e-mail: colin.hastings@mail.concordia.ca

J. Gruson-Wood
Department of Family Relations & Applied Nutrition, University of Guelph, Guelph, Canada
e-mail: jgrusonw@uoguelph.ca

M. Strang
Institute for Better Health, Trillium Health Partners, Toronto, Canada
e-mail: Matthew.strang@thp.ca

© The Author(s) 2021
P. C. Luken and S. Vaughan (eds.), *The Palgrave Handbook of Institutional Ethnography*,
https://doi.org/10.1007/978-3-030-54222-1_4

through texts and text-mediated relations. Institutional ethnographers empirically explore how our worlds are "put together," with a characteristic emphasis on how our lives and experiences are shaped by the activities of government, management, the professions, and other constituents of the relations that govern us.

From its beginning articulation as a sociology for women (Smith, 1987), institutional ethnography has broadened and become a sociology for people (Smith, 2005). A recent scan of institutional ethnographic research identified studies being carried out in over 16 countries exploring ruling practices at multiple empirical sites including heath care, social services, higher education, international migration, policing, and economic policy, among others (McCoy, Mykhalovskiy, & Gruson-Wood, 2017). A particular feature of the expansion of institutional ethnography is its uptake in disciplinary sites outside of sociology, particularly nursing, health sciences, education, and social work. While we view this as a welcome development, we are concerned about the fate of IE within the disciplinary space that is its intellectual origin—sociology.

In this chapter we respond to that concern by writing about the possibilities and challenges of teaching IE in the context of graduate sociological education. Our goal is to strengthen discourse about teaching IE as an alternative sociology. While there is a large corpus of published institutional ethnographic research and considerable discussion of IE as a research practice (DeVault & McCoy, 2012; McCoy, 2006; Mykhalovskiy & McCoy, 2002; Rankin, 2017; Smith, 2006; Smith & Turner, 2014), much less has been written about teaching IE (although see Mykhalovskiy & Church, 2006; Naples, 2009; Rankin, Doyle, Waters, Fast, & Pomerleau, 2016; Vaughan, 2016). This chapter is structured as a dialogue that combines the perspectives of students and a course director involved in a graduate course on IE taught in the Graduate Program in Sociology at York University in Toronto, Canada. Our chapter is not meant to be a "how to" guide to teaching IE. Rather, we aim to surface some of the key tensions and challenges encountered in teaching and learning IE in the particular institutional context from which we write, as well as our responses to them, with the hope that doing so might stimulate further thought about how to integrate IE into graduate sociology education elsewhere. Our dialogue about teaching addresses the following issues: positioning IE as an alternative sociology; the role of theory in IE; orthodoxy and IE's relationship to other research approaches; and IE, politics, and critique.

INSTITUTIONAL CONTEXT

This chapter is grounded in experiences of teaching and learning IE in a graduate course that Mykhalovskiy has taught intermittently at York University over the past 15 years (hereafter the IE course). We draw on discussions we had over a series of meetings in the spring of 2019 about two occasions when the IE course was taught (in 2012 and 2015). While the chapter is not an institutional ethnography of teaching and learning IE, we are mindful of how our own experiences have taken shape within a particular set of institutional relations that organize how university-based graduate education is done.

One of our key assumptions is that a robust future for IE within the discipline of sociology relies on creating conditions which permit IE to be taught and learned within the academy. We recognize that scholars teach and learn about IE in various ways, including through conferences and the informal networks that arise out of them, structured workshops, and individual mentorship. In this chapter, we focus on teaching and learning IE through an organizational form familiar to scholars who work in university settings in North America—the graduate course. Graduate courses fulfill particular curricular requirements. They follow a standardized format often involving classes of a particular length of time that are scheduled on a regular, often weekly basis, for a set duration, such as 12 weeks. Graduate courses have particular objectives and are typically organized in terms of topics and associated texts that students are expected to read and discuss during class time. Most often, students are required to complete particular written assignments and are evaluated for their work.

York's Graduate Program in Sociology is one of the largest in Canada and has a reputation for encouraging critical, theoretically-engaged scholarship. The program attracts students with varied substantive, theoretical, and methodological interests. The broader institutional context shaping the IE course is one of declining resources committed to graduate education, few opportunities for teaching graduate sociology courses, and considerable competition among graduate students for "good grades" that play an important role in applications for scholarships that are increasingly required to complete the degree in a timely manner, while maintaining a standard of living above the poverty line.

The IE course fulfills students' methods course requirement and falls under the generic course title "Selected Topics in Empirical Methods."[1] The content of the Selected Topics course changes depending upon who teaches the course in a given year. Previous iterations have focused on narrative analysis strategies and community-based research. When the course is taught with a focus on IE, it attracts students who are interested in fulfilling a methods requirement and whose specific interest in IE may vary considerably. Only a minority of the students who have taken the IE course have gone on to conduct full-scale institutional ethnographic research. The integration of IE into York's sociology graduate curriculum as part of methodological training can produce particular expectations and understandings of IE among faculty and students. In order to mitigate against an overly narrow "methodological" orientation to IE, the course includes readings from Smith's broader oeuvre as well as her writings on IE, readings that help to locate IE as a practice of sociology,[2] and more standard methodological fare including readings on interviewing and observations, working with texts, doing analysis, and research ethics.

IE AS AN ALTERNATIVE SOCIOLOGY

IE is perhaps best understood as an approach to sociology rather than a method of inquiry in a narrow sense. Framing IE as an alternative sociology is a common rhetorical trope that traces back to how Smith (1987) describes the emerging project of IE as an alternative to the sociology she was exposed to as a University of California Berkeley graduate student. There are a number of defining features that distinguish IE as an approach to sociology. Among the most significant are developing inquiry from people's actual experiences, rather than from disciplinary concepts and categories; a materialist ontology of the social that concentrates on what people actually do and how their activities are concerted translocally; and commitment to exploring the social organization of text-mediated relations through which contemporary societies are governed, particularly as those relations are produced in what people do. As Smith (2002) puts it:

> Institutional ethnography's radical move as a sociology is that of pulling the organization of the trans- or extra-local ruling relations–bureaucracy, the varieties of text-medicated discourse, the state, the professions, and so on–into the actual sites of people's living where we have to find them as local and temporally situated activities. (p. 19)

Describing IE as alternative sociology presumes a more or less stable version of established sociology against which IE stands as an alternative. Since Smith's early writings, various approaches to social inquiry have been proposed that make claims to be significantly different from the objectifying forms of sociology that dominated the North American landscape in the 1960s and 1970s. These include, among others, relational sociology, actor-network theory, situational analysis, critical realism, critical race studies, postcolonial studies, and feminist sociologies. One might argue that there are important resonances between IE and some of these approaches. For example, IE, situational analysis (Clarke, Friese, & Washburn, 2018), and the governmentality tradition in sociology (Burchell, Gordon, & Miller, 1991) share a common concern with discourse, language, and representation. Translocal processes are not a concern of IE alone, but appear as objects of analysis for global ethnographies (Burawoy, Blum, George, Gille, & Thayer, 2000; Marcus, 1995) and relational sociologies (Depelteau, 2018). While the recent proliferation of alternative sociologies might suggest the need for a more nuanced and complex differentiation between IE and other approaches to sociology, we are mindful of the ongoing specificity of IE as an intellectual project. In our experiences of teaching and learning IE at York, an environment where students are routinely exposed to novel theoretical and methodological approaches to social inquiry, IE continues to represent an alternative to what students typically know to do. Eric recalls:

I've taught the IE course on five occasions. While each year has brought different experiences and challenges, I've found that students, despite their exposure to all manner of alternative approaches to sociological inquiry, find IE's ontology of the social hard to grasp. The idea that sociology can be about understanding the world as it is actually put together in people's concerted activities is something almost entirely foreign to them.

As Matthew suggests, the shift toward studying social organization can open up new ways of approaching sociology.

I came to the IE course looking for a different way to do sociology. I had been disenchanted with other critical sociologies where I found I lost sight of people. Some of those other forms of sociology seemed to prioritize critique in ways that left me unsatisfied and thinking "ok and now what?" Despite this priming before the course, I struggled in the beginning. In many ways, IE countered what I had learned about how to do research. In the course, I was encouraged to "bracket" my previous understanding of sociological concepts and theories. It felt a bit like many of the intellectual tools I possessed could not be wielded within this framework. I think the lightbulb moment occurred when I realized that IE's focus is not on people themselves but, instead, on what people actually do and how people's activities are organized in ways that connect with what other people are doing elsewhere and "elsewhen." This focus was very different from sociologies that directed me to theorize people's experiences. The move towards investigating how people's experiences are socially organized has been one of the most useful shifts for how I think about doing research. In my ongoing study of living organ donation, I am exploring how organ donors and recipients do emotion and body work that is shaped by institutional relations of hospital-based organ transplant clinics, but that also conflicts with the clinics' organizational imperatives.

THE ROLE OF THEORY IN IE

Clarifying IE's relationship to social theory can be one of the most challenging aspects of teaching IE to graduate students. The Graduate Program in Sociology at York advertises itself as one of the most "dynamic centers of social theory" in Canada.[3] Through their training, students are exposed to a hierarchical division of intellectual labor that frames theorizing as an apex activity. As such, they often come to the course with an understanding that theorizing about the social is what they should spend their time doing.

That expectation can make it difficult for them to grasp IE, particularly given IE's cautious, at times hostile, relationship to sociological theory. Smith is very careful to establish that IE is not a project of theorizing in the conventional sociological sense. In fact, she treats sociological discourse in a manner that parallels her critique of objectified modes of knowledge. Smith (1990) notes that, much like formal discourses of management and professional expertise, sociology "transposes the actualities of [people's] lives into the conceptual currency with which [they] can be governed" (p. 14). Scholars working in the institutional ethnographic tradition often present or publish their research in ways that convey that IE is not a theoretical project. While this framing of IE may have some appeal in professional education settings, it can falter in the context of graduate sociology education, where students value opportunities to read, think about, and engage in contemporary theoretical debates in sociology.

One response to this teaching predicament is to be clear with students that IE draws from theoretical traditions that have been formative of sociology. Exposing students to Smith's reflections on feminist thought, ethnomethodology, phenomenology, and Marxism—particularly the ontology of the social as expressed in the *German Ideology* (Marx & Engels, 1976)—and her discussions of their significance for IE, is an important way to demonstrate that IE has theoretical roots and is not simply a technical method of inquiry. Engaging students with Smith's writing on Foucault's notion of discourse (Smith, 1999), Mead's theory of mind and self (Smith, 1999), and the notion of speech genre as developed by Bakhtin (Smith, 2005) can further help students understand how engaging with the work of social theorists is crucial to the ongoing development of IE as a project of inquiry.

Once it is established that IE is a theoretically-informed sociology, it is equally important to clarify how its engagement with social theory is distinguished from other forms of sociological inquiry. IE does not seek to generate social theory, as is the case in the grounded theory tradition (Glazer & Strauss, 1967), nor does it try to elaborate on an existing theory as does the extended case method (Burawoy, Burton, Ferguson, & Fox, 1991). IE's approach to exploring translocal relations does not rely on theoretical speculation as do some approaches to global ethnography (Burawoy et al., 2000) where theorizing about the global economy is used to connect empirical gaps produced through the locally-bound nature of ethnographic observation (Smith, 2005).

One way to concretize these differences is to invite students to analyze original data. In every year the IE course has been taught, students have conducted interviews, transcribed them, and interpreted them through individual analytic writing and, especially, through in-class exercises where they collectively read and analyze their interviews. Through their interview projects, students come to learn that what mistakenly gets taken up as IE's rejection of abstractions or dismissal of theory (Connell, 1992; Tummons, 2017) is, in fact, a rejection of a particular mode of theorizing in which concepts or categories internal to a particular theoretical tradition are projected onto interview transcripts in ways that obscure the experiences people have recounted.

Students are asked to contemplate what, from an IE perspective, are problematic forms of theorizing by considering what their analysis of transcripts might look like were they to try to make sense of their interviews from a critical realist, actor-network theory, or critical race theory position. What would Judith Butler, Michael Burawoy, or Nikolas Rose say about their transcript? In contrast to such moves, they are encouraged to follow an IE approach to the analysis of transcripts that focuses on reading for social organization (Mykhalovskiy & McCoy, 2002). Reading for social organization is an analytic practice that seeks to uncover how people's activities are coordinated translocally. It rests on the assumption that such forms of social organization "are already implicit in how people talk" about what they do (Smith, 2002, p. 31). Julia describes her way of working with this insight in her research on applied behavior analysis:

I took my experience in the IE course and applied it to composing and analyzing interviews with autism-based applied behaviour therapy providers as a way to understand social coordination and ruling relations. If not for the course, I might have engaged with the interview process as a way to learn about my participants' thoughts, views, and feelings. Instead, I approached my interviews with the goal of understanding the everyday work my participants completed and how their work was structured by translocal texts that governed from a distance and at the level of their moment-to-moment actions. In my analysis of interview transcripts, I focused on how my participants talked about standards, protocols, forms, regulations, rules, guidelines, and policies. I then analysed how working with these texts shaped their bodies, actions, and affects, their social conditions, and even their consciousness. The class taught me that—because texts are translocal regulatory objects—to talk about texts is to talk about the organization of our feelings, thoughts, views, subjectivity, discourse, and culture.

Using IE to analyze interview transcripts is not a practice that is disengaged from theory. Rather, it engages with concepts that help us to identify, understand, and put into view extended social relations. Many of those concepts, such as work and social relations, which have been described elsewhere in this volume, are internal to the existing corpus of IE. But it is also the case that they may be borrowed and transformed from elsewhere.

IE, Orthodoxy, and Other Research Approaches

Much scholarly writing about IE is methodologically focused. It emphasizes that IE takes a unique approach to formulating research problems, doing interviews, and analyzing textual materials, and takes great care and detail in demonstrating what those approaches look like (Campbell & Gregor, 2004; DeVault & McCoy, 2012; McCoy, 2006; Mykhalovskiy & McCoy, 2002; Smith, 2006). As we have already noted, IE also makes strong claims to be something quite different from established approaches to sociology. IE is represented by practitioners as at odds with, and highly critical of, mainstream sociological inquiry. One tends to encounter scholarly accounts of how IE is unique and distinguished from, rather than related to, existing sociologies (DeVault, 2006; Rankin, 2017; Smith, 1990, 2005; Smith & Turner, 2014).

Narratives of IE's methodological exactitude and uniqueness are important but, when taken to an extreme, they can contribute to an orthodox, almost ossified orientation to institutional ethnography. By orthodoxy we have in mind relations of thought, research, and writing that rigidly police intellectual boundaries and promote fidelity to a canonical formulation of a given approach to social inquiry. Such relations can produce IE as a sociology that is insular and self-sufficient, with little interest in other approaches to social research, and that can only be done in one way. The perils of orthodoxy are not unique to IE. They can be faced by any form of social inquiry that has a fairly high degree of internal coherence, a foundational methodological or theoretical literature, and a name—grounded theory, the extended case method, situational analysis, and so on—by which it is known to others.

What counts as an example of a given approach to social inquiry? Is this study a good example of institutional ethnography? How to make sense of an author's claims to have done research informed by IE when it appears to read otherwise? We are concerned about the rigid policing of such questions and the effects that can result when answers to them are constrained by orthodoxy. We have each experienced orthodoxy in relation to IE. We have seen it happen at conferences when the work of junior scholars—most often graduate students—is responded to by seasoned institutional ethnographers in ways that suggest they have not done IE, or not done IE the "right way." We have experienced it when we have been afraid to claim to do IE because we feel that our work does not look sufficiently similar to what are routinely treated as exemplars of institutional ethnographic research. We are worried about how a public impression that IE is rigidly policed can damage the continued growth and creative development of IE. Leigha suggests how this way of thinking about IE can create problems for teaching IE at the graduate level:

I have to say that the reputation of IE that I have heard from other graduate students is that it is closed off and that if you do not do IE exactly to the standards of the "gatekeepers," who determine what counts as IE and what does not, then there is no space for you. It's also the case that when boundaries are too rigidly policed, the consequences of failing to meet certain standards or expectations can be severe, especially for student researchers. The word orthodoxy means "conforming to established doctrine especially in religion" (Merriam-Webster, 2019). It's interesting that graduate students would often speak of IE as requiring a conversion. After the IE course, when I told other students that, moving forward, I would be doing IE, they would often tease me and say that I had been "converted." It seemed that one either subscribed fully to IE's tenets, creeds, and values, or one rejected them entirely. I'm concerned that this kind of policing and orthodoxy can lock students into overly formulaic conceptions of IE and can alienate students who are interested in IE but are wary of its reputation. I think this reputation has come, in part, from students' experiences at conferences and other situations where they meet experienced IE researchers. When I was going to attend my first IE conference, I was warned by other students to make sure that my work conformed to the "right" kind of IE. That was extremely intimidating for me. I think there's a fine line between teaching students the core tenets of IE and making sure they've thought through how they understand IE without restricting them as researchers. It's difficult for students to see where they fit in when IE is presented as a pre-defined project to which they can only contribute by reproducing its existing form. Instead, I think new researchers would benefit from conversations in which they're asked about how they orient to IE, what aspects of

IE they look to include in their research and which they might reject, how they weave other approaches into their work, and ultimately, what they perceive to be the core of IE. In my experience, those conversations have been much more fruitful than simply telling students "you aren't doing IE" or "that isn't an IE project."

The experiences Leigha recounts are typical of York's graduate sociology program, where students and faculty place a premium on creating "original" theoretical discourse and eschew sociologies that give little room to novelty when engaging in data collection and analysis. Two strategies for teaching IE have been key to negotiating the problem of orthodoxy in the context of this particular intellectual culture.

The first strategy involves balancing an orientation to IE as an unfinished and open project with methodological exercises and discussions of readings that engage students in what might be considered to be the formative characteristics of IE. Structuring the course in this way is a matter of emphasizing that IE does have boundaries, but that what gives IE its contours is evolving and something to which students can make an active contribution.

While the course changes from year to year, it generally treats IE as a theoretically-embedded empirical sociology of contemporary forms of ruling that seeks to understand how the world is put together. It emphasizes that IE focuses on ruling relations as an object of inquiry and does so in ways that are committed to a materialist ontology of the social. The course further emphasizes that IE is not about individual experiences, but commits to exploring how people's experiences and activities are socially organized, that is, coordinated across time and place. Finally, the course tries to instill among students an "ethics of empirical investigation" (Mykhalovskiy & Church, 2006, p. 77) that guides institutional ethnographers to discover how institutional relations actually operate and with what implications, rather than simply confirming what they think they already know about how the world works.

This formulation of the specificity of IE is something open to discussion and debate. Over the years, students have called it into question. Some have sought to broaden the sense of what written IE studies look like. For example, students have turned to Pence's (2001) work on supporting women who have faced domestic abuse as an example of writing that focuses not simply on explicating ruling relations per se, but on using IE to create alternative institutional practices for people subject to problematic bureaucratic processes. Others have called into question IE's ontology of the social and wondered whether and how it might be extended to incorporate the agency of nonhuman actors. Drawing on scholarly developments such as relational sociology (Depelteau, 2018) and actor-network theory (Corman & Barron, 2017; Latour, 2007) and on their own awareness of how, in our present, all life on the planet is threatened, they have tried to square IE with approaches to research that more fully attend to how the "social" is created, sustained, and transformed through networks of association that connect humans with other animals, things, artefacts, and natural phenomena. What such efforts might make of IE's humanist focus and articulation as a sociology of "people" remains an open question.

Promoting pedagogical dialogue about tensions between the foundational dimensions of IE and IE's openness to change can extend to other dimensions of IE practice such as how interviews are conducted and how text analysis is done. It can also take up the question of the forms of IE research that have risen to prominence within the field. Eric explains:

I want graduate students to get excited about IE and I try to make that happen by emphasizing that IE is an unfinished project, rather than some kind of ready-made, paint-by-number approach that they are asked to simply apply to a chosen topic. Part of what I try to do is tell students that what they often imagine IE to be, and here I have in mind the many recent important studies of managerial relations in the public sector focused on health care, education, social work, and so on (Griffith & Smith, 2014), is not all that IE is or can be about. Students often think that doing IE requires working with in situ managerial texts or producing detailed textual maps of one sort or another. I actively try to unseat those assumptions. I encourage students to apply IE approaches to novel topics—in particular, relations of capital (although I have had little success on that front). I invite them to revisit and work with earlier traditions of observation and ethnographic writing exemplified by the work of Timothy Diamond (2009) over the more text-heavy types of analytic writing that are now common in the field. I want students to breathe new life into how IE inquiry is conducted in order for the approach to continue to be able to grasp and make sense of the massive and accelerated proliferation of communications technologies, knowledges, and practices that are translocally coordinating our lives.

The second strategy involves recognizing that there are many ways that students can orient to IE. In our experience, it is important to teach IE in ways that permit graduate students to make choices about how they will relate to it. Some students will choose to fully engage with the approach and produce institutional ethnographies. Others may draw on aspects of IE in their research or combine it with other approaches. A goal of the course is to provide a level of introduction to IE that can enable multiple options, recognizing that for many reasons, including a lack of expertise in IE among prospective thesis supervisors, most students often only draw on IE in their dissertation research, rather than conduct full institutional ethnographies.

Of course, this raises questions about how to think about IE's relationship to other sociologies and how IE might be connected with them. Orthodoxy discourages such questions by framing IE as self-sufficient. It is not uncommon for seasoned practitioners of IE to dismiss other approaches with the refrain "I don't see why you need" Bourdieu, or actor-network-theory, or governmentality. One possible response to such objections is to suggest that thoughtful engagement with other approaches to the social analysis of governance or power might actually strengthen institutional ethnographic research.

IE can be taught to graduate students in ways that create a space for articulating principles of combination or of relationship between IE and other approaches to social inquiry (Lund & Nilsen, 2019). One way this can occur is by encouraging students to consider whether concepts from neighboring forms of inquiry can be enlisted in IE inquiry in ways that contribute to the exploration of ruling relations.

Elsewhere, Mykhalovskiy (in Grace, 2019) has argued that

> it is important for…institutional ethnographers to be conversant with a range of theoretical and research perspectives in the social sciences and to draw on them when they are helpful. The question of how to productively engage with other critical research traditions while holding to the epistemological and ontological commitments of IE is a challenging one. But, in the end, I do think…concepts used in other intellectual projects…can be useful for IE and…can assist with the work of exploring how ruling is actually put together. They can be used in ways that do not produce the mode of theorizing [that is problematic for IE]. (p. 121)

Colin offers an example of how he used concepts from Foucauldian scholarship to inform the study he undertook in the IE course:

An especially valuable aspect of the course was the occasion to experiment with producing an IE analysis that worked with concepts that are external to the IE corpus. For the culminating assignment of the course, I interviewed representatives of community-based organizations that facilitated "HIV disclosure interventions" that encouraged people living with HIV to widely disclose their HIV-positive status. I found that the theoretical conception of biological citizenship was helpful for articulating the normative character of these types of interventions, and attending to ways that such initiatives may produce a new ethic of how one is to disclose his or her HIV-positive status. However, rather than reproducing an analysis of self-governance, typical of Foucauldian scholarship, I read interview transcripts for social organization in order to explore how these interventions are actually organized by, and hooked into, broader social relations, such as the criminal law. This part of the IE course offered space to conduct and transcribe interviews, and to make sense of how to evoke theoretical concepts within IE projects that endeavour to study social organization with a view to providing reflexive, critical engagement with social movements.

For those concerned with preserving the foundational characteristics of IE, the question of IE's relationship to other research approaches may largely be one of how to draw on the intellectual resources of other forms of inquiry without transforming IE into a theory making endeavor or lifting analysis out of the realm of people's coordinated activities (Mykhalovskiy in Grace, 2019; Rankin, 2017). In teaching the course, posing the question of how IE might connect with work outside the IE corpus has been a matter of guarding against insularity, while also balancing questions about the specificity of IE and what might be lost or gained by relating IE research to other sociologies. An important goal for the IE course is to promote reflexivity among students about how drawing on work beyond the IE corpus shapes their scholarly practice and with what effect. Julia suggests some of what that can involve:

I came to IE through Science and Technology Studies and anthropology, which stress the diffuse nature of power and the multiplicity of truth. That background did not make IE an easy fit for me. I initially experienced IE's methods as overly proscriptive and rigid. Yet, I was also compelled by IE's insistence that power can be explored by focusing on people's actual work and how that work is shaped by translocal institutional and bureaucratic relations. I was growing disenchanted with my academic training, where theorizing inequitable social relations seemed more like a way to acquire academic capital than to create social change. The course engaged with my reservations and excitement about IE and guided me to apply it in a way that made sense with my training and interests. Through our weekly reflections on readings I considered how to use rich description and the analysis of culture, not as an antithesis to a social organization approach, but as a critical aide to unearthing institutional forms of governance. I explored how to do IE-informed work on texts without drawing on metaphors of mapping, with their vestiges of colonial pursuits. In my work on the use of behavioral therapies to "treat" autism, I continue to pursue interdisciplinary scholarship that combines an anthropological focus on meaning, intimacy, and culture with an IE approach to governance, textual coordination, and social organization (Gruson-Wood, 2018). My training in IE was pivotal in shaping my research framework in that I centered my fieldwork on studying the everyday work of behavior therapy providers as a way to uncover the relations of ruling that govern the lives of autistic people who receive such therapy.

INSTITUTIONAL ETHNOGRAPHY, CRITIQUE, AND POLITICS

There are many varieties of critical analysis available within sociology and many ways to produce sociological research that can be considered to contribute to struggles against oppression, injustice, and marginalization (Carroll, 2004; Hale, 2008; Mullins, 2011; Mykhalovskiy & Namaste, 2019; Sayer, 2009). York's graduate sociology program has a reputation for encouraging public, critically-engaged scholarship, particularly of the sort that connects with popular movements for social change. The IE course often attracts students who are interested in a practice of sociology that commits to progressive social transformation. As such, teaching and learning IE in ways that explore its relationship to critique and political engagement have been an important dimension of our shared experience of the course.

George Smith's work offers an exemplar of the political character of IE scholarship that can serve as an anchor for students as they consider IE's relationship to critical scholarship. George's work on the police regulation of gay men's sexuality (1988) and on the social organization of the Canadian state's response to the HIV epidemic (1995) formulate IE as political activist ethnography (1990). He offers an example of IE as research that explores how ruling is put together in people's activities that can extend social movement activists' working knowledge of the institutional relations they wish to transform. Even the seemingly simple gesture of demonstrating to students that they can do research on the relations that social movements confront rather than study the movements themselves opens up new spaces for thinking about critical sociological practice.

George Smith's work locates IE, in an uneasy way, within certain modernist traditions about the use of knowledge. He demonstrates how IE presumes a world that can be known through research and how that research can be used by activists to create better futures. However, at the same time, he shows how IE offers a form of critique focused on the problem of authoritative knowledges. His examination of how policing practices constitute men's sex at bathhouses as an "indecent" act punishable under the criminal code is a powerful testament to the emphasis IE places on the critique of objectifying discourses. It helps demonstrate how IE's critique of the social explores the workings of institutional relations, while underscoring the ongoing radical move of ensuring that people's everyday experiences form the ground of IE inquiry.

George Smith practiced IE as research that can assist social movement activists. His work offers an important basis from which to explore with students issues related to the political nature of IE in the face of growing expectations for scholars to engage with communities beyond the academy and to produce and write research that reaches wider publics (Fassin, 2017). For example, questions arise about how IE can preserve its specific approaches to sociological inquiry in the face of expectations within community-based and participatory traditions for all aspects of research to be subject to negotiation among research partners. How IE can be written in ways that register with multiple readers is an important question to pose of students who face new career expectations in the context of a post-truth society with changing literacy skills and growing demands for entrepreneurial scholarship that reaches publics through social media outlets and other innovations in knowledge translation (Hastings, Comer, & Mykhalovskiy, 2018). IE is not about poststructuralist deconstruction and the political moves associated with it, nor is it principally about identity-based forms of critical discourse that center politics in particular forms of social difference such as race, class, gender, or their intersection. Posing questions about how IE might connect with such forms of critical practice is an important area of discussion for graduate students, as Nancy Naples (2009) suggests in her work on using IE in teaching about intersectionality. Colin offers his own reflections:

Throughout my MA in Cultural Studies, theoretical discourse seemed like a necessary starting point to inquiry, one that had little resonance in community-based HIV advocacy organizations of which I was a part. I couldn't help but feel left behind as fellow grad students appeared to so easily and comfortably relate to theoretical texts, find and link to other Foucauldians, or develop novel and interesting applications for Deleuze and Guattari's rhizome theory. I valued social theory for how it pushed my thinking in challenging and exciting ways; however, I often struggled to understand what it meant to effectively apply theoretical concepts to the everyday social worlds that I and fellow HIV activists were experiencing and trying to change. An important feature of the IE course was that it foregrounded discussions about ways that our activism or experience can shape knowledge, an insight that Nancy Naples (2009) suggests "is often lost when theoretical approaches are institutionalized in the academy" (p. 574). Through our collective reflections on IE readings, I came to better understand how to produce knowledge for activists. I especially appreciated writing from institutional ethnographers who relate to studies of ruling relations as a way to "enlarge the scope" of what people can see from their everyday social worlds (McCoy, 2006, pp. 704, 706; G. Smith, 1990, pp. 629, 631). Conceptualizing sociological research as an effort to extend people's knowledge of how the social world is put together, with a view to transforming it, seemed like a way out of the gymnastics of trying to apply theoretical concepts to describe people's everyday experiences.

Conclusion

Institutional ethnography is an important alternative sociology that, in recent years, has grown in popularity in the health sciences, social work, education, and other disciplinary and professional sites external to sociology. This popularity has not been matched within sociology, where IE's particular approach to social theory, its critique of established forms of sociological discourse, and its engagement by some practitioners in ways that support relations of scholarly orthodoxy can misfire among sociology graduate students and emerging sociologists.

While we applaud the uptake of IE in sites beyond sociology, we also worry about the place of IE in its disciplinary home and wish its reach, appeal, and uptake within established sites of sociological training and publication were stronger. In our view, a stable and active presence of IE within sociological practice is important for its ongoing development. With a view to encouraging that development, this chapter has explored some of what makes teaching IE in the context of graduate sociology education challenging, but also rewarding and important.

We write from our collective experiences of a particular graduate program, one in which theorizing the social is presented to graduate students as the apogee of sociological practice and in which mainstream, objectifying formulations of sociological inquiry have a minor presence.

Graduate school is an intellectually formative period. The theories and methodologies students learn about during graduate school often remain key touchstones throughout their careers. How IE is taught in graduate schools of sociology is, therefore, of particular importance for its presence in the discipline and should be a matter of concern, care, and deliberation.

There can be no general recipe for how best to teach IE at the graduate level. In our collective experience, teaching and learning IE can invite and, perhaps, require, disrupting the separation of theory and methods that typically structures graduate curricula. At a time when sociological analysis (particularly of qualitative data) is so easily instrumentalized by coding practices of one sort or another, learning to analyze IE data as a matter of reading for social organization can help demonstrate for students what is unique about IE's analysis of the social. While graduate students benefit from rigorous in-depth exploration of IE, we emphasize that careful engagement with other areas of sociological scholarship has been central to the development of IE and need not be viewed as a threat to its specificity. Indeed, it may be critical for its ongoing development and for securing its place within sites where sociology is practiced and taught. Graduate students are curious about a range of sociological approaches and about the relationship of IE to other forms of scholarship. IE will not thrive if it is taught defensively or in ways that close down such curiosity. Thankfully, students have access to many examples of IE scholarship that, in different ways, engage with other traditions of social inquiry (Campbell & Teghtsoonian, 2010; Hastings, 2020; Lund & Nilsen, 2019; Mykhalovskiy, 2001; Reid & Russel, 2017; Weir & Mykhalovskiy, 2010).

Of course, we recognize that those who teach or are poised to teach IE in other settings of graduate sociology education may face rather different issues than those we have emphasized. Our hope is that our discussion offers them food for thought, encourages them to teach IE, and strengthens scholarly discourse about teaching IE as an alternative sociology.

Acknowledgements We thank Paul Luken and Suzanne Vaughan for their editorial guidance. We also thank the reviewers for their suggestions as well as Liza McCoy, Kathryn Church, and Marj DeVault for their constructive feedback on earlier versions of this chapter.

Notes

1. Professor Himani Bannerji has also taught "Selected Topics in Empirical Methods" with an IE focus. Bannerji's course explores the relationship between Smith's approach to IE and Bannerji's interconstitutive method for exploring the concrete nature of the social. Bannerji's version of the course does not include the practical methodological exercises that are central to Mykhalovskiy's version.
2. For example, previous versions of the course have included sections that compare and contrast IE with the extended case method and various approaches to global and multi-sited ethnographies.
3. See http://sociology.gradstudies.yorku.ca/

References

Burawoy, M., Blum, J. A., George, S., Gille, Z., & Thayer, M. (2000). *Global ethnography: Forces, connections, and imaginations in a postmodern world*. Berkeley: University of California Press.

Burawoy, M., Burton, A., Ferguson, A. A., & Fox, K. J. (1991). *Ethnography unbound: Power and resistance in the modern metropolis*. Berkeley: University of California Press.

Burchell, G., Gordon, C., & Miller, P. (Eds.). (1991). *The Foucault effect: Studies in governmentality*. Chicago: University of Chicago Press.

Campbell, M., & Gregor, F. (2004). *Mapping social relations: A primer for doing institutional ethnography*. Walnut Creek, CA: AltaMira Press.

Campbell, M., & Teghtsoonian, K. (2010). Aid effectiveness and women's empowerment: Practices of governance in the funding of international development. *Signs*, 36(1), 177–202.

Carroll, W. K. (2004). *Critical strategies for social research*. Toronto, ON: Canadian Scholars' Press.

Clarke, A., Friese, C., & Washburn, R. (2018). *Situational analysis: Grounded theory after the interpretive turn*. Thousand Oaks: Sage.

Connell, R. W. (1992). A sober anarchism. *Sociological Theory*, 10(1), 81–87.

Corman, M., & Barron, G. (2017). Institutional ethnography and actor-network theory. In J. Reid & L. Russel (Eds.), *Perspectives on and from institutional ethnography* (pp. 49–70). Bingley, UK: Emerald.

Depelteau, F. (2018). Relational thinking in sociology: Relevance, concurrence and dissonance. In F. Depelteau (Ed.), *The Palgrave handbook of relational sociology* (pp. 3–34). New York: Palgrave Macmillan.

DeVault, M. (2006). Introduction: What is institutional ethnography? *Social Problems*, 53(3), 294–298.

DeVault, M., & McCoy, L. (2012). Investigating ruling relations: Dynamics of interviewing in institutional ethnography. In J. A. Holstein, J. F. Gubrium, A. B. Marvasti, & K. D. McKinney (Eds.), *The Sage handbook of interview research: The complexity of the craft* (pp. 381–396). Thousand Oaks: Sage.

Diamond, T. (2009). *Making gray gold: Narratives of nursing home care*. Chicago: University of Chicago Press.

Fassin, D. (Ed.). (2017). *If truth be told: The politics of public ethnography*. Durham, NC: Duke University Press.

Glazer, B., & Strauss, A. (1967). *The discovery of grounded theory: Strategies for qualitative research*. New York: Aldine.

Grace, D. (2019). Institutional ethnography as critical research strategy: Access, engagement, and implications for HIV/AIDS research. In E. Mykhalovskiy & V. Namaste (Eds.), *Thinking differently about HIV/AIDS: Contributions from critical social science* (pp. 103–133). Vancouver: UBC Press.

Griffith, A., & Smith, D. (Eds.). (2014). *Under new public management: Institutional ethnographies of changing front-line work*. Toronto: University of Toronto Press.

Gruson-Wood, J. (2018). Dissertation: *I'm a juggling robot: An ethnography of the organization and culture of autism-based applied behaviour therapies in Ontario, Canada*. Doctor of Philosophy, York University, York Space, Institutional Depository. Toronto, Ontario, Canada.

Hale, C. (Ed.). (2008). *Engaging contradictions: Theory, politics and the methods of activist scholarship*. Berkeley: University of California Press.

Hastings, C. (2020). Dissertation: *Writing for digital news: The social organization of news stories about HIV criminalization in an age of convergence journalism*. Doctor of Philosophy, York University. Toronto, Ontario, Canada.

Hastings, C., Comer, L., & Mykhalovskiy, E. (2018). Review: Didier Fassin (Ed.) (2017), If truth be told: The politics of public ethnography. *Forum Qualitative Sozialforschung/Forum: Qualitative Social Research*, 19(2), Art. 17. http://dx.doi.org/10.17169/fqs-19.2.3044.

Latour, B. (2007). *Reassembling the social: An introduction to actor-network-theory*. Oxford: Oxford University Press.

Lund, R., & Nilsen, C. E. (Eds.). (2019). *Institutional ethnography in the Nordic region*. New York: Routledge.

Marcus, G. E. (1995). Ethnography in/of the world system: The emergence of multi-sited ethnography. *Annual Review of Anthropology, 24*(1), 95–117.

Marx, K., & Engels, F. (1976). *The German ideology* (3rd rev. ed.). Moscow: Progress Publishers.

McCoy, L. (2006). Keeping the institution in view: Working with interview accounts of everyday experience. In D. Smith (Ed.), *Institutional ethnography as practice* (pp. 109–127). Lanham, MD: Rowman and Littlefield.

McCoy, L., Mykhalovskiy, E., & Gruson-Wood, J. (2017). *Reading institutional ethnographies, 1996–2016*. Paper presented at the Society for the Study of Social Problems Annual General Meetings, Montreal, Quebec.

Mullins, P. (2011). Practicing anthropology and the politics of engagement: 2010 year in review. *American Anthropologist, 113*(2), 235–245.

Mykhalovskiy, E. (2001). Troubled hearts, care pathways and hospital restructuring: Exploring health services research as active knowledge. *Studies in Cultures, Organizations, and Societies, 7*(2), 269–296.

Mykhalovskiy, E., & Church, K. (2006). Of T-shirts and ontology: The pedagogical legacies of George Smith. In C. Frampton, G. Kinsman, A. K. Thompson, & K. Tilleczek (Eds.), *Sociology for changing the world: Social movements/social research* (pp. 71–86). Toronto: Fernwood.

Mykhalovskiy, E., & McCoy, L. (2002). Troubling ruling discourses of health: Using institutional ethnography in community-based research. *Critical Public Health, 12*(1), 17–37.

Mykhalovskiy, E., & Namaste, V. (Eds.). (2019). *Thinking differently about HIV/AIDS: Contributions from critical social science*. Vancouver: University of British Columbia Press.

Naples, N. A. (2009). Teaching intersectionality intersectionally. *International Feminist Journal of Politics, 11*(4), 566–577.

Orthodox [Def.1]. (2019). *Merriam-Webster Online*. Retrieved July 19, 2019, from https://www.merriam-webster.com/dictionary/orthodox.

Pence, E. (2001). Safety for battered women in a textually mediated legal system. *Studies in Cultures, Organizations and Societies, 7*(2), 199–229.

Rankin, J. (2017). Conducting analysis in institutional ethnography: Guidance and cautions. *International Journal of Qualitative Methods, 16*(1), 1–11.

Rankin, J., Doyle, E., Waters, N., Fast, O., & Pomerleau, S. (2016). *Teaching institutional ethnography across disciplines*. Paper presented at the Society for Studies in Social Problems Annual General Meeting, Seattle, Washington.

Reid, J., & Russel, L. (Eds.). (2017). *Perspectives on and from institutional ethnography*. Bingley, UK: Emerald.

Sayer, A. (2009). Who's afraid of critical social science? *Current Sociology, 57*(6), 767–786.

Smith, D. (1987). *The everyday world as problematic: A feminist sociology*. Toronto: University of Toronto Press.

Smith, D. (1999). *Writing the social: Critique, theory, and investigations*. Toronto: University of Toronto Press.

Smith, D. (2002). Institutional ethnography. In T. May (Ed.), *Qualitative research in action* (pp. 17–52). London: Sage.
Smith, D. (2005). *Institutional ethnography: A sociology for people*. Walnut Creek, CA: AltaMira Press.
Smith, D. (Ed.). (2006). *Institutional ethnography as practice*. Lanham, MD: Rowman and Littlefield.
Smith, D. E. (1990). *The conceptual practices of power: A feminist sociology of knowledge*. Boston: North Eastern University Press.
Smith, D., & Turner, S. M. (Eds.). (2014). *Incorporating texts into institutional ethnographies*. Toronto: University of Toronto Press.
Smith, G. W. (1988). Policing the gay community: An inquiry into textually-mediated social relations. *International Journal of the Sociology of Law, 16*, 163–183.
Smith, G. W. (1990). Political activist as ethnographer. *Social Problems, 37*(4), 629–648.
Smith, G. W. (1995). Accessing treatments: Managing the AIDS epidemic in Ontario. In M. Campbell & A. Manicom (Eds.), *Knowledge, experience, and ruling relations: Studies in the social organization of knowledge* (pp. 18–34). Toronto: University of Toronto Press.
Tummons, J. (2017). Institutional ethnography, theory, methodology, and research: Some concerns and some comments. In J. Reid & L. Russel (Eds.), *Perspectives on and from institutional ethnography* (pp. 147–162). Bingley, UK: Emerald.
Vaughan, S. (2016, July). Making institutional change in small ways: Introducing institutional ethnography to first generation university students. International Sociological Association, Vienna, Austria.
Weir, L., & Mykhalovskiy, E. (2010). *Global public health vigilance: Creating a world on alert*. New York: Routledge.

CHAPTER 5

Exploring Institutional Words as People's Practices

Dorothy E. Smith

The recognition of texts that are or can be reproduced has been central to the possibility of an ethnographic project of exploring ruling relations and/or the objectification of institutions and large-scale organization as they are brought into being as people's everyday doings. Replicated texts can carry the same message across different times and places and reach different people. They may not be read and taken up in the same way, but the text itself is generalized. What we have not developed, however, is a recognition of how words carried in such texts are brought into play as they organize people's local work.

I originally opened the door to exploring words as practices because it seemed to me that what people say, or think, or write, in words was not properly available to us ethnographically. I set aside the grand accumulation, in multiple disciplines, of investigations of language that I had been dutifully exploring and learning from in the hopes of discovering somewhere a recognition of language that would work for institutional ethnographies. I never found that. In this and in my earlier paper taking up words as people practice them (Smith, 2016), I made a decision to set aside this technically highly developed and multiply theorized literature. I want to move away from more technically developed modes of investigating and theorizing language, to an approach that allows us to see words as what people do and are doing and to be able to attend to words as people practice them.

D. E. Smith (✉)
University of Victoria, Victoria, BC, Canada
e-mail: desmith@uvic.ca

© The Author(s) 2021
P. C. Luken and S. Vaughan (eds.), *The Palgrave Handbook of Institutional Ethnography*,
https://doi.org/10.1007/978-3-030-54222-1_5

I am proposing to open up our ethnographic research practices to words people actually use or have used. It may be the words they are using when we are making observations; it will be, of course, the words that come into play as the texts that coordinate their work are activated—which may be in writing as well as reading and may not be spoken for us to hear. Texts are fundamental to the very possibility of exploring relations of ruling as people's local practices and we have much to gain, I believe, from also bringing into focus how people practice the words those texts carry in organizing people's work.

Working with words as practices is, for me, grounded first in the work of George Hebert Mead (1962). Mead was a philosopher linked to the American approach known as pragmatism. He was also a scientist, a social psychologist, influenced by behaviorism but departing from it significantly. While behaviorism focused on individuals and individual behavior dumping the concept of mind, Mead theorized mind as fundamentally social, as a human activity fundamentally connected to people's use of what he called *vocal gestures* or *significant symbols* and we might call *words*. He elucidated the social dimension of words by drawing a contrast between vocal gestures and gestures as they express feelings as *truncated acts* to which the other responds as s/he feels. Gestures express people's feelings and emotions; we respond to them in recognizing what a person may be expressing—someone shaking his fist in our face is expressing an anger with us that may scare or simply offend us, but we do not share it. What Mead called vocal gestures or significant symbols (I think of words) are radically different; the conventionalized sound evokes the same response in both speaker and hearer. I meet with a friend for supper at a local restaurant. As we arrive, she says, "Let's sit at that little table downstairs in the unused section of the bar so that we can hear each other." I know right away what she is talking about; I am visualizing where we are going and start to move in that direction. I do not have to puzzle about what she is saying; her words are already in my mind and I am responding. Mead's thinking is of language, or the significant symbol, not only as essentially social but as coordinating our doings, including our thinking, our consciousness, with those who are hearing or reading the same words. Mead's understanding of words as social in this sense is the grounding of the approach being developed and put forward here.

While his conceptualizing of vocal gestures (or words) is the grounding of the ethnographic approach we are working through here, Mead's work goes much beyond in his discoveries of social interchange as integral to human beings as we are. Here, however, we build on his understanding of words as essentially social; they coordinate people's consciousnesses as they organize in speaker and hearer the same response; no complicated accounts of how *meaning* is transmitted in a communicative act from one speaker to another is needed. In my earlier paper (Smith, 2016), I gave as a specimen my own experience of how words as practiced in my head organized consciousness; the words happened; I was talking to myself though not out loud; the words spoken in-skull organized a distinctive sequence of responses. Here is my little story again.

> I was out walking my dog in Vancouver when I met my grandson near the sports field. He'd been coaching a junior rugby team. We stopped to talk at the corner of 12th Avenue and Vine Street. While he was telling me about what he'd been doing, I happened to glance East on 12th and saw a bus passing across a street two blocks away. The 'in-skull' dialogue went on as shown below. The words in bold are those that I can remember actually practicing. In brackets are those aspects of the 'in-skull' dialogue that were not explicitly verbal.
>
> [a bus crosses 12th Avenue] **bus** [unuttered question: what street?] **Arbutus** [unuttered question: what bus?] **number 16** [unuttered question: where does it go after 12th?]
>
> It was as if the word *bus* that kicked in when I was actually seeing its referent generated further words that had at that moment no visible referents. It went into practice organizing a sequence of connections to transit buses—they travel definite routes along nameable streets. All this was fast, a momentary distraction from my conversation with my grandson.

So I am shifting from terms like *response* or *meaning* to using the verb *organize*. I use this notion partly because I see it as drawing attention to aspects of how words are practiced both among us and just in our heads that organize our subjectivities in specific ways. It orients our research awareness of how what is brought to consciousness when a word is spoken to others or when it is read by different readers, *organizes* what becomes relevant to how what they do is coordinated (including what they do in words). My own bus story can even be seen as coordinating my consciousness with the Vancouver transit system.

INSTITUTIONAL LANGUAGE GENERALIZES

In the earlier paper on words as practices (Smith, 2016), I was focusing on specimens of words in practice that named objects—some concrete and material, *table,* for example, others institutional, the *chemistry lecture, the body count* used by the US to evaluate the progress of the Vietnam war. I was concerned to bring into view how the relevant words could be recognized as organizing people's doings, including what goes on in our heads. This paper looks toward the practices of words that are integral to the textual coordination of institutional sequences of action. To frame this focus, I start with Alexander Luria's (1961, 1976; Luria & Yudovich, 1971) observations of how, when they come into play, words for objects standardize perception of the named object.[1]

> The word, connected with direct perception of the object, .. makes the perception of this object permanent and generalized. (Luria & Yudovich, 1971, p. 23)

Here is Luria's and his associate, Yudovich's description of how children in learning to name objects learn also to focus on generalized features of named objects.

> The mother's very first words when she shows her child different objects and names them with a certain word, have an indiscernible but decisively important influence on the formation of his mental processes. The word, connected with direct perception of the object, isolates its essential features; to name the perceived object "a glass," adding its functional role "for drinking," isolates the essential and inhibits the less essential properties of the object (such as its weight or external shape); to indicate with the word "glass" any glass, regardless of its shape, makes the perception of this object permanent and generalized. (Luria & Yudovich, 1971, p. 23)

Naming as organizing the generalized perception of objects establishes what Luria calls *verbal generalizing systems*. I came across a vivid experiential description of just what might be meant by such a notion in my incidental reading. James Prosek's (2013) account of his learning the names of trees provides a vivid instance of the generalizing organization of naming:

> I remember when I was a child my father taught me the names of the trees in our local woods. Before he did, the forest was like a beautiful green blob. Learning the names, helped me compartmentalize the world and see things more clearly. Each name was like a file folder into which I could store the tree's characteristics: those of leaf size, color, and shape, or texture of the bark. As soon as I learned the word "sugar maple," whenever I spoke it, or heard it spoken, I saw that tree's shaggy bark, the shape of its leaves, the twisted branches of a particularly beautiful specimen that had gnarled itself over a stone wall by my favourite trout stream. The world was altered now, with the names—no less perhaps, but different. (pp. 376–377)

Prosek's organized perception of the sugar maple is an extended account of how naming organized his recognizing of a particular tree as a tree of a particular kind, sharing features with others to be recognized as the same. Luria's identifying of such verbal generalizing systems (his phrase) focuses on words for material objects and that is what Prosek's experience illustrates. Institutional language, however, has no referents organized perceptually. Yet somehow, in practice, institutional language refers to what people do and have done and what has and is happening.

In moving toward recognizing ethnographically words as uttered (spoken, written, read), we encounter the problem of our implicit dialogue with discourses in which what people are doing in words gets expressed as nominals that dispense with their presence and actual doings. We want to be able to make observations of words as people practice them; we want to be able to see how they are working; we want observations both of what people say, write or read, but also of words as they go on inaudibly and invisibly inside the bony walls of the skull. What we have somehow to do is to avoid displacing the presence of people by replacing them with nouns such as *meaning, sense, thought, mind,* and so on. They are odd terms because although they can be assigned grammatically to work as the subjects or objects of sentences, they have no referents as objects beyond the texts operative in a particular situation in which they are uttered.

The very possibility of exploring ruling relations ethnographically means attending to the institutionally specified and authorized wording that generalizes across multiple actual sites and situations. As people become active in a given sequence, they practice the words that organize their local work, as we will learn from Gerald de Montigny's (2014) account in a later section. This is not difficult or fancy, but it does enable the ethnographic move in which particular observations or experiential accounts can be recognized as coordinated within the framework of an institutional course of action. The generalizing categories and concepts of the relevant institutional texts organize what people do to coordinate with others engaged in and with the same sequence. At the same time, we can recognize as ethnographers that those active in the sequence are not doing it exactly the same as others do or as they have done on different occasions. This is not a performance—Harold Garfinkel (2002) in his ethnomethodological account of how *social order* is reproduced uses the notion of *performance* for such an occasion as *the chemistry lecture*. It is a limiting notion, confining people's doings to a specific local setting and time, rather than opening up how what people are doing is engaging them in sequences of action extending beyond any particular occasion.

Institutional naming, however, unlike the physical objects in which Luria's observations are grounded, does not have definite objects, events or actions as their referents. What is named when institutional words are practiced does not organize a generalized perception, a perceptually standardized object, and yet generalized practices of reference to standardized objects, events and actions are integral to institutional process. Alison Griffith told me that, when she was still teaching teachers in the Faculty of Education of York University, she encountered a problem in talking with teachers who would use the word *levels* in talking about their work. She had no idea what they were talking about (she calls this *institution talk*). She learned from them that they were identifying an aspect of how their classes were organized that is derived from the standardized testing evaluating and ranking students (and schools) that is done at the provincial level in Ontario. Levels, as part of classroom organization, are arrangements of students according to test scores into five levels of achievement. Teachers could only refer to levels as what they took into account in their everyday work if they knew how the kids in their classes had been defined by the texts of the standard testing and its complex practices and authorization processes as well as how to take different levels into account in their teaching work. Notice that institution talk is common in research interviews. If the talk is familiar, you may take for granted that you know what your informant is talking about and indeed you may. But it will not be there in your interview when you get it home and transcribe it. Getting past the taken-for-granted *shells* found in institutional discourse to learn about the everyday concrete occurrence of what is going on is essential for institutional ethnography.

INSTITUTIONAL LANGUAGE ORGANIZES

Institutional powers, agency, courses of action, objects and events are specified in an objectifying language independent of particular times, places, and people. The project of exploring words as practices is to move from the inertia of the text as such to making visible how institutional courses of action are actually organized as an ongoing process. When the institutional words are not practiced or are not yet invented and authorized, what people do may be much like what later becomes institutionally specified, but it does not count in and does not connect and coordinate with what can come next institutionally. In a previous paper (Smith, 2001) I took up how the official introduction of a grade appeal procedure in a university department worked. I pointed out that before the grade appeal procedure had become official, the chair of a department might be willing to respond to a student's complaint that her/his completed assignment had not been properly evaluated and might ask the help of a faculty member with relevant knowledge to read and review it. Without official authorization there is no *Grade Appeal Procedure*. Ingenious ways must be found to make changes in the Registrar's record of the original grade. Once such a procedure is made official, what people actually do in carrying out the procedure will never be exactly the same from one instance to another but will get done so that it can be recognized as fitting the official categories. It becomes a Grade Appeal.

If I begin to explore what I have learned about institutional language as it is actually practiced, I can see that there is much in the IE literature that addresses this. I think of Gerald de Montigny's (1995) remarkable study of how his own experience of the professional discourse of social work as it was imposed upon him in his training. It was deeply in contradiction with what he knew and understood as a young working-class man and how it then entered into and organized his professional work when his training was completed. His book details his experiences with deep conflicts between what his working-class experience understood of the world and how he had to take up and work with people's problems using the discourse of social work imposed by his training. From an account of the process of being trained as a social worker he goes on to describe how the language of social work's professional discourse organized his work practices as a professional. His story is essentially an investigation of the experience of practicing institutional language; it is extraordinary and powerful—all too little recognized and drawn upon. In the following section,

I draw on his vivid account (de Montigny, 2014) focused on his child protection work to show just how his practices of the institutional language of child protection organized his work on a particular occasion.

Another and rather different uncovering of the distinctive properties of institutional language was developed in Gillian Walker's (1990, 1995) examination of concepts as social organizers in her study of the *conceptual politics* of the women's movement's struggle to achieve government response to violence against women. At the time of the early organization of women's initiatives to secure government action in relation to the endemic character of men's use of physical force on women there were no concepts: no *domestic abuse*, no *wife assault*, no *violence against women*. Walker explored the process of arriving at communities of struggle among organizations arising in different parts of the country and out of different experiences. Yet, as the grassroots struggle was articulated to the ruling relations through actions aimed at limiting violence against women, concepts became the avenue through which that struggle could be carried forward and also eviscerated. Walker (1995) wrote, about halfway through the book that records her discoveries, that she has been

> ... tracing a crucial progression whereby the anger and mobilization of feminist activists concerned with wife beating have been transformed and absorbed into existing institutional capture. The result of this process is that, although we may still be working, struggling, and angry, the sites of our struggle are dispersed, disconnected, and depoliticized. (p. 95)

At the first stage of the conceptual organization of women's struggle against male violence, concepts were needed to frame women's experience:

> The process of making the experience of oppression in our own homes visible to ourselves and then getting it accepted as a matter of public concern was one that involved defining it as an issue or problem in our own terms. The language we have available to us to do this kind of work presents us with a contradiction: it is the 'oppressor's language,' controlled by those who have the power to define its content and meaning. We have, however, to use it to express our cases. (Walker, 1995, p. 95)

Institutional concepts referring to violence against women differed depending on which government department was aimed at—the concept of *family violence* aimed at departments for responsible health and welfare; the concept of *wife assault* aimed at justice departments. Walker shows how in this second process government concepts reorganized and reframed what women's groups had been bringing forward. She describes how the concept of family violence "operated as an 'ordering procedure' for assembling" (1995, p. 75) a report and recommendations that came out of a legislative standing committee. The concept transforms and absorbs (her terms) what women's groups had been putting forward, displacing their distinctive orientation to the violence that was specific to women's experience.

> The new language displaces [women's] distinctive experiential orientation. The institutional concepts articulate to the functions of departments and committees as they were embedded in the formal standardizing language of the government authorization. (Walker, 1995, p. 95)

We can see in Walker's account, how the concepts developed to articulate to *bureaucratic* forms of governance displace women's own experience of male violence as they are reshaped to fit the pre-existing languages of relevant departments. Governmental standardizing language disconnected the concepts held by the women's organization seeking for governments to take responsibility for acting in relation to violence against women as women experienced it. The government-devised concepts such as family violence or domestic abuse established authorized frames displacing the authority of women's experience as spoken by women.

Institutional Words in Practice

So now we are making a shift. We're no longer just recognizing how institutionally named "objects" are built out of selected aspects of actualities encoded as *textual realities* or how people get done what can be recognized as the moments of an institutionally mandated and named sequence of action. Just how the institutional categories in practice organize what people do is very well described in Gerald de Montigny's (2014) fascinating account of how, in his child protection work, he went about determining whether and how he could make a case for removing a child from its home; notice here this concept, the very notion of a *case* relies on the existence of the formalized text that organizes the transtemporal continuity of identity to be built upon.

De Montigny was called out when a caretaker reported a commotion—breaking glass, shouting—in one of the apartments. What he sees, smells, hears, when he arrives, he treats selectively in terms that fit the categories of child protection law and of the discourse of social work that specifies and supplements it. As he goes through the apartment, he is now looking for evidence. He is looking for what will fit the categories of the provincial law on child abuse and neglect at that time (1980s). Here are some of his observations and how he brings them into relation with his projected institutional course of action—to make a temporary removal of the child to a group home to be followed up by court action granting custody of the child. The institutional course of action becomes observable in his account of how he practiced its words "in his head."

> As I walked into the back bedroom I found an infant, ...perhaps 10 or 12 months old, lying asleep on top of filthy sheets . . . . I looked at the child's body to note that she was wearing only a feces-soiled and urine-soaked diaper. Feces had dried, and caked her torso and face. I could see that she had been left unattended for several hours without attention to her needs.

Even more disturbing to me was that when I picked her up I saw that the back of her skull was flattened. I assumed that the flattened was not natural. I guessed that it signified the parent's failure to attend to her, and rotating her while sleeping or to pick her up when awake. The flattened skull could be an invaluable piece of evidence before the court. It would serve as a powerful and graphic sign of abnormality resulting from serious neglect. It showed that the child had been left alone lying on her back hour after hour and day after day.... As I stood in a dimly lit room and breathed in putrid air, I held a groggy child who was beginning to emit frightened cries, yet, my mind was focused on an institutionally defined problem of making a case. I had to establish that this was a child in need of protection. I had to compile sufficient evidence of neglect to make a case, that is, to justify my apprehension, and to be granted custody before the judge in court. (de Montigny, 2014, pp. 176–177)

De Montigny describes vividly his work of fitting the disturbing experiencing of the child's situation and condition into the categories that articulate what he is doing and thinking—the words in-skull that organize his present awareness—to fit an institutional course of action: he is making a *case*; he looks for *evidence of neglect* and to justify being *granted custody before the judge in court*. We can see here how the institutional terms, as he practices these words in his head, are organizing what he does as part of an institutionally mandated course of action, reaching from his work there with the child in its home to what follows as he initiates the course of action that aims as securing custody in court. "[M]y mind," he tells us, "was focused on an institutionally defined problem of making a case. I had to establish that this was a child in need of protection. I had to compile sufficient evidence of neglect to make a case, that is, to justify my apprehension, and to be granted custody before the judge in court" (de Montigny, 2014, pp. 176–177). This is his work but it also draws in others whose active parts in the sequence de Montigny brings into view are also institutionally defined.

Notice that all this organizing of de Montigny's consciousness is in his head. It is his local practice of the words that organize his present awareness in orienting to what he will aim at doing and achieving within the institutional settings. This is the language of the professional discourse which he was trained to activate in his professional work (de Montigny, 1995). The organizing done with words in his head is relating him to an institutionally defined course of action. His word-organized work is becoming the opening moments of the mandated course of action concluding with the court process and securing custody of the child and its final removal from its home. The institutional words *organize* what de Montigny was doing in one place in relation to the subsequent moments in an institutionally recognizable sequence.

Textual Realities

Earlier on in my pursuit of words as practices, I encountered the work of Hans-Jörg Schmid (2000), who introduced me to a type of noun that lacks specific content—for example, thing, fact, case, reason. Such nouns can be seen as waiting to be filled. He calls them *shells* (Schmid, 2000). Schmid's observations are only of English abstract nouns, but what he describes and analyzes can be applied to how the categories and concepts of institutional language are actually brought into action as people take them up.

Institutional ethnographers have investigated the work of producing textual realities by procedures selecting from actualities that source the representation of what will fit the shell of the institutional category. Schmid's treatment of shells and how they are filled is confined to sentence structures or sequences, but his account suggested as an analogy how the categories of the authoritative or, more casually, boss texts of institutional discourse are also waiting to be filled with substance extracted from the actualities of people's lives and doings. The fillings are not the original actualities shaped perceptually but they are realities constructed in texts to fit the shells of institutional discourse. While actualities can only be known by people experientially, textual representations are accorded the authority of words that are independent of the particularities of subjectivity; they are not only verbal generalizers but are also standardized as the same for different subjects and situations. They constitute realities independent of those who may have been experiencing and acting in the original actuality out of which the textual representation has been constructed. Instead of the perceptual standardization that Luria describes, what we have is a standardization built into the practicing of institutional words whether spoken, written, on the computer or in-skull. In courses of institutional action, such as we saw in de Montigny's account earlier, the institutional wording of what is to get done has also the problem of the Schmidt shell. What people do, how they act in such sequences, has to be organized so that it can be fitted properly, not only in the particular instance but as a component in a sequence coordinated with others whose work can be referred to and expected to fit to the institutional words that frame and organize the *mandated sequence*, to use George Smith's term (1988). The institutional words brought into play in any particular situation, organize how what is to get done engages in sequence with what is mandated to follow.

In de Montigny's account we can also see the beginning of coordinated work which will produce in the course of the proceedings of the court a "textual reality." What was actually going on, the child's actual situation, becomes displaced by the work of selecting from actualities just what will fit the categories that make the actual actionable in the terms of an institutional course of action. De Montigny describes how he selects from what is going on with the child what can count as evidence when he makes the case to the court. Producing textual realities to fit the shells (Schmidt) of the institutional categories built into the texts defining the institutional course of action is integral to how actual courses of action move forward.

George Smith (1988) wrote a detailed account of just how undercover police visiting a gay bathhouse while active sex was going on made observations and wrote their report so that it would fit the categories of Ontario's *bawdy house* law and enable charges to be brought against those involved.

Smith's account and analysis show just how passages in the police report are designed to fit what was observed into the categories of the law and hence setting up the basis on which those "found in" the bathhouse at the time of the later police raid could be charged. Their account fitted sections of the law defining criminal behavior and, on this basis, charges were laid. Here is one of the sections of the law that passages of the police report could fit: "A common bawdy house is a place ... that is kept ... for the practice of acts of indecency" (Smith, 1988, p. 175).

The category of *indecency* is in practice hard to define. In general it refers to sexual activity performed publicly in a public setting. The police report fitting what was observed to this way of defining indecency shows sexual activity going on when anyone who was around could observe it—a way of interpreting what could be seen as *public*. We can see here how the category of "acts of indecency" operate as a shell for selective accounts drawn from actual situation and described to fit. Here is a passage quoted by Smith from the police report. I have italicized the part specific to the above quote from the bawdy-house law.

> Constables Coulis and Proctor attended at the premises, entering separately, where they approached the cash area.... When the officers first entered the premises they walked around and noted the lay-out of the premises as well as any indecent activity that was taking place at that time. *It was at this time that both officers saw a number of men laying* [sic] *nude in the private booths with the door wide open. Some of these men were masturbating themselves while others just lay on the mattress watching as other men walked about the hallways.* The officers took periodic walks about the premises and they saw that the same type of indecent activity was taking place each and every time (as quoted by Smith, 1988, p. 169).

Other passages address other aspects of the law and overall the police report became the basis for laying charges against those found in the bathhouse as an institutionally mandated course of action.

Ethnographic Significance of Recognizing Institutional Words as Practices

In putting forward the idea of recognizing the institutionalized language vested in texts as people's local practices, I am not suggesting that we develop a whole new theoretical account of language. Rather I am thinking we should become more aware of—and make more ethnographically observable—how people are using words in coordinating institutionally governed actions. What researchers have observed or discovered in talking with informants/respondents can begin to advance for us our recognition of an important dimension of institutionally defined social relations/sequences of action. In the institutional ethnographic instances drawn on in the previous sections, we can see how institutional language organizes people's work in institutionally mandated sequences. Incorporating people's practices of institutional words into the ethnographic moment of the research dialogue entitles our ethnography to reach beyond particularities to the generalizing powers of institutional relations. I emphasize how the institutional words brought into practice generalize sequences of action across multiple actual sequences done by different people and never exactly the same. As institutional words carried in authorized texts are practiced in particular sequences of people's works, they generalize across the particular moment when it is happening, translating its local particularities into relevant moment in the institutional or mandated course of action. Here is a grounding for writing the ethnography that finds, in what people tell from their experience or what the ethnographer observes, the particular ways people are bringing the institutional into actuality. Attending to the language as it comes into play in the observations we make or the interviews connecting us with those doing the work, shows us how the particularities of any actual work can be discovered as it articulates sequences of actual activities as local language practices. People's actions are never exactly the same, but the institutional language coordinating the sequence represents the different moments of the mandated sequence vested in texts.

It is fairly usual in sociology to find written into its accounts terms like *social structure, organizations,* and so on that can be represented as *acting* or causing people to act. Michael Billig (2013) has argued that we "should try to undo the power that nouns seem to have over social scientists" and that "we should try to express ourselves in clauses with active verbs" (2013, p. 236). This is not just a matter of style; it is a matter of how we go in writing from what we have learned of what is going on among people to a written representation that goes beyond any one individual's doings to bring into view a complex of coordinated doings that is ongoing. From time to time in writing institutional ethnographies we have used words such as *organize* to suggest something of how the verbal mandating of sequences of action coordinate people's doings. We have also made it clear that we do not want to get hung up on notions such as *social organization*, even though they may seem entirely appropriate when we have brought our institutional ethnography to the point where its institutional standardization is fully visible in particularized people's doings. But now we are making a shift. We are no longer just recognizing how institutionally named "objects" are built out of selected aspects of actualities encoded as "textual realities." We are now beginning to make observable how institutional courses of action are vested in words that, as they are practiced, name the particularities of what people are doing as the actions, outcomes, etc., identified in the authorizing texts.

Starting out in the same world where we ourselves are in our bodies means that we are in a world that is always in process, building on a past that is never concluded as such and moving into a future that is never just the same as it was it is developing from. What I suggest we are discovering as we bring people's practices of institutionally authorized words into view is just such a grounding for our ethnography. I have emphasized and demonstrated, using de Montigny's study, how institutional words as they are practiced generalize courses of action that are institutionally mandated. We are not interested in one-time only accounts of what people do; we want to bring into view how institutions work, how institutional courses or sequences of action are actually put together, how what we might describe as social organization or social relations or however we make that move from the particularities of what actually goes on to a generalized and generalizing account of the workings of ruling or institutional relations. That institutional language as it is brought into practice generalizes across particularities—what is getting done or will be done can be recognized and treated as the same as what has been and will be done within the same jurisdiction (a term which clearly points to a region for further exploration). In a sense, the practices of institutional language as they become observed in actual settings as people's actual practices are valuable as grounding ethnographic representations drawing on particular and varied accounts of what is getting done. This paper is a move toward our making the generalizing powers of institutional words as people practice them more visible in explicating such relations as they become organized in what people do.

Note

1. Luria originally observed this phenomenon incidentally to an experimental study of children. I was unable to locate the original observation since it was not itself the topic and Luria's experimental work has been more or less buried—perhaps because his experimental procedures do not test hypotheses but aim rather at isolating and making aspects of children's learning observable.

References

Billig, M. (2013). *Learn to write badly: How to succeed in the social sciences*. Cambridge, UK: Cambridge University Press.

de Montigny, G. J. (1995). *Social working: An ethnography of front-line practice*. Toronto, CA: University of Toronto Press.

de Montigny, G. J. (2014). Doing child protection work. In D. E. Smith & S. M. Turner (Eds.), *Incorporating texts into institutional ethnographies* (pp. 173–194). Toronto, CA: University of Toronto Press.

Garfinkel, H. (2002). *Ethnomethodology's program: Working out Durkheim's aphorism*. A. W. Rawls (Ed.). Lanham, MD: Rowman and Littlefield.

Luria, A. R. (1961). *The role of speech in the regulation of normal and abnormal behavior*. New York, NY: Pergamon Press.

Luria, A. R. (1976). *Cognitive development: Its cultural and social foundations*. Cambridge, MA: Harvard University Press.

Luria, A. R., & Yudovich, F. I. (1971). *Speech and the development of mental processes in the child*. New York, NY: Penguin Books.

Mead, G. H. (1962). *Mind, self, and society from the perspective of a social behaviorist*. Chicago, IL: University of Chicago Press.

Prosek, J. (2013). What's in a name: Or unnamed in the forest. In S. Carson (Ed.), *Living with Shakespeare: Essays by writers, actors, and directors* (pp. 371–382). New York, NY: Vintage Books.

Schmid, H.-J. (2000). *English abstract nouns as conceptual shells: From corpus to cognition*. Berlin: Mouton de Gruyter.

Smith, D. E. (2001). Texts and the ontology of institutions and organizations. *Studies in Cultures, Organizations, and Societies, 7*(2), 159–198.

Smith, D. E. (2016). Exploring words as people's practices. In J. Lynch, J. Rowlands, T. Gale, & A. Skourdoumbis (Eds.), *Diffractive readings in practice: Trajectories in theory, fields and professions* (pp. 23–38). London, UK: Routledge.

Smith, G. W. (1988). Policing the gay community: An inquiry into textually mediated relations. *International Journal of Sociology and the Law, 16*, 163–183.

Walker, G. (1990). *Family violence and the women's movement: The conceptual politics of struggle*. Toronto, ON: University of Toronto Press.

Walker, G. (1995). Violence and the relations of ruling: Lessons from the battered women's movement. In M. Campbell & A. Manicom (Eds.), *Knowledge, experience and ruling relations: Studies in the social organization of knowledge* (pp. 65–79). Toronto, ON: University of Toronto Press.

PART II

Developing Strategies and Exploring Challenges

CHAPTER 6

Mapping Ruling Relations: Advancing the Use of Visual Methods in Institutional Ethnography

Nicole K. Dalmer

Mapping out ruling relations that extend beyond the local and the everyday is a central feature of institutional ethnography (Smith, 1987, 2005; Waters, 2015). This mapping, as both an action and as a metaphor, permeates institutional ethnographic inquiries, with maps serving "as a guide through a complex ruling apparatus" (DeVault & McCoy, 2002, p. 754).

As Waters[1] (2015) explains, for the majority of institutional ethnography (IE) investigations, "the term *mapping* is commonly used in institutional ethnography research to describe the empirical tracing of sequences of work and texts from a starting place in peoples' accounts into institutional work process and action" (p. 134, emphasis in original). These maps take shape over the duration of the study, progressively tracing and revealing the ruling relations uncovered throughout the investigation. Susan Turner (2003, 2006), for example, has developed a number of rather iconic maps within IE as she revealed the text-based work sequences to map the coordination of institutional action to understand how municipal planning comes to organize land development. To be clear, such maps provide an orientation not to a physical landscape, but to a social landscape that comprises the problematic under investigation. Traditionally, such maps are the result or outcome of the study, with the map used to make visible the many different mechanisms through which informants are linked and hooked into ruling relations (Smith, 1999).

N. K. Dalmer (✉)
Department of Health, Aging and Society, McMaster University, Hamilton, ON, Canada
e-mail: dalmern@mcmaster.ca

Smith (1999) goes on to remark that the results of an institutional ethnography should, in fact, be as "ordinarily accessible and usable, just as a map is" (p. 95).

As a complement to these traditional institutional ethnography maps, in this chapter, I provide an overview to a mapping exercise I carried out with family caregivers of older adults who are living with dementia. Rather than mapping out ruling relations and using the map as a final product or outcome of my investigation, the integration of this visual method served as a data elicitation tool, used to both support and visualize caregiver informants' exploration and articulation of their often-invisible care-related information work.

The Everyday Experiences of Family Caregivers: Contextualizing the Study

The work and findings in this chapter are part of a larger institutional ethnography study that sought to understand the character of and the social relations that give shape to family caregiving (Dalmer, 2018). More specifically, through conversations with family caregivers and dementia care staff (Dalmer, 2019a), an aging in place policy analysis (Dalmer, 2019b), and a critical review of the ways in which formal research organizes the way we think about and understand family caregivers' information activities (Dalmer, 2020), I explored how family caregivers' experiences of their information activities become shaped by institutional texts, practices, and processes related to the trend of aging in place. I was initially intrigued by a quote that I came across from Dementia Friends Canada, a collaborative, national awareness campaign that was launched in 2015 between the Canadian federal government and the Alzheimer Society of Canada. They stated, "The more you know about dementia, the more prepared you'll be to help people with dementia live better" (Dementia Friends Canada, 2015). The stark contrast between this quote and the tensions that arose in my own, everyday experiences as a librarian and as an information scholar ultimately formed the direction for this institutional ethnography inquiry.

Eighty-five percent of individuals living with dementia rely, at least in part, on family, friends, or neighbors for support for a number of tasks, including: transportation, managing appointments or finances, meal preparation, housework, taking medications, and personal care, including dressing, bathing, toileting, and eating (Wong, Gilmour, & Ramage-Morin, 2016). Information activities (including finding information, making sense of it, sharing it, and storing it) underpin each of the above-mentioned care tasks to which family caregivers lend their time, finances, support, and work. This might include seeking out information about medication delivery times or side effects, sharing information about where to access home-delivered meals, sorting through information about in-home modifications, or making sense and processing the implications of information about the progression of dementia.

With changing patterns of information provision and consumption, family caregivers are increasingly encouraged to actively and independently seek out information as part of being a "good" caregiver, as evidenced in Dementia Friends Canada's above quote. The provision of information is a key component in enabling a caregiver to be actively involved in the health and wellbeing of the older adult in their care. This push to use information to be prepared for or to meet the complex medical and social needs of a growing older adult population is tempered by family caregivers' continued reports of feeling inadequately prepared, informed, and supported (Allen, Cain, & Meyer, 2020; Bookman & Harrington, 2007; Washington, Meadows, Elliott, & Koopman, 2011). Despite the increasing availability of care-related information in online and print formats, a majority of family caregivers report that their information needs are largely unmet (Morris & Thomas, 2002), with more than 80% of family caregivers desiring more information on caregiving topics (AARP & National Alliance for Caregiving, 2015). In their examination of various documents from the Department of Health in England, Barnes and Henwood (2015) have similarly reported a prevailing "belief in the transformative power of information, with good care being positioned as a natural by-product of the widespread availability of good information" (p. 148), ultimately obscuring much of family caregivers' work that is needed to manage, gather, share, and keep track of information to complete or negotiate different care tasks.

Outlining the Interviews

Institutional ethnographers learn by talking with individuals who are directly experiencing the problematic under investigation (Smith, 2008). As a result, interviews with informants "who participate in such a regime to explore with them the work they are doing and to make visible in this way how the institutional regime enters into the organization of that work" (Griffith & Smith, 2005, p. 4) are a common method in IE. As previously mentioned, as one component of this larger institutional ethnography, I conducted interviews with family caregivers. For these interviews, I recruited the majority of informants from a dementia care facility that hosted adult day programs as well as weekly caregiver support meetings and education sessions. My recruitment was helped in large part through a research coordinator and a social worker who both worked at a dementia care facility. Following approval from The University of Western Ontario's Research Ethics Board, I spoke with 13 family caregivers who self-reported as the primary, unpaid caregiver for an older adult (over the age of 65), who had a formal diagnosis of dementia (of any type), and who was aging in place in Ontario.

Institutional ethnographers avoid abstracting or theorizing what people do, instead detecting and making visible the ruling relations that have generalizing effects. I therefore grounded the interviews in family care providers' actual, ongoing experiences and activities, organized around the 13 informants' experiences of work (using Smith's [2005] generous definition), including informants' associated work knowledges (Smith, 2005). I spoke with family caregivers, using empathetic listening to listen to what was latent in caregivers' talk to make visible and understand what information work they do and how they conceptualize this work. One structuring device in the interviews was to ask caregivers to run through a typical day as a means to construct and extract descriptions of the work they do in relation to caring for their aging family member. In another structuring device, I asked caregivers to think about when they first noticed changes in their family member, and where (and why) they decided to go to learn more about these changes.

Talking about information as it weaves in and out of family caregivers' everyday and every night lives proved difficult during initial, pilot conversations with informants. DeVault (1999) explains the potential difficulty in extricating informants' experiences: "most members of society learn to interpret their experiences in terms of dominant language and meaning; thus, women themselves (researchers included) often have trouble seeing and talking about their experiences" (p. 66). The characteristics of family caregivers' information activities pose particular challenges for data collection; first, because the work may be invisible to the people who do it, second, because keeping the interviews grounded in informants' everyday work and resisting generalizing informants' work knowledges can be a difficult task (McKenzie & Dalmer, in press), and third, both information and care are often vague and hazy concepts, constructed and interpreted differently between individuals. Care work is in many ways, "a nebulous and ambiguous concept and a part of everyday life which is taken for granted" (Phillips, 2007, p. 1), making the underlying, and often gendered and classed work of care often invisible to those doing, receiving, organizing, and legislating care. Information is likewise a vague concept with slippery borders (Buckland, 1991). Greyson and Johnson (2016), for example, list a number of often-invisible activities that might comprise families' information activities, including: blunting, accessing, seeking, assessing, monitoring, avoiding, recalling, encountering, processing, sharing, and sense-making. As informants may not have the occasion or opportunity to consider the role of information in their everyday lives, they may, understandably, have difficulty articulating activities such as these.

DeVault (1991) found that the vocabulary of *work* brought to light the workful character of providing sustenance, including cooking and feeding, which "is often unrecognized even by those who do it" (p. 228). As researchers, the language we use can impact the visibility of the activities we study, and thus our findings and their implications. So too can the methods that we elect to employ or not employ. As I sought some sort of tool, technique, mechanism, or method by which to guide the interviews and to more easily elicit memories, frustrations, or tasks related to information, I embedded an information world mapping exercise within the interviews. Not only did this visual method keep the interviews grounded in family caregivers' actual and ongoing activities and experiences (Smith, 1999), it provided an alternative way to extract and elicit caregivers' understandings and descriptions of their care-related information work. Ultimately, this exercise served as a helpful data elicitation technique to make visible "what is getting done and how" (Turner, 2006, p. 159), including the often-hidden work of finding, using, sharing, and dealing with the implications of information.

Detailing the Mapping Exercise

Visual methods and the use of visual materials in the research process, whether that be visual techniques, visual material culture, or researcher-initiated production of visual data, are gaining traction and popularity across disciplines (Pauwels, 2010). The integration of visual research methods challenge traditional researcher-participant dynamics, are helpful for researchers exploring the inner mechanisms of the ordinary and the everyday, and can engender abstract and unexpected meaning making from participants (Martin, 2015; Rose, 2016). Knowles and Sweetman (2004) underscore visual methods' "capacity to reveal what is hidden in the inner mechanisms of the ordinary and the taken for granted" (p. 7). The integration of visual methods or techniques with informants in an institutional ethnography investigation is fairly new, though not novel. In particular, Photovoice[2] has recently emerged as a popular visual method embedded within institutional ethnography studies (Newell, 2018; Ollerton & Kelshaw, 2011; Padilla, Matiz-Reyes, Colón-Burgos, Varas-Díaz, & Vertovec, 2019; Puddu, Nykiforuk, Kafara, Barrera, & Boyle Street Community Services, 2018). Puddu et al. (2018), for example, explain that the data generated through the use of Photovoice in their project were instrumental in providing helpful insights into the youth informants' daily experiences and ultimately helped provide direction regarding which institutional practices and policies to then explore. As these existing arts-based institutional ethnography investigations reveal, the integration of arts-based methods when engaging with informants about their experiences provides "the entry point into a set of institutional relations" (McCoy, 2006, p. 109).

Before moving forward with an articulation of the information world mapping exercise, it is imperative to emphasize that the objects of analyses in an institutional ethnography are the ruling relations. As such, the outcomes of a visual or arts-based method (whether these may be maps, photos, videos, or drawings, among others) are not to be considered as the objects of analysis or as the research findings in an institutional ethnography. Nichols, Griffith, and McLarnon (2018) have helpfully articulated the fit and the frictions when integrating community-based and participatory approaches in institutional ethnography, noting that they are of greatest use during analysis. This chapter argues that arts-based and visual methods are integral for their ability to secure and ground the research in the actualities of informants' lives. As institutional ethnographers are often searching through unwaged, unnoticed, and marginalized forms of work that are required to carry out leisure, domestic, or other everyday activities, this chapter advances that visual methods are especially useful during the data collection phase, used particularly in data elicitation with informants. What follows is an overview of the information world mapping exercise itself, including examples of the informants' maps, and three overarching advantages of embedding similar visual data elicitation tools in institutional ethnography interviews.

As I researched a structure or modality through which to talk about or elicit examples or experiences regarding family caregivers' care-related information activities, I ultimately created an information world mapping exercise, based on Sonnenwald's information horizons (1999; Sonnenwald, Wildemuth, & Harmon, 2001) and on subsequent mapping exercises outlined by Freund, Hawkins, and Saewyc (2016), Greyson, O'Brien, and Shankar (2010), Greyson, O'Brien, and Shoveller (2017), Huvila (2009), and Lingel (2011). While caregivers' information activities may occur in a broader, more generalizable context or situation than that prescribed by Sonnenwald, this concept served as a useful framework to ground caregivers' experiences of their information work.

Near the mid-point of the interview with each of the family caregivers, I asked informants if they would be comfortable participating in a mapping exercise. Twelve of the 13 caregivers agreed to take part in this exercise[3] and proceeded to map, write, doodle, sketch, and draw the information activities they described in their interview in addition to any other information work-related resources or tasks that came to mind as they drew out their own map. While I offered informants the option of creating the map alone (I offered to leave the room), all informants allowed me to stay with them as they created their map. This proved particularly helpful as I was able to ask for clarification as informants created their map. Prompting questions included asking informants why they drew their map in a certain order and asking for further clarification for resources, people, or places that appeared on the information world map but that had not yet been mentioned during the interview. Following the completion of an initial series of pilot interviews, I created a template information world with the goal of making the mapping exercise less onerous. Informants could choose to work from a blank paper (as Sylvia[4] did, as illustrated in Fig. 6.3[5]) or from a template that Alice and Marge used, in Figs. 6.1 and 6.2, that blocked out: (a) what resources families used, (b) from or with whom caregivers sought or shared information, and, (c) where caregivers went for information.

Informants maintained a large degree of control over the design, creation, and interpretation of their information worlds. Maps varied considerably between caregivers, particularly in degree of detail, as is evident in Figs. 6.1, 6.2, and 6.3. Sparsely populated maps, though, should not be mistaken for a lack of information conveyed. For some caregivers, such as Alice (Fig. 6.1), writing out the information they simultaneously verbally relayed was a helpful strategy, whereas for others, such as with Marge (Fig. 6.2), jotting down a few, key names, places, or resources served as a trigger to remember, identify, or link other lines of work or other people involved in completing or navigating their various care-related tasks.

6 MAPPING RULING RELATIONS: ADVANCING THE USE OF VISUAL ... 87

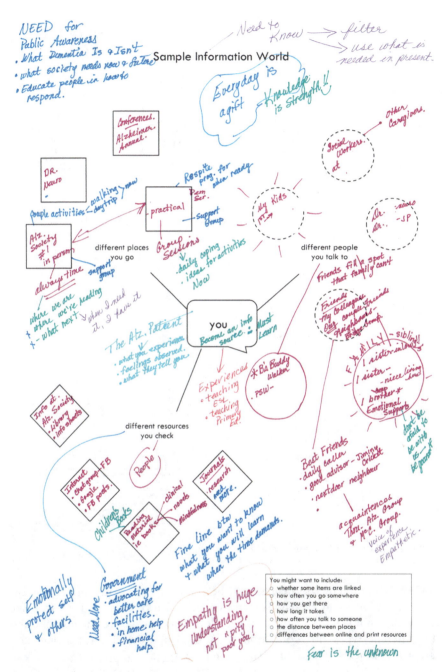

Fig. 6.1 Alice's information world

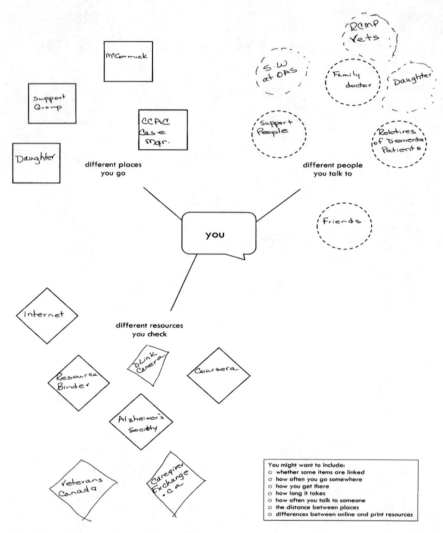

Fig. 6.2 Marge's information world

Given the difficulty in delineating the boundaries of both care and information, the mapping exercise served as a helpful tool for caregivers to make visible the complexities of their information work, including the amount and the different types of information work they performed throughout their caregiving trajectory and the barriers encountered and inventive strategies they employed to access, use, and translate information needed to guide and support their care work. Each map depicts the caregiver's unique understanding and experience of their everyday lives, representing the information resources (family members, health care professionals, agencies, texts, tools, and

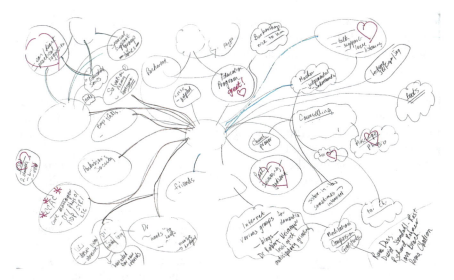

Fig. 6.3 Sylvia's information world

websites) they accessed within their care context. In addition to mapping information sites and resources, caregivers included relationship dynamics, quotes, and self-care activities, revealing how information more broadly intersects with and may both support and complicate their care work. As the informants completed the mapping exercise, they articulated their surprise at and sense of validation in seeing this particular type of work they do. Perhaps as a result of this visual display of an often-unrecognized form of work, a majority of caregivers asked for scanned copies of their maps to keep for themselves.

As demonstrated by Alice's information world map in Fig. 6.1, maps depict differing constellations of items, places, mantras ("knowledge is strength," "fear is the unknown"), and formal and informal relationships that shaped and guided their information activities. As these information world maps were not constrained to depicting one specific place or one particular point in time, a fuller complement of families' information work emerged. Alice's detailed map guided the conversations we had in person, helping to make visible the many networks of places (including non-profit organizations and internet sites), social relations (including friends and family and a myriad of health care professionals), and resources that jointly provide support for both her and her husband, who was diagnosed with early onset Alzheimer's disease. Each of these relations required work that would not have been brought to light without the integration of this mapping exercise in our interview: work to navigate the information received, work to assemble that information into existing knowledge, and, in Alice's case, work to determine how to translate this information to different family members, including her grandchildren. As a number of informational activities are often invisible even to those who perform them, such visual elicitation techniques allow for the mapping of individuals' work on many planes—in terms of the actual type or content of work and its spatial and temporal aspects. The act of filling out one of the circles, squares, or diamonds on the template map would prompt Alice to draw in the next sequence in her care work, leading her to fill in another shape. This process made visible, for example, the effort needed to travel physically and virtually between different information resources. In completing her map, Alice came to identify certain lines of information-related care work that had been previously invisible to her.

Sylvia (Fig. 6.3) was the sole informant who created her very own map, working from a blank piece of paper. Sylvia, in fact, contacted me a few days after our interview as she realized she had missed including her paid work on her original map and later emailed me a scanned addendum map she had made by herself. In addition to the relations that inform, support, and complicate informants' care-related information activities (key components to all family caregivers' information worlds and everyday care experiences), Sylvia's information world illustrates the information work needed to schedule and keep track of her many self-care activities she takes part in (swimming, prayer, tai chi, counseling, and internet support groups, among others). Quite significantly, as we discussed the activities she had included in her map, she quietly revealed that these self-care activities were not necessarily for her own benefit or pleasure, but she viewed these activities as necessary in ensuring that she could be a better (or even best) care provider for her husband for as long as possible.

Importantly, as Sylvia and the other informants crafted their maps, they simultaneously provided key clues as to which individuals, organizations, or documents I would need to investigate next (including, for example, provincial funding models as well as geriatricians, social workers, and dementia care staff). The mapping exercises, therefore revealed, where or with whom to collect level-two data (Campbell & Gregor, 2004), that is, data that are "positioned outside the setting" (Deveau, 2008, p. 15). Collecting level-two data allowed me to work back to see how informants' experiences happened as they did. By following the different institutions, texts, and actors on the informants' maps, I was able to progressively reveal "how people's everyday lives may be organized without their explicit awareness but still with their active involvement" (Campbell & Gregor, 2004, p. 43).

Descriptions of family caregivers' work knowledges, illuminated through a combination of interviews and mapping exercises, guided my investigation into the networks and coordination of other people, systems, and texts that are hooked into larger institutional complexes (including the aging in place complex) and that enter into and shape family caregivers' information-related work knowledges. For example, Sylvia's explanation of her many lines of work that support her need to be a "best" or "better" caregiver provided an entry point to progressively examine how the ideals of familism, or a family ethic, centered on "traditional" family values (Hooyman & Gonyea, 1995) and a neoliberal mindset of individualization (McGregor, 2001) underpin aging in place as an ideological code (Smith, 1993).

Moving Forward: Proposed Affordances of Visual Methods in Institutional Ethnography

This chapter is but a starting point in advancing the utility of embedding visual methods, such the mapping exercise described in this chapter, within existing institutional ethnography methods, such as interviews. The mapping exercise has highlighted the following three interconnected affordances in integrating visual methods within an institutional ethnography. These three advantages may serve as helpful starting points for further conversations as the use of visual methods is brought up and discussed among institutional ethnographers:

1. Grounding in Informants' Everyday Experiences

    Visual methods provide an alternative mechanism through which informants can make visible those aspects and experiences of their every day (and every night) lives that are significant to them. The information world mapping exercise was a tool that served as a visual reminder that institutional ethnography investigations are to remain intimately rooted in informants' everyday actualities. Relatedly, as rigor in institutional ethnography is established through transparent and accurate descriptions of "what is actually happening within the social relations" (Prodinger, 2012, p. 89), such visual methods can be mobilized to ensure the authenticity of informants' descriptions is maintained and respected.

    For institutional ethnographers, the social can only be discovered among actual people and the ongoing moment-by-moment concerting of their activities (McCoy, 2008; Smith, 2006). By grounding my interactions with family caregivers in their actualities and by privileging their work knowledges, this exercise was instrumental in helping me avoid institutional capture (when institutional discourse subsumes everyday experiences, trapping writing in specific institutional language and thinking [Smith, 2005]) and from imposing my own generalizing thoughts. Maintaining this grounding in informants' everyday experiences was particularly important given my past professional and scholarly work as a librarian and an information scholar. I was acutely aware of the ease by which institutional capture could invade my thinking and interpretation of family caregivers' descriptions of their information-related everyday and every night experiences.

2. Privileging Informants' Work Knowledges

Smith's (2005) concept of work knowledge, that is, "a person's experience of and in their own work, what they do, how they do it, including what they think and feel" (p. 151), is rooted in institutional ethnography's social ontology and focus on descriptions of the social world as it is actually happening (Rankin, 2017; Smith, 2005, 2006). Each caregiver's work knowledge is steeped in their own experiences and is based within their local setting. Work knowledges are considered authoritative, not open to reinterpretation. The mapping exercise not only served as a reminder to ground interactions with informants in their actualities, but by turning the mapping exercise over to informants and by purposefully privileging their subjective work knowledges, the expertise was placed in the hands of those caregivers that are doing (and knowing, feeling, and experiencing) the information activities at the focus of this research. The mapping exercise therefore prompts a reconsideration of the informant's agency and expertise in the research interaction.

This consideration of informants' agency and expertise is particularly crucial for investigations that are examining the social organization of invisible or hidden forms of work, as so many IE studies do. Minnich (1990), for example, speaks to the challenges and opportunities of measuring and highlighting unpaid work, in that it requires the transformation of knowledge beyond traditional boundaries or categorization: "rethinking mystified concepts, ideas, notions, categories and the like that are so deeply familiar they are rarely questioned" (p. 51). Within the context of this particular study, Mol, Moser, and Pol (2010) argue: "if care practices are not carefully attended to, there is a risk that they will be eroded. If they are only talked about in terms that are not appropriate to their specificities, they will be submitted to rules and regulations that are alien to them" (p. 7). Accordingly, if an informant's expertise regarding their work knowledges is not privileged, the language that is used to describe or support families' experiences of their hidden care work might not reflect their actual, lived realities.

3. Revealing Invisible, Background Work

The integration of visual methods within interviews can offer an alternative mechanism through which different types of work knowledges can be brought to the fore. Certain aspects of people's work have a tendency to fade into invisibility. This may occur when the work is so routine as to be unremarkable or may be the result of the low social status of those conducting it (Star, 1991; Star & Strauss, 1999). Drawing, doodling, or writing out experiences can be used as a tool to expose the invisible, background work that supports so much of people's everyday (and every night) lives. DeVault (2014) has advanced four different analytic strategies in examining invisible work, including: (1) look at everyone's work (and how it's divided); (2) look at work that facilitates access; (3) look behind policy and procedure; and (4) look at work that's done "under the radar". As it is difficult to both identify and articulate which or how many lines of work invisibly comprise our days, visual methods can be used as a tool to support these four different analytic strategies. As I was rooted in caregivers' actualities, their information world map not only served as a tool to respect and cultivate caregivers' expertise, but it made tangible how caregivers went from one point to another (making visible "what happened next") and made visible the sequencing of actions and activities that can often be difficult to bring to focus.

Conclusions

DeVault (2014) notes that "as we see more of people's invisible labors, we find more work that needs to be done—projects in which we can apply the tools of our discipline and our craft" (p. 788). Indeed, this paper is a starting point in reflecting how the "tools of our discipline," including the methods institutional ethnographers select and apply, can impact which and what types activities (and the people doing those activities) are brought to the fore. Visual methods, such as the information world mapping exercise outlined in this chapter, can be a collaborative tool that contributes toward a rich understanding of the ruling relations that permeate informants' everyday (and every night) lives. Such visual methods can be mobilized as a mechanism to support informants as they articulate their often-hidden work, can keep interviews grounded in informants' actualities, are an opportunity to refocus on the informants' expertise regarding their work knowledges, and can help institutional ethnographers avoid institutional capture throughout the research process.

Notes

1. Nicola Waters (2015) has provided an excellent overview to the differences between the concept, understandings, and uses of maps within an institutional ethnography context and maps within other disciplines and for other purposes.
2. Developed by Wang and Burris (1994, 1997), Photovoice is a participatory action research method in which participants are given cameras and are asked to take photos of their everyday experiences in their communities. Using their photos, participants then "identify, represent, and enhance their community through a specific photographic technique" (Wang & Burris, 1997, p. 369), describing and explaining to the researcher why photos hold different meanings. Photovoice has been used to highlight a range of experiences and perspectives that have been historically and systemically silenced, providing marginalized or vulnerable populations a voice through photographs.

3. One family caregiver indicated that they felt they did not have the time to participate in this additional mapping exercise. With the many known demands (paid work, familial responsibilities, etc.) on family caregivers, I was initially anxious when asking informants to take on this additional task and was quite surprised that so many informants graciously agreed to try out this mapping exercise.
4. Informants in this study selected their own pseudonym to ensure confidentiality.
5. Information world maps featured in this chapter have had identifying materials blurred or removed.

References

AARP & National Alliance for Caregiving. (2015). *Caregiving in the U.S.* Retrieved from https://www.aarp.org/content/dam/aarp/ppi/2015/caregiving-in-the-united-states-2015-report-revised.pdf.

Allen, F., Cain, R., & Meyer, C. (2020). Seeking relational information sources in the digital age: A study into information source preferences amongst family and friends of those with dementia. *Dementia, 19*(3), 766–785.

Barnes, M., & Henwood, F. (2015). Inform with care: Ethics and information in care for people with dementia. *Ethics and Social Welfare, 9*(2), 147–163.

Bookman, A., & Harrington, M. (2007). Family caregivers: A shadow workforce in the geriatric health care system? *Journal of Health Politics, Policy and Law, 32*(6), 1005–1041.

Buckland, M. K. (1991). Information as thing. *Journal of the American Society for Information Science, 42*(5), 351–360.

Campbell, M., & Gregor, F. M. (2004). *Mapping social relations: A primer in doing institutional ethnography*. Walnut Creek, CA: Altamira Press.

Dalmer, N. K. (2018). *Informing care: Mapping the social organization of families' information work in an aging in place climate*. Doctoral dissertation. The University of Western Ontario.

Dalmer, N. K. (2019a). Considering the local and the translocal: Reframing health information practice research using institutional ethnography. *Aslib Journal of Information Management, 71*(6), 703–719.

Dalmer, N. K. (2019b). A logic of choice: Problematizing the documentary reality of Canadian aging in place policies. *Journal of Aging Studies, 48,* 40–49.

Dalmer, N. K. (2020). 'Add info and stir': An institutional ethnographic scoping review of family care-givers' information work. *Ageing & Society, 40*(3), 663–689.

Dementia Friends Canada. (2015). *Dementia 101.* Retrieved from https://dementiafriends.ca/dementia-101/.

DeVault, M. L. (1991). *Feeding the family*. Chicago, IL: The University of Chicago Press.

DeVault, M. L. (1999). *Liberating method: Feminism and social research*. Philadelphia, PA: Temple University Press.

DeVault, M. L. (2014). Mapping invisible work: Conceptual tools for social justice projects. *Sociological Forum, 79*(4), 775–790.

DeVault, M. L., & McCoy, L. (2002). Institutional ethnography: Using interviews to investigate ruling relations. In J. F. Gubrium & J. A. Holstein (Eds.), *Handbook of interview research* (pp. 751–776). London: Sage.

Deveau, J. L. (2008). Examining the institutional ethnographer's toolkit. *Socialist Studies/Études socialistes, 4*(2), 1–19.

Freund, L., Hawkins, B., & Saewyc, E. (2016). Reflections on the use of participatory mapping to study everyday health information seeking by LGBTQ youth. *Proceedings of the Association for Information Science and Technology, 53*(1), 1–4.

Greyson, D. L., & Johnson, J. L. (2016). The role of information in health behavior: A scoping study and discussion of major public health models. *Journal of the Association for Information Science and Technology, 67*(12), 2831–2841.

Greyson, D., O'Brien, H., & Shankar, S. (2010). Visual analysis of information world maps: An exploration of four methods. *Journal of Information Science, 46*(3), 361–377.

Greyson, D., O'Brien, H., & Shoveller, J. (2017). Information world mapping: A participatory arts-based elicitation method for information behavior interviews. *Library & Information Science Research, 39*(2), 149–157.

Griffith, A. I., & Smith, D. E. (2005). *Mothering for schooling.* New York: Psychology Press.

Hooyman, N. R., & Gonyea, J. G. (1995). *Feminist perspectives on family care: Policies for gender justice.* London: Sage.

Huvila, I. (2009). Analytical information horizon maps. *Library & Information Science Research, 31*(1), 18–28.

Knowles, C., & Sweetman, P. (2004). *Picturing the social landscape: Visual methods and the sociological imagination.* New York: Routledge.

Lingel, J. (2011). Information tactics of immigrants in urban environments. *Information Research, 16*(4). Retrieved from http://informationr.net/ir/16-4/paper500.html.

Martin, W. (2015). Visual methods in aging research. In J. Twigg & W. Martin (Eds.), *Routledge handbook of cultural gerontology* (pp. 93–104). London: Routledge.

McCoy, L. (2006). Keeping the institution in view: Working with interview accounts of everyday practice. In D. E. Smith (Ed.), *Institutional ethnography as practice* (pp. 109–125). Toronto: Rowman & Littlefield.

McCoy, L. (2008). Institutional ethnography and constructionism. In J. A. Holstein & J. F. Gubrium (Eds.), *Handbook of constructionist research* (pp. 701–714). New York, NY: The Guilford Press.

McGregor, S. (2001). Neoliberalism and health care. *International Journal of Consumer Studies, 25*(2), 82–89.

McKenzie, P., & Dalmer, N. K. (In Press). "This is really interesting. I never even thought about this." Methodological strategies for studying invisible information work. *Nordic Journal of Library and Information Studies.*

Minnich, E. K. (1990). *Transforming knowledge.* Philadelphia: Temple University Press.

Mol, A., Moser, I., & Pols, J. (Eds.). (2010). *Care in practice: On tinkering in clinics, homes and farms.* Bielefeld: Transcript.

Morris, S. M., & Thomas, C. (2002). The need to know: Informal carers and information. *European Journal of Cancer Care, 11*(3), 183–187.

Newell, F. (2018). *Exploring the link between food insecurity, social stigma and social marginalization among low-income lone mothers.* Doctoral dissertation. Mount Saint Vincent University.

Nichols, N., Griffith, A., & McLarnon, M. (2018). Community-based and participatory approaches in institutional ethnography. In J. Reid & L. Russell (Eds.),

Perspectives on and from institutional ethnography (pp. 107–124). Bingley, UK: Emerald.

Ollerton, J., & Kelshaw, C. (2011). Inclusive participatory action research: Rights, camera, action! In J. Higgs, A. Titchen, D. Horsfall, & D. Bridges (Eds.), *Creative spaces for qualitative researching: Living research* (pp. 267–280). Rotterdam, the Netherlands: Sense.

Padilla, M., Matiz-Reyes, A., Colón-Burgos, J. F., Varas-Díaz, N., & Vertovec, J. (2019). Adaptation of PhotoVoice methodology to promote policy dialog among street-based drug users in Santo Domingo, Dominican Republic. *Arts & Health*, *11*(2), 147–162.

Pauwels, L. (2010). Visual sociology reframed: An analytical synthesis and discussion of visual methods in social and cultural research. *Sociological Methods & Research*, *38*(4), 545–581.

Phillips, J. (2007). *Care: Key concepts*. Cambridge: Polity Press.

Prodinger, B. (2012). *Being an Austrian mother with rheumatoid arthritis: An institutional ethnography about the social organization of everyday life*. Doctoral dissertation. The University of Western Ontario.

Puddu, C., Nykiforuk, C., Kafara, R., Barrera, S., & Boyle Street Community Services. (2018). *Voices from the street: Stories of vulnerable youth in the shadow of urban development*. Homeward Trust Edmonton. http://homewardtrust.ca/wp-content/uploads/2019/03/Puddu-2018.-Stories-of-vulnerable-youth-in-the-shadow-of-urban-development.pdf.

Rankin, J. (2017). Conducting analysis in institutional ethnography: Analytical work prior to commencing data collection. *International Journal of Qualitative Methods*, *16*(1), 1609406917734484.

Rose, G. (2016). *Visual methodologies: An introduction to researching with visual materials*. Thousand Oaks, CA: Sage.

Smith, D. E. (1987). *The everyday world as problematic: A feminist sociology*. Toronto: University of Toronto Press.

Smith, D. E. (1993). The Standard North American Family: SNAF as an ideological code. *Journal of Family Issues*, *14*(1), 50–65.

Smith, D. E. (1999). *Writing the social: Critique, theory, and investigations*. Toronto: University of Toronto Press.

Smith, D. E. (2005). *Institutional ethnography: A sociology for people*. Lanham, MD: Altamira Press.

Smith, D. E. (Ed.). (2006). *Institutional ethnography as practice*. Oxford, UK: Rowman & Littlefield.

Smith, D. E. (2008). Institutional ethnography. In L. Given (Ed.), *The SAGE encyclopedia of qualitative research methods* (pp. 433–437). Los Angeles: Sage.

Sonnenwald, D. H. (1999). Evolving perspectives of human information behavior: Contexts, situations, social networks and information horizons. In T. Wilson & D. Allen (Eds.), *Exploring the contexts of information behaviour* (pp. 176–190). London: Taylor Graham.

Sonnenwald, D. H., Wildemuth, B. M., & Harmon, G. L. (2001). A research method using the concept of information horizons: An example from a study of lower socioeconomic students' information seeking behaviour. *The New Review of Information Behaviour Research*, *2*, 65–86.

Star, S. L. (1991). The sociology of the invisible: The primacy of work in the writings of Anselm Strauss. In D. Maines (Ed.), *Social organization and social process: Essays in honor of Anselm Strauss* (pp. 265–283). Hawthorne, NY: Aldine de Gruyter.

Star, S. L., & Strauss, A. (1999). Layers of silence, arenas of voice: The ecology of visible and invisible work. *Computer Supported Cooperative Work, 8*(1), 9–30.

Turner, S. M. (2003). *Municipal planning, land development and environmental intervention: An institutional ethnography*. Doctoral dissertation. University of Toronto.

Turner, S. M. (2006). Mapping institutions as work and texts. In D. E. Smith (Ed.), *Institutional ethnography as practice* (pp. 139–162). New York: Rowman & Littlefield.

Wang, C., & Burris, M. A. (1994). Empowerment through photo novella: Portraits of participation. *Health Education Quarterly, 21*(2), 171–186.

Wang, C., & Burris, M. A. (1997). Photovoice: Concept, methodology, and use for participatory needs assessment. *Health Education & Behavior, 24*(3), 369–387.

Washington, K. T., Meadows, S. E., Elliott, S. G., & Koopman, R. J. (2011). Information needs of informal caregivers of older adults with chronic health conditions. *Patient Education and Counseling, 83*(1), 37–44.

Waters, N. (2015). Towards an institutional counter-cartography of nurses' wound work. *Journal of Sociology and Social Welfare, 42*(2), 127–156.

Wong, S. L., Gilmour, H., & Ramage-Morin, P. L. (2016). Alzheimer's disease and other dementias in Canada. *Health Reports, 27*(5), 11–16.

CHAPTER 7

Discovering the Social Organization of Perinatal Care for Women Living with HIV: Reflections from a Novice Institutional Ethnographer

Allyson Ion

It was in 2009 while completing my Masters of Science in Health Research Methodology at McMaster University in Hamilton, Ontario, Canada, that I first heard about institutional ethnography. I attended a seminar facilitated by Dr. Christina Sinding at McMaster University called "Qualitative Research on Health Care Disparities: Contributions from Institutional Ethnography." My interest was immediately stimulated with the ontological and epistemological orientation to examine people's work practices within institutional settings. Moreover, I was intrigued by how taking such an approach could uncover how the conditions are created in which people experience challenges when navigating and receiving health services; and explicating how such challenges occur because of how healthcare practices are organized and routinized. Dr. Sinding used an analogy of creating visible threads within and across institutional contexts; that is, institutional ethnography could be employed as a research strategy to thread together the experiences of individuals, work practices and the coordination of work, and regimes of ruling and governance. The idea that there was something connecting people's experiences with how care practices themselves were organized and coordinated was appealing and stayed with me.

A. Ion (✉)
McMaster University, Hamilton, ON, Canada
e-mail: iona@mcmaster.ca

An Opportunity to Ask New Questions About HIV, Women, and Perinatal Care Through Institutional Ethnography

Since 2001, I have been involved in the HIV movement in Canada as part of community development and education projects and more recently community-based, participatory research initiatives. Through my involvement with various projects, and through relationships forged with people living with HIV, community activists, and researchers, I have increased my knowledge of and appreciation for the activist movements of "nothing about us without us" (Charlton, 1998) and the greater involvement of people living with HIV/AIDS (or GIPA) (UNAIDS, 1999, 2004), as well as feminist HIV advocacy (Carter et al., 2013; Loutfy, Sonnenberg-Schwan, Margolese, Sherr, & Women for Positive Action, 2013). In coming to know these movements, I now place significant value and importance on partnering with women living with HIV in community education and community-based research initiatives, and grounding community development, practice, and policy in the needs and priorities of women living with HIV. Because of my connection to different projects and established relationships with women living with HIV and community activists, I take seriously their invitation to be an ally and advocate as it relates to healthcare access, and collaboratively identifying recommendations to ensure women have positive interactions with health and social care providers.

Through the HIV Mothering Study (Greene et al., 2015b, 2016, 2017; Ion et al., 2016; Khosla, Ion, & Greene, 2016), the Positive Parenting Pilot Project (Greene et al., 2016, 2018), and the Women, ART, and the Criminalization of HIV study (Greene et al., 2019), I have had the privilege to sit with many women living with HIV and learn about the challenges, tensions, and roadblocks they have encountered when navigating health and social services, in particular as pregnant women and new mothers. These qualitative research endeavors have created space for women to share their stories and have focused on shaping policy and offering practice recommendations based on women's perspectives and experiences. For example, the HIV Mothering Study illuminated valuable insights into women's interactions within maternity care and child welfare, and identified important issues related to infant feeding, HIV-related stigma in medical settings, and how women respond to perpetual monitoring and surveillance of their bodies as pregnant women and mothers living with HIV (Greene et al., 2015a, 2015b, 2016, 2017; Ion et al., 2016; Khosla et al., 2016). Multiple studies have illuminated the challenges that women encounter related to disclosing their HIV-positive status to family, friends, intimate partners (Adam et al., 2015; Vyavaharkar et al., 2011; Women's Health in Women's Hands, 2017), and moments when their HIV status was shared by healthcare providers to people they did not intend to disclose, and how they were left to manage these situations (Ion, 2019; Ion et al., 2016). Contributing to these projects has significantly shaped my own and others' ways of knowing about HIV in the context of pregnancy and motherhood.

Sinding (2010) reminds us that qualitative research makes "apparent the layered consequences of inclusion and exclusion as they unfold...[yet] studies often have not detailed the processes by which some women come to not have [relevant] care resources" (Sinding, 2010, p. 1657). A body of social science research, including the studies noted above, has examined, described, and categorized peoples' subjective experiences of living with HIV; however, minimal research has been done to explicate how and why these experiences come to be and how the systems that produce the conditions for such experiences actually work. Some important notable exceptions are the work of George Smith (1995), the Making Care Visible project team (McCoy, 2002, 2005, 2009; Mykhalovskiy, 2008; Mykhalovskiy & McCoy, 2002), Laura Bisaillon (2011), and Daniel Grace (2015).

Qualitative research exploring the disparities encountered by women living with HIV in the healthcare system has focused on women's narrative accounts. Research grounded in narrative, interpretive qualitative traditions, and critical feminist paradigms are vitally important to raise awareness about women's experiences and elevate the voices and perspectives of mothers living with HIV. This research, however, has not necessarily critically examined institutional work processes nor connected women's experiences to regimes of ruling and governance. In learning about institutional ethnography, I became increasingly aware of the practical utility and distinct form of analytic description that was possible through such a research strategy. Rather than construct meanings or theories from people's individual experiences, institutional ethnography could be employed to map organizational processes and make visible social relations (Grace, 2019).

Given my history in the women and HIV research community in Canada, I felt it was important to investigate the work and regulatory structures of healthcare providers to uncover how women's experiences are produced in the routine operation of perinatal health services (Sinding, 2010). I started to question whether there were particular policies or day-to-day practices that were creating gaps in care or producing certain conditions for women living with HIV during the perinatal period. The gap in published literature and lack of institutional ethnographic investigations into this particular topic were evident; the perinatal health systems that women living with HIV interact with had not been critically examined, nor had any investigations been conducted regarding if and how women's perinatal care experiences may be connected to institutional work processes and broader institutional arrangements. This catalyzed my doctoral studies to begin to explore this problematic. As I increased my familiarity with Dorothy Smith's scholarship, a sociology *for* people, and institutional ethnography, in particular the ontological origins and grounding in critical feminist scholarship and activist movements, the appeal to be an ethnographer, to track a particular territory, and to ground my doctoral research in this paradigm deepened. Institutional ethnography was selected as my mode of inquiry for my doctoral research because it begins from women's experiences and can identify possibilities to direct action and organizational change in ways that take seriously and amplify women's voices and experiences.

Reflections as a Novice Institutional Ethnographer

Having an orientation to Dorothy Smith's scholarship and developing a foundation in the theoretical and philosophical tenets of institutional ethnography were critical for me to begin to fully understand how and why to conduct an institutional ethnographic inquiry, and to unlearn and shift my ways of thinking about research. Keeping in view Smith's alternative sociology was important throughout my dissertation to not stray off course or to return to familiar territory of conducting research from a traditional sociological orientation or positivist paradigm. I have had to unlearn and reorganize my usual ways of thinking and doing including what I know about and how I do research. I believe this is a common experience for those of us who embark on doing institutional ethnography.

Institutional ethnography is not prescriptive as a method of inquiry, and burgeoning ethnographers can gain insights about what an inquiry might entail from numerous published examples. A how-to guide does not exist about what George Smith refers to as the ontological shift (Smith, 1990) in coming to know a sociology for people and institutional ethnography. I did not know what this ontological shift might look or feel like. It was through the actual doing of my research, and reflecting back on my own journey, that I fully appreciated the moments that were pivotal in my development, and that subsequently influenced various stages of my doctoral research. I hope by offering this detailed personal account that I might provide some motivation and guidance to others embarking on similar investigative journeys. Through this chapter, I offer some reflections and ideas about my experience of conducting an institutional ethnography beginning from the standpoint of pregnant women living with HIV. This chapter includes three sections: (i) the importance of ethnographer reflexivity to ground an inquiry; (ii) reflections about interviewing women for an institutional ethnographic inquiry; and (iii) what story is told through institutional ethnography, specifically thinking through the scope and sociopolitical implications of what is discovered through an inquiry.

Reflecting on What You Know: Reflexivity and Locating the Ethnographer in the Inquiry

An institutional ethnographic inquiry begins from the standpoint of an embodied subject who is located in a particular setting and in the particularities of their experience (Smith, 1987). This entry point is distinct from traditional sociological approaches that prioritize objectified forms of knowledge and reify literatures as the rationale and starting point for discovery

(Smith, 1990). Dorothy Smith's early writing encouraged sociological inquiry to begin from the standpoint of women. For Smith, beginning inquiry from the standpoint of women was transformational for sociologists who advocated for such an approach (Smith, 1992). Women's standpoint located inquiry in women's embodied and everyday experiences, and this was a departure from traditional research approaches that were steeped in male control, domination, and oppression of women's bodies (Smith, 1992).

Reflexivity is a critical element of doing research from the standpoint of women and making visible the ruling relations that organize and coordinate women's local realities, and numerous feminist scholars have written about the concept of reflexivity (Neitz, 2014; Smith, 1987, 1990; Taber, 2012; Walby, 2007). Reflexivity has been critical to my development as a community-based researcher in terms of thinking about my power, privilege, positioning, and social location in relationship to the research; engaging in a reflexive practice has also been central to thinking through my role as a researcher and advocate. In coming to know institutional ethnography, I have broadened the practice of reflexivity and taken to heart Smith's assertion to begin with our experiences as women and how we know *in our bodies* (Smith, 1992)—not only for the participants that I have engaged in research projects, but also for myself as the ethnographer.

The practice of reflexivity can be helpful to think through a research problematic and how one is taking up the notion of standpoint in their research. As Neitz (2014) argues, reflexivity is built into feminist standpoint epistemologies as a way to consider the positionality of knowledge and to attempt to understand how the position of the researcher might reflect structures of power. Through reflexivity, the researcher can contemplate how not to reproduce problematic ideologies, discourses, and systems of ruling that may objectify the real people involved in the construction of knowledge (Neitz, 2014; Smith, 1987).

I believe that the everyday world of the ethnographer is an important point of reflection when thinking through the starting point of an inquiry, as well as the relationship between the ethnographer and the standpoint and positioning of individuals or community from whom the inquiry will begin. Ethnographers are encouraged to ask themselves reflexive, critical questions at the beginning stages of the research. For example, what knowledge, understanding, and viewpoints do you bring to the inquiry as the researcher? What organizational knowledge, discourses, and institutional terminologies might you draw upon, reify, and/or take-for-granted in developing an inquiry? How do you see the research problematic as the ethnographer?

Importantly in institutional ethnography, reflexivity is essential for the ethnographer to keep in check how they are going about their exploration and discovery, and how they are uncovering the actualities of the everyday world by those who are experiencing, speaking, writing, and living such actualities (Smith, 2005a). Reflexive practice in institutional ethnography involves a commitment to and constant engagement with what is actually going on in the social of people's lives, and it is through a dialogic process of engagement and reflection with people in their social worlds that the researcher learns, evolves, and changes (Smith, 2005a). In an institutional ethnographic inquiry, "people remain the subjects, the knowers, or potential knowers" (Smith, 2005a, p. 52). As such, the researcher is guided by the ontology of the social regarding what they observe, listen for, and make visible; and it is through dialogue and engagement with people in their local worlds that we make sense of and uncover the social relations that produce our experiences (Smith, 2005a).

Reflexive writing can be a helpful exercise for institutional ethnographers to deeply reflect on what they know, how they know it, and how their ways of knowing may shape their aims, goals, and research direction. Reflecting upon one's positioning within the research as the ethnographer can help to articulate how you understand the research problematic, what is discussed and emphasized with study participants, and what becomes the findings or story of the research. Reflexive writing is also helpful to make sense of what constitutes the social in your inquiry, and to ensure that conceptual frameworks and theoretical concepts are not being attached to or used to explain such actualities (Smith, 2005a). What follows is an example of my reflexive writing as a novice institutional ethnographer.

Noticing Disconnections: Women and Their Healthcare Providers Know HIV Infection Differently

I became interested in the social organization of perinatal care for women living with HIV because of my experience working in an HIV clinic in Ontario, Canada. Rather than take for granted the ways that I have come to know and understand HIV, I have developed an appreciation for and have learned to see how different and competing social relations influence and organize my own consciousness, and are built into my everyday world as a research coordinator, graduate student, and cis-gender woman (Campbell, 2016; Smith, 1990). This realization surfaced once I became acquainted with Dorothy Smith's work. Reflexivity, therefore, has been integral to thinking critically about what I have witnessed and felt in the space where women receive HIV care, as well as what I have learned from women and healthcare providers about how they know HIV.

In projects such as the HIV Mothering Study, I have learned directly from women about the various concerns, challenges, troubles, and worries they have faced as pregnant women and new mothers, and the multiple practicalities involved to participate in their HIV and maternity care including traveling distances, taking time off work, arranging childcare, and balancing numerous responsibilities to attend appointments (Ion, 2019; Ion et al., 2016).

Being situated within an HIV clinic, I have also witnessed institutional ways of knowing HIV. I attended team meetings (or rounds) to hear client assessments. I witnessed the work practices of specific healthcare providers, and the technological and textual infrastructure that facilitated such work practices. I became intimately familiar with the systems of communication and electronic health records that were used to track, document, and advance both the care provided to women living with HIV and the work of healthcare providers who were based within the HIV clinic. I began to see how women living with HIV were identified as part of institutional practices and texts, and how this representation was different from how women identified themselves and expressed their identities and experiences.

I learned the medical jargon and institutional language used within clinical spaces and as part of the institutional processes to provide care to women. For example, clinicians in the HIV clinic often referred to people living with HIV as patients and were focused on medication regimens, adherence to antiretroviral therapy, viral load suppression, clinical markers of the CD4 count and HIV viral load,[1] and the use of these clinical markers to determine effectiveness of HIV treatment. This language and jargon could be heard in team conversations and as part of dialogue between healthcare providers, and it is language that I too became accustomed to while navigating medical records and interacting with the team.

Patients were understood as bodies using health services, and bodies supplying information to understand treatment effectiveness vis-à-vis blood tests and other biological markers. Bodies were also counted to justify funding to different health services, to ascertain which populations were receiving care within the institution, and to enable surveillance and monitoring of the HIV clinic population.

As part of my research coordination work, I learned how to navigate the medical record system, which included an electronic and hard copy chart. It was through notes dictated by their healthcare providers, through prescriptions and orders for specific treatments, and through blood tests, specifically their HIV viral loads and their CD4 cell counts, that women's bodies and their HIV-positive status became visible and known. Requisitions were produced to order these blood tests and then clinical test results (in the electronic record and in hard copy format) were generated to communicate the results to nurses, pharmacists, HIV specialists, and obstetricians. Test results, dictated notes, and prescriptions directed the activities of various healthcare providers operating within the healthcare institution. For example, dictated notes recommended actionable next steps for the person to whom it was addressed, and prescriptions activated pharmacists to fill and dispense medications. It was through my shifting ontological frame toward a sociology for people that I began to see how institutional texts mediated relations and activities between providers and catalyzed the work of various healthcare providers within a particular institutional setting.

What I was observing as a research coordinator based within the HIV clinic was a disconnection between what women were sharing about their care experiences and how healthcare administrators, managers, and providers talked about HIV. There was a disjuncture between women living with HIV and those who provided healthcare to women whereby HIV infection was understood in different ways, and these different groups came from different places of knowing, experiencing, and understanding HIV infection. What I began to see in my local context was Smith's notion of a bifurcated consciousness (Smith, 1974, 1990). On the one hand, I was experiencing embodied knowing—knowing that was located in my body and arose from my direct experiences of interacting with and coming to know women living with HIV, and hearing their stories of navigating and accessing care as pregnant women and mothers (Smith, 1974, 1990). On the other hand, I was witnessing an abstract world that included the activities and administration of the HIV clinic, which was disconnected from thoughts, emotions, and embodied experiences (Smith, 1974, 1990). In this abstracted, institutional world, knowing constituted factual accounts of externalized and objectified relations (Smith, 1990). Exposure to these different ways of knowing not only opened my eyes to how people working in healthcare go about their work and how healthcare institutions operate, but also stimulated questions about what policies, routinized daily practices, and institutional arrangements may be creating the conditions for the types of experiences that women expressed during the HIV Mothering Study (Greene et al., 2015b, 2016, 2017; Ion et al., 2016; Khosla et al., 2016).

A Case Example: Tanya's Viral Load

As I noted earlier, people who are new to institutional ethnography may find it challenging to make the ontological shift to a sociology for people. I now offer an extended reflection about a situation involving an HIV Mothering Study participant that was significantly formative in my intellectual journey. I do this to show how informants' stories can become defining moments in understanding an institutional complex. The story of Tanya (a pseudonym) contributed to my ontological shift where I moved from a theorization and abstraction of the social to actually being able to see the everyday world as it is constituted in the actions and practices of individuals (Smith, 1990). I describe how I drew on this new seeing to orient my doctoral research and reflect on the significance of institutional ethnography in doing social justice-oriented projects.

For the HIV Mothering Study, our team relied on laboratory results, discharge summaries, and clinic notes dictated by multiple healthcare providers to obtain the data we were interested in, and to keep track of a women's clinical trajectory during pregnancy, at the time of childbirth, and early postpartum. While extracting information from women's charts I learned that any notes that healthcare providers dictate are automatically uploaded to the medical record system following dictation. Laboratory results, on the other hand, take more time to be uploaded depending on the time it takes to process the person's blood work, run the laboratory test, and send the results back to the institution. For example, an HIV viral load test is processed by a provincial laboratory and it can take up to seven business days for the results to appear in the chart after the blood has been drawn from the pregnant woman.

One day I was collecting information from the medical record of Tanya, a study participant. A resident in obstetrics had dictated a discharge summary of the care Tanya had received leading up to, during, and immediately following childbirth. The resident noted that Tanya had not gone to get her blood work done immediately prior to her delivery as there was no HIV viral load recorded in the chart at the time of dictation; the resident also implied that Tanya had not followed her physician's orders to complete her blood work, and as such information was missing from her chart to direct care for Tanya and her baby.

I discovered the information stated by the resident to be false. Tanya had gone for blood work, and an HIV viral load result had been uploaded into her medical record the day after her delivery, which was also the day after the resident dictated her note. Furthermore, Tanya had gone for blood work multiple times leading up to her delivery, and the multiple test results showed an undetectable HIV viral load coinciding with adhering to her treatment and reducing the likelihood of perinatal HIV transmission.

Importantly, the information in Tanya's chart had significant implications for her care at childbirth. The HIV viral load is an important marker of the effectiveness of HIV treatment, and the test result directs the decision-making of multiple members of a healthcare team at the time of childbirth including how the baby will be delivered (i.e., vaginal vs. Caesarian section delivery), what medications will be administered to the pregnant woman, and what medications will be administered to the infant postpartum. The laboratory result of an undetectable viral load means that a vaginal birth, not a C-section, is the recommended mode of delivery. I learned from Tanya, however, that she had an unplanned C-section and not the vaginal birth that was planned during her prenatal care. Tanya did not offer much explanation or information about why the C-section was performed, and we did not meet with her healthcare providers to hear their perspective about the rationale for the C-section. We cannot rule out, however, that the absence of a text (i.e., viral load result) and the healthcare providers' participation in objectified forms of knowledge (i.e., medical chart) produced the conditions in which Tanya had a C-section.

At the time, I was struck by how the information that was recorded in the resident's dictated note pertaining to Tanya's blood work and HIV viral load result was false and misleading, and how this text harnessed much power to influence and produce particular circumstances—for Tanya, for her baby, and for the healthcare team providing care to Tanya and her baby. Later, reading and coming to know Dorothy Smith's work, I came to appreciate how the language and concepts that the resident articulated were constituted as "discrete phenomena in the institutional contexts of ruling" (Smith, 1990, p. 15), and that the expression of these terms and the production of a specific text (i.e., dictated note) could activate people's work and set into motion a particular care trajectory for Tanya and her baby. It was through this relationship between text and work in Tanya's case that I came to see how people can participate in objectified practices of knowing (Smith, 1990), and how this can have particular implications or consequences for people on the receiving end of these practices. It was objectified knowledge that came to be seen as truth in Tanya's chart and directed Tanya's care. The text that was produced through the resident's work activities was a property of institutional organization and became a form of objectified knowledge that institutional actors engaged with and took cues from in order to subsequently direct their work activities (Smith, 1990).

Furthermore, Tanya's voice and experience as a woman and mother were absent and not represented in her medical records. The discharge summary was produced by someone who was involved in Tanya's care, and through the production of this institutional text, Tanya was objectified as a patient, a viral load, and a woman delivering a baby. During study visits with Tanya for the HIV Mothering Study, however, she shared her concerns about the health and well-being of her baby and talked about her efforts to take her medication to keep an undetectable viral load to reduce the chance of perinatal HIV transmission. She also talked about her motivations to "cut down" smoking and to change the people she interacted with and the places she frequented to stay "clean and sober." The disjuncture between how I came to know Tanya's story and experiences in her own words versus how she was represented through her medical record was stark. Tanya's thoughts, intentions, desires, hopes, feelings, and actions were absent from her chart; and Tanya had become represented through texts constructed by others which made it very difficult to contextualize her story, her history, and her experience (Smith, 1990). When I read Tanya's medical records, I thought about what her textual record meant *about* her—as a mother, as a woman, as someone interacting with perinatal health services, and as someone living with HIV. I also thought about how Tanya's textual representation in her medical record could have significant implications for how her life would be organized into the future.

Tanya's story highlights how we all participate in social processes and ruling relations that reach beyond the scope of our local, everyday worlds (Smith, 1987). These systems that we encounter can be in tension with our own ways of knowing and operating in the world because they are connected to discourses and ideological frames not of our making, nor that are relevant to our daily, local experiences (Campbell & Gregor, 2008; McCoy, 2006; Smith, 1987, 1990, 1999). When I read Tanya's chart, I observed not only a textual conversation between healthcare providers acting through the medical record, but also a conversation happening inside of me as the reader and someone standing beside Tanya watching the events unfold (Smith, 1990, 2005a). I was uncomfortable, angry, and empathetic toward Tanya; and I felt paralyzed by my limited role as the HIV Mothering Study coordinator and ill-equipped to act on the discrepancy in Tanya's chart.

Tanya's story highlights how we all participate in ruling discourses as part of our work—as individuals receiving healthcare, as employees within institutional and organizational settings, and as actors who engage with texts (Smith, 1999). Women like Tanya do not necessarily participate in the creation of these ruling discourses (Smith, 1987). Instead, the social relations that women like Tanya participate in overshadow their thoughts, experiences, actions, and dreams because perinatal care for women living with HIV, similar to medication adherence, is "steeped in relevancies of medical power and social control" (McCoy, 2009, p. 129). Through regimes of ruling, women like Tanya have been repressed and stifled to assert her authority of knowledge, voice, and experience (Smith, 1978, 1987).

An important part of the story is when a social worker based in the HIV clinic who knew that I was frequently meeting with Tanya as part of the HIV Mothering Study, and who was also supporting Tanya throughout her pregnancy and interactions with the child welfare system, also came across the error in the resident's discharge summary. She approached me one day, wondering if I had also seen the discrepancy while completing study data extraction. In appreciating how the information in Tanya's chart could influence her care and future, the social worker took it upon herself to follow-up with Tanya and the obstetrics clinic. This social worker was also activated by the resident's discharge summary, but the text-reader conversation (Smith, 1990, 2005a) that she was engaged had a different meaning compared to other institutional actors. This social worker put into action a different text-work-text sequence (Smith, 2005a) that was underpinned by values inherent in social work that prioritized Tanya's dignity and self-realization (Swigonski, 1994), and ensured that not only was the information in Tanya's chart correct, but that she was supported.

What I have come to believe is that institutional ethnography becomes a mechanism through which we can illuminate the experiences of people who are objectified and ignored by ruling discourses, and expose relations of power that shape our worlds while preserving the doings of active individuals like Tanya (Grace, 2019). Reflecting upon Tanya's story and learning about the challenges that women living with HIV can have when interacting with healthcare providers motivated my interest to investigate how and why these circumstances occur in the first place; and my involvement in the HIV Mothering Study was a formative experience that deepened my commitment to do so.

Interviewing Women

Given my involvement in numerous research projects and work as a research coordinator, I have had the privilege of conducting a large number of qualitative interviews (Greene et al., 2015b, 2015c, 2016, 2017; Ion, Greene,

MacMillan, & Smieja, 2013; Ion et al., 2016, 2017; Khosla et al., 2016; Sunderji et al., 2019). Choosing institutional ethnography for my doctoral research, however, required that I critically reflect upon my interview practice and think carefully about what I would be asking during my conversations with women living with HIV and healthcare providers. For example, I am used to conducting interviews that follow a narrative approach to inquiry and do not follow a structured interview guide, but rather, begin with one question and allow the participant to tell her story on her terms (Greene et al., 2015b, 2015c, 2016, 2017). Using this approach, my role has been to gently probe and seek clarification as the participant tells her story. I have also conducted interviews that follow a structured interview guide where participants are asked to respond to specific questions that the researchers are attempting to answer, and I, as the interviewer, orchestrate and direct the conversation to closely align with the research objectives.

Regardless of the approach I am taking, I have always viewed qualitative interviews as conversational where there is dialogue between myself and the participant, and the speaking time is shared between us. For example, narrative interviews may play out with an approximate ratio of 1:3 where the participant speaks three times more than I do having room to articulate and share their story in the way they feel comfortable. For more structured interviews, the ratio has typically been 1:1 where the speaking is balanced between the participant and me.

As I have reflected on my conversational interview style, I do believe that appropriate space and time has been created for participants to share intimate details of their lives and to respond to the questions in a way that fostered a sense of comfort and ease. At the same time, I realize that my interviewing approach has not always produced periods of silence or lengthy pauses for participants to just be without me probing, acknowledging their emotions, or seeking clarification about the details of their story. I have viewed my role as the interviewer to gently lead and steer the interaction to satisfy the research objectives and aims while at the same time valuing and honoring the information being shared.

Embarking on an institutional ethnography and thinking about the interviews and explorative inquiry as dialogic (Smith, 2005a) required that I take a serious look at my interviewing practice. Despite my engagement in reflexive practice as a community-based researcher, and attending to issues of power, privilege, and social location in relationship to the people I interview, I have had to critically think about how I take up airtime and space in an interview, and how this may shape the study in ways that are both congruent and in tension with institutional ethnography as a method of inquiry.

I first had to wrap my head around what interviewing is all about when doing institutional ethnography and what, exactly, the ethnographer is trying to learn about and listen for in an interview. As Rankin asserts, the ethnographer needs to "get from 'contradictions,' 'tensions,' 'disquiet,' or 'unease'—to interrogating what is going on. You need to train yourself to see how informants' everyday life is being organized through an institution's ruling practices" (Rankin, 2017, p. 5). I quickly realized in coming to know institutional ethnography that my experience of interviewing for my doctoral research would be distinctly different from the other projects I had been a part of.

In previous projects that followed a narrative approach to inquiry, women were the object of the investigation (e.g., Greene et al., 2015b, 2015c, 2016, 2017; Ion et al., 2016; Khosla et al., 2016), and the emotions and feelings that women expressed were salient to our team's analysis and interpretation of the phenomenon of interest. In institutional ethnography, however, women are not the objects of the investigation. Rather, it is "the aspects of the institutions relevant to the people's experience, not the people themselves, that constitute the object of inquiry" (Smith, 2005a, p. 38). When conducting institutional ethnographic interviews, I have given space for emotions to be expressed, and to honor how participants choose to talk about their experiences. And, I have also been listening for clues about how their experiences connect to institutional arrangements and regimes of ruling. Within these interview encounters I have kept in mind the goal to uncover social processes that organize and produce local situations and reach beyond the scope of any one individual and their local, everyday world (Smith, 1987).

Therefore, I had to train myself to see things organizationally, that is, to listen for terminologies, discourses, and activities that were clues about the participants' work, how their work was connected to the work and activities of others, and how their actions were produced by ruling relations. This often meant that I had to sit back and actively listen to what participants were saying without interruptions, without probing, and without leading the conversation. I would often begin my interviews by asking participants to teach me about their work, for example, to tell me about the health services and healthcare providers they interacted with and navigated as a pregnant woman and mother living with HIV. Or, I would indicate that I wanted them to tell me about their job activities related to caring for women living with HIV during pregnancy and early motherhood. I began the interviews by letting participants know that I wanted to learn from them – the exact and concrete details about what they do, how they do, and what their actions actually look and feel like in their local setting and context either as women living with HIV or healthcare providers.

The notion that participant accounts are "windows onto extended sequences of activity that are only partially visible in the accounts themselves" (Mykhalovskiy & McCoy, 2002, p. 29) was a helpful mantra in how I thought about and engaged in my interview process. Thinking about participant accounts as one node or interchange in a complex circuit of activities that included work processes and institutional texts was helpful to remind myself to think organizationally before, during, and after each interview. This analytic thinking needed to happen at all stages of the research to begin to thread together and make visible women's experiences, healthcare providers' work activities, and ruling relations.

I also had to think about how I would present this form of interviewing to my institutional ethics review board before the iterative ethnographic inquiry even began. Research ethics boards (REBs) typically require a detailed list of questions that participants will be asked so they can assess the level of risk and get a comprehensive understanding of the various ways that participants will be engaged in the research. Through in-person consultations with Dorothy Smith, she suggested that I outline a series of topics, rather than a rigid interview guide, that would be covered with participants. Covering a series of topics enabled flexibility with how the interview could proceed, and what territory could be covered with each participant, and it satisfied the expectations of the REB. This was especially important given the heterogeneity and diversity of the participants I aimed to involve in the research, and the fact that as the ethnography evolved new information about institutional arrangements would become apparent that I would want to review and explore with participants.

The last issue that came to light as I embarked on this research was how we as researchers produce accounts through our interview exchanges. Reading Dorothy Smith's article "K is Mentally Ill" (Smith, 1978), in which Smith critically analyzes an interview where a woman called K is defined by her friends as mentally ill, completely disrupted how I think about analyzing and interpreting interview data and forced me to question what I know about qualitative inquiry. I first had to think about how I was framing the topics that I planned to cover with study participants including the language and terminologies that I was using, and the assumptions that might be embedded in the topics I was presenting to participants. Smith asserts that "the form of the question tells the respondent what sort of work she is being asked to do. It asks her to operate on her knowledge, experience, etc., in a particular way" (Smith, 1978, p. 27). Because my interviews began with me presenting a topic for discussion, I am mindful about how this could set into motion a particular response and engagement by the participant. As an interviewer, I always come from a place of respect and positioning the participant as the expert of their own life and their work within the institutional complex that I want to know more about. I am now much more aware, though, about how the framing of questions can lead to particular answers. As Smith (1978) outlines, the phrasing of questions and the setting in which they are asked taps into particular knowledges and experiences of the participants. With this in mind, I always began interviews with the intention to place the participant in the driver's seat so that I could observe, be fully present, and listen carefully for organizational clues.

I also wanted to be respectful of participants' time, and it was often a challenge to learn about their complex experiences and concrete work activities within a limited timeframe. Women typically preferred to schedule their interviews when they were attending clinic appointments, especially if they did not live close to the hospital where the study was situated, and they were often juggling their return to work, catching their ride, rushing home to pick up their kids, etc. Healthcare providers typically agreed to meet with me during their workday and told me about their work activities in between seeing patients, while on break, or before or after their shift. I believe that it is imperative that institutional ethnographers reflect upon and keep in mind how "the actual events [that we want to know about are] much richer, much less orderly, simply much *more*, than those arranged into an interview of an hour or so" (Smith, 1978, p. 27). Realizing this motivated me to think carefully and strategically about my data generation. This involved speaking with a range of women living with HIV to ensure a comprehensive picture of the services, procedures, and providers that all women living with HIV interact with as part of a particular institutional complex during pregnancy, childbirth, and early motherhood, and to ensure that my research problematic resonated with the wider women's HIV community. I scheduled interviews when and where it worked for them and used their preferred communication channels (e.g., text messaging). I also built in mechanisms to follow-up with, validate, and fill in the gaps across the group of healthcare providers whom I interviewed. This involved triangulating, verifying details, and connecting the dots across the provider participants in terms of the infrastructural supports used in their daily work, forms and texts to which they responded or produced through their work, and checking in about the concerns and issues that women raised about their perinatal care experiences. Doing so ensured that I was carefully, critically, and methodically tracking the institutional territory and connecting women's experiences to institutional arrangements and objectified forms of knowing.

Telling a Story Through Institutional Ethnography: Scope and Sociopolitical Implications

As I mentioned earlier, my inquiry began from the standpoint of women living with HIV. Although my ethnographic process was iterative and informed by the data that I was gathering, I made decisions along the way about what organizational clues and texts to focus on. It can be difficult, however, to always see a clear path and stay focused on the research problematic once all the data has been collected and accounts have been obtained from multiple people who perform multiple tasks and activities within the institutional complex. Careful decisions must be made about what aspects of the institution will be explicated, and what story will emerge from the inquiry.

Lisa Watt, a fellow graduate of the McMaster University Social Work Ph.D. program, once used an analogy of a ski hill to offer some guidance about how to wrestle with the scope of a doctoral institutional ethnographic inquiry. Looking at a ski hill map, the runs become visible by the color-coded system that explains the routes to follow and their level of difficulty. As an ethnographer, we have to decide what trail we are going to take. Lisa always encouraged fellow ethnographers to pick one trail, to examine it closely, and to not steer off path. Although institutional ethnographic inquiries are always open-ended, Lisa offered the advice to pick a start and finish line because of the limited time and resources that are available to us as doctoral students.

In keeping with the tenets of institutional ethnography, I kept in view the women living with HIV from whom the inquiry began as active and experiencing subjects and preserved their presence as knowers and actors (Smith, 1987); it was their stories and experiences that stayed with me and directed what I prioritized and paid attention to. Based on my history and connection to the women's HIV and community-based HIV research communities, I viewed my research as connected to a particular political project and feminist agenda to tell a particular story about a particular group of women. I knew going into the research that I wanted to be strategic about what I was exploring, writing about, and publishing. I wanted to ensure that the story I was sharing, and the discourses to which I was contributing, elevated the voices and experiences of women living with HIV. I wanted to reaffirm women's experiences as legitimate forms of knowledge that could contribute to alleviating the oppression and marginalization of women and mothers living with HIV (Smith, 1987). In a way, I wanted to stay true to the relationships or sisterhood (Smith, 2005b) that I had forged with women, as well as the commitments we had articulated through our shared research and community development endeavors.

For Dorothy Smith, sisterhood is an important tenet of feminism that resonated with her own experience and her development of women's standpoint and a sociology for people (Smith, 2005b). Sisterhood is a multidimensional concept that goes beyond "a sentimental basis for relations among women" and refers to a connection that is realized between women prior to taking on a political aim or project (Smith, 2005b, p. 227). Sisterhood directly relates to the positioning of the researcher relative to other women and articulates "the change from being an outsider...to women in their struggles and suffering, to locating yourself on their side and in their position" (Smith, 2005b, p. 228). I will always respect and acknowledge the differences that exist between myself as a white, cis-gender woman who does not have HIV and the women living with HIV with whom I work as colleagues and research participants.

I also recognize the synergies between our ways of knowing, living, and being in the world. We share a similar political project and aim for liberation as it relates to supporting women living with HIV and contributing to the improvement of health and social care for families affected by HIV. As we have come to know each other, we have found ourselves on the same side, on the same team, speaking the same language, and fighting for the same goals. This relationship goes beyond our sentimental appreciation for the contributions each of us are making; it is about our shared history and trajectory. It is this connection and history that enables us as a group of women to take on a political project, to think about our collective contributions to social justice and social change.

My experience of sisterhood is embodied in the relationships that I have with the women I work with who have become a part of my everyday world. Sisterhood is not only about the work we're engaged in, but also about connecting as women and attending to our needs beyond those that are intellectual. Marjorie DeVault talks about her own relationship with her doctoral supervisor and how her supervisor recognized that her intellectual work was "best sustained through attention to emotional, as well as intellectual needs" (DeVault, 1999, p. 13). They shared meals, went shopping together, attended similar seminars and conferences, and did not confine their relationship to discussions focused on DeVault's dissertation (DeVault, 1999). This relationship pulled DeVault into a feminist community that her supervisor was affiliated with. I too have experienced and benefited from a similar relationship with my colleague and doctoral supervisor Dr. Saara Greene who always considers my emotional, social, physical, and intellectual well-being equally. We have and continue to support each other in our shared work and have also supported the women around us who have been leaders and contributors to that work. What we have created is a supportive environment of mutual respect, dialogue, and friendship that goes beyond titles, categories, and positions on a research team or employment contract; we are connected as women and as human beings.

Sisterhood is a beacon that orients me to the standpoint that I support, to the side of those being ruled (Neitz, 2014; Smith, 2005b); it is a lens through which the character and form of oppression materializes and relocates me to the side of those who are oppressed and are positioned outside of the ruling apparatus (Smith, 2005b). Sisterhood is an important grounding principle that encourages me to always be reflexive about my research and to think about what it means to be on the side of women living with HIV. Throughout my doctoral research and as I continue in my journey as a community-based researcher focused on women's health, HIV, pregnancy, and motherhood, I am fueled by sisterhood, relationships, social justice, and the words of Nason-Clark who eloquently argues "while passion without data can be misguided and even dangerous, passion based on empirical validation can be powerful. And that power has the potential to shape not only the path the data travels but also the heart of the researcher" (Nason-Clark, 2005, p. 228).

NEXT STEPS AND POSSIBILITIES

As I learned during that first seminar led by Dr. Christina Sinding, institutional ethnography offers tremendous practical utility to guide action by offering people an "intellectually reliable way to 'talk back' to the objectified forms of health care knowledge being authorized by...[for example,] the evidence-based practice and 'outcome measures' through which hospital efficiency is managed" (Rankin & Campbell, 2009, p. 2). Because of my ontological orientation toward social justice and sisterhood, as well as my longstanding relationships with women living with HIV, I remain committed to mobilizing my doctoral research and working with people in decision-making capacities to identify and facilitate change within the spaces that women living with HIV receive maternity care and beyond.

Since completing my Ph.D. in September 2019, I have been corresponding with staff in the HIV clinic to plan an information session where I can share my research and engage in dialogue about how the findings can be integrated into clinic work practices and institutional procedures. From that initial session and in collaboration with the HIV clinic leadership, I will explore possibilities to connect with maternity care providers and decision-makers and examine how my research could inform policies and procedures within perinatal care services.

My inquiry identified a number of concrete recommendations to shift and improve care practices from the standpoint of mothers living with HIV. For example, I discovered during my inquiry that perinatal care providers are interested to update the checklist that guides care provided to pregnant women living with HIV during childbirth and early postpartum. It was noted that the checklist could include concrete steps healthcare providers can take in response to women's sociocultural needs and concerns that go beyond the need for antiretroviral therapy during labor and postpartum for the infant. My doctoral research identified concrete steps that could be included in this checklist to enhance women's care experiences including mechanisms to respond to women's concerns about HIV disclosure in healthcare settings (Ion, 2019).

Lastly, I believe that there is an opportunity to develop educational materials and resources for mothers living with HIV who are navigating perinatal care. These resources could provide women with concrete information about what responsibilities healthcare institutions have to protect their private health information, and what women can do if their privacy and confidentiality are breached. These resources could also outline what steps women and their healthcare providers can take to respond to women's concerns about disclosure of their HIV status within healthcare settings (Ion, 2019). I will be exploring ways to collaboratively develop these resources with women living with HIV and healthcare providers within the hospital where my research occurred and as part of my provincial and national knowledge translation activities.

Conclusions

This chapter provides a critical reflection about my journey of coming to know about and do institutional ethnography for my doctoral research. I offer some points for consideration and reflexivity for burgeoning institutional ethnographers and connect my decisions and reflections to Dorothy Smith's work, the tenets of a sociology for people, and feminist knowledges. It is my hope that by accounting for my experiences and decisions as a graduate student researcher, I can inspire and motivate others who choose to employ institutional ethnography as their critical research strategy.

Note

1. The CD4 count is one of the most important measurements used to assess HIV disease progression and immune system strength. CD4 cells are one type of immune cell; these cells activate and direct other immune cells. Because they help to coordinate and lead the body's immune response, CD4 cells are an essential part of a healthy immune system. The CD4 count is measured in number of CD4 cells per cubic millimetre (mm^3), or microlitre (μl), of blood. A normal CD4 count ranges from 400 to 1200 cells/mm^3 in men and 500 to 1600 cells/mm^3 in women. Viral load measures the amount of HIV circulating in the blood. The viral load is measured in copies of HIV per millilitre (ml) of blood. A higher viral load will cause greater damage to the immune system. The goal of HIV treatment is to achieve an "undetectable" viral load of less than 40 copies of HIV per ml of blood. For more information, see http://www.aidsmap.com/about-hiv/basics/cd4-and-viral-load.

References

Adam, B., Corriveau, P., Elliott, R., Globerman, J., English, K., & Rourke, S. (2015). HIV disclosure as practice and public policy. *Critical Public Health, 25*(4), 386–397.

Bisaillon, L. (2011). Mandatory HIV screening policy & everyday life: A look inside the Canadian immigration medical examination. *Aporia, 3*(4), 5–14.

Campbell, M. L. (2016). Intersectionality, policy-oriented research and the social relations of knowing. *Gender, Work & Organization, 23*(3), 248–260.

Campbell, M., & Gregor, F. (2008). *Mapping social relations: A primer in doing institutional ethnography*. Toronto: University of Toronto Press.

Carter, A. J., Bourgeois, S., O'Brien, N., Abelsohn, K., Tharao, W., Greene, … Loutfy, M. (2013). Women-specific HIV/AIDS services: Identifying and defining the components of holistic service delivery for women living with HIV/AIDS. *Journal of the International AIDS Society, 16*(1), 17433. https://doi.org/10.7448/IAS.16.1.17433.

Charlton, J. I. (1998). *Nothing about us without us: Disability oppression and empowerment*. Berkeley, CA: University of California Press.

DeVault, M. (1999). *Liberating method: Feminism and social research*. Philadelphia, PA: Temple University Press.

Grace, D. (2015). Criminalizing HIV transmission using model law: Troubling best practice standardizations in the global HIV/AIDS response. *Critical Public Health, 25*(4), 441–454.

Grace, D. (2019). Institutional ethnography as a critical research strategy: Access, engagement, and implications for HIV/AIDS research. In E. Mykhalovskiy & V. Namaste (Eds.), *Thinking differently about HIV/AIDS: Contributions from critical social science* (pp. 103–133). Vancouver: UBC Press.

Greene, S., Ion, A., Elston, D., Kwaramba, G., Smith, S., Loutfy, M. (2015a). (M)othering with HIV: Resisting and reconstructing experiences of health and social surveillance. In B. Hogeveen & J. Minaker (Eds.), *Criminalized Mothers, Criminalizing Motherhood* (pp. 231–263). Toronto, ON: Demeter Press.

Greene, S., Ion, A., Kwaramba, G., Mwalwanda, M., Caswell, J., Guzha, E., et al. (2015). "Trust me, it's different": Experiences of peer case management of women living with HIV in Ontario, Canada. *Canadian Social Work Review, 32*(1–2), 73–93.

Greene, S., Ion, A., Elston, D., Kwaramba, G., Smith, S., Carvalhal, A., & Loutfy, M. (2015b). "Why aren't you breastfeeding?": How mothers living with HIV talk about infant feeding in a "breast is best" World. *Health Care for Women International, 36*(8), 883–901.

Greene, S., Ion, A., Kwaramba, G., Lazarus, L., & Loutfy, M. (2017). Surviving surveillance: How pregnant women and mothers living with HIV respond to medical and social surveillance. *Qualitative Health Research, 27*(14), 2088–2099. https://doi.org/10.1177/1049732317725219.

Greene, S., Ion, A., Kwaramba, G., Mwalwanda, M., Caswell, J., Guzha, E., & Carvalhal, A. (2015c). "Trust me, it's different": Experiences of peer case management of women living with HIV in Ontario, Canada. *Canadian Social Work Review, 32*(1–2), 73–93.

Greene, S., O'Brien-Teengs, D., Dumbrill, G., Ion, A., Beaver, K., Porter, M., et al. (2016). A community-based research approach to developing an HIV education and training module for child and family service workers in Ontario. In H. Montgomery, D. Badry, D. Fuchs, & D. Kikulwe (Eds.), *Transforming child welfare: Interdisciplinary practices, field education, and research* (pp. 163–185). Regina, SK: University of Regina Press.

Greene, S., O'Brien-Teengs, D., Dumbrill, G., Ion, A., Beaver, K., & Vaccaro, M. (2018). It's better late than never: A community-based HIV research and training response to supporting mothers living with HIV who have child welfare involvement. *Journal of Law and Social Policy, 28*(1), 61–80.

Greene, S., Odhiambo, J., M., Cotnam, J., Dunn, K., Frank, P., Gormley, R., ... Kaida, A. (2019). How do you prove that you told? How women living with hiv react and respond to learning about Canadian law that criminalizes HIV non-disclosure. *Culture, Health and Sexuality, 21*(10), 1087–1102. https://doi.org/10.1080/13691058.2018.1538489.

Ion, A., Greene, S., MacMillan, H., & Smieja, M. (2013). HSV-2/HIV co-infection, health-related quality of life and identity in women. *The Canadian Journal of Human Sexuality, 22*(3), 123–133.

Ion, A. (2019). Keeping secrets, disclosing health information: an institutional ethnography of the social organisation of perinatal care for women living with HIV in Canada. *Culture, Health & Sexuality.* https://doi.org/10.1080/13691058.2019.1604996.

Ion, A., Greene, S., Mellor, K., Kwaramba, G., Smith, S., Barry, F., ... Loutfy, M. (2016). Perinatal care experiences of mothers living with HIV in Ontario, Canada. *Journal of HIV/AIDS & Social Services, 15*(2), 180–201.

Ion, A., Sunderji, N., Jansz, G., & Ghavam-Rassoul, A. (2017). Understanding integrated mental health care in "real-world" primary care settings: What matters to health care providers and clients for evaluation and improvement? *Families, Systems, & Health, 35*(3), 271.

Khosla, P., Ion, A., & Greene, S. (2016). *Supporting mothers in ways that work: A resource toolkit for service providers working with mothers living with HIV.* Hamilton, ON: The HIV Mothering Study Team and the Ontario Women's HIV/AIDS Initiative. Available at http://www.catie.ca/en/resources/supporting-mothers-ways-work-resource-toolkit-serviceproviders-working-mothers-living-hiv.

Loutfy, M. R., Sonnenberg-Schwan, U., Margolese, S., Sherr, L., & Women for Positive Action. (2013). A review of reproductive health research, guidelines and related gaps for women living with HIV. *AIDS Care, 25*(6), 657–666.

McCoy, L. (2002). Dealing with doctors. In M. Bresalier, L. Gillis, C. McClure, L. McCoy, E. Mykhalovskiy, D. Taylor, & M. Webber (Eds.), *Making care visible: Antiretroviral therapy and the health work of people living with HIV/AIDS* (pp. 1–36). Toronto, ON: Making Care Visible Working Group. Retrieved from https://www.academia.edu/3644765/Making_Care_Visible_Antiretroviral_Therapy_and_the_Health_Work_of_People_Living_with_HIV_AIDS.

McCoy, L. (2005). HIV-positive patients and the doctor-patient relationship: Perspectives from the margins. *Qualitative Health Research, 15*(6), 791–806.

McCoy, L. (2006). Keeping the institution in view: Working with interview accounts of everyday experience. In D. E. Smith (Ed.), *Institutional ethnography as practice* (pp. 109–126). Lanham: Rowman & Littlefield.

McCoy, L. (2009). Time, self and the medication day: A closer look at the everyday work of "adherence". *Sociology of Health & Illness, 31*(1), 128–146.

Mykhalovskiy, E. (2008). Beyond decision making: Class, community organizations, and the healthwork of people living with HIV/AIDS. Contributions from institutional ethnographic research. *Medical Anthropology, 27*(2), 136–163.

Mykhalovskiy, E., & McCoy, L. (2002). Troubling ruling discourses of health: Using institutional ethnography in community-based research. *Critical Public Health, 12*(1), 17–37.

Nason-Clark, N. (2005). Linking research and social action: Violence, religion and the family. *Review of Religious Research, 46*(3), 221–234.

Neitz, M. J. (2014). Doing advocacy from a feminist standpoint. *Religion, 44*(2), 259–275.

Rankin, J. (2017). Conducting analysis in institutional ethnography: Guidance and cautions. *International Journal of Qualitative Methods, 16*(1). https://doi.org/10.1177/1609406917734472.

Rankin, J., & Campbell, M. (2009). Institutional ethnography (IE), nursing work and hospital reform: IE's cautionary analysis. *Forum qualitative sozialforschung/forum: Qualitative social research, 10*(2). Available at http://www.qualitative-research.net/index.php/fqs/article/view/1258.

Sinding, C. (2010). Using institutional ethnography to understand the production of health care disparities. *Qualitative Health Research, 20*(12), 1656–1663.

Smith, D. E. (1974). Women's perspective as a radical critique of sociology. *Sociological Inquiry, 44*(1), 7–13.

Smith, D. E. (1978). 'K is mentally Ill': The anatomy of a factual account. *Sociology, 12*(1), 23–53.

Smith, D. E. (1987). *The everyday world as problematic: A feminist sociology*. Boston, MA: Northeastern University Press.

Smith, D. E. (1990). *The conceptual practices of power: A feminist sociology of knowledge*. Toronto, ON: University of Toronto Press.

Smith, D. E. (1992). Sociology from women's experience: A reaffirmation. *Sociological Theory, 10*(1), 88–98.

Smith, D. E. (1999). *Writing the social: Critique, theory, and investigations*. Toronto, ON: University of Toronto Press.

Smith, D. E. (2005a). *Institutional ethnography: A sociology for people*. Lanham, MD: Altamira.

Smith, D. E. (2005b). Feminism and Marxism—A place to begin, a way to go. In S. P. Hier (Ed.), *Contemporary sociological thought: Themes and theories* (pp. 225–232). Toronto, ON: Canadian Scholars' Press Inc.

Smith, G. (1995). Accessing treatments: Managing the AIDS epidemic in Ontario. In M. Campbell & A. Manicom (Eds.), *Knowledge, experience, and ruling relations* (pp. 18–34). Toronto, ON: University of Toronto Press.

Sunderji, N., Ion, A., Zhu, A., Perivolaris, A., Rodie, D., & Mulsant, B. H. (2019). Challenges in conducting research on collaborative mental health care: A qualitative study. *CMAJ Open, 7*(2), E405–E414.

Swigonski, M. E. (1994). The logic of feminist standpoint theory for social work research. *Social Work, 39*(4), 387–395.

Taber, N. (2012). Beginning with the self to critique the social: Critical researchers as whole beings. London, UK: InTech Open Access Publisher. https://doi.org/10.5772/35336. Retrieved from http://cdn.intechopen.com/pdfs/31538.pdf.

UNAIDS. (1999). From principle to practice: Greater involvement of people living with or affected by HIV/AIDS (GIPA). Geneva: UNAIDS. Available at http://www.infocenter.nercha.org.sz/taxonomy/term/283.

UNAIDS. (2004). *2004 Report on the global HIV/AIDS epidemic* (4th Global Report). Geneva: UNAIDS.

Vyavaharkar, M., Moneyham, L., Corwin, S., Tavakoli, A., Saunders, R., & Annang, L. (2011). HIV-Disclosure, social support, and depression among HIV-infected African American women living in the rural southeastern United States. *AIDS Education and Prevention, 23*(1), 78–90.

Walby, K. (2007). On the social relations of research: A critical assessment of institutional ethnography. *Qualitative Inquiry, 13*(7), 1008–1030. https://doi.org/10.1177/1077800407305809.

Women's Health in Women's Hands. (2017). Negotiating disclosure: The HIV serostatus disclosure toolkit. Available at http://knowyourstatus.ca/wp-content/uploads/2017/11/HIV-DISCLOSURE-TOOLKIT-2017.pdf.

CHAPTER 8

IE and Visual Research Methods: An Open-Ended Discussion

Morena Tartari

This chapter aims to open a discussion on the intertwining between Institutional Ethnography (IE) and visual methods in sociology. It does so by analyzing and discussing a number of studies. IE considers visuals (photographs, paintings, sculptures, videos, CDs, etc.) like texts (laws, regulations, reports, translations, articles, pamphlets, and so on): these are indispensable elements for exploring text-mediated relations of ruling (Smith, 1990). The current *Zeitgeist* (spirit of the age) is characterized by people's increasing use of visuals in their everyday practices that affect doing research and its dissemination. Societal changes have made visual texts more usable, available, widespread, and sometimes more persuasive. However, a limited number of IE studies explicitly discuss the utilization of visuals and visual research methods in IE research practices. This is the reason why researchers who use IE could benefit from wider discussion about its intertwining with visuals and visual research methods. The analysis of people's visual and sense-making practices and the utilization of visuals and visual research methods in IE are connected aspects. However, this chapter will focus mainly on the latter topic. Therefore, it will illustrate how researchers have to date employed visual data, visual research methods and visual dissemination methods in IE, what the other potential uses in the future are, and the aspects in regard to which the debate remains open.

The chapter is organized into three parts. The first consists of an introductory overview of what visual methods are, the societal changes that affect

M. Tartari (✉)
Department of Sociology, University of Antwerp, Antwerp, Belgium
e-mail: Morena.Tartari@uantwerpen.be

© The Author(s) 2021
P. C. Luken and S. Vaughan (eds.), *The Palgrave Handbook of Institutional Ethnography*,
https://doi.org/10.1007/978-3-030-54222-1_8

their rise, and their intertwining with IE. The second part presents exemplary IE research studies, which use visuals and visual methods for different purposes and employ different research practices. The chapter concludes with an open-ended discussion about the strengths and weaknesses of utilizing visual methods in IE.

Visual Methods, Societal Change, and IE

It is useful to begin by considering what visual methods are, then the reason for their importance in our society and finally to consider how visual methods intertwine with some aspects of IE.

Although visual methods in sociology involve many different approaches, Van den Scott (2018, p. 720) provides a list useful for understanding what visual methods are. These comprise the following: photo-elicitation, photo-voice, photography, and autophotography, family photos, mental or cognitive mapping, GIS mapping, interviews with video or photography, grounded theory mapping, mapping of social groups, art making and its analysis, study of material culture, graffiti, ethnographic content analysis of visual materials like cartoons, movies, paintings, drawings, photographs, and so on. A wide range of visual methods exists with different degrees of collaboration and involvement of the participants and of the researcher. These methods are usually applied in anthropology, psychology, and sociology, in qualitative research and classical ethnography, and they can be profitably transferred to IE and adapted to its ontological framework.

Generally, qualitative researchers utilize visuals in three ways: as *data*, as *tools to gather data*, as *tools to record data*. The first case—visuals as *data*—concerns the situation in which researchers conduct content analysis of visual materials that are already available in the social world (e.g., advertising images become data to analyze). The second case—visuals as *tools to gather data*—concerns the situation in which researchers use visual methods to elicit data from participants. In this case, visuals may be created by the researcher or by participants or by researchers and participants working together. The classic example of this second case is when researchers gather data from participants by means of photo-elicitation. The third situation—visuals as *tools to record data*—regards the case of researchers who use visual methods in order to register data in a more detailed and material form, for example when researchers take photographs with the purpose of enriching fieldnotes and memos and representing the material aspects of the problems that they are studying. A fourth situation should be added: when researchers use visual materials from their fieldwork to present, explain and disseminate findings to an academic public or a broader general audience. In summary, ethnographers can (1) analyze visuals, (2) use visuals in order to gather or generate data, (3) use visuals as means to present findings. These three different ways to employ visuals in IE can be combined to generate hybrid uses, as we will see.

The second aspect to be considered concerns why the visual methods are increasingly applied. This has its roots in the extraordinary social and cultural changes that have occurred in recent decades, most notably the transition from logocentrism to imagocentrism. The term *logocentrism* (Klages, 1972) concerns the conception of words and language as fundamental expressions of everyday reality. Logocentrism can be considered an umbrella term that describes not only the relationship between thought, speech, and writing, but also the centrality of that relationship in everyday life. The term *imagocentrism* was coined to describe a culture in which the image is an epistemological referent. De Sousa Santos (2015) explains that logocentrism is related to social and territorial matrices (space and time), while imagocentrism is based on *mediatrixes* (a media-driven culture) in which space and time are replaced by velocity and superficiality. In imagocentrism the processes of relation and communication are mainly enacted by images. Even if these -*centrisms* might seem *blob* ontologies, it should be considered that the materiality of digital technologies has redefined "how images operate in society" (Harper, 2016, p. 246), how people think and act, and, consequently, how research can be done. Within sociology, this has generated a progressive affirmation of visual research methods that are considered fundamental for investigating societal and cultural changes in an everyday life, which is increasingly *thick* with images (Mirzoeff, 2009). Visual research was underestimated for a long time (Spencer, 2010), and only at the beginning of the current century did scholars recognize the value of this approach. Pink (2006, 2012) considers that the attention paid to visual methods is due to theoretical changes in social sciences, as well as new attention paid to social practices, to the multisensorial nature of knowledge processes, and to the spatial dimension of everyday life. Van den Scott (2018) observes that the affirmation of visual methods was possible only with the reflexive turn in social sciences, and this affirmation was enhanced by the spread and affordability of digital technologies. According to Van den Scott, visual methods can support public sociology from data collection to the dissemination of findings. Herzog (2020) adopts a similar position: visual research methods are fundamental in a society that is using "visual representation as a primary form of communication" (p. 184).

The third aspect to be considered concerns how visual research methods intertwine with some aspects of IE. First of all, IE responds effectively to the *linguistic turn* in the social sciences, directing attention back to people, their quotidian experiences, their everyday-life materiality, their practices in relation to cultural representations. As Smith and Turner (2014) argue, texts are all material objects that convey a message. A text cannot be separated from the concrete relations that it coordinates in people's everyday activities. A text can be reproduced many times and its replicability is central. This sensitivity of IE to texts and their social settings enables researchers to work with the materiality of visual texts and discover how this materiality can be linked to discursive dimensions through the lived experience. It follows that IE enables researchers to investigate and demonstrate the translocal ruling relations functions of visual texts, both when visuals are considered as *data* and when they are conceived as *tools to gather* and *record data*. For example, when visuals are tools to gather data, seeing how images are taken up and acted upon by participants makes the application of visual methods to IE effective in understanding the participants' point of view. Indeed, the sensitivity of IE to materiality, joined to the visual methods, enables researchers to make the participants' standpoint and their everyday work more visible, displayable, and understandable in the concrete details.

Furthermore, IE can contribute to the study of visual-mediated practices, for example, by analyzing how people look at images, the role of images in their daily lives, their effects, and the acts of meaning attribution. Visuals activate different sensorial modalities and symbolic mechanisms, and considering these practices and mechanisms is necessary during research. Even if IE can certainly make valuable contributions to the study of these visual-mediated practices, the main focus of this chapter is broader.

Above all, a crucial point is the role of visual research methods in enhancing IE's attitude of being a sociology *for* people that promotes social and political activism and that engages in change-making practices with regard to social problems. The explanations of Herzog (2020) about how visual methods can significantly contribute to the study of social problems by integrating visual methods into social problems studies can be applied to the intertwining between visual methods and IE. Herzog argues that visuals yield a better understanding of aspects of social problems that are too abstract and that can benefit from the materiality of visuals; they are of great help when interpreting social problems; they make it easier to call the public audience's attention to social problems.

A Selection of IE Research Studies with the Focus on Visuals

The following selected IE research studies will be analyzed considering the four main categories of visuals and visual methods utilization (as *data*, as *tools to gather data*, as *tools to record data*, as tools to *disseminate* findings), the distinctive nature of the IE research approach, and Herzog's suggestions about visual methods and social problems' analysis.

Some of these studies utilize visual methods in more than one of the four above-mentioned categories of application. Furthermore, these studies do not exhaust all possible applications of visual research methods in IE, since there are many such research methods.

It is useful to begin with the study by Luken and Vaughan (2006), an example of how visuals can be utilized as *data* in IE. Walby (2005) provides another example of visuals as *data* that activate the text/reader conversation and that can be observed by the researcher in their natural setting. The study by McCoy (1995) is an example of application of photo-elicitation as a *tool to gather data*, while my study (2018) provides a hybrid use of visuals as data and as tools to gather data. Finally, my study on the transition from double to single motherhood (2019) and the study by Puddu (2018) are examples of the hybrid use of visuals as tools to gather data and to disseminate findings to an academic public or a broader public outside academia.

Archival Visual Data (Help) to Unpack Institutional Discourses

Luken and Vaughan (2006) use visual texts including historical photographs to explicate the social relations shaping housing and family practices in early twentieth-century United States. The aim of the study is the exploration of "the processes by which an institutional discourse combining childrearing and housing practices was formulated through the work practices of three state-affiliated organizations between 1900 and 1930" (Luken & Vaughan, 2006, p. 300). Beginning with the oral histories of older women, the authors analyzed how parents took up the discourse of the Standard American Home (SAH) as a form of housing suitable for raising infants and children elaborated by three state-affiliated organizations. They collected documents on childrearing and housing between 1890 and 1930 from the U.S. National Archives and Research Administration (NARA), the Library of Congress, historical societies and museums in cities where the interviewed women lived as children and parents, and library repositories across the United States. Using historical investigative methods to connect the documents to the local experience of these women, as "texts-in-use", the authors, for example, collected and examined brochures from The Better Homes in America movement—a campaign started in 1922 at a national level—whose demonstration projects and brochures were in the cities in which the women lived. From these brochures, the authors discovered photographs of houses advertised as a part of the annually sponsored Better Homes Week. The use of two of these photographs by the authors allows us to understand how the SAH discourse operated. These photographs show a home before and after the work of remodeling and decoration. The authors argued that the images, their accompanying texts, the contrast between the two appearances of the home posed by the ordering discursively construct the aspiration of the working class, modeling it by an image of a middle-class home. Images and their order of presentation work by argumentatively producing class differences. Through these materials, Luken and Vaughan demonstrated that the SAH discourse universalized and typified aspects and appearances of the homes and furniture and defined home and home ownership as fundamental goods for the construction of a balanced personality in children.

In this example, historical photographs—produced in standardized and replicable forms—are texts-in-use that contributed materially to organizing the responsibility of parents. Through these photographs and their accompanying texts, the institutional ideological code produces a standardization of visual norms and is able to organize the interviewees' narratives even decades later. This process of organization of knowledge can be activated not only through photographs but also through other visual texts, like posters, newspaper ads, paintings, as these authors demonstrated in other studies (e.g., Luken & Vaughan, 2005).

In conclusion, in light of the above-mentioned suggestions by Herzog (2020), one observes that in the study by Luken and Vaughan (2006) the materiality of visuals is constitutive of the institutional discourses that they analyzed, so that these visual data cannot be neglected either in the analysis or in the discussion of how some concerted ideological codes affect the everyday practices of people. For this reason, it is essential to include the visual texts in the presentation of the results of these studies.

CCTV Texts as Visual Data to Integrate with Participant Observation

Walby (2005) studied how institutional discourses affect the practices of interpretation of CCTV (closed-circuit television) visual texts performed by the camera operators in control rooms and how these practices give rise to forms of racialized discrimination. CCTV, also known as *video surveillance*, is a television system whereby video cameras are used to transmit a signal to a specific number of monitors in the control room, where operators watch images on the monitors, write logbooks and reports to send to other control agencies, in order to a make a specific place, person or activity secure. Walby conducted unstructured interviews with CCTV operators and observed them in their workplace in three organizations in Victoria, British Columbia.

Visual texts shown by the monitors can be considered as *visual data* observed during Walby's fieldwork. He considered a visual text on the monitor as a *rolling text* (a sequence of events in real time on the monitor) or as an *initiating text* (a sequence of events that can be rewritten and reinterpreted). The rolling text enables operators to catch the act of shoplifting. The initiating text reports the act of the offender to the various institutions involved in the process of surveillance, risk detection, and risk communication. The operators interpret stimuli from the rolling visual texts and discriminate between people deemed to be suspicious and not suspicious. They transcribe the visual text into a sequence of written texts, which activate processes (like reports and arrests) at local level and far away in translocal organizations. The video can be freezeframed, extracting pictures of suspects to send to other stores, or to attorneys and courts to report an incident, becoming "a form of text which is central to the coordination of peoples' activities" (Walby, 2005, p. 191).

Walby observed that initiating visual texts have a *replicable* form because they can be sent to various institutions, to various readers who can differently activate the fragments from videorecordings, referring to ruling (written) texts that are different from the ruling text of the camera operators. These visual texts are subject to activation through intertextual circles, passing through different activations and interpretations, also after years. The materiality of the CCTV text, because it is activated by diverse subjects (from the camera operators up to the judges), allows one to make visible the involvement of the subject in reproducing institutional discourses. The study's findings show how operators participate in reproducing the dominant institutional discourse using the CCTV videos. Walby argued that the operators aim to protect the practices of contemporary consumerism from the deviant behavior that they commonly identified in Aboriginal shoppers' activities.

Walby's study is interesting because it shows how an institutional ethnographer can observe the process of activation of visual texts in a workplace (see also Walby, 2006). These visual data can be combined and compared with other data collected through observation, interviews and document analysis.

In conclusion, in regard to Herzog's (2020) suggestions, this study yields, through the materiality of visual data, better understanding of abstract aspects of the social problems generated by so-called surveillance society and it enables interpretation of how institutional discourses affect the everyday practices of surveillance and racialized profiling.

Photo-Elicitation to Make the Text/Reader Conversation Visible

McCoy (1995) examined visual texts embedded in the social situations of their use with the aim to discover how people give meaning to these texts and how the interpretive practices of their activation occur. She argued that the practice of "looking at" and interpreting photographs in daily life is socially organized. McCoy analyzed diverse visual texts; but, for the current analysis, the most interesting part of her work concerns study of the sense-making process related to wedding photographs and the institutional discourses that affect this process.

To study this process, McCoy proposed an innovative method using the materiality of visual texts. She made "the text-reader conversation observable by getting three people together (she was one of the group) to talk about the photographs of the wedding of one of them" (Smith, 2005, p. 106). She did not control the conversation, but she followed its natural development. She applied a kind of *photo-elicitation* in which photographs belong to the wedding album of one of the participants, and photographs are produced by a professional photographer. Photo-elicitation is a method of research that consists in using photographs (or other visual materials) during an interview or a focus group with the aim of activating a discussion with the participants, gathering data on social processes and practices, and exploring different interpretations and reactions by the participants. The visual materials for the photo-elicitation can be chosen among those collected by the researcher or among those collected or created by the participants.

McCoy analyzed how wedding pictures are activated in the talk and by the relations among the viewer, the picture and the owner. These relations and talk show the ability of actors in reading the photographic album as a record of "real events." In doing this, they apply the ruling interpretive scheme of the ideal wedding discourse. She (1995) observed that "at a wedding people organize a series of actions that aim at discursive ideals of love, romance, family, and so forth" (p. 187). Images, created on and with the bodies, produce the local realization of the wedding's discursive forms on the basis of those ideals.

Therefore, the small focus group conducted by McCoy made visible the text/reader conversation as a situated activity in the course of action. This means that the act of interpreting during the text/reader conversation connects the visual text to the situation in which that reading is happening and is embedded. In other words, without the presence of the bride in the group, in her study McCoy would have collected a different interpretation of the visual texts.

In conclusion, even if McCoy's research study appears not to be related to the field of social problems and visual methods as discussed by Herzog (2020), it provides an example of how IE can investigate, through the materiality of visual texts, how people organize their actions, at what discursive ideals they aim, what kind of local realization of these discursive forms is produced. This approach makes it possible to analyze social processes in detail, so that it can be utilized for a deeper interpretation of social problems.

Photo-Elicitation to Investigate the Accountability Strategies of Court Experts

A research study that I conducted (Tartari, 2018)[1] on court-appointed psychologists as experts illustrates another possible use of photo-elicitation in IE. I investigated the everyday social practices that regulate and coordinate the work of court experts within the judicial context of child custody evaluation from their standpoint, and the strategies that these professionals use to show their responsibility and accountability during these evaluations. I applied a hybrid visual method: I used photograms from previously videorecorded sessions as *visual data* in my autoethnography and as *tools for photo-elicitation* in interviews and focus groups with the participants. The photograms were extracted from a corpus of videorecorded sessions from my professional work, since, for about 20 years, I had worked as a court expert in Italy in the area of psychological assessment of parental responsibilities in order to help courts to decide child custody arrangements.

The research study began with a visual auto-ethnography, where I used visuals as data; then, in a second phase, I conducted interviews and a focus group with court-appointed experts, where I used visual data for a photo-elicitation.

The first phase of the study, the visual auto-ethnography, provided better identification of the research question: that is, how the everyday practices of the experts were textually mediated and shaped by the discourses on responsibility and accountability during psychological assessment of the parents. I analyzed the last ten court-appointed evaluations that I had conducted before leaving my professional job for my academic career. They consisted of ten written reports and of videorecorded meetings I had with parents and children. On analyzing the videorecorded sessions, I found that the discourses about accountability and responsibility propounded by the judicial system and the professional community induced me increasingly to express my responsibility and reliability in different ways, both verbally and visually, during the process of evaluation. My work was ruled by various texts (code of conduct, guidelines for psycho-forensic evaluation, family law) and by the interpretations that parents, lawyers and (private experts) colleagues made of these texts. Since the autoethnography did not yield sufficient findings, I extended my study to psychologists who were used to working as court-appointed experts and as private experts for parents (in Italy, the legal procedure for the court-appointed expert's evaluation prescribes that each parent may be accompanied by a private expert—a psychologist of their choice—during all sessions of the evaluation).

In this second stage of the research, I conducted a focus group with three experts (as in McCoy, 1995) and some in-depth interviews (because many experts refused to discuss the topic of responsibilities and professional practices in a group with other colleagues). The interview and the focus group followed the same design: a first part with open-ended questions about the procedures that the participants applied to be accountable in the most recent evaluations they had conducted for courts; and a second part concerning the discussion of the images extracted from my work. In this second part, I used a show-and-tell procedure. I selected participants to include a variety of professional experiences, particularly experts with different psychological approaches to the evaluation of parents. Informed consent was provided by the participants and for the data I reused from my professional practice. In addition, I applied a masking technique so that parents and children were not recognizable in the images.

Regarding the selection of the images, I freeze-framed the videorecordings pertaining to the last ten evaluations that I had conducted for courts, extracting some pictures. I selected images that represented practices related to professionals' accountability and responsibility in different phases of the evaluation. For example, I selected images where the setting between the consultant/s and me showed details about how the expert used audio and videorecording, took notes, and discussed these procedures with the parents. The images in Figs. 8.1, 8.2, 8.3 and 8.4 are examples of those that I proposed to the participants.

The first image shows me at the desk with a child during a meeting and the technological devices that I used. The second image shows me at the one-way mirror while I am explaining to a father and his daughter the role of the mirror and the presence of other colleagues behind the mirror.

The third image shows me with a parent and his son while I am explaining to them the role of the room with CCTV and of the colleagues in that room. The fourth image shows a technical error concerning operation of the CCTV in the other room resulting in the loss of many minutes of the recording.

Fig. 8.1 Me at the desk

Fig. 8.2 Me at the one-way mirror

When I presented the images to participants, I explained to them that the images came from my professional practice and that we could discuss them together. I told them that at the start of the research I had worked on my personal experience, trying to reflect critically about it. I presented the images one at a time, describing each of them briefly.

During the first part of the interview and focus group, the participants provided more off-topic accounts, focusing the narratives mainly on the qualities of the relationship between parents and children, rather than on their

8 IE AND VISUAL RESEARCH METHODS: AN OPEN-ENDED DISCUSSION   131

Fig. 8.3 Me explaining the role of CCTV

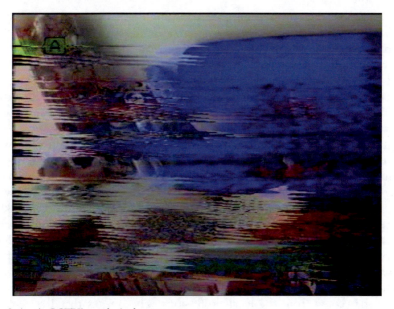

Fig. 8.4 A CCTV's technical error

practices and strategies concerning accountability and responsibility. However, the photo-elicitation was more fruitful since the second part of interviews and focus groups allowed the experts to discuss, in detailed terms, *disjunctures* between their practices and the institutional discourses. Through the photos, experts were able to focus better on changes in their own practices, differences between their practices and those of other colleagues, and on how discourses from the legal/judicial field and from the psychologists' professional community affect the need to show and perform responsibility and accountability through specific practices.

The findings of the study can be summarized into two issues. The first is a disjuncture between the discourses from the legal and the psychological fields: the former indicates some practices as accountable and responsible practices, but the latter—in particular the clinical psychology discourse—does not consider some of these practices as responsible. For example, commenting on the first image, an expert considered that audio and videorecording pertain to the legal field that needs evidences and proofs, but not pertinent to the field of psychology. She explained that the use of devices compromises the relationship of trust between parents and experts, which is a kind of relationship defined by the field of the clinical psychology profession and not by the field of other professions involved.

Second, the discourses from clinical psychology failed to promote in the experts a sense of awareness about accountable and responsible practices. Since these discourses maintain the focus on the trust relationship between expert and client (adult or minor), they failed in making the experts aware of the need to keep the focus on the entire process of evaluation, on the institutions involved, and on the projection of the effects of their practices into the future. In other words, participants emphasized that experts have different degrees of *awareness* about the issue of the subsequent *potential* reactivation of the (written or visual) texts collected during the evaluations. When this awareness is present to a large extent, it affects how experts collect data during the evaluation. Because they know that at a different level of the process and in different institutions, other people with similar or different roles can watch their videos or read their reports, they enhance and underline certain kinds of practices. Some participants commented that the more aware an expert is of the subsequent reactivations of the text, the more s/he acts accordingly in order to anticipate some consequences of this. They commented that this awareness had made necessary, over the years, an increasing "rigidity" of their practices. Such awareness was ruled by the ideals of accountability and responsibility that come from the legal professions. The images that I selected, in their opinion, reflected this rigidity very well.

In conclusion, it is to be observed that in this study visuals are used in a hybrid way: *as data* in the autoethnography and then as *tools to gather data* by the photo-elicitation in the interviews and focus group. In regard to Herzog's suggestions (2020), this study highlights how visuals can be used to improve the understanding of abstract aspects related to responsibility and accountability as increasingly perceived as problems in professional practices. Visuals contributed also to improving the interpretation of such practices and the social processes related to them.

Using Visuals to Disseminate Findings and Promote Social Justice

Visuals can be utilized for dissemination purposes to an academic or a broader public outside academia. Explaining how people act and how institutions work can become more ethnographically accessible to a broader public if visuals are used. This is the case of an IE project which I am currently conducting (Tartari, 2019) and of a study conducted by Puddu (2018).

My ongoing study[2] focuses on single mothers' everyday strategies and social practices to claim inclusion and to negotiate—or not negotiate— the dominant definition of family and parenthood proposed by institutions and professionals and the less legitimated definitions of single parents and their families. In particular, the analysis considers the transition from double parenthood to single motherhood, paying attention to the period of judicial evaluation for child custody and judicial decisions in regard to allowances and other obligations. The research conducted for the study collects data in Belgium, Italy, Spain, and in the UK through discursive interviews with single mothers, judicial professionals, and gender issues activists, participant observations, and photo-voice sessions involving mothers and professionals. Interviews and photo-voice sessions are audio and videorecorded (after participants have signed an informed consent form) and are usable for the audio and visual dissemination. Participants can choose to make available to the video-dissemination only some fragments from their video interviews conducted by the researcher. Furthermore, participants have a third option: a voluntary non-professional actor can videorecord the excerpts from the interview, lending his/her face for the recording. A detailed informed consent form concerning the dissemination is submitted to the participants and images, and voices are masked when the participants request it.

The research is hybrid in its use of visuals: (1) Each mother collects pictures of her everyday life with the EthnoAlly[3] app (Favero & Theunissen, 2018) on her mobile phone. These pictures are interpreted by the researcher, but they are also discussed in the photovoice session with mothers as participants and in the focus groups with judicial system professionals. Hence, visuals are used *as data* and *as tools to gather data* by photo-elicitation and by the focus groups. (2) Then, they are used *as tools to disseminate findings*. Indeed, visual fragments from the videorecording of the interviews, from the photovoice, from the focus groups, and pictures collected by the mothers are utilized for the visual dissemination of the findings. The visual dissemination is structured into short videos produced by the researcher (with her explanations, image, and voice) which include video excerpts from the interviews with the participants, pictures collected by the mothers, and video excerpts from the photovoice sessions and the focus groups. In addition, videos provide an explanation of the maps created during the research fieldwork. Maps are a typical tool of IE, and showing and commenting on them can improve people's understandings of some processes. Maps are graphic objects that can be shown through digital animations with specific software, enhancing the understanding of abstract aspects of practices or social processes.

In this ongoing study, the visual dissemination aims to reach an academic public, a non-academic public (such as policy makers, stakeholders, professionals) and a broader general public. Videos and pictures are shared through different platforms like a dedicated channel on YouTube, a website, Twitter, and Facebook. This kind of dissemination is intended to explain, through the visual materials from the research fieldwork, the standpoint of the single mothers in different countries and the invisible and taken-for-granted forms of governance that rule their everyday lives. In this study, the choice of investing energies and time in a visual video dissemination has the purpose of impacting on a broader non-academic public, sensitizing policy makers, professionals, and citizens to single mothers' problems.

A second example is provided by an IE study conducted by Puddu (2018) that used visuals *as data* and *as tools to disseminate findings*. Puddu's study explored how vulnerable youths' lives are socially organized during urban revitalization in Edmonton, Canada. This community-based participatory research project utilized participant observation, field notes, open-ended interviews, focus groups and photovoice. Using the photovoice method, Puddu asked street-involved youths to collect photographs about how urban revitalization shaped their experiences in order to gain better understanding of their daily lives and their perspectives on the impact of the fast growing district. Outputs of the photovoice study were a photographic booklet and a public exhibit by means of which the youths concerned were able to present their photographs and stories to citizens, stakeholders, and local authorities. In the booklet, pictures taken by the participants were accompanied by fragments from the interviews and author's comments. These outputs made it possible to connect youth with policy makers and the community.

In conclusion, following the considerations of Herzog (2020) about the intertwining of visual methods and social problems research, it is possible to argue that the two research studies presented above mainly aim to use visuals to direct the *public audience's attention to social problems*.

An Open-Ended Conclusion

This chapter has illustrated some aspects of visual methods and their intertwining with IE. Then, by illustrating various studies, it has shown how researchers can utilize visual materials as data, as tools to gather data, as tools to record data, and as tools to disseminate findings. This conclusion summarizes the intertwining between visual research methods and IE and the possibilities that it offers to social problems research, highlighting its strengths and weaknesses.

A first strength concerns the *adaptability* of visuals and visual methods to the IE approach. Visual materials and different visual methods can be brought into an IE project and adapted to its specific theoretical and methodological characteristics. The study by Luken and Vaughan (2006) provides an example of this adaptability using visual data as second-level data in IE (see also Campbell & Gregor, 2002), which are data collected outside or beyond people's experiential accounts. In the aforementioned study, these visual data enable explanation of the linkages among local accounts, local actions and social relations of ruling, and they reinforce the explanation and the interpretation of those processes. Furthermore, the study by McCoy (1995) provides an example of how photo-elicitation can be adapted to the IE approach, as the researcher organizes a small group to discuss the interpretive processes of the activation of the bride's pictures.

On the other hand, IE shows *flexibility* by including visual research methods but retaining its own methodological and theoretical characteristics, as in the study on court-appointed experts' practices (Tartari, 2018). In other words, an IE project can flexibly integrate visuals as data and as tools to gather, to record and to disseminate data. Since the IE approach is a sociology in itself (DeVault, 2020), fruitful integrations and exchanges are possible in relation to visual methods.

Furthermore, one of the most important strengths seems to be the link among the *materiality* of visuals, the focus of IE on materiality itself, and the *sensitivity* of IE to people, their standpoints, their everyday experiences, and the concrete aspects of discursive and cultural representations. The utilization of visuals and visual methods, which help to maintain the focus on the real social world and its materiality, enhances this kind of IE sensitivity. For example, in the study on court-appointed experts (Tartari, 2018), it is precisely the materiality of the visual text that enables participants to keep the focus on their actual practices, describing, and discussing them in detail. Bringing the materiality of visual texts into IE also makes it possible to achieve greater *richness* in narrating experiences (Rose, 2016). For example, in the study on court-appointed experts, the visual texts used for the photo-elicitation were able to generate processes of identification and differentiation by the experts that would not be activated in the same way by a verbal question of the researcher. The materiality of visual texts enables participants to explain aspects of the social world that could be difficult to express or show verbally; then, they enable researchers to grasp these aspects. An example of this process of *overcoming verbal limits* can be found in the study by Puddu (2019) where, through pictures collected by the participants, a stigmatized condition like youth homelessness can be analyzed, displayed, and communicated by the participants and the researcher.

Puddu's study affords explanation of another strength of involving visuals in the research process: *equalizing power*. Visuals enable a horizontal approach to be taken between interviewer and interviewees, reducing power inequalities. Therefore, visuals are recommended when researchers are in situations where the power between them and the participants is particularly unequal, for instance, research with children (e.g., Mannay, 2010), with immigrants, or with disadvantaged groups, like the vulnerable youth in Puddu's work. Indeed, visuals become an excellent instrument when researchers study intersections and use the intersectionality approach. Therefore, when there are power inequalities in the relation between the researcher and the participants and/or when participants come from life experiences of inequality and stigma, visual methods can facilitate the dialogue between researcher and participants, both when visuals are used as tools to gather data and when they are used to record them.

Finally, implementing visual methods in IE improves *effective action to disseminate research results and involve* stakeholders and policy makers. Firstly, these methods allow communication with participants and different audiences using means that are meaningful to them, as Herzog (2020) suggests. In a society that uses visual representation as a primary form of communication, visual research methods and visual disseminations (like, for example, short videos, booklets with photographs, photographic exhibitions) are important tools. An example of dissemination practices of this kind can be found in my study on single mothers and judicial system (Tartari, 2019). Furthermore, mapping—a typical tool of IE—can be displayed in videos with animations in order to explain social processes to a non-academic public. Visual dissemination can be done through social media platforms (like YouTube, Facebook, and Twitter) and it can reach different audiences and sensitize them, achieving one of the main aims of IE. This kind of dissemination does not replace the traditional form of written dissemination through academic journals, but it can constitute a parallel channel.

Visual research methods and visual practices of results dissemination can be properly included in IE studies, strengthening the social mission of IE as a sociology for people. In regard to the social mission of IE, to be considered is what Vannini (2019) states about public ethnography and visuals: "In our digital age, multimodality is not an option for ethnography but a necessity" (p. 4). Vannini explains that a multimodal message concerns not a single mode of communication, but more than one. In other words, (academic) writing is not enough to reach a wider audience. Researchers need to use other modes of communication and to learn other effective strategies for communicating, following the examples of other disciplines like human geography and anthropology. Vannini underlines the potential of ethnographers in developing visual disseminations: they are sensitive and able to involve themselves directly in the life world of participants and to interpret these experiences, describing and explaining such interpretation to different audiences. Even if Vannini considers other kinds of ethnography, his suggestions can be usefully applied to IE. Concluding, the use of visuals, in many of the forms analyzed in this chapter, contributes *to giving voice to the participants*, who are often without voice, as in the studies by Puddu (2018) and Tartari (2019). If Van den Scott (2018) suggests that visuals are a form of answer, I argue that the use of visuals in IE as tools to disseminate findings consists, above all, in questions and answers that can generate forms of dialogic reflexivity in dealing with social problems.

The use of visuals in IE as data, as research methods, and as tools for dissemination has also some potential weaknesses. The first of them concerns *how to define visual texts as appropriate* for use in an IE. Replicability and "incorporation" are the necessary characteristics of such texts, as explained by Smith and Turner (2014). It follows that a critical analysis should be conducted on visual texts to ensure that they are suitable for use or interpretation. Analyzing visuals as data and/or selecting them as tools requires practice, critical thinking, and a good theoretical knowledge of IE. As in other kinds of ethnographies, researchers should manage visual data like textual data: internal patterns and/or links to the external data should be sought. This search should be systematic and reflexive (Van den Scott, 2018). The study by Luken and Vaughan (2006) provides a good example of visual data that are effective in showing how discourses affect social practices. The authors made an extensive collection of materials like brochures from different sources assuring the quality of historical archival data that they analyzed, and then linked them to the interviews that they conducted.

However, the problem of the appropriateness of visual texts concerns mainly the situation when visuals are tools for gathering data, as in photo-elicitation. A visual text used for photo-elicitation should be selected with attention to its replicability and incorporation in the actual settings of people's everyday lives. For instance, in the study on court-appointed experts, the selection and creation of images that represented recurrent situations in work processes needed critical attention to my personal and professional practices of looking, because that "looking" could generate biases in selecting the images. The way in which researchers "look" is socially organized; it is not a neutral practice. Furthermore, visuals are embedded in social settings and situations, and their uses can be culture-sensitive, age-sensitive, gender-sensitive and generation-sensitive. For this reason, critical attention is necessary to determine when and how the selection of images can be biased.

Another important weakness of the intertwining of IE with visual methods concerns the *ethics*. The more the aim is to give voice to the participants and make ethnography *public* through the use of visual materials, the more the use of visuals in research and dissemination requires careful consideration of ethical issues. Pictures and videos of the participants (collected by the researcher or by themselves) can be shown to a small group (for example in a focus group or in a photovoice session), but also to a wide public audience. Some ways of preventing rejections by ethical committees regarding showing images and videos for the dissemination include: (1) the preparation of a detailed information sheet and consent form to protect participants and researchers by stating clearly the use of the images before, during, and after the research study and how they will be manipulated; (2) the application of audio and visual masking (i.e., the masking of faces, bodies and voices) in videorecordings, pictures, or podcasts that will be used to disseminate findings; and (3) the utilization of semi-fictional methods involving volunteers as non-professional actors (an actor who lends his/her face and voice to the participant), as in the study on single mothers and judicial system (Tartari, 2019).

It is useful to conclude by highlighting that other strengths and weaknesses can be found in the theoretical and methodological intertwining between IE and visual methods. Therefore, the discussion remains open.

Acknowledgements I am grateful to the anonymous peer reviewers and to Dr. Jackie Gulland (University of Edinburgh) for their comments on the earlier drafts of this chapter.

Notes

1. This IE project is a self-funded research study, carried out by myself in collaboration with the University of Padua for the recruitment of the subjects and the conduct of the study. Regarding ethical issues, the study complies with the code of conduct elaborated by AIS - Associazione Italiana di Sociologia, and meets international legal and ethics requirements.
2. The IE research project "Study on TRansition and Exclusion in Society of Single-Mums (STRESS-Mums)" has received funding from the European Union's Horizon 2020 research and innovation programme under the Marie Sklodowska-Curie grant agreement no. 843976. This study received ethical approval from the Ethical Committee "Ethische Adviescommissie Sociale en Humane Wetenschappen" of the Universiteit Antwerpen, host institution of the project.
3. EthnoAlly is a mobile application that enables researchers to create and organize multimodal field notes for ethnographic studies. It can be downloaded for free on smartphones—by iOS and Android—and it produces GNSS-tagged multimodal material that can be archived, organized and analyzed on a cloud application server. EthnoAlly is a research tool designed specifically for the purpose of helping anthropologists and other social scientists conducting sensory, participatory, and multimodal ethnographic research. EthnoAlly is also a participatory research tool. Participants can download the app onto their smartphones and generate images, text notes, sound files and geolocative and temporal metadata to share with the researcher. In this way, the app can work as an extension of the ethnographer's fieldwork.

References

Campbell, M. L., & Gregor, F. M. (2002). *Mapping social relations: A primer in doing institutional ethnography*. Toronto: University of Toronto Press.
de Sousa Santos, B. (2015). *Epistemologies of the South: Justice against epistemicide*. Abingdon: Routledge.
DeVault, M.L. (2020). Institutional ethnography: A mode of inquiry and a strategy for change. In A. B. Marvasti & A. J. Treviño (Eds.), *Researching social problems* (pp. 83–101). Abingdon: Routledge.

Favero, P. S. H., & Theunissen, E. (2018). With the smartphone as field assistant: Designing, making, and testing EthnoAlly, a multimodal tool for conducting serendipitous ethnography in a multisensory world. *American Anthropologist, 120*, 163–167. https://doi.org/10.1111/aman.12999.

Harper, D. (2016). The development of visual sociology: A view from the inside. *SocietàMutamentoPolitica, 7*(14), 237–250. https://doi.org/10.13128/SMP-19704.

Herzog, P. S. (2020). Visual research methods. Integrating images in the study of social problems. In A. B. Marvasti & A. J. Treviño (Eds.), *Researching social problems* (pp. 172–187). Abingdon: Routledge.

Klages, L. (1972). *Der Geist als Widersacher der Seele* (1929–1932). Bonn, 746, 81.

Luken, P. C., & Vaughan, S. (2005). "… be a genuine homemaker in your own home": Gender and familial relations in state housing practices, 1917–1922. *Social Forces, 83*(4), 1603–1625.

Luken, P. C., & Vaughan, S. (2006). Standardizing childrearing through housing. *Social Problems, 53*(3), 299–331.

Mannay, D. (2010). Making the familiar strange: Can visual research methods render the familiar setting more perceptible? *Qualitative Research, 10*(1), 91–111. https://doi.org/10.1177/1468794109348684.

McCoy, L. (1995). Activating the photographic text. In A. Manicom & M. Campbell (Eds.), *Knowledge, experience and ruling: Studies in the social organization of knowledge* (pp. 181–192). Toronto: University of Toronto Press.

Mirzoeff, N. (2009). *An introduction to visual culture* (2nd ed.). Abingdon: Routledge.

Pink, S. (2006). *The future of visual anthropology: Engaging the senses*. Abingdon: Routledge.

Pink, S. (Ed.). (2012). *Advances in visual methodology*. Los Angeles: Sage.

Puddu, C. (2018). *Voices from the street: Stories of vulnerable youth in the shadow of urban development. Community Research Project Final Report.* Homeward Trust Edmonton. https://www.homewardtrust.ca/wp-content/uploads/2019/03/Puddu-2018.-Stories-of-vulnerable-youth-in-the-shadow-of-urban-development.pdf.

Puddu, C. (2019, August 10). How youth banning policies shape the lived experiences of homeless youth. In M. DeVault (Chair), *Session 121: Illuminating the Social Through Institutional Ethnography* [panel presentation] Annual Meeting of the Society for Study of Social Problems 2019, New York. https://www.sssp1.org/file/2019AM/SSSP_Program_2019.pdf.

Rose, G. (2016). *Visual methodologies: An introduction to researching with visual materials*. Thousand Oaks: Sage.

Smith, D. E. (1990). *The conceptual practices of power: A feminist sociology of knowledge*. Boston, MA: Northeastern University Press.

Smith, D. E. (2005). *Institutional Ethnography: A sociology for people*. Lanham: AltaMira Press.

Smith, D. E., & Turner, S. M. (Eds.). (2014). *Incorporating texts into institutional ethnographies*. Toronto: University of Toronto Press.

Spencer, S. (2010). *Visual research methods in the social sciences*. Los Angeles: Routledge.

Tartari, M. (2018, July 19). Responsibility and accountability of parents and professionals in judicial contexts: a research study with the institutional ethnography approach. In D. Talbot (Chair), *Responsibilisation, Accountability and Assessment Practices in Systems, Institutions and Homes* [panel presentation] The XIX ISA World

Congress, Toronto. https://isaconf.confex.com/isaconf/wc2018/webprogram/Session8144.html.

Tartari, M. (2019, September 2). *Study on TRansition and Exclusion in Society of Single-Mums (STRESS-Mums)*. European Commission. https://cordis.europa.eu/project/id/843976.

Van den Scott, L. K. (2018). Visual methods in ethnography. *Journal of Contemporary Ethnography, 47*(6), 719–728. https://doi.org/10.1177/0891241618806972.

Vannini, P. (2019). *Doing public ethnography*. Los Angeles: Routledge.

Walby, K. (2005). How closed-circuit television surveillance organizes the social: An Institutional Ethnography. *Canadian Journal of Sociology, 30*(2), 189–214. https://doi.org/10.2307/4146130.

Walby, K. (2006). Locating televisual and non-televisual textual sequences with Institutional Ethnography: A study of campus and apartment CCTV security work. *Culture and Organization, 12*(2), 153–168. https://doi.org/10.1080/14759550600683005.

CHAPTER 9

And Then There Was Copyright

Suzanne Vaughan

Since the passage of the U.S. Digital Millennium Copyright Act in 1998, which amended the U.S. Copyright Revision Act of 1976 in response to the availability of new digital media, debate about the ownership of culture has circulated among academics and policy makers alike. Discussions include cautionary tales about infringement of copyright. In this chapter I examine the social re/organization of ownership of textual materials in the digital age as it relates to researchers in academic settings. I present discoveries made in the process of collaborating with my colleague, Paul Luken, on the preparation of a manuscript on the subject of housing policy in the United States that was destined for publication in an academic journal. Using institutional ethnography as my mode of inquiry, I discuss the work I did in response to documents we received from the publisher of the academic press to which we submitted our article. Our research shows how changes in policy and the legal environment in which the law is interpreted have transformed the everyday world of researchers working within the knowledge industry. As a follow-up, I include a postscript on the copyright work with Palgrave to publish this chapter.

S. Vaughan (✉)
Arizona State University, Phoenix, AZ, USA
e-mail: svaughan@asu.edu

© The Author(s) 2021
P. C. Luken and S. Vaughan (eds.), *The Palgrave Handbook of Institutional Ethnography*,
https://doi.org/10.1007/978-3-030-54222-1_9

Copyright in the Digital Age

Critical studies of the knowledge industries and U.S. copyright law drawn from diverse intellectual traditions in legal studies (Boyle, 1996; Litman, 2006), communication studies (Bollier, 2005; Gillespie, 2007; Lessig, 2004; Vaidhyanathan, 2004), information and library sciences (Varian, 2005), and policy studies (Klein, Lerner & Murphy, 2002) suggest that the 1998 U.S. Digital Millennium Copyright Act radically alters the balance between users and owners of copyrighted material that has existed in the United States under copyright legislation and case law. In so doing, the law establishes a capitalist market model by commodifying copyrighted work and transforming the interpretive framework of legal terminology from infringement to liability. According to Healy (2002), historically the legal justification for copyright law was to represent "a bargain between the interests of authors and the public" (p. 488) by granting temporary control of copyrightable material to authors to encourage creativity and monetary rewards for their efforts, but control was relinquished to encourage creativity in the long run "by not privatizing the common stock of culture" (p. 488). Although the U.S. Digital Millennium Copyright Act continues to permit fair use, critics argue that the trajectory of the law points toward greater copyright control over scientific and artistic materials (reproduction of journal articles, techniques, methods, images, photographs and so on) by the information industries, more restrictive interpretations of fair use rights where the burden of proof lies with the user, and diminishes access to knowledge within the public domain. For example, Vaidhyanathan (2001, 2005) speculates that these transformations will have a profound stifling effect on all users, but particularly on scholars, librarians, and researchers since the law grants total control over access to work to producers or publishers of that work. He argues that until recently work was fairly accessible, and scholars, librarians, and researchers used this copyrighted work fairly confidently under fair use exceptions.

Historically, fair use has been a common practice in the United States under which researchers did their work without asking permission or making payment. The 1976 Copyright Revision Act, which first codified fair use, and the Digital Millennium Copyright Act, which further refined fair use as applied to the digital environment where virtually everything is now copyrighted, outlines four factors to be used in tandem in determining the use of copyrighted work: the purpose and character of use, the nature of the copyrighted work, the amount and sustainability of the portion of the work used as a whole, and the monetary effect of the use upon the potential market for the copyrighted work (Wherry, 2008).

Although many accounts of the erosion of these fair use provisions discuss court cases brought by major corporations or theorize about intellectual property within the knowledge economy (Bettig, 1996; May & Sells, 2006; McLeod, 2001), we know little about what is happening at the ground level where conventions and expectations of use emerge (Healy, 2002). As I stated above, while there is wide agreement that work practices will be transformed in the university, none of these accounts describe how institutional relations and local processes are changing researchers' everyday work. Few empirical studies exist which have as their focus the textual practices of copyright work done by researchers. The purpose of this article is to make visible the actual copyright-related work processes researchers must undertake to publish and to explore the social determinants of these activities.

This is an institutional ethnographic investigation of the social relations oriented around copyright (Smith, 1987, 2002, 2005). Following Turner (2002) in her analysis of the municipal planning process and land development in Canada, I argue that numerous participants, particularly authors, photographers, journal editors, copy editors, typesetters, academic and commercial presses, university and media legal departments, librarians, and media agents are active in coordinating the regulation of copyright work across a number of institutional settings. These participants are connected through texts, the interpretative frames of institutional and professional discourses, and the organizational features of their work across a complex of institutional relations as the copyright work of agents in the publishing industry is transported from one organizational setting to another. Although the relations of copyright work practiced by us in the university are locally accomplished, these relations are transferred and continuously made subject to modes of extra-local coordination, regulation, specialization, differentiation, and objectification (as per Smith, 1999).

Research Problematic and Method

While residing in Phoenix, Arizona, in the 1990s, Paul Luken and I began collaborative research from the standpoint of women on the transformation of housing in the United States during the twentieth century. As part of this project, we interviewed older women and collected textual materials about their housing histories. In 2002, we received a letter from the editor of *The Sociological Quarterly* (*TSQ*) accepting a manuscript that we had submitted for publication. This letter elaborated the process that the manuscript would undergo during publication. Included with this letter was a publication agreement form from University of California Press, publisher of the journal, which we were instructed to read, sign, and return to their offices office along with the copy-edited manuscript we would receive for review in several weeks.

The text of the publication agreement outlined the contract between us, the authors of the text, and the sponsor, the Midwest Sociological Society, and the publisher of the journal, University of California Press. The form included several sections including the agreement, author's rights, licenses to the sponsor/publisher, subsidiary rights and compensation, and warranties. Although this text was a standard agreement form both of us have signed many times before, our *TSQ* manuscript included reproductions of parts of documents produced by others. These verbal texts and images played a key role in the manuscript that explored the textually mediated discourse on independence and old age by using newspaper and magazine advertisements, magazine articles, professional conference brochures, requests for proposals, cartoons, photographs, and advice columns as exhibits to explicate the line of fault between women's experience and the ruling discourses on old age (Luken & Vaughan, 2003). As we read and discussed signing this document that transferred our rights to the article to the publisher (a fairly common practice in academic publishing), what was of particular concern to us was the paragraph on warranties where a sentence focused on artwork stating, "The Author warrants... that the Author's work does not infringe any copyright... [and] The Author guarantees that if the article, or any artwork therein, has been previously published in whole or in part, permission has been obtained to reproduce such article/artwork in The Sociological Quarterly..." (Publication Agreement, 2003, p. 2).

Either this clause was something recently added to copyright agreements or we had simply ignored what the clause intended in the past. We did not know for sure whether our work *infringed* on any copyright law or whether we needed to obtain permission for use of *artwork*, but we concluded that acknowledging these images in the article was no different than other standard citation practices in academic writing under fair use. We signed and returned the form with our copy-edited manuscript to *TSQ* editor.

Several months later we received an email forwarded to us from the managing editor of *TSQ* from the company in charge of typesetting for the journal. The email asked whether we had **reprint** permission for all the images included in the article. Further down in the original message of the email, the typesetter for our article noted that the figure captions did not indicate copyright holder or permission to reprint. She was most concerned about the *Life* cover and article included in the article and stated that source information should be included in the legend. She also told us that we should file the permissions for reproductions with the University of California Press, the publisher.

We were presented with an unexpected obstacle to disseminating our research. We needed to secure reprint permission for the materials that comprised much of our data. We were forced to discover how to go about getting permission in a format that would satisfy the publisher. At the same time, we wondered what was at work producing this new requirement, one that is not intrinsic to scholarly work. Although we did not recognize it immediately, as we worked to secure the contact information of copyright holders, I became aware of a new research opportunity.

In this institutional ethnographic investigation the standpoint is that of researchers within a university setting in the United States working to have a manuscript published. The problematic is to explicate the ruling relations controlling the use of copyrighted materials as these relations are of consequence to academic researchers. The data are our own experiences as we took up securing reprint permission (Campbell, 1998), and the texts that we encountered while doing this work.

Texts, whether they are words, images, or sounds in material form that can be read, seen or heard and replicated, play a crucial role in institutional ethnographic analysis. Texts themselves are not the focal point of this research. Rather, texts are examined as courses of action or how they enter into and coordinate the work people are doing at different times and places. The objective in institutional ethnography is to discover how texts "articulate our local doings to the translocally organized forms that coordinate our consciousness with those working elsewhere and at other times" (Smith, 2006, p. 66). In other words, an examination of texts as courses of action allows us to unfold the ways in which the work activities of people in locally observable settings are controlled and transformed by translocal social relations and organization.

One research procedure for examining textual practices as coordinators of sequences of action involves tracing ethnographically what Smith (2005) calls the act-text-act sequence. Attending to this sequence allows researchers to discover how the textual work of copyright that is done in one setting of the research enterprise is transported at different times and places to other settings. Analysis of this sequence focuses attention on the how the text was produced, including its reading, interpretation, and discussion, and "explicating what it [the text] projects as organization for what comes next" (Smith, 2006, p. 68).

Regulation is an important dimension of the textual organization of institutional processes and ruling relations. In examining the design, language, and institutional discourse of text in the act-text-act sequence, regulatory texts—laws, administrative rules, and policy—are often identified as framing this intertextual coordination. A distinctive feature of this coordination is its hierarchical form in which texts at one level establish frames, concepts, and categories that come into play in other settings. Thus, as Smith notes, regulatory frames "established from the positions of power in the institutional regime, control facticity; they control and are specified as the categories and concepts that come into play at the front line of building institutional realities" (2005, p. 191). Although these texts do not achieve their capacity to regulate by their mere existence, the location of the regulatory text and the frames it establishes helps us make sense of conversations and email exchanges (subordinate texts) between others and ourselves doing the work of copyright and its enforcement.

Texts involved in publishing processes concerning copyright do not achieve their capacity to monitor or regulate by themselves. Rather, as Smith notes, "That it [the text] is activated by the reader means that the activity or operation of the text is dependent upon the reader's interpretative practices. These too are constituents of social relations rather than merely the idiosyncrasies of individuals" (1990, p. 121). As researchers read, interpret, and act upon the text, their activation is bound up in interpretative and subjective processes of human consciousness, reading and action shaped extra-locally. As the act-text-act sequence is set in motion, those involved in copyright work use interpretative frames organizationally relevant to their work to read and act upon the text.

Copyright Work as Practice

As discussed, we read, interpreted, and acted upon the copyright agreement form sent to us as novice readers relying upon knowledge of academic practices and our own experience of publishing research. The text, however, entered us into new discursive practices organizing contractual law and copyright work of which we were unaware.

A close reading of the contract agreement brought into focus a standardized vocabulary of legal words and phrases used to talk and write about copyright in the publishing industry in the United States including, *author, sponsor, publisher, rights, licenses, and warranties*. The first paragraph of the contract agreement included a statement about the importance of securing copyright to "protect unauthorized use of its contents" and granting copyright and licensing rights to the article "in any and all media, including electronic rights" (Publication Agreement, p. 1) Embedded in the third section on licenses was a phrase, *Copyright Law of the United States of America*, which elaborated that the law defines and regulates *exclusive rights* on use by publishers. As a reader of these paragraphs, my attention was drawn to the law as a regulatory text and how the law operates to hierarchically coordinate the secondary institutional texts we began to encounter in our interactions with other people and texts at different times and places as we sought copyright permission for images for our article. Under the section on subsidiary rights and compensation, the agreement discussed fees and the terms of compensation for reprinting either, "all or any portion of the Author's article… in any medium" (p. 1). The agreement noted that where appropriate, the publisher "will establish the amount of the fee to which the Publisher is entitled" (p. 1). The transfer of copyright monetized the social relation of distribution between the publisher and any subsequent user of the material.

The fourth section on warranties discussed infringement and guarantees by the author that the *work* does not infringe on copyright or *proprietary rights*, while at the same time *indemnifies* the publisher from any liability in any *claim, action or proceeding* that result from use, reuse, or licensing. The ordering of sentences and organizational syntax transforms the legal discourse of rights and infringement in the beginning of the text to a discourse about liability, authorizing the sponsor or the publisher to make the text actionable. This is reflected in the wording of the email exchange between the managing editor of the journal, the typesetter for the press, and the two of us as co-authors we discussed above.

The interpretation of texts as reprints or reproductions of originals by people working elsewhere began to coordinate our reading, interpretation, and work with other texts in a series of courses of action or act-text-act sequences. An early email exchange between us after receiving the email about copyright from the managing *TSQ* editor, noted the work we needed to do: "We were afraid this would happen. We have some scrambling to do." These sequences led us to unfold the complex of institutional relations organizing ownership within the publishing regime.

And we did scramble. Because my experience with these matters in my role on the University Intellectual Property Committee and the committee's work with Arizona State University's legal counsel office, I emailed that office requesting a copy of standard copyright agreement forms. Along with the requested forms, legal counsel sent a brochure entitled, *What You Need to Know about Intellectual Property,* which outlined our obligations as employees of the university. The brochure notes that "by accepting a University appointment, employees agree to be bound by all applicable U.S. copyright and patent laws and by the University Policies and the pronouncements of the Arizona Board of Regents, which are in-corporated by reference in all employment contracts" (Office of the Vice President for Research, 2003, p. 1). In addition, the brochure briefly noted that fair use policies have changed and requested that interested parties contact the office for the fair use guidelines for the university as specified by new U.S. copyright law. The brochure not only invokes the concepts and categories of the regulatory text such as *copyrightable work* and *fair use* policies, it also directly ties our work as employees of the university to our contractual obligations as specified by university policy.

We adapted for our purposes the request for copyright forms sent to us by the university legal counsel office; and I began to contact newspaper and magazine offices, funding agencies, pharmaceutical companies, and professional associations. The contents of the form we adapted are important. Our copyright permission form noted who was requesting copyright permission, our affiliation, what was to be reprinted, where the original document was produced, and where and when the reprint would appear. Most importantly, however, the text of our permission agreement drew on U.S. copyright law and the professional discourse about fair use for educational and research purposes in addition to the not-for-profit status, the circulation size, audience, the educational and research mission of the journal, and the lack of remuneration for the producers of the text. The interpretative frame of the text was the language of the legal profession organizationally housed within the university whose concern is liability. By adopting this discursive frame, our own text was conceptually coordinated with other legal texts about liability, generating terms and practices of how our text should be attended to and used in other places.

Our copyright permission work involved securing addresses, telephone numbers, and email addresses, and locating departments or persons responsible for signing copyright permission agreements in numerous organizations. In addition, we engaged in interpretive work as we corresponded with these persons and organizations. This was no easy task since many of these organizations were large corporations that channel communication with the public through customer service representatives who were prepared to answer questions about products and services rather than queries related to reprint permission.

Our first clue that legal and advertizing departments within these organizations were integral to interpreting, monitoring, and regulating the use of their organization's intellectual property emerged when I contacted our local newspaper where an advertisement for a senior apartment living community had appeared. The advertisement for Chris Ridge Village, an affiliate of Baptist Hospitals and Health Systems, Inc., included a photo of a smiling daughter and her mother along with the headline "She wants Independence. You want *Peace of Mind*" (*The Arizona Republic*, 1997, p. B3).

After I faxed the copyright permission form to the newspaper for signature along with a copy of the image we wished to use, the newspaper's advertising department replied that their legal counsel search indicated that they did not hold ownership. We needed to contact Baptist Hospitals for permission. On contacting the advertizing department of that hospital, we were directed to the hospital's legal department. After my telephone conversation explaining what we were requesting, I faxed the advertisement and the permission form to them. Several days later, we received an email notifying us that their legal department could not grant permission because the facility promoted in the advertisement, Chris Ridge Village, had been sold to another company, and both organizations were now in state receivership. We were given the State of Arizona's legal counsel email address and, although we requested permission to use the advertisement, the States Attorney replied that the office could not grant copyright permission because the advertisement was published prior to the sale of the property, an issue that could compromise the legal dispute between the companies.

We appeared to be at an impasse, but an email exchange between the University Legal Counsel Office and me advised us to retain our paper trail to document that we had made a "good faith effort" to obtain permission to reproduce the advertisement. They told us that we were probably protected from a suit. This email exchange with the University's legal counsel provided the interpretative frame through which our work of seeking copyright permission was coordinated. The legal counsel's writing and our reading/interpretation of the advertisement, particularly the use of words like *suit* and *good faith attempts* is embedded in both the organizational relevancies of the lawyer's work as legal counsel to the university and the discursive practices of law about liability and appropriate defenses for infringement.

A second image that we used in our original article was from a *LIFE* Magazine cover story, "Can We Keep MOM at HOME?: One Family Copes with the Anguish of OLD AGE" (Fineman, Mason & Dowling, 1993, pp. cover, 29–31). The image we wished to reproduce included the cover and several pages of an article with photographs and a story about how one family was coping with the aging of America. Our inquiries about obtaining copyright permission opened up an array of work practices and social organization in popular print journalism of which we were unaware. After locating the appropriate office, I faxed the image we wished to use and the copyright permission form to the advertising department of Time/Life Corporate Offices in New

York City. In a series of emails back and forth with the advertising department, we learned that Time/Life only owns rights to the cover logo, titles, and subtitles in the article, something the publishing world calls "text." We were informed that we would need to contact the photographer and the reporter or their respective agents to obtain permission for use of portions of the text including photographs. The trademark officer of Time/Life granted us permission for educational and research use of the cover logo, titles, and subtitles. However, we were charged a fee of $450 US for the text. The fee was based on percentage of the original text we intended to use, the size of reproduction of figures in our article, and the journal's circulation. We obtained dimension and circulation figures in an email from the managing editor of *TSQ*.

We learned through the Time/Life advertising department that the photographer, a well-known commercial photographer, licensed her pictures through Corbis, an imagining licensing company owned and established in 1989 by Bill Gates. Although the company was originally based on "the idea that people would soon decorate their homes with a revolving display of digital artwork" (Hafner, 2007, p. C4), the company has purchased a large number of historic collections including the famous image of Rosa Parks seated on the bus in Montgomery, Alabama; the familiar picture of President Kennedy's son under a desk; the well-known photo image of Albert Einstein sticking out his tongue; and the iconic photograph of Marilyn Monroe on a subway grate with her white skirt ballooning around her legs. Corbis also owns the digital reproduction rights of art from the Hermitage Museum in St. Petersburg, the Philadelphia Museum of Art in Philadelphia, and the National Gallery in London. The company has increasingly moved to what is called *rights clearance*, a practice of sorting out the "complicated questions of who owns what material and how much should be paid for its use" (Hafner, p. C5). At the time the company was developing an archive of stock photos and videos, such as children playing, people in business meetings, and persons running down the beaches. Newspapers, magazines, advertising and media clients, including corporate marketing departments, use stock materials provided by Corbis rather than use the services of in-house photographers for photo shoots.

Corbis, as it turned out, did not have a licensing agreement with photographer for the particular photographs in question. It also did not have any contact information for her because the company made a one-time purchase for each photograph she submitted. Through a *Google* search we found her most recent address was in Malibu, California, and through another search we found her telephone number. We called her to explain our predicament. She requested that we fax to her the copyright agreement form and a copy of the images we intended to use. We told her that Corbis charges between $75 and $1000 US for her work depending on the image. In a follow-up communication the photographer gave us permission to reprint her three images in our article for a fee of $300 US; the fee interestingly was routed through the Time/Life, Inc. patent office.

The breakdown of text into pieces—logos, headings, titles, work, and images—that can be copyrighted separately is a market process of assigning monetary value to discrete, measurable pieces of property. Time/Life inquiries about the percentage of text we would reproduce, the size of images the journal would reproduce, the circulation of the professional journal, and the photographer's queries about Corbis's charges are all embedded in capitalist social relations of the market and new copyright laws. According to fair use statutes, "If the use of protected material significantly affects the potential of that work to provide a monetary profit to its author, the use is infringement and not fair use" (Wherry, 2008, pp. 56–57). Time/Life, the reporter, and photographer used the monetary exception of fair use in U.S. copyright law to interpret and assess whether our request to reproduce images in our article warranted a usage fee or was an instance of fair use. Littman (2006) suggests that in the digital world, copyright has taken on a new meaning in the law and the U.S. Congress since it added over one hundred new pages to copyright statutes as a way to close loopholes. Littman argues, "Copyright is now seen as a tool for copyright owners to use to extract all the commercial value from works of authorship, even if that means that uses that have long been deemed legal are now brought within the copyright owner's control" (p. 14).

Another image we used in the original article in *TSQ* was an Evista advertisement by Eli Lilly and Company that was produced in the American Association of Retired Persons' *Modern Maturity* magazine (*Modern Maturity*, 1999, p. 130). The advertisement included a photograph of an older woman relaxing in a chair, arms behind her head, after gardening and proclaiming, "I like my independence! I'd hate to rely on family and friends for everything." At the bottom of the page was safety information that described Evista as a treatment for osteoporosis after menopause and not for everyone. Although we first emailed the advertising department of the magazine to obtain copyright permission, we were directed to the pharmaceutical company whom they said held copyright of the text in question. After faxing the advertisement, the copyright form, and a requested copy of our manuscript to the company, the trademark department sent a fax and letter granting us a revocable license to use, reprint, reproduce, or duplicate, but not to edit, modify or delete the image for educational and scholarly research purposes. Interestingly, this letter also noted that the company may rescind the license if the information contained in the copyright material is no longer medically accurate, or for any other reason. The letter also alerted us to prohibitions against any digital modifications that we might make and called our attention to a *revocable license* that may be rescinded *for any other reason*. The text of the letter alluded to the new digital technologies available to alter copyrighted work. If used, these may make the work subject to fair use if it is *transformative* in nature and to copyright laws defining and granting licenses for use. The letter, by noting what our work can and cannot include, organizes and regulates our actions as educators and researchers in relation to the copyrighted text and our work with others located elsewhere.

We requested copyright permission for four other images in our article. The requested images included one image of a Request for Proposals from the U.S. National Institute of Aging and another from the Commonwealth Fund. We also asked to reproduce the images of two brochures announcing conferences from the University of Wisconsin, Department of Engineering Design, and from the Mortgage Bankers Association of America. Each organization told us that they did not think we needed copyright permission provided that we cited the publication in question, which historically been the practice used by researchers. They commented to us that they were glad we were sharing their work with others. The organizational practices and relevancies of federal agencies, not-for-profit foundations, and professional organizations produce texts that are part of the *public domain*. However, after consulting with Arizona State University's general counsel officer and the managing editor of the journal who told us that we needed to be protected from liability of any work in *fixed* form, we again requested that officials authorized by the four organizations sign the copyright agreement forms and return them to us. All four returned the forms to us with the signatures from their general counsel offices. These signed documents satisfied the university general counsel office and the journal editor.

The final email exchange between *TSQ* journal editor and us instructed us to retain the copyright permissions we obtained for our records. *TSQ* journal editor noted that the publication agreement we signed was sufficient to protect the publisher and sponsor of the journal from copyright infringement.

Conclusion

This chapter constitutes an investigation into the social re/organization of ownership of images in the publishing industry. I have outlined the ways in which copyright permission work with journal publishers, editors, managers, legal and advertising offices, newspapers, magazines, and other businesses using images to advertise was produced, coordinated, and regulated through courses of action involving act-text-act sequences at different times and in different places.

This exploration has revealed an institutional complex of overlapping textually mediated social relations among those who are producing and selling texts for profit; those producing texts, but selling other products and services; and those producing texts as part of bureaucratic administration and as a product of rationalization (Weber, 1983). The textually mediated discourse of copyright permission produced by specialists working in universities, publishing houses, trademark offices, legal counsel offices, and advertising offices of corporations serves to monitor use and to protect infringement on property rights. The actual work of researchers as they attempt to disseminate their research is rendered invisible by the 1998 U.S. Digital Millennium Copyright Act and by the interpretative frames of liability and profitability used in the law and in the market.

There is a clear disjuncture between the dissemination of scholarly research and adherence to copyright regulations. We experienced this in our publishing activities, and it is evident by comparing copyright infringement to standard scholarly notions of plagiarism. While they both recognize ownership of texts, scholarly principles and practices do not recognize the transferability of ownership from the author/creator to another entity. When scholars mention the work they are reading, they commonly identify the texts by the authors' names, not those of the copyright holders. Also, scholarship merely requires that one give credit where credit is due, and this requirement is satisfied by the standard uses of references, footnotes, and quotation marks. Copyright regulation, however, necessitates being granted permission to use the work of others; and that permission comes at a price. Scholarly practice encourages becoming knowledgeable of the texts of others and borrowing and building from these texts. That is part of routine practices within a scholarly community. Copyright, on the other hand, turns scholars into individual entrepreneurs and undermines the advancement of knowledge as a collective endeavor.

Many policy critics have lamented the regulations and practices that have stemmed from 1998 U.S. Digital Millennium Copyright Act, particularly as industries that distribute knowledge have adopted technological fixes that impede access and infringement. Klein, Lerner, and Murphy (2002) note that there is "no inherent conflict between the courts and copy-holders with regard to particular uses [except] ...with regard to a technology that has both 'fair' and infringing use" (p. 205). This site is precisely the institutional location in which researchers do their work. Fitzgerald (2008) argues that given the knowledge afforded by current technologies, we need to promote seamless *access* and negotiability principles in the law by granting, with the owner's *permission*, the use and repurposing of copyrighted materials for non-commercial purposes. These solutions, however, contradict the traditional norms and work practices operating in science. In conversations with colleagues about the time and cost of doing copyright permission work, we have contemplated various strategies to make our work as researchers more visible, less time intensive, and less costly. Would eliminating the fair use principle about market effect in the law reduce our costs? Would resurrecting a centralized registry for copyright, now obsolete since any work upon creation in a fixed format is copyrighted, regardless of registration under the new laws, reduce our labor? Would the formation of a centralized office at universities charged with obtaining copyright permission facilitate our work? We do not know the answers to these questions, but we are certain they are worth contemplating in the context of our analysis.

Increasingly, the articulation of digital production processes with the market has expanded as *Google* and others digitize texts. Such practices will likely further transform traditional academic writing practices and publishing relations as academics coordinate their work and its enforcement.

POSTSCRIPT

Copyright work never ends and is even more complicated for academic researchers in 2020. An earlier draft of this chapter included seven exhibits of text/documents including our permission agreement contract with the University of California Press/*The Sociological Quarterly*, emails, permission to reprint letters from companies and organizations, and illustrative images for which we had already sought and obtained copyright permission to reprint. Well aware that copyright permission might well be an issue in publishing this chapter, I emailed our editor for the *Handbook* and provided copies of all the images, previously signed permissions to reprint, and background on each image I hoped to reproduce as exhibits in this chapter. I was told that the Palgrave legal department would require me to re-seek copyright permission using their forms and obtain original signatures. As I started this process again, several roadblocks emerged. First, unlike academic journals, Palgrave, the publisher of this volume, is a for profit company. University legal counsel explained that we could not claim fair use for educational and research purposes under current copyright law when publication is monetized. Second, I encountered numerous problems in trying to determine who actually held copyright and was authorized to give permission at this time. For example, The University of California Press is no longer the publisher of the sponsor, The Midwest Sociological Society and its journal, *The Sociological Quarterly*; another publisher has taken its place. It proved impossible to locate authorized personnel to sign the permission agreement form when these two entities were no longer under contract. Similarly, as is the practice in academic organizations, editor and managing editors of journals serve for limited terms and no longer preside in these positions while typesetters and their companies contracted by journal editors had gone out of business. Companies such as Corbis, Time/Life Inc., and Baptist Hospitals have been sold, merged, broken up or disappeared over the last decade and the question of who owns copyright to images or documents is not clear. Is it Getty, *Goggle* or some holding company located in another part of world? My search was endless often following circular trails from advertising and legal/patent departments where employees often metaphorically threw up their hands and declared, "I have no idea where to inquire next!".

So in this chapter I compromised by describing images, summarizing or quoting sentences from brochures, contracts, paraphrasing passages from personal correspondence and citing references to sources publically available to researchers. Although I am well aware that exhibits of documents/images play a major role as empirical data in institutional ethnography, particularly their form, syntax, vocabulary, context, and so on that can be seen by others in tracing ruling relations ethnographically, once again our work as researchers in the knowledge enterprise has been interpreted, organized, regulated and enforced by capitalist relations of how researchers at the local level must discover and document the social.

REFERENCES

The Arizona Republic. (1997). Advertisement for Chris Ridge Village Apartment Community, September 18, 1997, p. B3.

Bettig, R. V. (1996). *Copyrighting culture: The political economy of intellectual property.* Boulder, CO: Westview Press.

Bollier, D. (2005). *Brand name bullies: The quest to own and control culture.* Hoboken, NJ: John Wiley & Sons.

Boyle, J. (1996). *Shamans, software & spleens: Law and the construction of the information society.* Cambridge, MA: Harvard University Press.

Campbell, M. (1998). Institutional ethnography and "experience as data." *Qualitative Sociology, 21*(1), 55–73.

Fineman, D., Mason, J., & Dowling, C. G. (1993, August). Can we keep mom at home? One family copes with the anguish of old age. *Life,* cover, 29–31.

Fitzgerald, B. (2008). Copyright 2010: The need for better negotiability/usability principles. In G. Hearn & D. Rooney (Eds.), *Knowledge policy: Challenges for the 21st century* (pp. 52–161). Northampton, MA: Edward Elgar.

Gillespie, G. (2007). *Wired shut: Copyright and the shape of digital culture.* Cambridge, MA: MIT Press.

Hafner, K. (2007, April 10). A photo trove, a mounting challenge. *The New York Times,* pp. C4–5.

Healy, K. (2002). Survey article: Digital technology and cultural goods. *The Journal of Political Philosophy, 10*(4), 478–500.

Klein, B., Lerner, A. V., & Murphy, K. M. (2002). The economics of copyright "fair use" in a networked world. *The American Economic Review, 92*(2), 205–208.

Lessig, R. (2004). *Free culture: How big media uses technology and the law to lock down culture and control creativity.* New York, NY: Penguin Books.

Litman, J. (2006). *Digital copyright.* Amherst, NY: Prometheus Press.

Luken, P. C., & Vaughan, S. (2003). Living alone in old age. *the Sociological Quarterly, 44*(1), 109–131.

McLeod, K. (2001). *Owning culture: Authorship, ownership, and intellectual property.* New York, NY: Peter Lang.

May, C., & Sells, S. K. (2006). *Intellectual property rights: A critical history.* Boulder, CO: Lynne Rienner.

Modern Maturity. (September-October, 1999). Advertisement for Evista: Eli Lily. American Association of Retired Persons. p. 130.

Office of the Vice President for Research. (2003). *What you need to know about intellectual property.* Tempe, AZ: Arizona State University.

Publication Agreement (2003). University of California Press. Berkeley, CA, 1–3.

Richards, D. G. (2004). *Intellectual property rights and global capitalism: The political economy of the TRIPS agreement.* Armonk, NY: M. E. Sharpe.

Smith, D. E. (1987). *The everyday world as problematic: A feminist sociology.* Boston, MA: Northeastern University Press.

Smith, D. E. (1990). *Texts, facts, femininity: Exploring the relations of ruling.* London: Routledge.

Smith, D. E. (1999). *Writing the social: Critique, theory, and investigations.* Toronto, ON: University of Toronto Press.

Smith, D. E. (2002). Institutional ethnography. In T. May (Ed.), *Qualitative research in action* (pp. 17–52). London: Sage.

Smith, D. E. (2005). *Institutional ethnography: A sociology for people*. Landham, MD: AltaMira.

Smith, D. E. (2006). *Institutional ethnography as practice*. Landham, MD: Rowman & Littlefield.

Turner, S. M. (2002). Texts and the institutions of municipal government: The power of texts in the public process of land development. *Studies in Cultures, Organizations and Societies, 7*, 297–325.

Vaidhyanathan, S. (2001). *Copyrights and copywrongs: The rise of intellectual property and how it threatens creativity*. New York, NY: New York University Press.

Vaidhyanathan, S. (2004). *The anarchist in the library*. New York, NY: Basic Books.

Vaidhyanathan, S. (2005). Remote control: The rise of electronic cultural policy. *Annals of the American Political Science and Social Sciences, 597*(1), 122–133.

Varian, H. L. (2005). Copying and copyright. *Journal of Economic Perspective, 19*(2), 121–138.

Weber, M. (1983). The nature of modern capitalism. In S. Andreski (Ed.), *Max Weber on capitalism, bureaucracy and religion: A selection of texts* (pp. 25–44). London: George Allen & Unwin.

Wherry, T. M. (2008). *Intellectual property: Everything the digital librarian needs to know*. Chicago, IL: American Librarian Association.

CHAPTER 10

Invoking Work Knowledge: Exploring the Social Organization of Producing Gender Studies

Rebecca W. B. Lund

This chapter explores the production of *work knowledge*—more specifically, the work of producing gender studies—to explore the how epistemic inequalities are organized materially and socially, from the standpoint of feminist academics. The chapter is based on research I did on my own temporary academic community, Finnish gender studies. I chose this as a focus for my inquiries because Finnish gender studies have been characterized by significant internal epistemic and identity tensions, as well as struggles in and around its role, legitimacy, and position as an autonomous discipline (e.g., Dahl, Liljeström, & Manns, 2016; do Mar Pereira, 2017; Griffin & Braidotti, 2002; Hemmings, 2011; Korvajärvi & Vuori, 2016; Messer-Davidow, 2002; von der Fehr, Jonasdottír, & Rosenbeck, 1998). Gender studies, like other disciplinary fields in Finland, has witnessed major institutional shifts as a result of neoliberal reform processes following the *Academic Act* of 2009. With the reforms, gender studies did, however, face particular sets of challenges related to being (re)integrated as units into larger faculties in all Finnish universities. Simultaneously gender studies had to balance its interdisciplinary nature, with a managerial push to engage in disciplinary profiling as part of making

---

The *for people* signifies a manner of distinguishing the purpose of Institutional Ethnography from approaches that do research *about people*.

R. W. B. Lund (✉)
Center for Gender Research, University of Oslo, Oslo, Norway
e-mail: rebecca.lund@stk.uio.no

© The Author(s) 2021
P. C. Luken and S. Vaughan (eds.), *The Palgrave Handbook of Institutional Ethnography*,
https://doi.org/10.1007/978-3-030-54222-1_10

themselves accountable, comparable, and competitive (Korvajärvi & Vuori, 2016).

I illustrate the process of producing work knowledge through an account of my research journey from institutional capture to discovery. My initial plan for the research project—which had received three years of funding from the Academy of Finland—was to focus on how experiences of epistemic exclusion were organized by the Finnish reforms and hegemonic feminist epistemic orientations. This plan was inspired by my own participation and knowledge of feminist debates, conversations with feminist academics, and by existing literature (e.g., do Mar Pereira, 2017; Fricker, 2007)—a knowledge that would turn out to contain benefits for the process of discovery, but which also presented significant challenges. As I shall show, by taking people's embodied work knowledge seriously, I learned that my interests in exclusion and hierarchies of epistemic orientations blocked me from seeing people's actual activities, possibilities and challenges: rather this focus, I realized, directed me toward restating or confirming existing theory. In doing so I would privilege *relations of struggle and hierarchy* above *relations of collaboration and support*; and moreover, I would draw too straight a line between epistemic marginality and epistemic status within gender studies. The particular analysis I was able to produce, in the end, was only possible through a focus on concrete activities that allowed me to take seriously the complexities and contradictions of people's experiences and perspectives in a manner that a focus on epistemic hierarchies and exclusion would not.

In what follows I will, after an outline of my use of standpoint and work knowledge, explicate what my move from a focus on *exclusion narratives* to a focus on the work of producing gender studies from the standpoint of feminist academics meant for my process of discovery.

STANDPOINT AND WORK KNOWLEDGE

Institutional ethnography starts from the ontological premise that human beings are social beings who engage in actual *social relations* involving the ongoing coordination of activities. Each activity happens in a particular local time and space, but is at the same time is part of a larger sequence of action making it stretch beyond the confinement of the local sphere and bringing us into connection with people located elsewhere/elsewhen (Smith, 2005, 2006). The coordination that happens between everyday activities make up what in institutional ethnography is referred to as *social organization*. The ambition is to map out how the social is put together "…not […] as a way of discovering the everyday world as such, but of looking out beyond the everyday to discover how it came to happen as it does" (Smith, 2006, p. 3). The point of departure is that everything human beings engage with, and are organized by in turn, is socially constructed (Campbell & Gregor, 2004, p. 28). The manner in which things are interpreted and used is not fixed, but malleable over time and space and depending on the standpoint from which they are engaged.

The social ontology of institutional ethnography has consequences for what is rendered knowable. The institutional ethnographer looks to document actual people's everyday experiences and embodied practical activities. This approach does not simply seek to bridge mind and body, but rather to, in a Merleau-Pontyan sense, collapse the very distinction (Smith, 2005, p. 24). Collapsing this dichotomy is a necessity for engaging with and making sense of people as being radically entangled with the world, for making sense of their experiences as formed within social relations.

Epistemologically institutional ethnography is situated within standpoint feminism, holding that all knowledge production is political and embedded in historical struggles and processes. Non-epistemic values—such as moral and social values—do not only play a legitimate role in science, but also an "epistemically productive" role (Rolin, 2015, p. 11). However, as Dorothy Smith (Smith, 1997, p. 392) observes in her response to Susan Hekman in the 1997 debate in the feminist journal *Signs*, one should not make the mistake of thinking that Standpoint Feminists are univocal. As Smith notes, this is a "coherence invented for us" and thus one that "distorts the reality" of the difference between those categorized as standpoint feminists. I will therefore clarify how I read and have come to distinguish between Smith and other proponents of standpoint feminism.

Common among standpoint feminists is the insistence that knowledge production must take its point of departure in situated knowledges and actualities (Haraway, 1988; Harding 1993, 1995, 2007; Smith, 1987) of those whose perspectives are somehow excluded from dominant discourses, institutions and ways-of-knowing. Such a basis provides the point of entry for making visible and de-naturalizing the taken-for-granted order of things, hierarchies and structures that offer default privilege to certain people and perspectives, while simultaneously excluding and downplaying others. In opposition to the claims of some (e.g., Fawcett & Hearn, 2004; Hekman, 1997), the standpoint feminism of Smith does not grant an automatic epistemic advantage to women. Thus, who might help or enable me to scrutinize the order of things from a new perspective is "neither automatic nor all encompassing" (Wylie, 2003, p. 37). The epistemic justification always refers to a particular context in which particular "assumptions are likely to function as default entitlements" because they are hard to challenge (Rolin, 2006, p. 135).

Instead of starting, as Sandra Harding suggests, from a predefined social position or category such as gender, sex, class or race, the institutional ethnographer establishes a "subject position" that is open for anyone (Smith, 2005, p. 9). In other words, subjects are understood as particular people with varied perspectives, rather than "types" of people. This signifies a development within Smith's body of work, which began from and remained a wish to "Talk back to Sociology" (DeVault, 1996). In the wake of the Feminist Consciousness raising movement, Smith developed an alternative methodology for feminist knowledge by starting from "women's experience" (Smith, 1974, 1987). However, the ongoing development in feminist thought would problematize this starting point by revealing "the complex fragilities and resiliencies of this construction, which Donna Haraway characterizes as 'a fiction and fact of the most crucial, political kind'" (DeVault, 1996, p. 30). Consequently, Smith developed a Standpoint for People (Smith, 2005). Indeed, it would seem that starting from predetermined or universalizing categories, not unlike the insightful claims of Judith Butler, is, in itself, participation in "conceptual practices of power" that institutional ethnography seeks to scrutinize and denaturalize (Smith, 1990). "Conceptual practices of power" are defined by Smith as "accounts of the world that treat it selectively in terms of a predetermined conceptual framework" (Smith, 1990, p. 93). The category woman/women or man/men, involve the risk of blinding us to actual embodied activities, experiences and knowledge, because so much sociocultural baggage and assumptions are connected to these categories, ultimately resulting in objectifying accounts of people and the social. Such categorical points of departure hold the potential of neglecting the overlapping experiences that may exist across social categories, e.g., women and men; but also risks neglecting differences within and between women. The categorical fixation can furthermore blind us to how social relations are exactly relational, and thus to the fact that these are sites of negotiation, contestation, change and conflict. Predetermined notions of who provides me access to what would make me insensitive to such dynamics.

The standpoint established by the institutional ethnographer is, in principle, "open for everyone" and a position intended for directing attention to particular problems or questions in the institutional or ruling order (Smith, 2005, p. 9). Whether someone can direct my attention cannot be assumed (e.g., on the basis of their belonging to a particular gender, sex, race, or class category). This must be discovered by commencing the investigation from the everyday actualities of people's lives and work, and how this is coordinated and connected to activities of other people located elsewhere/elsewhen (Smith, 2005). As such the social positionality of people—which speaks more to the kinds of relations people are engaged in, than it speaks of a premature categorizing—may reveal certain patterns of (under)privilege that are classed, gendered, raced, or otherwise, with regard to the social positions embedded in ruling relations.

Feminism and feminist theory constitute ways of knowing differently, the attractions to which is rooted in an affectionate dissonance (Hemmings, 2012; Probyn, 2003). The dissonance is rooted in a deeply felt discrepancy between "ones embodied sense of self and the self we are expected to be in social terms" (Hemmings, 2012, p. 149). The work of feminism is, one might say, to negotiate and seek to shift this relationship, to make life more livable for more people. While feminist standpoint, as understood by Sandra Harding, for example, would involve a problematic generalization, downplaying the differences between feminists and their particular experiences and commitments, the standpoint taken here differs. It does not speak from a generalized feminist standpoint, but from the standpoint of people who identify as feminist (something that can never be one thing) and who work as academics in gender studies. These are embodied knowers, who can teach me about their work processes and point toward the ruling relations shaping their experiences. While I am also an embodied knower, a feminist academic based in gender studies, I am in the interview situation first and foremost seeking to learn from them and take their different perspectives seriously.

As already indicated above, central to learning from people and bringing forth the diversity of experiences, perspectives and social positionalities within a chosen standpoint, is the explication of *work* and *work knowledge*. In my project I named it the work of producing gender studies. This operates as an "empirically empty term" (Mykhalovskiy & McCoy, 2002, p. 24) to be filled when people tell me about their practices and experiences as feminists academics based in gender studies. This notion of work draws on Alfred Schutz' concept of work as "purposive, embodied action that gears into the social and physical worlds surrounding any one individual" (Mykhalovskiy & McCoy, 2002, p. 24). In Dorothy Smith (2005) this is translated to everything that people do which takes time, effort, emotions, and at least some degree of competence, as they (re)produce or resists institutional orders, and ruling relations. This has quite significant consequences for my inquiry, because it means allowing production of knowledge to be coordinated by the concepts and relations participants they introduce as relevant though their explicated actual work knowledge. It directs my attentions toward social and ruling relations I might not otherwise have seen.

Shaping Research: From "Exclusion Narratives" to Work Knowledge

As already mentioned above, my research was conducted in and with my own temporary academic community, gender studies in Finland, with a focus on learning from feminist academics how their possibilities for participating in the construction of gender studies was organized socially. By drawing on life-story interviews as my methodological approach (e.g., Atkinson, 1998) and combining it with the particular methodological procedures of identifying textual clues and "keeping institutions in view" (DeVault & McCoy 2006), I hoped to place current experiences in a broader temporal context. The life-story interview approach made it possible for people to narrate their lives (past and present) and would allow me to make better sense of the problematics related to epistemic inequality they faced in the institutional present (see Ylijoki, 2005). For instance, by asking how people had come to identify as feminist and eventually as feminist academics, and how they would position themselves now compared to then, I could more easily make sense of their reported experiences and embodied activities within gender studies.

I wanted to identify a wide a range of experiences through the life-story interviews. However, instead of selecting participants based on gender, sexuality, class and so forth, as in conventional sociological participant selection procedures, my selection was organized through my interests in the kinds of work feminist academics do and what this meant for their experienced possibilities for contributing to the production of gender studies (see also Mykhalovskiy & McCoy, 2002). I could base this selection in my own experience as a member of the feminist community and through everyday conversations with colleagues. Thus, I identified different kinds of experience and social locations based on the kinds of feminist commitments people had, the university of employment, the point of academic career and degree of employment security.

Beyond individual life-story interviews, I engaged in participant observation through my everyday belonging to a community where I had informal chats with colleagues and became embedded in particular institutional and organizational procedures, such as curriculum planning, thematic profiling of the unit, and conference participation. Through this I could place individual level stories in wider relations and it allowed me to engage with the various ways in which people's activities are coordinated, and how coordination is experienced in real time. As such the observational data became central for making sense of the contexts in which individual narratives and activities were located.

The interview situations were emotionally saturated with vulnerability. Many participants expressed fear that if they were "too honest" or if they were "too easy to identify" they would become *persona non grata* in the gender studies community; and they would check and double check to ensure that I would keep them anonymous. At other times I experienced direct hostility to me and my research project. One example stood out in particular and I mention it here because it would prove relevant for the direction of my project. Upon initiating my postdoc position in Finland, I made a visit to a senior academic in gender studies with whom I had hoped to work because I had noted certain interest overlaps. Despite knowing nothing of the amount of work I had put into my research proposal nor having seen my evaluation reports, she made clear that I had most likely had an advantage in terms of winning a prestigious research grant because of the current ambitions to internationalize Finnish academia. Furthermore, the senior scholar made it clear that, as far as she was concerned, I had nothing to do in Finland and the project was not relevant, as this kind of work had already been done, and the least I could do was learn Finnish quickly. I had several uncomfortable encounters with the same person during the years I worked in Finland. What relations were shaping these affective responses to me and my research? How was internationalization and tough competition for short-term positions and grants shaping Finnish gender studies? How were they (re)shaping social relations within gender studies? This also pointed me toward where people's everyday concerns were located.

One of the major challenges arising early in my data production and early stage analysis was that my interest in exclusion and hierarchies of epistemic orientations blocked me from seeing peoples' actual work. Everyone I spoke to told stories of how their commitments were marginalized or excluded. To give a sense of the diversity of stories I present some of them here. One feminist scholar told me how she, through co-authoring and discussions at research project meetings, learned what "correct gender studies" was. She experienced there being more emphasis on processes of categorization and the identification of societal discourses, than there was on experiences. It made her feel out of place and as if her expertise as a feminist scholar was not recognized, and she felt forced to work in a way to which she was not committed. Feeling that one's contribution was positioned as out of place was something another feminist academic reported in referring to "dominant" and "self-evident" theoretical perspectives within her gender studies unit. She pinpointed that these usually involved "a Foucauldian understanding of power, a Derridean understanding of language and meaning, combined with a certain Lacanian psycho-analytical twists." She told me how she, at seminars, had attempted to speak about "women" or "experience" and would immediately be put through a "deconstructive shredding machine" which involved accusations of being "essentialising" or otherwise. In other words, she was confronted by a certain epistemic wall which resulted in the exclusion of feminist knowledge labelled by her colleagues as "naïve or stupid or unpolitical or, some sort of realism or empiricism." Other participants in turn reported that the gender studies community found their work "boring" and not "core gender research," because it was more about equality and less about gender and sexuality. As a result, they found their collaborators mostly in feminist scholars based in other disciplines. Others again, found that gender studies was populated by "old school feminists" only interested in furthering equality between white privileged middleclass cis men and cis women and not engaged in activism benefitting the most vulnerable people. This had resulted in people dropping out of the gender studies program due to "disappointment," as one of my participants expressed it.

However, people are, I could see from their further reporting on their activities and work, divergently positioned in terms of drawing value from their epistemic commitments and they are divergently positioned in terms of being allowed to contribute on that basis to the production of gender studies. In the beginning I looked for ways of explaining the reported experiences of exclusion by pointing to hegemonic epistemic and theoretical positions within Finnish gender studies, as constituting a ruling discourse.

This was, however, an *institutional capture*, and it began to reveal itself to me as my efforts to identify a hegemonic feminism did not bring about answers I was satisfied with or which could be made relevant for the diverse and contradictory experiences of my participants. Firstly, the hegemony story resulted in a representation of Finnish gender studies that did not give sufficiently space to differences and nuances. It involved a representation of gender studies that emphasized struggles and hierarchy, but downplayed relations of support and collaboration that also existed between people and across diverging epistemic orientations and commitments. Secondly, it blinded me to what at first glance might appear as contradictions: the ways in which self-identified marginal epistemic commitments within Finnish gender studies, such as feminist fat-studies or feminist indigenous studies, could be ascribed a lot of value and legitimacy in terms of discursive space and funding; and epistemic positions with a historical stronghold in Finnish gender studies, such as those focusing on gender equality in work and politics, would increasingly have to enter themselves into an intersectionality framework to maintain legitimacy as proper feminist. Thirdly, it resulted (oddly enough) in what would seem like a repetition of theorizing about Nordic gender studies written 20 years ago (e.g., Griffin & Braidotti, 2002; von der Fehr et al., 1998), which did not seem relevant given the changed institutional conditions of gender studies today.

The conditions of gender studies in Finland and the work of producing gender studies today are marked by being highly internationalized and stretching far beyond Finland and the Nordics. Moreover, there is a wide range of sub-fields—including fat-studies, trans-studies, feminist indigenous studies, masculinity studies, queer studies, nature-culture/animal studies—with their own journals, conferences and other forums for debate and peer-feedback, each containing with their own layers and complexity of relations. International collaborations, communications, and exchange is integrated into the everyday lives of Finnish feminist scholars through possibilities afforded by email, social media, and Skype. In this way one cannot speak meaningfully of a uniquely Finnish, or even Nordic, gender studies, within which antagonisms, hegemonies, and hierarchies can be neatly located. Rather there are a diverse range of contradictory processes and debates in and around concepts of gender and feminism—within and beyond gender studies—which can be identified only through an empirically open approach. This means, for instance, that what might be privileged at the level of societal discourse and European funding schemes, such as the focus on increasing gender equality in academic leadership, might be considered "out dated" in feminist debates; at the same time studies of gender might be considered radical outside gender studies, but within feminist debates be perceived as reproducing gender binaries, cis-normativity and white privilege.

The exclusion narratives did, however, point me to something else, when read in the context of the complete interview transcripts and through my own everyday participation in the Finnish gender studies environment. They pointed to problems in the current institutional orders and provided insight as to the kinds of community people feel energized and sustained by. In that connection they also revealed what community was experienced as reduced to within the current conditions of academic work. People were differently positioned in terms having their needs met. Indeed, within conditions of perpetual short-termism, exacerbated by neoliberal reforms, some needs for community can be met more easily than others. Belonging and community easily become reduced to institutional belonging—funding and an office space—under conditions of perpetual short-termism. For some people this was experienced as a problem, while for others it was not. It depended on how they were otherwise positioned within the social relations.

In order to learn more about that positioning and its social organization, I had to base inquiry and analysis on the actual work and work-knowledge people engage when participating in the production of gender studies. I needed to avoid introducing categories and discourses into interviews, while at the same time noting when participants introduced them by themselves. Consider the following long excerpt from an interview. I have purposefully kept it long, because it illustrates so well the work of participating in the production of gender studies:

Iris: [...] I definitely got the sense that there exists a certain idea of what gender studies is and how things *should* be done when I began working here...

Rebecca: What is that idea? How did you learn how gender studies should be done?

Iris: ...I wrote the conference abstract and I sent to my colleagues for comments. When it came back it was a *completely* changed, with the explanation that it would be better for a gender studies conference. Then I felt like, *oh*, am I not capable of doing gender studies...

Rebecca: So you had placed the emphasis differently or?

Iris: I think mine was more focused on the data, and what came out of the stories our participants told, the cultural narrative, and what we ended up instead was an abstract that spoke more generally of societal equality discourses and category construction. [explains in more detail...] ...I think there is this difference, but they are sort of very small differences.

Rebecca: They seem quite significant to me.

Iris: Yes, they are.

Rebecca: So would you like to stick around in gender studies? Is it a place you would like to pursue your academic career?

Inga: I think so, yes. [...] I really like the community and gender studies people are not that afraid of taking political stance and there is a lot of collaboration beyond the academy. More so than in other disciplines.

Rebecca: How do you actually do that, *stay*? What do you have to do to make that happen?

Iris: I hate *it* [indicating that it refers to what we both know as formal performance standards]. I just try to resist it.

Rebecca: How do you resist it?

Iris: I just trying not to let it affect me too much and just trying not to care too much about the JUFO rankings [the Finnish journal ranking system], and not care too much about this pressure that we should only publish in international journals, in English, and not in national journals, in Finnish. I prefer writing in my own language. You cannot really capture cultural nuances in the translation. So that's really frustrating. I also try to avoid getting into this mode of always working too much and always being too busy. I am well aware that there is this competition, and performance pressure, but because of the length of my current contract I don't necessarily feel a pressure to get a permanent position *right now*. Maybe it will never happen either.

Rebecca: But so far you seem to have been doing quite well for yourself. You have never had periods of unemployment, right?

Iris: Yeah, that's really surprising.

Rebecca: So, you must have been doing something right? [laughter] What do you think that is? What do you think it is that you have done?

Iris: I am not sure. I think I have good multidisciplinary networks. I think my social skills have helped me. And sort of making sure to maintain the networks, by sending emails and keeping in touch, also. Not just forgetting people when one project or collaboration is over. I don't know. Just having enough publications. I mean, *barely*. That's two per year, or so.

The quote reveals some of the hidden work people engage in when participating in the production of gender studies. In the case of Iris, this involves navigating diverging approaches to doing feminist research and managing collaborative relations in the research team through the affective soothing work of downplaying differences as "very small" (at least to me), despite the fact that her account of what actually happens would suggest rather significant differences in procedures for engaging with the production and analysis of data. Thus, the work of collaborating and producing research for a project is not just a question of winning research funding and living up to the formal requirements that would land you a position in it, but involves navigating diverse perspectives through meetings and ongoing discussions. Iris' activities of downplaying differences for the sake of collaborating illustrates this.

The quote also highlights the work of translating performance standards—that is international publication outputs mediated via the Finnish publication forum ranking lists (JUFO)—into everyday activities. However, Iris' account reveals an outspoken resistance to these: she "hates it." In her own words she "barely" lives up to the requirements, but she does what she needs to do to secure her next contract, and emphasizes the importance of her "social skills" and the emotional work of "not forgetting people when one project is over."

By putting into view the activities obscured by dominant discourses of investment and success, I was able to highlight how people were differently positioned in terms of bringing their feminist and epistemic commitments into play while moving between research projects, disciplines, and universities. While some connected the performance pressure with a great degree of anxiety and "worked permanently on the verge of a burnout" and never said no to any job or collaboration that might add to the Curriculum Vitae, others tried to "have a life outside work," did not care "too much about rankings," and did not worry about saying no to jobs they found "boring" or collaborations that might involve compromising own commitments.

Finland's *Academic Act* of 2009 followed a strong normative discourse that reduced academic organization to managing themselves like a business—investing in the activities that would result in most returns and value (see also Gershon, 2011). A review report, made in the aftermath of a 20% academic staff reduction in 2016/2017 at the University of Helsinki, stated: "There is now a view that the University is no longer a public body in any sense but has become a private body and therefore is run like a business" (Scott, 2017, p. 16). This Act and report worked in very powerful ways in people's lives and laid out a normative discourse for academic success that I call a performance and investment discourse. But people have different abilities and opportunities to make such investments. If one does not have the abilities or opportunity to do this, one's experience of the possibility of contributing to the production of gender studies becomes very dependent on the local environment available. And there it can be difficult to gain the support and recognition needed for one's epistemic orientations because people move away as fast as they move in.

READING FOR THE SOCIAL ORGANIZATION OF WORK

So far, I have discussed the central role of the institutional ethnographic notion of work: how it came to organize my research and became central for moving away from the institutionally captured search for a hegemonic feminism normally invoked when exploring epistemic inequality within gender studies. I now turn to the analysis, to show how the accounts of work were socially and institutionally shaped, even when this was not reflected on in a direct sense in the accounts of my participants. Reading for the social organization allowed me to reconnect to my initial interest in epistemic inequalities, but, as I shall show, in a rather different way!

This involved careful reading of interview transcripts and looking for how activities are hooked into sequences of action, that is, how activities are connected to the activities of other people, and how these entered into or did not enter into ruling discourses of performance and career investment and what consequences this had for their epistemic commitments. For illustration, consider the following quote, which is an account of the kinds of work involved in securing employment and the kinds of work still involved after getting permanent employment.

Alexis: Getting a permanent position in gender studies is kind of like winning in the lottery [...] and then when you have the position you still have to continue applying for research funding [...] we are evaluated every year on how active and productive we are by the funding agencies, but also by the university. You have to perform, in terms of publications and funding applications and international collaborations [...] Previously I constantly had to think of getting things on my CV and I had to say yes to every single request and invitation to author, review, teach or otherwise. I think most of us probably have been working at the verge of burnout for many years because of that. [...] I have never had a partner who could provide for me. I have always been responsible for the economic side of the household. And now my mother is elderly and needs my economic support too. [...] It has not been a possibility for me to be un-employed. If I don't secure the next funding or the next contract, there would not be someone there to support me [...] So it has been a little bit tough and I have had to work in projects where I had a hard time seeing myself. Because I have a permanent position I am now in a position where I am able say *no* to some things...I don't *have* to do things just because of the CV ...That makes a *huge* difference and that's a *huge* privilege [...] But we still have evaluations all the time, and with new austerity measures and restructurings being introduced regularly there is no certainty. I can't be sure that I actually can work there for the next 20 years.

Reading for the kinds of activities represented in Alexis' talk and the relations implicated in it gives her experience and activities the form it does. It involves making decisions about working "at the verge of burn out" to live up to the performance standards: writing funding applications; getting the funding; publishing in the right journals; collaborating with the right people—building the right networks, even when it involves compromising one's own research interests. However, it also points to how her dependent partners and elderly mother add an extra pressure on her to be successful. She cannot afford to be unemployed. Thus, the work of living up to performance standards and compromising her own interests are tied into a variety of relations, within and beyond academia. Alexis' account is saturated with anxiety and worry that has shaped her career so far, and she displays little confidence in the future, despite having landed a permanent position. This anxiety is of course also closely connected to the austerity measures following the academic act, and the sense that another round of lay-offs may appear at any time.

As a second example consider the following excerpt from my interview with Saija, which focuses on the why she chose a short-term position over a longer-term position.

Saija: Even though I don't have a permanent position, I feel that I have a secure position. I have been able to choose where I work and with whom, and in which projects. And I was actually, I was offered a long-term position, and for much better salary than I get where I am now. But I still chose my current short-term position because it was an opportunity for me to do my own research, and there is much more freedom, [...] and I was advised by [a senior scholar] that this was more prestigious and better for my career. During the last couple of years I have many times been in a position where I have had to choose between several job offers. So, I have this sense that it's going to be OK.

Rebecca: So how have you managed to put yourself in that situation?

Saija: I'm quite productive. I have a lot of publications, and I have done lots and lots of things beyond publishing. I also have a good track record in teaching and pedagogy, and, in, this societal impact kind of thing – for me doing gender studies has never just been about doing research, but it's about politics, about making a difference in the world – and, I have good networks and, I think, in general, it's easy for me to collaborate with people, and I can kind of work with almost anyone. Including those that others find very difficult. So that also makes it easier. It's easy for me to become part of and build research groups.

Saija effortlessly activates discourses of performance and investment to explain her success. She has made the right choices and priorities and is surrounded by people who can give her professional advice on what is the best option for shaping her future career. While acknowledging the importance of research groups and receiving advice from seniors, she emphasizes that her success relates to her individual track record, and that she is ultimately responsible for her current success, and no longer feels that she has to worry about her future. Elsewhere in the interview, her account of her personal life teaches me that Saija is able to choose the short-term position with lower pay, but more prestigious and interesting to her in terms of research interests, above the long-term position with higher pay, because she has a partner with a good income.

While Alexis and Saija have diverging experiences and positionalities in terms of their social and economic circumstances in life and their feminist epistemic commitments, they both activate individualist ideological codes attached to the discourses of academic performance and investment.[1] These codes reorganize the local as they become accomplished there—time, effort and resources are devoted to their realization across gender, sexuality, class, and age structures. The more we see these codes as authorized and authorizing through their consolidation in local practice, the more naturalized they become and the more they obscure actual embodied activities, actual relationships, and political social consequences.

Success, in order to be made comparable and quantifiable within a university that is now "run like a business," must appear a result of their *individual* investments and choices. A particular individualist code must be activated for reading the discourses of success and investment. The individualist code marks a desirable ideal because it involves the promise of recognition and reward (and ultimately, perhaps even employment), although no one can ever fully attain it. Indeed, it is an understanding of the subject which "transcends its bodily sites of being and hence also its historical situation…it conceals the shift from activities of the individuated subject to the universalized functions" (Smith, 1999, p. 104). It makes invisible peoples actual work and relations, bypasses material relations of exploitation, and people's diverging positions in terms of accomplishing the supposedly neutral and objective standards of quality. However, some do come closer than others in accomplishing the publication productivity, mobility, flexibility and instrumentalizing relationship building it assumes. Particular ways of working, choosing how one wants to participate in the production of gender studies, and speaking about one's accomplishments as a result of smart individual investments, was easily available to certain people more than others. Part of the successful accomplishment of the code is to make it seem effortless and natural—in other words depoliticize it. Saija and Alexis clearly differed in that regard. The more effort one signals having to have put into approximating the individualist ideal, the more one also reveals having imperfections in need of mending. The possibility of downplaying one's efforts was, it seemed, organized locally in relations of class, sexuality, and gender. Those who struggled the most with reading the discourses of investment and success through an individualist code, as exemplified in the quote by Inga earlier, also reported feeling that they could not participate in the production of gender studies in the ways they would have preferred to. They flagged the luck of having networks and social skills, rather than recognizing network building and the nurturing of relations as work too.

Embedded in the local accomplishment and institutional reorientation of the discourses of investment and success is the work of interpreting what does not properly belong; and thus, involves an awareness of deviating from a norm. This in turn explains Ingas expression of surprise that she has not yet experienced unemployment given her resistance toward international publication performance standards. Her explicit focus on networks and social skills marks a kind of work that is indeed significant for all academics' everyday survival and career possibilities, but which if explicated alongside not having produced large amounts on standardized performance measures, comes with the risk of being recognized as not fully deserving her position.

When reading through interviews for their social organization, I remained attentive to the presence of ruling discourses in people's talk about their work. I became aware of how the experiences reported where organized in relations of class, sexuality, and gender. This only became visible when comparing the accounts of work by feminist scholars from different social locations. The exclusion narratives I mentioned earlier in this chapter could not, without the explication of the social organization of work, tell me much about what those exclusion experiences actually meant for the ability to participate in the production of gender studies.

Having identified the discourse of investment and success and the code of individualization, I could now describe how certain knowers and forms of knowing become downplayed or excluded from participation in the production of gender studies. I could take seriously the contradictory relations shaping the conditions of being a feminist scholar in gender studies today. Indeed, if one has the flexibility and the networks to find emotional support and research collaboration elsewhere, it is perhaps of less importance whether one's formal workplace provides it as long as that workplace does not actively work against the faculty member. However, if one does not have the flexibility and mobility, nor the options available to choose the job of most interest, it becomes much more important that the local workplace provides the support needed. Here stage of academic career also becomes significant, and it was clear in that regard that PhD scholars where more dependent on the local environment.

Conclusion

Through my research on the social and material organization of epistemic inequality within gender studies in Finland, I have sought to illustrate a research journey from institutional capture to discovery, made possible through invoking work and work knowledge of producing gender studies today. I have shown how these notions allowed me to take into account the contradictory processes as well as institutional local/translocal conditions shaping the position of gender studies and feminist research today.

Institutional ethnography offers some fruitful practices for engaging in research, ones that help complicate the ways in which power works, in this case within gender studies from the standpoint of feminist academics. Taking the nuances and contradictions seriously involves a number of choices concerning how interviews are done, what is sought after in the reading of data and in analysis, and the appropriate role of theory. By moving away from theoretically informed notions of exclusion and epistemic hierarchies, I was able to flag the work of producing gender studies as central in the coordination of my research and the path it took. Through this I was enabled to discover something new about how inequalities are organized in relations of class, age, gender, and sexuality, rather than confirming existing theories of hegemony and identity struggles.

Acknowledgment I would like all the people who have participated in this research. I would also like to thank Marja Vehviläinen, Päivi Korvajärvi, Louise Morley, Tiina Suopajärvi, Helene Aarseth, Ann Christin Nilsen, and May-Linda Magnussen for fruitful discussions and comments, as well as editors, Paul Luken and Suzanne Vaughan, for comments on the early versions of this chapter.

Funding Funded by Academy of Finland, project number 310795/326765.

Note

1. For more studies of what I have named the ideological code of the "ideal academic" (Lund, 2012, 2015, 2020; Lund & Tienari 2019).

References

Atkinson, R. (1998). *The life story interview*. New York: SAGE Publishing.
Campbell, M., & Gregor, F. (2004). *Mapping social relations: A primer in doing social relations*. Lanham: AltaMira Press.
Dahl, U., Liljeström, M., & Manns, U. (2016). *The geopolitics of Nordic and Russian gender research 1975–2005*. Huddinge: Södertörns högskola.
DeVault, M. L. (1996). Talking back to sociology: Distinctive contributions of feminist methodology. *Annual Review of Sociology, 22*(1), 29–50.
DeVault, M. L., & McCoy, L. (2006). Institutional ethnography: Using interviews to investigate ruling relations. In D. Smith (Ed.), *Institutional ethnography as practice* (pp. 15–44). Lanham: Rowman & Littlefield.
do Mar Pereira, M. (2017). *Power, knowledge and feminist scholarship: An ethnography of academia*. London: Routledge.
Fawcett, B., & Hearn, J. (2004). Researching others: Epistemology, experience, standpoints and participation. *International Journal of Social Research Methodology, 7*(3), 201–218.
Fricker, M. (2007). *Epistemic injustice: Power and the ethics of knowing*. Oxford: Oxford University Press.
Gershon, I. (2011). Neoliberal agency. *Current Anthropology, 52*(4), 537–555. https://doi.org/10.1086/660866.
Griffin, G., & Braidotti, R. (Eds.). (2002). *Thinking differently: A reader in European women's studies*. London: Zed Books.
Haraway, D. (1988). Situated knowledges: The science question in feminism and the privilege of partial perspective. *Feminist Studies, 14*(3), 575–599.
Harding, S. (1993). Rethinking standpoint epistemology: What is "strong objectivity"? In A. Linda, & P. Elizabeth (Eds.), *Feminist epistemologies* (pp. 49–82). London: Routledge.
Harding, S. (1995). "Strong objectivity": A response to the new objectivity question. *Synthese, 104*(3), 331–349. https://doi.org/10.1007/BF01064504.
Harding, S. (2007). Feminist standpoints. In S. N. Hesse-Biber (Ed.), *Handbook of feminist research: Theory and praxis* (pp. 46–64). London: Routledge.
Hekman, S. (1997). Truth and method: Feminist standpoint theory revisited. *Signs: Journal of Women in Culture and Society, 22*(2), 341–365. https://doi.org/10.1086/495159.
Hemmings, C. (2011). *Why stories matter: The political grammar of feminist theory*. Durham, NC: Duke University Press.
Hemmings, C. (2012). Affective solidarity: Feminist reflexivity and political transformation. *Feminist Theory, 13*(2), 147–161. https://doi.org/10.1177/1464700112442643.
Korvajärvi, P., & Vuori, J. (2016). A classroom of our own: Transforming interdisciplinarity locally. *Women's Studies International Forum, 54*, 138–146. https://doi.org/10.1016/j.wsif.2015.06.012.

Lund, R. (2012). Publishing to become an "ideal academic": An institutional ethnography and a feminist critique. *Scandinavian Journal of Management, 28*(3), 218–228.

Lund, R. (2015). *Doing the ideal academic: Gender, excellence and changing academia* (Doctoral Dissertations 1998/2015). Aalto University Publication Series, Helsinki.

Lund, R. (2020). The social organisation of boasting in the neoliberal university. *Gender and Education, 32*(4), 466–485.

Lund, R. & Tienari J. (2019). Passion, care, and eros in the gendered neoliberal university. *Organization, 26*(1), 98–121.

Messer-Davidow, E. (2002). *Disciplining feminism: From social activism to academic discourse.* Durham, NC: Duke University Press.

Mykhalovskiy, E., & McCoy, L. (2002). Troubling ruling discourses of health: Using institutional ethnography in community-based research. *Critical Public Health, 12*(1), 17–37. https://doi.org/10.1080/09581590110113286.

Probyn, E. (2003). *Sexing the self: Gendered positions in cultural studies.* London: Routledge.

Rolin, K. (2006). The bias paradox in feminist standpoint epistemology. *Episteme, 3*(1–2), 125–136.

Rolin, K. (2015). Values in science: The case of scientific collaboration. *Philosophy of Science, 82*(2), 157–177. https://doi.org/10.1016/j.shpsa.2015.10.008.

Scott, S. (2017). Helsinki University change review, beyond the changes: The effects of, and lessons from, the downsizing and restructuring process of 2015–2017. *Helsinki University Change Review Group.* Available from: http://yliopisto2020.fi/wp-content/uploads/2017/10/Beyond-the-Changes-SUE-SCOTT-fullreport.pdf.

Smith, D. E. (1974). Women's perspective as a radical critique of sociology. *Sociological Inquiry, 44*(1), 7–13.

Smith, D. E. (1987). *The everyday world as problematic: A feminist sociology.* Toronto: University of Toronto Press.

Smith, D. E. (1990). *The conceptual practices of power: A feminist sociology of knowledge.* Toronto: University of Toronto Press.

Smith, D. E. (1997). Comment on Hekman's "Truth and method: Feminist standpoint theory revisited." *Signs: Journal of Women in Culture and Society, 22*(2), 392–398. https://doi.org/10.1086/495164.

Smith, D. E. (1999). Telling the truth after postmodernism. *Writing the social* (pp. 96– 113). Toronto: University of Toronto Press.

Smith, D. E. (2005). *Institutional ethnography: A sociology for people.* Lanham: Altamira Press.

Smith, D. E. (Ed.). (2006). *Institutional ethnography as practice.* Lanham: Rowman & Littlefield Publishers.

von der Fehr, D., Rosenbeck, B., & Jonasdòttir, A. G. (Eds.). (1998). *Is there a Nordic feminism: Nordic feminist thought on culture and society.* London: University College London Press.

Wylie, A. (2003). Why standpoint matters. In R. Figueroa, S. Harding, & A. Wylie. (Eds.), *Science and other cultures: Issues in philosophies of science and technology* (pp. 26–48). London: Routledge.

Ylijoki, O. H. (2005). Academic nostalgia: A narrative approach to academic work. *Human Relations, 58*(5), 555–576. https://doi.org/10.1177/0018726705055963.

CHAPTER 11

Teaching Institutional Ethnography to Undergraduate Students

Kathryn Church

At Ryerson University in Toronto, two ceiling-high bookshelves dominate the south wall in the office of the School of Disability Studies. Sagging somewhat under the weight, the shelves hold a collection of white three-ring binders—more than 200 of them—organized chronologically from 2003 forward. These binders are a paper record of Independent Studies completed by program students as the final requirement for their degree. Many were done as ethnographies and some lay claim to Institutional Ethnography. What is the context for this production? Who are these students and how did they learn this approach? What are these studies and how were they done? Who am I to provide this account? These questions frame a discussion about teaching Institutional Ethnography that is offered as a companion reading for Mykhalovskiy, Hastings, Comer, Gruson-Wood and Strang (this volume). In this instance, the focus is on undergraduate rather than graduate students, in a different program and university context.[1]

Disability Studies is a relatively new and somewhat rare form of social justice education. Through decades of social movement organizing, it has been shaped by disabled people who are forging and claiming proud identities, and by multiple theoretical and methodological approaches.[2] More plentiful in Britain and the United States, there are only a handful of degree-granting academic programs in Canada. Ryerson University is home to one of them. Established in 1999, the program is mature for the field but youthful in

---

K. Church (✉)
Ryerson University, Toronto, ON, Canada
e-mail: k3church@ryerson.ca

© The Author(s) 2021
P. C. Luken and S. Vaughan (eds.), *The Palgrave Handbook of Institutional Ethnography*,
https://doi.org/10.1007/978-3-030-54222-1_11

comparison to more traditional disciplines in the social sciences and humanities. Foregrounding the lived experience of difference (bodies and minds), the curriculum challenges dominant assumptions of normalcy as "the legitimate way of being in the world and the only version of a good life" (Titchkosky & Michalko, 2009, p. 5). Committed to critical inquiry, it guides students in examining the ways that professional interventions are implicated in disabling social relations.

I was hired into Disability Studies in 2002, becoming one of just three full-time faculty members. After a decade of doing contract research with community groups, I valued the relative stability of the university as well as the program's location on the organizational periphery. In the first flush of growth, it was not weighed down by orthodoxies or managerial scrutiny; its fledging character invited experimentation. I have taught courses in community organizing and research methodology, and supervised students in their capstone studies: 125 in total. A strong tool for the project of radically rethinking disability, Institutional Ethnography has been a major influence in my practice. Like Mykhalovskiy and associates, I view it as a critical, feminist alternate sociology that starts in people's experiences, attends to their routine activities, and unfolds the mediation of texts that coordinate and govern their lives.

How Did I Learn?

I encountered Dorothy Smith and her work in the late 1980s in the Sociology in Education department at the Ontario Institute for Studies in Education (OISE), University of Toronto, Canada.[3] She was a faculty member, and I was a doctoral candidate studying the impact of psychiatric survivor organizing on community mental health policy in Ontario. I took the sociology of knowledge course that she taught with her colleague, George Smith (Hurl & Klosterman, 2019; Smith, 1990). It introduced me to a sociology for women (later reframed as a sociology for people) and gave me a sense of who the instructors were as people. The course was a turning point but left me with blank spots in understanding and a troubling confusion over making what they referred to as "the ontological shift" (Mykhalovskiy & Church, 2006).[4] While my doctoral study bears traces of reading Smith (1987), it was a more traditional ethnography with a strong embrace of critical autobiography (Church, 1993, 1995; Jackson, 1990).

In the years that followed, Toronto provided a rich context for further learning. I made a point of attending presentations, workshops, and conferences where I got to know and engage with other academics in similar pursuit. I was in Sudbury, Ontario, for a conference that marked the passing of George Smith and recalled his practice of political ethnography. In a panel with Eric Mykhalovskiy, I discussed my attempts to create a research program from outside a politico-administrative regime. These remarks later became a co-authored chapter (Mykhalovskiy & Church, 2006). A continuing connection, Eric's work has been invaluable—as has his inclusive networking.

At a conference in Toronto, Eric introduced me to Timothy Diamond who, at the time, was teaching in the sociology department at the University of Western Michigan. Tipped off by a friend, I had already read *Making Gray Gold*, his influential book on the American nursing home industry. Here was a unique translation of feminist materialist methodology: a rigorous analysis conveyed in an easy narrative style, full of people and complex interactions, implicitly rather than obtusely theoretical, and rich with the contradictions of being a worker in a service provision role. I understood the book immediately: as a former nurses' aide, a teacher of care-workers and as a narrative writer. It became a touchstone of my practice.

Timothy introduced me to the Society for the Study of Social Problems (SSSP), its annual conference and the section on Institutional Ethnography that it has hosted since 2003. SSSP was the context in which I made my first IE-related presentations: on creating disability sensitive research, on encountering societies within the care provider/receiver dyad, and on breaching corporate walls to study the learning strategies of disabled bank employees. In Toronto, (the late) Roxana Ng, Timothy Diamond and I organized an international event in 2004 titled "Celebrating a Legacy: A Teach-In on Institutional Ethnography". It fostered rich conversations among an array of associated researchers including students.

The years 2000 to 2010 mark a significant advance in my activation of IE within a research program. It was a decade of trying things out in dialogue with colleagues and in formal presentation. Collaborating on funded research into Personal Support Work gave me a firmer grip on how to design and implement a study (Church, Diamond, & Voronka, 2004). I rolled that experience into a study of the learning strategies that disabled employees use in corporate employment. Titled "Doing Disability at the Bank," it was constructed around the idea of work knowledge/s (Luken & Vaughan, 1999; Smith, 2005), and the way the Making Care Visible Working Group (2002) shaped their inquiry into the health work of people living with HIV/AIDS (Mykhalovskiy & McCoy, 2002).

In a funded network of scholars, the bank study was one of a dozen case studies that were positioned in relation to a large survey of work and learning (Church, Frazee, & Panitch, 2010; Livingstone, 2010; Livingstone & Scholtz, 2010). Nancy Jackson was part of this international initiative. An early student of Dorothy Smith, and a faculty member in Adult Education at OISE/University of Toronto, she argued that positivist and non-positivist research traditions could not be read into the same framework of results. Fruitful collaboration across paradigms is difficult because "while each is actively engaged in constituting the 'actual' they do so using disparate procedures, degrees of reflexivity and conceptions of 'validity'" (Jackson, 2005, p. 28; see also Church et al., 2010, p. 141). Her questioning about what "counts" as learning and for whom had a major impact on me. A strong academic leader, she gave me the courage of my feminist materialist heritage (Church, 2016; Jackson, 2004).

With continued reading, mentorship, and research practice, I made a shift, ontologically, to the kind of social analysis that Dorothy and George envisioned for the course they taught in the 1990s. Understanding from personal experience how slow this transformation can be is at the root of my pedagogy: a pedagogy of optimistic patience for a complex process. I channeled the conceptual and collegial resources I had acquired into many roles and tasks. By filtering IE into a study of disabling childhoods and schooling in Ontario (Underwood, Smith, & Martin, 2018), Henry Parada (Parada, 2011; Parada, Ibarra, Mulvale, & Limon, 2019) and I demonstrated how it can be activated without formal instruction as well as adapted in translation.[5] All Ryerson-based, our research team hosted institutional ethnographers attending the International Sociology Association World Congress in 2018. Beyond studies and events, however, the approach was an invaluable resource for me in thinking through the contradictions of directing Disability Studies during a period of intensified university managerialism.

How Shall I Teach?

While scholars in our field aspire to disability as a "fluid and shifting" set of meanings (Titchkosky & Michalko, 2009, p. 6), Disability Studies operates in bureaucratic organization. It is squared-off by hierarchical leadership, a myriad of governing policies and the non-standard way that university officials decided to structure the program. Designed solely for degree-completion, its two-year curriculum tops-up two years of previous training that students receive in community colleges. Addressing the education of full-time workers, most of whom are women, we work exclusively with part-time students in the tensions of applying new knowledge to established jobs. As a distance education program, with students living all over the province, we do much more teaching in virtual environments than we do in traditional on-campus classrooms. In both modalities, we are committed to moving continuously toward full accessibility.

In a confluence of tight and uneven timelines, virtual and geographic spaces, we teach research through two courses. DST 88 "Research Methods in Disability Studies" focuses on reading, discussing, and doing exploratory exercises. Reflective of my own learning history, DST 99 "Final Independent Study" offers students the opportunity to try things out. We counsel students to take these courses in close sequence so that the preparation of the methodology course underpins the work of doing a study.

In designing "Research Methods," I wanted students to acquire a broad understanding of social science research and how it might address the oppression of disabled people. I wanted them to acquire skills in data-gathering techniques but not without querying knowledge itself. Drawing from Nancy

Jackson, I structured the course around the question: What counts as knowledge? I side-stepped the quantitative/qualitative binary in favor of a "three-legged stool" approach where each leg signifies something significant. The course modules are: "Words that Count," "Images/Objects that Count," and "Numbers that Count." I placed the Numbers module last to ensure that quantitative thinking does not set the frame for the whole course.

With weekly posted lectures and discussion forums, the methodology course is delivered on-line with on-site classroom days at the start of each semester. Early course readings ask students to recognize their own presence as researcher. "You are here!" I insist, reinforcing the most basic premise of IE – and perhaps the most difficult to teach. "Who's in charge?" I ask, in relation to disability communities and their interests, as well as the university with its rules and requirements. We consider the tensions of these connections and the dynamics of participating with others especially if observing and field-noting are used as techniques (Emerson, Fretz, & Shaw, 1995).

C. Wright Mills' (1959) notion of intellectual craftsmanship is helpful for students whose paid work often involves watching others, whether for instruction, correction, or outright surveillance. His detailed advice for activating a sociological imagination shifts them toward witnessing the upheavals of our times: connecting personal troubles with public issues. Feminist anthropologist Ruth Behar (1996) introduces them to the "vulnerable observer" as a subject position for witnessing. I peel away the layers of "dressing" subjectivity (Church, Frazee, Luciani, Panitch, & Seeley, 2006) while Eric and I offer up the t-shirts and ontologies of George Smith's pedagogical legacies (Mykhalovskiy & Church, 2006). These resources support an assignment called Observing in the Field. Here are the instructions.

> Choose a site for observing for approximately 1 h. I recommend a coffee shop or a shopping mall. Wherever you pick, choose a place where you can observe rather unobtrusively – without staring. Keep some notes, openly, as if you are writing in a journal. Don't worry about specific focus. Just allow yourself to follow what is happening. Stay alert to sensory data. Length: 5 pages of notes, plus an introductory paragraph describing your preparations, and a final section that summarizes what you learned – both about observing and about the site itself. Try to separate direct observations from interpretations. Consider the difference between observing particular individuals versus observing the social organization of the site as a whole.

By placing observation at the heart of critical inquiry, I dislodged individual interviews from the taken-for-granted center of qualitative research. We take two weeks to think about listening and talking as techniques: with individuals and groups but also organizations and institutions. I assign Devault and McCoy (2002, 2012) to counterbalance the massive literature on individual interviews. Their articulation of interviewing for ruling relations guides students to begin in everyday life, with experience, to find the rules that are operating, and to listen for texts embedded in conversation. Given where our students make their living, I value their inclusion of frontline organizational work. For similar reasons, and for the clarity of her writing, I assign Nancy Jackson's "Notes on Ethnography as Research Method" (2004) for thinking about data analysis and interpretation.

Because disability arts and culture feature prominently in our program, arts-informed methods are a high priority for the Images/Objects module. The course readings feature excellent projects that were close at hand: on visual representation and documentary film (Church, 2006; Ignagni & Church, 2008), on working from material objects and public exhibit, (Church, Panitch, Frazee, & Livingstone, 2010; Frazee, Church, & Panitch, 2016) and on research-based theater (Gray, Ivonoffski, & Sinding, 2001; Gray, 2003). Students are intrigued by starting from material objects: a piece of clothing, a box of childhood trinkets, or the contents of people's pockets.[6] Even so, it is the narrative turn that defines the work we do in the second semester. I allot three weeks to narrative practices: from realist narrative to narrative fiction to auto-ethnography.

From start to finish, the course emphasizes writing, narrative writing in particular, and provides opportunities for students to try out alternate conventions. Sociologist Laurel Richardson (2000) sets the tone by asserting that "writing is not just a 'mopping up' activity at the end of a research project (but) also a way of 'knowing'– a method of discovery and analysis whereby we attempt to but can never fully capture the 'studied world'" (p. 923). Early on, I ask students to write about a potential research project. The assignment is required but not graded. Here are the instructions.

> Without censoring yourself too much, or over-thinking, describe a problem or a question or a situation that you would like to make the focus of a research project. Do not worry too much about form; that can come later. Simply get some ideas or thoughts or wonderings on paper. Our general topic area is disability and society but how you find your way into that general area will differ from one person to another: through your own experience, your family, your community, your work or through some other broader situation that you have been watching through newspapers or on television, on the streets (or social media). Let your mind go!

Months later, the final assignment reinforces this direction. It asks students to use narrative writing to produce an account of their journey through the course. Here are the instructions.

> Reflect on your discoveries and the major turning points in your own learning with particular attention to surprises created through engagement with course materials. Engage with the debates and issues that have been raised, as well as some of the traditions, methodologies, methods/techniques, and ethical considerations you have encountered. This assignment is an opportunity to read back over materials that perhaps you did not have the time to read previously – and draw them into view as part of your learning.

The overview that I have provided here is condensed and selective. It highlights elements of a course that incorporates multiple interpretive approaches with statistical concepts and techniques.[7] The assemblage meets the university's requirement for a research course in an undergraduate degree, and it anticipates admissions requirements for alumni applying to Masters programs. Caught between preference and regulation, my best option as course designer was to seed the syllabus with ethnographic practices that tilt students toward Institutional Ethnography, if not directly into it. Whether they seize that possibility for their Independent Study—and how far they take it—depends largely on supervision.

How Shall I Supervise?

In DST 99 "Final Independent Study," students work with a faculty supervisor to design and implement a small study. The syllabus lays out the major requirements and grading scheme for this year-long project: in the Fall, a study proposal addressing all the typical elements, and (if necessary) an Ethics Protocol; by the Spring, a complete thesis document and oral presentation. Early on there is an on-site day for proposal presentation and peer feedback after which the course shifts to student–supervisor interaction through in-person meetings where possible, email and telephone calls.

In her clearest instruction for an alternate sociology, Smith (1999) asks us to start "one step back before the Cartesian shift that forgets the body" (p. 4). Her studies all began with "some sensation of disquiet, a political discomfort that directed attention to a problem that I could not, at that stage, make explicit" (p. 3). In that spirit, I encourage students to bracket theoretical constructs in favor of finding that disquieting starting point. Somewhere along the way I began to speak of it as a "knot of trouble": the gut-wrenching feeling that something does not add up in a job, a situation, an organization, or a relationship.

As active practitioners, our students are tied up in knots, brimming over with complaints, worries and dilemmas that make great points of entry to broader inquiry.

- Danielle worked in a residence for people with intellectual disabilities in a small city. Her union organized a strike which, while legitimate, turned the sanctity of home into a fractious picket line. She went searching for government policies on wages for workers in community services and discovered not a single department that claimed responsibility. (Cheyne, "The Anatomy of a Black Hole," 2008).
- Lee worked as a communications specialist in a big city hospital. She walked miles of corridors looking for evidence of accessibility in her workplace. In the absence of any physical modifications, she discovered an in-house website with links to government legislation, organizational

action plans, annual reports, and a staff person who had no budget. (Armstrong, "Searching for Hospital Accessibility," 2018).
- Sheena worked as an American Sign Language (ASL) interpreter. To keep her deaf clients front and center, she wore dull clothes on the job. Talking to other interpreters, she discovered that dressing to disappear was common practice. Her analysis reclaimed it as part of the invisible work of women. (Vert, "Disappearing Acts," 2014).

Students are intimidated by the prospect of the Independent Study. Perhaps because it is the final stretch of a long journey, they feel compelled to reach beyond themselves to complete it. It is reassuring when I suggest that what they are looking for might be close at hand in their families or their own bodies.

- Jodie was pregnant and caring for a toddler. Finding it difficult to get around but needing to shop, she made multiple trips to two downtown stores in her community. Against a background of accessibility legislation, her fieldnotes documented physical barriers and demeaning social encounters arising from her own embodiment (Young, "Accessible to Whom?" 2010).
- Keri and her family faced challenges when her mother returned home after hip replacement surgery. Documenting the difficulties that arose day to day, she discovered a schism between hospital and home. Home care was available in theory but restricted by funding regulations. From building renovations to nursing care, it was family labor that closed the gap (Cameron, "Too Much Baggage!" 2008).
- Employed as a hospital-based health worker, Jennifer found herself caring for elderly family members at home. Her study made visible the carework she did as a daughter in a Canadian-Filipino family. Starting from the array of tasks that fell to her, she explored the "strife and concern" of her responsibilities, and the webs of support she tried to create (Manalac, "Living the Caregivers Life", 2014).

Although the timeline for completing their research is short, I encourage students to get physically active—to actually move their bodies—into the process of collecting data.

- Curious about how accessible transportation worked, Lerin got up early for many weeks to ride a Toronto Transit Commission (TTC) Wheeltrans bus. Bouncing along with the driver, he learned about hours of work, wages, seniority, working conditions and the regulations that govern pick-up and delivery of passengers. (Jones, "Riding Along with Smith," 2008).
- Ryan held conventional views on mental illness but was interested in body/mind connections. I hooked him up with someone who organized

a weekly run for psychiatric survivors involved in a local economic initiative. Ryan jogged with the group, and they jarred him into rethinking the diagnostic categories that were governing his worldview (Ali, "Walking into the World of Psychiatric Consumer/Survivors," 2010).
- Maria's interest in religion led her to wonder about the participation of disabled people in church. She attended every religious establishment within several blocks of her home—regardless of denomination. These places of worship had two things in common, she discovered: the absence of disabled people, and religious doctrines that fostered ableist views (Holland, "Get Me to the Church on Time," 2008).
- Karen visited suburban shopping malls regularly throughout the winter. With her fiancé in tow, she ran from door to door testing access door plates to see if they were working. Many were not. In spite of the Accessibility for Ontarians with Disabilities Act, she found no regulations holding malls and stores accountable for maintenance and repair (Da Silveira, "All Talk and No Action," 2009).
- A big sports fan, Rod wanted to find out about wheelchair basketball and the men who played it in the city where he lived. The locals let him join a team. He spent a winter in their court learning the revised rules of the seated game—and the demands a wheelchair makes on the body. "My hands are bleeding!" he wrote, as the first line of his thesis (Walsh, "Slamdunkin' in a Wheelchair," 2008).

In an activist program, some students want to move politically. Beyond the physical or geographic, they want to shift how they related to disability communities and histories.

- As a mental health worker, Angie was challenged by our *Mad People's History* course. To connect with her local mad community, she helped members of a peer support service prepare a weekly meal. She was surprised that the conversations they had over dinner were not about symptoms and treatment. They were about finding a decent place to live and how to get subsidized housing in the community (Snyder, "Sunday Night Dinners," 2007).
- Stifled by her job in a hospital, Joanne wanted to be directly involved with a community. During Mad Pride Week in Toronto, she pushed a hospital bed along Queen Street as part of an annual march. In lapel buttons, signs, slogans, t-shirts and protest paraphernalia she discovered a language of mad resistance (Byrne, "The Push to Mad Pride," 2009).
- Carolyn was curious about how people who identify as mad relate to the city and public space. She found four people who were willing to walk her along their passage through Toronto each day. These journeys helped her trace patterns of safety and risk that interrupt the established guidelines for urban planning (Lee Jones, "Walking with Strangers," 2016).

- Deaf student Joanne and her twin sister, Julia, were fascinated by the story of deaf twins who built and retreated to a treehouse in British Columbia in the late 1800s. In a pilgrimage to "entwine deaf lives, past and present," researcher and sister drove across Canada to visit the site, to analyze its reconstruction as a tourist attraction, and to assess the archive that preserved the story in the local library (Patterson, "In the Place of Trees, In the Paradise of the Imperfect," 2014).

As beginners, our students find it much easier to gather data than to analyze it. They tend just to report what they see and hear, to describe experience or to identify common themes: powerful tendencies for which I have some sympathy. I press them to read the data for social organization—where the term "social" refers to the ways that people's actions in a local site are "hooked into sequences of action implicating and coordinating multiple local sites where others are active" (Smith, 1999, p. 7). Because that move is accomplished, often, through texts (Turner, 2006), I ask students to attend to documents, standardized forms or formal rules that they encounter in the field.

- Mother of three young children, Shaunessey was concerned about disabled children needing adoptive parents. To get close to how that was happening, she engaged the process of becoming an adoptive parent. She attended and took notes at introductory meetings held by an adoption agency; she gathered and analyzed texts associated with that orientation (Bergeron, "Watching Others Be Chosen," 2009).
- Jennifer's study started with a difficult situation in her workplace for which she held a personal support worker responsible. By studying policies, procedures and especially training manuals, her initial explanation shifted to understanding how worker actions are situated in and governed by agency policies and procedures (Liberty, "Beyond Bad Apples," 2009).
- A hospital employee, Linh was diagnosed with an illness that threatened her ability to keep working. Reluctant to self-identify, she moved gradually into seeking time off. Her study identified and commented on the management encounters and documents that designated her officially as sick, and the intricacies of "living the organizational experience" (Chau, "Illness and Disability in the Workplace," 2017).
- Brandon had been badly injured in a bus accident in the United States. Caught up in the transnational disability insurance industry for a decade, he drew on documents embedded in his own claim: disclosures, examinations, assessments, compliance, applicant benefits and compensation (Arkinson, "Mapping a Quagmire," 2017).

A small portion of the school's collection, these studies are remarkable examples of undergraduate research. Through them, each student got a better grasp on a troubling problem. Taken together, they intersect in advancing our understanding of the oppressive relations of disability. Completing them was immensely satisfying for each student—but did not necessarily resolve the discomfort that sparked the inquiry in the first place. Each study had major implications for future action.

- Diagnosed with a degenerative disease, Jessica's body and her politics transformed simultaneously in our program. Her research probed the absence of peers from influential roles in the only organization that provided service to people with her condition. The organizing she did toward a Youth Council that would press formally for change felt like a betrayal (Dell'Unto, "Biting the Hand that Feeds," 2014).
- As a student organizer in a position of executive leadership, Francis explored student unions for their accessibility practices. He tussled with the ethics of insider observation, and the risks of pointing out shortcomings in a group that is relatively powerless. Laid out in by-laws, its relation to university administration includes whether and how the group will be funded (Pineda, "Missing In Action?" 2018).
- Marsha attended all events on the public schedule of a prominent disability activist—listening to him speak over and over and documenting what he was doing. She discovered strands of work that she had no idea were there—including a massive Twitter-feed which she mapped for core messages. These textual trails shifted her from curious onlooker to engaged advocate (Ryan, "Following David Lepofsky," 2017).

The prospect of producing an undergraduate thesis is daunting—especially when the writing required is more than an assemblage of long quotes from authoritative sources in the literature. I urge students to start writing from the first day—instead of waiting until the desperate weeks at end of term—and I offer to give feedback on chunks of text along the way. Even in projects that are grounded and creative, they tend to revert to traditional academic style. I prod them to remember the power of writing from "I"—not the biographical "I" but the ethnographic "I": first person political. I urge them to use active rather than passive voice—and to heighten rather than suppress the drama of their work.

I provide a draft Table of Contents to guide students in constructing their final document. It includes the standard headings but is offered as a pliable tool rather than a rigid template. "Play with it," I urge, and I provide a stack of examples from previous students who have experimented with formats. In listening to the colloquial ways that students describe their projects, I often hear possible titles—a catch phrase someone has used that crystallizes the subject. I flag these phrases early to see whether they hold up toward the end: many of them do. Using verbs is important throughout the document but especially for titles where the core idea needs to be communicated in a short hit.

Conclusion

This chapter is an account of teaching Institutional Ethnography to undergraduate students. In reviewing the core elements of two courses, I have beaten a path across the terrain of an organization that is not very receptive to a revolutionary feminist method of inquiry. Given the constraints, how can such an adventure be made to "count?" For undergraduate training, the substantive example of Disability Studies suggests that the best strategy is to ride tandem, quietly tucking the radical alongside the conventional to produce what universities take for granted as science.

This approach has worked well for our program but gives rise to its own struggles. Even without previous training, our students harbor all kinds of unspoken assumptions about research. Untangling them from a gnarl of positivist roots is a big task. It takes effort to push back and make space for another way of thinking; students do not simply glide in. And it takes time, sometimes all the time that we have just to get to the starting line. As working women with multiple responsibilities, they have no trouble recognizing invisible labor when they see it. They find it more difficult, however, to probe for external authorities, to make connections between rules and ruling, and to develop a sixth sense about texts. The documents and forms that permeate people's lives are difficult to yank out of the commonplace.

Through my own learning history, I know the impact of reading and re-reading Dorothy Smith, of inter-generational interpreters and generous mentors, of organized gatherings and informal conversations, of opportunities to try things out and opportunities to pass things along. In a field with radical aspirations, my quest was to channel a feminist materialist ontology into the lives of Disability Studies students. Over the years, they have given back as good as they received. The evidence is there in completed studies—row after row of white binders on sagging shelves—only some of which I have presented. It is a great discovery: that this alternate sociology is not too complex for undergraduate students—their scholarship, their practice, and their lives.

Notes

1. I am indebted to the skills and patience of editors Paul Luken and Suzanne Vaughan. Thank you. This chapter was written in dialogue with Timothy Diamond who also guided and sustained the work that it documents. Much honor is due.
2. I use the word disability to reference a wide range of bodies, minds, lived experiences, communities, and points of view. It would be more accurate and more

inclusive to say disabled/deaf/mad/neuro-diverse, to say deaf/Deaf where the capital D signifies cultural membership, and mad/neuro-diverse where "neuro-diverse" is preferable to "autistic." For more than fifty years, people with mental health histories have been active in challenging and enriching the discourse that defines them, the most recent edgy reclamation being the word "mad" (Reville & Church, 2012). As an ally, my preferences are "psychiatric survivor" and "mad."
3. Now called the Department of Studies in Social Justice.
4. It was not unusual for George Smith to show up for class wearing a t-shirt boldly lettered with the claim: "I have made the ontological shift!" A display of actual material—as well as materialism.
5. https://www.ryerson.ca/inclusive-early-childhood-service-system/.
6. Student studies from objects: Kira Michado, "Trying to Walk in his Shoes," 2007; Jessica Doberstein, "Quilting Identity: Out of the Box," 2016; Mary-Teresa Korkush, "Stuff Revealed: What do Possessions of Importance Tell us about People with Developmental Disabilities?" 2016.
7. Students have an assignment that requires them to discover a research tradition. The list of choices includes Indigenous methodologies, Queer methodologies, critical discourse analysis, ethnography, grounded theory, narrative inquiry, oral history, and community-based participatory research.

REFERENCES

Behar, R. (1996). *The vulnerable observer: Anthropology that breaks your heart*. Boston: Beacon Press.

Church, K. (1993). *Breaking down/breaking through: Narratives of psychiatric survivor participation in making community mental health policy in Ontario*. University of Toronto: Doctoral dissertation.

Church, K. (1995). *Forbidden narratives: Critical autobiography as social science*. New York: Gordon and Breach; (2003) Routledge.

Church, K. (2006). Working like crazy on "working like crazy": Imag(in)ing community economic development practice through documentary film. In E. Shragge (Ed.), *Community economic development: Building for social change* (pp. 69–82). Sydney, Nova Scotia: University College of Cape Breton.

Church, K. (2016). My dinners with Tara and Nancy: Feminist conversations on teaching for professional practice. In J. Gingras, P. Robinson, J. Waddell, & L. Cooper. (Eds.), *Teaching as scholarship: Preparing students for professional practice in community services* (pp. 75–87). Waterloo, Ontario: Wilfrid Laurier University Press.

Church, K., Diamond, T., & Voronka, J. (2004). *In profile: Personal support work in Canada*. Occasional Paper #2, Ryerson-RBC Institute for Disability Studies Research and Education, Ryerson University.

Church, K. with Frazee, C., Luciani, T., Panitch, M., & Seeley, P. (2006). Dressing corporate subjectivities: Learning what to wear to the bank. In S. Billett, M. Somerville, & T. Fenwick (Eds.), *Work, subjectivity and learning: Understanding learning through working life* (pp. 69–85). The Netherlands, Dordrecht: Springer.

Church, K., Frazee, C., & Panitch, M. (2010). Beginning from disability to study a corporate organization of learning. In D. W. Livingstone (Ed.), *Lifelong learning in paid and unpaid work* (pp. 137–154). Abingdon and New York: Routledge.

Church, K., Panitch, M., Frazee, C., & Livingstone, P. (2010). Out from under: A brief history of everything. In R. Sandell, J. Dodd, & R. Garland Thomson. (Eds.), *Re-presenting disability: Agency and activism in the museum* (pp. 25–53). Abingdon and New York: Routledge.

Denzin, N., & Lincoln, Y. (Eds.). (2000). *Handbook of qualitative methods* (2nd ed.). Thousand Oaks: Sage.

Devault, M., & McCoy, L. (2002). Institutional ethnography: Using interviews to investigate ruling relations. In J. Gubrium & J. Holstein (Eds.), *Handbook of interview research: Context and method* (pp. 751–776). Thousand Oaks: Sage.

Devault, M., & McCoy, L. (2012). Investigating ruling relations: Dynamics of interviewing in institutional ethnography. In J. A. Holstein, J. F. Gubrium, A. B. Marvasti, & K. D. McKinney (Eds.), *The Sage handbook of interview research: The complexity of the craft* (pp. 381–396). Thousand Oaks: Sage.

Diamond, T. (1992). *Making gray gold: Narratives of nursing home care*. Chicago: University of Chicago Press.

Emerson, R., Fretz, R., & Shaw, L. (1995). *Writing ethnographic fieldnotes*. Chicago: University of Chicago Press.

Frazee, C., Church, K. & Panitch, M. (2016). Fixing: The claiming and reclaiming of disability history. In C. Kelly & M. Orsini. (Eds.), *Mobilizing metaphor: Art, culture and disability activism in Canada* (pp. 25–53). Vancouver, BC: University of British Columbia Press.

Gray, R. (2003). Performing on and off the stage: The place(s) of performance in arts-based approaches to qualitative inquiry. *Qualitative Inquiry, 9*(2), 254–267.

Gray, R., Ivonoffski, V., & Sinding, C. (2001). Making a mess and spreading it around: Articulation of an approach to research-based theatre. In A. Bochner & C. Ellis (Eds.), *Ethnographically speaking: Autoethnography, literature, and aesthetics* (pp. 57–75). Walnut Creek, CA: Alta Mira.

Hurl, C., & Klostermann, J. (2019). Remembering George W. Smith's "life work": From politico-administrative regimes to living otherwise. *Studies in Social Justice, 13*(2), 262–282.

Ignagni, E., & Church, K. (2008). One more reason to look away? Ties and tensions between arts-informed inquiry and disability studies. In A. Cole & J. G. Knowles (Eds.), *Handbook of the arts in qualitative social science research* (pp. 625–638). Thousand Oaks, CA: Sage.

Jackson, D. (1990). *Unmasking masculinity: A critical autobiography*. London: Unwin Hyman.

Jackson, N. (2004). Notes on ethnography as research method. In M. E. Belfiore, T. A. Defoe, S. Folinsbee, J. Hunter, & N. Jackson (Eds.), *Reading work: Literacies in the new workplace* (pp. 277–290). Mahwah, New Jersey and London: Lawrence Erlbaum Associates.

Jackson, N. (2005). *What counts as learning? A case study perspective*. Unpublished manuscript. Work and Lifelong Learning Network Annual Meeting, June, Toronto, Ontario Institute for Studies in Education.

Livingstone, D. W. (Ed.). (2010). *Lifelong learning in paid and unpaid work: Survey and case study findings*. New York: Routledge.

Livingstone, D. W., & Scholtz, A. (2010). Work and learning in the computer era: Basic survey findings. In D. W. Livingstone (Ed.), *Lifelong learning in paid and unpaid work: Survey and case study findings* (pp. 15–55). New York: Routledge.

Luken, P., & Vaughan, S. (1999). Life history and the critique of American sociological practice. *Sociological Inquiry, 69*(3), 404–425.
Making Care Visible Working Group (Bresalier, M., Gillis, L., McClure, C., McCoy, L., Mykhalovskiy, E., Taylor, D., & Webber). (2002). *Making care visible: Antiretroviral therapy and the health work of people living with HIV/AIDS*. Ottawa: Canadian Public Health Association.
Mills, C. Wright. (1959). *The sociological imagination*. London: Oxford University Press.
Mykhalovskiy, E., & Church, K. (2006). Of t-shirts and ontologies: Celebrating George Smith's pedagogical legacies. In C. Frampton, G. Kinsman, A. Thompson, & K. Tilleczek (Eds.), *Sociology for changing the world* (pp. 71–86). Toronto: Fernwood.
Mykhalovskiy, E., Hastings, C., Comer, L., Gruson-Wood, J., & Strang, M. (this volume). Teaching institutional ethnography as an alternative sociology. In Luken, P. & Vaughan, S. (Eds.), *Handbook of institutional ethnography*. Palgrave /Macmillan.
Mykhalovskiy, E., & McCoy, L. (2002). Troubling ruling discourses of health: using institutional ethnography in community-based research. *Critical Public Health, 12*(1), 17–37.
Parada, H. (2011). *Etnografía Institucional del Sistema de Protección de la Republica Dominicana*. Santo Domingo: UNICEF Press.
Parada, H., Ibarra, A., Mulvale, E., & Limon Bravo, F. (2019). Children, youths, and resilience. In H. Bauder (Ed.), *Putting family first: Migration and integration in Canada* (pp. 197–212). Vancouver: University of British Columbia Press.
Richardson, L. (2000). Writing: A method of inquiry. In N. Denzin & Y. Lincoln (Eds.), *Handbook of qualitative research* (2nd ed., pp. 923–948). Thousand Oaks: Sage.
Reville D., & Church, K. (2012). Mad activism enters its fifth decade: Psychiatric survivor organizing in Toronto. In A. Choudry, J. Hanley, & E. Shragge (Eds.), *Organize! Building from the local for global justice* (pp. 189–201). Oakland, CA: PM Press.
Smith, D. E. (1987). *The everyday world as problematic: A feminist sociology*. Boston: Northeastern University Press.
Smith, G. W. (1990). Political activist as ethnographer. *Social Problems, 37*(4), 629–648.
Smith, D. E. (1999). *Writing the social: Critique, theory, and investigations*. Toronto: University of Toronto Press.
Smith, D. E. (2005). *Institutional ethnography: A sociology for people*. Walnut Creek, CA: AltaMira Press.
Titchkosky, T., & Michalko, R. (Eds.). (2009). *Rethinking normalcy: A disability studies reader*. Toronto: Canadian Scholars Press.
Turner, S. (2006). Mapping institutions as work and texts. In D. Smith (Ed.), *Institutional ethnography as practice* (pp. 139–162). Oxford: Rowman & Littlefield.
Underwood, K., Smith, A., & Martin, J. (2018). Institutional mapping as a tool for resource consultation. *Journal of Early Childhood Research*. https://doi.org/10.1177/1476718X18818205.

PART III

Explicating Global/Transnational Ruling Relations

CHAPTER 12

Using Institutional Ethnography to Investigate Intergovernmental Environmental Policy-Making

Lauren E. Eastwood

So, what essentially happened—well you have seen that the text came out at 9:00 in the evening, then there was a very short intervention saying that Parties now had two and a half hours to look at the text. And then they would convene in the square table format with three slots per delegation, and then having overflow rooms for Parties, but no transmission for observers. So, in terms of transparency it could have been better, obviously. So, then, essentially, at midnight, the session opened, and it lasted all night until 5:40 in the morning. I can now go through the critical things that happened, but let's first start with the conclusion…

—Field notes 11 December 2015, Paris, France: United Nations Framework Convention on Climate Change.[1]

To whom is the above language familiar? Surely, it is comprehensible to those present in the meeting room during the morning briefing for the Research and Independent Non-Governmental Organizations (RINGOs)[2] at the 15th Conference of Parties (COP) of the United Nations Framework Convention on Climate Change (UNFCCC) in Paris in 2015. These briefings are intended to update participants on the current status of the texts being negotiated by governments. Given that negotiations are complex and many different policy frameworks are often negotiated simultaneously, the briefings are an efficient way to share information on deliberations as they unfold. People present in the room during the briefing nodded knowingly, chuckled

---

L. E. Eastwood (✉)
SUNY College at Plattsburgh, Plattsburgh, NY, USA
e-mail: eastwole@plattsburgh.edu

© The Author(s) 2021
P. C. Luken and S. Vaughan (eds.), *The Palgrave Handbook of Institutional Ethnography*,
https://doi.org/10.1007/978-3-030-54222-1_12

at the subtle digs leveled at government delegations or at meeting Chairs, and asked probing follow-up questions, equally peppered with acronyms, that demonstrated their knowledge of the broader context of intergovernmental negotiations.

Those who had access to the meeting venue on 11 December 2015, the final official day of negotiations of text that would result in the Paris Agreement, had a solid sense of the range of topics covered during the RINGO briefing. These were participants in the process who were not confused by the language of "intervention," "transparency," and "observers." Nor were they surprised by the details that were reported on for clarification—such as the fact that governments spent the entire prior night deliberating a particular document that contained multiple points of contention for various government delegations. These were people who understood the points of contention. They were interested to know how those conflicts might be resolved so that the Paris negotiations could successfully end with a "consensus text"—a document on which all governments could agree.

Extending beyond those present in the room during the RINGO morning meeting, if a transcription of the entire briefing were to be made available, who would understand its content, or know how to make sense of the conversation? Those who regularly engage in policy-making processes that take place under the auspices of the UN would have the background to comprehend the broader context of the discussion, if not the specific acronyms, agenda items referenced, and other details germane to the climate negotiations processes. The particular work knowledges that are part and parcel of UN deliberations would be deployed by those who regularly engage in UN policy fora, whether they be focused on climate, biological diversity, forests, Indigenous Peoples, human rights, or any number of dynamics that are taken up under the auspices of the UN.

After more than 20 years of observing and participating in UN meetings around the world, the texts, prevalence of acronyms, and style of framing issues and debates—all of which are typical of UN deliberations—are familiar to me regardless of whether they pertain to one of the specific UN bodies I have been researching. While I may not understand the details, there are recognizable elements that typify UN deliberations.

I first entered the United Nations in 1998, arriving at the *Palais des Nations* in Geneva with the objective of conducting research on the Intergovernmental Forum on Forests (IFF) (see Eastwood, 2005). At the time, I was fascinated by the sheer volume of documents and agreements that came out of the United Nations Conference on Environment and Development (UNCED) held in Rio de Janeiro in 1992. Dubbed the "Earth Summit," the Rio meetings resulted in the framework for three legally-binding agreements, two of which—the United Nations Framework Convention on Climate Change (UNFCCC) and the Convention on Biological Diversity (CBD)—continue to provide the context for a substantial portion of my current data collection. These legally-binding agreements set in motion the subsequent processes of negotiation that regularly take place in various locations around the world. Governments come together to hash out the details as Non-Governmental participants, known as Observers or Major Groups, lobby government delegations in an attempt to influence the outcomes.

In addition to the legally-binding environmental agreements, the UNCED meetings also resulted in a non-legally binding "statement" on forests. This instigated a policy process designed to hash out the details of policy goals that were vaguely sketched out in the original statement. My goal in 1998 was to enter the post-Rio forest policy process and to investigate how it was that policy was negotiated under the auspices of the UN. Since then, I have attended over close to 50 official UN-based meetings of various sorts, including the massive "Conference of Parties" (COP) meetings of the legally-binding agreements, more focused "Working Group" or "Expert Group" meetings associated with the climate, biological diversity, or forest policy processes, and meetings of the United Nations Permanent Forum on Indigenous Issues (UNPFII). The UNPFII often takes up the intersections between environmental policy and indigenous concerns. I have accessed all of these arenas as an Observer or Major Group participant. In other words, my access to the meetings has been as a participant who is not credentialed on a government delegation. I note this as it has implications for where I can go and what I can see within the context of the meetings I attend. It also organizes the interactions that I have with other participants.

Throughout this chapter, using examples from data gathered in these settings over the past two decades, and providing ethnographic snippets to bring readers into the policy-making process, I aim to discuss the application of the ontology of institutional ethnography to the world of intergovernmental policy-making. From a research perspective, multilateral environmental agreements are more often analyzed through the theoretical frameworks of international relations or political science. I have occasionally encountered other sociologists who aim to analyze the intergovernmental arena. However, deploying an approach grounded in the ontology of Institutional Ethnography allows the researcher to make visible the actualities of policy work—actualities that are not represented in the final policy documents and in the texts that are produced for negotiation. In addition, the focus on textually-mediated organizations that is central to institutional ethnographic work is apt, as participants constantly orient to texts as they are produced in negotiations or to language in agreements that have previously been negotiated. Lastly, guided by the ontology of institutional ethnography, I have analyzed the discursive terrains that serve to organize the work of practitioners in important ways. In doing so, I situate the local (represented in my ethnographic data) within the context of the trans-local—the dynamics that coordinate the work of policy-making through the UN.

Throughout this process, I have focused primarily on the interests of members of civil society and Indigenous Peoples, as the UN, as an *intergovernmental* arena, is specifically organized for government participation. This results in a dynamic whereby participants who are not on government delegations must deploy particular strategies in order to influence policy. I refer to the work of participants as "strategy work," as participants strategically orient to the texts being produced in negotiations. An element of this strategy work for Civil Society Organizations and Indigenous Peoples Organizations involves gaining access to the meetings themselves, as non-governmental participants' participation is deemed important yet clearly secondary to governments' engagement. Thus, non-governmental participants' work begins long before the actual negotiations, as they must be recognized by and accredited with the UN body under which the negotiations are taking place. This is becoming increasingly difficult in the context of the climate negotiations as the urgency of the climate crisis has spurred intense concern among members of civil society and indigenous peoples' organizations, thus putting pressure on the capacity of UNFCCC meeting venues and raising larger questions about the logistics of participation in policy.

In this chapter, my goal is to first explain how and why I apply institutional ethnography to the research site of intergovernmental environmental negotiations. I demonstrate this application through providing some ethnographic snippets designed to bring the reader into various moments where the work of policy-makers can be documented and made visible. I then move outwards from the explication of the research site and in-depth description of participants' work to the realm of analysis. The work that participants do is organized by larger dynamics that merit investigation. As with all institutional ethnography, my goal is not only to describe but also to analyze. As the chapter moves toward conclusion, I illustrate several places where one can move from ethnography to analysis. In other words, after bringing the reader into the research site ethnographically, I demonstrate some of points of analysis and conclusions that I draw from my engagement in the various policy processes.

INSTITUTIONAL ETHNOGRAPHY IN INTERGOVERNMENTAL FORA

As I entered the arena of UN forest policy negotiations in 1998, I was drawn to institutional ethnography for a variety of reasons. On one level, I had been seeking a way to gain a greater understanding of the sorts of things that become invisible in the finalized policy documents. For example, one could do an analysis of textual changes that documents go through as they move from one set of meetings to another, and as they are worked on over the course of a given meeting. However, the texts themselves obscure the work that people do to create them. One could make note of changes in the language or terminology in the texts, but such a documentation would be disconnected from the strategic work that participants engage in to influence the language in the texts. In being present during negotiations, it is possible to document the ways in which participants work strategically to contribute to those negotiations, and how they orient to the evolving texts throughout the process.

Additionally, institutional ethnography appealed to me as I have endeavored to analyze the larger trans-local relations of ruling that serve to organize the production of texts and coordinate the work that practitioners do to engage in policy processes. Smith (2005) explains: "Institutional ethnography's modest proposal is to work from what people are doing or what they can tell us about what they and others do and to find out how the forms of coordinating their activities 'produce' institutional processes, as they actually work" (p. 60). In contrast to beginning from a theoretical standpoint, I maintained the stance of discovery that is central to institutional ethnography. Smith (2005) articulates the overarching ontology of institutional ethnography as follows:

> Institutional ethnography's program is one of inquiry and discovery. It has no prior interpretive commitment such as that which follows from concepts such as *global domination* or *resistance*. It means to find out just how people's doings in the everyday are articulated to and coordinated by extended social relations that are not visible from within any particular local setting and just how people are participating in those relations. (p. 36, italics in the original).

This stance of discovery that exists without a theoretical investment in any particular interpretive framework requires that the researcher be attentive to particular work practices in which participants in policy processes actively engage. By contrast, the researchers with whom I come in contact, and who are working from other research paradigms, are often interested in using theoretical frameworks to define and make sense of particular elements of the policy processes. It is not unusual to see such research organized around whether the "climate regime" is an example of "good governance," or whether NGOs have been effective in influencing policy outcomes, for example.

As DeVault develops (this volume), institutional ethnographers do not eschew theory. However, we do not attempt to place our research sites within the abstract realm of theoretical concepts and instead focus on the actual activities of those within the research site. The ethnographic elements of my work, as I illustrate below, allow me to bring the reader into the actualities of the negotiations in order to illustrate the work of making policy. In being attentive to the actual activities of participants, I simultaneously remain attentive to the various levels of broader social relations that serve to coordinate those activities, and, ultimately analyze the implications of those relations that are not immediately visible within the local setting, as I illustrate toward the end of the chapter.

Ethnographic Snippet: Copenhagen Climate Negotiations, 2009

Appreciating the free access to public transportation provided by the Danish government to all participants in "COP15" (the 15th Conference of Parties of the United Nations Framework Convention on Climate Change, or UNFCCC), I board the train from Sweden to Denmark without needing to purchase a ticket. Given the relatively short distance and the lack of affordable places to stay in Copenhagen during the two weeks of the COP meetings, I am not alone in taking this daily trip to the COP venue. Since the Conference of Parties format is structured for Parties to the legally-binding agreements (governments that have ratified the agreement) to negotiate policy, upwards of 30,000 people are in Copenhagen for the negotiations. This includes large government delegations and accredited members of Observer (civil society and Indigenous Peoples) organizations.

COP participants are recognizable by our baby-blue lanyards from which hang our identification badges. This badge not only legitimizes our use of public transportation but more importantly provides proof of credentials needed to access the actual meeting venue. Security is tight at the venue, and the barcode on our badges is scanned as we enter and again as we leave the site. Within the venue, access to particular areas is based on the category of credentials that each participant has. This category is visibly represented by a color-coded swath on the identification card, which provides a visual key for each individual's designation. Having gained credentials to attend the meetings themselves under the designation of Party (government), Indigenous Peoples Organization (IPO), Environmental NGO (ENGO), RINGO, etc., each participant's ability to enter certain spaces within the meeting venue is likewise organized by this designation. Negotiations that are listed as "closed" on the scrolling daily schedule inside the meeting venue are open only to those who have a particular authorized designation. As negotiations get more contentious some deliberations become closed to Observers as governments exercise their right to engage in debates without the watchful eye of non-governmental participants.

As a researcher, back on the train on my way to the meeting venue, I take note of the color-coded swaths to better understand who the people are as they cluster around seats and discuss various issues related to the deliberations. On our route, each stop the train makes increases the number of COP participants. Some enter the train alone and select seats that allow them to observe the scenery. Many participants, however, travel in groups knowing that even the time spent in transportation can be used to discuss the current state of various negotiating texts or different governments' positions. This is more pronounced once we arrive at the main station and switch to the local tram that goes past the Bella Center, the massive meeting center constructed specifically for the climate negotiations, complete with restaurants, postal service, offices for government delegations, space for side events, meeting rooms, and plenary halls. At the tram stop for the Bella Center, the vast majority of the occupants exit with many of them engaged in discussions with colleagues. I catch bits of conversations in various languages, peppered with acronyms and references to particular agenda items. Even when I do not understand what people are saying, actions such as retrieving texts from brief cases and pointing to particular segments or checking mobile phones for updates from colleagues and reporting back to others in the group—these are the sorts of things I have not only observed but participated in over the years as I have conducted UN research. The tram and the short walk to the conference venue from the tram stop are also sites where people are busily engaging in strategic policy work.

Ethnography and Global/Intergovernmental Institutions

In the segment above, I have attempted to use my experience in the actual research setting to bring the reader into a small slice of the work of making policy. Traditionally ethnography has been used as a tool for in-depth investigation of a particular location. The site of UN research can be described in some detail in order to flesh out the actual "doings" of individuals. As I mentioned earlier, rather than speaking abstractly about the policy outcomes, participating in and observing the work that people do allows for insights into processes that get made invisible in final texts. Here, "the local" is seen as significant in the sense that it provides the researcher with primary data. In Grahame and Grahame's (2017) description, "[c]lassical ethnographies tend to treat the everyday world as a local realm of culture, meaning, and face-to-face activity" (p. 1). Given this site-specific focus, how then would one ask questions about the intersections between the local and the global? It is clear that the site of UN research extends far beyond the walls of specific meeting rooms, and meetings take place all over the globe. Along these lines, Blok asks "when researching global-scale social relations, how exactly are we to 'map' such connections empirically, particularly if we aspire to ideals of localized ethnographic fieldwork?" (2010, p. 507).

A resolution to this apparent incongruity is found in recent critiques of the assumed dichotomy between the local and the global. As researchers have increasingly called into question the schism between the local and the global (Blok, 2010; Burawoy et al., 2000; Lapegna, 2009; Tsing, 2005), several research methodologies have been developed in an attempt to address these critiques. These methodologies are predicated on the local focus of ethnography, yet they aim to explicate dynamics that extend beyond the specific site itself. However, each articulates the resolution to this quagmire in somewhat different terms. Lapegna (2009) notes that Burowoy's global ethnography is effectively used as a critique of the grand theorists of globalization who "fail to identify how such processes are locally mediated with diverse effects on everyday life" (p. 5). Furthermore, "[a]s a method that requires immersion in a local setting and direct contact with informants, ethnography provides the ideal tools to investigate the diversities and heterogeneous manifestations of world-wide capitalism" (Lapegna, 2009, p. 5). I concur with Lapegna yet see important distinctions between what institutional ethnographers and global ethnographers attempt to illuminate in their work. Smith, for example, has argued that institutional ethnography differs in significant ways from global ethnography. For Smith, Burawoy's extended case method relegates data to conceptual categories, whereas institutional ethnography is instead predicated on explicating how social relations organize individuals' actions and work in specific locations and institutions (Smith, 2005).

Using Smith's orientation rather than the one represented in classical ethnographies as articulated by Grahame and Grahame above, the global/local divide no longer presents a problem for the researcher. Instead, in investigating the work that people do within a setting and understanding that such work is organized by trans-local ruling relations, the actualities of people's doings become the central focus. In approaching UN negotiations as a research site, it has been important for me to orient to the work that participants do, including the work they do to become knowledgeable about how to engage in this arena. Participants understand that in order to participate in the policy process, they need to become familiar with the specific texts under negotiation and to keep up with changes in the texts as they are transformed throughout the process. Participants understand that they need to work strategically to influence policy outcomes. The policy outcomes themselves are not my focus of analysis. Rather, the ways in which participants work to get particular language into the texts, or to keep particular language out, for example, becomes part of my data. The work of CSOs and IPOs has been marked by a sense of marginality and a clear understanding of the distinctions in status between Parties (governments) and Observers (everyone else). While discourses of transparency and participation require that governments engage in some way with people who are not on government delegations, people who represent CSOs and IPOs know that they need to constantly re-assert their rights to engage in deliberations to develop the substance behind the rhetoric of transparency and participation. At times this means using the discursive frames of transparency and participation strategically in order to push governments for greater access.

Beyond the focus on the work of practitioners in making policy, the primacy of the text in UN negotiations makes institutional ethnography a fitting approach, as long as the researcher maintains a particular orientation to texts and documents that is consistent with institutional ethnography. As Grahame and Grahame (2017) write, institutional ethnography emphasizes "(1) ethnography as an approach to studying social organization and (2) a conception of institutional processes in which text-based forms of coordination play a key role" (p. 1). Institutional ethnographers are interested in the manner in which texts serve to coordinate individuals' actions within particular institutional processes. Some institutional ethnographers have focused on the ways in which documents have organized or coordinated the work of front-line workers (e.g., Ridzi, 2009). However, within the context of UN negotiations, while texts are ever present, they do not appear as forms that need to be filled out. Instead, texts appear as policy briefs, negotiating texts, "white papers," "non-papers," Declarations, Agreements, Accords, and the like. They organize individuals' actions in significant ways, but they are also representative of larger ruling relations that likewise serve to organize what goes on beyond the UN.

Richard Harper's approach to his research on the International Monetary Fund (IMF) is useful here, given some caveats for how to apply his insights to institutional ethnographic work. As Harper (1998) immersed himself as an ethnographer in the policy-laden work of IMF bureaucrats, he too focused on "the organization of the organization" (p. 111), as institutional ethnographers would, in order "to draw attention to how the Fund organizes itself to do certain tasks" (p. 111). Influenced by the centrality of texts in Smith's work, Harper examined both the textually-mediated nature of the IMF as an institution as well as the background knowledge that practitioners needed to have in order to activate texts within work processes. Harper (1998) argues that "one way an ethnographer can get around an organization is by following the career of the key information in that organization" (p. 69). Here he points to the manner in which key information works its way through a particular pre-determined bureaucratic process. For Harper, seeing information as having a career, and as doing particular work, was a crucial manner of accessing the workings of the institution being studied. This technique allows for the researcher to develop a certain focus without losing sight of the larger dynamics that provide the context for that information.

However, what is crucial from an institutional ethnographic standpoint is to ensure that "information" does not take the place of individuals as they engage in their work. In other words, "information" does not have a career aside from how it is deployed through the work that practitioners do to strategically intervene in particular processes.

Below I bring readers into a recent meeting of the Convention on Biological Diversity, all of the legally-binding Multilateral Environmental Agreements (MEAs) that came out of the 1992 Rio UNCED process have subsidiary bodies through which details of the policy framework are negotiated. In the following segment of text, I demonstrate how participants draw on prior language to support their positions on how they think the final texts should appear. In addition, it demonstrates the strategic orientation of participants to the negotiating texts as they evolve.

Ethnographic Snippet: Montreal Biological Diversity Negotiations, 2018

The Plenary Hall at the International Civil Aviation Organization (ICAO), located in Montreal, Canada, provides the proper equipment and facilities for UN negotiations. Complete with concentric desks outfitted with microphones and earpieces that extend from the front of the hall to the back, delegates and observers have adequate space to engage in the work of deliberating texts over the course of the 22nd SBSTTA meeting. Earpieces are necessary not only for hearing whomever has the floor but also for translation of each speaker into the six official UN languages. At the front of the hall, facing the room on a raised platform—also outfitted with microphones and earpieces—sit members of the Secretariat, an elected Co-Chair of the SBSTTA meeting, and rapporteur. Flanking the back of the room are the glassed-in booths of the translators. I am often struck by how complex their work is as they are expected to keep up with speakers who are pressed for time. To keep interventions manageable, a bell sounds at the three-minute mark. The Chair has the discretion to cut the speaker off after this point, which often lends to hurried speech. In addition the translators must understand an incredibly complex and evolving vocabulary that is specific to each agenda item.

I check my watch and note that it is 10:17 a.m. The program has designated that particular items are to be addressed during the morning period, which extends from 10:00 a.m. to 1:00 p.m. However, in typical UN fashion, even after the designated start time, no one looks especially prepared to begin. In fact, very few delegates are at their seats, and it seems that many people have not yet even arrived at the Plenary Hall. Those who are in the room are talking with other delegates, or getting situated at their designated locations identified by country-named placards. The desks and chairs at the back of the Plenary Hall are marked by placards indicating the proper space for varying categories of Observers. When I entered the hall on the first day of negotiations, I located the sign for "Education," as that is the designation under which I obtain my credentials for attending meetings of the CBD, and therefore where I am authorized to sit.

Finally, it appears that people are settling down and preparing to get started on the official discussions of the agenda item. The Chair seats herself on the raised platform in front, presses the button on her microphone, and begins to speak.

> Distinguished ladies and gentlemen…if you could please take your seats, we will soon begin taking statements on the text you have before you. I would first, however, like to announce that there will be a Friends of the Co-Chairs group meeting on digital sequence from 10:00 to 12:00 in Conference Room 2. I would also note that CRPs have been developed with a view to taking previous interventions into account. I ask that you keep this in mind as you make your statements today, as I have had to reconcile the divergent views. Please keep this in mind and think about ways that your delegation can be flexible in the spirit of compromise, as we have limited time to address this agenda item. I already see a list of 13…no 14 speakers who have requested the floor. Experience tells me there will be more [slight laughter from the room]. Experience also tells me that some of you may feel constrained by the 3-minute time limit for interventions. Please do keep in mind that we must resolve these issues as SBSTTA comes to

a close soon, and please keep your comments short and direct. Finland—you have the floor.

As governments engage in commenting on the texts, many speakers deploy a fairly standardized formula for interventions. Interventions typically begin with a general statement of appreciation for the work that the Chair has done to compile the document being negotiated. This is often followed by an articulation of agreement or alignment with specific prior Parties' interventions. Lastly comes the particular addition of content that the speaker wishes to convey related to the specific item at hand. However, Finland diverges from this format as the first speaker.

> Thank you Madame Chair. We would like to go through this document para by para, but on the issue of IPBES as raised by UK, we are also of the opinion that we have new information that was not reflected in the COP decision nor the previous SBSTTA and would like to see that reflected in the document....

The lead negotiator for the Finnish delegation here has done several things that are consistent with the policy work being done, while also expressing concern about the overall content of the document. The language of "para by para" stands in reference to the fact that standard protocol is to go through each paragraph in succession in order to obtain "clean text"—text that does not contain brackets. Square brackets in the text indicate that governments have not come to agreement about the language in the document. The goal of any meeting is to pass on a consensus text to the subsequent negotiating session. Often, as the meetings move closer to conclusion, only the bracketed segments of text are up for discussion.

Additionally though, while aligning with the UK, the Finnish delegation has indicated that the "COP decision" and the "previous SBSTTA" provided the basis for the text that is being discussed. Both items referenced represent prior consensus text. Finland, following on the point made by the UK, wishes to point out that new language has been introduced. For both Parties, this new language is inconsistent with what has been agreed upon in previous negotiating sessions. This sort of attention to consensus language only merits mention when governments have concerns about the new language that is being introduced. At times, in order to move negotiations forward, Chairs take chances with Conference Room Papers (CRPs) that are still under negotiation. Understanding that there is some level of contention, Chairs need to make decisions regarding how to balance the concerns of delegations. This was referenced by the Chair in her introduction when she asked participants to "be flexible" in their positions "in the spirit of compromise." From time to time the risk pays off as Parties decide that the language is something that, as policy-makers say, they "can live with." At other times, Parties continue to raise concern in hopes that the next version of the Chair's text is more amenable to their position.

After hearing the Finnish intervention, the Chair again pressed the button on her microphone, enabling her to take the floor.

> Thank you Finland for your intervention, thank you also for the support of the process, and I hope my dear colleagues that you can be more flexible at this point in the process. I understand that the text does not represent each position. However, if we could please address these concerns in a systematic fashion, I believe we can come to an agreement. So we shall begin with the first paragraph of the chapeau—any comments?

While the interventions that follow this gentle admonition contain the appropriate level of diplomacy that is expected of UN negotiations, it becomes clear that many delegates are asking whether the issue at hand is one that appropriately falls under the mandate of SBSTTA. This is another technique that is often used when governments have concerns with the content of particular texts. Referencing the mandate of another body and suggesting that it would be a more appropriate venue for the discussion can help delegates to push discussions to an organizational location where different types of wordsmithing can take place. During these discussions, there is a suggestion by one government that the issue be moved to a different subsidiary body—the Subsidiary Body on Implementation (SBI), rather than being taken up in SBSTTA.

It is clear that the Chair is getting somewhat frustrated with the circular discussion, as she is tasked with getting governments to move forward. She notes that the UK has asked for the floor. "UK—is it on the same issue?" The UK negotiator presses the button on his microphone.

> Thank you Madame Chair. We've been listening to the various interventions and we feel there is a possible compromise that was suggested by Brazil. I don't necessarily have the language for that, but I don't know. It might be a possible compromise.

At this point the UK attempts to articulate the compromise language. The next government to take the floor, the Netherlands, also agrees: "Yes I'm very happy with the idea that was raised by Canada and the proposal made by Brazil that was supported by the UK looks very good to us...." Here governments have aligned themselves with others who have had similar concerns and have attempted to provide the Chair with particular language for the next version of the document.

As I listen to the interventions being made, in addition to attempting to document the content of the interventions as closely as possible, I am also attentive to the ways in which Observer participants—clustered around placards that identify them as various categories of non-governmental participants—are responding to the statements being made. Having attended meetings associated with the CBD since 2009, by 2018 I am familiar with many of the specific issues that are important to CSOs and Indigenous Peoples

Organizations (IPOs). The majority of the issues that governments deliberate are not of keen importance to most of the non-governmental participants. However, as the next segment of this chapter illustrates, there are several dynamics that become highly politicized for Indigenous Peoples and other participants who raise concerns about the implications of certain deliberations.

FROM ETHNOGRAPHY TO ANALYSIS

In the preceding segments of this chapter, I have introduced my orientation to the United Nations, illustrated ethnographically some of the aspects of the research site, and pointed to the fact that the UN represents a site that is simultaneously local and global. Applying the ontology of institutional ethnography to this site, I have maintained a sense of the local in the everyday actualities of people's work as they orient that work toward the various documents being negotiated. This is work that is made invisible in the final meeting documents or "policy outcomes." Simultaneously, though, I have kept an eye to the trans-local—those elements which transcend the actualities of people's experiences in the UN, yet which also serve to coordinate those actualities. In the following two sections, I move outward from the descriptive ethnographic snippets to briefly analyze the implications of some of the dynamics I have observed. In the two examples that follow, while I significantly gloss over many of the finer details in order to make a broader analysis, I point to some of the dynamics that strategy work is organized to influence as participants are invested in particular language for specific identifiable reasons.

FROM ETHNOGRAPHY TO ANALYSIS: CLIMATE, BIOLOGICAL DIVERSITY, AND DEFORESTATION

Leading up to the 1992 UNCED negotiations in Rio, participants perceived that global environmental problems could reasonably be separated into specific, discrete issue areas such as climate, biological diversity, or desertification. However, in the decades that have followed the historic establishment of the global MEAs that originated in the UNCED meetings, it has become increasingly clear that there are significant points of overlap between the various conventions. Increasing desertification is accompanied by biodiversity loss. A changing global climate leads to desertification as well as to other threats to biological diversity. Likewise, the solutions that are proposed under various fora can have implications for other policy-making processes. There have been several cases where the solutions proposed under the Climate Convention have had implications for the negotiations under the CBD. Within this context, the actualities of deforestation have been increasingly politicized, as forests have become pertinent to the climate deliberations in multiple ways.

The association of forests with climate policy negotiations has created a context where other intergovernmental bodies have attempted to assert their relevance in this area. The climate deliberations are clearly the most politicized of all of the UN environmental deliberations. These negotiations receive the most attention in the press, the most participation from Observer organizations, and heightened scrutiny by governments as well. The relative prominence of climate negotiations vis-à-vis other UN bodies has served as a point of leverage for bodies with a stake in forests to seek resources. Likewise, the negotiations have shed light on what some stakeholders consider to be problematic elements of the environmental negotiations. For example, the implications of viewing forests through a fairly narrow lens of carbon sequestration, and the potential human rights and land tenure issues that arise once previously disregarded forests become commoditized, are issues that organize the work of many Observer participants in climate policy.

Here, I use the politicization of deforestation—and avoiding deforestation—as a particular point of departure from which to elucidate the various interests that become entangled in global environmental governance—interests that are brought to the table by governments, Convention Secretariats, and other stakeholders. Specifically, forests have become the focus of increasing attention since their emergence as key components of UN climate negotiations under "Reducing Emissions from Deforestation and Forest Degradation" (REDD). In spite of the fact that a forest policy process also came out of UNCED, the focus on forests under REDD negotiations within the UNFCCC created a context whereby far more emphasis was placed on examining the existence of forests. However, this was not always done in a way that was consistent with the policy terrain of either the forest policy process or the Convention on Biological Diversity. Due to the relative lack of overlap between the various bodies, as I discuss below, the manner in which forests were becoming important to governments was being defined by the exigencies of reduction of greenhouse gas emissions.

To elaborate, in addition to deliberating ways to reduce greenhouse gas emissions from the burning of fossil fuels, the climate negotiations began to take a closer look at deforestation and other land use changes. This followed the 2007 report of the Intergovernmental Panel on Climate Change (IPCC), the science body associated with the UNFCCC, which confirmed that over 17% of anthropogenic greenhouse gas emissions were emanating from the forestry sector (IPCC, 2014, p. 36). This quantification merely added to the broad scope of research on carbon sequestration and land use change that has been conducted over the past several decades. However, exactly how forests are addressed under the negotiations has been a point of intense contention. For example, many participants in the climate negotiations have been concerned about the ways in which a focus on maintaining carbon sinks—the carbon-absorbing and retaining properties of forests—effectively lets governments off the hook as far as reducing fossil fuel-related emissions.

A "REDD regime," the framework under which REDD was emerging in the policy deliberations and in the programs designed to implement those policies, began to garner criticism from some participants in the climate policy process. Some participants noted that the negotiation and implementation of REDD policy frameworks was jeopardizing both biological diversity and land tenure of indigenous peoples. As forests became commodified under the REDD policies in order to incentivize their conservation, various outcomes were predicted or observed. Many Indigenous Peoples and local communities found that their access to forest areas and resources were being compromised now that forests were given an economic value under REDD frameworks. In addition, though, as "forests" were not clearly defined under the REDD protocols, governments could effectively engage in replacing "natural" forests with monocrop plantations. Oil palm and eucalyptus could effectively "count" as forests under this broad definition. With carbon sequestration as a goal, other ecosystem services of forests could be eliminated and the program would still be compliant with the REDD policy framework. Thus, Observer organizations (including Indigenous Peoples Organizations) began to mobilize to influence the REDD policy process as it was being negotiated under the auspices of the climate deliberations. REDD became a point of engagement for many organizations concerned about the rights of Indigenous Peoples and the destruction of forest biological diversity. Many engaged in this process are wary of the potential for the policies to exacerbate existing inequalities associated with access to resources. This point of analysis clearly moves beyond thick ethnographic description and into the realm of sketching out the implications of certain policy outcomes. The trans-local imperatives of economic growth have shaped governments' enthusiasm with REDD policies, as well as their implementation in ways that allow for transforming forests into plantations. This, then, is part of the broader terrain that becomes a point of contention for participants in the climate negotiations. The following example likewise explores some of the issues that have become contentious in the negotiations under the Convention on Biological Diversity. As with REDD, the analysis below is predicated on explicating the competing interests of various participants engaged in the negotiations. Thus, the strategic work of participants revolves around how it is that they attempt to influence the policy processes to reflect their concerns.

FROM ETHNOGRAPHY TO ANALYSIS: STRATEGIC USE OF LANGUAGE, THE CONVENTION ON BIOLOGICAL DIVERSITY, AND "INDIGENOUS PEOPLES"

When I first entered the negotiations associated with the Convention on Biological Diversity in 2009, several governments took issue with attempts to include the language of "Indigenous Peoples" in negotiating texts. Many governments argued that the agreed-upon language of the Convention was "indigenous and local communities," often abbreviated as "ILCs." When I say that governments took issue with this language, this is the sort of thing that becomes invisible in final texts. One can see what sort of terminology ends up in texts that are sent to the next deliberating body, but debates over terms and bracketed text are no longer visible.

As I illustrated in the ethnographic snippet related to the CBD SBSTTA in Montreal in 2018, there is much back and forth between governments during any particular negotiating session. In order to understand how a particular text comes to be, one must be present during the negotiations to listen to interventions and to query participants as to what the significance of particular language is. In the case of the language of Indigenous Peoples, the governments that rejected the terminology understood that the term was not a neutral one—it was not merely a case of changing the language from "indigenous and local communities" to "indigenous peoples." In fact, the term "indigenous peoples" has a much stronger association with sovereignty, self-determination, and many other elements that IPOs have been struggling to obtain within the intergovernmental system for decades. This is precisely why I choose to capitalize the term as it is more in line with the objectives of decades of work in which Indigenous Peoples have been engaging in order to advocate for self-determination. In the CBD in 2009, governments (Parties) that were not interested in fully recognizing the sovereignty of Indigenous Peoples were resistant to giving up the agreed-upon language of ILCs. Repeatedly, during negotiations that were relevant to Indigenous Peoples, such as those around the traditional knowledge associated with genetic resources and the rights of Indigenous Peoples, I witnessed the attempts by some participants in the process to get the language of "indigenous peoples" into the text, and the subsequent rejection of that terminology by other participants.

This particular example illustrates several things about intergovernmental negotiations. First, it illustrates the importance of documentary complexes that are established under a variety of disparate UN fora. Participants who want to strengthen the language of a particular text will often point to other negotiating bodies where Parties have signed on to agreements that contain stronger language. In addition, it represents the significance of language, as there is nothing necessarily inherent in the terms "indigenous peoples" versus "indigenous and local communities" aside from the meanings that are imbued in them within the context of the deliberations. Over the course of several years of observing meetings associated with the CBD I watched as this point of contention evolved.

The legacy of ILCs was established in the origins of the CBD, as it was negotiated in 1992 through UNCED. The text of the Convention uses language that Indigenous Peoples perceive to be weaker (ILCs versus Indigenous Peoples). Therefore, participants who wished to strengthen the language of the Convention regularly referenced agreed-upon language from other policy processes. Those who wished to maintain the language referenced the "consensus texts" that already existed in the CBD. In addition, those who wanted a strengthening of language aligned themselves with specific concepts, such as "Traditional Knowledge" (TK) or "Traditional Environmental Knowledge" (TEK), both of which are recognized and codified within a variety of agreements and work programs taking place under the auspices of the UN. The references to TK or TEK allowed participants to tap into policy processes where Indigenous Peoples often played more of a central participatory role as a result of their relevance to the agenda items. The original text of the Convention itself contains language associated with Traditional Knowledge, and thus opens up opportunities for Indigenous Peoples' participation in the work of the CBD. This language paves the way for participants to strategically work to strengthen the language in the texts in that it ties Indigenous Peoples as holders of knowledge about biodiversity into the conservation of that biodiversity. It opens opportunities for Indigenous Peoples to demand a more central role in negotiations and to thus have more power over strengthening the language in the texts.

At the third Conference of Parties of the CBD (COP3) in 1996, just four years after the original signing of the Convention, the International Indigenous Forum on Biodiversity (IIFB) was formed by Indigenous participants. They made the argument that many of the policy discussions related to biological diversity, and not only those related to TK, were also relevant to Indigenous Peoples. Thus, a strategic move was made by Indigenous participants to push for a coherent approach to policy in the name of participation of relevant stakeholders. Subsequently, the IIFB has been able to advocate as a block for particular policy positions. As many of the participants in the IIFB are also engaged in other UN fora, such as the United Nations Permanent Forum on Indigenous Issues (UNPFII), the passage of the United Nations Declaration on the Rights of Indigenous Peoples (UNDRIP) by the General Assembly of the UN in 2007 served as an important point of leverage for those engaged in CBD negotiations. As was articulated by the IIFB in their opening statement to the CBD COP10 in 2010,

> In 2007, the United Nations General Assembly recognized and affirmed that Indigenous Peoples have equal rights and freedoms to all other peoples of the world. ... Our status and our rights, as Indigenous Peoples, are universally recognized ...We do not want Parties to this Convention to dismiss our relevance or importance. When the Convention was negotiated and adopted in 1992 it did not take due account of our existence and importance as Indigenous Peoples nor our responsibilities for our own territories. Much has occurred in these past two decades to bring our issues to the fore so we do thank the Parties for that partial progress to date. (Field Notes, CBD COP10, 29 October 2010, Nagoya, Japan)

Clearly, governments did not immediately respond to the signing of UNDRIP by incorporating the same language in the CBD, as up until 2017 I still witnessed governments reject the inclusion of the language of "indigenous peoples" instead of "indigenous and local communities" in CBD negotiations. However, the years of efforts by Indigenous Peoples eventually resulted in a change since by the end of 2017 the term "indigenous peoples" remained uncontested in the texts. This does not seem earth shattering by any means. However, without engaging in the negotiations, one would be able to only follow the texts and see the change in terminology. What would be missing would be the actualities of work that are organized around the strategic attempts to influence policy processes. For example, the statements of Observers such as the IIFB cannot be included in the texts unless governments take up the language themselves. Without that support, observers can speak with passion and conviction, but there is no evidence of that position beyond the meeting room walls.

Conclusions: Putting the Pieces Together

I began this chapter asserting that the ontology of institutional ethnography can be applied to sites such as the UN in order to explicate and to make visible the work that people do to enact what is often relegated to global environmental governance. As individuals engage in the strategy work that is designed to influence policy processes, and as they deploy their complex work knowledges, the making of policy is done by actual people in identifiable locations. As these last two segments have illustrated, it is possible to move from ethnography to analysis—to identify broader themes and concerns that extend beyond the actual work of individuals, but that serve to coordinate that work. Here, I advocate for deploying methods that are consistent with ethnography in order to shed light not only on the work of practitioners, but also to speak to the significance of broader relations of ruling that serve to organize that work. I have endeavored to illustrate how institutional ethnography can be applied to sites that are often seen through the abstracting lens of global governance. Instead of starting in categories, I have pointed to the sort of understanding one can derive from putting all of the pieces together—from following policy processes over time, observing negotiations, talking to participants, reading documents that are relevant to the policy terrain, and multiple other methods deployed. These methods have allowed me to gain a strong sense of both the actualities of people's work as well as the broader terrain that organizes that work in important ways.

Notes

1. Throughout this chapter, I use examples from meetings and negotiations. These are close approximations of verbatim transcriptions based on the notes I have taken at the time.
2. For the purposes of readability for audiences who are less familiar with UN deliberations, I have chosen at some points throughout the chapter to maintain the full definition rather than just the acronym.

REFERENCES

Blok, A. (2010). Mapping the Super-Whale: Towards a mobile ethnography of situated globalities. *Mobilities, 5*(4), 507–528.

Burawoy, M., Blum, J. A., George, S., Gille, Z., Gowan, T., Haney, L., ... Thayer, M. (2000). *Global ethnography: Forces, connections, and imaginations in a postmodern world*. Berkeley: University of California Press.

Eastwood, L. E. (2005). *The social organization of policy: An institutional ethnography of UN forest deliberations*. New York, NY: Routledge Press.

Grahame, P. R., & Grahame, K. M. (2017). Institutional ethnography. In G. Ritzer (Ed.), *Blackwell encyclopedia of sociology*. New Jersey: Blackwell Publishing. Blackwell Reference Online.

Harper, R. (1998). *Inside the IMF: An ethnography of documents, technology and organisational action*. London: Taylor & Francis.

Intergovernmental Panel on Climate Change (IPCC). (2014). *Climate Change 2014: Impacts, Adaptation, and Vulnerability. Part A: Global and Sectoral Aspects. Contribution of Working Group II to the Fifth Assessment Report of the Intergovernmental Panel on Climate Change*. Cambridge, UK: Cambridge University Press.

Lapegna, P. (2009). Ethnographers of the world... united? Current debates on the ethnographic study of "globalization.". *Journal of World-systems Research, XV*(1), 3–24.

Ridzi, F. (2009). *Selling welfare reform: Work-first and the new common sense of employment*. New York, NY: NYU Press.

Smith, D. E. (2005). *Institutional ethnography: A sociology for people*. Oxford: Alta Mira Press.

Tsing, A. (2005). *Friction: An ethnography of global connection*. Princeton, NJ: Princeton University Press.

CHAPTER 13

Regulating the Duty to Consult: Exploring the Textually Mediated Nature of Indigenous Dispossession in Chile

Magdalena Ugarte

On June 28, 2018, the Supreme Court of Chile ruled to revoke the environmental permit for the construction of the Doña Alicia hydroelectric project on the Cautin River, Araucanía region. Several Mapuche communities cheered the decision, which was the result of years of social mobilization, grassroots activism, and legal action in order to prevent hydroelectric projects from damaging the river. For the Mapuche nation the river is sacred. In their ruling, the judges stated that the proposal's significant effects on surrounding communities had not been adequately considered by the government, despite the obvious impacts the project was going to have on the river's ecosystem. While that project was paralyzed, a year and a half year later another hydroelectric project is already in the plans, threatening the Cautin River once again. It seems like history keeps repeating itself.

This story is just a snapshot of the historically tense relationship between the state and Indigenous peoples. Frictions are not surprising given the ways in which policy and other forms of institutionalized state action have enabled

---

This research was supported by an International Development Research Centre (IDRC) Doctoral Award, a Social Sciences and Humanities Research Council (SSHRC) Doctoral Fellowship, and a Bottom Billion Fieldwork Fund from the Liu Institute at the University of British Columbia.

M. Ugarte (✉)
Ryerson University, Toronto, ON, Canada
e-mail: magdalena@ryerson.ca

© The Author(s) 2021
P. C. Luken and S. Vaughan (eds.), *The Palgrave Handbook of Institutional Ethnography*,
https://doi.org/10.1007/978-3-030-54222-1_13

Indigenous dispossession over the centuries. For the Mapuche nation, historical dispossession consolidated with the military occupation of their ancestral territory in the mid-1800, a few decades after Chile declared independence from Spain in 1810. Since then, the Mapuche have lost most of their traditional territory, being confined to just 5% of the lands they have occupied ancestrally (Comisión Económica para América Latina y el Caribe [CEPAL] & Alianza Territorial Mapuche [ATM], 2012).

State action has contributed to the structural impoverishment and dispossession of Indigenous peoples both through active land usurpation and displacement—where the discipline of planning has played a key role with tools like mapping, surveying, naming, and town building (Alvarado Lincopi, 2015; Boisier, 2007)—and through "softer" techniques of social and cultural control, like compulsory public schooling and competitive grants-based access to economic development funds (Antileo, Cárcamo-Huechante, Calfío Montalva, & Huinca-Piutrin, 2015; Castro, 2003). Today, while 12.8% of the population in Chile is Indigenous, 30.8% of them live in poverty (19.9% for non-Indigenous people), 4.7% are illiterate (compared to 3%), 23.5% experience malnutrition (compared to 17.2%), and almost 80% neither speak nor understand their traditional language (Government of Chile, 2017). Territorial conflicts and land claims have spiked in recent decades, and the ongoing presence of militarized police marks the everyday life of hundreds of Indigenous communities (Toledo Llancaqueo, 2005). Many tensions concern private or public investment projects on Indigenous lands, actively promoted by the government in a political-economic system that relies heavily on the export of commodities.

In this context, recent developments in international law have created expectations regarding potential institutional transformations. In 2007, the General Assembly of the United Nations (UN) passed the Declaration on the Rights of Indigenous Peoples (hereafter the Declaration) with Chile's vote in favor. One year later, the country ratified the International Labour Organization's[1] (ILO) Indigenous and Tribal Peoples Convention 169 (hereafter Convention 169). These two international agreements set standards regarding the protection and promotion of Indigenous rights, some of which have direct implications for state-directed planning. This chapter focuses on one of them: the duty to consult with Indigenous peoples. According to Convention 169, Indigenous peoples shall be consulted whenever a government administrative or legislative measure might affect them directly (ILO, 1989). The practice of consultation has thus become a key site where Indigenous and state planning interests meet.

Taking as a point of departure the experience of Indigenous peoples who are recurrently affected by the imposition of state policies, this chapter adopts an Institutional Ethnography (IE) stance to explore how state planning with Indigenous peoples happens today by focusing on the institution of consultation. Turner (2006) argues that contemporary "planning processes are often talked about by practitioners as a *conversation* or *consultation* where different actors *have something to say*," adding that "*consultation* is a peculiar governing work process" (p. 153, emphasis in original). In order to understand this peculiar governing work, instead of exploring how specific consultation processes have unfolded or how consultation regulations have been applied, I examine the creation of a key governing text that regulates the duty to consult in Chile, known as Supreme Decree 66 (hereafter DS66). I consider the process of regulation-making as a key space where the relationship between the state and Indigenous peoples gets enacted, where the ruling relations that shape planning practice become visible. My focus, then, is "how governing texts are brought into being" (Smith & Turner, 2014, p. 65) and the particular ways in which they organize the actions of government planners in relation to Indigenous peoples.

An examination of the text-reader conversations (Smith, 2005) shaping the creation of DS66 reveals how selective intertextual hierarchies—in particular references to the Chilean Constitution and to court rulings that confirm its supremacy—reaffirm the hegemony of state power and authority, despite the country's supposed adherence to stricter international human rights standards that reaffirm Indigenous self-determination. At the same time, the creation of legal categories that constrain what government measures should be consulted and what it means to affect Indigenous peoples directly, excludes many matters and people from being consulted outright, and abstracts "individualized [Indigenous] experiences into terminology that is recognizable as being part of the work of the [governmental] bodies" (Eastwood, 2006, p. 193). Through standardizing practices, consultation regulation serves to make Indigenous rights in Chile amenable to existing workflows and institutional frameworks, restricting potential courses of action to those that avoid disrupting economic activities and state operations, thus negating Indigenous self-determination. I now turn to explore how this happens.

The Context: Chile and the Landscape of International Indigenous Rights

Two international agreements are the most relevant to my examination of state planning in Chile today: Convention 169 and the Declaration. Convention 169 was adopted by the International Labour Organization in 1989 and endorsed by Chile in 2008. It promotes the full control of Indigenous peoples "over their own institutions, ways of life and economic development and to maintain and develop their identities, languages and religions" (ILO, 1989). The Declaration was adopted by the UN in 2007 by a majority in favor, including Chile. It reaffirms and expands Convention 169's spirit, affirming the human rights and fundamental freedoms of Indigenous peoples and individuals, and setting out specific rights with regards to identity, language, health, and education, among others (UN, 2007). It also highlights the right of Indigenous peoples to preserve and strengthen their own institutions, cultures, and traditions, prohibiting any form of discrimination against them.

As a legally binding agreement that becomes domestic law once ratified by a country, one of the key contributions of the Convention to international Indigenous rights is to establish the duty to consult (Anaya, 2006). According to Article 6.1 (a), countries shall "consult the peoples concerned, through appropriate procedures and in particular through their representative institutions, whenever consideration is being given to legislative or administrative measures which may affect them directly." Article 6.2 further adds that "the consultations carried out in application of this Convention shall be undertaken, in good faith and in a form appropriate to the circumstances, with the objective of achieving agreement or consent to the proposed measures" (ILO, 1989). Indeed, the ILO has referred to the duty to consult as the cornerstone of Convention 169, the foundational principle upon which all other provisions are based.

As this chapter will show, the practice of consultation in Chile is organized ideologically in relation to these and other governing texts. In order to meet this international standard, in 2011 the Government of Chile set in motion a process to create a mechanism to regulate the duty to consult. The result of that process is DS66, a domestic governing text that articulates the scope and depth of consultation adapting it to the country's reality.

Approaching Regulation-Making Ethnographically: Methodological Considerations

The analysis I present in these pages derives from my doctoral research, which involved a grounded investigation of state-led planning with Indigenous peoples in Chile. My inquiry started from a pragmatic concern for the foundational injustice of Indigenous dispossession in Chile. Departing from the overt marginalization described in the opening section, I wanted to explore how planning unfolds and if/how it contributes to perpetuating such injustice. Unlike much IE research (DeVault & McCoy, 2006), this work does not start by analyzing the grounded experience of Indigenous peoples who are the objects of consultation work as such. Instead, "the point of entry is in organizational work processes... studying how they are carried out, how they are discursively shaped, and how they organize other settings" (p. 22). According to Eastwood (2006), what is different about studying policy-making using IE is that most of the work revolves around producing new documents and texts, as opposed to activating specific forms or documents that are already embedded in particular work processes.

When I started my Ph.D., the Convention had entered into force in Chile just a couple of years before and conversations about how to implement the duty to consult dominated an important part of the Indigenous policy discourse. Given that the implications for planning practice seemed significant, I started to follow the process systematically. Examinations of consultation with Indigenous peoples in Chile often focus on the success or failure of specific consultation processes, or on general perceptions about consultation as an institution (Caniuqueo & Peralta, 2017). There are also analyses of the legal foundations of consultation as an obligation of the state, which delve into juridical debates, including the compensatory nature of Indigenous rights (Carmona, 2013). Other studies often focus on assessing implementation gaps, examining how well or how poorly the principles of consultation have been applied according to the ideal standards as expressed in international law instruments (Sanhueza, 2013).

Adopting a different angle, this inquiry is concerned with how the key governing text regulating Indigenous consultation in Chile was brought into being (Smith, 2006). How the process of implementation actually happened and the ways in which DS66 constructs consultation as an institutional practice. Grounded in IE's materialist ontology, I understand state planning as a set of institutional networks coming into being through the actions and activities of people, which are in turn mediated by the presence of texts that activate or prevent certain courses of action from becoming a reality. From this perspective, the practice of consultation is the result of "complexes of international agreements... and regulations implementing [it] at various levels of government" (Smith & Turner, 2014, p. 4).

In the context of the relationship between the Chilean state and Indigenous peoples, DS66 emerges as a key governing text. It directly affects how Indigenous policy will be carried out moving forward, defining the playing field regarding Indigenous involvement in decision-making regarding certain government measures, as I elaborate below. It acts as a regulatory text that assigns roles, allocates responsibilities, defines what is possible, and sets the limits for Indigenous and state action. It introduces specific terminology and establishes the duty to consult as an obligation of the state. Importantly, it outlines specific procedures, stages, and timelines, setting in motion government workflows.

Therefore, in order to understand how state planning in my country is socially organized and what the practice of consultation actually does for Indigenous peoples, I delved into how such governing text emerged in the first place. As Smith (2005) reminds us, regulatory texts establish agency, controlling and mobilizing the work of individuals through their provisions. It is only by unpacking the process by which DS66 was created that stories like the paralysation of the Doña Alicia hydroelectric project that opened the chapter can be more fully understood.

This research assumes that regulation-making is a space of struggle, contestation, and power. The negotiation of DS66 was to a great extent a negotiation of meanings about what futures would become possible at the expense of what others. Analyzing the negotiation and wording of a governing text meant to regulate future consultations, therefore, "make[s] visible the activities that have systematically been made invisible through the abstraction effected by the documentary reality" of institutions (Eastwood, 2006, p. 184).

REGULATING CONSULTATION: UNPACKING THE PRODUCTION OF A GOVERNING TEXT

DS66 was crafted over the course of three years, between March 2011 and March 2014, through a massive participatory planning process. The Government of Chile led a set of consecutive planning initiatives, which brought together the national government and Indigenous representatives with the explicit goal of creating a mutually agreed mechanism to regulate consultation. After an initial phase comprised of numerous meetings, information sessions, the presentation of government proposals and Indigenous counterproposals, a consensus table was established at the request of Indigenous leaders in order to draft together the wording of the regulation, article by article.

During all those years, I followed the process closely by collecting newspaper clippings, reviewing official documents and public statements, watching official videos of the consensus table sessions, and compiling a list of people who were directly involved in the process. The core of the analysis, however, draws on the seven-month fieldwork I conducted in Chile in 2014–2015, where I carried out extensive interviews with Indigenous leaders and government officials who were involved in the actual creation of DS66.[2] The fieldwork also gave me access to official documents and reports, including different versions of DS66 showing the evolution of its wording and the Consultation's final report, which summarizes the process in detail and justifies many of the decisions made. Following a methodological path similar to Eastwood's (2006) examination of UN policy development, I focused on the actual workings involved in policy-making. These included the participants' use of insider's knowledge during the negotiations, and how particular legal terms and categories seek to capture a diversity of people's experiences in the final texts produced.

When in August 2012 the government released the first draft of DS66, the document included 27 articles. As a result of the negotiation between the government and Indigenous leaders over more than 30 consensus table sessions, some articles were removed, others were added or merged, and still others were substantially revised and rewritten in light of the counterproposals presented by Indigenous peoples. When the consensus table ended, 17 out of 20 articles had been agreed upon,[3] most of which concerned procedural matters such as stages and timelines, and operational definitions (Government of Chile, 2013). Still, three substantial disagreements remained: the definition of what administrative measures should be consulted, what it means to affect Indigenous peoples directly, and how to go about consultation processes related to investment projects with environmental impacts on Indigenous lands.

In what follows, I examine how DS66 was brought into being. I pay particular attention to how practitioners and Indigenous peoples negotiated the scope and wording of the text. The analysis "breaks open the work concealed behind those governing or boss texts known as 'policy,' making visible the skills and contentions of negotiating the language that will come into play in the representations of actualities they will govern" (Smith & Turner, 2014, p. 11).

Analyzing the practitioners' accounts of how they created DS66 and reading through key documents sheds light into three key dimensions of the social organization of state-led planning and the practice of consultation. First, the analysis shows how government officials crafted certain selective intertextual relations while making the regulation, which reinforce the supremacy of state power and authority. I focus on the action of excluding the Declaration and the constant references to the Chilean Constitution, and how these text-reader conversations strengthen the unquestioned imposition of institutional structures and Chilean sovereignty upon self-determining Indigenous peoples. Second, the examination shows how the production of legal categories and definitions constrains possible courses of action in ways that negate Indigenous self-determination. I focus on the definition of measures to be consulted and what it means to affect Indigenous peoples directly, and how through these conceptual constructs "other possibilities disappear from view" (Wilson & Pence, 2006, p. 211) that have direct material implications for Indigenous peoples. Finally, the analysis reveals how consultation legislation standardizes and proceduralizes Indigenous rights, embedding the duty to consult within existing government workflows to avoid paralyzing state operations, and to minimize the chances that public and private investment projects—which are key to Chile's economic growth—are threatened by the exercise of Indigenous rights. The chapter concludes by reflecting on how these textual practices ultimately reproduce Indigenous dispossession today although under softer, more covert veils, now under the auspices of international law and human rights.

"The Declaration Is Not Binding": Selective Intertextual Relations

DS66 did not emerge from scratch. It was brought into being in relation to other pre-existing texts that were used as a baseline for its wording, some of which are explicitly acknowledged in the opening paragraphs of the document (Fig. 13.1). As Eastwood (2006) puts it, government organizations produce texts "that have clear connections both to prior negotiating processes and larger discursive terrains" (p. 189). The actual production of this governing text involved the initial definition of its scope—a sort of duty to consult playing field—as well as the specifics necessary to govern future courses of action regarding why, when, and how consultations should take place.

The Constitutional Tribunal's Ruling

The need for DS66 emerged directly from Convention 169, specifically from Article 6 that concerns Indigenous consultation, as explained earlier. The Convention is thus the key governing text behind the duty to consult from

REPÚBLICA DE CHILE
MINISTERIO DE DESARROLLO SOCIAL
SUBSECRETARÍA DE SERVICIOS SOCIALES
LGB/FIU/MJDV/MAM/HWO/TPP

APRUEBA REGLAMENTO QUE REGULA EL PROCEDIMIENTO DE CONSULTA ÍNDIGENA EN VIRTUD DEL ARTÍCULO 6 N° 1 LETRA A) Y N° 2 DEL CONVENIO N° 169 DE LA ORGANIZACIÓN INTERNACIONAL DEL TRABAJO Y DEROGA NORMATIVA QUE INDICA.

DECRETO SUPREMO N° 66

SANTIAGO, 15 NOV 2013

VISTOS:

Lo dispuesto en los artículos 32 N° 6 y 35 de la Constitución Política de la República; en el Decreto con Fuerza de Ley N° 1/19.653, de 2000, del Ministerio Secretaría General de la Presidencia que fijó el texto refundido, coordinado y sistematizado de la ley N° 18.575, Orgánica Constitucional de Bases Generales de la Administración del Estado; en la Ley N° 19.880, que Establece Bases de los Procedimientos Administrativos que Rigen los Actos de los Órganos de la Administración del Estado; en la Ley N° 19.253 que Establece Normas sobre Protección, Fomento y Desarrollo de los Indígenas, y Crea la Corporación Nacional de Desarrollo Indígena; en el decreto supremo N° 124, de 2009, del Ministerio de Planificación, actual Ministerio de Desarrollo Social, que reglamentó el artículo 34 de la Ley N° 19.253; en los artículos 6 N° 1 letra a) y N° 2 del Convenio N° 169 de la Organización Internacional del Trabajo sobre Pueblos Indígenas y Tribales en Países Independientes y en la Resolución N° 1600, de 2008, de la Contraloría General de la República, que Fija Normas sobre Exención del Trámite de Toma de Razón.

CONSIDERANDO:

Que, con fecha 27 de junio de 1989, la Conferencia General de la Organización Internacional del Trabajo, en su Septuagésima Sexta Reunión, adoptó el Convenio N° 169 sobre Pueblos Indígenas y Tribales en Países Independientes.

Que, el Congreso Nacional dio su aprobación al proyecto de acuerdo aprobatorio de dicho convenio; siendo depositado el instrumento de ratificación con fecha 15 de septiembre de 2008.

Que, el referido Convenio N° 169 de la O.I.T, fue promulgado por medio del Decreto Supremo N° 236, de 2008, del Ministerio de Relaciones Exteriores.

Fig. 13.1 First page of Supreme Decree 66 (DS66) (*Note* Some of the legal instruments the opening paragraphs of DS66 make reference to include the Chilean Constitution, the Indigenous Law, the Constitutional Tribunal's 2008 ruling, and the laws that govern the administration of the state, among other documents. *Source* Government of Chile [2014])

the time Chile ratified it in 2008. However, while Convention 169 was being discussed by the Chilean Congress prior to its endorsement there were several attempts by elected officials to delay, interrupt, or openly block its ratification. Its opponents argued that it ran against the Chilean Constitution and in 2000 requested the Constitutional Tribunal (TC), an independent government body whose main role is to ensure all laws adhere to the Chilean Constitution, to pronounce whether the agreement violated Chile's legal frameworks.

The Tribunal issued a ruling in 2008 and confirmed that the Convention did not contravene the Constitution. It further clarified that Article 6 was self-executing, meaning that it would automatically become domestic law once Convention 169 was ratified. However, the ruling also included several additional considerations that constrain consultation. Section 13 of the ruling (Fig. 13.2) explicitly states that the duty to consult:

> Shall not, *of course*, be understood as implying the exercise of sovereignty [by Indigenous peoples], since [sovereignty], as clearly stipulated in the [Constitution], essentially resides in the Nation and is exercised by the people through plebiscite and periodical elections, as well as by the authorities the Constitution itself stipulates. The method of consultative participation established in [Convention 169] shall not take the form of a plebiscite or a binding popular consultation either, since the [Constitution] regulates those modes of participation… *in a way that is incompatible with such a possibility*… It shall be understood that where Article 6 number 2 of [Convention 169] stipulates that the goal of consultation is to reach an agreement regarding the proposed [government] measures, it does not imply a mandatory negotiation, but *it constitutes a way of gathering opinions, which will not be binding nor will affect the exclusive power of the authorities the Constitution stipulates*… With this understanding, the [articles of Convention 169 under discussion] are fully compatible with democratic participation as established in… the [Constitution], and with the existence and exercise of [Chilean] sovereignty. (Government of Chile, 2008, emphasis and translation mine)

Bases Generales de la Administración del Estado, 19.175, sobre Gobierno y Administración Regional, y 18.695, de Municipalidades, respectivamente;

DECIMO TERCERO. Que la consulta a los pueblos interesados que dispone el N° 1 del artículo 6° del Acuerdo remitido no podrá, desde luego, entenderse que implique el ejercicio de soberanía, pues ella, conforme al claro tenor de lo dispuesto en el artículo 5° de la Carta Fundamental, reside esencialmente en la Nación y se ejerce por el pueblo a través del plebiscito y de elecciones periódicas y, también, por las autoridades que la propia Constitución establece. La forma de participación consultiva que la norma en examen contempla tampoco podría adoptar la modalidad de un plebiscito o de una consulta popular vinculante, pues la Carta Fundamental regula estos modos de participación, de manera incompatible con tal posibilidad, en los artículos 118 y 128 de la Constitución;

DECIMO CUARTO. Que ha de entenderse que al disponer el artículo 6, N° 2, del Acuerdo remitido, que la finalidad de las consultas es la de llegar a un acuerdo acerca de las medidas propuestas, no importa una negociación obligatoria, sino que constituye una forma de recabar opinión, misma que no resultará vinculante, ni afectará las atribuciones privativas de las autoridades que la Constitución Política de la República establece. En este entendido el precepto resulta plenamente compatible con la participación democrática que contempla el artículo 1° de la Carta Fundamental y con la radicación de la soberanía y de su ejercicio que contempla el artículo 5° de la misma Ley Fundamental;

Fig. 13.2 Article 13 of Constitutional Tribunal's ruling (2008) (*Source* Government of Chile [2008])

The Tribunal's ruling is thus another key text governing the duty to consult and shaping the development of DS66. Very importantly, the document reveals how the members of the Tribunal read and interpreted the overarching international governing text that is the Convention. What do the creators of the ruling do in practice? By mediating between the Convention's understanding of consultation and Chile's existing legal frameworks, they produce a sort of selective intertextual hierarchy, creating a constrained landscape that limits a deeper engagement with and reduces the scope of Indigenous rights.

The creators of the document place the Chilean Constitution as the unquestioned point of reference. In doing so, they reaffirm the supremacy of state power and authority, which actually takes precedence over international human rights standards such as the Convention. Despite the country's endorsement of the Convention and of its vote in favor of the Declaration, both of which reaffirm Indigenous self-determination, the ruling minimizes the potential impact of these agreements. First, the ruling explicitly brings Indigenous peoples under the veil of Chile's sovereignty. It assumes that ("of course") any discussion about Indigenous peoples' right to influence government decisions that affect them exists within the margins of Chile's supreme political power, and that the duty to consult will never affect the "exclusive power of the authorities the Constitution stipulates." Regarding consultation practice specifically, the creators of the ruling ensure that it remains at the level of "gathering opinions, which will not be binding," clearly subsuming Indigenous consultation within existing Chilean legal frameworks related to democratic participation. In doing so, they foreclose the possibility of creating a space for actual negotiation that might compensate for historical exclusion of Indigenous peoples from decision-making. Finally, by framing the discussion in terms of *compatibility*, the creators of the ruling grant Indigenous rights an inferior status in relation to "Chilean" rights established in the Constitution.

Leaving the Declaration Aside

The intertextual hierarchy just described connects to another selective intertextuality: the exclusion of the UN Declaration from the development of DS66. Chile's vote in favor of the Declaration was seen as a political indication that some movement regarding the protection of Indigenous rights was taking place in the country. There was an expectation among Indigenous rights advocates that Convention 169 should be read and interpreted in light of other relevant standards that were stricter and further strengthened Indigenous rights.

The government officials I interviewed described how they deliberately excluded the Declaration from the conversations. Government Planner 1 admitted that the Declaration "came up at the Consensus Table at the request of Indigenous peoples. But from the perspective of the state, *there was never a plan* to include it or to regulate it, or to use it as an input" (emphasis mine). He further added that "[Convention 169] is the applicable law. [The

Declaration] is not binding. One commits to it, *one tries to respect it*, but it is not an obligation for the state" (emphasis mine). This exclusion reveals the spirit guiding the practices of the government officials at the consensus table negotiations. The rules of the game were the jurisdiction of the state and were not up for negotiation. As Indigenous Leader 1 explained, "international agreements and international law were not touched [by government officials] because it wasn't favorable for them... They turned to the Constitution [instead, arguing] that they could not go [too far in the negotiations] because of the Constitution." This passage reinforces a crucial issue introduced in the previous section, namely the tautological nature of Chilean law—how legal decisions are recursively linked to and justified in relation to other pieces of legislation. The supremacy of state institutions superseded any consideration regarding the spirit of Convention 169. Government Lawyer 1 explained that leaving the Declaration aside was done "in [a] spirit of prudence."

Some readers could argue that this is not really an intertextual relation, since the Declaration is *not* a text directly shaping DS66. However, international agreements are not just referential. As Anishinaabe scholar Sheryl Lightfoot (2016) argues, the UN Declaration is meant to be "a persuasive moral and political tool to push state actors toward a new vision and new global imaginings that can accommodate Indigenous ways of being, and thinking beyond the existing international law and the constraints of state sovereignty" (p. 64). As such, the Declaration "is a political document that became part of the international human rights consensus and its principles are, in some sense, morally binding on all state conduct whether or not an individual state voted for it" (p. 66).

By placing the Declaration in the sphere of the ideal, government officials disregarded its spirit and substantial contributions to Indigenous rights standards, particularly all references to the notion of free, prior, and informed consent (FPIC), which goes well beyond Convention 169's notion of consultation. FPIC seeks to "restore to indigenous peoples control over their lands and resources, [... as well as] to redress the power imbalance between indigenous peoples and States, with a view to forging new partnerships based on rights and mutual respect between parties" (United Nations-Human Rights Council, 2018, p. 4). In doing so, FPIC openly engages with Indigenous self-determination. Very importantly, it "also suggests the possibility for indigenous peoples to make a different proposal or suggest a different model" (p. 5), something that terrified Chilean government officials.

Excluding the Declaration from the production of DS66 is not inherently problematic. It is problematic because it reveals the ruling relations shaping the duty to consult in Chile. It signifies the imposition of the government's will over Indigenous expectations for how consultation as *their* right should be approached and negates Indigenous political authority. The exclusion is also problematic because it openly seeks to limit the state's engagement with Indigenous self-determination, which includes territorial rights and the material consequences derived from Indigenous peoples exercising forms of social, political, and spatial organization that pre-date the state.

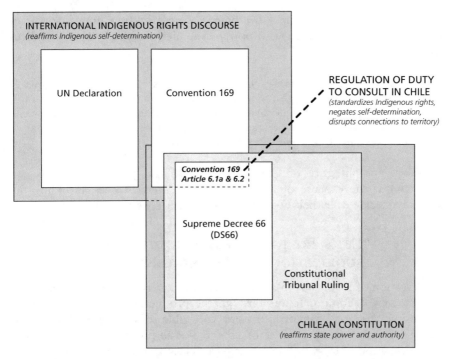

Fig. 13.3 Selective intertextual relations shaping the regulation of the duty to consult in Chile

As a whole, what do these intertextual relations mean in practice? Figure 13.3 outlines the key texts DS66 enters into dialogue with, and how these relations produce a constrained institutional and legal landscape for consultation in Chile. On the one hand, these selective relations reduce the scope of the duty to consult and limit engagement with Indigenous rights. The refusal to read Convention 169 in light of the Declaration and the insistence on referring to domestic legislation instead—in particular the Constitution and the Tribunal's ruling—show how the supremacy of state authority was never questioned. On the other hand, these decisions turn the duty to consult toward procedure as opposed to substance, as several clauses and conditions throughout the document constrain the spirit of Convention 169, as the next section will show. Government officials were able to move the conversation away from broader debates about Indigenous self-determination, FPIC, territorial control, and political authority. Instead, they placed the focus on operational matters and reduced debates about the duty to consult to negotiations about a usable consultation mechanism. Besides the obvious proceduralization, excluding the Declaration from the conversation also indicates the supremacy of western understandings of what legal agreements should be followed (i.e., binding ones) and which ones are just referential according to the Government, demonstrating how intertextual relations are always infused with power dynamics. Smith (2006) reminds us that:

> Texts don't achieve the capacity to regulate just by their existence... [A given text] would have no *force*, that is, no capacity to effect a change... had it not an authorization by some body established under [government] rules having itself *under these regulatory texts* been accorded the capacity to create and authorize such a procedure. (pp. 81–82, emphasis in original)

In short, the integrity of Chile's sovereignty and political authority are protected at the expense of Indigenous people's experiences, including the ability to decide over their own priorities on their ancestral territories.

"Let's Try to Be Very Specific:" Legal Categorization and Meaning Negotiation

The creation of DS66 was to a great extent an exercise in legal categorization and concept definition. It was through the production of categories that a governing text was brought into being to enable some courses of action to become a reality at the expense of others. Not surprisingly given the stakes, the negotiation of the wording article by article at the consensus table became a site of contestation, as government officials and Indigenous leaders sought to agree on key terms. As Eastwood (2006) argues, it is through text that actual experiences get abstracted into standardized language that institutions can recognize. Therefore, "unveiling the ideological nature of these concepts" (p. 184) and the process by which particular terms become abstracted in the first place was a key task in this inquiry.

As I mentioned earlier, in the end no agreement was reached regarding three articles of DS66, all of which revolved around particular legal definitions: what administrative measures should be consulted, what it means that a government measure affects Indigenous peoples directly, and how investment projects on Indigenous lands should be consulted. Taken together, these articles go to the core of what consultation should be about since they elucidate what, when, and whom to consult. As Government Lawyer 1 said, the work of government officials:

> Was basically to define, to specify what had to be consulted. And an analysis was done and the conclusion was reached that it was necessary to offer a definition of administrative measures, [and] a definition of affecting [Indigenous peoples] directly that made consultation reasonable.

Essentially, these articles sought to draw boundaries regarding Indigenous peoples' identity and unique status, about authority to determine what counts as impact, and about impact quantification. These are the issues that trigger Indigenous consultation or not.

Eastwood (2006) has used the term "intentional institutional capture" to describe how practitioners involved in creating governing texts strategically translate their experiences and preferences into terminology that organizations can recognize and absorb. The process demands active efforts in order to ensure that the final texts align as much as possible with the practitioners' expectations. After much debate, the articles about defining administrative measures and affecting Indigenous peoples directly were merged into a single article, while the government decided to divert the discussion about investment projects by creating a parallel consultation mechanism within the environmental assessment system, as detailed below.

Defining Administrative Measures That Affect Indigenous Peoples Directly

Indigenous peoples advocated to be consulted on all administrative measures that might affect them. Government officials sought to narrow down the scope. Drawing on legal distinctions present in Chilean Administrative Law, government officials differentiated between measures so-called regulated (*regladas*) and discretional (*discrecionales*), with only the latter being subject to consultation. Government Lawyer 1 explained how they did a series of analyses regarding the notion of administrative measures, because Convention 169 does not specify; "it just talks about administrative measures... And administrative measures... according to Chile's Law of Administrative Procedures are a vast number of things.[It] can be a letter, a written notice, a report, a procedure conducted by a public agency." When I asked him for more details about how they actually went about this discussion, he said:

> Administrative measures have to be consulted *in order to reach an agreement. You [can only] reach an agreement regarding those things that can be [legally] stipulated...* And that is when the distinction between ruled and discretional measures came to be. And [we took a position] that only discretional measures would be consulted. In other words, those where the [relevant] authority can pronounce... against or in favor, reject or approve... So, then we started leaving aside [government] organs... the measures of which [we thought] should not be consulted. (emphasis mine)

This move excluded several measures Indigenous peoples consider that potentially could affect them, such as the planning stages of investment projects with potential environmental impacts on their lands, which according to Chile's environmental legislation can only be consulted after a project enters the environmental impact assessment system if certain conditions are met, as described below. This categorization gave precedence to Chilean legal frameworks over respect for Indigenous rights, echoing earlier discussions about selective intertextuality. That is, the need to make consultation manageable and reasonable according to state standards comes to the foreground again.

Discussing the institutional use of categories vis-à-vis Indigenous peoples in the US legal system, Wilson and Pence (2006) understand categorization work as "a distinctively Westernized way of pulling highly individualized situations or events into clearly delineated categories to organize how... practitioners perceive, discuss, and handle institutional business" (p. 210). In this process, "the information selected... at the intersection of an institution and people's everyday lives [is] put into a category as an expression of a given rule or procedure" (p. 210).

The discussion presented here clearly illustrates this point. Following Eastwood (2006), the experiences of Indigenous Peoples at the table—which simultaneously were different and shared commonalities—"were intended to be 'reorganized' so that they could be effectively directed... However... the language of the policy-making regime is not that of Indigenous communities. An entire worldview is encapsulated in the texts" (p. 195). In fact, Indigenous representatives involved in the creation of DS66 wanted to include the term worldview in the regulation, in order to expand the notion of direct impacts to encompass effects that are hard to capture in discrete western policy language. While the government made changes to the original wording of DS66 to include what they saw as volitional and intangible aspects—such as spirituality, culture, and traditions—they declined to refer to Indigenous worldviews. Government Lawyer 2 described their work as follows:

> At the beginning we had a catalogue [of measures that affected Indigenous peoples directly] that resembled the impacts [found] in the environmental legislation. And in the end that was changed to more cultural aspects [on the one hand] and more objective [aspects on the other], which is when Indigenous lands are affected... [The goal] was to encompass [the Indigenous] worldview. Because we also had a discussion at the [consensus] table, what is the Indigenous worldview? Because one is not able to understand.

In addition to distinguishing between discretional and ruled measures, and to refusing to use the term worldview and instead breaking down the notion into discrete aspects, another categorization seems relevant. Government officials pushed for the duty to consult only getting triggered when the impacts of a government measure are "significant and specific" to Indigenous peoples. This definition further restricts the depth of Indigenous rights by limiting the kinds of measures to be consulted based on the government's perceived intensity and scope. What is key here is that the state decides what is significant and specific, challenging Indigenous peoples' authority and ability to determine impact level and quantification.

Going back to the opening story, the hydroelectric project on the Cautin River was initially approved by the government precisely because there seemed to be no direct and significant impact on the surrounding communities. It was only when Indigenous peoples pushed for their broader understanding of impact—which was inseparable from a worldview that conceives the river as sacred—that it was possible to paralyze the project.

Investment Projects as a Separate Consultation Category

Indigenous peoples at the negotiation table wanted DS66 to regulate consultations related to investment projects with environmental impacts that might affect them, their territories, and their ways of life. However, according to Chilean legislation these kinds of consultations fall under the environmental impact assessment system (SEIA). In practice, the government approached this third disagreement by creating two parallel consultation mechanisms: one for investment projects called Supreme Decree 40 (DS40) and DS66 for other government measures.

Indigenous peoples advocated for a single consultation regulation because in practice most consultations carried out in Chile since the endorsement of Convention 169 have concerned investment projects, oftentimes related to extractive activities (Abogabir, 2014), as the opening story illustrates. What is most important, most investment projects that reach the SEIA only trigger the duty to consult when it is too late, i.e., initial exploration has begun, territories have already been exposed to environmental damage, or the industry lobby is well advanced.

In practice, drawing this boundary delays and reduces Indigenous peoples' ability to participate in decision-making, and significantly reduces legal uncertainty for the state. Government officials capitalized on an existing institutional and procedural distinction: within the environmental impact assessment system the administrative measure to be consulted is the Environmental Qualification Resolution, which takes place after a project has already entered the system.

By splitting consultation into two parallel systems, government officials mutilate the application of Convention 169. They make a large percentage of consultations—which, not surprisingly, happen to be the most controversial ones (Abogabir, 2014)—subject to a process where consultation happens too late compared to other government measures. Wilson and Pence (2006) argue that "although practitioners may proceed entirely properly within institutional rules or guidelines, the categories used to define the relevance to the institutional mandate may obstruct rather than promote the protection of victims of ongoing abuse" (p. 210). In this case, while legitimate according to Chilean law, the move of government officials clearly violates the spirit of Convention 169.

"Not Everything Should Be Consulted": Consultation as Standardization Practices

Taken together, the practices I have described in the previous sections proceduralize Indigenous rights and put in place standardizing mechanisms (Smith,

2005). Legal categories in particular, while might not be new, are re-actualized in consultation legislation in ways that consolidate Indigenous dispossession under new veils. Focusing on discretionary measures only excludes important government initiatives that Indigenous peoples consider might affect them, while reinforcing state authority. Breaking down Indigenous peoples' worldviews into operational dimensions understandable to government officials' privileges bureaucratic comfort over Indigenous authority to decide what counts as impact. Finally, leaving investment projects aside excludes some of the most controversial government measures from DS66, especially those related to extractive activities that threaten the integrity of Indigenous territories. During the interview with Government Planner 2, he reflected on the government's approach in the following terms:

> Not everything should be consulted, not everything can be consulted. Why? … Because there are measures that are not possible to consult due to their nature… They are not subject to consultation not because we do not want to, but because they cannot be consulted. Because I can't follow an agreement I reached with you if it goes against the law.

The official's words reaffirm the supremacy of Chilean legal orders as the absolute and unquestionable frame of reference. Despite the public discourse about regulating the duty to consult to protect Indigenous rights, what really seems to have animated the process was the desire to reduce legal uncertainty regarding economic activities and to avoid what the government saw as "excessive" Indigenous consultation that would paralyze state operations.

As captured in Fig. 13.4, the negotiation and final wording of DS66 break down Indigenous rights into manageable procedures amenable to state workflows and consistent with existent regulatory frameworks, which are never examined as a construct subject to further analysis. In this way, Indigenous peoples are turned into subjects of consultation, but only to the extent that the practice of consultation does not threaten the stability of government processes. By ensuring the consistency of the recently acquired duty to consult with existing Chilean laws, DS66 reduces the duty to consult to a cosmetic exercise where the state always has the final word. Under the tacit veils of reasonableness and compatibility with Chilean legal frameworks, consultation legislation in Chile restricts the scope of Indigenous self-determination and reproduces a well-known pattern: what some authors have called "domination by imposition of Chilean law" (Burgos, Cabellos, & Luna, 2006).

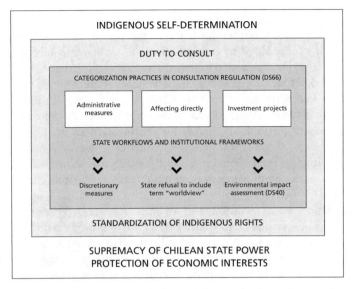

Fig. 13.4 The duty to consult and the social organization of state planning with Indigenous peoples

Conclusion: Uncovering the "Colonial Cultures" of Consultation

The duty to consult with Indigenous peoples has become an important site of encounter between state-led planning and Indigenous peoples' interests in Chile over the last decade, stirred by the country's recent engagements with international law. This chapter examined the implementation of consultation by analyzing the creation of a recently developed national consultation regulation: a governing text. By focusing on the process of regulation-making itself as a key site where the scope and contours of consultation are negotiated, the analysis aimed to examine the social organization of state planning with Indigenous peoples—in other words, how consultation happens.

The analysis shows how, when putting the duty to consult into practice, government officials selectively interpreted the international law agreements related to Indigenous rights the state has committed to. By turning to the binding nature of Convention 169 and to previous court rulings limiting its application to protect the Chilean Constitution, leaving aside the stricter standards the Declaration puts forward, DS66 essentially serves to reduce the scope of Indigenous rights in ways that run against the spirit of Convention 169 itself. In this way, the development of DS66 reveals how different forms of institutional dominance and power get enacted through the actions of government planners in the seemingly beneficial landscape of the international Indigenous rights discourse.

Specifically, the government's fears of legal uncertainty paralyzing the economy and state operations have translated into a proceduralization and fragmentation of the duty to consult. Such a compartmentalized approach has broken down Indigenous rights into manageable procedures amenable to state workflows, reinforcing the unquestioned supremacy of Chilean legal frameworks. The duty to consult in Chile acknowledges Indigenous presence and rights while trying to reduce, mutilate, and neutralize Indigenous self-determination through standardizing practices. In short, DS66 produces a textual universe where Indigenous worldviews, ways of planning, and making decisions, planning priorities, and sovereignty and self-determination are rendered marginal, if not non-existent. Where Indigenous concerns about territory and self-determination are dismissed with arguments that dress the conversation with technical and operational veils. Where Chilean law takes precedence essentially through the use of tautological intertextualities that arguably have no more intrinsic validity than international agreements endorsed by the country or than Indigenous laws. Consultation contains and delimits the possibilities of Indigenous rights by making them amenable to state operations.

In the end, while the creation of DS66 might look like an over-regulation of the duty to consult—in the sense of codifying consultation through detailed procedures—the government's actions actually contribute to a deregulation of economic activities on Indigenous territories. This has prompted wide Indigenous rejection of both consultation mechanisms, DS66 and DS40, and their application. This wide rejection suggests that the government's efforts to proceduralize Indigenous rights clash deeply with Indigenous expectations for self-determination. In a context marked by institutionalized Indigenous dispossession and historical power imbalances, as described in the introductory section, the state's urge to codify and fragment the duty to consult only feeds the already tense relations with Indigenous peoples.

In a critical examination of contemporary state-led planning in Australia, scholar Libby Porter (2010) coins the term the "colonial cultures of planning" to describe "the extent to which modern planning is constituted within colonialism itself, and... far from being merely an 'export' of [colonial powers], is the product of colonial relations" (p. 3). In other words, not only "the activities, readings, desires, philosophies, technologies and regulatory methods that the historical record shows actively and materially constructed colonies" (p. 47) fall within the realm of what today is called planning, but planning practice actively (re)produces social injustice for Indigenous peoples today.

Porter's (2010) notion directly echoes Smith's (2005) understanding of ruling relations. The phrase "not everything should be consulted" encapsulates well the continuity of a settler colonial logic and practices, which deeply infuse Indigenous-state relations in Chile and Indigenous policy up to this day, even in the apparently beneficial context provided by the international Indigenous rights discourse. As Porter argues, the social organization of state planning today is not only a historical artifact of colonial processes, but rather actively reproduces colonial ruling relations and Indigenous dispossession today under new, softer veils. And contemporary consultation legislation, in particular, further consolidates the state's long-standing approach toward Indigenous peoples. If state-led planning has historically dispossessed Indigenous peoples through overt land usurpation, displacement, and assimilation, the duty to consult re-enacts historical trends in Indigenous policy today by forcefully negating and reducing the exercise of Indigenous self-determination through the language of Western law. By reaffirming the supremacy of state power and authority, by disregarding Indigenous worldviews, and by fostering a detachment from land concerns DS66 reproduces colonial ruling relations in twenty-first century Chile every time a consultation process gets triggered.

While IE has not been widely used to explore the relation of state planning with Indigenous peoples—exceptions include Livesey (2017) and Barry and Porter (2012)—this chapter shows that institutional ethnographic research offers great potential to uncover colonial ruling relations in planning practice. Governing texts like DS66 are key vehicles shaping the relation between settler states and Indigenous people through policy. Understanding how they are negotiated and the sequences of action they activate or prevent is a crucial step in challenging existing planning practices that perpetuate Indigenous dispossession, opening the door to more emancipatory practices.

Notes

1 The ILO is a specialized agency of the United Nations dedicated to improving the working conditions of the citizens of its member states. Founded in 1919, it has developed and ratified two related international agreements aimed at improving the living conditions of Indigenous peoples worldwide: Indigenous and Tribal Populations Convention No. 107 (1957) and Indigenous and Tribal Peoples Convention No. 169 (1989).
2 In total, I conducted 56 semi-structured in-depth interviews with 49 people who were involved in or familiar with the process of regulating the duty to consult, including Indigenous leaders, government officials, Indigenous rights activists, and advocates. The quotes here are drawn from interviews with people who participated directly in the wording of the regulation only. All quotes are translated from Spanish by me.
3 The general matters the regulation oversees are the following: definition of general concepts, consultation principles, and consultation procedures.

References

Abogabir, M. (2014, October). *Estudio de caso Chile: Convenio N° 169 de la OIT y la consulta a los pueblos indígenas en proyectos de inversión*. https://www.cpc.cl/estudio-de-caso-chile-convenio-n-169-de-la-oit-y-la-consulta-a-los-pueblos-indigenas-en-proyectos-de-inversion-oit-actemp-octubre-2014estudio-de-caso-chile-convenio-n-169-de-la-oit-y/.

Alvarado Lincopi, C. (2015). La emergencia de la ciudad colonial en Ngülu Mapu: Control social, desposesión e imaginarios urbanos. In E. Antileo, et al. (Eds.), *Awükan ka kuxankan zugu Wajmapu mew. Violencias coloniales en Wajmapu* (pp. 107–140). Temuco: Ediciones Comunidad de Historia Mapuche.

Anaya, S. J. (2006). Indian givers: What Indigenous peoples have contributed to international human rights law. *Washington University Journal of Law & Policy, 22*, 107–120. Retrieved March 7, 2020, from https://openscholarship.wustl.edu/law_journal_law_policy/vol22/iss1/7.

Antileo, E., Cárcamo-Huechante, L., Calfío Montalva, M., & Huinca-Piutrin, H. (2015). *Awükan ka kuxankan zugu Wajmapu mew. Violencias coloniales en Wajmapu*. Temuco: Ediciones Comunidad de Historia Mapuche.

Barry, J., & Porter, L. (2012). Indigenous recognition in state-based planning systems: Understanding textual mediation in the contact zone. *Planning Theory, 11*(2), 170–187. https://doi.org/10.1177/1473095211427285

Boisier, S. (2007). *Territorio, estado y sociedad en Chile. La dialéctica de la descentralización: Entre la geografía y la gobernabilidad*. Doctoral dissertation, Universidad de Alcalá. Retrieved March 7, 2020, from https://ebuah.uah.es/dspace/handle/10017/2113.

Burgos, P., Cabellos, F., & Luna, P. (2006, December 31). *Historia mapuche durante la conquista y la colonia, la conquista, apropiación y reparto territorial del Pikun Mapu*. https://interculturalidadysalud.blogspot.ca/2006/12/.

Caniuqueo, S., & Peralta, C. (2017). *Taller sobre consulta indígena en Chile: Propuestas de reglamentos desde los propios actores: Apuntes y propuestas*. Temuco: ICSO Universidad Diego Portales. https://www.icso.cl/wp-content/uploads/2011/03/ICSO_DT32_Caniuqueo_Peralta.pdf.

Carmona, C. (2013). Tomando los derechos colectivos en serio: El derecho a consulta previa del Convenio 169 de la OIT y las instituciones representativas de los pueblos indígenas. *Revista Ius Et Praxis, 19*(2), 301–334. https://doi.org/10.4067/S0718-00122013000200009.

Castro, M. (2003). Desafíos de las políticas interculturales en Chile: Derechos indígenas y el desarrollo económico. *Boletín Antropológico, 21*(59), 231–252. Retrieved March 7, 2020, from https://www.redalyc.org/pdf/712/71205901.pdf.

Comisión Económica para América Latina y el Caribe (CEPAL) & Alianza Territorial Mapuche (ATM). (2012). *Desigualdades territoriales y exclusión social del pueblo mapuche en Chile: Situación en la comuna de Ercilla desde un enfoque de derechos*. Santiago: CEPAL-Naciones Unidas.

DeVault, M., & McCoy, L. (2006). Institutional ethnography: Using interviews to investigate ruling relations. In D. E. Smith (Ed.), *Institutional ethnography as practice* (pp. 15–44). Lanham: Rowman & Littlefield.

Eastwood, L. (2006). Making the institution ethnographically accessible: UN document production and the transformation of experience. In D. E. Smith (Ed.), *Institutional ethnography as practice* (pp. 181–197). Lanham: Rowman & Littlefield.

Government of Chile. (2008, April 3). *Tribunal Constitucional sentencia rol N° 1050-08. Control de constitucionalidad del proyecto de acuerdo aprobatorio relativo al Convenio N° 169 sobre pueblos indígenas, adoptado por la Organización Internacional del Trabajo, de 27 de junio de 1989*. Retrieved from https://www.tribunalconstitucional.cl/expedientes?rol=1050-08.

Government of Chile. (2013). *Informe final consulta indígena sobre la nueva normativa de consulta de acuerdo al Convenio 169 de la OIT*. Unidad de Coordinación de Asuntos Indígenas: Ministerio de Desarrollo Social.

Government of Chile. (2014, March 4). *Decreto Supremo N° 66 del Ministerio del Ministerio de Desarrollo Social. Aprueba reglamento que regula el procedimiento de consulta indígena en virtud del Artículo 6 n° 1 Letra a) y n° 2 del Convenio n° 169 de la Organización Internacional del Trabajo y deroga normativa que indica*. https://bcn.cl/1w1ac.

Government of Chile. (2017). *CASEN 2015 pueblos indígenas. Síntesis de resultados*. https://observatorio.ministeriodesarrollosocial.gob.cl/casen-multidimensional/casen/docs/CASEN_2015_Resultados_pueblos_indigenas.pdf.

International Labour Organization. (1989, June 27). *Convention No. 169 concerning Indigenous and tribal peoples in independent countries*. https://www.ilo.org/dyn/normlex/en/f?p=NORMLEXPUB:12100:0::NO::P12100_INSTRUMENT_ID:312314

Lightfoot, S. (2016). *Global Indigenous politics: A subtle revolution*. New York: Routledge.

Livesey, B. (2017). *Planning to develop land returned under Treaty settlement in Waikato, Aotearoa New Zealand: An institutional ethnography*. Doctoral dissertation, Massey University. Retrieved March 7, 2020, from https://mro.massey.ac.nz/handle/10179/11215

Porter, L. (2010). *Unlearning the colonial cultures of planning*. Burlington: Ashgate Press.

Sanhueza, C. (2013). La consulta previa en Chile: Del dicho al hecho. In H. Olea (Ed.), *Derecho y pueblo mapuche: Aportes para la discusión* (pp. 217–256). Santiago: Universidad Diego Portales.

Smith, D. (2005). *Institutional ethnography: A sociology for people*. Lanham, MD: AltaMira Press.

Smith, D. (2006). *Institutional ethnography as practice*. Lanham: Rowman & Littlefield.

Smith, D., & Turner, S. M. (2014). *Incorporating texts into institutional ethnography*. Toronto: University of Toronto Press.

Toledo Llancaqueo, V. (2005). Políticas indígenas y derechos territoriales en América Latina: 1990–2004. In P. Dávalos (Ed.), *Pueblos indígenas, estado y democracia* (pp. 67–102). Buenos Aires: CLACSO.

Turner, S. M. (2006). Mapping institutions as work and texts. In D. E. Smith (Ed.), *Institutional ethnography as practice* (pp. 139–161). Lanham: Rowman & Littlefield.

United Nations (UN). (2007). *United Nations declaration on the rights of indigenous peoples*. https://undocs.org/A/RES/61/295.

United Nations-Human Rights Council. (2018, August 10). *Free, prior and informed consent: A human rights-based approach study of the expert mechanism on the rights of Indigenous peoples*. https://documents-dds-ny.un.org/doc/UNDOC/GEN/G18/245/94/PDF/G1824594.pdf?OpenElement.

Wilson, A., & Pence, E. (2006). U.S. legal interventions in the lives of battered women: An Indigenous assessment. In D. E. Smith (Ed.), *Institutional ethnography as practice* (pp. 199–225). Lanham: Rowman & Littlefield.

CHAPTER 14

Transnational Power Relations in Education: How It Works Down South

Nerida Spina and Barbara Comber

We give Dorothy Smith (1993) the first word: "An ideological code is analogous to a genetic code, reproducing its characteristic forms and order in multiple and various discursive settings" (p. 50).

This chapter presents an audit of research done in Australia employing Institutional Ethnography (IE). It outlines key problems investigated and discoveries made so far, namely early 2020, across the different sectors of education, and identifies challenges ahead for frontline practitioners, including educational researchers in the South. Studies undertaken during this period document an unprecedented pace and magnitude of change. Reading across this research, we noticed a similarity in the organization and logic of texts across very different sites. The coherence of language, procedures, policies, vocabulary across media, policy, and other popular texts indicated to us that an advanced liberal ideological code now underpins ruling relations in contemporary Australian education. This ideological code has generated a conception of education in which childcare, schooling, and tertiary education are conceived as a part of an education market. Parents and students have the freedom to choose schools and sites, based on publicly available data, where the results themselves are based on indicators of quality such as large, standardized tests

N. Spina (✉)
Queensland University of Technology, Brisbane, QLD, Australia
e-mail: n.spina@qut.edu.au

B. Comber
University of South Australia, Adelaide, SA, Australia
e-mail: barbara.comber@unisa.edu.au

© The Author(s) 2021
P. C. Luken and S. Vaughan (eds.), *The Palgrave Handbook of Institutional Ethnography*,
https://doi.org/10.1007/978-3-030-54222-1_14

and quality rating systems. The role of the state is reframed such that individuals and families are responsible for making choices about where to send their children to school; teachers are also reframed as accountable for the quality of the teaching they deliver.

This chapter proceeds in three parts. We begin with an overview of global policy maneuverings in education and describe how some international trends rapidly took hold in Australia. We then provide an overview of IEs from early years through to post-secondary education as instantiations of IE's ability to retain a focus on embodied perspectives while mapping ideologically driven relations of ruling, including our own research projects. We conclude with some possibilities and suggest that IE can be an important part of the struggle for justice.

GLOBAL POLICY REFORM COMES TO AUSTRALIA

Global changes in governance from classical liberalism to "advanced liberalism" (Rose, 1999) have had a significant effect on teachers' work and subjectivities. Advanced liberalism emerged in the late twentieth century with a changing conception of the relation between people and the state. Rose (1999) describes:

> To govern better, the state must govern less; to optimize the economy, one must govern through the entrepreneurship of autonomous actors—individuals and families, firms and corporations. Once responsibilized and entrepreneurialized, they would govern themselves... (139)

These changes have reframed relations between students, parents, educators as experts, and governments. Where education was once characterized by educators working with students, this relation has been reconstituted into one of consumers (either parents or students) with new rights and expectations. In this context, the role of governments is transformed into one of providing standardized measures of education that quantify education (typically through large scale assessment programs) so that schools, teachers and systems are rendered comparable, and therefore commodifiable. Perhaps ironically, the explosion of calculative apparatuses that quantify education through the production of global and national datasets (such as student attendance and achievement) is largely possible because of the everyday work of educators and education bureaucrats who form a "calculative network" (Miller, 1994, p. 246). This work bridges the gap between vastly different schools, universities, childcare centers, and so forth, allowing them to become "comparable"; and making way for textually mediated translocal ruling, whereby educational workers continuously document quantifiable aspects of their daily practices, which can then be accessed by evaluators located elsewhere. These regulatory texts typically rely on New Public Management techniques such as the use of standards, targets, and audit procedures (Griffith & Smith, 2014, pp. 6–7), and are instantiations of governing as a "problematizing activity" (Rose & Miller, 1992, p. 279). That is, states generate norms through standards and benchmarks; these are used to determine the "problems" that states subsequently seek to address. Discursively constructing the conduct of educators as a problem to be addressed enables programs that purport to improve *quality* or *outcomes* or *national consistency* to flourish.

Education policy change in Australia has transpired alongside these wider global moves that Lingard, Rawolle, and Taylor (2005) characterize as an emergent global policy field. The Organization for Economic Cooperation and Development's (OECD) transformation into an authority on education quality has been assumed through its global assessment programs, most notably, PISA (Program for International Student Assessment). These transnational changes have been taken up in Australia through a series of reforms that have combined state and territory operated systems and regulations into a nationalized approach. This move toward "corporate federalism" (Lingard, 1991) enshrined corporate managerialist and economic rationalist approaches to education governance. It is within this policy assemblage that much of the institutional ethnographic research conducted in Australia has occurred.

Some of the sociological scholarship in education has established connections between *concepts* without making connections to social relations, or the embodied work and experiences of those within the institution. As Smith (1999) has argued, traditional sociological work tends to favor objectified and abstracted forms of knowledge represented in the kinds of theoretical concepts described above such as "benchmarks," "competition" and "school choice." This "dominance of theory" (Smith, 2005, p. 50) has precluded an understanding of how people's everyday lives happen. Abstracted concepts are apparent in much of education policy and research; which can become "a boundary to inquiry rather than a beginning" (Smith, 1990, p. 41). Smith's (1990) challenge to traditional forms of sociology has been to adopt an alternate sociology in which we "are called to explore the ground of a concept in the actual ordering of what living people do" (p. 41).

In education, the dominance of traditional sociological approaches that begin with abstracted concepts has created what Ball (1997) describes as a "policy-practice" research gap. Ball has explained that while *practice* oriented research claims to examine educators' work, it often does so by using dominant conceptual theorizations of education, that Smith (2005) warned against (such as whether or not teachers are providing "quality" instruction). Constituting educators' work according to these pre-theorized concepts means that research is inevitably bound to ideologically construed categories. This approach is at odds with developing an understanding of the actualities of people's lives, because it is based on taken-for-granted ways of thinking. These kinds of policy studies also tend to commence with an examination of educators' work that is out-of-context; ignoring the intersections between educators' lives and wider organizing forces. This approach has culminated in blame-based research where problems are seen to be "'in' the school or 'in' the teacher but never 'in' policies" (Ball, 1997, p. 265). An underlying assumption of this body of research is typically that there has been an "implementation failure" (p. 265) caused by teachers or principals who fail to implement policies "correctly." In this kind of research, teachers may (or may not) be objects of study, but are rarely constituted as subjects who have views that originate in their own embodied experiences of policy enactment, or whose social relations are shaped by relations of ruling. Thus, much education research has tended to ignore the everyday actualities of what real people do; or how *ensembles* of policies and texts interact with each other, and how they impact on the social relations and everyday work of educators. In contrast, institutional ethnographic research has provided a means of moving beyond conceptual boundaries, toward examining the intersections between the everyday lives of educators and wider relations of ruling.

A Picture of Ruling: IEs of Australian Education

Since Dorothy Smith and Alison Griffith's visits to Australia in the 1990s to work with educational researchers and social scientists, IE studies have exposed the significance of advanced liberal reform on educators, and the communities they serve. This body of work demonstrates how IE can make empirical links between relations of ruling, the underlying ideological codes that drive these relations, and people's everyday work. As Doherty (2015) points out, while an "orthodox ethnographic gaze of looking within a bounded setting or group" (p. 349) provides its own set of methodological affordances, IE adds the opportunity to look beyond the local, and instead, to map power relations that are typically accomplished via translocal institutional processes and texts (Smith, 2006).

An increasing number of educators in Australia have taken to social media to tell their stories of how performative pressures have changed the nature and work of education. One of the first to do so, Kathy Margolis, posted a private Facebook message that soon went viral, being shared tens of thousands of times. She described, "I get that teachers need to be accountable and of course that we need assessment, but teachers have an innate ability to know what kids need. A lot of it is data for data's sake" (cited in Dunn & Stinson, 2015, p. 97). This, and other stories that followed, articulated educators' unease stemming from their embodied understanding of what it is to be a teacher, and how these perspectives are silenced (yet coordinated) by education policy. Because IE affords researchers a method of inquiry that begins from, but ultimately looks beyond local settings, it is well suited to examining education in contemporary times, where relationships between the local and extra-local are not always visible. In the following sections, we provide examples of IEs that have been conducted from prior-to-school settings, through to post-secondary education, highlighting the similar ideological codes in play across systems and sectors.

Early Childhood Education and Care: The Quality Agenda

Educators in the early years sector in Australia work in a context that has undergone extraordinary change over the past decade. In 2012, Australia introduced the National Quality Framework which established licensing standards linked to a national assessment and rating system. Grant, Danby, Theobald, and Thorpe's (2016; Grant, Comber, Danby, Theobald, & Thorpe, 2018) IE began from the standpoint of kindergarten teachers as they implemented this new regime. It highlighted the enormous burden placed on educators, often working in single-teacher kindergartens, as they undertook significant work to document what the rating assessments counted as quality via representations of good teaching and good early year's settings. These dominant conceptual notions of quality and good teaching are a way of structuring understandings of early childhood educators' work, and prescribe what counts in both internal self-assessments and external reviews of quality, such as particular forms of communicating with parents or collaborating between educators and parents, which ignore the actual diversity contexts where the centers are situated. For instance, they take for granted an English speaking community with parents who are available to collaborate. They subordinate the embodied knowledge of educators as they work with babies, toddlers, and children. These policies, and their associated conceptual categories, are built on objectifying views contained in regulatory texts that espoused the view that "making children's learning visible" (ACECQA, 2012, p. 22) through documentation is an inherently valuable mechanism for improving teaching quality. Yet, as Grant et al. (2018) describe, documentation not only intensified workloads and stress; it also reoriented teachers' attention and time toward documentation. Ball (2003, p. 224) describes this as the "fabrication" of evidence that is "produced purposefully in order to be accountable," and not necessarily to inform parents or set directions for students' learning. Indeed ironically, teachers reported that the production of evidence took their time, energy, and attention away from children, families, and professional practice (Grant et al., 2016). These ideologically driven discourses around accountability changed social relations and produced standardized understandings around how care and teaching is valued and practiced in the early years of education.

Schools

A number of researchers have used IE to explore the effect of policy change in the school sector. Much like the early years sector, Australian schools have been subject to numerous reforms that have standardized and quantified education—creating an appearance of decentralization (for example, through policies that require self-evaluation); but ultimately allowing the "center [to maintain] control through its management and use of data" (Ozga, 2009,

p. 149). The most significant of these policies includes the 2008 introduction of an inaugural standardized testing program, the National Assessment Program—Literacy and Numeracy (NAPLAN); the introduction of a national website, *MySchool* that publishes school NAPLAN data; the 2009 introduction of an inaugural national curriculum (ACARA, 2009); the introduction of the inaugural Australian Professional Standards for Teachers (AITSL, 2011) and the Australian Professional Standard for Principals (AITSL, 2011); and the 2017 introduction of an inaugural system for funding students with disabilities (Australian Department for Education and Training, 2018).

As we discuss below, much of our own work has examined the translocal effects that occur when standardized testing data are used to manage schools. The following section presents the work of others who have used IE to explore how ideologically similar regulatory texts dominate and orchestrate teachers' work in schools.

The fabrication of evidence: a significant form of work. Talbot's (2016) IE explored teachers' work as it came under the auspices of the 2011 *Australian Professional Standards for Teachers*. Talbot followed teachers as they took up the new policy which required them to produce evidence of having met professional standards to maintain teacher registration. Talbot's research highlights the extensive time and energy this work required, and, revealed a significant disjuncture between teachers' everyday actualities and objectified ruling relations. While the stated policies goals were focused on ensuring teacher quality, Talbot's work revealed the opposite to be true. At the time of her data collection (prior to 2018), only some teachers were subject to these accreditation demands. By contrasting the lived realities of those who were subject to textually mediated ruling relations with those who were not, Talbot demonstrated the disjuncture between lived and objectified ways of knowing. In contrast to those whose development was organized through the standards, those operating according to their own professional knowledge worked productively in close dialogue with colleagues and students: "they did not require a set of professional standards to guide their professional learning" (p. 88).

Technology, texts, and the invisible spaces of teachers' lives. Hewson's (2013) research considered how the introduction of a new electronic database that managed curriculum, pedagogical design, and assessment have changed teachers' everyday/night work. The new system had been introduced by senior managers in her education sector with claims that digital processes would streamline and ease teachers' work. Yet, Hewson discovered that teachers' embodied experiences showed that official texts failed to account for the extent of work teachers undertook (such as responding to technical difficulties and system interruptions). Hewson's work showed how online systems that collect data were removed from the embodied work of teaching, yet still had the power to reach into the homes and family lives of teachers via a technology that is online 24 hours a day. Smith's (2005) generous definition of work brings this activity into view. This is especially important for educators whose work typically extends far beyond the classroom. Hewson's IE shows how technology (which is an instant means of transmitting replicable, ruling texts) authorized a great deal of new work that was accomplished in previously invisible spaces and times—for example, at home on nights and weekends. Her participants reported feeling that a teacher "worth their salt" would be "sleeping and breathing work" (p. 268), and hence that they had re-ordered their lives at school, and at home in order to take on this new work. In Hewson's accounts, we see how teachers' lives and social relations are shaped by textually authorized tasks that could only be completed when they worked longer hours on weekends, holidays, and at nights. The use of technology enabled local happenings to be standardized, inscribed, and recorded in the online database, with teachers translating their knowledge of students into the conceptual categories of the institution. Teachers knew their students as real people with human needs; they also knew themselves and their families as real people with human needs. The institutional demand for teachers' work and knowledge of students to be recoded meant a bifurcation of consciousness—with their bodily knowing subjugated by textually mediated institutional demands. This example illustrates the *reach* of the underlying advanced liberal ideological code which is apparent in the talk of teachers, their discursive positioning of teaching and teachers, and the subjugation of their bodily knowledge and personal lives.

Inclusive practice and ruling relations. Yet another reform having an effect on school educators' work is the introduction of a new national system of collecting data on school-aged students with disability, the *Nationally Consistent Collection of Data on School-Age Students with Disability*. The new system establishes a mandatory data collection process in which teachers categorize and report on the "level of educational adjustment" they provide to students with disability so that students can access education "on the same basis"[1] as their peers. Gallagher and Spina's (2019) IE, undertaken during the early phases of policy implementation, found that teachers' attention was increasingly oriented toward the production of evidence. As one of the teacher informants described "…it actually takes away… our time of being in that moment with the kids, and really having those deep conversations…" (p. 10).

Tait's (2013) exploration of inclusive education policies, and the work of registered teachers in hospitals who support, advise, and advocate for young people with long-term health needs illustrates how education policy can reach beyond school settings. Tait's work was conducted prior to the introduction of a new funding model, yet, it revealed many similarities in the institutional requirement for students to be inscribed into standardized categories of educational need. Because long-term health conditions do not always fit neatly into regulatory categories, these students and their families were often unable to access coordinated services. Smith's (1987) concept of *bifurcated consciousness* helps explain support educators' experiences of engaging in work that obscured embodied perspectives of disability and education. For example, the expectation that classroom teachers in mainstream schools manage the care of a student with a tracheostomy tube with little or no support was obscured by the objectifying focus on students' educational needs. Tait described that "the shift to focusing on the 'capabilities' of the child... re-affirm the decision that the support put into place will be sufficient to enable her to go to school" (p. 564). She argued that the "talking-up" of a system worked to reinforce a view that the system worked, despite educators' everyday, bodily experiences of working with real children and families indicating otherwise. The promotion (or "talking up") of objectifying views of life for young people with long-term health needs was accompanied by a subordination of educators' bodily, experiential knowledge, in what Tait described as "talking down" (p. 564) to lived realities. In refusing to engage with the messy and complex actualities of those living with long-term health conditions, ruling texts subordinated the need for additional services or support for students or educators within the school.

Post-Secondary Education: Equity in Policy and Practice

A number of IEs have been undertaken in higher and further education sectors. In the Australian Vocational Education and Training (VET) sector, Grace's (2005, 2014) work has examined ruling relations in contemporary times. Like the early years and school sectors, VET has undergone significant change, including the introduction of a national policy framework and changes to the structure of federal government funding (Nakar, Bagnall, & Hodge, 2018). Many students in the VET sector have had significant employment experience, but little formal training. This situation has led to a complex set of regulatory texts, for example, the creation of policies that seek to recognize prior learning. Students' engagement with VET qualifications can include an assessment of existing knowledge and skills, or completion of a new training program. Workers seeking recognition of prior learning for VET courses must meet detailed competency standards. Grace's work traced how educators' and students' work has been coordinated by ruling relations mediated by dense, abstract, and linguistically complex governing texts. Herself an experienced VET educator, Grace (2006) described that, "I have experienced a growing sense of disquiet as the texts themselves, and the processes they give rise to, have become so complex that they are virtually impenetrable to all but knowledgeable readers" (p. 2). Her informants described spending extensive time trying to understand the requirements for competency standards, before trying to help students understand and document these requirements, and, prepare for audit processes. As Grace (2014) described, "these texts establish an accountability circuit that governs almost every aspect of the professional work of educators in the VET sector" (p. 255). This complexity left many students feeling marginalized and vulnerable. One student said (after spending much time working to understand and document "units of competency"), "it made me feel really dumb. Really dumb" (p. 4).

Issues of equity and access for students in the post-secondary sector are not unique to VET. Peacock's (2014) research explored university student equity and outreach programs. His work demonstrated the everyday effects on university staff working in widening participation schemes governed by textual targets with indicators such as social inclusion, competition and collaboration. Peacock provides the example of an outreach program that illustrates how these ruling texts organized work in universities and community organizations, with material effects on students. The program, originally developed to support Pacific Island students, moved from "engaged outreach" to a "selective equity" focus that sought to "reward the higher achieving, 'deserving' students" (p. 109). This shift was driven by widening participation targets and resulted in a service which focused on the "deserving poor" (p. 113). *Deserving* students were textually inscribed as having met criteria such as performing to required academic standards, coming from *supportive homes* or from a low SES background. This research is significant, because although the changing policy landscape represented the largest investment in equity since the 1970s, the focus on abstracted categories diminished broad outreach, and often led to inadequate support and services for some students (such as those who fell outside the "deserving" category and those with disabilities).

Advanced liberal ruling relations also shape the work of lecturers, students and the professionals with whom they interact. Hosken's (2017) IE explored how ideological codes and standardized normative ideas around the "good social work student," the "good social work lecturer/professor," and the "good social worker" are constructed by dominant ideological codes. Hosken (2010) adopted a "mutual respect inquiry approach" (p. 3), working closely with a key informant who had migrated to Australia from South Sudan. Hosken's analysis traced how a field such as social work—that is characterized by discourses of social justice, equity and cultural competence—can function as an "inequality regime" (Acker, 2006, p. 443). Like many of the studies outlined above, her work revealed the operation of an ideological code that favored white, middle-class, professional values embedded in key regulatory texts, and highlighted the significant effect of this code on those outside of this normative ideal. For example, her key informant described how university assessment extension processes ignored cultural and social practices such as extended periods of mourning. These accounts, written by a South Sudanese refugee were poignant, and demonstrated the disjuncture between relations of ruling and everyday realities—even in a field that prides itself on valuing diversity and justice. Instead, this work shows how education remains a space where racialized, gendered, and classed relations oppress and discriminate. The ideologically driven reasoning apparent here works to privilege notions of merit while constraining what can be said about diversity and justice.

The IE studies summarized above illustrate how discourses of accountability, quality, collaboration, even equality, have been appropriated, translated, and recontextualized into a regime that hooks educators into advanced-liberal rule. These relations of ruling have material effects on educators' work and subjectivities; and have changed social relations between educators, students, and communities. What follows is a discussion of our own research, where we further tease out translocal effects in contemporary education.

OUR PROJECTS

We now turn to our research projects—two in the state of South Australia and one in Queensland—to further reveal how key aspects of teachers' work are orchestrated by external social relations through series of texts that flow from governments to bureaucrats and ultimately into schools.

South Australia

In 2008, Australia introduced its first ever program of national testing in literacy and numeracy, called NAPLAN. Testing was made compulsory for students in Years 3, 5, 7, and 9, unless parents decided to withdraw their children. With the threat of NAPLAN and a federally funded website called *MySchool* that would publish NAPLAN results in an online league table, a group of Australian researchers invited Dorothy Smith and Alison Griffith to mentor us in conducting an Institutional Ethnography. Entitled *Mandated literacy assessment and the reorganization of teachers' work*, this project was conducted in two states of Australia in contrasting school communities and was funded by the Australian Research Council.[2] Schools included private and public, rural and suburban, high schools and primary schools, and were located in a mix of affluent and poor locales.

In proposing the grant, we argued that policies which prioritize standardization take little account of the fact that teaching is work, done in real time, with wide variations in material conditions and school cultures. The work of teachers in schools in different locations, grade levels, and with contrasting student profiles is not the same; hence it could not be assumed that policy imperatives will have a uniform result. At that time, no systematic research had been done in Australia to ascertain the actual effects of standards-based reforms on the reorganization of teachers' work and the effects of such reforms on teachers and students' learning in contrastive school settings. This is despite the fact that the policy developers who promote the value of standardized testing often see teachers as central to making a difference to student learning and achievement. The study explored this unknown terrain, with the central question guiding our inquiry: How does mandated literacy assessment and reporting reorganize the work of teachers in contrastive school contexts?

The term "teacher" included school-based educators (teachers and school leaders) allowing us to examine how standardized assessment and reporting policies coordinate professional decision-making and work within individual classrooms and distinctive school contexts. It also investigated teacher responses to mandated literacy assessment and reporting within the broader context and expectations of local school communities and school systems.

The inclusion of a variety of schools—including those recording high performance, and those recording low performance on national literacy tests results was designed to deliver a nuanced understanding of the way that standards-based reforms mediate the everyday professional practice of teachers. Inspired by Griffith and Smith's (2005) *Mothering for Schooling*, we were determined that the normative frames associated with standardization did not bracket out diversity and disadvantage, in terms of gender, poverty, class, race, and location.

The research team published a range of articles and presented widely on the project in Australia, Sweden, New Zealand, US, UK, and Canada (e.g., Comber, 2012, 2016; Kerkham & Nixon, 2014; Kostogriz & Doecke, 2011), with Comber presenting to Australian Education Union national events on the dangers of NAPLAN and other mandated standardized tests. Most worrying was the not-surprising finding that NAPLAN and other compulsory testing (decided by state and regional authorities) had the most dramatic effect on the work of teachers and school leaders working in poorer and regional areas (Comber, 2012; Comber & Cormack, 2011; Cormack & Comber, 2013). In other words, mandated literacy assessment reorganized educators' work most profoundly in areas where socioeconomic disadvantage and cultural diversity already made education complex, unpredictable, and challenging—including in schools with low student attendance and where it was difficult to recruit and retain experienced teachers. This led to a range of changes in teachers' practices—time spent on literacy was increased and time on other curriculum areas such as art, physical education, and even science was reduced. Time rehearsing for testing was inserted into the timetable. Classroom tasks and activities came to replicate test items. Time spent on data-entry and basic analysis took the leadership team away from other areas of priority, for instance, in one case from a time allocation for liaising with Aboriginal community members. The effects were substantial and daily. In terms of students' lives, many schools started to prioritize literacy skills (as evident in the tests) from early childhood, in the belief that it would take these children a long time to catch up with their more affluent peers. Teachers began setting NAPLAN type tests for homework practice and many parents began buying NAPLAN-like workbooks from local post-office shops and supermarkets. In short, there was a chain reaction. At the government level, NAPLAN became high stakes because states, systems, and sectors could now be compared across Australia (Comber, 2012, 2016). Various educational consultants and tutoring businesses began to emerge or grow as there was now a significant market for teacher and student coaching (Doherty & Dooley, 2018). Some research findings are now treated as the "evidence" and some are marginalized when it comes to interpretations of student performance and school quality.

Importantly, this project demonstrated what it was like for teachers in different schools to experience the effects of a national standardized test, as the change was being introduced. This meant that we were able to capture the actions of school leaders, teachers, and to some degree students and parents before NAPLAN became business as usual and, as a result, less visible to the practitioners actually doing the frontline work—the purchase of new data storage software, NAPLAN-like workbooks, the appointment of new "data-people" in schools and sectors. We also documented how this mandated test changed teacher–student relationships. For example, many teachers reported the painful ideological wrestling they suffered when they were not able to help children on the days of the tests, or even to speak with them. They had to follow set scripts or else they might be accused of cheating. Many baby boomer teachers reported retiring earlier than they had intended and significant numbers of recent graduates left the profession in the first five years of teaching, alienated from the vocation they had believed they were entering.

While NAPLAN and other mandated testing have reshaped education in Australia, the negative effects were most acutely experienced in schools located in areas of high disadvantage, with culturally and linguistically diverse student cohorts, inexperienced and frequently changing staff, and students. These were often in regional, rural, and remote communities. In other words, the need to improve and sustain NAPLAN performance may be nigh on impossible; yet an unavoidable goal for some school communities.

Queensland

As the IE described above highlights, standardization, measurement, and the introduction of New Public Management techniques have failed to provide significant improvements in equity and parity of participation in education. In 2015, a diverse group of academics[3] in Queensland undertook a research program to explore how ethical decision making could exist in a landscape that prioritizes competition and improvement. The research team was intentionally diverse, bringing together a range of scholarly backgrounds and theoretical interests including institutional ethnography, inclusion, school change, leadership, assessment, statistical analysis of school data and critical inquiry. Each of the researchers came to the project with a commitment to improving schooling for all young people, regardless of our theoretical or methodological preferences. The work was funded by the Australian Research Council and conducted in six geographically and socially diverse schools.

The university research teams worked with teachers and school leaders at the six schools on a series of small-scale critical inquiries, providing opportunities for educators to share their experiences across vastly different school settings. Much of this work is documented in a book *Promoting Equity in Schools: Collaboration, Inquiry and Ethical Leadership* (Harris, Carrington, & Ainscow, 2018).

Having worked with Dorothy Smith and Alison Griffith on the project described above, Barbara Comber led the institutional ethnographic work, including working as a doctoral supervisor for Nerida Spina, who undertook a Ph.D. as part of the project. Spina's work examined how Australia's high-stakes literacy and numeracy testing regime, NAPLAN was being taken up as part of school improvement policy, and how this was shaping the everyday life of teachers.

Through tracing chains of texts from teachers' work out to school leaders, regions and wider government policy, this work demonstrated how teachers' work was largely coordinated from beyond. Many of these textual chains flowed from global discourses and policies (such as PISA) through to federal and state governments and ultimately into schools and classrooms. For example, national legislative[4] moves to shift the focus of education funding from outputs and outcomes rather than inputs, and the inclusion of targets in international standardized achievement tests flowed down into multiple state government, departmental, regional and school policies. The use of NAPLAN targets in managing the performance of school principals (Spina, forthcoming), flowed into teachers' work as school principals retained a strong focus on school improvement. Aware that (at the time), principals' jobs were highly dependent on meeting targets (in particular, NAPLAN), it is not surprising that principals made comments such as:

> As a leader I don't think we can get away from the accountability of that indicator [NAPLAN]. I don't know what it's like in any other regions, but it sure—it's front and center in our region.... there's this balance between the political and the educational...

Principals and school leaders talked extensively about performative pressures, and their attempts to shield teachers from these. However, principals were also aware that this was not always possible, as their own work was textually mediated by wider relations of ruling. One principal said:

> In our region, the regional director has an A3 spreadsheet... and some of my colleagues know all about this... and that's our performance. It's based on NAPLAN. [Pause]. That's it. [Pause]. Right.... So if you [are achieving above your target] then you are free. You are what they call a "free principal". You journey along, and you charter your own journey in your school. [Pause]. If you're... less than that.... Well then you're supervised with different levels of supervision...

He went on to describe a scenario in which much of his autonomy was curbed by a range of regional programs that insisted teachers at his school undertake new pedagogical practices. This included teaching focused around NAPLAN requirements, more frequent assessment and data collection, mandated conversations between principals and teachers (known as "data conversations"). Regional surveillance meant that principals activated departmental and regional texts by authorizing the development of new school-based texts. These included school assessment calendars, and processes such as "data grabs" every four or five weeks, data walls, "data placemats" that mapped student progress and so on. These texts had a profound effect on teachers' work. Data grabs were an institutional process requiring teachers to conduct standardized assessment of their students (in literacy and numeracy), with the resultant data to be entered into the departmental database every four or five weeks. What was produced in data grabs was done so using an inscription of students according to text-based categories. Teachers' embodied knowledge of students—as young people or children with very real needs and wants was subjugated by textually mediated institutional demands. These processes required teachers to regularly and publicly display these objectified inscriptions about students using abstracted categories. For example, in activating the texts known as "data placemats" and "data walls", teachers were required to produce a visual display of students' achievement on standardized literacy and numeracy assessments. Data walls were the public display of these representations—typically found hanging on classroom walls or in staff rooms, while data placemats were visual displays (similar to a placemat used on a table when dining) shared and discussed with school principals, supervisors and colleagues.

The translocal effects—including how teachers spent their time in class and at home—were evident in multiple ways. This included the "proletarianization" (Apple, 2013) of teachers' work as they followed scripted lessons and lesson sequences, a narrowing of the curriculum toward the kind of literacies and numeracy assessed in standardized testing (Spina, 2021); a resurgence of ability grouping and other practices known to exacerbate inequity (Spina, 2019); and the intensification of work, driven by ever-increasing requirements for documented evidence of student improvement.

Transnational Ruling Relations from the Standpoint of Australian Educators

The purpose of this chapter has been to examine Australian education across multiple sectors so as to piece together the fabric of transnational ruling relations. By exploring the advanced liberal rationalities and the vast changes that have taken place in Australian education, a growing field of IE scholars have contributed to our understanding of underlying ideological codes and the similarity of frustrations experienced by frontline educators across the country. The examples of IE research assembled in this chapter exemplify how the method of inquiry developed by Smith and colleagues has been practiced and elaborated on, and provides a way of understanding how globalized neoliberal policy ensembles have put pressure on national education systems; and how this has reconstituted educators' work. As Griffith and André-Bechely (2008) argue, "to understand the intersections between globalization and work in local settings, research must attend to the social relations of ruling that are coordinated textually" (p. 46). By revealing how things work as they do across a wide variety of educational settings, this chapter has demonstrated the power of an advanced liberal ideological code in achieving translocal change. This has changed the everyday realities (and subjectivities) of educators and the students they serve.

POSSIBILITIES

Making educators' work visible and explicating the effects of the dominant ideologies that drive ruling relations creates opportunities for "speaking truth" to ourselves and to others (Ball, 2016), and to inspire both activism and collegiality. This is important, because, as Smith (1987) stresses "methodological strategies… do not transform in and of themselves…. they do not work magic" (p. 144). In other words, without sharing this work, including with those who are involved in education (educators, students, policy-makers and so on), the ideological codes and discourses shaping relations of ruling are unlikely to change. As can be seen from the research presented in this chapter, a significant proportion of IE research in Australian education has been undertaken sparked by educators with a sense of disquiet between what they know from their own lives and work with children, young people, and families; and who have sought to contest the assumptions and practices of ruling.

Because IEs uncover the lines of fault between embodied knowledge and official textual representations, they frequently resonate strongly with educators. Inviting educators to read this scholarship creates a space for them to consider how their own work is coordinated translocally. In our experience with Master of Education students, encouraging them to read and engage with IEs that begin from the standpoint of educators, and to trace ruling relations, can be a powerful and life-changing experience. Sharing IEs and talking to these experienced, practicing educators, who are enrolled in an introductory sociology unit as part of their studies has been an important way of raising consciousness, and of encouraging them to think about how their work is governed translocally. In Australia, many students complete Master of Education degrees online part-time, while working full-time. There are also students who enroll while on maternity leave. In our experience, these discussions become an important moment of discovery for educators who are geographically isolated, and unaware of how their work and social relations are textually coordinated from beyond their local settings. In one of Master of Education units we have worked in, students are encouraged to use their assessment tasks to explore the socio-cultural context in which they work, consider power relations and how this changes everyday work and lives, and develop ideas for activism or refining their own practice. The kinds of activism these educators have considered include adjustments to their leadership, pedagogy and engagement with their employers.

This is also the case for Master and Doctor of Philosophy scholars, many of whom are also experienced and accomplished educators in their own right. The majority of IEs presented in this chapter grew out of a sense of unease that researcher/educators had with the rationalities and policies that dominated their lives. For example, Hewson (2013) was in a leadership position at a school when she undertook her Doctor of Education. In her concluding remarks, she noted:

> I have aimed to be critically reflective and to make visible the ruling relations in which I am implicated. I am aware that this goal is beset with difficulties but my own learning has been significant... More than ever, I believe that it is critical to provide time and space to dialogue with teachers about their work, to respect teacher judgement, professionalism and individuality whilst generating a shared understanding of the purpose of policy enactment and its impact on practice. (p. 274)

This reflection demonstrates the power of IE for educators as a tool for reshaping their own work, as well as providing a language for ongoing dialogue about the extent and nature ruling relations. A number of the other researchers whose work is documented in this chapter have used the knowledge gained in their IE research to inform practice in their workplaces. We do, however, note that few of the researchers have gone on to undertake and publish further explorations, or written about the activism they have undertaken based on their findings. The work of Ellen Pence (2001) in the US serves as an example of what can be achieved when IE is used to advocate for change, and to draw attention to the workings of power. We believe this would be a fruitful direction for IE research in education into the future. The dominance of ruling relations and advanced liberal mentalities demonstrates the importance of activism in working alongside administrators and practitioners to re-evaluate practices and consider more just ways of working.

Our vision for developing the potential of Institutional Ethnography in education research includes the possibility for longitudinal studies, re-visiting IE graduates and developing a national network of Institutional Ethnographers, perhaps through our professional research associations in education and sociology. One of the ironies of IE studies is that they tend to make visible the trouble front-line practitioners experience without providing solutions. No one study can do it all. We are aware that our IE colleagues work differently in their day-to-day professional practices and in their future research studies as a result of taking on this standpoint and approach to analysis. Yet this has yet to be systematically documented and analyzed. Longitudinal studies could incorporate a change/action stage in their design, but this is easier to write than it is to enact, as power relations frequently limit what individuals can do, especially in the short-term. It could be timely to conduct studies which revisit both IE researchers who are still working in their professional contexts and also participants of IEs to retrospectively and critically examine what if anything the research has enabled. Another important move for us is to develop a national network of IE researchers who can conduct some meta-analyses of their work and its implications for future policy and practice. We are also moving toward transdisciplinarity by connecting with IE researchers in other fields, in particular, health. Working in IE reading groups with colleagues across health and education fields has provided a useful means of broadening our understandings of translocal ruling relations, and how ideological codes operate in different settings.

We provide a word of caution, given that higher education itself operates under increasingly advanced liberal rationalities. Ironically, for IE scholars and their supervisors, much of the textually coordinated work of undertaking a Ph.D. does not sit neatly within the parameters of university policy. Fixed timelines set within a project management approach toward research (typically with set milestones and associated textual requirements across the course of the program) create disjunctures for IE researchers in neoliberal university structures. As Doherty (2015) explains, even the textual requirements for human research ethical approval can prove a challenge for IE researchers as they are expected to provide set lists of participants, planned interview questions and so on. These expectations, of course, fail to meet the requirements of a method of inquiry that begins from the standpoint of people, and reaches up and out in the spirit of genuine inquiry, to map ruling relations.

We have also found IE to be a useful means of engaging bureaucrats into dialogue that helps them understand the effects of policy change. Following on from the project described above (see Harris et al., 2018), Spina has commenced worked with a small research team that includes researchers from *both* the university and Queensland Department of Education to further explore the effects of data, particularly focusing on school reviews. Using IE data allowed the research team to illustrate for the department how institutional texts and processes are implicated in local activities. Drawing on these accounts, the team held a day-long workshop in 2018 where departmental policy-makers, regional directors, school reviewers, and school principals were invited to learn how departmental policies were experienced in schools. Together, the participants developed ideas for further inquiry, with a focus on how the lowest-performing schools' performance is reviewed and managed. Smith's (2002) suggestion that bringing these power relations and processes into critical consciousness is highly relevant here. By making the coordination of principals' work visible, it is hoped that the department can introduce incremental changes. Smith (2002) writes that such changes do not need be revolutionary or radical, but rather, allow for gradual, achievable modification. Smith (1987) stresses that IE was always intended to be a collective endeavor that might lead to activism. Working with her own feminist colleagues including Alison Griffith and Susan Turner opened up multiple opportunities for Smith to engage in such research-led activism. We hope that by drawing together a collection of IE scholarship by Australian scholars provides a worthwhile contribution to a collective effort that is making ruling relations visible to the educators, students, and families whose lives are coordinated by advanced liberal technologies; opening up new and different analytic windows, as well as opportunities for activism and change.

One of the features of advanced liberal rule is the dismantling of the state apparatus. Relations of rule are fragmented, textually- mediated and subject to rapid change. The take-up of complex and ever-changing technologies in education has dominated education, making ruling relations the site of the struggle for change. However, this form of rule also affords new possibilities for "making change from below" (Smith, 2008, p. 8). Drawing on the work of Gramsci, Apple (2001) argues that education policy change has been made possible by conservative forces that have adopted a broad program of advanced liberal reform, and who have reshaped subjectivities and social relations in a way that convinces people that the current set of ruling relations is inevitable. He posits that "oddly enough, it gives reasons for hope. It forces us to ask a significant question. If the right can do this, why can't we?" (p. 194).

Conclusion

Smith (1987) argued over four decades ago that sociology "must provide for subjects the means of grasping the social relations organizing the worlds of their experience" (p. 174). The body of IE scholarship in this chapter makes visible ways that educators practices are shaped by what Smith (1992) describes as the social relations that organized from beyond local sites, often through texts that are imbued with a dominant ideological code. As can be seen in the work presented in this chapter, these ruling structures cascaded into educators' work in multiple ways organizing their doings both inside and outside of their educational settings, often with significant implications for students. Bringing this body of scholarship together demonstrates the magnitude of ruling structures driven by ideological ideals.

Transnational ruling relations are evident across a vast proportion of Australian education sectors. As Griffith and Smith (2014) describe, many of these changes have happened "behind our backs" (p. 8). The advanced liberal ideological codes underpinning these power relations have "sought to develop techniques of government that created a distance between the decisions of formal political institutions and other social actors" (Miller & Rose, 2008, p. 212). It is striking for us in Australia, who came later to the dominance of standardized testing than many other western nations, to note how quickly neoliberal audit cultures have transformed our educational landscape. Those of us who were the beneficiaries of a democratic equitable national policy scene through scholarships to university and high-quality public education have been staggered at the pace of change. Clearly international media pundits, publishing giants and translocal political entanglements meant that the machinery to deliver this transformed approach to education was already in place. All that was needed was the political will; in other words, it needed a government to authorize such approaches and indeed require them.

Yet, as the body of work presented in this chapter also demonstrates, IE exposes the realities of these regimes for frontline educators and students, and ultimately creates space for new possibilities as educators and scholars argue that different versions of educational governance and practice are possible. We as Institutional Ethnographers need to engage in grassroots action at the frontline to turn this tide and in the meantime work locally wherever we can to offer different ways of working. This might include public work as educational activists, mentoring early career colleagues, teaching teachers other ways of operating, co-researching with front-line teachers, and demonstrating a repertoire of practices framed in ethics and justice.

Notes

1. Australia's *Disability Standards for Education* 2005, requires educators to make adjustments to teaching so students with disability have the same or similar choices and opportunities as students without disability.
2. Mandated Literacy Assessment and the Reorganization of Teachers' Work is an Australian Research Council Discovery Project (No. DP0986449) between the University of South Australia, Queensland University of Technology and Deakin University in Australia and York and Victoria Universities in Canada. The chief investigators are Barbara Comber, Philip Cormack, Helen Nixon, Alex Kostogriz and Brenton Doecke. Partner investigators in Canada are Dorothy Smith and Alison Griffith. The views expressed in this paper are those of the authors only.
3. Ethical Leadership: A collaborative investigation of equity-driven evidence-based school reform was an Australian Research Council (ARC) Linkage Project (no. LP 120200647). This project involved collaborative work between researchers at the Queensland University of Technology (QUT), six Queensland schools and the Queensland Educational Leadership Institute undertaken between 2013 and 2015. The Chief Investigators were Lisa Ehrich, Barbara Comber, Val Klenowski, Suzanne Carrington, and Judy Smeed (QUT). Mel Ainscow (University of Manchester) was Partner Investigator; Jessica Harris was Research Associate; Nerida Spina was a doctoral researcher. The views expressed in this paper are those of the authors only.
4. For example, the *Schools Assistance Act Regulations* (2.7, subsection 19 (4) of the Act) required that every child in Years 3, 5, 7 or 9 who attends school must sit a common national test in literacy and numeracy. The 2009 Regulations made direct reference to international data (e.g., Regulation 3.1 refers to "The percentage of students achieving at or above the standard in the PISA mathematical literacy assessment for 2009 and 2012").

References

Acker, J. (2006). Inequality regimes gender, class, and race in organizations. *Gender & Society, 20*(4), 441–464.

Apple, M. W. (2001). *Educating the right way: Markets, standards, god and inequality.* London, UK: Routledge.

Apple M. W. (2013). *Knowledge, power, and education: The selected works of Michael W. Apple*. New York, NY: Routledge.

Australian Children's Education and Care Quality Authority. (ACECQA). (2012). *Assessment and rating instrument.* Retrieved May 12, 2019, from http://files.acecqa.gov.au/files/National-Quality-Framework-Resources-Kit/NQF-Resource-03-Guide-to-NQS.pdf.

Australian Curriculum Assessment and Reporting Authority. (2009). *The shape of the Australian curriculum.* Retrieved from http://www.acara.edu.au/verve/_resources/Shape_of_the_Australian_Curriculum.pdf.

Australian Department of Education and Training. (2018). *Nationally consistent collection of data: School sudents with disability*. Australian Department of Education and Training. Retrieved from http://www.schooldisabilitydatapl.edu.au/data-collection-steps/introduction-to-the-steps.

Australian Institute for Teaching and School Leadership (AITSL). (2011). *National professional standards for teachers*. Canberra, ACT: The Ministerial Council for Education, Early Childhood Development and Youth Affairs (MCEECDYA). Retrieved from http://www.aitsl.edu.au/australian-professional-standards-for-teachers/standards/list.

Ball, S. J. (1997). Policy sociology and critical social research: A personal review of recent education policy and policy research. *British Educational Research Journal, 23*(3), 257–274.

Ball, S. J. (2003). The teacher's soul and the terrors of performativity. *Journal of Education Policy, 18*(2), 215–228. https://doi.org/10.1080/0268093022000043065.

Ball, S. J. (2016). Subjectivity as a site of struggle: Refusing neoliberalism? *British Journal of Sociology of Education, 37*(8), 1129–1146.

Comber, B. (2012). Mandated literacy assessment and the reorganization of teachers' work: Federal policy and local effects. *Critical Studies in Education, 53*(2), 119–136.

Comber, B. (2016). Poverty, place and pedagogy in education: Research stories from front-line workers. *Australian Educational Researcher, 43*, 393–417.

Comber, B., & Cormack, P. (2011). Education policy mediation: Principals' work with mandated literacy assessment. *English in Australia, 46*(2), 77–86.

Cormack, P., & Comber, B. (2013). High-stakes literacy tests and local effects in a rural school. *Australian Journal of Language and Literacy, 36*(2), 78–89.

Doherty, C. (2015). Making trouble: Ethnographic designs on ruling relations for students and teachers in non-academic pathways. *The Australian Educational Researcher, 42*(3), 353–370.

Doherty, C., & Dooley, K. (2018). Responsibilising parents: The nudge towards shadow tutoring. *British Journal of Sociology of Education, 39*(4), 551–566.

Dunn, J., & Stinson, M. (2015). Media informed or research informed? Some reflections on changing the game of education. *NJ, 39*(2), 97–100.

Gallagher, J., & Spina, N. (2019). Caught in the frontline: Examining the introduction of a new national data collection system for students with disability in Australia. *International Journal of Inclusive Education*, 1–15. https://doi.org/10.1080/13603116.2019.1614231.

Grace, L. (2005). *Language, power and ruling relations in vocational education and training*. Doctoral dissertation, Deakin University, Deakin, Australia. Retrieved from http://dro.deakin.edu.au/eserv/DU:30023271/grace-languagepower-2005.pdf.

Grace, L. (2006, August). *Mapping the social relations of the Australian vocational education and training sector*. Paper presented at the annual meeting of The Society for the Study of Social Problems Montreal, Quebec, Canada.

Grace, L. (2014). Accountability circuits in vocational education and training. In A. Griffith & D. E. Smith (Eds.), *Under new public management: Institutional ethnographies of changing front-line work* (pp. 255–262). Toronto, ON: University of Toronto Press.

Grant, S., Comber, B., Danby, S., Theobald, M., & Thorpe, K. (2018). The quality agenda: Governance and regulation of preschool teachers' work. *Cambridge Journal of Education, 48*(4), 515–532.

Grant, S., Danby, S., Theobald, M., & Thorpe, K. (2016). Early childhood teachers' work in a time of change. *Australasian Journal of Early Childhood, 41*(3), 38–45.

Griffith, A. I., & André-Bechely, L. (2008). Institutional technologies: Coordinating families and schools, bodies and texts. In M. DeVault (Ed.), *People at work: Life, power and social inclusion in the new economy* (pp. 40–56). New York, NY: New York University Press.

Griffith, A. I., & Smith, D. E. (2005). *Mothering for schooling*. New York, NY: RoutledgeFalmer.

Griffith, A., & Smith, D. E. (2014). *Under new public management: Institutional ethnographies of changing front-line work*. Toronto, ON: University of Toronto Press.

Harris, J., Carrington, S., & Ainscow, M. (Eds.). (2018). *Promoting equity in schools: Collaboration, inquiry and ethical leadership*. New York, NY: Routledge.

Hewson, S. (2013). *Control, shift, insert: Living and enacting policy in teachers' day/night work*. Doctoral dissertation, Queensland University of Technology, Brisbane, Australia. Retrieved from https://eprints.qut.edu.au/63495/1/Sandra_Hewson_Thesis.pdf.

Hosken, N. (2010). Social work and welfare education without discrimination: Are we there yet? *Practice Reflexions, 5*(1), 3–16.

Hosken, N. (2017). *Exploring the organization of social injustice in Australian social work education*. Doctoral dissertation, University of Tasmania, Tasmania, Australia. Retrieved from https://eprints.utas.edu.au/27194/1/Hosken_whole_thesis.pdf.

Kerkham, L., & Nixon, H. (2014). Literacy assessment that counts: Mediating, interpreting and contesting translocal policy in a primary school. *Ethnography and Education, 9*(3), 343–358.

Kostogriz, A., & Doecke, B. (2011). Standards-based accountability: Reification, responsibility and the ethical subject. *Teaching Education, 22*(4), 397–412. https://doi.org/10.1080/10476210.2011.587870.

Lingard, B. (1991). Policy-making for Australian schooling: The new corporate federalism. *Journal of Education Policy, 6*(1), 85–90.

Lingard, B., Rawolle, S., & Taylor, S. (2005). Globalizing policy sociology in education: Working with Bourdieu. *Journal of Education Policy, 20*(6), 759–777.

Miller, P. (1994). Accounting and objectivity: The invention of calculating selves and calculable spaces. In A. Megill (Ed.), *Rethinking objectivity* (pp. 239–264). London, UK: Duke University Press.

Miller, P., & Rose, N. (2008). *Governing the present: Administering economic, social and personal life*. Boston, MA: Polity Press.

Nakar, S., Bagnall, R. G., & Hodge, S. (2018). A reflective account of the VET FEE-HELP initiative as a driver of ethical dilemmas for vocational education teachers in Australia. *The Australian Educational Researcher, 45*(3), 383–400.

Ozga, J. (2009). Governing education through data in England: From regulation to self-evaluation. *Journal of Education Policy, 24*(2), 149–162.

Peacock, D. R. (2014). *Practising equity: The activation and appropriation of student equity policy in Queensland higher education*. Doctoral dissertation, University of Queensland, Brisbane, Australia. Retrieved from https://espace.library.uq.edu.au/view/UQ:337500.

Pence, E. (2001). Safety for battered women in textually-mediated legal systems. *Studies in Cultures, Organisations and Societies, 7*, 199–229. https://doi.org/10.1080/10245280108523558.

Rose, N. (1999). *Powers of freedom: Reframing political thought*. Cambridge, UK: Cambridge University Press.

Rose, N., & Miller, P. (1992). Political power beyond the state: Problematics of government. *British Journal of Sociology*, 173–205.

Smith, D. (2008). Making change from below. *Socialist Studies/Etudes Socialistes, 3*(2), 7–30.

Smith, D. E. (1987). *The everyday world as problematic: A feminist sociology*. Boston, MA: Northeastern University Press.

Smith, D. E. (1990). *The conceptual practices of power: A feminist sociology of knowledge*. Toronto, ON: University of Toronto Press.

Smith, D. E. (1992). Sociology from women's experience: A reaffirmation. *Sociological Theory, 10*(1), 88–98.

Smith, D. E. (1993). The standard North American family SNAF as an ideological code. *Journal of Family Issues, 14*(1), 50–65.

Smith, D. E. (1999). *Writing the social: Critique, theory and investigations*. Toronto, ON: University of Toronto Press.

Smith, D. E. (2002). Institutional ethnography. In T. May (Ed.), *Qualitative research in action* (pp. 17–51). New York, NY: Sage.

Smith, D. E. (2005). *Institutional ethnography: A sociology for people*. Lanham, USA: Altamira Press.

Smith, D. E. (Ed.). (2006). *Institutional ethnography as practice*. New York, NY: Rowman & Littlefield.

Spina, N. (2019). "Once upon a time": Examining ability grouping and differentiation practices in cultures of evidence-based decision-making. *Cambridge Journal of Education, 49*(3), 329–348.

Spina, N. (2021). *Data cultures and the organization of teachers' work: An institutional ethnography*. Abingdon, UK: Routledge.

Tait, B. L. (2013). "Talking up and talking down": The presentation of educational need in an age of inclusive education policy reforms. *International Journal of Inclusive Education, 17*(6), 555–570.

Talbot, D. (2016). Evidence for no-one: Standards, accreditation, and transformed teaching work. *Teaching and Teacher Education, 58*, 80–89.

CHAPTER 15

The Struggle for "Survival" in Contemporary Higher Education: The Lived Experiences of Junior Academics in Taiwan

Li-Fang Liang and Yu-Hsuan Lin

It was a typically hot and humid Taipei afternoon in early summer, and we had met, as we often do, in a cozy coffee shop. Conversation quickly turned to our struggles with career transitions. At the time one of us was a second-year assistant professor at a private university and the other a doctoral student on the academic job market. Much as we had many other times, we talked about stress, anxiety, guilt, depression, and self-reproach. We both feel like surviving, rather than successful, academics, and we struggle to be the daughters and romantic partners and intimate friends we would like to be. We feel besieged with a great deal of complications that we do not understand, let alone know how to solve. Why do we feel so driven and so inadequate?

In the past two decades, a growing body of literature has focused on how and why academics in contemporary higher education face high demands and long work hours. The explanations vary from individuals' choice, such as work devotion (Blair-Loy, 2003) to structural factors (Jacobs & Winslow, 2004), including state policy, university regulations, and neoliberalism (Chubb & Watermeyer, 2016; Leišytė & Dee, 2012; Sousa & Brennan, 2014). The impact of the emergence and development of neoliberalism has drawn particular attention from researchers.

L.-F. Liang (✉)
Department of Sociology, National Dong-Hwa University, Hualien, Taiwan
e-mail: lfliang@gms.ndhu.edu.tw

Y.-H. Lin
Department of Applied Sociology, Nanhua University, Chiayi, Taiwan
e-mail: yuhsuan@mail.nhu.edu.tw

© The Author(s) 2021
P. C. Luken and S. Vaughan (eds.), *The Palgrave Handbook of Institutional Ethnography*,
https://doi.org/10.1007/978-3-030-54222-1_15

The meaning of being an academic is contested, and it has shifted over time. Most research treats neoliberalism as a force that has replaced autonomy, purpose, intellectual value, and academic freedom in scholars' lives with efficiency, performativity, and accountability. Market-oriented logics, rather than public interest value, drives many decisions in higher education, including those that reward faculty (Rutherford, 2005; Teelken, 2012; Wright, 2008). University administrations widely use auditing and measurement systems to evaluate, manage, and monitor academics' performativity, as well as to demonstrate accountability in order to sell a university itself and its "brand." Past discussions of neoliberal influences on higher education in Taiwan have generally emphasized how neoliberal ideology drives state policy toward universities and faculty's measurement of performativity (e.g., Chiang, 2015; Sun, 2007). These studies focus on how neoliberal discourses objectify academics' bodies, minds, and labor.

The problems involved in academic work provide us with an entry point for this study. Thus, the investigation is anchored in our lived experiences as intellectual laborers and moves beyond personal experiences to discover how extended social relations and the social organizations of academic work mediate our daily activities in the current context of the new economy. Relying on institutional ethnography (Smith, 1987, 2002, 2005), we interviewed 21 junior academics who work in both public and private universities in Taiwan. This study explores how these junior academics experience the disjuncture between what they are doing and how they are laboring in their everyday and everynight life and what the university administration counts as work, driven by the institutional discourses, such as efficiency, productivity, accountability, and performativity.

In this chapter, first, we portray the everyday actual activities and work of interviewees, giving a concrete account of how their lives and work are arranged and organized in different spaces and at different times. This study uses Dorothy Smith's broad understanding of work: anything people do intentionally, under definite conditions, that takes time, effort, and thought (2005, pp. 151–152). Thus, it considers many unpaid and invisible activities that the capitalist economy does not recognize as work. Rather than beginning in the theoretical framework of neoliberalism, the section that follows analyzes the disjuncture between this institutional discourse and the respondents' lived experiences and everyday work. It demonstrates that translocal relations of ruling in contemporary higher education are governed by the ideology of new management that mediates the everyday/everynight lives of study participants. This chapter concludes by discussing on how gender relations organize female and male academics' lives differently in the neoliberal context.

The use of generous concepts of work orients this study to move forward from local lived experiences to discovering the extended social relations that organize the local particularity, as well as mapping out institutional connections. In contrast to past studies that understand neoliberalism as a hegemonic value or a grand theory (e.g., Archer, 2008a, 2008b; Berg, Huijbens, &

Larsen, 2016; Mountz et al., 2015; Münch, 2014; Shore, 2010), this study treats neoliberalism as a constant constructing process where people are at work to (re)construct and (dis)construct it.

Research Design and Methods

We interviewed 21 academics who had worked as university professors less than five years, 11 women and 10 men. Their age ranged from 34 to 44 years old. Four of the women were married and three of these had children. Six of the men had ever married and four of them had children. One of the fathers was divorced. These demographic characteristics reflect, in a general way, the differences between female and male academics in the current Taiwanese academic context, in that it is far more common for men to have married and had children. Participants' institutional affiliations were geographically diverse within Taiwan, and 12 were teaching at private universities and the rest taught at public institutions. One respondent worked in the natural sciences and the rest worked in the humanities or social sciences. Nine were assistant professors and the remainder was an associate professor.

Instead of organizing interviews with explicit questions, we sought to explore participants' lives in three dimensions: personal information (e.g., educational background, professional training, career choices, family background, intimate relationships), work lives (e.g., specific work tasks and details, work responsibility, university policy, administration regulations), and the arrangement of work and personal life (e.g., daily schedule, family responsibility and care work, intimate relationships and friendship, personal habits and leisure). The length of each interview varied from 1.5 hours to 5 hours. Informants' work schedule and family responsibilities tended to impact interview length; those who had more time gave it. While most of the interviews took place in July and August at the time when respondents were not teaching, the majority of our informants were still doing their academic work seven days a week.

In addition to interviews, we examine the texts our informants referenced during the interviews and explore how the institutional texts they mentioned mediate their embodied work and make them accountable to administrative processes. The incorporation of texts and the processes of textualization excavates ideological codes (Smith, 1999) around the language of "academic work" and "university professor" that are woven into state policy, university regulations, academic discourse, and everyday practices.

Unpacking Institutional Categories

When we asked our informants about their work and its content, most of them answered without thinking: teaching, research, and service work (TRS). Linda remembered learning this TRS formulation at her university's orientation for new faculty. This institutional language amounts to a process of textualization, through which textual reality and institutional discourses replaces individual actuality (Smith, 2005). At the end of her first year as a professor, Linda was required to enter information in an online system quantifying her academic performance on TRS. The system uses a formula to calculate every professor's individual "points" on each of the three dimensions based on their academic performance. For example, the score calculates teaching points according to course credits and number of students enrolled. The system Linda encountered is a performative technology. Such technologies audit and evaluate, document and measure individual performance (Lynch, 2010, 2015; Shah & Sid Nair, 2012). When used in the university context, they subsume individuals' actualities under the institutional discourses of academic work. The every day doing is subject to institutional capture (DeVault & McCoy, 2002; Smith, 2003), which obscures what happens in particular locales and at particular times. In this section, we unpack the work categories defined by institutions to understand academic work based on people's work knowledge and their everyday lived experiences as well as to make the invisible work visible.

Teaching

Teaching involves a myriad of physical and emotional tasks. The work of teaching includes in-class time, organizing and preparing for class, grading, and advising students and resolving their questions. In many in-person and remote settings, students might also seek help with issues unrelated to a given class. Teaching may offer greater autonomy than many other kinds of work, but university administration and academic measurements nonetheless regulate it. In this section, we describe the regulation and how it impacts what faculty are actually doing in the work processes that organize and accomplish teaching.

Planning Courses

Teaching includes a sequence of pre-class activities which are harder to document than physical presence in a class. Each activity not only demands quantities of time, but also involves a wide variety of mental and emotional tasks (Chang, 2009; Gilmore & Anderson, 2016). However, quantitative assessment systems that rate professors do not treat these activities as academic performance.

Amy typically plans the theme of a course on her own, then develops a course syllabus, which discloses an effort to plan and organize the teaching. She puts in hours finding and selecting "appropriate" readings and supplemental materials, such as videos and clips, for her students. It was common for participants to use terms such as proper and appropriate, which are anchored in their understanding of students' learning conditions. Andrew's experience suggests determining what might be appropriate for his students takes work and time. He explained:

Now I am aware of students [meaning, students' ability level]. When I design a course, I know their demands better. In other words, it is because I notice their level and the responses they might have [that I am able to determine what is appropriate].

A syllabus displays the process of structuring a course. It not only implies the embodied work behind it, but also indicates how the university administration intervenes in teaching. Maggie's university provides a regular syllabus format that faculty members must use. The format consists of the elements of a course from the administrative perspective. At the end of each semester, Maggie and her colleagues must upload the standardized version of their syllabi in order for students to register for their classes. The version uploaded is always different from the final one used in classes, because the participants usually are busy during the semester and do not have time to work on the syllabi. While students learn to expect this, Maggie feels uploading an inaccurate syllabus has limited utility for students. Thus, she says, its only function is to fulfill the administrative requirement.

Such processes do not account for class planning tasks such as mastering the assigned readings and creating lectures, handouts, and slides with which to teach them. Most respondents use PowerPoint, which they described as a better way of engaging students than older tools. Janet explained that assembling presentation materials is very time consuming:

> The students emphasize multimedia effects. You need to have PowerPoint, YouTube clips, and music. I found out that it does not take much time to go through the textbooks or readings, but it is time-consuming to look for the supplemental materials.

Respondents said they spend a great amount of time searching for interesting class materials. They described always being alert for cultural products that might be useful in their teaching; even while out shopping for their families, they might spot an advertisement for an upcoming movie relevant to their lectures. They scour YouTube and perform many web searches. They watch for clips they might use in lectures even while watching television. Thus the work for class preparation is integrated with their personal lives, such as entertainment or leisure time.

Beyond preparation, junior academics describe being ever-alert to how to improve their teaching from interactions in the classroom. Andrew has gradually revised his teaching methods based on his class experiences and seeks frequent follow-up to determine if students are learning. He has learned to use examples to explain abstract concepts or theories. While he feels this process has improved his teaching, it is extremely time-consuming. Christine described how she observes students' responses to her teaching in class and how their responses affect her:

> While I am lecturing, I pay attention to students' reaction. I look at their facial expression and notice if they are bored or fall into asleep. I still feel little bit hurt if they don't participate actively [in class].

Christine updates reading materials, the content of her lectures, and in-class activities based on both direct and indirect feedback she receives from students. The assessment system the university administration uses never accounts for the labor and the time that these adjustments to her teaching require.

Supporting Students Outside of the Classroom
The administration of respondents' institutions requires professors to have posted office hours devoted to students. Some universities also require them to be on campus for a certain number of hours per week in addition to class time and office hours. But respondents said the time they spend interacting with and counseling students is hard to calculate. At the end of each class professors answer students' questions. Susan said this can take one or two hours of her time after every class meeting.

Professors who advise theses work with students spend time working intensively on this as well. While most graduate students in Taiwan may not be fully confident in reading English, they must at a minimum engage with English-language scholarship. Mike named this as one reason that advising master students is very exhausting:

> Advising graduate students includes assisting them in finding a research topic, relevant literature, teaching them how to do research, revising their writing, and so on. It is extremely tiring work. The students do not have the ability to search for literature, especially in English. In the early years, I even searched for the relevant literature for them. I did the library search…. I would directly edit students' writing in Word. Some of them have difficulties in writing. I had to do the revision. Their writing is not readable. You do not consider that it is the complete work.

Sometimes, advising students also includes resolving students' emotional burdens. Amy said that because she looks warmer than some of her colleagues, students looked to her for help with personal issues and she found it difficult to refuse. She described bringing a student out to lunch to talk about his personal situation and losing an entire afternoon, which she could ill-afford. "And then he expected that I could resolve his life for him," she said ruefully. Steve divorced a few years ago, and he feels this encourages students to bring their romantic problems to him. He said:

> If I did not care [about my students], my life would be very easy. When students come to me, what I only say is: "Sorry, I do not have time [to talk with you]." But, if I want to talk to them, two or three hours are gone. It will impact [my] later scheduled work. I have a student who comes to see me every two weeks.

He discusses his online friends with me. He knows a girl through the internet. He feels that she is too fat and thinks of encouraging her to lose weight. But at the same time, he worries that he might harm her after telling her his thought. This is the stuff they bring to me. What can I do? He does not have friends, and he trusts me.... Sometimes, I tell my students that I am extremely busy and do not have time to talk with them. I tell them to rearrange the time for meeting. But then I usually feel very bad.

Steve tries to draw boundaries, but it is clear he has often failed. He described receiving midnight phone calls from students who have difficulty falling asleep.

The relationships between professors and students are not only bound by their position in institutions and personal affections. All of the institutions employing respondents had developed mentorship systems that monitor teacher–student relations. As junior academics, respondents are assigned to mentor 20–50 students each term. The university administration pays for activities with their mentees but does not compensate junior academics for their time to organize and participate in these activities. Alan and Peter arrange regular lunch meetings with mentees every week. Janet brings her students to the restaurants she thinks they will like even if university funds will not cover the cost; she pays the difference from her own pocket.

A few universities require mentors to fill out a counseling form to record the number of students who consult with them. The form is one of the technologies developed to make junior academics' performativity accountable and measurable. Steve described this administrative requirement as a significant burden:

[Recording mentorship] is so funny. There are many students knocking on my door and coming in and out. It is impossible [to count the number]. The university administration also requires us to fill out the form of counsel record. Please! I spend two hours talking with students and put my own work away. After they leave, I have to work on my own stuff. I do not have time to write up the form.

Peter's university requires him to not only name students but also the issues he discusses with them in counseling. He must summarize the conversation after the fact. Such forms transform the embodied work respondents do into quantitative numbers and official discourses recognized by the institutions as performativity. It also represents an additional drag on their time, and research constantly competes for such time.

Research

The contemporary corporate university administration emphasizes two key products for faculty: external research grants and "high-quality" publications (Archer, 2008a, 2008b, p. 389). Taiwan's Ministry of Science and Technology (MOS) provides grants to academics that have become an indicator of academic performance. Their grants not only bring money into the university, but also signify the viability and success of individuals and institutions in institutional discourses (Archer, 2008a, 2008b; McWilliam, 2004). The university administration develops various technologies to assess and audit the performativity of institutions and individuals (Acker & Webber, 2017; Olssen, 2016). This section addresses how respondents organize and reorganize their daily lives to respond to the governance of ruling relations.

Prioritizing Research
Institutional discourses consider research as more important than teaching or service work. Respondents learn this through observation of academic assessment processes and university regulations and from their senior colleagues. Linda's university explicitly weighs research as three times as important as teaching or service in tenure promotion. She was told when she interviewed for her job that if her research did not merit promotion within six years the school could fire her. Reflecting such pressures, respondents said that the assessment of performativity and the institutional discourses of being a successful academic drive their research as much as individual interests and passion. Within this context, faculty are always evaluating themselves according to the imposed standards (Acker & Webber, 2017; Lund, 2012).

Pressure to submit the MOS grant applications likewise creates stress. In addition to the funding itself, the university administration regards the MOS grant as an indicator of a university's reputation, productivity, and performativity, which are evaluated when a university strives for ranking. Therefore, universities audit the number of grant applications members of departments and colleges submit. As a result, Maggie and Amy said their departments and colleges require them to submit a proposal for an MOS grant—or a report explaining why they are not. Those who fail to submit grant proposals for three years cannot teach classes at the graduate level. Alan's university administration informed him of a particular MOS submission for new faculty in his first year and he felt pressured to submit that year even though he felt the project was not ready and simultaneously he had three conference papers to write. He felt that rushing had made denial inevitable and had no way to know if submitting when he did had even helped his chances. As a result of having to teach, adjust to a new environment, and prepare the grant proposal and the conference papers, he said, "My first semester was really awful. My research was terrible.... I felt ashamed."

The institutional discourse of the MOS grant is imposed on respondents through everyday interactions and practices. Christine described how the senior colleagues in her institute within the university push her to apply for the grant as soon as possible:

> Most senior colleagues in my institute have several grants at the same time. They often remind me how it's important to have funding, such as hiring

research assistants, buying equipment, and so on when we meet at the institute's corridor or regular meetings. Most important is that we need to have at least one national-level grant when we are evaluated by the university administration. In addition to my personal performance, the number of my grants affects the institute's record too. It may impact our annual budget distributed by the university administration.

Like Alan and Christine, all respondents see how the organizational norms work and affect their life.

Comments about publications reflected a similar mindset. Peter learned the importance of publication at the orientation for new faculty, from university regulations, and from his senior colleagues:

> When you apply for promotion, the university administration emphasizes your publication. You need to have "strong" publications. [This] means SSCI [Social Sciences Citation Index] and SCI[Social Science Citation Index][-listed journals].... When you accumulate enough credits, you are able to convert the credit to the position of associate professor. [He laughed.]

A number of respondents mentioned SSCI, SCI, or the Art and Humanity Citation Index (AHCI). Journals listed in these indexes are perceived as publishing "excellent" research, and have greater prestige indexed by the citation databases Web of Science and Scopus (Vessuri, Guédon, & Cetto, 2014). In contrast, articles published in journals that are not on the SSCI, SCI, and AHCI lists, receive less recognition in research assessments as institutions assume they have lower accountability of quality and excellence.

The decision-making of submitting and publishing academic work in particular journals has been driven by the university's audit system rather than by the academic spirit of intellectual exchange and communication. A few respondents mentioned the idea that a particular study might be best suited to a particular journal but their livelihood depends on impact factor. Writing for mainstream-recognized publications has become a measure to acquire the institutional recognition of performativity, which viable academics must enact. The institutional discourse of doing research is embedded in performativity and accountability, which are alien to respondents' everyday experiences of doing research. The primary experience of doing research is feeling they did not have enough time.

Doing Research in Limited Time

Respondents find it hard to do research "efficiently" according to the institutional standard. They frequently sacrifice personal life and abstain from care responsibility to obtain it. Some people experience more struggles than others, and gendered patterns emerge in the data (Lund, 2012).

Andrew uses weekends to conduct observations in the field and leaves his family at home. Sean describes summer and winter breaks as the "perfect" time for doing research. Maggie gets on a high speed train when her weekly classes end to go to her field site; the two hours on the train are her "free time." Because she lacks personal connections with those who run her field site, Maggie has spent enormous amounts of time building trust. Acquiring permission to enter her field research site took a long time. She described frustration, anxiety, anger, sadness, and hopelessness that made it difficult to continue the pursuit. Sean maintains relationships with his research informants through phone calls, e-mails, and social media when he is not in the field. He spends time listening to their personal troubles and talking with them.

Research involves myriad tasks after fieldwork, including interview transcription, typing up fieldnotes, data analysis, literature review, manuscript composition and editing, identifying journals for submission, submitting work, and addressing the response. Peter goes to his fieldwork often when he does not have classes. He is used to finishing his notes on the same day he does fieldwork. He said, "After my kids go to bed, around nine or ten o'clock, I work on my stuff [research] intensively. Sometimes, it is very painful if I have class [to prepare for] the next day. The time is not enough."

Some people are finding they have no time for research. Susan described stress because of the delay of her research progress. She is always busy with teaching and the endless grading, and teaching took up all of her energy and time in her first two years as faculty. Linda explained that she has a little time for research, but it is always in short segments and other obligations easily distract her. She has to care for her aged father, who has severe Parkinson's disease, and, she said, administrative work can "fall down from the sky" suddenly from her department or university.

Christine is a mother of a two-year-old boy. During the interview, she described how she handles her university work, household chores, and her mothering work at the same time. She is disappointed in herself as an academic, a wife and a mother: "I feel that I am a loser in many regards. I am an unqualified academic. It's even hard for me to maintain my routine teaching; not to mention doing research." These junior academics feel they should be carefree individuals with constant availability to fulfill institutional requirements, but in reality they struggle with various kinds of work and care responsibility.

Service Work

Service work is the third dimension of academic work in the institutional discourse and evaluation of performance. While service is not rewarded as highly as research, respondents feel they must cooperate with the administration in order to demonstrate that they are "good" faculty members. In the hierarchal university, they struggle with recognition, security, and promotion, aware of the prominence of measurement tools. In addition, they feel pressure to establish a sense of belonging to their department, the university, and the community through sharing administrative work. Andrew said that he valued the sense of affections binding his department as a team through shared administrative tasks. The discourse of teamwork is also promoted by university administration to impose responsibility on each individual.

The work of service is hard to measure. Respondents may attend various committees and administrative meetings, organize conferences and talks, review journal articles, edit departmental publications, recruit prospective students, write funding proposals and reports, attend meetings hosted by the government or social organizations, participate in advocacy activities, and do many other things. They feel that countless unexpected tasks swamp them. Linda gave an example:

> The department assigns me for some particular tasks or to attend meetings. For example, organizing students' events, attending a public speech, especially when there are few people in the audience, hosting visitors, and so on. During the last academic year, I was on three different committees, including the department and school committees, and curriculum committee. I did not have any idea before I was assigned to these representatives and did not know what my responsibility for these different positions should be…. Once in a while, the department would ask me to attend the meetings. I had at least one regular meeting every week.

Maggie spent more than a half hour describing the work she did to organize a conference with a hundred attendees. It included many embodied tasks, beginning with writing the funding proposal submitted to the Ministry of Education and ending with publication of conference articles. The publication represents the outcome of performativity. Maggie emphasized accountability and performativity when she explained the pressure she experienced.

The implementation of administrative work and academic and social services demands countless e-mail exchange. This technology does not reduce workload. Instead, it adds a new dimension to the content of academic work. Maggie relies on e-mails to do her academic and social services work. She explained:

> I need to respond to a great quantity of e-mails every day. If I do not respond to e-mails immediately, the senders would think I had died or had an accident. They [would] think that I did not do my work because my work depends on e-mails to contact and communicate with others.

Maggie's experience exemplifies why and how the invention of e-mail increased the workload for academics. It is easier and quicker to send out a message through e-mails, and this results in an increasing numbers of e-mail exchanges. In addition, people expect prompt responses to e-mail.

The Formation of Neoliberal Subjects

Strongly advocating accountability, performance, and consistent surveillance, the university education reform led by the ideology of neoliberalism dramatically increases faculty workload. Interviewees often referenced having "not enough time," "no time," "fragmented time," and "loads of things to do" as well as being "very busy," constantly interrupted, and forced to focus on "trivial" things. Since there is always not enough time, they have to develop various ways to be more efficient and productive according to the university administration's accounting. Personal beliefs, commitment to work, personal physical and mental condition, family situations, and school systems drove their ways of coping. All respondents described a system that squeezes their time for fostering intimate relationships, the need to shrug off responsibility for care work, and the competition logic of pursuing personal performativity. In this section, we illustrate how the institutional discourse and arrangements mediate respondents' everyday lives, and how they have gradually developed the literacy to identify how the relations of ruling work and construct their ways of participating in that domination.

Pursuing "Efficiency"

Assistant professors new to the academic profession are often not familiar with the everyday world of organizations and the duties involved and have yet to establish work procedures to manage. Linda, who had been in her job just a year, described feeling like she "had to hold a bucket to collect water all the time" without knowing "where the water would be coming from." Being constantly ready (to work) is just one of the strategies respondents have developed to cope.

Making Wise Use of Fragmented Time

In addition to classes, respondents described frequent interruptions including a ringing phone, students seeking help, and procedural requirements. They had to develop ways to make good use of their fragmented time. For example, Angel takes Mass Rapid Transit. She uses this commuting time to correct her students' assignments and read the newspaper, searching for news or topics she can utilize in class. She also has two children in their teens. While they are in after-school class (*buxiban*), she meets graduate students under her supervision in nearby cafés, wrapping up the meetings in time to pick up her children. Peter, a father of two, described waking up at six o'clock every morning so he would have an hour to read, prepare classes, or go over his lecture for the day before his older child gets up at seven. Christine, a mother of a two-year-old boy, shared how she multi-tasks:

> I am used to handling several things at once. For example, when I prepare breakfast for my little boy, I utilize the waiting time to collect clothes to launder.

After I come home from his babysitter's place, usually the laundry is done. I can hang out the laundry to dry in the sun.

Through the entire interview, Christine talked about her tips for better time use. Like Christine, the other respondents change their habits of time use to sustain their daily lives with limited time resources.

Minimizing Unrewarded Work
When the university evaluation lists out the number of points each journal article, conference paper, or even book chapter represents, the efforts of publication become quantified numbers and ranks. Accordingly, academic professionals have little choice but to consider insignificant the labor that cannot be converted into points and try to reduce the time and energy these tasks take so as to invest in the work that can be directly converted and contributes to meeting the criteria. Those who have been at their jobs longer have learned to avoid work that would consume significant time without producing a commensurate reward. For example, some people decide to give up qualitative research in favor of text analysis or re-analyzed the field data they gathered for their dissertations to avoid having to gather new data. Some are strategic in supporting graduate students, which they see as very time-intensive and garnering minimal professional reward.

When planning a course, respondents try not to design assignments that would be very time-consuming to grade or involve significant discussion with students. They use materials they have read recently for their own research or articles they have already read before rather than doing new research for a course. Andy said he had recognized that evening school students were less interested in theoretical knowledge. He briefly considered converting the existent teaching materials to make them more concrete and relevant to students' daily lives, but immediately recognized how much work it would require and decided not to. The effort it would require seemed unequal to the expected reward from improved course evaluations. The negative impact on his students of this calculus is obvious, but Andy felt he had no choice.

Minimizing Personal Relationships

Overwork inevitably impacts respondents' relationships with their families, partners, children, and friends. Almost every respondent's partner has complained about their excessive working. Mike took work on his honeymoon. Peter had to cancel family travel at the last minute due to an unexpected meeting. Andy has been working for more than sixteen hours a day since he met his wife, and she knows to make an appointment in advance if she wants his attention. Alan's wife gets angry about the time he spends on work. He said that he told her:

> I can't even be counted as the hardworking type. I just try to meet the requirements to survive. I am not spending all the time on it. There are extreme cases out there. And I don't do that. I come back for dinner every night; at least we have a meal together.

Although many respondents (especially men) give their priority to their career, they try hard to maintain their intimate relationships with minimum efforts. They expect their partners to understand during their period of transition from untenured to tenured, and from junior to senior scholar.

Couples who have to live apart because of different work locations are under even more stress. Judy and her husband lived apart for a period of time, one in the eastern Taiwan, the other in the western region. Visiting required a half day's travel involving a bus, a train, and a taxi. As a result she seldom visited her husband, and he began visiting her every two weeks. Susan and her partner, a woman, also lived apart. They had seen each other every two weeks before the current semester, but Susan was busier than ever, and could only see her partner once a month. When they did get together, Susan's tenseness from her considerable work pressure affected how they spent their time. She recalled:

> [My partner] was joking with me today. She said that I only talked more gently in summer vacation; and that when the school began, I would tell her not to come, to get lost, to stop bothering me. I asked, "[is it] that obvious?" She said, "Of course!"

When asked whether she wished to have more time to be with her partner, Susan said that under her conditional six-year contract, she would rather spend her time writing papers, publishing articles, instead of getting together with her partner. Making work a priority seemed like the only way to survive.

As for the respondents who are now single, all of whom are women, they do not imagine being partnered in the future. It is stressful enough to deal with their lives as they are. They cannot imagine how they would have time to build a close relationship with another person. Linda explained:

> I have plenty of work, and—how to describe it—I have a busy schedule, and even if I have spare time, I want to take a break and make it a personal leisure time. It is very valuable. It's time when you can read by yourself, or plant flowers by yourself, or take a walk by yourself, and you don't need to take another person into consideration. Right, I suddenly feel this is so valuable.

These women academics understand that they face greater barriers to establishing an intimate relationship than their male counterparts. This is because the current gender system is organized such that partnered women must prioritize their male partners' careers and emotional health (Baker, 2010; Erickson, 2005).

Care(Less) Workers

Contemporary organizations are designed as if workers are unencumbered by any needs unrelated to their work or limitations. This assumption is problematic for workers, especially those who are mothers and caretakers (Acker, 1990, 2006; DeVault, 2008, p. 3). A mother of two teenage children, Angel gets up at 6:30 every morning to hang the laundry that she washed overnight. She then leaves home by 7:00 to drop off her children at school. Her commute by Mass Rapid Transit to the university takes another hour and a half. In the afternoon, she usually needs to leave the office at four to pick up her children at school at five-thirty to take them to an after-school class, although her mother occasionally provides that transportation. When the class is dismissed, she takes her children home, arriving home past 9 p.m. She then oversees her children's homework and studies alongside them. The whole family goes to bed around midnight after Angel puts the laundry in the washing machine.

All this might seem to suggest that Angel is single, but in fact she is married. Her husband might be willing to share some of this labor, but he works in a university administrative position, which carries enormous pressure to work all the time. Men who can rely on women for care work have a better opportunity to enter leadership roles (Lynch, 2010). Angel's husband often attends meetings and activities in the afternoon or evening, which makes him unavailable for the critical period between school and bedtime.

Like Angel's husband, Andy does considerably less care work than his wife. She and their infant live with her parents while he rents an apartment near campus and goes home on weekends and on some weekday evenings to see them. He said honestly that he was a very lucky man. Unlike his wife, who worked full-time while taking care of the baby, he could enjoy a good sleep almost every night in the rented room. His wife is suffering sleep deprivation, although having her parents to take care of their child during the day is a relative blessing. He called his rented room "heaven" by comparison, acknowledging that his wife never gets even three hours of uninterrupted sleep.

Peter and Mike are also depending on their wives and/or wives' parents to take on the role of main caretaker. A mother of a little boy, Christine's comments suggest it is more difficult for her than her male counterparts to disengage from her care responsibility and routine care work. She mentioned that if she had to work on weekends she always negotiated with her husband in advance. Sometimes she still felt considered herself an irresponsible mother and wife:

> I try to avoid the work scheduled on weekends and keep the time for family life. But usually I don't have choice. For example, when I have a [writing] deadline, weekends are the only time I have for writing. Sometimes, I have to attend academic or administrative meetings. It's part of my work. I feel bad if I reject my colleagues and academic friends too often. At the same time, I also feel bad

if I cannot spend weekends with my family. My husband complains a lot if I cannot join the weekend family activities along with them.

Christine experiences more struggles for a compromise between her academic job and her care responsibilities. The broader gender relations shape the care situations of female and male academic professionals differently. While men can avoid primary care work by relying on the moral imperative on women to care, women have no such option. Being defined as the default carers in society, women are care's foot soldiers while men are care commanders (Lynch et al., 2009).

In addition to childcare, care for aging parents is another important issue for respondents who are in their middle age. Steve's divorce was several years ago and he has remained single. He has a daughter with his ex-wife but she lives in another city; his weekly routine was to drive 40 minutes to another city to get his daughter so they could spend the weekend together every Friday. However, six months before the interview Steve's mother was diagnosed with cancer. To help his mother receive the best medical resources, he transferred her from Taichung to Taipei, the capital city of Taiwan. Whenever he has no classes to teach, he stays in the hospital in Taipei to keep his mother company during her chemotherapy treatments. When he has classes, he goes back to Taichung to teach. He reschedules his time with his daughter to Thursday and Friday evenings. As soon as he gets off work on those days, he drives 40 minutes to have dinner with his daughter and then goes back to school or the hospital.

Steve had been planning to build his academic curriculum vitae and apply for a promotion when his mother got sick. But, he said, because of his mother's illness, "everything was stuck there. Just stopped." His university continues to evaluate his performance, so he completed an academic article in the hospital. He paid for a private room at the hospital for his mother and there was a small dressing table. He said, "It's a small table, but it's alright. I was not staying in a hotel, and I could adapt myself to that easily. Right there, an article was finished, submitted, and [now it is] published." He sighed, saying:

> But I really think that the whole thing about my mother's hospitalization is, I am not saying she became my burden, that's not what I mean, but a burden to a family. For the work of our kind, it has always been…[your job] doesn't do something [to accommodate your needs] just because of your personal reasons. You still have to teach classes. If you can't, you have to swap with another teacher. And your research has to go on, or else. You have to work for promotion, or else others will laugh at you. That's the reality.

Steve's words indicate how he and the other academics experience disjuncture between the institutional expectation and their daily actuality, and between the careless workers and the real human being with all the responsibility connecting to his or her loved ones. Difficult times in personal life, differences in resources, and the load of care work are all unified in treatment, and performance of each worker is assessed using the same set of criteria. Consequently, the outside world of work follows the masculine ethic: a tough-minded approach, a capacity to set aside personal, emotional considerations in the interest of task accomplishment (Acker, 1990, p. 143), a continuously demanding cycle.

Individualizing Rhetoric

Higher education adopts various quantitative calculations of points and scores to assess a person's performance. These points or evaluation not only impact the definition of academic work but change the everyday world of universities. With these measurement tools and technologies, universities find a way to monitor each academic's performance. University surveillance leads to a reflexive surveillance of the self in personal life (Lynch, 2010, p. 55), also called a governmentality of the soul (Archer, 2008a, 2008b, p. 389). For example, many interviewees see the MOS evaluation criteria as unreasonable or arbitrary, but they still felt ashamed when the MOS rejected their research proposals, because of the evaluation rules and institutional discourses. Steve, for example, said he had to submit a MOS proposal or it would be "too shameful."

> [E]veryone has to submit theirs, and if yours is not accepted [he paused]— I think there will be peer pressure. People would ask if the MOS—no, my proposal is not accepted. Why ask? And their response would be: What? You submitted it but in vain! Then you would feel even more ashamed. It implies that others' proposals were submitted and accepted without difficulty. Right?

When asked where this pressure comes from, Steve answered definitively:

> The peers in the department. We are in the same field and this group of people would inevitably compete with each other. For instance, they would say that we are in the so-and-so field, and you are local [trained], and I am of foreign background. Your papers, my MOS projects, etc. are all objects for comparison. And people toot their own horn, that's true, and you have to have a strong heart for this.

Respondents also use "How many papers now?" as a standard greeting to their colleagues. Since Christine received her doctoral degree four years before the interview, she had published three academic articles; two were in journals on the SSCI list and another one was published in a peer-reviewed English journal not on a prestigious index. During our interview, Christine teased herself about her "unproductivity":

> My son was born in my second year [as an assistant professor]. The time spent for raising a child is much more than I expected. In addition to childcare, I am swamped with my teaching work. It's difficult [for me] to find the time for writing academic papers. Sometimes, I write some memos and diaries for childcare. That's all. Nothing I have accomplished. I often doubt myself if I don't have the capacity [for academic work].

The institutional discourses of contemporary higher education, such as efficiency, productivity, and accountability, have become the standard language for university administration to communicate with these junior academics in terms of institutional performance. Further, they have taken upon these institutional demands as the reference when they evaluate themselves. Although most of our interviewees identified the broader institutional context in which they are situated to some degree, they also often blame themselves, feeling like a failure and unqualified to survive in institutions.

Conclusion

We started this study with our embodied experiences of being junior academics who always work hard and for long hours, but still feel that we always fail to achieve the requirements of our jobs as defined by the institutional discourses, which act as the ideological code (Smith, 1999) woven into governmental policy, institutional regulations, media reports, daily practices, and so on, to (re)shape our lives in particular settings and at particular times. In the current context, the objectified knowledge of neoliberalism dominates almost every aspect of human life, including higher education in developed countries. The ideology of neoliberalism transforms our everyday embodied practices into the abstract market logic that emphasizes performativity and accountability measured through technologies of auditing and textualized accounts. For example, the teaching performance of junior academics is measured in quantitative indices and is abstracted from what they really do every day. The efforts they devote to research are simplified into the number of publications and grant recipients they produce. In the processes of abstraction and simplification, the current measurement and auditing system marginalizes the embodied work done to accomplish teaching, research, and service work, rendering it invisible.

The ideology of neoliberalism assumes that the ideal worker is unencumbered (Acker, 1990), devoid of responsibilities outside the job. The corporate university regards these junior academics as available 24/7, as unlimited working machines and isolated individuals without family bonds and emotional ties. Yet if workers are to continue in their jobs, their bodies must be sustained in households and through services of various kinds of work (DeVault, 2008, p. 2). In most situations, women perform the supporting and sustaining work, due to the division of labor shaped by gender relations. In our study, the female junior academics shoulder more of the responsibilities of household chores and care responsibilities than their male counterparts. The unequal division of household labor and care responsibility creates a disadvantage for female junior academics in the context of contemporary higher education.

Based on the lived experiences of female and male junior academics, we argue that the university as an organization is not gender neutral. The university administration looks for a free, rational, independent, and autonomous subject who is capable of working efficiently 24/7 without other responsibilities and needs outside the work settings. Within this context, individuals are only assessed via their work performance counted by the organizations. Women and who have responsibilities to care for are excluded from the ideal subject desired by the university administration and institutional discourses.

By studying how the institutional discourses of contemporary higher education, including efficiency, performativity and accountability, and the auditing system applied to measure them, affect junior academics' lives, we have sought to demonstrate what is missing, marginalized, devalued, and invisible in the pursuit of institutional goals and the implementation of measurement systems. In this study, we deal with real lives where people work hard to sustain organizations, their families, and themselves. We argue that reforms of higher education must center on individuals and their various needs. Such reforms should create a friendlier and more inclusive working environment for all academics, regardless of their care responsibilities. Students, the academic inquiry, institutions, and scholars themselves will reap the benefits.

REFERENCES

Acker, J. (1990). Hierarchies, jobs, bodies: A theory of gendered organization. *Gender & Society, 4*(2), 139–158.

Acker, J. (2006). Gender and organizations. In J. Chafetz (Ed.), *Handbook of the sociology of gender* (pp. 177–194). Boston, MA: Springer.

Acker, S., & Webber, M. (2017). Made to measure: Early career academics in the Canadian university workplace. *Higher Education Research & Development, 36*(3), 541–554.

Archer, L. (2008a). Younger academics' constructions of "authenticity", "success" and professional identity. *Studies in Higher Education, 33*(4), 385–403.

Archer, L. (2008b). The new neoliberal subjects? Young/er academics' constructions of professional identity. *Journal of Education Policy, 23*(3), 265–285.

Baker, M. (2010). Motherhood, employment and the "child penalty". *Women's Studies International Forum, 33*(3), 215–224.

Berg, L. D., Huijbens, E. H., & Larsen, H. G. (2016). Producing anxiety in the neoliberal university. *The Canadian Geographer/Le Géographe Canadien, 60*(2), 168–180.

Blair-Loy, M. (2003). *Competing devotions: Career and family and women financial professionals*. Cambridge, MA: Harvard University Press.

Chang, M. L. (2009). An appraisal perspective of teacher burnout: Examining the emotional work of teachers. *Educational Psychology Review, 21*(3), 193–218.

Chiang, T. H. (2015). Why do higher education policies in Taiwan incline towards neoliberalism? A critique on this approach. *Taiwan Journal of Sociology of Education*, 15(2), 131–165.

Chubb, J., & Watermeyer, R. (2016). Artifice or integrity in the marketization of research impact? Investigating the moral economy of (pathways to) impact statements within research funding proposals in the UK and Australia. *Studies in Higher Education*, 24(2), 1–13.

DeVault, M. L. (Ed.). (2008). *People at work: Life, power, and social inclusion in the new economy*. New York, NY: New York University.

DeVault, M. L., & McCoy, L. (2002). Institutional ethnography. Using interviews to investigate ruling relations. In J. F. Gubrium & J. A. Holstein (Eds.), *Handbook of interview research* (pp. 751–76). London: Sage.

Erickson, R. J. (2005). Why emotion work matters: Sex, gender, and the division of household labor. *Journal of Marriage and Family*, 67(2), 337–351.

Gilmore, S., & Anderson, V. (2016). The emotional turn in higher education: A psychoanalytic contribution. *Teaching in Higher Education*, 21(6), 686–699.

Jacobs, J. A., & Winslow, S. E. (2004). Overworked faculty: Job stresses and family demands. *The Annals of the American Academy*, 596, 104–129.

Leišytė, L., & Dee, J. R. (2012). Changing academic practices and identities in Europe and the US: Critical perspectives. In J. C. Smart & M. B. Paulsen (Eds.), *Higher education: Handbook of theory and research* (pp. 12–22). Dordrecht: Springer.

Lund, R. (2012). Publishing to become an "ideal academic": An institutional ethnography and a feminist critique. *Scandinavian Journal of Management*, 28(3), 218–228.

Lynch, K. (2010). Carelessness: A hidden doxa of higher education. *Art & Humanities in Higher Education*, 9(1), 54–67.

Lynch, K. (2015). Control by numbers: New managerialism and ranking in higher education. *Critical Studies in Education*, 56(2), 190–207.

Lynch, K., Lyons, M., & Cantillon, S. (2009). Time to care, care commanders and care footsoldiers. In K. Lynch, J. Baker, & M. Lyons (Eds.), *Affective equality: Love, care and injustice* (pp. 132–157). Basingstoke, UK: Palgrave Macmillan.

Mcwilliam, E. (2004). Changing the academic subject. *Studies in Higher Education*, 29(2), 151–163.

Mountz, A., Bonds, A., Mansfield, B., Loyd, J., Hyndman, J., Walton-Roberts, M., Basu, R.et al. (2015). For slow scholarship: A feminist politics of resistance through collective action in the neoliberal university. *ACME, International E-journal for Critical Geographies* Advance online publication. https://www.academia.edu/12192676/For_Slow_Scholarship_A_Feminist_Politics_of_Resistance_through_Collective_Action_in_the_Neoliberal_University.

Münch, R. (2014). *Academic capitalism: Universities in the global struggle for excellence*. New York: Routledge.

Olssen, M. (2016). Neoliberal competition in higher education today: Research, accountability and impact. *British Journal of Sociology of Education*, 37(1), 129–148.

Rutherford, J. (2005). The market comes to higher education. *LATISS: Learning and Teaching in the Social Sciences*, 2(1), 5–19.

Shah, M., & Nair, C. S. (2012). The changing nature of teaching and unit evaluations in Australian universities. *Quality Assurance in Education*, 20(3), 274–288.

Shore, C. (2010). Beyond the multiversity: Neoliberalism and the rise of the schizophrenic university. *Social Anthropology*, 18(1), 15–29.

Smith, D. E. (1987). *The everyday world as problematic: A feminist sociology*. Boston, MA: Northeastern University Press.

Smith, D. E. (1999). *Writing the social: Theory, critique, investigations*. Toronto: University of Toronto Press.

Smith, D. E. (2002). Institutional ethnography. In T. May (Ed.), *Qualitative research in action* (pp. 17–52). London: Sage.

Smith, D. E. (2003). Resisting institutional capture: A research practice. In B. Glassner & R. Hertz (Eds.), *Our studies, our selves: Sociologists' lives and work* (pp. 150–161). New York: Oxford University Press.

Smith, D. E. (2005). *Institutional ethnography: A sociology for people*. Lanham, MD: AltaMira Press.

Sousa, S. B., & Brennan, J. L. (2014). The UK research excellence framework and the transformation of research production. In C. Musselin & P. N. Teixeira (Eds.), *Reforming higher education* (pp. 65–80). Dordrecht: Springer.

Sun, C. L. (2007). Accountability control or professional development? A dilemma of faculty evaluation in university. *Journal of Education Practice and Research, 20*(2), 95–128.

Teelken, C. (2012). Compliance or pragmatism: How do academics deal with managerialism in higher education? A comparative study in three countries. *Studies in Higher Education, 37*(3), 271–290.

Vessuri, H., Guédon, J. C., & Cetto, A. M. (2014). Excellence or quality? Impact of the current competition regime on science and scientific publishing in Latin America and its implications for development. *Current Sociology, 62*(5), 647–665.

Wright, S. (2008). Knowledge that counts: Points systems and the governance of Danish universities. In M. L. DeVault (Ed.), *People at work: Life, power, and social inclusion in the new economy* (pp. 294–337). Toronto: University of Toronto Press.

PART IV

Making Change within Communities

CHAPTER 16

Building Change On and Off Reserve: Six Nations of the Grand River Territory

Susan Marie Turner and Julia Bomberry

This is an account of how the authors worked together on two projects in Canada that begin from the standpoint of, and working *for*, the Six Nations of the Grand River Territory community and Haudenosaunee people.

Many people on Six Nations of the Grand River Territory supported our work. Ganohkwasra Family Assault Support Services and Executive Director Sandra Montour did community-minded work for the Haudenosaunee people long before this, with the goal of realizing Ganohkwasra (Love Among Us). Project researchers Gabriella Salazar and Amye Werner, Doris Henry, Staff at Ganohkwasra, and Six Nations Police Service Officers, Policy Analyst, and Chief Glen Lickers, contributed substantially to the work and its success. Off-reserve justice and service providers generously participated, telling us about how they do their everyday work and joining our Final Gathering presentation and conversation at Ganohkwasra. Nya:weh.

Quotations throughout this chapter are the words of the speaker but in some cases lengthy quotations have been condensed for clarity and in order to succinctly convey and highlight the points speakers are making and formulating in conversation.

Thank you to Liza McCoy, Suzanne Vaughan, and Paul Luken for helpful comments on earlier versions of this chapter. Its shortcomings are the writer's responsibility.

S. M. Turner (✉)
Guelph, ON, Canada

© The Author(s) 2021
P. C. Luken and S. Vaughan (eds.), *The Palgrave Handbook of Institutional Ethnography*,
https://doi.org/10.1007/978-3-030-54222-1_16

The chapter describes how we adapted Institutional Ethnography concepts, methods, and techniques in order to prioritize the community's and partner organization's goals, work with Haudenosaunee principles, fit the concrete realities of the community, and work in politically charged settings on highly sensitive topics: police investigations and services for Six Nations victims of sexual violence.

Six Nations of the Grand River Reserve is the largest First Nations reserve in Canada with 26,034 registered band members, 12,436 living on reserve; its 46,000 acres is just 5% of the land set out in a 1784 Treaty. Previously the Cayuga, Mohawk, Seneca, Onondaga, Oneida, and Tuscarora nations' Territories covered much of Southwestern Ontario and New York State. The creation of reserves and residential schools was part of centuries of governing strategies to create a Canadian nation and eliminate First Nations (see Castellano, Archibald, & DeGagne, 2008; Wesley-Esquimaux & Smolewski, 2004). Located in Southwestern Ontario, Six Nations sits adjacent to the Montreal–Windsor highway corridor that is one of the highest risk areas for drugs and human trafficking. The former Mohawk Institute residential school in nearby Brantford that operated for 139 years is now the Woodland Cultural Center.

Six Nations people are Haudenosaunee (People of the Longhouse). The clan system is the traditional government preserved over centuries. Williams (2018) describes how many centuries ago a message of peace and system of law—Kayanerenko:wa—was brought by one individual known as The Peacemaker to the original five nations, in order to build peace and a structure based on their clan systems that would maintain peaceful relations among them. Its elements are first, that everyone is capable of a rational "Good Mind" that chooses peaceful ways, and that all people are related and therefore obligated to help one another (see also Cousins, 2005). Once bound together as one family in one structure, the nations called themselves Haudenosaunee. Following "The Great Law," individuals are peacemakers. Spoken at gatherings, the law is something that people actively know and live in relationship to others. The second element is the constitution and governing processes of a civic society of nations under The Great Law of Peace.[1] Longhouse communities extend all around Lake Ontario. Every Haudenosaunee citizen is a member of a clan that extends into the past and future. The obligation to help one another is integral to the Haudenosaunee worldview of being in relationship in a web of all living things: the laws are "natural" laws of responsibility for upholding peace and order in all relations.

Our research began from the experience of Ganohkwasra Family Assault Support Services (Ganohkwasra), the Six Nations organization that has sheltered and worked with victims of violence on the Territory for over thirty

---

J. Bomberry
Six Nations of the Grand River Territory, Brant, ON, Canada
e-mail: jbomberry@ganohkwasra.com

years. Ganohkwasra's goal for the project was to learn the work of the Six Nations Police Service (SNPS) in order to strengthen relationships with them and within the community and improve services for the Haudenosaunee. This account provides a just glimpse into the process, work, and learning involved this project that has resulted in significant changes on and off reserve.

Our work was an ongoing dialogue and conversation. How this chapter is written is part of how we work together. The use of "we" reflects that and refers to the collectivity of the researchers. Both are authors of this work. Susan is the writer here, however, our approach, learning, work, and outcomes were developed together in ongoing conversations over several years. Julia's voice appears separately in italics as her words also may: (1) draw on the relevancies of her experience as Haudenosaunee or Onkwehonweh (Cayuga language meaning Original People here); (2) refer to Ganohkwasra and their relevancies as a non-profit First Nations on-reserve organization; or (3) reference Six Nations as a community of First Nations whose original laws and teachings endure as a reference point of principles for the Haudenosaunee.

We completed two projects under provincial Aboriginal Sexual Violence Action Plan (ASVAP) Programs. The first was part of a province-wide 2012–2015 Aboriginal Community Response Initiative funded by the Ontario Women's Directorate. Ganohkwasra was one of four Indigenous organizations invited to undertake research in their community. The provincial Indigenous organization that received the funds wanted to use institutional ethnography (IE). Susan and Dorothy Smith gave a 3-day workshop on IE to organization leaders. Susan was hired to train community researchers in institutional ethnography and assist them in their projects. Julia and Gabriella Salazar interviewed Six Nations residential school and sexual violence survivors, police and service providers (Werner, in consultation with J. Bomberry, 2016). The second project (Bomberry, Turner, & Werner, 2016) was funded by the Ontario Ministry of Community Safety and Correctional Services 2016 Police Responses to Sexual Violence and Harassment Against Aboriginal Women and Girls' Program. Ganohkwasra's Executive Director Sandra Montour asked Susan to apply for funding with Ganohkwasra as partner in affiliation with Six Nations Police. Ganohkwasra wanted to go deeper with the Police into sexual assault investigations and services, from Six Nations' standpoint, work with IE and Haudenosaunee principles, and produce the (Ministry-required) best practices for investigations that were *culture-based*. The proposal was explicitly IE and to achieve real outcomes for the community. Ganohkwasra orients beyond projects to goals of building reciprocal knowledge relations among agencies, strengthening them and relationships in the community and outside it. We refer to our work as one project.

We first describe how Susan, a non-Indigenous institutional ethnographer, and Julia, Haudenosaunee, Cayuga Nation Clan Mother and Manager at Ganohkwasra, developed the research from the standpoint of Ganohkwasra and the Six Nations Police. That in itself is remarkable. When Susan first came to Ganohkwasra to discuss if they would join the province-wide project,

Julia and Executive Director Sandra Montour asked, "How is this going to be different? We have been researched to death and nothing has changed much." It had to "not be another form of oppression." When we began, sexual violence was a taboo topic on reserve and Police did not talk about their work.

Next we describe how we did the work, talking with people and graphically mapping to track and show what we were learning from them. We illustrate the map-building process. Mapping showed where significant issues arose for Six Nations officers who "navigate" Criminal Code categories and Great Law principles and are accountable within text-based procedures geared to "hand it over" to a criminal justice system that does not "fit" Six Nations. Mapping showed how providing culture-relevant services simply could not happen within the existing city-centered "well-integrated response" that precluded Six Nations victims "getting to healing." We describe how we used mapping to discover and talk about what we were learning as we went along and the significance of using the map at a final gathering of people we had interviewed showing how we had learned from them and how their work fit into a big picture.

Our discoveries led us to call for profound changes to how services were delivered. We list our "calls to action" to government ministries and describe major changes that resulted. In conclusion, we comment on Institutional Ethnography's potential going forward for learning from and with Indigenous communities and in research prioritizing assisting them in achieving their goals for their people and building real changes in ways of knowing and relationship and the world.

Developing the Project from Ganohkwasra's Standpoint

Ganohkwasra (Love Among Us in the Cayuga language) is a non-profit Six Nations organization. Haudenosaunee principles are integrated into programs, management, frontline work, job descriptions, therapeutic practices, and trainings. From the start, we were building a working standpoint from Six Nations' knowledge, experiences, views, and practices—that are often conflated as *culture*. Six Nations' worldview and physical location was our place in the world from which to explore the externally organized policing and services delivery system.

To start, we discussed and changed funder, government, and IE language and terms to suit Six Nations realities. Before Ganohkwasra signed on to the province-wide *Aboriginal* project, we had to agree that their project would not take on its *Violence Against Women and Girls* framework that does not fit Haudenosaunee worldview and laws. Julia explains,

We (Ganohkwasra, Haudenosaunee) don't label women as victims and men as perpetrators. Our belief is that everyone has the possibility of being either victim or

perpetrator. We had to clear that up if we were going to participate and continue to help our men and boys in that first project.

We did not want to be taking on any words that could mistakenly be taken to stand in for our people, our realities, our views, laws, and ways of working for our people. Haudenosaunee teachings emphasize listening. That was foundational to us building a trusting relationship for moving forward. It had to not be another form of oppression.

We (the researchers) talked over how we were thinking and talking about things; what were the words we'd use and practices; what were the beliefs and assumptions behind the words we would use. We had to clarify IE terms before proceeding. And how and when to interview police officers and sometimes we had to wait. What could they be comfortable with, what were their circumstances and difficulties? That kind of conversation occurred throughout. We negotiated through a difficult path, stayed with the dignity of IE and with what Ganohkwasra wanted and knew.

It was a process of tuning into words that are active in two different worldviews and worlds, how words carry consciousness, thinking, ways of being in relationship. Ganohkwasra knew from experience how words organized relationships and people's experiences of oppression, and what needed to be changed. Western words were, and are still, integral to attempts to eradicate First Nations and their laws.[2] Haudenosaunee laws passed down orally, preserved in text, and spoken at gatherings, actively organize relations differently.

Julia and Sandra knew also what was needed in carrying out the research,

Because of the amount of intergenerational trauma within our community, as a result of colonization, residential school, the 60s Scoop—where First Nations children were taken from their families and put into foster homes—things that went on in this region, sexual violence is still a taboo topic in our community, it's not spoken about. For Ganohkwasra to take the lead, have a way to open that conversation and be gentle about it was crucial. It couldn't be intrusive; it had to be done in a safe way. Not scare people. That would have happened with a different research approach. It didn't happen. Talking to people about their work helped open that conversation in a mindful and respectful way.

Changing the language to what best suited us was important for Ganohkwasra taking that first project into our Territory and our community. For us to talk to the police, who provide services and work with Six Nations community and experience violence and risk every day the way they do, it was crucial for us to use language that they could connect with. We hammered out how we could talk to them in terms that would work for them. We typed it up and hung it on the wall in all our offices. It helped keep us clear and focused on our goals that aligned with our community, knowing as we completed that first project that it was in our terms.

We agreed at the start Ganohkwasra would lead; it was their project, their data. We used *focus and direction* to talk about what we wanted to learn more about that would be useful to know for making change. It would mean listening and learning what that was along the way.[3]

We did not talk about *social relations*; the Haudenosaunee understand relations are among all living things, not only human beings. Talking to Six Nations police, Julia spoke of learning about their work, listening for, in what they were telling us, the procedures and processes they worked in, and hearing what was known, relevant, and of concern for them in how things were organized, and what they knew could be different and wanted to be changed.

Nor did we use IEs term *boss texts*, that could be heard generally to mean texts were all-powerful. We spoke only concretely about particular texts as we learned about them in people's work, and as external institutional texts that have no power over the Haudenosaunee teachings. Julia discovered online, for example, the Major Case Manual, a text Six Nations officers mentioned when describing their work of determining *severity* of an offense and how to proceed with a case of sexual violence. As Julia read it out loud, we could see how it was authoritative in that specialized course of action; how it *spoke to* police who take it up and entered into their work, its categories into how they think what to do and to speak about it—as we learned, mapped, and illustrate later in the chapter.

Developing an understanding of what Ganohkwasra knew also was a process of learning some of the everyday operating realities they knew, as a Haudenosaunee non-profit organization, on reserve, providing shelter and healing services to their community, in the vivid context of government administration of health and social services delivery that discriminates against them. Julia had said "In the imposed systems, the Haudenosaunee knowledge practices among our people can't get to us. When we get through the institutional barriers, then we can get to healing." That led us to explore how that happened in the organization of support services and policing. When reading the call for proposals and application guide for the second project, Susan phoned Ganohkwasra Executive Director Sandra Montour about what to do, "the Ministry wants us to develop best practices for policing sexual violence." Sandra replied, "How can province-wide best practices for addressing sexual violence exist when First Nations communities have no sexual assault funding?" That question led to reading about Aboriginal shelter funding (Riggs & Sault, 2014) and asking off-reserve service providers about their funding. Put simply, agencies in the region counted Six Nations population among those they provided services to; ministry funding formulas added Six Nations' numbers and dollars to those agencies' funding. Off-reserve agency managers however, did not know how many Six Nations victims they saw; one said "we don't do a good job" of serving them. All agencies were asking the Province for more funds to expand their services.

Hearing that major provincial funding was going to hospitals' Sexual Assault Domestic Violence units, the Executive Director spoke about the current organization of services. Drawing on layers of knowledge and expertise in relationship and dialogue with government and neighbor agencies, *she defines the problem here: it can be corrected "if they'd just watch and listen,"*

> They are still way back there when it comes to Indigenous populations on reserve. There is a lot for them to learn ... if they stop, and rather than trying to pull and trying to take, if they just watch and listen there is a lot they can learn. There are a lot of social issues that can be corrected. If they just put the resources in the right place rather than giving it to our neighbors – that's not the right place. That continues to foster the problem and make our situation worse. If they want to help our people, give the resources to the communities, don't give it to our neighbors.

These moments helped us refine our focus and direction: to learn how Six Nations people were not, as Julia said, getting to healing; to explore with service providers and police the existing organization of services, their work and funding; and to ask *Ganohkwasra's* questions.

Going into the Community: Talking with People About Their Work

When Dorothy interviewed me in the training, it was with genuine interest and kindness. I saw how to do research differently. It was a conversation. It was interesting, respectful; it delved into and valued what I do; I was the teacher and Dorothy was the learner. It was a powerful teaching. I saw how talking with people about their work can be non-threatening and non-judgmental. We built from that how we talked to people. The Six Nations Police get criticized and judged every day for their work and we were able to learn from them and build a relationship with them in doing that.

Flexibility with how we worked together and talked to people was very important; Susan joined interviews when we knew it would be safe for people and we could set the pace that was needed to really be "community-minded." Community-minded is how we at Ganohkwasra do our work and the police do theirs—that is, with our community in mind. We ask, "What can we do that will help our people who are working for Six Nations victims and community?"

Building on our previous work together, our project went roughly as follows. This is not intended as a formula, nor did it happen in a linear or timely way:

1. Review and discuss previous interviews with Six Nations survivors and others, our direction and focus, and ministry, police, professional and legal texts and literatures relevant to: (i) police reporting, (ii) responses and support services, and (iii) investigative practices.
2. Interview: (i) Six Nations Police constables, sergeants, inspectors, policy analyst, and chief, (ii) off-reserve agencies and Crown Attorneys, (iii) Six

Nations Police High-Risk Committee members, Ganohkwasra Executive Director and manager.
3. Meet to *debrief* and map throughout, where to go next, work and *sites for change*.
4. Bring together participants with our big picture map; talk through it with them, check its accuracy, what we had learned from them about their work, how it fits in producing the complex of investigation, reporting, support services, criminal justice processes, and where could be sites for change that emerged for us in the research and that could engage them going forward.
5. Debrief, discuss, and write report and Community Minded Best Practices.

Our strategy for practice throughout was:

1. Be community-minded. How we interviewed followed Julia's knowing who to talk to, when, how, and so on.
2. Listen to interviews, meet, and debrief every few interviews to go over what we were hearing, learning, and where to follow up.
3. Build maps from interviews, continually come back to our focus and direction, and find ways to talk about what we were discovering.
4. Identify what we were hearing in everyone's talk what it was to keep the community in mind and where issues arose for doing that.
5. Identify our *key practice issues* and *sites for change*: specific *work-text-work procedures*, standardized *institutional language* in use; where and how we heard it in police officers' and service providers' talk, and in texts they used that regulated and were integral to doing the work.

The *institutional response* to sexual violence comprises multiple agencies' processes including police investigations, hospital treatment and care, sexual assault center counselling, victim services, and justice processes. Our interviewing varied. Julia approached the Six Nations Police and interviews with officers were done by Ganohkwasra researchers, Gabriela Salazar and Amye Werner. Susan listened to the recordings and we all met to map and talk through what we were hearing and learning, going back and forth between the interviews, the wall map being built, and flip chart notes we were making to see what to ask next, sort and gather what we were hearing into *discoveries*. Other interviews were small group conversations, the three of us visiting off-reserve agencies, meeting with the SNPS Chief, the policy analyst, and with Ganohkwasra's Executive Director. Conversations were more than two hours long. Susan did not join the Crown Attorneys meeting but did a follow up phone interview. We navigated all along when and how to go, drawing heavily on Julia's knowledge of the community and agencies, and on Susan's of IE. Using interview data is shown in the accounts of maps later in this chapter.

Six Nations Police (SNPS) Work in a Sexual Assault Investigation Process

The Six Nations Police Service (SNPS) mandate is to provide "culturally appropriate policing," enforce the Ontario Criminal Code, and provide 24-hour service for everything in the community. SNPS is a self-administered First Nation police service, recognized as an excellent service with strong leadership, funded 48% by the provincial and 52% by federal government through a First Nations Policing Policy and Program with limited resources. Sexual violence in particular presents the Six Nations Police with challenges. The Police Chief told us: "We see the peripheral stuff, the family stuff, the damage that it does, and unfortunately, all we can do is the police stuff… to pay the attention to it that it needs, we just don't have the capacity to do it."

We learned from officers what it was to work in conditions of underfunding and with standardized texts that exclude providing culturally appropriate ways to help community members according to their laws: how basic Police College training in sexual assault investigation procedures and interviewing was inadequate for the complexities of violence and traumas they deal with on the reserve; how when a call comes, there was no sexual assault officer or unit; the road officer who takes the call may have worked back to back shifts and overtime, must work and think using categories of the Criminal Code, and will know the victim or the suspect or their families. Officers described "navigating two worldviews" (Werner in consultation with Bomberry, 2016) and "balancing" external imposed laws and methods with Haudenosaunee laws and principles of justice: "We have The Great Law; we have policing through the Criminal Code now, but with that, we have to make it fit for Six Nations." Their everyday work is constructing a fit.

Some officers envisioned agencies in the community helping one another according to the Great Law; knew the new SNPS High-Risk Committee was doing that; knew "there's a reason" for violence in the community, and how their people cannot access the help they need. The Police Chief told us SNPS wanted to "reach out to the families; is that crossing the line? We need something there, that keeps the victims and the families safe and in the community." SNPS had contracted their policy analyst to write "culture-based practices" into SNPS Policies and Procedures. Officers are accountable for their actions in investigations in its terms; SNPS were actively incorporating Haudenosaunee laws and practices into these types of operational texts that mediate between regulatory texts such as Policing Standards and local practices. The policy analyst describes some challenges,

> Officers do some community-based practices; they're very cognizant of that, but it doesn't always translate into *good policy*. If the victim is Longhouse and the officer understood that, they'd say "this or this," trying to help make them feel safe, secure, calm, protected, in order for them to share what happened to them. But that wouldn't be on that (sexual assault procedure) list. The amount

of time they spend speaking with a victim, doing smaller things that our people will respond to, are also not reflected in any of the policy or procedures that we have. It's "interview the victim." Period. At that initial stage, where they gather information and first speak with the victim, they want to help: they know "this might not be the best thing, but what other tool do I have?" Often times they really want other avenues to be able to deal with something.

Being underfunded, SNPS officers did not have time to sit and talk with the policy analyst about what they do. The Chief and policy analyst knew officers were navigating regulated textual terrain and actual circumstances on reserve. An officer describes succinctly the standard investigation process, key integral text production, and activities to "do the initial work of it." The organization of a complex of institutional sequences is evident in his description.

> Road officers always have to do the initial: you get that call; you have to go. You get the initial: you get everything going; you get the information and the evidence there; and gather the evidence. You call in the SOC (scenes of crime officer) to get the photos. Get them going to the hospital for their sexual assault kit to be performed. All that gets going with the road officer; you do up the report and then generally it'll get called, the sergeant or if there's no in-charge officer working, they'll contact the inspector, let him know what's happened and then he'll assign a CIU (Criminal Investigation Unit officer) to follow-up.

As we learned the concrete practices, we were mapping how their work of "dealing with the victim" and "having the evidence" will go into connected work sequences that will determine *severity* of what happened to the victim, what happens next, and assess what the officer puts into the Police Report and Brief that the Crown Attorney will take up for going to court.

Map Building: An Oral Collaborative Conversational Approach

We built our inquiry and map of the sexual assault investigation process and linked services throughout the project; as we were learning and exploring, we were meeting and mapping. We listened and relistened to interviews, going back and forth among them, hearing where texts entered and were integral to people's work, moved to a next step and connected up with others' work. We would meet at Ganohkwasra or Susan's home for full debriefing days with transcripts, legislation and procedure texts, large wall size mapping paper and flip chart paper to clarify our discoveries.

Knowing people's work is behind every step shown in the maps shown and described in the next section. Mapping graphically what we were learning as we went, helped us build a deep knowledge of the work organization and a full map showing a complex of intersecting work sequences and texts integral to them: officers interviewing victims; building a police file; procedures, concepts, and textual practices integral to key process work sequences. We began with depicting an officer doing things in words and texts, where a Six Nations victim, in time and space *at the initial*, is taken up in a SNPS officer's work, into *preliminary investigation*.

Mapping is selective. A map does not stand alone; it must be accompanied by an oral or written account that guides the reader or listener to seeing what the map is meant to show. It is never a final text. Its accuracy can be checked with people, it can be added to. We presented the full map to a gathering of SNPS police officers and service providers we had talked to and others from their organizations. Knowing their work, having learned from them, we could talk through it with them so they could see we had listened to them, see their work, see where and how it fit in the big picture of investigations and services, and how it affected Six Nations victims and community, and talk with them about how it might be changed.

This way of using graphical mapping is different from that in Turner's (2003, 2006) land use planning study in which *text-based work process* mapping was developed to show *sequences of institutional action* as work and texts. Here map building is an interactive process. Still, we used the conventions (Turner, 2003, p. 167): texts appear as a rectangle and work actions as a circle or written in as mundane activities—asks, observes, writes, fills in checklist form. Actions go on in *work settings*, done by people in their bodies and in space and time (see Turner, 2001, 2014). In this mapping we show in the following section the police officer and victim as stick figures to emphasize this and our focus. A *time line arrow* indicates temporality. Phases of the larger process are indicated—for example, *first police contact*, *Crown prosecution process*. A hierarchical organization is shown; *work sequences* also accomplish reporting and accountability (shown as upwards) to managers, ministries, sector databases. The work shown participates in multiple intersecting processes.

The Sexual Assault Investigation Process Maps

We discovered five "institutional moments"—shown as circled numbers on the maps—where issues arose for victims, SNPS officers, and the community. Much can be said about each, however, our focus in the following brief map-by-map accounts that describe the map-building process, is on what happens when a victim reports, and at the initial contact with police. The markings and words we wrote on the map appear in each Figure's account in italics.

Figure 16.1 is a section of an early mapping. It shows how we were seeing the multiple *lines*—ways a victim may report what had happened to her. A map legend upper left distinguishes what we were tracking in different color markers: *SNPS work*, *boss texts* and *external processes*, off-reserve victim services (Victim Services and Victim Witness Assistance Program shown on the map as *VS, VWAP*), and *key action sites*. The *stick figure* victim, *family*, *friends*, *Ganohkwasra*, and *community agencies* are bottom left. The *time line* marks our discovering the actual institutional work and work sequences as going

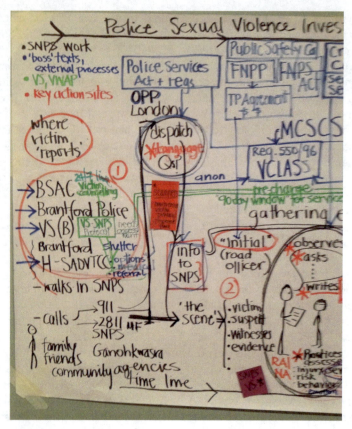

Fig. 16.1 Where a victim reports

on in time and space, and notes that what happens for victim, families, and community, goes on differently.

We tracked every *sequence line* where a *victim "reports:"* each service agency is shown with *action arrow* and how the victim reports written as: *calls, walks in, 24/7 line, protocol, needs assessment, options, referral*. We were learning service providers' work in each setting (hospital, sexual assault center, Victim Services (VS) or Brantford police, the nearby municipal police or shelter). Drawing those lines showed how every sequence—including where the victim reports to *SNPS*—took victims off reserve, with consequences for them and community. Geography matters: we knew from interviews with survivors and Ganohkwasra staff, it was an issue for victims who must travel—without bus service–to the city; we had just learned from officers how, for example, when a Six Nations victim calls the Emergency *911* number, it goes to an Ontario Provincial Police (*OPP*) center in urban *London* over an hour away, where a *dispatcher* who does not know Six Nations people or reserve geography asks standard questions (*language Qs?*); the call may be bumped down the OPP queue, delays occur, an OPP sequence of work is activated; and it was not clear how information reached SNPS. We used color sticky notes to indicate where issues emerged for SNPS police (*info to SNPS?*).

This early map also shows national laws and provincial regulations that, we were learning from officers, with underfunding, organize their work. We were hearing officers use *institutional terms—the scene, the initial, CIU*—when telling us what they did. They gathered information but would give a victim time to come to the station to make a formal statement if "she wasn't ready." They saw people experiencing trauma; knew what "historical trauma" and "lateral violence" looked like in the community and did not have a way within standard procedures to offer or take a victim to services in the community. SNPS wanted that.[4]

At the scene an officer must *assess injury, severity, risk, behavior, and emotion*, take notes, and take the victim to hospital and a *safe place*. Doing so orients to future work filling in provincially standardized *forms* in the data management system. One form asks if the victim is "credible," if she "cooperated." The officer is shown on the map gathering evidence to develop the occurrence report; *observes, asks* about *victim, suspect, witnesses*, looks for physical *evidence, writes notes*, according to procedure.

SNPS officers and Chief spoke of keeping the victim and families and community safe. We learned from them the major issues of services being off reserve, where was a safe place, and having no means to assess or address safety and risk according to the actualities for their people (See also Wilson & Pence, 2006 on risk).

Figure 16.2 shows a later mapping and our learning progress that recognizes the significance of officers' textual work at the scene, when we'd learned more about and included the texts that regulate officers' work (national *Criminal Code of Canada* and provincial *Evidence Act, Policing Standards and guideline*s, *Reg.550/96, Guidelines, LE-024 DV*) and that, with Police College training, enter officers' assessment and interviewing practices at the scene. We were drawing, with *double lines*, where we saw this entry into practice occur (the line from *Policing Standards* and *LE-024* guideline for domestic violence occurrences, to what the officer does and says at first contact with the victim). We were highlighting with stars, the officer's actual activities, adding to the map sticky notes where community-minded interventions based on Haudenosaunee principles could be inserted to help officers' safety assessments and referrals.

Figure 16.2 shows two spots on the map as sites for change, indicated with circled numbers: *(2)* the officer *observes, asks,* and *writes notes*; and *(3)* the intersecting moment in which the officer then *refers* and *reports* (*double lines* upwards in multiple sequences). Officers spoke of the importance of the SNPS High-Risk Committee (*SNHRC*) to them and the community: where officers refer to victim services (*VS* refer) we mark with a star where they can *report to SNHRC* in addition to SNPS *sergeant*. Proceeding, the officer *inputs notes*

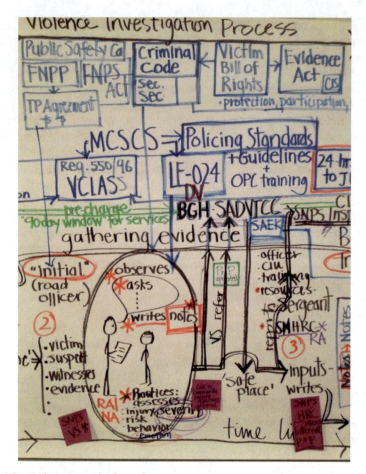

Fig. 16.2 Policing standards at the scene

(3) from the scene and initial into the file management system and Crown Brief, practices some called "writing for the Crown."

We were identifying as issues, the standard procedure requirement for officers to refer to off-reserve victim services (*VS refer*) and standard risk assessment texts (**Practices*). SNPS identified two gaps here for road officers: assessment texts and methods do not fit Six Nations realities or needs; no policy or procedure written into SNPS Policies and Procedures that applies to the initial investigative practices regarding sexual violence.

We were learning from interviews and examining the actual texts officers used, how different risk assessment questions miss the complex kinds and layers of violence and sexual violence SNPS officers and Six Nations agencies and community know and experience. For example, checklists had 13–20 questions requiring Officers to check "Yes" or "No" if they have "offered Victim Services," "taken them to a place of safety," and "did they accept."

Also, "What is their reaction, are they cooperative?" Checkboxes limit how the officer observes, talks to, and interprets what is going on with the victim. Julia knew that a victim from Six Nations may not make direct eye contact, may appear passive, and may have many good reasons to not want to go to Brantford at that time, not call off-reserve Victim Services, and not know in that moment what would be a safe place for her or him. She may appear uncooperative if, per the checklist, she declines to go to the hospital or to answer multiple questions the form asks.

We at Ganohkwasra know that what is happening for the victim, if it is historical (that is, the experience of sexual violence happened in the past, over a year previous) and she is reporting in the present, is that she will have just experienced a triggering event. Traumas are layered. She may have seen the perpetrator, there may have also been a current episode of violence, and she is dealing with post-traumatic stress disorder (PTSD) symptoms such as sleep disorder, self-harming, anxiety and panic and depression. She may be using alcohol or other drugs to mask the pain from a range of traumas and these symptoms are part of her/his life.

When interviewing sexual assault victims, all police officers including SNPS need to understand PTSD symptoms, and the kinds of things—words, questions, ways of asking and body language—that can act as triggers. This includes the investigation language that police are using (Werner in consultation with Bomberry, 2016). *Police officers need to understand the behaviors that a victim of sexual violence and lateral violence will exhibit—the victim in front of them may be frozen or dissociative, leave their bodies, or she may be angry. She may be also be continuing the fear-based decisions and lifestyle she's been living and will not be able to problem-solve or she may decide to report and may not be able to take the action to do so.*

SNPS officers spoke to us about putting the focus on victims, their safety and experience, including the safety of their families and the community. And while they knew that helping the victim right there in the moment was paramount, they did not have the means or ways to do it.

We saw that taking into account what officers knew about families, extended families and friends and inter-family relationships that might be unique risk factors for the victim and others, should have a way to be brought in and recognized as significant risk factors for Six Nations victims. Six Nations community agencies have that kind of community-based knowledge. At that initial conversation with the victim, evidence-gathering practices using Criminal Code categories of crime and severity, often do not help. They shift the focus from the victim and her or his actual multi-layered injuries, circumstances and risks, to what happened that can be seen and taken up by officers in the terms of the criminal code as evidence of a crime by a perpetrator. SNPS navigated complex text management work with a lack of resources and specialized sexual violence training and no way to make cases move forward in ways that make sense to Six Nations victims and community.

Figure 16.3 shows how we focused in—Dorothy Smith calls it *laying your magnifying glass over a spot in the map of the terrain you're exploring*—to talk about what we'd learned about what *NO FIT* looked like in practice at the scene and the initial. We were looking to identify where changes could be made to practices. We used two colors of sticky notes to identify who could make changes: SNPS in their *Policies and Procedures* and *Directives*, and Ministries in their funding (shown on the map as $$$$). Having learned First Nations Policing Program funding language, we asked for recognition for SNPS actual working conditions, dollars for equitable, plus "rural," and "high-risk" funding. Knowing SNPS day-to-day and other agencies' work from interviews, we drafted Community-Minded Best Practices for Sexual Assault Investigations (CMP) as a prototype protocol for frontline workers and to fit their policies and procedures. Julia would go on to seek SNPS and agencies'

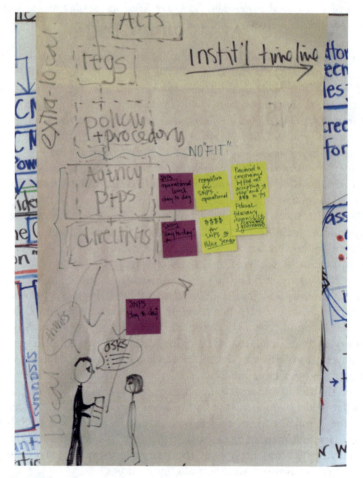

Fig. 16.3 No fit

approval and incorporate the CMP into Ganohkwasra's sexual assault training for frontline workers. We drafted a Safety Risk Assessment and Referral sheet for use at the initial for SNPS and agencies' consideration.

When police lay a charge, all the documents of the case go to the *Crown (prosecuting) Attorney*. Figure 16.4 shows how we were focusing on the actualities of what the Crown wants and considers, how that is done and police officers know that (*pre-charge consult, collaboration, CA screens files*). Crown Attorneys spoke about what happens in court and what they must consider and assess prior to going to court. The work involves screening and assessing everything they have that will have to be put before the judge (the texts in the Crown Brief and evidence submitted by police). This is textual work, shown on the map as *screening form, assesses, quality, sufficiency of evidence*. Crown Attorneys assess all with a view to what can and will be *heard* in court; will the victim be seen as a credible witness and knowing the victim will be, in legal parlance, "whacked" by defense lawyers (see Tanovich, 2015). The Victim's Statement,

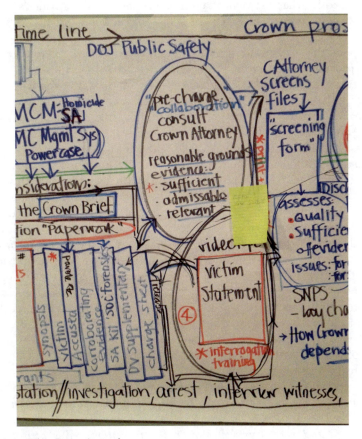

Fig. 16.4 The Crown's work

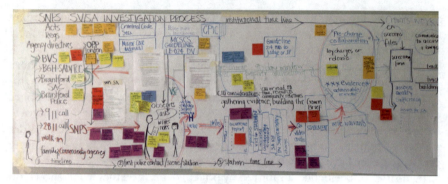

Fig. 16.5 Mapping, discovery, and working with texts

a text produced by the police formally interviewing the victim (*Victim Statement*) will be part of "full disclosure" to the defense lawyer. Its content will be compared to what the victim says in court and any discrepancies attacked. Hence, Crowns want that Statement at the initial, not when the victim "felt ready."

Mapping this work and drawing on interviews with off-reserve victim service providers also revealed issues for Six Nations victims and community in two areas not addressed here: how Victim Services (VS) who provide "pre-charge" services and Victim Witness Assistance Program (VWAP) who work for the Crown "post-charge," assess trauma, risk, and eligibility for their services; and the forms of bail hearings and releases that did not fit Six Nations realities. Further, getting to court could take one to three years.

Figure 16.5 shows working with the actual regulations and texts taped directly onto the map. We were making and identifying with color sticky notes, our discoveries of what got in the action and what could become action items for the ministries responsible for the processes we had explored. Different colors identify regulatory level texts, texts integral to procedures, guides, and potential changes that were do-able in the terms of the actual *institutional complex of work processes* we were coming to know our way around in; and what actions would build working relations and knowledge that would ultimately be useful for Six Nations. Mapping *institutional procedures* as courses of action with the actual integral administering and regulating texts stuck onto the map, allowed us to discover and recommend to the Ministry, for example, that SNPS get "violence and risk pay," equitable pay, funding for a sexual assault officer and new Six Nations victim services.

Figure 16.6 shows the full map.

Our successes really came from building and using that map: presenting it in-person to all the stakeholders who each could see the reality differently from how they had, even though they work in it every day. They saw for themselves where they fit and what their work did for the institution and what it did to the victim—they could see what it was for the victim to experience.

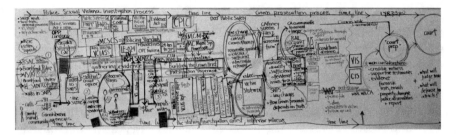

Fig. 16.6 The map used at the final gathering

We put the story to each section of the map: we discovered this, this, this from you. The map showed that we had listened to them, we heard them, and we had put together what they told us about their work and their working conditions and concerns and hopes. It is complex, but they can see the relations and can talk about that.

It is a great visual tool. The map and the stories go hand in hand; essential is knowing the work and seeing how what they can do is limited, how each connects and their concerns. There are misunderstandings of processes. Seeing people's work this way, with the map, increased understanding and compassion for the victim.

Our final gathering brought together the people we had talked to with the map: talking through the mapped sequences, checking if we had gotten right what we had learned from them. They said it was powerful "seeing the big picture," "how our work is connected," that it helped, "it broke down silos." Some said seeing "what their work did and how it fit," would help them talk to colleagues and do their work better. This gathering was a continuation of how we worked—orally and collaboratively learning together—in conversations that were not an easy path, but that were powerful for showing and building in-common ground and for making change.

CALLS TO ACTION: STRENGTHENING SIX NATIONS AGENCIES

Further working with the community and off-reserve service providers, we researched what other police forces were doing about sexual violence and best practices (Government of Alberta, 2013) and what legal and judicial practice advocates were debating and doing (Randall & Haskell, 2013; Tanovich, 2015). At Crown Attorney trainings, we listened with police and Crowns to Tanovich, Randall and forensic experts on evidence criteria and defense lawyer practice and to speakers including Julia on sexual assault services. Seeing the talk and texts as discourses going on among people, we saw how their operating concepts of "best practices" and "trauma-informed" excluded Six Nations realities; how our work was unique in Ontario and Canada; how to state its distinctiveness within relevant active discourses and strongly speak from Six Nations' standpoint. Speaking to Ministries in our final report: We said, "*Listen…*"

Six Nations had built a net of services and procedures to establish a High-Risk Committee (HRC) and *Community Safety Response* to high-risk situations. The community process was led by Ganohkwasra and the Six Nations Police; some situations involved sexual assault. *Response* processes and procedures are based on Haudenosaunee values and principles: the focus is the safety of the whole community; frontline practices are *culture based*. The procedures that agencies follow in high-risk situations link the work of Six Nations and off-reserve agencies. As agencies carry them out in high-risk situations, SNPS leadership and relationships among agencies are built and strengthened. The HRC in its first year of existence developed an in-common Risk Assessment-Needs Assessment checklist and community safety protocol. The HRC and protocol were developed to assist community agencies in providing services and protection for all community members. Agencies request the assistance of all agencies, share information and develop case-specific High-Risk Joint Safety Action Plans. Here was an inter-agency model for building a SNPS Victim Services on Six Nations Territory and a model for inserting a safety assessment and referral procedure to community safety planning agencies right at the initial that could keep victims safe and on reserve (see Fig. 16.2, *SNHRC*). And Ganohkwasra was building a Haudenosaunee Response to sexual violence.

Community-Minded Practices: A Haudenosaunee Response

Ganohkwasra's goal was to strengthen community agencies and their working together to help sexual violence victims and the whole community. Having a text that was an active ongoing, renewable agreement among agencies would assist that goal. We submitted to the Ministry—rather than generic *best practices*–the *Community-Minded Practices for Investigating Sexual Violence on Six Nations of the Grand River Territory*. It was a prototype for a protocol that would guide the on and off-reserve frontline practitioners' work we knew was connected to sexual assault investigations. It was already changing work relationships among agencies on and off reserve that had signed on. Julia emphasizes how the text enters, in language, Haudenosaunee principles into people's thinking and practice,

A Haudenosaunee response doesn't focus on a victim but also on perpetrators and secondary victims. This is how relationships are restored and healed. Agencies signing our Community-Minded Practices protocol agree to respond to sexual violence based on the Haudenosaunee values and principles that we included in the text in the Mohawk and Cayuga language and explain, that come from our teachings and our texts that guide our work and how we support our community.

Our report to the Ministry (Bomberry et al., 2016) addressed Six Nations underfunding and the discriminatory organization of service delivery. It is ethnographic. It does not impose categories. It spoke directly to the Ministry, told them what we discovered, showed where there were built-in discriminations. It called on them to recognize the expertise of Six Nations leaders and to listen to them; to work with other ministries under their mandates to effect the changes we were asking for. The map was appended, shown whole and in five sections. We used "Calls to Action," echoing Senator Murray Sinclair (Truth and Reconciliation Commission of Canada, 2015). We called on government to recognize the expertise and initiatives already happening on Six Nations that ministries could support. It provided a framework for their action, *Going Forward: Tools and Actions for Changing the Relationship, and Respectful Practices Framework*, and identified these priorities:

- Equitably fund Six Nations Police Services (SNPS).
- Fund a Six Nations Police Services Sexual Assault Unit or special officers.
- Establish and provide secure funding to a Six Nations Sexual Assault Centre and recognize Six Nations sexual assault counselors (disentangle funds from off reserve).
- Work with ministry partners to fund and provide secure funding for more SNPS officers, training, initiatives related to sexual assault, human trafficking, missing and murdered Indigenous women and youth.
- Support SNPS High-Risk Committee initiatives, Community Minded Practices Protocol (CMP) and SNPS safety Assessment tool.
- Establish and fund SN Victim Services (disentangle funds from off reserve).
- Establish and fund SN Victim Witness Assistance Program (disentangle funds from off reserve).

Changes and Outcomes

All of our priority items were acted on:

- SNPS officers received a raise.
- SNPS received dedicated funds and has a sexual assault officer.
- Six Nations now has an Indigenous Victim Services on Territory.
- Six Nations has a funded Sexual Violence Healing Centre—something Ganohkwasra had been fighting for since 2001.

Other major changes took place in and for the community: Ganohkwasra now works directly with various ministry partners; Ganohkwasra participated on six Ending Violence Against Women provincial committees where before they did not; Ganohkwasra is funded to give trainings with SNPS to other communities on their high-risk initiative; community and off-reserve agencies are signing on to the CMP Protocol.

Continuing the project, Ganohkwasra was funded to design, produce, and deliver a sequence of Sexual Assault Prevention Training modules for community and off-reserve frontline workers in the region including in the justice system.[5] Several hundred attended. The training increases frontline workers' understanding of Indigenous experiences of sexual violence; it offers Haudenosaunee cultural-aware words and practices that are relevant in the regional context; practices for healing that, when we began, people could not "get to." It incorporates what we learned: attendees' actual everyday work and the standardized language and textual practices that reproduce *institutional responses* and exclude Six Nations' realities; "culture-aware practices" that would help frontline workers help Six Nations victims.

We presented this work with co-researcher Amye Werner to institutional ethnographers at a Special Forum for the Institutional Ethnography Division of the International Sociology Association at Ryerson University, Toronto, Canada, July 2018. We are glad that Dorothy sat in front to see the fruitions of our work using her teachings.

Conclusions

In our second project there were three very special things: Ganohkwasra lead; we kept central Haudenosaunee values and principles; we could speak with the authority and expertise of Ganohkwasra and the Six Nations Police who work for their people.

Our work was inclusive, our interviews conversational. Our report shows our cultural distinctiveness; it gives the authoritative voice to our people, not to outside researchers looking at us. Truly, no harm was done to people and we are proud of this.

How we knew about people's work by using IE was key. We learned their language for doing their work and that was really helpful for us. Using IE, you have tools to learn the practices and language of those who can help and those who make decisions; learn how their work is connected and how each participates in these processes; and be part of being able to change what happens and how it goes on.

We at Ganohkwasra continue to use what we learned. We knew how frontline workers were in relation to victims and we could show that. We used IE to get the whole story of people's work and that is behind the map. For some workers it was filling in a form; for others—like Ganohkwasra—victims walk in the front door. The mapping was a profound tool for us to see how to help other frontline workers, which we've been able to do since. Without IE and the mapping work we did, that we presented to everyone so they could see their work, we wouldn't have been able to do that.

Our biggest success is we're still using it and what we learned doing it. It is in our sexual assault prevention training to frontline workers. We have built relationships with the Six Nations Police and with off-reserve workers. We can call them and talk, and it is because I use their terminology and relate to their concerns and work because of knowing their work. It was not just a research project. Our work continues.

Institutional ethnographers can make significant institutional changes and can expand institutional ethnography's range of possibilities for explorations of ruling in projects that learn from and with Indigenous people. New ways can be developed for putting institutional ethnography into practice as Dorothy Smith began it–as a collective project of research *with people and for change*. We investigated areas of exploration familiar to institutional ethnographers using IE, however our ethnographic methods and ways of proceeding were designed to learn and effectively explore from the standpoint of Six Nations Grand River Territory, work with Haudenosaunee principles, and prioritize the community's interests and goals for changes. Our success was that combination and Ganohkwasra's integration into everyday work practices.

In this chapter we illustrated mapping as an oral and collaborative conversational approach in which we were constantly learning and developing knowledge together. Using this mapping method helped us from beginning to end, refine our focus and direction, explore complex work, come to know and be able to say what was wanted for the community, and bring people together for making change effectively.

We developed a full map of institutional processes from what we (Ganohkwasra) knew and what we learned from our police and on and off-reserve services. Making the full IE map gave us a lot of understanding about where gaps were and where there were barriers, but also things that were working in our community. This process and how we had been able to go about it really helped us build our relationship with them. Listening and learning from people was different. It was amazing. Hearing about their work, learning how you go about talking about someone's work on something that is a highly sensitive topic, something not talked about in our community, and finding how we could talk about it through that process—that in itself was healing our relationships. We are continuing, talking with the police and our other agencies about their work with the goal we share of helping our community. And we are planning mapping training workshops.

Notes

1. The original Haudenosaunee society of five nations—known as the Iroquois Confederacy—dated to the 1100s (the Tuscarora joined in 1720) is the oldest participatory democracy on earth. Its active democratic principles and organization set out in The Great Law of Peace were the model for the 1788 confederation of the 13 colonies into one United States republic.
2. Six Nations people experienced multiple governing attempts to assimilate and eliminate Indigenous people and their Territories: governments "stole" their land (Wright, 1992); took children into residential schools built to "take the savage out of the Indian," where sexual abuse and starvation were common and children were taught to hurt one another, resulting in disproportionate numbers of Indigenous children in the child welfare system (Castellano, Archibald, &

DeGagne, 2008); disproportionate numbers of Indigenous youth, men, and women experience, disappear, and die by violence and are taken into a justice system that is biased against them and causes them harm (Royal Commission on Aboriginal Peoples, 1996; Truth and Reconciliation Commission of Canada, 2015). Blatant discrimination in funding to Indigenous organizations and provision of infrastructure and services to communities persists, as do government attempts to take First Nations' lands, all going on in seemingly innocuous institutional forms (Legislative Assembly of Ontario, 2015; McGillivray & Comaskey, 2012).
3. Sally Hacker (Smith, 1990) described her methods as "being with people" and "listening so you pick up what is really important…what is bothering people." The goal was making changes that people wanted to inequitable and unjust conditions they were in. Smith writes:

> I radically altered my methods of interviewing and analysis, and I find myself…describing what I'm now doing as "listening:" Beyond being attentive to the surface features of what people are saying…it's an attentiveness to the shape or form or organization that the "material" is beginning to inform you about. The woodworking sculptor describes the "soul" of the tree coming to meet him as he cuts, carves, and polishes. Listening is that kind of practice – a tuning-in of a capacity to find, hear, what that is already there. (5)

4. Instead, officers are required to offer and/or take the victim off reserve to hospital, the investigative focus being forensic evidence on her person. The hospital gathers medical information then funnels victims through "community referral" processes to a network of urban "City Response" agencies who use different, standardized risk assessment tools; the medical evidence and information into hospital databanks and health and police nation-wide databases (hospitals' "anonymous reporting option"). An institutional organization of services that discriminated against Six Nations victims, community and their healing services, became visible.
5. A 2017 needs assessment (Johnston Research, 2017) had indicated that 77% of these frontline workers wanted to learn wellness strategies for working with Indigenous community members impacted by sexual assault.

REFERENCES

Bomberry, J., Turner, S. M., & Werner, A. (2016). On-reserve first nations police reporting, responses and support services, and investigative practices. Toronto, Ministry of Community Safety and Correctional Services, Ontario Police Responses to Sexual Violence Against Aboriginal Women and Girls, 2015–2016 Program.

Castellano, M. B., Archibald, L., & DeGagne, M. (2008). *From truth to reconciliation: Transforming the legacy of residential schools* (pp. 119–140). Ottawa. Aboriginal Healing Foundation.

Cousins, M. (2005). Aboriginal justice: A Haudenosaunee approach. In W. D. McCaslin (Ed.), *Justice as healing indigenous ways: Writings on community peacemaking and restorative justice from the Native Law Centre* (pp. 141–159). St. Paul. Living Justice Press.

Government of Alberta. (2013). *Best practices for investigating and prosecuting sexual assault*. Edmonton. Alberta Justice and Solicitor General Criminal Justice Division. https://open.alberta.ca/publications/9781460110249.

Johnston Research Inc. (2017). *Grand River of the Six Nations Territory sexual assault needs assessment*. www.johnstonresearch.ca.

Legislative Assembly of Ontario. (2015). *Final report. Select Committee on Sexual Violence and Harassment*. https://www.ola.org/en/legislative-business/committees/sexual-violence-harassment/parliament-41/reports/final-report. Ontario Legislative Assembly.

McGillivray, A., & Comaskey, B. (2012). *Black eyes all of the time: Intimate violence, aboriginal women, and the justice system*. Toronto: University of Toronto Press.

Randall, M., & Haskell, L. (2013). Trauma-informed approaches to law: Why restorative justice must understand trauma and psychological coping. *The Dalhousie Law Journal, 36* (2), 501–533.

Riggs, J., & Sault, M. (2014). *Aboriginal family violence in Ontario needs assessment*. Aboriginal Shelters of Ontario.

Royal Commission on Aboriginal Peoples. (1996). *Report of the royal commission on Aboriginal peoples*. https://data2.archives.ca/e/e448/e011188230-01.pdf. Ottawa, Canada. Retrieved October 15, 2020.

Smith, D. E. (1990). On Sally L. Hacker's method. In S. L. Hacker, D. E. Smith, & S. M. Turner (Eds.), *Doing it the hard way: Investigations of gender and technology* (pp. 1–17). London. Unwin Hyman Inc.

Tanovich, D. M. (2015). "Whack" no more: Infusing equality into the ethics of defence lawyering in Sexual Assault Cases. *Ottawa Law Review, 45*(3), 495–525.

Truth and Reconciliation Commission of Canada. (2015). *Final report of the truth and reconciliation commission of Canada: Summary: Honouring the truth, reconciling for the future*. Winnipeg: Truth and Reconciliation of Canada.

Turner, S. M. (2001). Texts and the institutions of municipal planning government: The power of texts in the public process of land development. *Studies in Cultures, Organizations, and Societies, 7*(2), 297–325.

Turner, S. M. (2003). *The social organization of planning: A study of institutional action as texts and work processes*. Unpublished doctoral dissertation, University of Toronto.

Turner, S. M. (2006). Mapping institutions as work and text. In D. E. Smith (Ed.), *Institutional ethnography as practice* (pp. 139–162). Lanham, MD: Rowman and Littlefield.

Turner, S. M. (2014). Reading practices as decision processes. In D. E. Smith & S. M. Turner (Eds.), *Incorporating texts into institutional ethnographies* (pp. 197–224). Toronto: University of Toronto Press.

Werner, A. in consultation with J. Bomberry. (2016). *Exploring the gaps and barriers experienced by sexual assault survivors from Six Nations of the Grand River Territory: Aboriginal sexual violence community response initiative report*. Ganohkwasra Family Assault Support Services.

Wesley-Esquimaux, C., & Smolewski, M. (2004). *Historical trauma and aboriginal healing*. Ottawa: Aboriginal Healing Foundation.

Williams, P. (2018). *Kayanerenko:wa: The Great Law of Peace*. Winnipeg: University of Manitoba Press.

Wilson, A., & Pence, E. (2006). U.S. legal interventions in the lives of battered women: An indigenous assessment. In D. E. Smith (Ed.), *Institutional ethnography as practice* (pp. 199–225). Lanham, MD: Rowman and Littlefield.

Wright, R. (1992). *Stolen continents: The "new world" through Indian eyes*. Boston: Houghton Mifflin.

CHAPTER 17

Mapping Institutional Relations for Local Policy Change: The Case of Lead Poisoning in Syracuse New York

Frank Ridzi

Syracuse, New York, is a major refugee resettlement community in the United States, possibly in part due to its very affordable housing stock. With this advantage, however, comes the challenge of maintaining housing safety amid a flooded market that commands only low rental fees. While this can include a variety of problems ranging from insulation and infestations to tripping and fire hazards, in this paper I focus on the issue of lead poisoning. The federal government outlawed lead in residential paint in the 1970s but, due to costs, people have largely remediated it by painting over it rather than removing it. While this is a relatively inexpensive and effective strategy (with painting over costing in the neighborhood of $5000 as opposed to removal which may reach as high as $50,000), it means that this approach is not a permanent solution. As homes continue to age the paint once again begins to chip and expose young children to the harmful effects of lead.

Researchers have linked lead with a wide variety of deleterious effects, especially with exposure during the first few years of life. High friction surfaces such as windows and doors are particularly dangerous because they are easy for children to reach and once dust gets on their hands it can easily find its way into their mouths. Lead poisoning is linked with delinquency, ADHD, disruptive classroom behavior, repeat teen pregnancy, and tobacco use among other things (Gump et al., 2017; Lane et al., 2008).

F. Ridzi (✉)
Central New York Community Foundation, Le Moyne College, Syracuse, NY, USA
e-mail: ridzifm@lemoyne.edu

© The Author(s) 2021
P. C. Luken and S. Vaughan (eds.), *The Palgrave Handbook of Institutional Ethnography*,
https://doi.org/10.1007/978-3-030-54222-1_17

Using an IE Approach to Address the Issue

The origins of the IE approach are as an action-oriented ethnographic method that strives to make visible broader structures and relationships that influence our daily lives (and that we may wish to change) but that are not immediately evident to people from where they are situated (Hussey, 2012; Nichols, 2016). In this paper, I examine how this approach, and specifically the mapping of institutional relations (Pence, 1997, 2001; Prodinger & Turner, 2013), can and has been used to identify, coordinate and keep track of the many complementary activities of a community coalition (Kania & Kramer, 2011; Ridzi & Doughty, 2017) of service providers, community activists, policy decision makers and institutional leaders.

I proceed by presenting the mapping diagram I created as a player in this mix, an academic, a philanthropic professional, and a coalition member seeking to figure out how best the resources at my disposal could contribute to positive systems change (see Kania, Kramer, & Senge, 2018; Kramer, 2017). In this way, I endeavored to do what IE researchers such as Nichols (2016) and Mykhalovskiy and Church (2006) have advocated by packaging the insights that an Institutional Ethnography yields in ways that are recognizable and actionable to practitioners.

Point of Departure

The point of departure for this exploration is the perspective of refugee parents as voiced during a subcommittee meeting of the Syracuse Common Council (the legislative branch of city government that makes laws and passes ordinances). At this meeting several members of Syracuse's refugee community stood before council members and shared, in broken English, their fears for their children and their children's future due to lead contamination in their rented homes. On public display was the wicked irony of people traveling thousands of miles with an unknown destination other than to escape war, persecution, and repression, only to find a new terror in the homes where they had resettled.

Lead exposure, long known to be correlated with insidious and permanent effects on cognitive ability, classroom behavior, emotional behavior, and delinquency, lacks any telltale odor or color (Gump et al., 2017; Lane et al., 2008). Rather, a family can inspect and inhabit a home for years or even decades before they realize it has poisoned them. In Syracuse, where winters are unforgiving, there are many other things to be concerned with, such as insulation, heating and the overall safety of the neighborhood. It is too easy to overlook the possibility of lead contamination when renting a home, especially since the United States outlawed lead paint in housing back in 1978 and anyone who is new to the nation would certainly not have any recollection of our efforts to ban it from things like leaded gasoline and paint on toys. Furthermore, anyone who has noticed the tribulations of Flint Michigan in the news due to lead leaching into the water supply (CNN, 2019) might assume that water is the main source of poisoning. In Syracuse, it is not water at all but rather the lead paint that lines the interiors and exteriors of homes built before 1978 in this legacy city.

Syracuse is merely a microcosm of a larger statewide problem. In 2016 New York State was the worst state in the nation in children with elevated blood lead levels (i.e., BLL over 5 µg/dL) (CDC, 2019) with 17,745 New York children (5610 from New York City alone) (National Center for Healthy Housing 2018). As with Syracuse, the problem across the state is older homes since "79% of New York housing was built before 1978 and New York has the highest percent of housing built before 1950 of any state" (Curtis, 2019).

In recent years awareness has grown about the fact that this toxin is not gone but merely forgotten until paint begins to chip and shed dust particles that once again put families in contact with what landlords had painted over many years before. It is this awareness that brings these mothers to the Common Council, fearful that their children are crawling through lead dust particles and then putting their dusted fists in their teething mouths. It only takes a split second and a shockingly small amount of dust to do irreversible damage to the brain including loss of IQ points and elements of concentration and self-control (Gump et al., 2017; Lane et al., 2008).

To these new American mothers it seems just as horrible that lead poisoning is 100% preventable. Why are they so vulnerable to this unseen monster when our country has been aware of it for decades? Why are their homes not safe? Who is to blame and what can we do, if it is not already too late?

In this lived experience we see a disjuncture between the idealized notion of finding political refuge in another country and the actual lived experience of these refugees. With the concept of refuge and in the international political structures established to create it, there is a sense of safety and of being better off. But this is not necessarily what happens when families enter into a poisonous domicile. In this situation we find the problematic that guides this exploration.

From the vulnerable standpoint of a resettled refugee, it is beyond frustrating that one can find oneself in the midst of such danger after fleeing to the "land of opportunity," a nation that leads the world in many ways yet places its asylum seekers within the clutches of a long known and completely preventable danger. It may seem like environmental racism or a form of structural racism in which no one person is acting out of racial intent but specific racialized and ethnic groups, because of their newness to the nation, and economic and political vulnerability, end up disproportionately affected. Indeed, it is not only refugees but also lower income, less white, residents of the city who tend to live in the neighborhoods that have the highest poisoning rates. Countywide, through the diligent work of local government, the rate of children exposed to lead poisoning has dropped to approximately 5%. However, when looking at the city, where most of the poverty is concentrated, that rate rises to 11%.

Furthermore, zeroing in on specific neighborhood census tracts the poisoning rate is as high as 24% (Onondaga County Health Department, 2019). In such neighborhoods, some of which are primary resettlement targets for refugees, family after family walks unknowingly into a new type of warzone.

Combining IE with Coalition Work to Unpack the Problematic Relations Governing the Situation

How then is this possible? What are the institutional relations of governing and ruling that either cause lead poisoning to happen or prevent our community from solving it? From the standpoint of new American refugee parents, the solutions are opaque because no one has clearly mapped out the institutions.

The solutions were also not clear to those in the audience. How could resettlement agencies place people in danger? How could the federal government be so negligent? Who was to blame and what do we need to do to fix this? None of this seemed clear to the Common Councilors or the audience.

As other IE studies reveal, this case is not unique. It is a facet of modern life that the relationships that produce our day-to-day experiences are often not visible from where we stand. Instead, it takes diligent work to trace the connections between what we experience and the many factors holding that experience in place and re-creating it again and again.

A common goal with an institutional ethnography is making these connections visible or, in the metaphor of Dorothy Smith, turning a sweater inside out so that we can see the stitching that holds it in place (1987). One way to do this is through mapping daily interactions as they begin with a person's standpoint and extend out to implicate the actions and patterns of behavior of the many other actors that together comprise an institution.

In this case I begin with this shared experience of refugee mothers and rely on a larger research project in which I am investigating the collaborative work of community coalitions by using ethnographic approaches of observation, conversations and interviews (such as described by Hussey, 2012; Smith, 1990) to figure out and indeed map out both the multiple components of the way society is presently organized and how community groups take action to improve them.

Community coalitions often involve people from multiple sectors working together toward a common agenda (Kania & Kramer, 2011, p. 36). They are basically activist movements for positive community change. For this research I attended community meetings in which collaborations were developing as a participant. I then invited some other participants in collaboration meetings to participate in in-depth, open-ended, unstructured interviews about the role and nature of collaborative efforts. As with other IE work, one of the strategies for organizing what I learned is creating a diagram that, much like a map, helps a person understand the many factors beyond their view that create their lived experience (Pence, 1997, 2001; Prodinger & Turner, 2013). Also like a map, this research can point to places where the community can make improvements to rectify the disjuncture that constitutes our problematic. As a participant observer who is both researching collaborative community efforts and serving as a professional within the philanthropic sector, the mapping of institutional relations has the added advantage of identifying and pointing out where philanthropic and collaborative actors can most strategically make efforts in order to transform the institutional relations that govern the situation for the better. Since these mapping practices begin from the standpoint of new refugee parents, it also has the quality of being accountable, ultimately, to them as opposed to an abstract accountability to the general public or some form of government entity.

You Are Here—Mapping the Existing Relations that Perpetuate Lead Poisoning Among Children

Dorothy Smith describes the metaphor of a map within IE as similar to "…being in the malls in Toronto and you can find a map that says, "You are here." And it is that kind of finger pointing off the text, into the world in which you stand, looking at the map or reading it" (Carroll, 2010, p. 27; Rankin, 2017). Part of the value of an IE approach is that, prior to investigation, much of these institutional components that produce a negative experience, such as that of our refugee mothers, are not visible from their daily lived experiences. This is indeed the case here. As one community official shared, "None of this is visible to the renter. We barely understand it so they wouldn't!"

The experience of the refugee mothers (unfortunately) typically begins not with concern over lead but with startling news from a pediatrician. Sometimes this is in response to overt and frightening symptoms. One refugee family recalls not remembering exactly when their child became ill with extreme diarrhea and uncontrolled vomiting. After taking the child to the hospital his mother learned he had a blood lead level of 32 micrograms per deciliter, which was much higher than the warning threshold of 5. "I kept saying 'what is lead?' to the doctor, …I was confused because in my country we don't have lead.'" (CNY Vitals, 2019).

Other times, the discovery of lead is much less dramatic, but just as scary. One family learned during a routine doctor's visit that their 2-year-old son's blood lead level had risen dramatically due to lead paint after only four months in a new apartment. Seeking a cause, they found paint flakes along the baseboard near their children's play area. They furthermore realized in horror that their practice of putting a fan in the window was blowing the toxin into their children's mouths (Breidenbach, 2018, December 20).

Yet another family learned that the carpeting on their porch did not have a rubber backing which allowed the lead paint underneath to rub off with the friction of foot traffic and poison their children as it permeated the rug.

This sense of horror, only after the fact, has led some in the medical profession locally to liken children to the canaries that coal miners would bring

Fig. 17.1 Map of the initial institution that did not prevent lead poisoning

into caves with them to test for noxious gasses. If the canary stopped singing and died, they would know to be wary and evacuate quickly before they also perished.

One local physician commented, "This is like the canary in the coal mine. You're using the children as the canary to find the problem" (Messineo, 2018). Another health care provider shared, "I think of children and I think they are not canaries …That should not be the way we use children in this country at this time" (Breidenbach, 2018, October 24).

While families learn of lead poisoning from their physicians, the pediatrician is actually just one part of the broader apparatus that relates to lead. Following the map above (see Fig. 17.1) we learn that physicians test for lead because the county health department requires it and monitors reporting.

Importantly, from this map, we realize that, other than physicians, the main point of contact for families with the institutional apparatus around lead is through their landlords. If we were to point on a map and say "you are here" these refugee mothers find they are in a contentious and scary situation in which they are pitted against their landlords.

As one new American and mother of three shared, "We need to talk to the government and really do something. The landlords of these homes already know that their properties have a problem with lead. If something is done, we can put an end to this" (CNY Vitals, 2019).

As another renter explained, "He had the opportunity…He never had a late payment of rent. He had enough time and enough money to get it fixed. We were eligible for lead programs, so he could get new windows. I don't know what was on his mind" (Breidenbach, 2018, November 14).

Though some landlords are doubtlessly vigilant, others promise to fix peeling paint but fail to follow through. This is not an issue in Syracuse alone, but rather a situation that is choreographed by extra local relations that exist in cities across New York State, and for that matter the northeast, in which older housing stocks and an overabundance of housing, due to declining populations, have created a complex series of market challenges.

Landlords purchase properties in order to make a profit. But, because of market conditions, they can only charge a certain level of rent. In order to be profitable there is an inherent tension when it comes to renovations that would improve safety and security for tenants. There is a common practice in which, due to existing legislative policies, owners can sell homes without conducting a test for lead and hence there is a perverse incentive not to test for this toxin to avoid having to disclose.[1] However, when families find from the health department testing of their children that the home is likely the cause of lead poisoning, this triggers local reaction from government. The county health department is required to test the home for a source of the lead exposure and, if they find it, they notify the city which can issue a citation for a code violation.[2] In this equation the proclivities of tenants are important since they can invite the testing themselves. As one official explains: "Tenants can consent to an interior inspection, that's how we get in the majority of places, tenants call and make a complaint and let us in."

Having children that might test positive for lead or families that may request lead testing from county health departments become things that landlords would rather not have to deal with.

In this situation landlords have even been known to screen potential tenants by whether or not they are likely to have children or to give them warnings that they should not have children while in these apartments. In some cases landlords even have potential tenants sign an agreement that they will not get pregnant while in that property. The incentive is not to protect children but to avoid them. This creates a situation in which parents are less likely to be vigilant about testing since they do not want to be evicted or face other retaliation from landlords.

This interpersonal tension between residents who are renters and their landlords is further held in place or reinforced by governing relations in the manner in which they are enforced.

Specifically, the city has a rental registry that landlords participate in by registering with the city. This rental registry is part of the broader codes enforcement efforts of the city that are reinforced by the legal department but this has historically been problematic for several reasons. First, lead itself is not a violation so the city has to issue citations for chipping paint or other hazards. Second, it has historically lacked a robust enforcement mechanism. In the past the rental registry only required landlords to vouch on paper for their housing being safe; registering did not prompt an internal inspection. Simply attesting to the safety of their apartments placed the power squarely in the hands of landlords. Furthermore, if the city issued a citation, it was up to the legal department to take the landlord to court. Over time a large backlog virtually assured that legal cases would not make it to court.

On the surface it is hard for the typical resident to see how these things fit together and what is problematic about them that contributes to frustration in daily lived experience. But through IE we can begin to see behind the scenes. In this case, what we encounter is a set of institutional relations that are in flux. Rather than an impregnable bureaucratic maze designed to keep residents in the dark, we see a flurry of action by seemingly disparate actors that are intended to bring about positive changes that will benefit community residents such as our refugee families. However, to the casual observer, these activities appear in news snippets and public announcements that do not seem to coalesce into a coherent whole.

It is not until we use IE style mapping to sketch out how things work now and how a continuously evolving system could be improved that realistic and meaningful courses of philanthropic and policy actions become visible. In the following sections I explore in greater detail how mapping of texts and processes can and has guided policy, philanthropy, and programming to make things better for refugee families.

Following the Map to Chart the Course for Future Policy Advocacy

Using this technique, the diagram below (see Fig. 17.2) maps out the broader situation that the refugee mothers (and indeed any Syracuse resident) find themselves within. Beginning on the left and reading to the right we quickly noticed that there are two distinctive types of residents. The first are homeowners and for them there has existed a Green and Healthy Homes coalition that has been working to coordinate services in order to remediate unsafe conditions as well as ensure that renovations are done in an environmentally friendly way. Being a member of this coalition was my first introduction to this issue and, as I will discuss in the conclusion, my understanding of the problem and ways in which concerned coalition members could take action benefited immensely from the wisdom of this structure and the members within it. However, for the purposes of this paper I will focus more on the

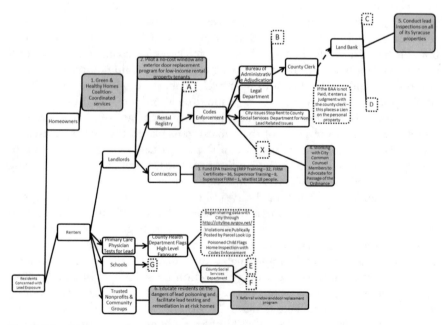

Fig. 17.2 Mapping of revised institution evolving to prevent lead poisoning

renters since this is the group that pertains more to the situation faced by the refugee mothers that have given us our point of departure.

In order to transform the situation multiple community entities have sought to transition toward a new set of institutional relations in which landlords and tenants are not pitted against one another and children are not used as "canaries in the coal mine," so to speak, to identify lead hazards.

City officials in the mayor's office, elected councilors, grassroots groups, and a network of funders and housing service providers (many of whom are part of the coalition I mentioned earlier) have embarked on a series of changes that promise to transform these relations, but their activities are complex and to see their coordination and potential areas for improvement requires mapping.

In order to be proactive there needs to be a system that prevents lead poisoning rather than responds to it. The city itself has taken several steps to put components into place that will help to make this a reality.

Looking at the map I begin with the resident or refugee family. When they are searching for an apartment, they typically connect directly with landlords or homeowners and the Division of Code Enforcement in the Department of Neighborhood and Business Development regulates these homes. Their home inspectors are the ones who examine the situation and determine whether a location is habitable.

In the past landlords could renew their membership on the rental registry with a postcard and by vouching for the safety of their dwelling in writing along with their annual fee. Any inspections conducted were only on the exterior of the building. This situation, however, changed in March 2018 when internal inspections were included in order for the city to add a location to the rental registry. It also required inspections at a 3-year interval, but at this point lead is not a violation. Rather homes that the city cites for lead-related infractions need to be cited for chipping or peeling paint (a point of discussion later in this paper). Finally, this change made a failure to register with the Rental Registry a code violation.

- Policy Change A: In March 26, 2018, The council amended the city's rental registry to mandate[3] an interior inspection every three years for all one- and two-family rental properties (Baker 2018a).

As the policy change was taking shape, March 2018, state and local officials were collaborating in the creation of a new entity, the Bureau of Administrative Adjudication (BAA). The BAA altered the way in which the community addressed code violations making them more powerful. Historically, the city could only enforce payment of housing code violation fines by suing the landlord, but this seldom happened because of the excessive financial and time costs associated with litigation. Landlords were for the most part free to ignore code violations. The new BAA restructured this so that fees are now addressed by a city office instead of in court (much like parking tickets) that would put a lien on the home if the fines are unpaid, hence making it harder for landlords to sell the property.

- Policy Change B: In the past people could ignore violations, but now a Bureau of Administrative Adjudication (BAA) has been created so that the city does not have to go to litigation to address less serious cases of code enforcement (Magnarelli, 2018).

Several months later, legislative change enacted by the governor with local support made it such that municipalities could add unpaid code violations from the BAA to a landlord's tax bill.[4]

- Policy Change C. On Aug 1, 2018, Governor Cuomo signed a law letting Syracuse add unpaid housing violations to tax bills (Baker, 2018b).

The creation of a land bank several years earlier magnified the significance of this legislation. The land bank was launched as a charitable organization with the goal of acquiring, repairing, and then returning vacant, abandoned, underutilized, and tax-delinquent properties to productive use in ways that support the community's long-range vision for its future. This entity provided a critical link since the land bank is empowered to accept any properties that the city seizes due to unpaid taxes. Furthermore, it has the staff and resources to rehabilitate these homes and place them back on the market as a strategy for avoiding urban blight.

- Policy Change D: A Land Bank was created in 2012. If landlords do not pay taxes, property can be taken over by the city and given to the Land Bank (Greater Syracuse Property Development Corporation, 2012).

The following year the County Executive (who is the Chief Executive Officer and the Chief Budget Officer of Onondaga County Government) announced that the Social Services Department under his jurisdiction would halt rent subsidies "from any landlord whose property is found to have lead violations. If a landlord owns multiple units or properties, the county can withhold the rent on all of them, even if just one has lead violations" (Advance Media NY Editorial Board, 2019). In order for this to happen, "The health commissioner will implement a program providing for a lead-free certification process, including educating tenants to demand a lead-free certification as a condition of any rental agreement" (Knauss, 2019).

- Policy Change E: County Executive withholds rental assistance from landlords with violations (Knauss, 2019).

Following this more aggressive approach, the District Attorney's (DA) office (the DA is the chief prosecutor for the county) responded to greater public awareness about lead exposure by charging landlords in the most egregious cases of not fixing lead problems with "willfull [sic] violation of health laws," a misdemeanor charge that can include fines totaling $10,000 and a year of jail time (Mulder, 2019).

- Policy Change F: Onondaga County District Attorney grand jury investigation into lead paint violations (Mulder, 2019).

Even with all of the above policy changes, there was one that was glaringly missing—a city ordinance that would make lead in homes a code violation. The city could do this by simply mandating dust wipes to check for lead-contaminated dust during the interior inspections that they recently added.

- Policy Change X: The new lead ordinance would rely on interior inspections to make lead in dust, bare soil and deteriorated paint violations.[5]

As one interviewee explained, "I think the lead ordinance is a really key piece to give more leverage to the process. The hope with the new ordinance is that codes would be able to test for lead and if there is lead and they are not compliant in fixing it you could kick it to the Bureau of Administrative Adjudication or to the legal department for enforcement."

Even with this new ordinance, it may still be a challenge to have enough staff to implement these policies. There are, however, avenues, such as the use of an Environmental Impact Statement,[6] that would enable the city to target neighborhoods for extra focus and enforcement due to higher than average rates of poisoning among children.

In the shifting relations of governance we do not see a static system of rules and regulations designed to stymie the concerns of our refugee parents. Rather, we see a dynamic set of governance relations that are steadily marching forward toward progressive community change that would benefit these parents. In mapping them out I begin to see a logic whereby we ensure safer homes through more thorough interior inspections (potentially including dust swipes to detect lead before children are poisoned), stricter penalties for failed inspections through the BAA, and more intentional enforcement of polices even up to confiscation of property (Fig. 17.3).

Following the Map to Find a Niche for Philanthropy

Historically when we think of changing relations of governance, we think of policy changes. However, philanthropy presents another avenue for taking action. Furthermore, IE mapping can help to guide this in such a way that funders can address the need as expressed by community members and with

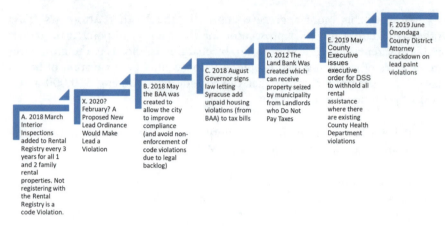

Fig. 17.3 Policy progress

the input of those who are expert at the different levels of institutional functioning. As with the policy changes above, we can once again use the IE map to make sense of a series of thematic investments within the larger picture of institutional functioning.

The first opportunity for funding that appears is for the Green and Healthy Homes Coalition. This group began in 2015 with $1 million in funding from the State Attorney General's Office and intended to streamline programs that address health, safety, energy efficiency, and weatherization. The initiative braids local, state, federal, and philanthropic investment into an integrated, comprehensive approach to better serve low- and moderate-income families in Syracuse. In practice this translates into more weatherized and safer (including lead remediation) houses for low income homeowners. This is something that the Central New York Community Foundation, where I serve as a staff member focusing on strategic investments in addressing community needs, has contributed to funding since its inception. Perhaps more importantly, in this case, however, is that this network of community organization representatives has formed the foundation for understanding the broader institution that surrounds the lead poisoning situation shared by local refugee mothers.

- Philanthropic Action 1: Fund the Green and Healthy Homes Coalition. $45,000 in support for coalition efforts that assist low- to moderate-income Syracuse homeowners in using less energy and creating homes free of health and safety hazards.

Following the map along a different pathway, that of renters, we see that there is an opportunity to provide incentives to landlords to improve their housing. Whereas most of the policy discussed in the preceding section pertained to penalties or "sticks," funding things like subsidized window and door replacement can offer incentives or "carrots" to bring about positive changes. One local article acknowledged as much: "Onondaga County takes carrot-and-stick approach to remove lead from Syracuse homes" (Knauss, 2019).

- Philanthropic Action 2: Fund $150,000 for pilot renovation of existing homes to make them lead safe. Efforts include the removal of lead paint in high-traffic friction areas and the replacement of windows and doors. This was also paired with funding the construction of new, affordable housing that is free of lead and other safety hazards commonly associated with deteriorating housing.

While some have resisted doing such renovation so as not to benefit landlords (through enhancing their property values), this approach de-emphasizes those worries by prioritizing immediate action to avoid lead exposure for young children. These differences, however, do not preclude collaboration as these investments have helped to encourage a follow-up $4.1 million grant from the U.S. Department of Housing and Urban Development, the national entity tasked with overseeing housing (Advance Media NY Editorial Board 2018). The community can use much of these funds to fill the gaps left in Community Foundation funding.

Continuing to follow this pathway we see that a third opportunity for action through funding emerges in the lack of EPA-trained contractors in the community. The EPA, or Environmental Protection Agency, is the federal department charged with protecting human health and the environment. As a result, landlords who want to improve their properties have a hard time doing so without running the risk of having contractors make things worse by failing to take proper precautions that end up exposing children to more lead.

- Philanthropic Action 3: $20,000 to train contractors and landlords to be EPA certified for properly completing lead safe home renovations.

Ensuring that there are enough trained contractors and offering incentives, as noted above, is most likely to result in change if the penalties noted in the policy section are fully in place. This can be more complex than it at first seems since some communities have enacted lead ordinances only to have landlords rally with legal challenges to have them overturned. To avoid this, members of the community discerned that they would need an Environmental Impact Statement (EIS) to fully vet the proposed ordinance. Such evaluations are not cheap, which revealed another opportunity for funding.

- Philanthropic Action 4: Support local elected officials with promise of support for an Environmental Impact Statement (if needed) as they design and vet the new Ordinance.

Beyond the promise of support, the foundation also contributed to the effort by publicly articulating the rationale and meaningfulness of the proposed policy options (Willis, 2019).

The next stop on the map points out the potential of reaching out to the land bank to ensure that they conduct optional lead tests on their properties before they are sold to new owners.

- Philanthropic Action 5: $43,750 to enable the Greater Syracuse Land Bank to Conduct lead inspections on all of its Syracuse properties.

Finally, while many of these opportunities have involved outreach to landlords, the IE map makes us accountable to the people from whose perspective we began, the residents (and particularly refugee mothers). This presented an opportunity to fund local nonprofits to serve as trusted messengers to refer specific homes to window and door replacement programs, to educate residents on the dangers of lead poisoning, and to facilitate lead testing and remediation in at-risk homes.

- Philanthropic Action 6: $30,000 to educate residents on the dangers of lead poisoning and facilitate lead testing and remediation in at-risk homes
- Philanthropic Action 7: $1000 to Identify weatherization service applicants for referral to window and door replacement program

While these efforts are already in progress, the mapping process has also revealed a series of future opportunities ranging from providing small business loans to individual contractors who have completed EPA certification to targeted outreach to encourage internal inspections in high exposure neighborhoods (particularly if the ordinance is passed).

Conclusion

I began our IE exploration with the point of departure of the lived experience of refugee mothers speaking in front of the Syracuse Common Council. While this may seem to be obscure, it is representative of a larger pattern. According to local physicians studying lead exposure, some of "the worst cases this year were in refugee children. Families survived civil war and extreme poverty in developing nations only to be sickened by lead paint in dilapidated American homes" (Breidenbach, 2018, October 24). Furthermore, recent research on Syracuse has found lead exposure upon arrival and post-resettlement in approximately 17% of newly resettled pediatric refugees (Lupone et al., 2019).

Lead exposure can be considered to be a "wicked" social problem (Head, 2008; Rittel & Webber, 1973, p. 155) since it is entangled with other social problems (such as poverty), implicates a variety of community actors, and may arguably not be completely solvable (Wahl, 2017). In this paper I explore how we can deploy Institutional Ethnographic mapping techniques to make sense of and keep track of the steps that communities (such as Syracuse) take to address such challenges.

Institutional Ethnography has long utilized mapping as a tool for understanding how processes work in order to figure out what needs to change in order to make life better from the standpoint of those who experience the problematic aspect of society. This study continues in that tradition but there is a key distinction that sets this approach apart from other studies that are less action-oriented. In this case, I am not simply tracing things as they are in order to provide insight and constructive criticism. Rather, I take the mapping a step further by using it to keep track of how the various portions of the institution could and perhaps should fit together as we collaborate with others in its creation and re-creation with the betterment of society in mind. In her recent work, Nichols (2016) writes:

> Critical researchers have produced a legacy of research that illuminates social problems, failing to participate in conversations about how a problem might be solved. This legacy continues to shape our interactions with service providers, policy decision makers and institutional leaders. If we seriously want our research to make a difference, we need to 'ratchet up the sophistication' of our work (Russell & Tieken, 2011). Our challenge is not to engage in further or more robust analysis, but to work with others (e.g., community organizers, policy analysts, institutional leaders) to strategically and collectively apply what we know to create change. (pp. 20–21)

Other Institutional Ethnographers have indeed begun blazing such a trail. Most notably George Smith (1990) used IE mapping to more strategically direct the focus of activism around homophobia and policing and Hussey (2012, p. 18) produced an action guide from his work in Vancouver to support "community-driven change" in municipalities. In the present case I illustrate how mapping institutional relations can serve as a tool for engaging in collaborative work with "community organizers, policy analysts, [and] institutional leaders… to strategically and collectively apply what we know to create change" (Nichols, 2016, pp. 20–21). More specifically I draw attention to ways in which private dollars (rather than government resources) can be used to bring about change.

Mapping what needs to change in this type of scenario, (i.e., as a funder working among others seeking the common good) is substantially more dynamic and fluid than other mapping in which researchers see themselves as examining a more established institution. In this case, mapping is more akin to figuring out how the actions of one group of people can fit together like puzzle pieces to complement the work of others in the same community.

Kramer (2017) argues that "Community leaders have long advocated for systemic change to overcome structural racism and other complex barriers" (p. 2). What is new about this is the use of IE as an approach to help plan and bring about such change. This present paper reflects on one concrete instance of how IE can be used in this type of work by people who are in and of the community trying to make change, rather than standing on the sidelines. In this way, it is a departure from the internal critique of IE scholars who bemoan the difficulties the field has had with "knowledge translation" from academic research to policy and decision makers (Mykhalovskiy & Church, 2006, p. 84) and packaging their findings in "ways that are institutionally actionable or salient" (Nichols, 2016, p. 21). In the words of Marie Campbell (2006):

> For activist researchers, that means learning a set of research strategies beyond critiquing differing perspectives and their appearance in public policies. Activists must also learn how to understand and engage with the actions of public administration whereby policies are planned, implemented and evaluated. (p. 91)

Similarly, Hussey (2012) asserts that, "to make research results understandable and useful, political activist ethnographers should improve their ability to write up their research in plain language as well as continually seek out ways to disseminate research results through various forms of media" (p. 11). In the current case, I have tried to evolve toward the goal of packaging findings in "institutionally actionable" (Nichols, 2016, p. 21) ways by striving for a hybrid style of communication that mixes the genres of IE research and the forms of speaking that my colleagues in the community philanthropy and policy field use. Importantly though, and perhaps most unusual to the policy professionals who encounter this paper, I have striven to keep the entire analysis anchored in the lived experiences of the refugee mothers that provide us with our point of departure.[7] As Nichols (2016) urges:

> Institutional ethnographers need to deliver on the promise of a sociology for people, adding to the visibility and navigability of a particular complex of social relations. To proceed as such would also require an open admission that the institutional ethnographic mapping process is necessarily ongoing, requiring a wiki-like orientation to co-construction, revision, debate and reformulation. And like any other cartographic enterprise, our sociological maps would be designed to be engaged and used to navigate and change the very world within which they get created. (p. 21)

This paper is indeed an exercise in wiki-like mapping, comprised of not only my understandings garnered from being an engaged community member and philanthropic professional, but also from interview discussions, newspaper clippings, and stories shared with me in multiple formats. It was not uncommon for me to hear of someone's experience only to later find them being quoted in the local newspaper sharing similar thoughts. In this sense, the mapping was not a lonely experience, but rather an ongoing process in which person after person would help me refine my understanding. Herein lies another key takeaway lesson: IE and community coalitions are natural partners. It was my involvement in community coalition work that assembled most of the people that I needed to learn from in order to make sense of the complex web of institutional relations that were not immediately evident (but nevertheless immensely present) in the lives of our refugee mothers. In this respect, this paper is less an endpoint of a research study, and more a waypoint along a collaborative journey of community change that acquires direction and progress milestones through the discipline of IE mapping.

Notes

1. "In 1992, the federal government passed a law that requires the disclosure of known lead hazards in properties for sale or lease. But the law does not require any cleanup and does not provide funding" (Breidenbach, 2018, October 24).
2. As we will explore further in future pages, without the passage of a new Lead Ordinance (which at the time of this writing was being proposed and supported by the foundation and is now passed) the city can only issue a citation for peeling paint or other hazards (since lead is not at present a violation). Another consideration is the challenge of gaining access to the home since they must be let in by either the landlord or the tenant. Nevertheless, having a "red flag" that children have been exposed to lead in a particular location can prompt the codes department to seek a warrant (though this is not yet common).
3. Though newspapers reported that interior inspections are mandated, in actuality landlords have the option the opt out in which case codes would need to apply for a warrant to compel an interior inspection. However, if the County has an open lead case, Codes will not issue a rental registry certification. Assuming there is no County open lead case, Codes will issue a rental registry certification despite the landlord not consenting to an interior violation as long as there are no exterior violations.
4. As one interviewee explained, this is not happening at the moment but needs to be looked at more in depth on a legal level. Changes may need to be made to make it work but "That is the goal, eventually we will get there. Ultimately we need a mechanism like that to make it work."
5. Draft & meeting with Common Councilor 3/11/19.
6. This is a type of study that is typically commissioned before passing a new policy to assess the level of impact it will have on the environment (including living organisms and people).
7. In the words of Nichols (2016), "I suggest we return to its origins as an activist ethnography, used to discover foci, objectives and methods for change that are not immediately evident to people from where they are situated in the daily unfolding of their lives" (p. 21).

References

Advance Media NY Editorial Board. (2018, December 13). Scrutiny, funding reignite Syracuse's fight against lead poisoning (Editorial). *Syracuse.com*. Retrieved from https://www.syracuse.com/opinion/index.ssf/2018/12/scrutiny_funding_reignite_syracuses_fight_against_lead_poisoning_editorial.html.

Advance Media NY Editorial Board. (2019, May 29). Finally, Onondaga County pressures landlords to fix lead hazards (Editorial). *Syracuse.com*. Retrieved from https://www.syracuse.com/opinion/2019/05/finally-onondaga-county-pressures-landlords-to-fix-lead-hazards-editorial.html.

Baker, C. (2018, March 26). After 2 years of trying, Syracuse council passes rental inspection law. *Syracuse.com*. Retrieved from https://www.syracuse.com/news/2018/03/after_2_years_of_trying_syracuse_council_passes_rental_inspection_law.html.

Baker, C. (2018, August 1). Cuomo signs law letting Syracuse add unpaid housing violations to tax bills. *Syracuse.com*, Retrieved from https://www.syracuse.com/news/2018/08/cuomo_oks_law_letting_syracuse_add_unpaid_housing_violations_to_tax_bill.html.

Breidenbach, M. (2018, December 20). Syracuse children are poisoned by lead paint even when taxpayers pay the rent. *Syracuse.com*. Retrieved from https://www.syracuse.com/news/2018/12/syracuse-children-are-poisoned-by-lead-paint-even-when-taxpayers-pay-the-rent.html.

Breidenbach, M. (2018, October 24). Syracuse's lead-poisoning crisis: For hundreds of poor kids, home is making them sick. *Syracuse.com*. Retrieved from https://www.syracuse.com/health/2018/10/hundreds_of_syracuse_children_are_still_poisoned_by_lead_paint_every_year.html.

Breidenbach, M. (2018, November 14). Lead paint scofflaw leaves Syracuse with a vacant house, poisoned children. *Syracuse.com*. Retrieved from https://www.syracuse.com/news/2018/11/lead_paint_scofflaw_leaves_syracuse_with_a_vacant_house_poisoned_children.html.

Campbell, M. (2006). Research for activism: Understanding social organization from inside it. In C. Frampton, G. Kinsman, A. K. Thompson, & Kate Tilleczek (Eds.), *Sociology for changing the world: Social movements/social research* (pp. 87–96). Halifax, NS: Fernwood Publishing.

Carroll, W. K. (2010). You are here: Interview with Dorothy E. Smith. *Socialist Studies, 6*, 9–37.

CDC. (2019, July 30). *CDC national childhood blood lead surveillance data*. Centers for Disease Control and Prevention. Retrieved from https://www.cdc.gov/nceh/lead/data/national.htm.

CNN. (2019, July 2). *Flint water crisis fast facts*. Cable News Network (CNN). Retrieved from https://www.cnn.com/2016/03/04/us/flint-water-crisis-fast-facts/index.html.

CNY Vitals. (2019, March 26). *Lead poisoning in Syracuse: Bea's story*. Central New York Community Foundation. Retrieved from https://cnyvitals.org/lead-poisoning-in-syracuse-beas-story/.

Curtis, K. (2019, April 1). *NYS budget protects children from lead*. Clean and Healthy New York. Retrieved from http://www.cleanhealthyny.org/single-post/2019/04/01/NYS-Budget-Protects-Children-from-Lead.

Greater Syracuse Property Development Corporation. (2012, July 2). Launching of the Greater Syracuse Property Development Corporation. Press Release. Retrieved from http://syracuselandbank.org/wp-content/uploads/2014/03/2012-07-02-GSPDC-Press-Release.pdf.

Gump, B. B., Dykas, M., MacKenzie, H. A., Dumas, A. K., Hruska, B. Ewart, ... Bendinskas, K. (2017). High normal lead and mercury exposures: psychological and behavioral problems in children. *Environmental Research, 158,* 576–582. Retrieved March 19, 2019, from https://www.ncbi.nlm.nih.gov/pmc/articles/PMC5562507/.

Head, B. W. (2008). Wicked problems in public policy [online]. *Public Policy, 3*(2), 101–118. https://search.informit.com.au/documentSummary;dn=662880306504754;res=IELFSC. ISSN: 1833-2110.

Hussey, I. (2012). "Political activist as ethnographer" revisited. *Canadian Journal of Sociology, 37,* 1–24.

Kania, J., & Kramer, M. (2011). Collective impact. *Stanford Social Innovation Review, 9*(1), 36–41.

Kania, J., Kramer, M., & Senge, P. (2018). *The water of systems change.* FSG. https://www.fsg.org/publications/water_of_systems_change.

Knauss, T. (2019, May 16). Onondaga County takes carrot-and-stick approach to remove lead from Syracuse homes. *Syracuse.com,* Retrieved from https://www.syracuse.com/news/2019/05/onondaga-county-takes-carrot-and-stick-approach-to-remove-lead-from-syracuse-homes.html.

Kramer, M. R. (2017, April 11). Systems change in a polarized country. *Stanford Social Innovation Review.* Retrieved from https://ssir.org/articles/entry/systems_change_in_a_polarized_country.

Lane, S. D., Webster, N., Levandowski, B., Rubinstein, R., Keefe, R., Wojtowycz, M., ... Aubry, R. (2008). Environmental injustice: Childhood lead poisoning, teen pregnancy, and tobacco. *Journal of Adolescent Health, 42,* 43–49.

Lupone, C. D., Daniels, D., Lammert, D., Borsuk, R., Hobart, T., Lane, S., & Shaw, A. (2019). *Journal of Immigrant Minority Health.* https://doi.org/10.1007/s10903-019-00880-y, https://link.springer.com/article/10.1007/s10903-019-00880-y.

Magnarelli, T. (2018, May 9). Syracuse Municipal Violations Bureau to take effect this summer, freeing up work in law dept. *Syracuse.com.* Retrieved from https://www.wrvo.org/post/syracuse-municipal-violations-bureau-take-effect-summer-freeing-work-law-dept.

Messineo, D. (2018, November 19). *Federal and local leaders push to curb child lead poisoning.* Central New York Community Foundatiom. Retrieved from https://cnycentral.com/news/local/federal-and-local-leaders-push-to-curb-child-lead-poisoning.

Mulder, J. (2019, Jun 27). 7 Syracuse landlords charged in crackdown on lead paint scofflaws. *Syracuse.com,* Retrieved from https://www.syracuse.com/health/2019/06/7-syracuse-landlords-charged-in-crackdown-on-lead-paint-scofflaws.html.

Mykhalovskiy, E., & Church, K. (2006). Of t-shirts and ontologies: Celebrating George Smith's pedagogical legacies. In C. Frampton, G. Kinsman, A. K. Thompson, & K. Tilleczek (Eds.), *Sociology for changing the world: Social movements/social research* (pp. 71–86). Halifax, NS: Fernwood Publishing.

National Center for Healthy Housing. (2018, September). *New York Healthy Housing fact sheet*. Retrieved from https://nchh.org/resource-library/fact-sheet_state-healthy-housing_2018_ny.pdf.

Nichols, N. (2016). Investigating the social relations of human service provision: Institutional ethnography and activism. *Journal of Comparative Social Work*, *11*(1), 1–26. Retrieved from http://journal.uia.no/index.php/JCSW/article/view/360.

Onondaga County Health Department. (2019). *Lead poisoning prevention data*. Retrieved from http://www.ongov.net/health/lead/data.html.

Pence, E. (1997). *Safety for battered women in a textually mediated legal system*. Ph.D. Dissertation, University of Toronto.

Pence, E. (2001). Safety for battered women in a textually mediated legal system. *Studies in Cultures, Organizations and Societies*, *7*(2), 199–229. https://doi.org/10.1080/10245280108523558.

Prodinger, B., & Turner, S. M. (2013). Using institutional ethnography to explore how social policies infiltrate into daily life. *Journal of Occupational Science*, *20*(4), 357–369. https://doi.org/10.1080/14427591.2013.808728.

Rankin, J. (2017). Conducting analysis in institutional ethnography: Guidance and cautions. *International Journal of Qualitative Methods*. https://doi.org/10.1177/1609406917734472.

Ridzi, F., & Doughty, M. (2017). *Does collective impact work? What literacy coalitions tell us*. London: Lexington Books.

Rittel, H., & Webber, M. (1973). Dilemmas in a general theory of planning. *Policy Sciences*, *4*(2), 155–169.

Smith, G. W. (1990). Political activist as ethnographer. *Social Problems*, *37*(4), 629–648.

Wahl, D. C. (2017, April 29). Facing complexity: Wicked design problems. *Age of Awareness*. Accessed online June 21, 2019, from https://medium.com/ageofawareness/facing-complexity-wicked-design-problems-ee8c71618966.

Willis, S. (2019, March 22). *Syracuse's stubborn lead problem: Collaborative effort aims to help families, landlords*. Retrieved from https://www.waer.org/post/syracuses-stubborn-lead-problem-collaborative-effort-aims-help-families-landlords.

CHAPTER 18

The Institutional Analysis: Matching What Institutions Do with What Works for People

Ellen Pence

The challenge of actively listening and responding to people who have been pushed to the margins of society is one of the most difficult tasks confronting managers of large institutional processes, such as those of the child welfare, human services, healthcare, and court systems. Institutional interventions frequently leave marginalized populations unprotected, poorly served, or even harmed. Increasingly, administrators of legal and human service agencies are turning to the Institutional Analysis (IA) developed by Praxis International to help identify how the work of practitioners is configured in ways that might contribute to these unintended outcomes. Praxis International is based in St. Paul, Minnesota, USA, an internationally recognized technical assistance provider for advocacy groups and jurisdictions working to improve their responses to victims of gender-based violence and abuse.

The IA provides a method of analyzing institutions that process people and situations as cases. It offers a practical agenda for change to guide the reform of institutional processes that do not work well for the people they are intended to serve. This paper introduces the IA method by describing its

---

Correspondence concerning this article should be addressed to: Kata Issari, Praxis International, 179 Robie St. E., St. Paul, MN 55107, United States. Email: kata@praxisinternational.org.

E. Pence (✉)
Praxis International, St. Paul, MN, USA
e-mail: kata@praxisinternational.org

© The Author(s) 2021
P. C. Luken and S. Vaughan (eds.), *The Palgrave Handbook of Institutional Ethnography*,
https://doi.org/10.1007/978-3-030-54222-1_18

beginnings and purpose, discussing its ethnographic origins and methodology, and showing the way it serves to identify and change problematic institutional practices. In this article we also talk about IA in relation to legal and human service institutions processing "cases," but the same methodology can be used to analyze schools, which process students; hospitals, which process patients; and prisons, which process inmates. We use the rather awkward phrase "people who are being processed as cases" because depending on the process into which they are drawn, their "institutional names" might be litigants, clients, suspects, defendants, victims, or patients.

Origins and Purpose

When used in an Institutional Analysis (IA), the word "institution" is defined not as a particular agency or even group of agencies in a community but as that apparatus of disciplines, agencies, and organization of work that comes together under a specialized function, for example, family law (Smith, 2006). Institutions such as the criminal, family, and juvenile court systems include locally organized agencies whose workers do the daily tasks of processing people's unique situations as institutional cases: the 911 call taker working for the county communications center, the patrol officer working for the city's police department, the child protection worker working for the county. The situations in which they intervene (crimes, divorces, acts of neglect) occur in particular settings—families, neighborhoods, and communities. However, these local agencies and organizations are linked to a system that is typically a combination of governmental, community, and private entities that are themselves linked to organizations and entities outside of local communities that define the character of institutions and their ways of acting.

To understand how any institution operates, one must view it both at the local case-processing level and at the level of the extended relations that are part of directing what happens locally, i.e., the extra-local. These extended relations include regulating entities such as federal, tribal, state, and city legislative bodies; insurance companies; funding agencies; accrediting and professional organizations; and fields within academia and research. They also include bodies that produce discourses, set standards, and train and credential professionals to take up responsibility for a distinct type of work whether it is as a social worker, police officer or attorney. Figure 18.1 depicts the connected relations that make up the institutions vis-à-vis gender violence, beginning with people in their everyday settings.

When an institution's intervention in people's lives produces consistently positive results, we take for granted that the institution "gets it right"—it brings to bear its resources and powers of social management in ways that improve the everyday lives of the people. In contrast, when an intervention generally produces negative results, there has to be something amiss in how workers are organized to act on people's situations as cases.

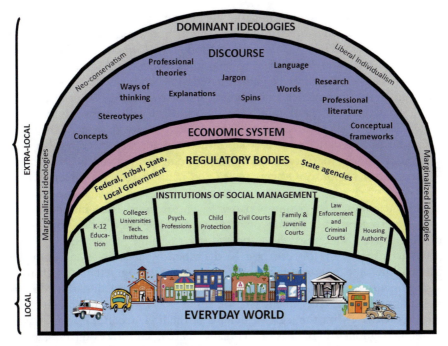

Fig. 18.1 Institutions of social management

When an institutional response seems to be particularly unsuccessful in matching the intervention to what is actually going on in the lives of a specific group of people, such as people with disabilities, victims of battering,[1] families of color, or migrant workers, an IA can help to identify how the intervention is implicated. An IA focuses on the gap between what is actually happening in people's lives and what the institution is doing as it processes them as cases. It seeks to identify how the mismatch occurs and the methods of institutional action that might be reorganized to what actually works for people. While IA begins by describing the interchanges between a person being processed as a case and a local practitioner acting on that case, it extends to all relations that shape those interchanges.

IA was developed as an alternative to what activists seeking institutional change saw as the limitations of reform efforts that focused on training individual practitioners (or workers) to think differently about cases. Attributing institutional failures to the attitudes, personal beliefs, biases, or ignorance of individual workers leaves unchallenged and unaltered all the ways institutions do not adequately connect the intervention to what is actually going on for people. IA was developed as an application of an emerging sociology, known as institutional ethnography (IE), founded by Dorothy Smith. IE explores "how individual behavior [of institutional workers] in one situation is tied into networks of control and power outside that immediate setting" (Hale,

2010). The IA as a defined data-gathering and analysis process was developed by Ellen Pence, Ph.D., director of Praxis International and a longtime student of Dorothy Smith. Praxis has used the methodology (formerly called the *Praxis Safety and Accountability Audit*) to help jurisdictions assess and address the gaps between what victims of gender-based violence needed and what legal and human services agencies intervening in their situations actually did. IA was initially designed to examine how the various legal processes into which battered women are drawn account for the violence they experience. The more ambitious projects attempted to take on every major step in criminal justice case processing. Some focused on a specific point in the process, such as the 911 or patrol response. Others applied the method to the problems faced by specific groups, such as Native women, battered women who use violence against their abusers, or victims of battering who are mothers. A number examined the problems of battered women drawn into the child protection system or who accessed supervised visitation and safe exchange programs.

What is meant by this can best be described by a family court example. Most of the time, a couple who is divorcing comes to agreement on custody arrangements on its own. If the issues cannot be worked out, the court is called upon to intervene. In these cases, family court judges making custody-related orders rely on the legal arguments of the litigants and, in many cases, recommendations and reports of guardians ad litem, custody evaluators, mediators, and/or psychologists. These reports are critical in the court's decision as to whether both parties can share legal custody of the children and whether physical custody can be shared, and if not, to which party it should be awarded. The court also uses the reports in deciding the non-custodial parent's access to the children.

Certain cases are considered "high-conflict" cases—cases that seem irresolvable: the parents do not get along, cannot agree, and will not cooperate. Cases involving domestic violence, in which one parent is often the object of coercion, intimidation, and abuse, are frequently included in this category and treated as a variation of it. In this court system, there are no generally agreed-upon assessment tools, interviewing processes, or formats that help differentiate among the uses, implications, and severity of violence in cases. Thus interveners are unable to see significant distinctions in the nature of parental conflict—for example, whether the conflict is embedded in a history of violence, is part of an ongoing pattern of abuse, is a manifestation of a parent's mental illness, or is connected to one or both parents' philandering ways.

In domestic violence cases, treating all of these kinds of conflict as the same thing can be dangerous. It means the court fails to address whether ongoing coercive domestic violence is occurring and, if so, its specific scope and pattern; if/how the children have been drawn into the violence and how the violence has affected them, their relationship with each parent and each other, and their daily well-being. Those making recommendations do not have a way of addressing basic questions: for example, how might a particular father, who has battered his partner, be prepared to share legal custody without using it as an instrument of control over her?

Even when there is a history of domestic violence, most evaluators use generalized data-gathering and reporting processes linked to the concepts and theories governing high-conflict cases that results in them frequently failing to "get it right." This results in a failure to identify the risks of harm presented by various court decisions (sometimes including misguided decisions to either terminate or increase contact with a parent). Thus, a wide gap is created between what is going on in the actual lives of the children and parents and the institutional frame within which the court acts in resolving the case. IA aims at uncovering just this institutionally organized mismatch between what goes on in people's lives and how the institution "knows" and acts on their cases.

The IA's primary contribution to institutional change work has been to identify how the everyday work of practitioners, coordinated across various settings, produces unintended harmful outcomes. In the last ten years, several well-publicized IA reports have drawn attention to IA as a methodology, and it has subsequently been applied to other institutional processes and to the experiences of people other than battered women. When data showed that not a single rape case involving a Native woman had been prosecuted in more than a year, police, advocates, and prosecutors in St. Louis County in northern Minnesota used IA to examine the prosecution of rape cases involving Native women. In Minneapolis, Minnesota, IA was used to examine police practices that led to African Americans being subjected to traffic stops at seven times the rate of Caucasians. Change agents interested in reducing racial inequities in the child welfare system, such as the Center for the Study of Social Policy (CSSP), the Annie E. Casey Foundation, and the Center for Regional and Tribal Child Welfare Studies with the Department of Social Work at the University of Minnesota Duluth, have looked to the IA method as an effective tool to identify specific measures to reduce negative child welfare outcomes for Native children and children of color.

INSTITUTIONAL ANALYSIS'S ORIGINS IN INSTITUTIONAL ETHNOGRAPHY

Institutional Analysis (IA) is grounded in the field of institutional ethnography (IE), a form of sociology that produces accounts of institutional practices. These accounts describe in detail how workers are organized and coordinated to act on institutionally constructed "realities" or cases. Ethnographers observe and interview. Their work is characterized by the rich and descriptive accounts they provide of what actually happens in the world. IE extends the observation by introducing a way of identifying and describing how texts are used to coordinate institutional work. For the IA analyst, this means using institutional texts to fully explicate what is done at each point of interaction with people who are being managed as cases. In this sense IA is focused on the institutional processing of cases, which is not necessarily the focus in most studies using institutional ethnography. These texts are not necessarily produced locally and are often the key to showing how extra-local entities within the institution drive local practice.

IE seeks to clarify how work is organized. In turn, it shows how practitioners are institutionally directed to talk or write about what they are empowered to deal with. IE explores the real world and makes visible how the work of a practitioner is institutional as opposed to independent actions. Institutional actions do not just happen once, they are not always done by the same person, and they do not always happen in a particular spot. Both IE and IA want to see how what workers do is put together to produce what can be seen as an institutional process. As part of this process, IE aims, among other matters, to uncover the discourse of the institution. In legal and human service institutions, this discourse is largely embedded in and transmitted through standardized texts used in case processing, such as a pre-sentence-investigation report-writing format, a child protection workers' risk-assessment tool, a rule or law, or a parental-bonding evaluation.

And so, IE, when applied to examining case processing, allows us to discover and then map out how workers at various points of taking action are organized and coordinated to act in institutionally directed ways. An IA map is not simply an organizational chart illustrating a sequence of institutional actions. For each interchange between the institution and the person being managed as a case, the IA map illustrates how the worker acting on the case is coordinated and organized to act in an authorized way.

Analysis of Institutional Texts

Texts are material things that carry messages. They articulate the assumptions, operating theories and concepts, and priorities of the institution. They serve as the primary tool for directing the action of workers. They shape the frameworks and categories the institution intends workers to use in processing cases. Their required use solidifies and codifies the prevailing discourse and institutionally authorized ways of doing things. Texts used to process cases can be grouped accordingly:

- **regulating texts**: include funding regulations, federal and state laws, and definitions of phenomenon such as parental neglect, physical abuse, sexual abuse, best interests of the child, failure to protect, probable cause, and self-defense. They also direct agencies and practitioners to do certain things under certain conditions. They delineate the factors that require an officer to make an arrest, a worker to remove a child from the home, and the court considers in determining a child's best interest in custody cases. Other examples of regulating texts are tests administered during psychological evaluations, e.g., the Minnesota Multiphasic Personality Inventory (MMPI) (Hathaway, 1982), actuarial tools to determine

dangerousness (such as the Ontario Domestic Assault Risk Assessment (ODARA) (Hilton, Harris, & Rice, 2010), or Method for Objectively Selecting Areas of Inquiry Consistently (MOSAIC) (De Becker, 2010), and the structured decision-making tools used in child welfare work.
- **administrative texts**: include tools and forms such as risk-assessment report formats, screening tools, police-report-writing formats, parenting assessment forms, and psychological-assessment formats. Typically these texts are designed to help practitioners consistently put regulations into practice on a given case.
- **evaluative texts and reports**: include police reports, psychological evaluations, guardian ad litem recommendations, caseworker recommendations, custody evaluations, and pre-sentence investigations. They are typically produced by practitioners at a local level but standardized by the practitioners' professional associations (probation, psychology, policing). Professions are legally credentialed bodies of specialists whose training and practical experience produce a scientifically or technically developed way of knowing that they bring to their practice in a local setting. The regulating text guiding the individual worker is produced, for the most part, by these professional groups. Through them, professions direct members of their fields in ways of conceptualizing and acting on cases: they guide how practitioners put meaning to information, connect to a discourse about the case, and draw conclusions about what is going on. In the IE field, institutional actions are continuously linked to how the institution organizes workers to establish institutionally recognized realities. Doing this presents the moments and opportunities to either capture or fail to capture what is actually going on. The institutional need to fit people into pre-determined groupings or categories (uncooperative client, recanting witness, failing to protect) almost always means that only those things that can be fitted into an institutional category will be selected for documentation and representation of who the client is and what they are doing. This process can leave enormous gaps in what the institution captures and what is actually going on.
- **case files**: are the collections of texts related to individuals' histories with one or more institutional agencies. A case file provides an ongoing institutional account about what has been done by the institution and by the subject of the file in relation to the case.

Texts are not inert objects. They are dynamic—they screen, prioritize, categorize, and define. Every time an institution places a text between a worker and a person being processed, the interchange is shaped by that text. The inclusion of text analysis in IE, and as a core element of the IA, allows the analysts to recognize and examine the ways in which texts become actively involved in coordinating practitioners' work, including their actions at a particular point of case processing, their interactions with people being managed as cases, and their connection to others acting on the case. These texts are not necessarily produced locally and are often the key to showing how extra-local entities drive local practice.

Consider for example, the experiences of two parents arriving at different supervised visitation centers. Each meets with a worker for a half an hour and learns how, when, and under what conditions they will be allowed to have contact with their children. In many cases, these parents have been living with their children just days or weeks earlier. The idea of a stranger telling them under what conditions they can see their children or what they can or cannot talk about is intolerable for some parents. At one center, the worker has been told her job is to get to know the visiting parent, establish a working relationship with her, and explain how the center works. The worker has not been given an intake or orientation form to use during the intake but has been instructed to fill out a short form at the end of the interview.

At the other center, the worker has been instructed to use a specific intake form to conduct an interview with the parent. The intake form is a standard supervised visit intake form adapted from a national organization that provides training and professional conferences for supervised visitation centers. It has two sections to be completed: information about the parent and court case and information about the child. The third part of the intake is a list to be checked off as the worker reviews the agency policies and rules with the client. It is obvious how this intake form will standardize what the worker says and does, control the conversation between the visiting parent and the worker, and capture only that information required by the form.

Each intake process will presumably meet the agency's needs; only one is likely to meet those of the parent as well. The intake form described above is one text of the dozens and dozens used to process a single case through most legal and human service procedures. The goal here is not to eliminate the use of such texts in institutions but to ensure that they do not contribute to the institutional failure to capture what is actually going on in cases and then contribute to interventions that do not work for people.

Discovery of the Institutional Discourse

An institution's practitioners belong to certain disciplines and professional organizations that have ways of conceptualizing the work they do, the people they work with, and the circumstances of people's lives. Professionals engage in a discourse that helps them conceptualize, define, and understand cases. They fit the people whose cases they are processing into that discourse. For example, Karen, a woman who has been beaten by her husband, attends the arraignment hearing that will set the conditions for his release. She tells the judge, "Your Honor, I don't want to have a no-contact order while this case is being processed. I want to be able to have ongoing contact with my husband and have him return home when he's released today."

The prosecutor argues that the court should deny the request because such contact is likely to result in the intimidation of the witness. After all, studies show that over 30% of women are re-assaulted during the period between charging and conviction. The social worker reading the criminal court file notes that Karen, a mother of three, has just asked to have a known abuser allowed back into the household, an action that places her children at some risk of exposure to violence. In child welfare discourse this amounts to "failure to protect," a form of neglect. After all, studies show that children are harmed by repeated exposure to domestic violence.

Neither of the intervening practitioners in this example knows what is actually going on for Karen. Each respond by fitting her into and operating from a discourse about her and her situation. Their respective discourses may or may not reflect what is actually happening in her life or what will work for her at this point to manage the actualities of her lived situation. Does she need her husband to care for the children while she goes to work? Does she know that he will go to stay with his brother, where he is likely to start using drugs again? Is his car the only transportation for getting the kids to school and her to her job? Is she aware of the fact that she may get pushed, shoved, or hit but believes the alternative is worse? Does she feel safer when she actually knows where he is and what he is doing?

The IA uses institutional ethnographic methodologies to make "discourse mismatches" visible. They show how discourse mismatches are produced by the way practitioners are organized and coordinated to talk about and act on cases, including ways the workers come to know the people being processed. It requires that analysts identify and describe the way recognizable discourses are directing the work of practitioners. The analysts' four-part task is to (1) identify what discourse/s is/are operational in the processing of the case; (2) identify when and where the institution has embedded a particular discourse into the work organization of the practitioner doing a specific job; (3) ask if that discourse has an actual connection to the individual circumstances of the people being managed as cases; and (4) identify the technologies (e.g., tests, assessment tools, matrices) being used to hook into specific discourses and ask if it is more likely that they are capturing or that they are misrepresenting what is actually going on in cases. The IA asks, "What is the situation of the people being processed? How are they being represented institutionally at key points of intervention?" The analysts attempt to discover when the institutional representation and the actuality diverge and to identify the institutional practices that produce this divergence. At the same time, they are exploring how the institution manages to match what it does/offers to what a person is experiencing and what might work for their circumstances.

Discovering How the Worker Is Coordinated and Organized to Act

As noted earlier, an institutional process does not happen just once, or only in one place, and it is not always carried out by the same people. Processes carried out in a courtroom in Saint Paul, Minnesota, look and sound similar to those carried out in San Francisco or Memphis or Jacksonville, Florida. Similarly, psychological reports produced in each of these cites by professionals whose paths have never crossed read eerily alike. Regardless of the practitioners—social workers, judges, prosecutors, probation officers, custody evaluators—not one of them simply walks into work at their respective agency and asks, "How shall I go about my tasks today?".

For the most part, practitioners in these vast institutions of social management are themselves managed to talk about and act on cases in highly directed ways. Institutions generally want practitioners to treat similarly-situated cases similarly and to act within accepted conceptual boundaries for good reason. To ensure that a person's institutional fate is not determined by the idiosyncratic behaviors and beliefs of a particular practitioner, institutions both at a local level and on an extra-local level deploy managerial methods to standardize ways of talking about and acting on cases.

IA analysts always look for eight common ways institutions organize workers to act on cases as the possible culprits in the mismatch between what is going on and what the institution represents the "case" to be. These methods are not meant to put a boundary around what analysts look for in trying to explicate how workers are organized. Analysts may find additional methods at work. The IA is designed to point analysts to those that have been repeatedly found in various studies. These eight methods are listed below, followed by Fig. 18.2:

1. Adopting a mission, carving out a job function, and assigning workers' responsibilities and duties.
2. Producing regulating texts to standardize how certain situations are treated at certain points of institutional intervention.
3. Requiring the use of administrative processes or tools such as assessment forms, which organize and coordinate the workers' actions and ways of talking about the case.
4. Creating linkages between workers in a specific job and others within the institution and coordinating the work between and among intervening practitioners.
5. Selecting and allocating resources for both workers and people being processed as cases.
6. Holding workers accountable for some actions but not for others.
7. Providing mandated training for workers that is both skill-based and intended to solidify certain operating discourses in workers' approaches to cases.
8. Giving currency and authorization to particular discourses, concepts, assumptions, and theories and embedding them in regulations and administrative case-processing tools.

Fig. 18.2 Eight methods institutions use to coordinate worker's actions (*Source* Pence & Sadusky, 2005)

A disconnect between what practitioners write about in texts and what is actually going on in people's lives is almost always linked to how the worker has been conceptually and administratively organized to carry out the task of collecting and documenting information. It is also almost always linked to problematic organization of their interventions.

For example, an IA analyst observes a pre-sentence investigation processes in criminal court domestic violence cases. The probation officer reports to the court that his client, Greg Hansen, admitted to him in the pre-sentence investigation (PSI) interview that he assaulted his wife on September 6th in their home and that he caused injury to her shoulder and bruising to her face. The probation officer goes on to report that Mr. Hansen is willing to go to the domestic abuse class offered by the local mental health center. He further informs the court that Mr. Hansen works at Arco Coffee, makes $17.45 an hour, is current in his house payments, has no known problem with drugs or alcohol, coaches a youth hockey team, and has no other convictions. The IA analyst asks, "If the probation officer has just a few short minutes to tell the court what kind of a domestic violence offender Mr. Hansen is, why does he report these particular facts?".

The analysts come to understand how such a report is produced and entered unremarked into the sentencing proceedings by reading domestic violence PSIs, watching the proceedings in the courtroom, and talking to victims, defendants, and probation officers. In the case of Greg Hansen, and of all the other defendants that for years have been sentenced in that courtroom, the analyst discovers that the primary organizing mechanism of the PSI was a court-approved generic PSI form. Probation officers were required to use this form for their reports on all misdemeanant offenders. It was known as the "fine'em and find'em" form, reflecting its basic purpose: to tell the court whether the defendant can pay a fine if one is imposed and whether, if the defendant fails to return for subsequent hearings, the court can locate him. Filling out this form, then, became the primary responsibility of the probation officer.

The PSI format requires only this information because it is what the court uses to make a sentencing decision in most misdemeanor cases. It does not require that for a domestic violence offender the probation officer ascertain the scope, severity, or pattern of abuse. Instead, the statement "no prior conviction" substitutes for such an inquiry in the institutional record. As a result, the report fails to tell the court what kind of risk Mr. Hansen might pose to his wife—arguably critical information for the judge deciding the conditions for his release and his sentence.

Analysts understand that practitioners operate within the frameworks of the various legal, professional, psychological, and other discourses that regulate and standardize local practice. They recognize that an institutional worker's actions must always fit (or be fitted into) an institutional frame and institutional categories—categories that may or may not adequately connect to the lives of people being processed as a case.

In the IA, it is the making of the case that analysts watch and fully describe. The phrase "watching the making of a case" is meant quite literally. For example, an analyst might sit beside a dispatcher in a 911 center and listen in as a child calls, crying: "My dad is saying he's going to kill himself. He says if anyone tries to stop him, he'll shoot us all." The call taker enters the girl's words into the computer and assigns a code to the call. If the 911 worker codes the call as a domestic with the threat of a weapon, the man is likely to spend the night in jail; if she codes it suicide threat, he is likely to spend the night in a hospital.

The difference in what this means to the child and her father and mother is immense. The way practitioners are organized to fit people into these institutional realities is a key concern of the IA. Analysts explore in detail how the worker is directed to respond through regulations, administrative tools, routine documentation practices, requirements of completing certain tasks, and other institutional expectations. The inability of the system to take up this particular case as both a mental health and a possible family violence issue is a crucial limitation that an IA will likely discover. The IA works to make visible the mechanisms put in place by managerial systems to direct workers in their decisions; through this process of explication, they seek to determine the relation of these mechanisms to the production of problematic outcomes.

Every tool designed to coordinate workers in an institutional setting carries the assumptions and conceptual frameworks of the institution. The IA goal is to identify when those assumptions and concepts get in the way of understanding what is actually going on in people's lives. As Dorothy Smith suggests, an institution's account or their "official story" about a case will often be incomplete and may therefore misrepresent the realities of people's lives, particularly survivors of gender-based violence (Smith & Pence, 2011).

Smith notes that standardization of practices is ensured through the professionalization and related forms of training of those who are responsible for institutional action (Smith, 1989). Professions are legally credentialed bodies of specialists whose training and practical experience participate in a scientifically and/or technically developed way of knowing; professionals bring this way of knowing as a practice to the local settings of institutionalized work organization. Yet the versions of the world they apply, however, validated by professional bodies of knowledge, may be at odds with people's everyday knowledge and experience of the actualities of their lives.

Mismatched versions happen at every level of case management. For example, in some families, notably African American and Native American families, childrearing may be shared among kin in a fluid pattern over time. This collection of uncles, aunts, cousins, grandmothers, brothers, and sisters, together with the biological parents, constitute the children's caretakers and immediate family. However, this is not the family that the child welfare institution looks to when searching for the single person or couple within one home who will step in as a temporary or permanent replacement for the biological mother who is unable to care for her children. What is often missing in interventions in both African American and Native American families is not the availability of kinship care, but the ability of the institution to link children to the way kinship care occurs in their communities.

In addition, every administrative tool used to process a case is framed by assumptions and concepts and relevancies that its authors have embedded within it. A therapist who is asked to examine parenting performance as part of a custody study or child welfare assessment uses an agency form riddled with assumptions about appropriate and inappropriate parenting indicators. Therapists are directed to answer such questions as "Did the parent arrive on time? Did the parent bring age-appropriate games or toys for the child? Did the parent make appropriate eye contact with the child? Did the parent engage in age-appropriate talk with the child? Did the parent redirect the child's play when the child exhibited frustration?" The assumption of the universality of a particular view of parenting becomes an ideological representation that does not represent any group well, but when applied to some groups will definitely reveal parents as deficient, if not completely incompetent. Is it not valid to assume that Somalis, Native Americans, middle-class African Americans, working-class Irish Americans, German Americans, and lesbians and gays of all classes and races might appropriately parent in different ways? These examples show why the IA gaze is not on individuals, but on the way the institution has standardized and authorized the work they are doing. Of course, IA encounters cases in which an individual practitioner is acting from a racial, class, or other bias, or whose actions are not in line with administrative rules or the law. In these instances, the IA interest is on whether managerial systems are in place to locate and address such individual bias or error. In other words, what systems of accountability protect clients from these kinds of unauthorized behaviors?

The investigative focus is on routine work and on the taken-for-granted modes of coordinating and organizing workers, such as the required use of an institutionally authorized parenting assessment form. Both IE and IA seek to show how common understandings are generated and sustained simultaneously in many different work sites that regulate and coordinate specific institutional interventions. The IA seeks to make visible to institutional workers the ways in which they are unknowingly implicated in creating the problems experienced by their clients, and thus makes it possible to see how such an organization of work might be changed.

Conducting an Institutional Analysis: Objectives and Methods

An IA is built one step at a time. The analyst may not know what to look for until certain basics have been covered. The process of data collection is one of learning—learning from system users about the issues and problems they are experiencing and from institutional workers about work routines relevant to those problems. It means exploring how work is organized, including how the work of those who deal directly with the people in each case is supervised, made accountable, and managed. Thus, it is necessary to work with the agency being analyzed; without the participation of the agency working the cases at the local level, such an analysis would be difficult. An overall objective is to map the relevant work organization at every significant point of case processing so that possibilities for change become visible.

Talking to and observing the way people interact with these work processes is a crucial part of gathering information. The case does not exist without clients, victims, defendants, patients, and what they do; through their actions, interactions, and inaction they make the case, too. That interchange between the person and the institutional process, and how the interchange is shaped by the institutional design of work routines, is part of what the IA seeks to discover. Hearing how people experience these interchanges is typically where the analysis begins.

Identifying the Problematic

In an IA, the problematic is the question that guides the inquiry from the standpoint of the people being processed as cases. The problematic is the foundation of an IA, which starts with uncovering and understanding institutional clients' experiences of negative outcomes. The focus on the problematic differs from that of a research project, which uses variables; an IA does not. The problematic encompasses many levels of organization and requires gathering a large body of information. This happens primarily through individual or group interviews with people who are being managed as cases and with their formal and informal advocates. Those selected to participate in focus groups and interviews are chosen to provide a range of experiences that are taken up in different institutional settings; it is these experiences that can help point to how the problems come about. Individuals are never objects of study.

The task of the IA is to thoroughly investigate how people being processed in an institution describe the gap between what might work for them and what is being done. It is also important to note that an IA is not necessarily looking for satisfaction levels of people being processed as cases. Few offenders, for example, are satisfied with a sentence to jail. The question is more how the sentence was reflective of what actually happened.

Information from these initial interviews directs the next stages of exploration. For example, data and the initial interviews CSSP conducted in one community suggested a number of processes for analysts' investigation. In a parents' focus group, they heard stories that made them pay attention to bonding studies, the process used to determine whether a parent was bonded to their child. It also made them watch for how practitioners dealt with the emotions of parents and children. Interviews and brief talks with the people whose cases the analysts observed in court directed their attention to how workers determined and then reported to the court whether a child was faring well in foster care. In focus groups with attorneys representing parents, analysts learned to watch for and explicate how the funding of legal representation shaped the quality and scope of contact between the client and the attorney. These early interviews are pointing fingers for analysts: "Here, pay attention to this!".

Choosing Sources of Data

As discussed, the IA locates problematic practices at the interchanges between the practitioner and the person being processed as a case, asking how those workers are organized to act in certain ways and not in others. As such, it is designed to observe as many of these interchanges as is practical and follow these observations with interviews about what was seen, as well as reviews of relevant texts.

The choice of which cases to review, which texts to analyze, and which interchanges to describe depends on what has been established as the problematic of the IA. In making their selections, analysts consider (a) the types of cases and points of intervention analysts will need to review to understand the practitioners' range of actions and their considerations in processing the cases; (b) the number of cases and points of intervention necessary to determine the range of institutional actions and decisions relevant to the type of case specified in the problematic, as well as the range of problems, obstacles, and situations that workers take on in processing this category of cases; and (c) the means of ensuring that the cases chosen and processes observed and explicated include a relevant range of institutional outcomes, including a number of cases that result in negative outcomes for differing reasons as well as cases with neutral or positive results.

Making Observations

Whenever practical, analysts observe practitioners in the work settings at the common interchanges generated by institutional action. For example, to analyze the decision to retain a child in foster care, the observable points of institutional action might include a worker's interview with a parent, a home visit, the administration of a parenting assessment tool, and an agency staffing on the case. Observations consume time, but in some settings, such as courtrooms and police patrol "ride-alongs," this work is invaluable, because the analyst is able to see several cases processed within three or four hours. Obviously, the cooperation (or lack thereof) of the institution being analyzed is critical to the way the IA is designed.

Unless analysts can see the conditions in which practitioners are doing their work, it is hard to imagine how it could be reorganized in helpful ways. Restricting the analysts' picture of what actually goes on in these interchanges to information gathered in interviews creates a problem. One reason is simply that in interviews, practitioners tend to use organizational language, such as, "We removed the child but first secured the premises." The analysts want to know exactly what that sequence of actions looks like. They ask for more details, but it is hard to completely capture what really occurs from a practitioner's description alone. For example, the police securing a premises may actually involve a SWAT team; observing a worker physically remove a child from a woman's home while trying to deal with the needs of the mother, the child, and the waiting police officers is invaluable in understanding why the family and the worker experience the intervention in the ways they do. Observations are crucial to understanding the conditions in which workers perform their duties.

Conducting Interviews

Learning from practitioners themselves how they put things together and how they go about coordinating what they do with others is a key method of IA data collection. Those who become cases managed by the institution are also experts in how they participate in the institutional processes. In the IA, analysts interview the people being processed, practitioners working with the cases, advocates, and local and national experts on the problem being explored. Not all interviews are alike. They seek different understanding and require different methods of asking. "Each interview provides an opportunity for the [analyst] to learn about a particular piece of the extended relational chain, to check the developing picture of the coordinative process, and to become aware of additional questions that need attention" (Devault & McCoy, 2006). The IA uses four kinds of interviews and trains analysts in conducting each. The kind of interview depends on the person to be interviewed and the information sought.

1. **The macro picture interview** is conducted with experts and administrators to document the issues influencing local practice and ascertain what the informant sees as the scope and causes of the problem under investigation. Some interviews conducted after data collection are used to help interpret what was seen, heard, and read in texts.
2. **The work practice interview** is conducted with practitioners to obtain a detailed description of how they engage in specific processes such as conducting intakes, carrying out investigations, writing evaluative reports, creating documentation, providing counseling, responding to the trauma of clients, and appearing in court. In these interviews, the interviewer simply asks the practitioners to describe how they do their work: "If I had to do your job tomorrow, what would I do, step by step?"
3. **The text-based interview** is conducted with a practitioner or supervisor to discover how a particular text is produced and used, including who created it, who reads and acts on it, what comprises an adequate report, what its purpose is, and what extra-local influences shape it.
4. **Focus groups** are conducted with the people being processed as cases, their advocates, and intervening practitioners to learn how people experience various aspects of the practitioner-person interchange. From them, analysts seek description and insider knowledge, insights into the problem, and thoughts on the ways work is organized that produce poor outcomes. In the early stages of an IA, focus groups help define the problematic. Later, focus groups provide an opportunity to ask, "Why are we seeing what we're seeing?"

Together, observations and interviews provide a window into the ways in which institutions construct and manage people's experiences as cases.

Analyzing Texts

As discussed previously, institutional work is organized by documents and texts. The problematic of the research helps to decide which texts are relevant to examine. Texts are generally not analyzed in isolation from the actual work relations and organization they coordinate. The IA is concerned with texts as they enter into, organize, and coordinate practitioners' work. This means analysts ask practical questions of the text: Who reads this? For what purpose? How does the writer establish the authority to comment? What other texts and sources of information were used to produce this text? It does not mean that analysts engage in some kind of discourse analysis speculating as to the meaning of the text. The analysis is focused on how the text is entering into a sequence of actions, drawing from what has gone before and creating a framework for subsequent interveners to act.

Taking the time to examine each type of text—regulating, administrative, evaluative, and case files—is important in the IA because of the way each: (1) carries the discourse that defines the case; (2) coordinates how practitioners talk about the case and apply to it certain assumptions, concepts, theories; (3) coordinates the workers' actions on a case; and (4) selects from the world of actual experience only those occurrences significant to the institution and represents them in terms that can be taken up by it, which may or may not accurately reflect the real situation. Thus one set of analysts found that a 14-year-old girl in foster care who violates the rules by calling her mother every night is, under standard organizational management routines, far more likely to be labeled as having "oppositional behavior" than as having "a strong bond with her mother."

Some texts, such as an initial police report or a psychological evaluation of a parent, may become visible as key in coordinating actions among specialized and sometimes separate units that make up an institutional setting. Others, such as a parental-bonding study, may seem less central in directing a case but still constitute part of an accumulation of data used to justify institutional actions.

In institutional settings where the problematic focuses on outcomes for individual clients, the case file is a major textual focus for the IA. Though it is always produced from the institutional standpoint and uses the categories and concepts of institutional discourse, the client has also participated and is in a sense present in the case file, which documents some of what the client did and said. Perhaps more importantly, the case file tracks the institutional actions of practitioners. Reading it can raise specific questions bearing on the organization of work in relation to a client. What is the practitioner held accountable to? What aspects of interchanges between the client and the practitioner are taken up as institutionally significant? What might be missing for the person whose case is being processed? The IA moves from the front line, where institutional workers engage directly with clients, to the extra-local levels of institutional organization when it takes up a review of regulatory texts such as laws, government directives, and policies and protocols. Analysis of texts at the extra-local level of organization is most productive when it focuses on how the texts are used in specific work settings. The IA seeks to discover how regulating texts act to do such things as raise issues of accountability, determine whether a given action by a worker can be properly treated as part of an institutional course of action, select information from client actualities to constitute the textual reality of the client (which becomes the institutional reality of that individual), and drives a particular course of action to be taken in processing a case.

Administrative texts are almost always involved in shaping the way cases are processed because they are the primary means of standardizing how workers carry out regulations and policies. They actively screen, prioritize, define, assign risk to, and categorize cases. No matter what task we observe, we almost always find an attached administrative text guiding the accomplishment of that task and linking that aspect of case processing to previous and subsequent actions.

A primary purpose of administrative texts is to coordinate future interventions in the case. The text does not fit only into this single point of case processing, but extends to subsequent actions, and often to actions not at all intended by the practitioner who produced it. Police reports are a classic example of a report produced with one process in mind—the prosecution of a crime—but used in many other institutional settings. The IA team frequently sees that a text is operating in a significant and perhaps problematic way. This observation does not mean that a better text is obvious, but it can point to what the designers of a replacement text need to consider. The analysis team note, for example, that a particular parenting assessment form is permeated with concepts and ideas that do not match the actualities of particular groups of people (e.g., recent immigrants, people with disabilities, members of the GLBT community), but is nevertheless taken for granted as a useful commentary on families. The team can frequently identify how this assessment form has worked in cases in ways that caused problems for family members.

Evaluative reports are a critical source of information showing how the discourse enters into and shapes the actions in cases. The IA holds these reports up against what is known about the actual experiences of the family and asks, "Is this a match?" For example, a psychological report is the object of inquiry in many kinds of legal cases. The analysts ask for a detailed description of the work that went into producing the report. They want to know how the psychologist made the observations incorporated into the final product, asking, "What was the basis the psychologist used in making these claims about the parent or child or defendant? What was the basis for selecting some aspects of the situation for commentary? What was the connection between the tests administered and the issues in the case? What was the basis of using one frame as opposed to another to link what was learned about the family to the portrait the psychologist has drawn?" And always they ask: Can we see how this report is acting to portray to the court—accurately or inaccurately—the person at the heart of the case?

For some evaluative reports, the IA analysts have access to the client and can therefore ask people to weigh in on the question of whether the conclusions actually represent what was going on for them. In other cases, analysts may have enough information to offer an alternative explanation to the one in the report and ask, "How is it that this particular representation of reality wins out over the other?" In doing so, they keep in mind that the IA definition of problematic practices is not that the subject of a case did not like what the practitioner did or the outcome of the case, but that the institutional actions did not adequately account for what was actually going on in the subject's life.

Of course, this is not to say that if the institution simply got it right about what is going on, then there would be no problems with institutional interventions. Getting an accurate account of what is going on is a crucial task of the institution, but not the only one. It must then match its intervention with what will work to resolve the problems it is charged with solving.

Organizing and Coordinating the Methods IA Analysts Use to Collect and Analyze Data

The analysts' charge is to describe in detail the everyday workings of case processing and the way workers' actions are coordinated. Like the institution it hopes to change, the IA uses an organized process that directs and coordinates its workers, the analysts. IA technologies focus the analysts' attention on institutional workings as opposed to workers' beliefs, attitudes, or idiosyncratic ways of going about their practice. As an investigative tool, the IA provides a method to coordinate and organize how analysts conduct their interviews, report on what they learned, and document their observations and insights.

The IA uses "shell maps" (see Fig. 18.3) to ensure that analysts consistently gather and document similar information about how specific interventions are

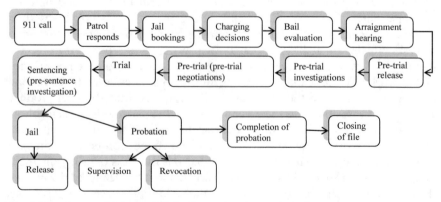

Fig. 18.3 Sequential layout of the key points in a criminal court case

carried out. The note-taking forms focus analysts on the eight key methods of standardizing work, described earlier, as they conduct interviews, read case files, and observe interchanges. A directed form of debriefing after observations and interviews makes certain that they consistently attend to institutional processes and work organization over the idiosyncratic ways individual practitioners take up cases. The IA also provides tools for reading and analyzing texts to determine how a particular text is acting in the case (Pence & Sadusky, 2006).

Forming and Training a Team

The investigation is carried out by a team which includes people who have a specific interest and knowledge of the problems that are the basis for the "making change" objective. A small core group with academic training and experience in IA provides leadership expertise and methodological guidance but relies on a larger group of people who are concerned with the issue—members of community organizations, advocates, and institutional practitioners among them to put meaning to what the group uncovers. The makeup of a team varies from one IA to the next and is determined by the local group initiating the IA. When making change is likely to involve discussion of national policy, the team may also include people who are experts in the field or participate in national work on the issue, such as child welfare or family or criminal law practices.

The selection of team members is critical to the IA success. It benefits from the presence of advocacy groups for people who are being processed as cases, for community members, and from people who work inside the institution being examined. Yet each of these groups might put forward a person(s) who become obstructionist in the process of knowing. Institutional practitioners who feel the need to justify or defend every action of the institution are not helpful; similarly, advocates who use this forum to be critical of practitioners who they observe or interview miss the opportunity to do what the IA does best—locate and change systemic organizational problematic practices. Analysts can of course be passionate about their beliefs, but during this process their goal is to learn what they do not know, to describe what happens, to explicate how things are put together the way they are that causes problems for people.

IA training sessions introduce the team members to the features and analytical orientation of the process and prepare them to use the ethnographic methods of interviewing, observing, and analyzing text. In addition to learning basic skills in data collection and debriefing, team members learn to (1) focus on how workers are organized to talk about and act on cases, rather than on the individual actions and idiosyncrasies of individual workers; (2) discuss the concept of discourse as it is used in institutional ethnography and IA; and (3) recognize when they are relying on their institutional or ideological language to describe, comment on, and arrive at conclusions.

Talking with People Being Managed as Cases and to National Experts

"Talking with" includes conducting interviews with individuals and focus groups and reading about people's institutional experiences. For example, CSSP conducted a number of background interviews and literature reviews as a part of its child welfare IA studying the negative experiences and poor outcomes for African American children in foster care. The focus groups with parents, children, extended family, and advocates were scheduled early on in the data-gathering process and continued throughout. The early interviews identified the disconnects (and the connections) between what was going on in peoples' lives and how their cases were being processed. They also identified the particular points of case processing that carried meaning to their cases or to the disconnects with the intervening institution.

Talking with people is the point at which analysts first document how those being managed experience institutional interventions and their outcomes. One analyst describes this step:

> In the first focus group of parents I sat in on, I listened to people talking about how completely discounted and controlled they felt whenever they expressed any emotion in court or to their worker. The next day when I was in court, reading a file and observing an initial interview with a father, I saw this apparent lack of care in every interchange. I'm not sure I would have picked up on it if I hadn't been in that focus group. I could see how the workers were interacting with deeply traumatized parents. That made me want to ask the workers about it. And they had lots to say that was crucial to understanding how the gap between the worker and "client" can so quickly form.[2]

This inquiry helps identify specific points of intervention at which people experience the gap between what is going on in their lives and what the institution is saying and doing about their situation. At the same time, the analysts also consult national experts in the area of the IA inquiry who can help guide the analysts and identify policies, frameworks, or specific administrative tools that may be active in producing poor outcomes.

Focus groups and interviews conducted later in the process give the analysts the opportunity to describe what they seem to be finding and ask whether and how it matches the experiences of those being processed in the system. This ongoing consultation provides additional insights and gives meaning to the data gathered in the IA's observations, interviews, and case file reviews.

Drawing the Map of Institutional Action

Drawing the map involves discovering relevant aspects of work organization. It begins with the key interchanges between the institutional workers and the people being managed or the case file that represents the people being managed. The IA team seeks to analyze institutional actions that lead to the

18 THE INSTITUTIONAL ANALYSIS: MATCHING WHAT INSTITUTIONS DO … 351

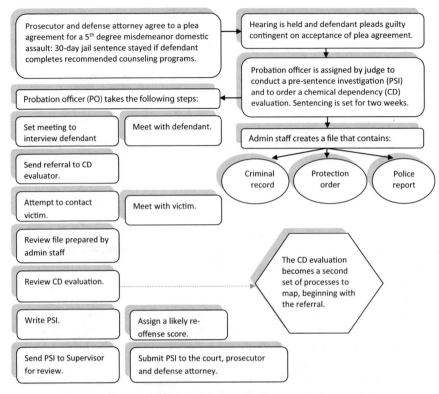

Fig. 18.4 Detailed map highlighting the sentencing stage of a criminal court case

problems people experience. Maps produced in the early stages of the inquiry sequentially lays out key points of intervention as in Fig. 18.3.

Because so many intersecting processes are carried out in different agencies that all become a part of producing the case outcome, this is not always simple. For example, a chemical dependency evaluation may be ordered by the court before sentencing a man convicted of assaulting his partner and teenage son. This is an intersecting process in the sequential layout of a criminal court case. These initial maps are produced during the planning phase of an IA. A person knowledgeable in the local system helps the IA leaders create the preliminary maps. As the analysis continues, the team discovers new points of intervention and adds them to the map as depicted in Fig. 18.4.

Explicating the Methods of Organizing and Coordinating Work

The team analyzes the data it has collected in interviews, observations, and text reviews by following the eight methods commonly used by institutions to standardize the way workers carry out their duties, described earlier (see Fig. 18.2).

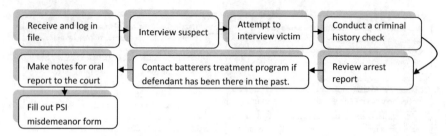

Fig. 18.5 Specific steps of conducting a misdemeanor pre-sentence investigation

Analysts put their data on the map to display what they have seen and read and heard. The team leaders keep the mapping focused on institutional ways of organizing and coordinating workers. The use of the eight core methods of standardizing workers is a key tool to keeping this focus. It is here that problematic practices and managerial processes are more closely examined. For each point of intervention in the original map, analysts create a picture of what actually happens in the interchange. They describe the methods institutions use to coordinate how workers conceptually and administratively act on a case.

The initial maps may look something like case-processing flow charts, but they merely create the shell to be filled in. As illustrated in Fig. 18.5, each point on the map, such as pre-sentence investigation, is to be further broken down to show how workers are organized.

Each worker is organized to act in institutionally authorized ways and to connect to others working on the case. The mapping process illuminates which instruments (methods) the institution uses to coordinate that work: a rule, a form, a limited set of resource options? A way of training workers to accomplish a task? A limited or expanded job description? These methods of organizing the workers are where the problems and solutions are found and thus are the focus of the analysts' investigation.

Notice that the production of a PSI in Fig. 18.5 is just one of many steps in the sentencing phase of a criminal case, and sentencing is just one of over 100 distinct steps in the processing of a criminal case. Analysts must select a handful to thoroughly analyze. Selecting what appears to be significant points of determining a case outcome is a crucial step of the IA. But in the end managers who seek to make the changes indicated by the IA need to reorganize almost every practitioner's work on some level.

Identifying and Proposing Changes

In the final step of the IA, the team of analysts puts forth proposals for changing work organization so that the outcomes for people are changed. The eight methods of coordinating a worker which characterize much of the data collection become the framework for recommending these changes.

To the greatest extent possible, the analysts make specific recommendations for altering current practice. Table 18.1 shows such a chart excerpted from a final map, recommending changes in the writing of a PSI. The full map was much more detailed, but this shows the kinds of practices the IA uncovers and attempts to fix. It illustrates how an IA can provide an agenda for change that gives administrators clear direction in how to embed reform into the routines of workers' actions. Doing so ensures that the changes are not dependent on the goodwill of people in the agency whose departure might result in the reversal of the reforms.

The final product of an IA may include a formal, detailed report. At a minimum, it provides a narrative description of the practices identified on the map that appear to be implicated in the negative experiences of people being processed as cases and specific recommendations for change. It also suggests the general direction that reform efforts might take, giving administrators and reform activists a detailed road map to changes that will likely make these interventions work better for people.

Conclusion

Institutional analysis (IA) is a method of identifying how institutional practices have been organized and coordinated to produce outcomes that often no one intends and that can be harmful to the people being managed as cases. It is a directed application of institutional ethnography, carried out by a team of local practitioners in the institution under scrutiny, community members concerned about how current practices are impacting the community, national or local experts in the issue being addressed, and consultants proficient in the use of the IA method. The IA produces a map of each of the key steps of case processing under scrutiny, showing just how the institution has both conceptually and administratively organized workers to intervene in ways that are at least partially responsible for poor case outcomes experienced by an identified group of people being managed in the institution.

The IA provides administrators seeking to improve their interventions with a particular group of people in a particular kind of case with concrete suggestions on altering local practice to reduce negative outcomes. It also identifies changes needed at the extra-local level (federal, tribal, state, or within a discipline) to reduce problematic outcomes. Inevitably the problems identified and explicated in an IA will clearly show any mismatches between what an institution is designed to do and what people need. It will show how institutions can so frequently fail to understand the actualities of the lives of those whose situations are managed as cases. It will show if and when the institution is creating a partial and often inaccurate picture of its practices.

The IA will unveil the mismatches between what kind of interventions actually work for people and what the institution actually does, both in terms of requiring people to do certain things and in how it seeks to provide services and assistance. And it will almost always show that these institutions of social

Table 18.1 Identifying problems and solutions in the writing of a pre-sentence investigation

Methods of standardizing workers responses	Problems observed	Beginnings of solutions
Mission, duties responsibilities	PSI writers very reluctant to try to determine whether the defendant is engaging in a pattern of coercion and control (a batterer), resisting violence by a batterer, or using violence unrelated to coercive control (perhaps attached to mental illness, alcohol use, etc.).	Require PSIs to paint a picture of the full scope of abuse and violence to whatever extent possible; see PSI as attached to an ongoing case not only the current crime.
Rules and regulations	PSI writers reluctant to make recommendations in their report regarding victim contact as they have little contact with victims and do not feel equipped to assess this, despite the legal requirement that the PSI include this information.	Include in the PSI writer's protocol a requirement to make diligent efforts to contact the victim and to consider: -The victim's wishes regarding contact. -Any hardship the victim might experience if contact is prohibited. -The level of risk and danger if contact is permitted.
Administrative tools	PSI format is generic to all crimes.	Make a new PSI form that guides writer in specifics of how to document domestic violence cases.
Resource allocation	Most agents find it hard to find the time to locate victims.	Set up better linkages between victim witness and community based advocates with PSI writer to help connect with victim.
Lines of accountability	Supervisor reads each PSI before it goes to court.	Develop a supervisory checklist to include: -Adequate attempts to locate victim. -Attempts to locate related documentation from criminal and civil courts. -How to summarize violence and related forms of abuse.

(continued)

Table 18.1 (continued)

Methods of standardizing workers responses	Problems observed	Beginnings of solutions
Concepts and theories	Domestic violence reported as incidents, not seen as a pattern of control of violence.	Have working knowledge of three kinds of domestic violence: -Coercive controlling (battering). -Resistive violence. -Non-battering related domestic violence.
Training and education	Main training focused on interviewing skills (i.e. motivational interviewing) but no specialized training on interviewing victims or offenders in domestic violence cases.	Offer two immediate trainings: -How to identify and respond to risk in domestic violence cases. -How to interview offenders and victims to obtain a good history of abuse.
Linkages	PSI writer does not have electronic access to: -Past police reports on defendants. -Affidavits for protection orders. -CAD reports.	Work out MOU with police department to resolve access to police reports. Work out methods for psi writer to have easy access to jail records, police reports, CAD reports, affidavits for orders for protection, etc.

management lack the full capacity to complete their mission. Lack of resources, complementary national policy, the ability to intervene in causes of social problems as opposed to individuals affected by problems such as poverty, racism, sexism, violence, and so forth all show up in this kind of an analysis. The IA is a powerful tool of reform in the hands of the right administrators working with a committed team of analysts. It can sidestep the main obstacle to institutional reform, the inability of reformers to look past individuals' actions and see that most workers do not intend these harmful outcomes.

IA may challenge cherished discourses and long-standing practices, but it does not assign blame to individual workers or even to the operating agency. Instead, it identifies routine practices that accomplish the institutional tasks, but not the agency intent to offer effective interventions. Finally, the IA offers a clear and logical means of achieving both.

Notes

1 The term "battering" connotes an ongoing pattern of coercive and controlling abuse in an intimate relationship.
2 Interview with analyst from racial disparity analysis, January 2011.

References

De Becker, G. (2010). *MOSAIC (Method for Objectively Selecting Areas of Inquiry Consistently)*. G. De Becker & Associates. https://www.mosaicmethod.com/.

Devault, M., & McCoy, L. (2006). Using interviews to investigate ruling relations. In D. E. Smith (Ed.), *Institutional ethnography as practice* (pp. 15–44). Toronto, ON: Rowman and Littlefield.

Hale, S. M. (2010). *Contested sociology: Rethinking Canadian experience*. New York: Pearson Education Canada.

Hathaway, S. R. (1982). *Minnesota multiphasic personality inventory*. Minneapolis, MN: Distributed by National Computer Systems Inc.

Hilton, N. Z., Harris, G. T., & Rice, M. E. (2010). *Risk assessment for domestically violent men: Tools for criminal justice, offender intervention, and victim services*. American Psychological Association. https://www.waypointcentre.ca/cms/one.aspx?portalId=10043&pageId=52600.

Pence, E., & Sadusky, J. (2005). *The Praxis safety and accountability audit toolkit*. Praxis International. https://praxisinternational.org/institutional-analysiscommunity-assessment-2/.

Pence, E., & Sadusky, J. (2006). *Text analysis as a tool for coordinated community response: Keeping safety for battered women and their children at the center*. St. Paul: Praxis International.

Smith, D. E. (1989). *The everyday world as problematic*. Boston, MA: Northeastern University Press.

Smith, D. E. (2006). *Institutional ethnography as practice*. New York: Rowman and Littlefield.

Smith, D. E., & Pence, E. (2011, August). *Institutional analysis: Making change from below*. Annual Meeting of the Society for Social Problems. Las Vegas, NV.

PART V

Critiquing Public Sector Management Regimes

Professional Talk: Unpacking Professional Language

Ann Christin E. Nilsen

Professional language is commonly filled with words, concepts, phrases, and abbreviations that give some kind of meaning within a specific professional context, while for an outsider they might appear theoretical and abstract. This happens because the professional language is embedded within institutional discourses in which experience is left out of view. For instance, a word such as *casework* does not indicate anything about what actually happens, to whom and by whom. Uttered in the context of, for example, child protection services, a phrase gives more specific associations; yet, unless it is linked to the agency of a subject and a verb in action (someone does something), it remains meaningful only by association. Smith (2005) claims that institutional discourses are predominated by nominalization, thus dissolving the intimacy between word and experience. The words and phrases that are used, therefore, function as *shells*, in themselves devoid of substance and agents. Nevertheless, institutional discourses provide the terms under which people's actions are rendered accountable. For professionals, using a professional language is inevitable. In order for these discourses, and the words, concepts, and phrases they invoke to give meaning and be linked to the empirical world, we have to unpack them, i.e., resolving nominalizations into an active verbal form.

The purpose of this chapter is to address why and how we can unpack professional language in institutional ethnography (IE). Drawing primarily on

---

A. C. E. Nilsen (✉)
Department of Sociology and Social Work, University of Agder,
Kristiansand, Norway
e-mail: ann.c.nilsen@uia.no

© The Author(s) 2021
P. C. Luken and S. Vaughan (eds.), *The Palgrave Handbook of Institutional Ethnography*,
https://doi.org/10.1007/978-3-030-54222-1_19

my own experiences from research on early childhood institutions in Norway, I address the following questions: What are the challenges of interviewing professionals? What is there to discover in the unpacking of professional language? And lastly: How can we go about unpacking professional words, discourse, and jargon when interviewing professionals?

The Conditions for Professional Practice Under New Public Management

Let me start by recollecting some of the insights developed within professional studies. Talcott Parsons is frequently referred to as the founding father of the sociology of professions. Associated with the functionalist paradigm within sociology, Parsons argued that modern societies are characterized by increasing differentiation and specialization. These changes threaten the social order unless they are accompanied by an integration of values within different societal sub-systems, such as family, education, etc. Such integration requires a consensual agreement about specific values, and according to Parsons (1939), professionals play a crucial role in that respect. Parsons saw professionals as mediators of specific values and knowledge, and as such, they function as a corrective force to the market and are imperative for the smooth functioning of society. In contrast to his American contemporaries, he argued that it is the professions, and not capitalism, that advance society.

When New Public Management (NPM) emerged in most Western societies during the 1980s, it was in an effort to make the public services more efficient, goal-oriented, and businesslike. The idea was that private sector management models would lead to higher quality and a more cost-effective delivery of public services. This turn, which is associated with neo-liberalism, required governments to develop standardized management instructions, such as procedures and routines, intended to minimize the risk of arbitrary and inefficient service delivery. A government's ruling hence occurs at a distance, and is mediated by an abundance of documents providing guidelines, procedures, indicators and so on that regulate professionals' practice, and against which they are held accountable. The concept of *accountability* has, therefore, entered the discourse in a way that sensitizes us to how government and management rule through measurable results that inform and influence people's activities. Institutional ethnographers have used the concept *institutional circuit* (e.g., Griffith & Smith, 2014; Nilsen, 2017a) to describe how sequences of text-coordinated actions render people's realities representable, and thereby actionable or accountable (Smith & Turner, 2014). A subcategory of institutional circuits is *accountability circuits* (e.g., DeVault, Venkatesh, & Ridzi, 2014), which describe the work done to make performance or outcomes produced at the frontline accountable in terms of managerial categories and objectives (Griffith & Smith, 2014).

In a narrow sense, accountability is used with reference to the presentation of auditable accounts. However, in a broader sense, accountability involves a moral responsibility, connoting "being answerable to" (Biesta, 2004). This ambiguity can be captured in Bauman's (1991) distinction between the concepts of ethics and morality. He describes morality as the genuinely human ability to distinguish between right and wrong, while ethics are the rules and norms that regulate and codify what counts as moral action. With reference to these concepts, Gert Biesta (2004) argues that the accountability culture is governed by ethics, and nurtures behavior that suits the accountability *system*, rather than commeasuring professional action with moral action. Arguing along the same lines, Julia Evetts (2009) refers to two ideal types of professionalism. Organizational professionalism is about following the rules, procedures and regulations embedded in the organizational structures. On the other hand, occupational professionalism resembles Parsons' notion of the role of professions, and is oriented toward professional integrity and autonomy. With the neoliberal turn, the demand for quality assurance, assessment, and revision has invoked a priority for organizational professionalism at the cost of occupational professionalism, Evetts argues. Others have analogously warned against the power of the "rituals of verification" (Powers, 1997) and the "corrupting power of institutions" (MacIntyre, 1984, p. 194). Steven Brint (1994) asserts that the professions, "as a source of collective moral force in public life," (p. 209) are on the decline. Today, professionals increasingly define themselves strictly in terms of their command of technical matters and by their marketable knowledge and skills.[1]

Conforming to this, *evidence* is another concept that has increasingly entered the discourse of professionalism after the neoliberal turn. In the context of professional practice, the concept is normally used with reference to science or scientific knowledge, epitomized in the "gold standard" of Randomized Controlled Trials (RCT). When a model or intervention is presented as evidence-based, one can assume that it has been tested with a scientific method, usually of an experimental kind that produces quantitative data (such as a controlled experiment). The purpose of evidence is to claim trust, and as such it is seductive. However, as suggested in the title of a book addressing how neuroscience and epigenetics have come to shape social policy in a particular direction, science can also "blind us" (Wastell & White, 2017). Moreover, Andrew Abbott, the author of the seminal book, *The System of Professions* (1988), asserts that interventions' allegiance to academic knowledge tends to the symbolic, rather than the practical. When claims of evidence are used to gain authority, it rarely reveals how scientific knowledge is negotiated, critiqued, and disputed, but rather tends to treat science as *truth*.

It is within this context that professionals have to make decisions and act. On the one hand, they have assumptively adopted a certain *professional ethos*[2] brought forward through academic systems and professional institutions; whereas, on the other, they have to abide by organizational rules and regulations, passed on by the government from a distance. How they do their work, how they reach decisions, and how they navigate between external demands and what they genuinely believe in, is a matter for empirical exploration. In this chapter, I will put the focus on professionals in the frontline of the welfare state, the *street-level bureaucrats* (Lipsky, 1980). Their role is to be the extended arm of the state vis-à-vis its citizens, and to "represent government to the people" (Lipsky, 1977, p. 196). According to Abbott (1988), what characterizes professionals, including street-level bureaucrats, is the use of abstract knowledge to solve specific issues. Abbott claims that in order to understand how professions function and change, we need to study the actual acts and activities of professionals, and not structures or culture as simply abstract phenomena.

Institutional ethnography is a line of inquiry that expands this view by acknowledging that the acts and activities of professionals cannot be disentangled from the abstracted discourses and institutional arrangements of which they are part. Institutional ethnographers study the processes that come to shape people's everyday/everynight acts and activities, and how their acts are also constitutive of the social organization of the institution. The concepts of *work/work knowledge* are useful in this respect. By exploring what professionals do, how they do it, what they think and feel about what they do, and importantly, how they coordinate their doings with other peoples' doings, mediated in texts, institutional discourses, and ideological codes, we can understand more of the institutional processes in which they are embedded. Exploring people's work is, therefore, often the starting point of an institutional ethnography.

When studying professional work, the researcher has to be particularly aware of *institutional captures*. These occur when the informant and researcher share a familiarity with an institutional discourse and come to lose touch with experience. Institutional captures thus typically involve the nominalization of verbs, drawing the attention away from what is actually being done, by whom and to whom, such as the example of *casework* in the introduction. Professional language potentially involves many institutional captures, thereby requiring the researcher to be specifically alert to his/her own usage of and familiarity with specific phrases, words, and concepts that circulate in a professional field.

CHALLENGES WHEN INTERVIEWING PROFESSIONALS

The examples I am using in this chapter are all taken from my own research on professionals in Norway who work within institutions targeting children and their families, such as kindergartens and the child welfare service (CWS). In Norway, as in the Nordic region at large, the public sector is comprehensive and trust in the state is high (Lund & Nilsen, 2019). As a consequence, the state can be said to play an important role in the policing of families (Donzelot, 1979), e.g., by providing guidelines and defining requirements, both for professional practice and for the academic education of professionals. The empirical examples I am presenting are selected because they illustrate how professional language comes to shape professional practice in specific ways. In order to maintain the anonymity of the informants, I am not disclosing any details about the organizations they work in or their identities, and all the interviewees are given pseudonyms.

In the interview below, the social worker Sara tells us about how she works with the young, single mother, Karen. The quotes are taken from a part of the interview where Sara talks about the different initiatives the CWS have taken to help Karen, which appear to have been very successful. Karen receives regular home visits from social workers in the CWS and has attended a parental training, which is based on a model called the *Circle of Security* (COS). Sara has attended several professional courses, including one on the COS, from which she has gained a certification to use specific methods.

> *Sara*: Children need to explore and to become independent individuals, but they still need a lot of help to regulate their emotions. She [Karen] struggled with that. When the child was crying a lot or got angry and she didn't know the cause, she found it difficult to know how to handle it. It made her stressed out, and her behavior became brusque. There were some difficult episodes when she had tried her best but was unable to calm him down. We talked a lot about helping her understand his emotions and helping her with self-regulation, because the mother should also receive help to regulate her own emotions. That would contribute to developing a safe attachment, which we [the CWS] are very concerned about.
>
> *Ann*: What does it mean to regulate emotions? How do you help a person with that?
>
> *Sara*: All children are dependent on their caretakers. Particularly during the first years of their lives, children depend on sensitive adults who know how to help a child. That concerns both physical and emotional care. It is imperative that children have sensitive adults that understand children. Her child was less than one year old and will not yet have developed personal strategies. If he was overwhelmed by his emotions and does not master what he is trying to do or does not get the candy, if he gets frustrated, angry or disappointed, they are dependent on external regulation because they have not yet established their own strategies. Adults help them with that.

In the interview, Sara uses terms such as *self-regulation, personal strategies, safe attachment,* and *sensitive adults*. All these concepts are part of a professional jargon and represent potential institutional captures. Despite their limited reference to any empirical content, they are used to express an assumptively shared notion. They belong in a sphere of academic language, in this case within psychology. Used in this context, where Sara is describing a line of reasoning, these words connote academic authority. Within one sentence Sara shifts her perspective from talking about one specific child ("if he was overwhelmed by his emotions"), to a general notion of children ("they are dependent on external regulation"), and the tense of the verb changes accordingly. This signals that Sara uses her professional knowledge to analyze the situation of the particular child, while simultaneously devoting a specific meaning to her observations. Now, this is of course part of the professional craft, as Abbott (1988) describes it, using abstract knowledge to solve specific issues. However, what is striking is how suddenly the shifts happen. Moreover, having studied professionals working with children within different institutions, I was struck by how similar Sara's account was to that of other professionals I had interviewed. It was almost as if someone had pressed a repeat button, using the same words and the same arguments to describe quite different situations and different people. So, I was left wondering: What does Sara actually think and feel about the situation? Would she be able to verbalize her thoughts and feelings if she did not have an academic language to rely on? And if so, would her analysis look different?

From a methodological perspective, the question is how to get behind the academic jargon and unpack the professional language. On several occasions during the interview I tried to ask questions that might open up a different way of talking, for instance, by asking "stupid" questions ("What does it mean to be certified?"), asking her to elaborate ("Can you tell me exactly what happened?"), and asking about her own opinions ("Do you think it is useful yourself?"). Nevertheless, the answers soon drifted back to the professional and institutionally captured way of talking.

This example illustrates some of the challenges of interviewing professionals. DeVault and McCoy (2006) assert that professionals are taught to use institutional words and phrases, and, thus, can be difficult to interview. The challenge is to identify such concepts in action, seeing in what ways they are capturing and being able to discover how they relate to the actualities of people's everyday activities. At the same time, the researcher's sensibility toward such concepts harbors a potential to discover institutional discourses and ideological codes often taken for granted, which tacitly come to shape professional practice.

What Is There to Discover in Professional Talk?

Professional words and phrases are embedded within institutional discourses and ideologies, and form part of ruling relations. As such, they offer a viable pathway into discovering the ruling relations of institutional complexes. As it is used in IE, the conception of discourse originates with Foucault in whose work it refers to "an assemblage of 'statements' arising in an ongoing 'conversation,' mediated by texts, among speakers and hearers separated from one another in time and space" (Smith, 1990, p. 121). Insisting on preserving the active presence of subjects-in-discourse, Smith (1990, Chapter 6) argues that "discourse and ideology can be investigated as actual social relations ongoingly organized in and by the activities of actual people" (p. 121). People are not subsumed by discourse, but participate in discourse. In order to discover how discourses coordinate actions, we have to explore how people activate, negotiate, and navigate between different abstracted and textually mediated discourses in their everyday lives.

When professional words and phrases come into play, they denote specific academic discourses. In Sara's case, she makes references to a set of evidence-based models and mapping tools that have been developed within developmental psychology. One example is the above-mentioned COS model, which is rooted in attachment theory (Marvin, Cooper, Hoffman, & Powell, 2002). The model is intended to improve the relationship between children and their caregivers by bringing attention to how a child signals his/her needs for protection, comfort, and exploration. The words Sara uses ("attachment," "sensitivity," "regulation") can be traced to this model. The COS model has been widely recognized, both in Norway and internationally, with many CWS offices offering parents training in COS. Moreover, it is a common assumption within this theory that parents construct their parental behavior on patterns deriving from their own childhood experiences. In the interview, Sara says:

> We know something about how parents' own childhood experiences have an impact on their own care practices. She [Karen] had experienced that she was not allowed to reveal anger as a child. She could see that this was a pattern she had reproduced.

However, in my interview with Karen, she says that she does not remember much from her own childhood. Instead, she describes a pregnancy impaired by pain and anxiety, and a current situation characterized by fear of losing the child and of a limited social network. She describes how the birth of her child involved a break with the child's father, who had a drug addiction, and how her own mother came to comfort her and help her out. Sara and Karen's accounts of Karen's parenting practice are similar in some respects, but are also strikingly contrasting. Where Sara shifts between specific descriptions of Karen's parenting practice and generalized descriptions of good parenting, Karen talks about specific incidences in which she felt that she either failed or succeeded as a parent, and about her fears and struggles. Having attended the COS training, she also depicts how her behavior as a mother changed for the better. She says that, "When you get a confirmation from the authorities that what you do is right, you feel lighter."

There are two main points of interest here. First, we can see how Sara interprets the empirical observations of Karen's behavior in a way that fits into an institutional discourse. This resembles the cutting-out-procedure Smith eloquently describes in the essay "K Is Mentally Ill" (Smith, 1978). Empirical observations ("her behavior became brusque," "she was unable to calm him down," "not allowed to reveal anger as a child") are cut out and combined with discursive features ("poor self-regulation," "unsafe attachment," "insensitivity"), and the result is a coherent image of a mother-child relationship characterized by a pre-defined set of risk factors. It represents an example of an accountability circuit in which Sara strives to align her empirical observations with managerial categories. Secondly, the example reveals how disciplinary the institutional discourse of good mothering is. Karen describes how she aligns her behavior to the expectations expressed within the COS model, and how she feels confident when she succeeds in that respect. The COS model is an example of a textually-mediated conceptual framework that organizes people's everyday lives. Within this framework is a unified understanding of what it means to be a good parent. The notion of "the good parent" is an ideological code, that is, a replicable schematic understanding that structures the language of texts and textually mediated discourses (Smith, 2012, Chapter 8). Ideological codes provide a discursive framework that organizes people's talk and actions, and to which people hold themselves accountable. That does not necessarily imply that people conform to the ideological codes. But even when they reject the codes or oppose them, people still organize their work in relation to the code (Luken & Vaughan, 2006; Smith, 1990). The "good parent" code, mediated through the COS model and the professional words and phrases used by Sara, thus have a direct implication on Karen's everyday parenting practice and confidence.

The example illustrates how professional language mediates translocal and ruling relations. In addition to that, professional words, categories, and phrases sensitize us to lines of inquiry worth following. They signal a disjuncture between academic theorizing and local actualities. In order to understand what is being done by whom and how it comes about, one cannot rely on professional words alone. Understood as institutional captures, they restrain us from seeing people's everyday *doings*. In order to empirically trace what kind of acts and activities the concepts refer to locally, we have to unpack them. Furthermore, unpacking such words and phrases can also enable us to discover acts of opposition and resistance, rendering into view a double subject: the appearingly passive *subject-in-discourse* and the active and competent *subject-at-work* (Smith, 1990, p. 152). Sørensen, Nilsen, and Lund (2019) argue that everyday resistance carries a transformative potential even in contexts such as the Nordic, where resistance seems out of place and where power dynamics are concealed as intentions of doing good. Unpacking professional language not only enables us to discover modes and relations of ruling, but also how ruling is opposed and contradicted by people set to be the extended arm of the state. In turn, this sets us in a position to address the problematics involved in nurturing a mindset where accountability and evidence are used almost synonymously with quality.

Unpacking Professional Language in Empirical Research

The methodological question emerging from this is how to go about unpacking professional language in empirical research. In the following, I will give some examples and suggestions based on my own experiences. These experiences form part of my work knowledge as an institutional ethnographer. I will primarily focus on how to unpack professional language in interviews. The reason for this is quite straightforward: Interviews are the most widely used method by institutional ethnographers. Yet, it has to be mentioned that ethnographic approaches that involve observation or a combination of interviews and observational data are very well-suited to obtain insight into professional practices and how professional talk is put into play. For instance, De Montigny's autobiographical account of a child protection case provides an excellent example of how professional discourse subsumes not only intuitive reactions, but also sensory responses (e.g., smells and sights), and informs what professionals should do and say/write in order to appear accountable (De Montigny, 2014).

In my research on early childhood intervention in Norwegian kindergartens, I was interviewing professionals about their *concern work*. Inspired by the so-called life-mode interview, I was able to acquire detailed descriptions of everyday life in the kindergartens. The life-mode interview, as developed by the Norwegian psychologist Hanne Haavind (1987), is structured along the chronology of an ordinary day. Important questions are, for example "What happened?" "Who were involved?" "Is this typical?" "What do you think about that situation?" and so on. The purpose is to make the participants talk as freely as possible about their everyday lives while at the same time allowing the researcher to probe into topics of interest. In the interviews with people working in kindergartens, I used a similar approach, but rather than asking the participants to talk about an ordinary day, the introductory question was, "Have you ever been worried about a child in the kindergarten?" If the participant said yes—and in fact, they all did—I then encouraged him or her to tell me about one such incident, while probing into details. During these accounts, I was particularly sensitive to professional words and phrases. For instance, the word "screening" was frequently used when the kindergarten teachers talked about children for whom they were worried. During the first interviews, I was genuinely curious about what screening was. I soon learned that when they used this word the kindergarten teachers were talking about a number of tests they used to assess children's abilities. I learned that the assessments most commonly conducted were by pedagogical leaders, that they were built on a set of indicators of mastery along different domains, that the scores of the children were based on the discretionary judgment of the person conducting the assessment, and that they normally would build their assessment on random observations, rather than having the child sit down across from them at a table. Sometimes, the participants showed me concretely how this work was done, which allowed me to ask even more detailed questions. After some interviews, I had a quite clear impression of which assessment tests were being used, what they looked like and how they were meant to work. Nevertheless, I asked the same "stupid" questions each time a participant used the word screening: What does that mean? Can you explain how it works? Can you show me? What do you think about it? and so on. This enabled me to get detailed accounts, to discover variation, and most importantly, to probe into the participants' thoughts and feelings about their work and thereby also tracing opposition or disagreement.

During these interviews I combined different techniques. By structuring the conversation around a situation that occurred in a chronological sequence, a story was told by the participants. Later in the interview, these stories could be used as reference points that enable comparison and elaboration. In addition, the stories revealed a complexity of social relations—there were references to colleagues, parents, texts, and documents—and the participants gave detailed accounts of their involvement in these diverse relations. Since the conversation started off with them telling me about a feeling ("worry"), the accounts were usually personal. Instead of depicting a formal case process procedure, the participants told me about their uncertainties and fears, their opinions and experiences, and about disagreement and differences. I noticed that the stories tended to focus more on the formalities of the case process (descriptions of how to do it) the closer the participant was to management and the more educated the participant was (e.g., the pedagogical leaders). Put differently, the disjuncture between word and experience appeared larger the more distant from the everyday life of the child the professional was. Whereas the kindergarten teachers who interacted directly with the children every day told complex and detailed stories of individual children, the stories told by the pedagogical leaders were about categories of children, for instance, "children with delayed language development" or "children with behavioral problems." I soon realized that the pedagogical leaders more readily adopted the standardized professional language used in formal documents and reports, hence appearing as subjects-in-discourse. As leaders in the kindergartens, it is their responsibility to report concern to the child welfare service or the educational pedagogical service if a child is not developing properly or does not receive proper care, which requires them to classify the child as a specific type of child. As a consequence, the pedagogical leaders had to coordinate their work in relation to specific professional discourses and codes.

By asking "stupid" questions, I attempted to get behind such standardized ways of talking. By stupid questions, I mean questions about actions and words used in an everyday and taken for granted way, and that the interviewees assume you are familiar with. My goal was to discover subjects-at-work, tracing how various social relations organized their work. It was to my advantage that I am not educated as a kindergarten teacher, and did not have to pretend to be unknowledgeable. However, as the data collection progressed, I became familiar with the professional language, and because I spent much time in the kindergartens the interviewees were aware of that. Asking stupid questions is difficult the more of an insider you are to the field of study. Even identifying what to ask stupid questions about can be difficult from that position, as you share the institutional discourse with the informant.

Finally, bringing texts and materiality into the interview, for instance, by asking to see forms, documents, and objects that the participants made reference to, enriched the data material. This made it possible to witness how the professionals did the screening in practice, how they had to estimate how well a child at a given age knows a given skill, and how they had to align their assessment to the preferred categorical outcome (for instance, making sure to depict a child as "delayed" if they think (s)he needs pedagogical support). This made me aware of accountability circuits where local, subjective, and discretionary judgements were transformed to a seemingly objective textual representation of the child, which was subsequently given an authoritative role as it was circulated among professionals responsible for implementing the proper intervention for the child.

The interviews made visible the kindergarten staff's work across fault lines, in the intersection between rules and values that sometimes contradict the rules. On the one side, the kindergarten teachers would fill in the forms, use the models and follow the guidelines, while on the other, they constantly found reasons to bypass these demands, or to twist and bend the guidelines out of a concern that they were not in the best interest of the children. This made me curious. If they were critical of the system, why did they not oppose it? Turning my attention to this question in the analysis of the interviews, I discovered that there was more opposition among the kindergarten staff than I could see at first glance. Let us have a look at one example.

In the interview below, the kindergarten teacher, Lisa, tells me about a program they use in the kindergarten in order to stimulate language development in children under three years of age. The program is referred to as a game and is conducted as a station-based play, led by an adult, in 10–15 minutes sessions (Rasmussen & Rosnes, 2019). Accentuating how a stimulation of language promotes brain development, the program is inspired by neuroscientific theories and makes reference to an investment logic that has become well-known through the Heckman-curve.[3] As such, it is part of a textually-mediated institutional discourse that is not only prominent in kindergartens in Norway, but also in transnational organizations such as the Organisation for Economic Co-operation and Development (OECD) and the World Bank, relying on a combined developmental-psychological and socio-economic rationale (e.g. Marope & Kaga, 2015; Nilsen, 2017b; Penn, 2011; Qvortrup, 2009). Accordingly, the program was implemented in the kindergarten due to a political decision in the municipality to increasingly enhance early childhood learning in kindergartens, in order to improve social welfare outcomes in the municipality at large.

> *Lisa*: We are supposed to use it several times a day, but we have chosen to do it once a day. Ugh, we cannot say that we don't have time, because we actually do have time. But we do something else instead.
> *Ann*: So, what do you do then?
> *Lisa*: Well, we spend a lot of time outdoors, now in the summer. We go for walks and pick flowers. There is a farewell dinner for the six year-olds tomorrow, so we have to find some decoration.
> *Ann:* Yes...?
> *Lisa:* I think we spend a lot of time on documentation. But children's natural element is play. They play—like roleplays, song games—well, all kinds of games. Children's natural element is playing. They play their way into the adult world, and indeed, they [experts, people] do say that role playing is a way to find out what you want to become.

It is clear that Lisa and her colleagues disagree with how the program has been implemented. But rather than openly oppose it, they twist their way around it and spend time on the activities they think are best for the children, such as playing outdoors. Being attentive to opposition, I discovered how Lisa and her colleagues activate different institutional discourses which come to organize their work. Outdoor activities, and free time for children to play without adult inference, are ideals that remain strong in Norwegian kindergartens (Nilsen, 2008; Seland, 2009; Synodi, 2010). As part of an institutional discourse, these ideals can justify different actions than the discourse of early language stimulation mediated by the program. When discussing, making decisions and working to organize their everyday lives in relation to the discourse of play, Lisa and her colleagues make the discourse accountable to themselves and others in a local setting. However, despite their rejection of the program, the discourse it mediates still codifies and organizes the kindergartens teachers' work. Later in the interview, Lisa tells me that the children she is most concerned for are the ones who fall out of games and struggle to find other children to play with. When describing this, she returns to language:

> *Lisa*: You cannot beat your way into a group. Because that's what happens, children beat their way in. If they are not allowed to join, they just hit. And then it is important to be in the situation, to tell them that they can't do it that way. But that you can use your words. You can ask, "Can I join you?" Or you can turn to an adult and tell her that you would like to join the others in their game. "Can you help me?" or "I need help."
> *Ann*: Yes...
> *Lisa*: But it's... It has to be learned over time... So it takes time. And then there is someone who cries earlier than others, and you also have to teach them how to use their words. Say, "Stop that, I don't like it." Small sentences like that, that they can remember. Instead of crying, because there is always someone who thinks it's funny when you start to cry.

The account shows us that even though Lisa is critical of the program that has been implemented in the kindergarten, and even though she does not use academic language, she is genuinely dedicated to enhancing children's language skills and social skills. Thus, even despite her tacit opposition to a particular way of enhancing children's language skills, she conforms to the institutional discourse of early language stimulation. Here is an example of a subject-at-work. Lisa's work knowledge is that children learn language best in naturally occurring and real-life situations, rather than in simulated situations controlled by adults. However, she does not tell me this directly. It is through detailed accounts of specific situations that this message is brought forward, as well as through my active listening for oppositional talk.

Final Reflections

The examples presented in this chapter illustrate how professional talk can be unpacked through different strategies. Many of these strategies are well-known to ethnographers, such as encouraging people to tell stories about their work, asking "stupid" questions and combining interviews with observation. Such strategies are well-suited to bring people's doings into view and are used by scholars who are informed by, for instance, grounded theory and symbolic interactionism. For an institutional ethnographer, however, the aim is to explore institutional processes, thereby bringing translocal and ruling relations into view. For that purpose I found it particularly useful to activate texts in the interviews, and to actively look for traces of oppositional talk which point to the social relations organizing their opposition.

Professional language carries institutional discourses that harbor a potential for swallowing perspective, the local and subjective experience of workers (Smith, 2005). Identifying phrases, words, and concepts that function as shells is imperative to avoid being subject to institutional capture. In order to bring the experiential knowledge of professionals into view, there is a need to reconnect the intimacy between word and experience by unpacking professional language. Moreover, professional language, which tends to be textually mediated, coordinates experience, and institutional discourses. Indeed, texts, used in a generous sense that comprises professional phrases, words, and concepts, function as social coordinators in at least two ways: As they enter into and coordinate a course of action, and as they coordinate a particular course of action with social relations extending beyond the local (Smith, 2005). I have discussed how professional language can be unpacked in interviews, and thereby bringing experience into view. That being said, professional phrases, words, and concepts, even when dissolved from experience, are interesting in themselves as they denote institutional discourses that form part of ruling relations. The quest for an institutional ethnographer is thus twofold: To identify how professional language is connected to both subjective local experiences and to translocal institutional discourses. Accordingly, encountering a concept such as *safe attachment*, *self-regulation* or *casework* raises two questions: How is it linked to experience and people's doings? and: How is the concept used in authoritative texts and institutional discourses?

The increasing managerialism and implicit standardization of modern welfare states require both professionals and researchers to be attentive to how language is used in ways that reproduce and reinforce specific narratives of knowledge. When professional words and concepts are used as tokens of accountability and evidence, they denote scientific authority and are often left unquestioned. They enter into institutional circuits in which professionals work to align empirical observations with managerial and standardized categories, thereby contributing to justification loops in which experience, critique and opposition are left out of view (Nilsen & Steen-Johnsen, 2019). This explains why certain strands of science remain authoritative and "blind us"

(Wastell & White, 2017). Consequently, institutional ethnography is a suitable approach to explore topics and assumptions embedded in professional talk and practice, and that tend to be taken for granted, as these may not be as straightforward and uncontested as they seem at first glance.

Notes

1. There is of course contextual variation. In the Nordic countries, for instance, where the social democratic welfare states are comprehensive, most professionals in the "soft" sectors (e.g. schools and social welfare) are employed by the state. However, the introduction of New Public Management has arguably also involved an increasing marketization and commodification of the public sector in these states.
2. *Ethos* is a Greek word used to describe the beliefs, ideals, and fundamental values that characterize, e.g., a community, a person, a corporation, or a movement. Professional ethos thus denotes the moral character, values and dispositions of a particular professional community. In rhetoric, the word is frequently associated with Aristotle, signifying one of his four modes of persuasion (the other three are pathos, logos and kairos).
3. The social investment logic targets children as engines for societal development and increased human resources. The internationally recognized and highly influential Heckman curve epitomizes this investment logic (Heckman, 2006). According to this theory, there is a multiplier effect of early investment: early learning fosters more learning, thus the highest rate of economic return results from the earliest investment in children.

References

Abbott, A. (1988). *The system of professions*. Chicago: The University of Chicago Press.
Bauman, Z. (1991). *Modernity and ambivalence*. Ithaca, NY: Cornell University Press.
Biesta, G. J. J. (2004). Education, accountability, and the ethical demand: Can the democratic potential of accountability be regained? *Educational Theory*, 54(3), 233–250.
Brint, S. (1994). *In an age of experts: The changing role of professionals in politics and public life*. Princeton, NJ: Princeton University Press.
De Montigny, G. (2014). Doing child protection work. In D. E. Smith & S. M. Turner (Eds.), *Incorporating texts into institutional ethnographies* (pp. 173–194). Toronto: University of Toronto Press.
DeVault, M., & McCoy, L. (2006). Institutional ethnography: Using interviews to investigate ruling relations. In D. Smith (Ed.), *Institutional ethnography as practice* (pp. 15–44). Lanham, MD: Rowman & Littlefield.
DeVault, M., Venkatesh, M., & Ridzi, F. (2014). "Let's be friends": Working within an accountability circuit. In A. Griffith & D. E. Smith (Eds.), *Under new public management: Institutional ethnographies of changing front-line work* (pp. 177–198). Toronto: University of Toronto Press.
Donzelot, J. (1979). *The policing of families*. New York, NY: Pantheon Books.

Evetts, J. (2009). New professionalism and new public management: Changes, continuities and consequences. *Comparative Sociology*, 8, 247–266.

Griffith, A., & Smith, D. E. (2014). *Under new public management: institutional ethnographies of changing front-line work*. Toronto: University of Toronto Press.

Haavind, H. (1987). *Liten og stor: Mødres omsorg og barns utviklingsmuligheter*. [Small and big. Maternal care and children's developmental potential]. Oslo: Universitetsforlaget.

Heckman, J. J. (2006). Skill formation and the economics of investing in disadvantaged children. *Science*, 312(5782), 1900–1902.

Lipsky, M. (1977). Toward a theory of street-level bureaucracy. In W. Hawley & M. Lipsky (Eds.), *Theoretical perspectives on urban politics*. Englewood Cliffs, NJ: Prentice Hall.

Lipsky, M. (1980). *Street-level bureaucracy: Dilemmas of the individual in public services*. New York, NY: Russell Sage Publications.

Luken, P. C., & Vaughan, S. (2006). Standardizing childrearing through housing. *Social Problems*, 53(3), 299–331.

Lund, R., & Nilsen, A. C. E. (2019). Introduction: Conditions for doing institutional ethnography in the Nordics. In R. Lund & A. C. E. Nilsen (Eds.), *Institutional ethnography in the Nordic region*. Abingdon: Routledge.

MacIntyre, A. (1984). *After virtue*. Notre Dame, IN: University of Notre Dame.

Marope, P. T. M., & Kaga, Y. (Eds.). (2015). *Investing against evidence: The global state of early childhood care and education*. Paris: UNESCO Publishing.

Marvin, R., Cooper, G., Hoffman, K., & Powell, B. (2002). The circle of security project: Attachment-based intervention with caregiver–pre-school child dyads. *Attachment & Human Development*, 4(1), 107–124.

Nilsen, A. C. E. (2017a). When texts become action: The institutional circuit of early childhood intervention. *European Early Childhood Education Research Journal*, 25(5), 918–929.

Nilsen, A. C. E. (2017b). Bekymringsbarn blir til: En institusjonell etnografi av tidlig innsats som styringsrasjonal i barnehagen [Concern children are "made up." An institutional ethnography of early intervention in kindergartens]. Unpublished doctoral dissertation, University of Agder. Retrieved from https://uia.brage.unit.no/uia-xmlui/bitstream/handle/11250/2435426/BEKYMRINGSBARN+BLIR+TIL+2017.pdf?sequence=2.

Nilsen, A. C. E., & Steen-Johnsen, T. (2019). The ECCD mission and the institutional circuit of evidence. *Journal of Early Childhood Research*. https://doi.org/10.1177/1476718X19860558.

Nilsen, R. D. (2008). Children in nature: Cultural ideas and social practices in Norway. In A. James & A. L. James (Eds.), *European childhoods: Culture, politics and participation* (pp. 38–60). London: Palgrave.

Parsons, T. (1939). The professions and social structure. *Oxford Journals*, 17(4), 457–467.

Penn, H. (2011). Travelling policies and global buzzwords: How international non-governmental organizations and charities spread the word about early childhood in the global South. *Childhood*, 18(1), 94–113.

Powers, M. (1997). *The audit society: Rituals of verification*. Oxford: Oxford University Press.

Qvortrup, J. (2009). Are children human beings or human becomings? A critical assessment of outcome thinking. *Rivista Internazionale Di Scienze Sociali, 117*(3/4), 631–653.

Rasmussen, I., & Rosnes, O. (2019). *Evaluering av språkleken Bravo* [An evaluation of the language game Bravo]. Report no. 15. Vista analyse. Retrieved from https://www.ferd.no/resources/fse/publikasjoner/VA-rapport-2019-15-Evaluering-av-Bravoleken.pdf.

Seland, M. (2009). Det moderne barn og den fleksible barnehagen. En etnografisk studie av barnehagens hverdagsliv i lys av nyere diskurser og kommunal virkelighet [The modern child and the flexible kindergarten. An ethnographic study of kindergarten's everyday life in light of recent discourses and municipal realities]. Unpublished doctoral dissertation, Norwegian University of Science and Technology. Retrieved from https://core.ac.uk/download/pdf/52110039.pdf.

Smith, D. E. (1978). "K is mentally ill": The anatomy of a factual account. *Sociology, 12*(1), 23–53.

Smith, D. E. (1990). *Texts, facts and femininity*. London: Routledge.

Smith, D. E. (2005). *Institutional ethnography: A sociology for people*. Lanham, MD: AltaMira.

Smith, D. E. (2012). *Writing the social: Critique, theory and investigations*. Toronto: University of Toronto Press.

Smith, D. E., & Turner, S. (2014). Introduction. In D. Smith & S. Turner (Eds.), *Incorporating texts into institutional ethnographies* (pp. 3–14). Toronto: Toronto University Press.

Sørensen, M., Nilsen, A. C. E., & Lund, R. (2019). Resisting the ruling relations: Discovering everyday resistance with institutional ethnography. In R. Lund & A. C. E. Nilsen (Eds.), *Institutional ethnography in the Nordic region*. Abingdon: Routledge.

Synodi, E. (2010). Play in the kindergarten: The case of Norway, Sweden, New Zealand and Japan. *International Journal of Early Years Education, 18*, 185–200.

Wastell, D., & White, S. (2017). *Blinded by science: The social implications of epigenetics and neuroscience*. Bristol: Policy Press.

CHAPTER 20

Frontline Interpretive Work of Activating the Americans with Disabilities Act

Erik D. Rodriguez

In the United States, federal laws intended to promote educational access and equity for students with disabilities have generated structural changes and management policies that impact the provision of student services. Educational institutions have modified building structures, implemented universal design principles, incorporated adaptive technologies, and provided academic accommodations. As colleges and universities follow public service organizations toward New Public Management principles that emphasize efficiency, accountability, effectiveness, and customer service (Dobbins, Knill, & Vögtle, 2011), compliance with federal disability law falls to professionals in designated disability services departments who are responsible for interpreting the imprecise language of federal regulations, activating them at the local level through institutional policies and texts. While ostensibly created to help students with disabilities, the procedures arising from the associated requirements cause additional work for the students served. The interpretive work of the disability services professionals is largely invisible, and the burden on the students unrecognized.

The first official services for college students with disabilities began in 1948 when the University of Illinois started the Division of Rehabilitation Education Services to assist U.S. veterans of World War II. There were few others until after the U.S. Rehabilitation Act of 1973 required entities receiving federal funds to accommodate individuals with disabilities (Haller, 2006). Even then,

E. D. Rodriguez (✉)
Department of Education, Gwinnett Technical College, Lawrenceville, GA, USA
e-mail: ERodriguez@gwinnetttech.edu

© The Author(s) 2021
P. C. Luken and S. Vaughan (eds.), *The Palgrave Handbook of Institutional Ethnography*,
https://doi.org/10.1007/978-3-030-54222-1_20

few U.S. colleges broadened their programs and services until the Americans with Disabilities Act of 1990 (ADA) expanded the legal definition of disability. Now, as a protected category under the law, people with disabilities living in the United States are afforded certain entitlements and services.

In colleges and universities, students seeking accommodations for disabilities are typically served by dedicated disability services offices. Disability service providers ensure that colleges comply with laws governing services and accommodations for college students with disabilities while maintaining academic and program standards and institutional priorities. This chapter examines the day-to-day activities of disability services providers at one U.S. community college who performed the work of interpreting, implementing, and complying with federal laws at the local level, including the development of texts that represent the institutional policies and procedures regarding students with disabilities.

The language of the ADA is vague, with words like "reasonable accommodations" and "undue hardship" loosely defined, requiring local entities to interpret these terms. In this analysis, I examine how The Office of Disability Services (ODS) staff were able to articulate their implementation and compliance responsibilities in light of the fact that the interpretive work was largely unrecognized. I also show that these textually mediated policies and procedures placed most of the responsibility for obtaining and using academic accommodations on the students, adding to their work and potentially limiting the usefulness of this assistance. Finally, I show that there was a linear, top-down flow of information originating from the legal texts and regulations at the highest translocal level to students at the local level, with the ODS serving as an intermediary. There was a noticeable absence of an upward flow of information or feedback loop.

The Function of Texts

Texts play an essential role in the coordination of modern societies. As forms of ruling, they mediate social relations and coordinate everyday experiences. Texts are interpreted at multiple sites and coordinate the work activities of people translocally (Luken, 2008). Front line workers produce textual representations conforming to authoritative texts that enable action at the institutional level. These "boss texts" include such things as laws, policies, and administrative mandates. Griffith and Smith (2014) maintain that, "Once a textual representation fitting the categories/concepts established by the authorized or boss text has been produced, the actuality (as textually represented) becomes institutionally actionable" (p. 12). As frontline workers, the ODS staff perform the work of bringing the governing texts to life through a process of interpretation and implementation that influence people's lives in a multitude of ways. An examination of their work must include consideration of the students served by the ODS who "put in time and energy and are active in actual local settings as they engage with or are caught up in institutional process" (Griffith & Smith, 2014, p. 11).

In the United States, the ADA, as amended in 2008, defines an individual with a disability as someone who: (a) has a physical or mental impairment that substantially limits one or more major life activities; (b) has a record of such an impairment; or (c) is regarded as having such an impairment (Americans with Disabilities Act of 1990 as Amended, 2008). The ADA serves as the authoritative document from which state, college, and departmental policies and texts emerge. The ADA does not list eligible disorders, focusing instead on their functional consequences. The original act was amended in 2008 after legal challenges sought to limit its scope (Heekin, 2010). The amendment clarified the ADA definitions and criteria for inclusion and "emphasizes that the definition of disability should be construed in favor of broad coverage of individuals to the maximum extent permitted by the terms of the ADA and generally shall not require extensive analysis" (U.S. Department of Justice, n.d.). This amendment expanded "major life activities" to include concentration, thinking, and communication (Rothstein, 2018), solidifying the inclusion of cognitive disorders such as Attention Deficit Hyperactivity Disorder (ADHD) as a protected category eligible for support services and special accommodations (Heekin, 2010).

Another piece of legislation, the Individuals with Disabilities Education Act (IDEA), governs how state and public agencies provide early intervention, special education, and related services in elementary and secondary schools (Individuals with Disabilities Education Act, 2004). This law is more prescriptive than the ADA. Primary and secondary schools must develop individualized educational plans (IEP) for students with disabilities based on a multidisciplinary evaluation. This plan includes annual goals and re-evaluation, progress tracking, and special education services. In high school, the IEP must include goals and resources for postsecondary planning. By contrast, colleges and universities are not required to provide evaluation, counseling, tutoring, or personal aids, nor must they "fundamentally alter" their programs or incur "undue hardship" (Office of Special Education and Rehabilitative Services, 2017). The ADA does not require changes to programs that could result in lower academic standards, or that would cause the college undue financial hardship (Thomas, 2000, p. 255). The imprecise language of the ADA allows for the law's intended inclusivity and affords colleges and universities the flexibility to interpret the text in ways that are reflective of their local priorities, comply with the letter of the law, minimize disruption, and control costs associated with implementation (Jung, 2003).

METHODOLOGICAL CONSIDERATIONS

The data presented here is derived from a larger ethnographic study of 14 community college students diagnosed with Attention Deficit Hyperactivity

Disorder (ADHD) as they tried to adhere to the schedule and time expectations of their college coursework. ADHD is a complex condition associated with organizational and time management challenges that can impact academic performance. The Diagnostic and Statistical Manual of Mental Disorders (American Psychiatric Association, 2013) includes ADHD as a neurodevelopmental condition, purportedly legitimizing it as a medical/mental disorder with potentially disabling characteristics eligible for academic accommodations.

Informed by institutional ethnography, I approached my original research from the standpoint of the students, whose everyday lived experiences were the cornerstones of the study. I explored how the students' work was linked to the processes and activities of the college and other translocal sites of action, including the college's Office of Disability Services (ODS). The focus of this chapter is on the work of the ODS staff, especially the disability services coordinators who managed the department. I analyze the social relations that organized the ODS as the entity responsible for accommodating students at a local site of action, while simultaneously interpreting and implementing legal and procedural frameworks at the institutional, state, and federal levels. I also explore how these linkages impacted the day-to-day work practices of the ODS frontline workers, shaped the students' own experiences, and did or did not ultimately affect institutional or public policy.

Conceptually, institutional ethnography supported the following assumptions about work important to my research: (a) investigation begins with "the standpoint of actual individuals located in the everyday world" (Smith, 1987, p. 159); (b) everyday experiences are organized by the activities of people (DeVault & McCoy 2002); (c) people are competent knowers of the work they do on a daily basis (Smith, 2005); and (d) "work knowledge" includes a person's experience of work and the coordination of this work with the work of others (Smith, p. 151). Methodologically, institutional ethnography supported the use of texts and interviews to bring these work processes to life.

The local site of action for the study was a 2-year community college, hereafter known by the pseudonym Southern Pines Community College (SPCC). I use pseudonyms throughout this report for locations and people. I use actual names for accrediting, regulatory, and governmental bodies. Southern Pines Community College consists of a main campus and several smaller satellite branches resulting from a merger of nearby community colleges. The college is part of a statewide system regulated by a governing body that establishes standards, regulations, and policies. In turn, this system is regulated and influenced by larger institutions at the national level such as governmental, regulatory, and accrediting agencies.

In the original study, I interviewed two groups of informants, students with ADHD who had registered with the ODS and two college disability services coordinators who did the frontline organizational work of providing accommodations to eligible students. At the completion of the study, and in preparation for the current analysis, I conducted two additional interviews with college administrators. These were useful in bridging the gap between the college and translocal bodies that shaped the work of staff and students. I also examined several types of texts, including the ADA, other federal laws regulating disability services in education, and institutional texts that guided the ODS work processes.

I initially viewed the coordinators primarily as conduits of information about the students. As the interviews progressed and I analyzed the data, I found that their day-to-day work was rich and complex. At SPCC, the work of interpreting, implementing, and complying with the ADA fell almost exclusively to the coordinators. These individuals served as critical intermediaries between the ADA and the students, who could not access the federally mandated services on their own. The coordinators primarily described their routine activities in terms of ADA implementation and compliance, but it was clear that they also performed important interpretive work that was influenced by personnel changes, management styles, and institutional priorities. I address each of these in subsequent sections of this chapter.

Frontline Disability Services Work

Rather than viewing institutions as representing specific social organizations, Dorothy Smith (1987) describes the institution as an "intersection and coordination of more than one relational mode of the ruling apparatus" (p. 160). Viewed from this perspective, SPCC is not an independent entity; it is a "node or knot" in an organizational system informed by the larger social narrative of what is expected from colleges by those who set the expectations. For example, if those who create the larger narrative believe that colleges and their students should be informed, orderly, and efficient, the college will construct policies to coordinate those beliefs with their local policies and actions to create a "functional complex" (Smith, 1987, p. 572). In this study, SPCC sought to coordinate its own practices with those of the ruling apparatus, developing policies that align with the norms of higher education in general and laws regulating disability in the larger society. The final task was to translate these policies into a procedural form and language that simultaneously upheld those ideologies while assisting individuals who sought help for a disability. According to Smith (1987), "Integral to the coordinating process are ideologies systematically developed to provide categories and concepts expressing the relation of local courses of action to the institutional function" (p. 160). At SPCC, the Office of Disability Services was tasked with coordinating multiple sites of action and ideologies. The college had its own set of practices; however, it was an institutionalized representative of the translocal agencies of social control dictating the authorization procedures required in the provision of accommodations for ADHD and other disabilities. Therefore, this analysis begins with a description of the Office of Disability Services at SPCC.

The disability services staff at SPCC was responsible for complying with the ADA by handling requests for student accommodation, verifying the diagnoses, and prescribing the accommodations. In some instances, such as monitoring tests or assigning note takers, the staff provided the accommodation. During our interviews, the staff were clear that their responsibility ended at the college doors. Compared to large U.S. universities, the scope of services at SPCC was limited. Its main purpose was to facilitate accommodations for documented disabilities, ADHD among them. According to one of the disability services coordinators, the largest group of students served in their office had learning disabilities. She guessed that students with ADHD comprised the second largest group, although she did not have statistics to support her statement, instead saying, "That's what I feel like I've come across."

The ODS staff changed over the course of the study. My initial interview was with Ms. Beasley. She had been running the department for 15 years, largely by herself. The department was in a state of transition during the study's first year due to a merger of several colleges in the state system. The structure of the department changed, and additional staff were hired. During most of her tenure, Ms. Beasley presided over one of the smaller colleges that was more traditional and less bureaucratic. The consolidation profoundly changed the hierarchy, priorities and management practices of the smaller colleges as they merged into a large, multi-campus organization. This impacted the ODS in subtle but important ways.

Halfway through the study, Ms. Beasley left the college and Ms. Santos took over as the coordinator for all SPCC campuses. She described her responsibilities as managing the staff, completing intakes, proctoring tests, meeting with students, keeping track of equipment inventory, and approving the budget. In her dual role as the "504 Coordinator," she was also responsible for monitoring compliance and investigating complaints associated with Section 504 of the Rehabilitation Act of 1973, a federal law that protects qualified individuals from discrimination based on their disability. Additional disability specialists and assistants traveled among the campuses proctoring tests and meeting with students. Office personnel processed documentation and student records. Despite each position having specific job responsibilities, Ms. Santos said they "kind of divide and conquer depending on the students' needs and when their appointments are."

The hierarchy of the department was fairly flat. The specialists, assistants, and part-time employees all reported to the Disability Services Coordinator. The Disability Services Coordinator reported to the Director of Student Engagement, who reported to the Vice President of Student Affairs. There was a consultant at the central office of the state system presiding over special populations and disability services. If a problem were to escalate beyond the college level, it would ultimately be reviewed by this person. No one could recall that ever happening. There was no standardized set of policies from the central office, so the responsibility for interpreting, implementing, and complying with ADA expectations occurred at the local level. This is noteworthy because most other operations in the state system were highly regulated and standardized.

Reporting and Compliance Responsibilities

Although the stated mission of the ODS was to serve students with disabilities, its fundamental purpose was compliance with federal laws governing access and equal opportunity for people with disabilities. The U.S. Department of Justice and the Department of Education Office of Civil Rights (OCR) provide guidance through written regulations, answers to frequently asked questions, OCR opinions, and the interpretation of case law (Rothstein, 2018). In higher education, OCR has the authority to enforce the relevant parts of the ADA and Section 504 of the Rehabilitation Act of 1973 through its administrative processes or through the federal court system (U.S. Department of Education, 2020). The OCR does not review student placement or educational accommodations, leaving assessment and implementation to the individual colleges. Federal entities are tasked with investigating complaints of discrimination and responding to potential noncompliance.

Day-to-day activities of the ODS are largely self-monitored and self-contained. Both coordinators reported there being very little, if any, regular oversight and little involvement from administration in the college. There was also no consistent written reporting mechanism between the ODS and college administrators or between the college and the state system. A vice president I interviewed at the conclusion of the study reported that a review process used to occur every three years. Written reports and supporting documentation were provided by all the college departments, compiled by the college administration, and sent to the state governing agency. Subsequently, central office staff visited the college for a compliance review. This practice was stopped after all colleges in the system were required to obtain regional accreditation. Accrediting institutions offered little guidance on services for students with disabilities and included only vague references in its standards and guidelines about providing activities and programs that meet the needs of the learners. Therefore, at the time of the study, few accountability systems were in place.

Nationally, the OCR visits only two colleges or universities nationwide each year for routine compliance checks, making it highly unlikely that a given institution will be visited. No one in the ODS knew the last time SPCC was visited, if ever. In the United States, primary and secondary schools are required to complete the biennial Civil Rights Data Collection Survey that gathers and publishes information on such things as demographics, enrollment, retention, staffing, and the number of Individualized Educational Plans for students with disabilities. There is no such reporting requirement for colleges. Rather, the ODS provides data to other departments where reporting requirements do exist. For example, colleges receiving certain federal grants must demonstrate that they serve nontraditional students such as full time workers, single parents, students who return to school after an absence, and students without a high school diploma. According to the Vice President overseeing the ODS, in some instances, students with disabilities are considered nontraditional students and can therefore be counted in the compliance reports. The financial aid office might also request data on enrollment and retention of ODS students. These data are quantitative and used to meet performance benchmarks required to receive continued federal funding in the form of student aid.

Aside from occasional meetings of disability services staff from different colleges in the state system, the ODS functioned autonomously. Reports of the work of the frontline personnel in the ODS, and by consequence, the work of the students, rarely, if ever, moved beyond the walls of the institution. Therefore, it was the coordinator's job to interpret ADA discourse, convert it into policy, and develop procedures that fit the values and priorities of the state system and the college itself, then apply those policies to the most local of levels; the students. The ODS coordinators inhabited a position of power and responsibility as the sole conduit between the lived experiences of students with ADHD and state/federal policies. This was clear in ODS work processes, texts, and interviews with both coordinators.

Implementation Work Processes

I obtained information about the work processes of the ODS from the coordinator interviews and my own observations. The first coordinator was Ms. Beasley, who I interviewed prior to meeting with the students. Until the merger, she ran the department herself with the help of an assistant who covered a satellite campus. She did not know how many active students the department served since she did not routinely close student files when they were no longer using ODS services. Ms. Beasley's focus was on providing accommodations to the students, but she acknowledged a new push from administration toward student retention, saying:

> The big focus for us is retention, so I'm supposed to contact all of the students that we had spring of 2015 if they're not here in spring 2016 and find out why they're not here and be as specific as we can. Did you graduate? Did you transfer to another school? Did you drop out? We're trying to get more information. We can get students here easily but retaining them is a bit harder. The people who are above me and above my boss are saying that they want disability services to figure out why they're not retaining their students and get as much information as they can.

This statement presumes that the ODS was not retaining students, yet Ms. Beasley did not know their actual retention rate because they did not collect these statistics in the first place. She believed that pressure from administration to retain students was mostly due to the state funding model. Fewer students meant less money from their funding sources. Ms. Beasley supported the retention efforts but for a different reason saying, "I'm glad. It's never made me happy that we get them in and then don't care if they stay or not." Until the merger, they did not have access to an electronic database. Given a shortage of staff, and the coordinator's admitted lack of follow through, records on the retention of disability services students did not exist. The new coordinator, Ms. Santos, reported that retention was still a priority, but no specific plan was yet in place to track it. She was also not aware of the retention rate, although she "felt like" it had gotten better.

According to Ms. Santos, the departmental work processes had changed little since she arrived except to provide more consistency among the satellite branches of the college. The department reviewed forms and procedures annually. While the policies, procedures, and texts may not have changed considerably, their interpretation and implementation had. There was a noticeable difference in the degree of flexibility and individuality afforded students after the change in the coordinator position as seen below in how each coordinator verified the diagnosis, enrolled students, and assigned accommodations.

Verifying the ADHD Diagnosis

The ODS collected documents verifying that students had been medically evaluated for ADHD in order to determine whether they fit the criteria envisioned in the enabling ADA legislation. In my first interview with Ms. Beasley, she described a somewhat informal process for verifying a diagnosis of ADHD, requiring only a letter from a clinician rather than a formal evaluation. This illustrates the local level of decision making, even on something as seemingly important as assuring that students met the ADA criteria for an eligible disability. She reported:

> We are much less demanding than a Regents school [she is referring to the state's university system] as far as documentation of a disability. We can use testing from the high school system as long as it's within five years. If you are going to a Regents school, you would probably have to go through testing. I can take that they are ADHD from their family doctor or a clinical psychiatrist. I'm not requiring testing.

As noted earlier, The Individuals with Disabilities Education Act governs how U.S. state and public agencies provide services in elementary and secondary schools. Before the student reaches the age of 16, high schools must develop an Individualized Educational Plan (IEP) that includes a plan for the transition to postsecondary education. Despite this requirement, there is no formal communication of that plan between high school and college personnel. Students are responsible for obtaining and providing a copy of their IEP to college personnel if they choose to do so.

Ms. Beasley gave the students a full semester to provide documentation, but at her discretion, they could start receiving some accommodations immediately. She admitted to having a hard time keeping up with students who still needed to submit documentation. At the time of the interview, Ms. Beasley reported that there was about to be a "crackdown," which she expected to cause a disruption that she was not comfortable with, saying:

> I have to have some documentation. There's a stack about this big [motions to about three feet high] of students that we started with some accommodations, and we will do that, but they have the semester to come to us with the full documentation. I have never cut them off. We're cutting them off in the spring. If I got audited, I'd be in a world of trouble because of students who aren't qualified.

Ms. Beasley favored flexibility over rigid adherence to the ODS verification policies. This changed when Ms. Santos took over as coordinator. Although Ms. Beasley's approach was arguably more student friendly and individualized, the process was less efficient and trackable, lending itself to possible abuse by the students. Ms. Santos made the students more accountable, requiring them to provide documentation before receiving any accommodations. She reported, "They have to have some sort of physical tangible proof from a medical professional." Like Ms. Beasley, Ms. Santos decided what documentation was acceptable and from whom.

Enrolling Students
As part of the ODS intake process, students received a folder containing information and documents for them to complete, the first of which was a "Request for Assistance." This was the student's official request to enroll with the ODS. Students were responsible for seeking information and services, as well as providing documentation of an eligible "disabling condition." The bottom half of this form had a list of approved accommodations and was completed by disability support staff after considering the student's needs. Students also completed a "Student Memo of Understanding." This form reiterated the importance of starting the enrollment process before the semester begins. It also pointed out that an instructor could not modify accommodations assigned by the ODS. Assumed, but not explicitly stated, was that students could not request, modify, or use any accommodation that had not been approved by the ODS. Only the ODS staff had the authority to give or change accommodations. An "Authorization to Discuss" form gave disability services personnel permission to talk about the accommodations with faculty involved in the student's coursework, although in practice, they had little to no contact with instructors aside from sending a form letter with the student's accommodations. This document also emphasized that it was the student's responsibility to ensure instructors received the accommodation form and contact disability services if they had not.

A "Request for Testing Form and Procedures" outlined the departmental policies on testing accommodations. Of note, students had to request testing accommodations no later than three days before the test was to take place. This could only be completed online. One important caveat to this policy was that the ODS was closed on Saturday and Sunday. Therefore, if students needed testing accommodations on a Monday, they had to request them by the preceding Wednesday. Unscheduled classroom assessments were particularly difficult to manage.

The "Student Rights and Responsibilities Form" explained that students had a right to equal access, "reasonable, appropriate, and effective" accommodations, and confidentiality of information. By contrast to these three rights, the form listed 15 student responsibilities, several of which stressed the importance of communicating with instructors and staying actively involved with the ODS throughout the semester. The form emphasized that students must read their student e-mail daily and respond to any ODS e-mail as soon as possible. The stated mission of the ODS includes promoting independence and self-advocacy, and this is evident in their processes. Yet, students coming out of high school are accustomed to a great deal of assistance and are frustrated by the autonomy required of college disability offices (Scott, 2019). A "Final Confirmation Form" summarized the other forms and verified understanding of the information. The student signed this document and returned it to the Office of Disability Services. Research shows that students with disabilities may not have a clear understanding of the supposed benefit of the accommodations, nor can they accurately predict the degree to which the accommodations helped them (Jansen, Petry, Evans, Noens, & Baeyen, 2019). They are often confused by the paperwork and have difficulty with self-advocacy. The ODS staff did not know how many students received the initial paperwork but failed to return and therefore did not receive assistance.

Assigning the Accommodations

The Office of Disability Services used a software program called SAMS to enroll and track students. SAMS is a program for managing long-term services for aging and disabled populations (WellSky, n.d.). According to Ms. Beasley. "We didn't start using SAMS as our database until the merger. It was clear that if we were going to have that many campuses, we were going to need a database. And that's how we do our intakes." SAMS has accommodations built into it. It is worth noting that SAMS is designed for long term care agencies, primarily as it relates to reimbursement for services. The motto, "Save time, Save money, Improve efficiency" can be seen throughout the product webpages. No one in the ODS could recall exactly how or why SAMS was selected, or questioned its efficacy, although other education specific accommodation software is available.

A list of accommodations was generated by entering the student's diagnosis into SAMS, or by using a customized category entered by the staff.

Once the list was generated, a staff member reviewed it with the student and adjusted it as needed. Ms. Beasley said, "We want to be flexible. It's always a case-by-case basis and there's always a work around. It's really important that we be flexible and individualized. The more individualized we can get, the better." Despite her desire to be flexible, Ms. Beasley, and later Ms. Santos, noted that accommodations must be reasonable and that students must not get an unfair advantage. Language regarding fairness, unfair advantage, and leveling the playing field appears often in the literature on accommodations (Barger, 2016; Thomas, 2000). Ms. Beasley gave several examples of what she considered an unfair advantage:

> There are times that we have to say no. We have people with a learning disability in reading and they can use a spellchecker except in allied health. That is a no. And I'll tell them that in the meeting. Another thing is, some people with traumatic brain injuries want open book tests. They can't have that. That's an unfair advantage.

She also provided a few examples of her meetings with students to review their accommodations. In the first example, she was working with someone right out of high school. In the second, it was a 42-year-old man who was returning to school.

> Well, we talk about the accommodation needs. Sometimes they bring in an IEP [referring to the Individual Educational Plan completed in K-12 for students with disabilities] and I don't bother looking at it. I'll ask the student, "what did you get in high school that you need here?" And we'll talk about whether that's an accommodation that they should have. I met with a guy yesterday who is 42 now. And he says he's had a lot of diagnoses. I go with what they say, and he says he's really ADD. I can go through the list [of possible accommodations] and I know what typically works for people with ADD or ADHD. I didn't do that with him. We just kinda talked about what might be happening. I didn't feel like taking him through the whole test. He's an adult. I don't feel like he needs all that stuff.

In both examples, Ms. Beasley used her own judgment and work knowledge more than the actual documents available to her. She did not look at the IEP, which presumably would have information that could be useful in deciding appropriate college accommodations. Instead, she asked what the student used in high school and what he thought was needed in college. It was interesting that Ms. Beasley did not "bother to look at it." In the second example, she again decided what the student needed to know about accommodations rather than "go through the list" since he was an adult and did not "need all that stuff." According to Ms. Santos, restructuring the Office of Disability Services led to more consistency and assured "fairness." Ms. Santos relied more heavily on the standard accommodations provided by the SAMS software.

Once a student's information was entered into SAMS, and accommodations selected, the software generated a form letter that was sent to instructors by e-mail. According to Ms. Beasley, "We send out accommodation letters. It is not the best way to do it, but that's what we do." There is no other contact unless the instructor calls them for clarification. The student's disability is not noted on the accommodation form. Only the ODS staff can log on to SAMS and access the student's medical information. Both coordinators said there was little resistance from instructors about the accommodations, and that this had improved over the years.

STUDENT USE OF ACCOMMODATIONS AND FOLLOW UP

I asked both coordinators about follow up throughout the semester and during the student's tenure at the college. On the initial paperwork, students signed a form agreeing to check their e-mail at least once a week for messages from disability services. Otherwise, it was up to the students to contact the office if they needed anything, which seemed counterproductive to their retention efforts. Ms. Santos reported, "We put the responsibility on the student." She continued:

> As long as they're enrolled and have completed all the documentation, their accommodations will continue semester to semester even if they don't reach out to us. But it's up to them to reach out to us if they have questions or concerns that we can help with. They can reach out to us if they want or need something, but we tell them that if we don't hear from you, we're assuming you are fine, so we won't do anything.

College students with ADHD have fewer support systems and are less likely to seek support or use accommodations than when they were in high school. They may no longer identify as having a disability (Soutra, 2018), be reluctant to accept accommodations for fear of being stigmatized, or want to succeed on their own without any special assistance (Denhart, 2008). In my study, students used their accommodations inconsistently or not at all. I had not yet interviewed the students when I first spoke with Ms. Beasley, but she mentioned that, "More frequently [than asking for additional accommodations], they end up not using most of the accommodations. I've had people who have 16 or 17 accommodations and don't use many of them. A lot of students don't use them." She didn't explain why. I asked Ms. Santos about this as well. She was not sure how many students made initial inquiries but did not actually enroll with the ODS. Of students who were enrolled, she also was not sure how many did not use the accommodations or why. She did venture a guess:

> It's hard to say. This semester, we probably have 105 brand-new students. I would say out of those hundred and five, I probably hear from half of them

about something and I would say a majority of that half will enroll, but either don't need the accommodations, or they just don't need it this particular semester. They might need it when they take anatomy. It's hard to say an exact number, but probably about half of them don't need or require any services within the semester.

When asked why she thought students with ADHD might not follow through, she reported, "It's hard to say if a student isn't coming back to us, whether it's related to ADHD or if it's something else. Could be the anxiety or depression. Could just be a family issue. It's hard to say just what would keep them from coming back, but I don't know that I necessarily notice." Despite the reported emphasis on retention, there was no mechanism in place to track this information, nor was there a process to assess the appropriateness or effectiveness of accommodations once they were assigned. The "Student Rights and Responsibilities" form identifies the student's right to "reasonable, effective, and appropriate" accommodations. The coordinators appeared to accept at face value that standard accommodations for ADHD were valid and therefore effective and appropriate. Their discretion was primarily manifested in their interpretation of "reasonable."

Assessing effectiveness was not the direct focus of the ODS. Its primary function was compliance with laws governing equal access to educational programs. These laws allow great flexibility among institutions. As one department among many, the ODS is part of a bureaucracy with competing interests and priorities which is reflected in their work processes and texts. Decision-makers create and rely on texts to organize what happens in people's everyday lives. The challenge lies in reconciling the needs of the decision-makers themselves with administrative constraints and student interests. Griffith and Smith (2014) note that, "Working with people is always in some way or another at odds with producing the standardization imposed by the institutional circuits in which the coordinated work on both sides of the 'front line' gets represented as the textual reality" (p. 347). So, where does that leave the student?

There is a surprising lack of research on the effectiveness of accommodations for ADHD, or on students' experiences with them. Existing studies often use research designs that cannot draw conclusions specific to students with ADHD, either because they are included in broader groups of students with emotional, behavioral, or learning problems, or because the research does not compare students with and without ADHD. Despite a lack of evidence as to their benefit, the students in my original study were offered common accommodations for ADHD such as extended time on tests, a quiet testing location, permission to audio record lectures, note takers, and the opportunity to stand or move about the classroom. Only half of the students used their accommodations, either because they did not understand how the accommodations could help or did not think they were necessary. For those who used them, the accommodations did not always address the complex and overlapping challenges they faced. Aside from extra time on tests, the accommodations did not especially help them outside of the college environment, where most of the work took place. For example, a quiet room to test reduced distractions at the college but may not have been available at home. The students were aware that these accommodations would not be available to them in the "real world," so some chose not to use them while at college.

All college students engage in familiar forms of work as they navigate their college experiences. For example, they apply to the college, register for classes, attend classes, study, and take tests. In my research, the students who used academic accommodations had additional layers of work that went largely unrecognized by the ODS, other college support systems, the larger social institutions that inform that office, and the students themselves. For example, at SPCC, most of the burden of obtaining and using accommodations fell on the student. They were responsible for all initial and follow-up contact with the ODS and for assuring that instructors received the accommodation letter and made the necessary changes. Students who used testing accommodations described having to frequently remind instructors to send their exams to the ODS and to set the online exams for extra time. One student reported, "I will sit down to take a quiz and see that the instructor forgot to set it for time and a half. I have to stop what I am doing, contact the instructor, wait for a response, and then for him to set the quiz correctly which could take a whole day. Then I have to find another time to take it." For those using the testing center, the procedures and limited hours made rescheduling difficult. These unforeseen obstacles often required the students to change work schedules or find additional childcare.

The entities charged with mandating and providing accommodations for students with ADHD do not see this invisible work or understand its impact. According to Smith (1987), categories of discourse (e.g. writing a paper, taking tests, completing homework) have "boundaries of observability beneath which a subterranean life continues" (p. 162). In her example of writing up a science experiment, she explains:

> Clearly things were done around the doing of the experiment that were essential to, but not entered into or made accountable within the "experimental procedure." Its boundaries were organized conceptually to select from a locally indivisible work process, some aspects to be taken as part of the work process and others discounted. All were done. All were necessary. But only some were to be made reportable-observable within the textual mode of teaching science. (p. 162)

Using accommodations afforded to the students required "anchorage in an economy of material conditions, time, and effort" that "does not appear as work" Smith (1987, p. 163). For my study participants, there were additional layers of work above and beyond what was necessary to complete their course work. Above the procedural maintenance work of navigating the ODS, the students also took on the work of executing the accommodations themselves. The students did not expect anyone to help them with this work or change anything to make it less difficult. They just accepted it. For them, ADHD was an individual problem. As one student said, "I just coped on my own and figured it out by myself."

Discussion

While the day-to-day activities of the ODS frontline workers appeared highly routinized, there was also significant interpretive work. As previously noted, the language of the ADA is often vague and open to interpretation. Every college or university operates within its own social context and, ideally, on behalf of the students they serve. Therefore, I could argue that this elasticity is necessary and useful. However, is also creates a lack of continuity between the quality and number of services provided by different disability services offices, even those within the same system. The quality and quantity of services a student receives is a direct product of the interpretive work performed by those responsible for transforming the ADA from a lifeless text into a living entity. Of concern is that this work was largely invisible to the frontline workers, who saw themselves as following standard practices that they "reviewed annually."

This was evident in the contrasting approaches of Ms. Beasley and Ms. Santos, which can be read as a metaphor for western society's evolution from a way of living that stressed ingenuity and adaptability into one that stresses routinization and bureaucratically controlled efficiency. Ms. Beasley represented an old school approach to management. She made it clear that her processes for providing accommodations were developed as a result of her many years of experiences in the coordinator position. She prioritized flexibility and concern for the student over conformity and strict adherence to policies. She expressed discomfort with the new expectations for consistency and accountability resulting from the merger and change in management priorities. Ms. Santos, by contrast, represented a style referred to as "New Public Management," where public institutions adopt private sector management approaches that emphasize cost reduction and efficiency (Griffith & Smith, 2014). These practices change how frontline workers, such as the ODS coordinators, interact with the people they serve. Ms. Santos stressed that every student who registered for accommodations must have proper documentation. She was more unswerving and uniform in her expectations of the students. Using SAMS more consistently, she standardized the process of student intake so that all workers in the office provided consistent accommodations to the students. When discussing the impact of technologically based systems on health care organizations, Rankin and Tate (2014) explain how these systems can be, "understood as forms of coordination and control that operate on the basis of information constructed systematically, most often for the purpose of numerical calculation" (p. 122), and note that, "an improvement in organization can become a source of trouble for practitioners" (p. 122). They conclude that the dominant role technology plays for decision-makers is not neutral, promoting some interests and subordinating others, while limiting the ability of educators to respond to students' individual needs. The same could be said for the ODS coordinators and the students served by this office. Ms. Beasley tried not to give unfair advantage to students with disabilities over their nondisabled peers while still affording them the most comprehensive services possible. While not discounting the importance of an individualized approach, by embracing the technology, Ms. Santos could more closely address her concern that students with disabilities not have unfair advantage over each other.

There are advantages and disadvantages to both approaches. Ms. Beasley's approach appears more student friendly and helpful given its individualized nature, but this admittedly led to a lack of consistency and efficiency. Outcomes were difficult to track and students with similar disabilities could receive different levels of assistance. There was also the potential for students to abuse the system. Ms. Santos' approach brought more structure to the process, making it easier to keep track of work processes and ensure every student received the same level of accommodation. Still, despite the emphasis on uniformity and accountability, Ms. Santos had not yet developed a plan to retain students, or even track the retention rate. The ODS changed, but without a tracking mechanism in place, it was hard to determine if these changes garnered the intended results.

The ODS was limited in how they could assist the students. The purpose of the office was to comply with the Americans with Disabilities Act. In doing so, the staff sought to "level the playing field" for students with disabilities. The ODS offered tools within its authority to serve the students in this study. Nevertheless, the scope of the accommodations was situated firmly in the hierarchical structure of the department, the college, the ruling bodies the college reported to, and the federal government through its ADA and IDEA requirements. Even for students who used them, the accommodations did not always address the complex and overlapping challenges they faced. The structures and laws set forth to provide "equal opportunity" for students with ADHD place most of the responsibility on the students, sometimes creating additional work and taxing their ability to adhere to the course requirements. Furthermore, there was no official structure in place to report information on the efficacy of the accommodations up the hierarchal chain. Unless there was a complaint, the flow of information was almost exclusively downward. Historically in education, amendments to the Rehabilitation Act of 1973 and the Americans with Disabilities Act of 1990 resulted from individual complaints of discrimination which were adjudicated through an OCR review or through the court system. Even then, the issue was compliance with existing law, not the quality or efficacy of services provided at the local level.

Ironically, by requiring the students in this study be enrolled with the ODS, I found myself navigating in and out of the same educational and disability discourses I just described. In doing so, I left out the students with ADHD (officially or self-diagnosed), who chose not to enter the system of ruling relations exemplified by the ODS. There is no way of knowing why they made that choice. The students who are enrolled with the ODS are visible, even if their experiences are reduced to a name or number. At least their experiences *could* be gathered and understood in ways that might lead to more effective support and accommodations. However, the experiences of students with ADHD who are not enrolled for services are doubly invisible. They are not counted at all, even though these individuals are present in the college. Nevertheless, they remain anonymous as long as they continue to work outside the boundaries of the ODS.

When everyday lived experiences morph into objectified knowledge, information that does not fit neatly into the language of policies, procedures, and discourses can be lost. This was apparent throughout the study on several levels. ADA discourse filtered down to the state and college levels, eventually resting with the ODS coordinators who interpreted and implemented ADA requirements. Compliance with the law was expected, but how the ODS staff executed this responsibility appeared to receive little attention by the governing bodies. Except for the texts, there was no direct channel of communication between the translocal forces responsible for shaping ADA discourse and those responsible for its implementation. The flow of information was top-down, originating from the legal regulations at the federal level and ending with the students at the local level, with the ODS serving as an intermediary. A feedback loop was noticeably absent. Those responsible for the translocal discourses gathered little quantitative, and virtually no qualitative data on how the ADA regulations were being implemented at the college level or on the direct benefit to the students, nor did the ODS record or report student experiences with accommodations to any translocal entity. The ODS and student experiences were usurped and subsequently lost by the overarching narrative of compliance.

At the time of the interviews, the ODS staff did not keep specific data regarding the use of accommodations for any of the populations they served. Specific to ADHD, Ms. Santos provided a rough estimate of how many students with ADHD enrolled but did not follow through. She had no knowledge of why they did or did not. She was not sure how to get this information, which is a valid dilemma. It is difficult to track retention, progression, and graduation rates of students with disabilities in higher education who must self-disclose in order to be counted. Much of the existing research uses special education language and categories that are not appropriate for higher education (Avellone & Scott, 2017). As such, the lack of information sharing between the ODS, state, and federal entities mirrored the lack of communication between the ODS and the students it served.

When embarking on this study, I expected to see strong connections between the Office of Disability Services and the students but found little involvement between the two aside from the standard accommodations provided by the ODS within the physical boundaries of the college. Referring to the specific requirements of the ADA, the coordinator explained, "this is what we must provide for the students," emphasizing that their work was confined to what occurred "under our roof." Those statements did not seem significant at the time of the coordinator interviews, but after talking with the students, I realized how limited the relationship was. There was a decided lack of information sharing between the students and the ODS staff who assumed that everything was fine if the students did not reach out to them. The aforementioned forms of knowledge and experience inherently existed, yet there were no mechanisms in place for this information to transfer from one node of the institutional network to the other. It was only attainable by exploring the everyday lived experiences of the students and understanding how those experiences were shaped by, and reinforced, the same translocal discourses that governed the frontline work of the ODS. The work and experiences of the students were evident in their stories, but they will remain invisible to ODS staff, college administrators, and federal agencies as long as compliance with extra local discourse is prioritized over the everyday work of all involved.

How well a college performs its duty to serve students is largely measured by quantitative indicators such as retention, graduation, and job placement rates. These statistics are relatively easy to obtain for the general student population. It is harder to collect similar data on college students with disabilities. This is especially true for students with "invisible" disorders such as ADHD who must self-disclose to be counted. It is also questionable as to whether these numbers are valid indicators of functional policies enacted to serve students on a local level, or if these measurements are designed to reinforce a form of institutional compliance focused on ensuring the next round of state or federal funding and accreditation. Without qualitative analysis based on a free flow of information between the various entities involved, understanding how well a college is serving students with disabilities is speculative at best. It is important to explore how these constructs intersect to create policy. Sociological research using institutional ethnography serves to examine how legislation prescribed by translocal bodies are interpreted and implemented at the local level, and how this impacts the individuals it was designed to help.

REFERENCES

American Psychiatric Association. (2013). *Diagnostic and statistical manual of mental disorders* (5th ed.). American Psychiatric Publishing. https://doi.org/10.1176/appi.books.9780890425596.

Americans With Disabilities Act of 1990 as Amended. (2008). https://www.ada.gov/pubs/adastatute08.html.

Avellone, L. & Scott, S. (2017, March). *National databases with information on college students with disabilities*. National Center for College Students with Disabilities. *1*(1), 1–17. http://www.nccsdonline.org/research-briefs.html.

Barger, T. (2016). ADA compliance across campus: Providing accommodations to level the playing field for students with disabilities. *University Business*. https://universitybusiness.com/ada-compliance-across-campus/.

Denhart, H. (2008). Deconstructing barriers: Perceptions of students labeled with learning disabilities in higher education. *Journal of Learning Disabilities, 41*(6), 483–497. https://doi.org/10.1177/0022219408321151.

DeVault, M., & McCoy, L. (2002). Institutional ethnography: Using interviews to investigate ruling relations. In J. F Gubrium & J. A. Holstein (Eds.), *Handbook of interview research* (pp. 751–775). Sage. https://doi.org/10.4135/9781412973588.n43.

Dobbins, M., Knill, C., & Vögtle, E. M. (2011). An analytical framework for the cross-country comparison of higher education governance. *Higher Education, 62*(5), 665–683.

Griffith, A. I., & Smith, D. E (Eds.). (2014). *Under new public management: Institutional ethnographies of changing front-line work*. University of Toronto Press. https://doi.org/10.3138/9781442619463.

Haller, B. A. (2006). Promoting disability-friendly campuses to prospective students: An analysis of university recruitment materials. *Disability Studies Quarterly, 26*(2). https://doi.org/10.18061/dsq.v26i2.673.

Heekin, J. (2010). ADHD and the new Americans with disabilities act: Expanded legal recognition for cognitive disorders. *William and Mary Policy Review, 2*, 171–192. https://drive.google.com/file/d/0B8oTW8Fs0rVEV2JYZTUtTGFwWDA/view.

Individuals with Disabilities Education Act as Amended, U.S.C. 33 § 1400 (2004) et seq. https://sites.ed.gov/idea/statute-chapter-33.

Jansen, D., Petry, K., Evans, S., Noens, I., & Baeyen, D. (2019). The implementation of extended examination duration for students with ADHD in higher education. *Journal of Attention Disorders, 23*(14), 1746–1758. https://doi.org/10.1177/1087054718787879.

Jung, K. (2003). Chronic illness and academic accommodation: Meeting disabled students' unique needs and preserving the institutional order of the university. *Journal of Sociology and Social Welfare, 30*(1), 91–112.

Luken, P. (2008). Institutional ethnography. In V. N. Parrillo (Ed.). *Encyclopedia of social problems*. Sage. https://doi.org/10.4135/9781412963930.n287.

Office of Special Education and Rehabilitative Services. (2017). A transition guide to postsecondary education. *U.S. Department of Education*. https://sites.ed.gov/idea/files/postsecondary-transition-guide-may-2017.pdf.

Rankin, J. & Tate, B. (2014). Digital era governance: Connecting nursing education and the industrial complex of health care. In A. I. Griffin & D. E. Smith. *Under new public management: Institutional ethnographies of changing front-line work*. University of Toronto Press. https://doi.org/10.3138/9781442619463-009.

Rothstein, L. (2018, June 28). A primer on disability discrimination in higher education. *Laws, 7*(3), 1–33. https://doi.org/10.3390/laws7030025.

Scott, S. (2019, April). *Access and participation in higher education: Perspectives of college students with disabilities*. National Center for College Students with Disabilities 2(2), 1–25. http://www.nccsdonline.org/research-briefs.html.

Smith, D. (1987). *The everyday world as problematic: A feminist sociology*. Northeastern University Press.

Smith, D. (2005). *A sociology for the people*. Boston: Alta Mira Press.

Soutra, M. (2018). On-campus support, accommodations, and mentorship for learning disabled and ADHD students. *Journal of the American Academy of Child and Adolescent Psychiatry, 57,* S93. https://doi.org/10.1016/j.jaac.2018.07.393.

Thomas, S. B. (2000). College student and disability law. *Journal of Special Education, 33*(4), 248–257. https://doi.org/10.1177/002246690003300408.

U.S. Department of Education, Office for Civil Rights. (2020, January 10). *Protecting students with disabilities*. Retrieved February 7, 2020, from https://www2.ed.gov/about/offices/list/ocr/504faq.html.

U.S. Department of Justice. (n.d.). Amendment of Americans with Disabilities Act Title II and Title III regulations to implement ADA Amendments Act of 2008. https://www.ada.gov/regs2016/504_nprm.html.

WellSky. (n.d.). WellSky Aging & Disability (formerly SAMS). https://wellsky.com/aging-disability/.

CHAPTER 21

Contested Forms of Knowledge in the Criminal-Legal System: Evidence-Based Practice and Other Ways of Knowing Among Frontline Workers

Nicole Kaufman and Megan Welsh

A movement promoting the use of "evidence-based practices" (EBP) has gained popularity in recent decades in the United States, with proponents calling for scientific approaches to the processing of clients across human services fields. As a result, front-line workers are increasingly required to use risk assessment tools, case management techniques, and other purportedly data-driven approaches to the administration of justice, and these methods have become the basis for the evaluation of individual practitioners, programs, agencies, and policies. These new tools comprise the primary, institutionally sanctioned forms of knowledge used by front-line workers to know about their criminalized clients, despite extensive critiques about their actual effectiveness (e.g., Harcourt, 2007), built-in biases (Benjamin, 2016, 2019; Eubanks, 2017; Hannah-Moffat, 2004, 2019), and social control uses (e.g., Simon 1993).

This movement has particularly impacted front-line community supervision workers, the over 100,000 individuals who supervise community-based clients in the United States (Gayman & Bradley, 2013). Their work is characterized by changing expectations and caseload size, contradictory policy aims, and frequent tension based on what is in the interest of the criminal-legal system,

N. Kaufman (✉)
Department of Sociology, Ohio University, Athens, OH, USA
e-mail: kaufmann@ohio.edu

M. Welsh
School of Public Affairs, San Diego State University, San Diego, CA, USA
e-mail: mwelsh@sdsu.edu

© The Author(s) 2021
P. C. Luken and S. Vaughan (eds.), *The Palgrave Handbook of Institutional Ethnography*,
https://doi.org/10.1007/978-3-030-54222-1_21

the community, and supervisees (Gayman & Bradley, 2013; Werth, 2012). The work is hierarchical and oriented around reporting information upward (Cheliotis, 2006). This division of labor effectively ensures their conformity, limits their responsibilities, and prevents them from grasping broader organizational goals and strategies (Cheliotis, 2006; Werth, 2012).

In these circumstances, workers are faced with various choices of how to respond to the evidence-based mandate as they make assessments about clients' dangerousness and ability to change. They can adhere to the rules of this mandate, or they can subvert them by relying on ways of knowing like intuition and experience developed on the job (Cheliotis, 2006; Lynch, 1998; Werth, 2012). Yet, as Werth (2019) notes, "even in cases where field-level personnel do not trust risk assessments, these tools exert bureaucratic and automatic effects that ascribe risk into assessed individuals" (p. 10).

This chapter follows the tension between the required implementation of evidence-based practices and the use of what Foster (2015) calls a "practice-based evidence" as we ask what community supervision agents know and do. Institutional ethnography (IE), an alternative sociology that couples "descriptive ethnographic accounts of people's everyday lives with a critical analysis of the social and institutional relations that give shape to personal embodied experiences" (Nichols, 2017, p. 3), provides an especially useful lens through which to understand this dynamic.[1] As a mode of inquiry, IE starts with an exploration people's everyday experiences, but then "goes beyond the local and the individual to a broader set of relations that organize both the micro context and people's experiences of it" (Doll & Walby, 2019, p. 150). IE illuminates workers' organization and production of knowledge in ways that inform their work with clients. Recent institutional ethnographies across a variety of disciplines have highlighted the tensions inherent in policies requiring evidence-based practices, many of which are evaluated through quantifiable outcome measures (see Mykhalovskiy et al., 2008; Waters, 2015).

IE serves as a tool to critically examine the criminal-legal system, as a small but growing group of studies has shown (see Doll & Walby, 2019). Naomi Nichols' (2017) work illuminated how racialized and "at risk" young people are marginalized and misrepresented by an array of public institutions. The criminal-legal system collects and uses evidence that constructs some youth as "unsafe" or "untrustworthy" (p. 8), allowing youth no avenue through which to account for how they accrued criminal charges in opposition to "official" accounts. After the institutional designation of some youth as unsafe or at risk, these designations characterize youth widely, and the assumption of their criminality then becomes self-fulfilling (p. 9). Walby (2005) conceptualized closed circuit television camera surveillance (CCTV) as a televisual text that coordinates the work of CCTV operators and shapes who is determined to be suspicious, often in racialized ways. Goodman (2008) examined how racial segregation occurs in "negotiated settlements" between California state prison inmates and correctional officers, mediated by a housing form that is filled out as inmates are categorized at intake.

These studies have used IE to understand the production of official forms of knowledge. Through the texts that govern how workers do their jobs and how people (clients, patients, criminal suspects, prisoners) are processed through systems, some information or experiences are captured and held up as objective knowledge, while others remain invisible. Building on this work, in this chapter we investigate how people working in the criminal-legal system construct and consume knowledge. To illuminate these processes, we employ what Dorothy Smith calls the "text-reader conversation" (2005, pp. 104–105), in which workers interpret texts and activate them through applying them to their work. An IE lens is especially valuable here, given that some scholars have suggested that defenders of risk assessment tools, like many algorithms, claim they are objective and minimize the role of subjectivity in decision-making (Werth, 2019; see also Benjamin, 2019; Hannah-Moffat, 2005; Harcourt, 2007; Isard, 2017).

Our analysis emerges from a larger project rooted in the standpoint of criminalized women in California, USA (see Welsh, 2015, 2019a; Welsh & Rajah, 2014). Through interviews and fieldwork with women who were working to rebuild their lives post-incarceration, it became clear that there was a disjuncture between women's needs, the stated goals of community supervision agencies, and the evidence-based tools of supervision. For example, women's experiences of supervision did not seem to align with their assessed level of riskiness for a return to criminal offending, and this also had the effect of women being excluded from opportunities to partake in services that could have helped them. Similar to Nichols' (2017) findings discussed earlier, no avenue existed through which women could offer an alternative narrative of their needs. Our problematic, therefore, is this tension; in an arrangement where there are misalignments of goals and missions of parole and probation in contrast with women's experiences, we analyze how parole agents and probation officers describe knowing about their clients. We are especially interested in how they work creatively to use alternative ways of knowing that do not rely on official forms of knowledge, particularly in a process that we term *learning from clients,* and how they may also merge these two broad methods of learning about clients in what we call *hybridized knowledge*.[2]

COMMUNITY SUPERVISION IN THE ERA OF THE "NEW PENOLOGY"

Discourses focused on actuarial risk and the probability of future criminal behavior dominate the contemporary correctional arena in the United States (Cheliotis, 2006; Feeley & Simon, 1992). The work of correctional administrators and workers is oriented around the assessment and management of risk through evidence-based practices, or the adoption of scientific approaches in the processing of clients across human services fields. In contrast to a view of the malleability in both individuals and their motivations for engaging in crime that dominated corrections in the middle of the twentieth century, a paradigm that Feeley and Simon (1992) term the "new penology" has taken hold and has replaced the "old penology." Motivated by the principle of waste management, the new penology employs techniques to categorize and manage the criminalized poor and groups deemed risky, at low cost (see also Garland, 2001; Lynch, 1998; Simon, 1993). Neoliberal practices, anxieties over fiscal stability and crime, and research questioning the effectiveness of rehabilitation have all fueled this transition, as has an interest in reducing bias based on race and gender in discretionary decision-making (Cheliotis, 2006; Feeley & Simon, 1992; Garland, 2001).

The risk predictions involved in the new penology are forecasts based on whether other criminalized individuals (as contrasted to the immediate individual under supervision) committed crimes while under supervision (Electronic Privacy Information Center, 2019; Harcourt, 2007; Werth, 2019). The newest iterations of tools, in fact, known as "risk-need-responsivity" models, rely on the principle of responsivity, or matching service styles and modes to individual clients based on the statistical correlation of client attributes with recidivism in a broad database (Andrews, Bonta, & Hoge, 1990, p. 20). States have required that staff use these tools, which are designed to provide more accurate assessment than the judgment of clinicians (Andrews et al., 1990; Turner, Hess, Bradstreet, Chapman, & Murphy, 2013). Another key feature of the new penology is the minimal devotion of resources to supervision. Lynch (2000) observes that "[a]gents are given a social work directive without the resources to fulfill it" (footnote 18, p. 62). Even while agents may approach their work with parolees with rehabilitative ideals, Lynch writes that the operating assumption is that changes necessary for desistance from crime can only come from the individual parolee; the agents can and should do little to advance this goal.

Requirements for the use of algorithms in pre-trial services, on parole boards, and in community supervision typically come from legislatures, administrative rules, or other state-level directives and policies (EPIC, 2019). These assessment tools demonstrate how evidence-based practices or EBPs have become the texts that coordinate much of the everyday work of workers responsible for the supervision of criminalized clients. Assessment tools and the data gathered through them thus become official forms of knowledge that workers generate and use. These algorithms prioritize risk and the protection of public safety over rehabilitation, which accordingly shapes interactions between agents and supervised clients.

Two commonly used proprietary assessment tools are the Correctional Offender Management Profiling for Alternative Sanctions (COMPAS) and the Level of Service/Case Management Inventory (LS/CMI).[3] As these tools are used widely, critics—from defendants and supervisees to think-tanks and academics—have raised concerns about fairness, particularly given these tools' opaque nature (Angwin et al., 2016; Benjamin, 2016; EPIC, 2019). Some of these critics have also shown that evidence-based tools do not necessarily lead to more effective practices (see further discussion in Angwin et al., 2016; EPIC, 2019; Turner et al., 2013).

There are also problems with the way tools guide front-line workers to determine whether and how to allocate more resources to their supervisees. They reinforce notions that risk—and the management of social problems more broadly—is comprised of individual problems with individual solutions (Hannah-Moffat, 2004, 2005). These algorithms collapse the needs of and risks posed by people convicted of crimes. For example, one widely used supervision model defines the principal (or Big Six) criminogenic needs as including "antisocial values, criminal personality, low self-control, criminal peers, dysfunctional family ties, and substance abuse" (Change Companies, 2014b); models use measures like these to predict recidivism (Hannah-Moffat 2004). The narrow parameters through which supervision clients are viewed may also produce ideas of need in terms of risk reduction that are distinct from the self-perception of people being supervised, leading to unmet needs once resources and supervision are assigned (Hannah-Moffat, 2004, 2005; Welsh, 2019a).[4]

The lack of resources within agencies where personnel are expected to implement these tools further minimizes their effectiveness. Policies requiring the use of EBPs presume departments will maintain certain caseload sizes that are seldom achieved (see, e.g., Flores, 2014). DeMichele and Payne (2007) found that parole and probation officers reported that they were open to using research findings to guide decisions, yet that training to use evidence-based tools was inadequate.

Not surprisingly, administrators who add new assessment processes to already overloaded employees are often met with resistance that could undermine the effectiveness of these tools. For example, Harris (2012) describes built-in suspicion or mistrust of data-collection efforts in law enforcement officers. Such resistance may manifest in low commitment to fidelity in implementation, such as using other, often individualized and experiential forms of knowledge in lieu of or in addition to actuarial assessments (Cheliotis, 2006; Viglione, Rudes, & Taxman, 2015; Welsh, 2019b; Werth, 2017). Furthermore, research on welfare workers has shown that when requirements for additional documentation are introduced into the supervision of caseloads, the nature of the work changes, without necessarily improving the ability of workers to address core problems faced by people they serve (Taylor, 2013).

Bias based on race, gender, and other social attributes also significantly limits the effectiveness of these tools. Purportedly objective or scientific knowledge is often laden with assumptions and biases (Isard, 2017), so that even seemingly neutral algorithms or technological systems are designed, created, and implemented in ways that activate biases based on race and gender. Despite claims to be race-neutral, predictive scores are still characterized by racial bias (Angwin et al., 2016; Barabas, Dinakar, & Doyle, 2019; Benjamin, 2016).[5]

Assessment results differ based on clients' gender, as well, when there are separate tools used with women and men (EPIC, 2019). Although lawmakers and administrators claim that tools are gender-neutral, researchers have shown that they cannot be, particularly as risk tools purported to be gender-responsive are based on standards designed with men in mind and employ stereotypical notions of femininity (Hannah-Moffat, 2006). One further reason that scores are shaped by race and gender is due to the input questions: demographic factors such as family and socioeconomic background are used to calculate scores are correlated with race, which likely leads to disparate scores based on race (EPIC, 2019); they are likely to be correlated with gender, as well. Dropping questions about poverty or joblessness, which correlate with race (and possibly gender), may further weaken the risk assessment (Angwin, Larson, Mattu, & Kirchner, 2016).

These tools, with all their flaws, powerfully shape the interactions that criminalized people have with their supervising agents or officers. Yet these tools alone do not sufficiently explain how workers form relationships, gather information, and make decisions. As Viglione et al. (2015) found, although probation officers frequently conduct risk assessments on their clients, their decisions about how to supervise their clients do not consistently follow from the results of these assessments. Front-line workers may not prioritize notions of actuarial risk that dominate community supervision policy. In fact, in addition to and at times in lieu of scientifically validated forms of knowledge about clients, probation officers, and parole agents who are faced with these mandates continue to rely on intuition (Lynch, 1998), "gut feeling" (Werth, 2012), and experiential knowledge (Welsh, 2019b). Front-line personnel express agency by using these varied forms of knowledge and not merely their mandated risk tools (Cheliotis, 2006). For these reasons, researchers must move beyond these assessments to gain a broader picture of supervision practices amidst requirements to use EBPs.

Our examination of how workers on the ground form relationships, gather information, and make decisions on case is guided by three questions:

1. How do workers obtain knowledge about their clients?
2. How do their discourses reflect required assessment tools (LS/CMI, COMPAS) or alternative discourses?
3. How could the mobilization of both these forms of knowledge contribute to existing social inequalities, biases, and disparities?

We find that while agents rely on official knowledge through using and contributing to reports and assessments, they also employ alternative techniques. We locate one set of strategies in the production of knowledge through interactions and relationship-building, which we term *learning from clients*. Furthermore, we demonstrate that agents can combine multiple ways of knowing about clients in what we call *hybridized knowledge*; we find that nearly all workers report using some form of experiential knowledge in lieu of or in addition to the official tools. We caution, however, that these alternatives to official forms of knowledge can, like official tools, produce bias based on gender and race.

DATA AND ANALYSIS

As part of a study of criminalized women's post-incarceration work (Welsh, 2015, 2019a), Welsh conducted in-depth interviews with 19 California state parole agents and county probation officers in 2013.[6] All agents and officers interviewed were working in the same geographic area as where the women in the study lived. The interviews were conducted after a lengthy examination of the post-incarceration process from the standpoint of criminalized women. The goals of the interviews were to enable analytically pairing the perspectives of the front-line workers and the women, to better understand the formation of the gaps and tensions between women's self-reported needs and official forms of knowledge.

California is a notable study setting for two reasons. First, law-makers and corrections departments are particularly concerned about risk and public safety during parole in the aftermath of prominent cases where parolees committed violent crimes that were widely covered by national press (see Werth, 2011). In the Jaycee Dugard case, a parolee, Phillip Garrido, kidnapped an 11-year-old girl and held her captive for 18 years, beginning in 1991. Garrido was under parole supervision for 10 out of these 18 years. Another prominent case was that the kidnapping, rape, and murder of 12-year-old Polly Klaas by Richard Alan Davis, a parolee, in 1993. This case was later used as a catalyst for three strikes legislation in California in the 1990s (see Lynch, 1998). As in national discussions, popular discourse on parolee dangerousness in California has long been connected to recent focusing events like these, which contributes to ongoing concerns in corrections departments about further, extreme events in which individuals on supervision threaten public safety.

Second, a massive legislative change in how criminalized people are supervised in California, known as Realignment, occurred within two years of the interviews.[7] State parole supervision is typically imposed on people who have served a prison sentence, while probation supervision is conventionally a punishment in lieu of incarceration. Realignment, however, created a new form of probation (Post-Release Community Supervision, or PRCS) for criminalized people who may also have served a prison sentence. The consequences of this shift are visible in how the workers interviewed for this project described their work, which is related to respondents' work history; this study's sample of parole agents is heavily skewed toward veteran agents.[8] The majority of probation officers interviewed for this study, in contrast, were very new to adult probation, as PRCS had to be newly staffed.[9]

In the interviews, which averaged one hour in length, the second author asked workers to describe their daily work activities, as well as probing questions about how workers used client case records, assessment tools, and other forms of documentation. Orienting the interview around work created a space for interviewees to reflect on their daily work lives that they otherwise rarely were able to do (see also Mykhalovskiy & McCoy, 2002; Welsh, 2019b). Each interview was audio-recorded and transcribed.

Both authors then conducted an inductive, iterative analysis of the interview transcripts loosely based on Doucet and Mauthner's (2008) listening guide approach. This technique, which has been shown to be compatible with IE, involves reading through transcripts multiple times to "see the organizational in the individual" (Walby, 2013, p. 151). We drew especially on the IE concept of textual mediation: how workers construct texts then activate them through use. In this case, we examine how officers describe the texts that coordinate their work—assessment and case management tools—and whether and how these texts shape what officers know about their clients. During these close readings, we engaged in open coding for official knowledge/tools and other ways of knowing, and we noted when accounts of interview respondents reflected the use of both these forms of knowledge together. We then followed a more deductive approach to coding in which we identified passages of text using key words related to the specific texts that coordinate supervision work.[10] The worker narratives presented here offer illustrative examples of these themes.

Results

Our analysis places workers' narratives in juxtaposition with official texts, which we show organize and shape their work but do not fully prescribe or determine how workers manage their caseloads. The following sections first demonstrate how texts shape worker knowledge about their clients before and during interactions. Next, we illustrate when and how workers stray from the script of the texts by drawing on other forms of knowledge, and at times even reject official tools. Finally, we examine how workers use what we call hybridized knowledge that is developed both through text and other sources, and the implications for these practices to mobilize their own bias and the bias built into tools.

Producing Knowledge Through Reports and Assessments

Community supervision entails both field work and office work. Interactions with supervisees occur through interviews, home visits, contact related to clients' criminogenic needs, and random drug tests. Before and during interactions, texts shape how workers form knowledge about new clients. A common theme in the narratives of both parole agents and probation officers was the importance of documentation, or the understanding that they must prioritize knowledge produced through prior reports on clients received from other agencies, as well as the required assessment and reporting mechanisms generated by supervision workers. In workers' accounts, doing so was a means to "CYA" (Cover Your Ass) and to demonstrate that they were meeting the "specs" prescribed by each client's risk assessment. However, there was institutional variation in how the language of the texts entered into respondents' description of their work.[11]

Under the new form of probation supervision (Post-Release Community Supervision, or PRCS) implemented through Realignment, new clients are assessed at a probation "hub" office, which may not be the field office where the client's assigned probation officer works. At the hub, the client receives an orientation to the PRCS program, and the LS/CMI (Level of Service/Case Management Inventory) assessment instrument is administered. The client's probation officer receives the client's prison file, other criminal history information, risk level determination, and information about any other issues, and develops a case plan based on these risks and needs. In an initial meeting with the client, the probation officer creates an individualized treatment plan, using the *Courage to Change* curriculum created by the Change Companies.[12] It is at this point that the officer is to identify the appropriate "dosage" of rehabilitative activities to meet the case plan goals.

For parole, in contrast, approximately 210 days before a prisoner is to be released, pre-release planning begins and the prisoner's risk level is assessed using the California Static Risk Assessment tool (Turner et al., 2013). Agents refer to this phase as "pre-parole." A prisoner's agent can review the pre-parole information and the prisoner's criminal and incarceration history before the first meeting, and during the first meeting they conduct the Correctional Offender Management Profiling for Alternative Sanctions (COMPAS) assessment. According to Turner et al., "COMPAS has a dropdown menu that links specific programs to specific criminogenic needs" (2013, p. 20). As one agent put it, "It's the plan that we set up. How are we gonna supervise 'em, conditions of parole… we assess 'em, you know their risk factors and all that other stuff. See what their needs are." Based on a parolee's identified needs, the agent produces a quarterly "goals and progress report" which prescribes that the parolee spends a certain number of hours over the course of the following three months to address the need. For example, if a parolee has no source of income, a goal will be to apply for cash aid and food stamps; if a parolee is homeless, they might be required to complete a certain number of hours to work toward finding housing.

For both parole agents and probation officers, work is thus fundamentally shaped by the assessment scores that accompany each new client's case file (LS/CMI for probation; COMPAS for parole), and their own agency's reporting procedures. Workers use these official forms of knowledge because of accountability to supervisors and administrators. When workers and supervisors are evaluated based on risk tools, their time and effort must go into managing domains of their clients' lives that directly pertain to the foci of these tools. Importantly, even though they may stray from the official tools at key points, agents and officers must still distill their interactions down to "what counts" as legible knowledge to supervisors. These dynamics thus shape what and how workers claim to know about their clients.

For example, when parole agents were asked in our interviews how quickly they can tell if a parolee will succeed or fail on parole, not one of them directly referenced the risk score produced by COMPAS as factoring into this assessment. However, some, like Harrison, did mention common what are known as static risk factors such as age:

> When you do their pre-parole investigation, when you go through their file, you kinda can get a feel of that. And their age. That's a big factor. It seems like the age of 50 is the magic number. Ha. It seems like if you're a lifetime criminal, if you're someone that's been in and out of jail most of your life, one of those guys that are habitual drug users or something like that, it seems like 50 is that magic number for some reason. One guy told me, he says, you know, "Harrison, I'm tired of going back. I got into it with this youngster and it's not the same." So, what he's saying is he got beat up. Ha. That's what he's saying. So, he's not able to move like he used to.

As Harrison indicates, agents rely on multiple forms of information to assess parolees' risk of future criminal behavior. Much of this information, in addition to age, is available prior to meeting the parolee.

When agents read through a parolee's file prior to release from prison, they will review their "prison file," which includes information about the parolee's behavior while incarcerated as well as their criminal history ("rap sheet") and prior risk assessments. During the pre-parole investigation, the individual is also interviewed regarding their post-release plans. Most questions on actuarial risk assessment tools assume that these plans are linked to objective, scientifically based predictors of risk. Although no agents described avoiding the use of these forms of official knowledge altogether, agents varied considerably in how much they described relying on this information to build an understanding of their clients prior to meeting them.

Probation officers were somewhat more likely than parole agents to directly mention risk scores and how this shapes their work. Officer Armstrong, for example, recognized that because she is unarmed, for her own safety she must limit her home visits to clients who were categorized as lower risk (the LS/CMI score range is from 0 to 43): "I can guarantee you one thing: I will not be going to see those clients that have a LS/CMI risk score of 26–29. Those will not be the guys I go and see. I will be seeing my clients who are working. I will be going to the transitional homes." Here, the assessment tool produces a number that helps her determine what settings will be safe and where she will devote her time.

In contrast, Officer Napier does not directly reference the LS/CMI, but its themes and terminology emerge in how he evaluates new clients. During our interview, Napier pulled out the file of a client with a long history of incarceration to show the different sorts of information he uses to develop an expectation about new clients:

> People like that, you gotta study them and know how to approach them... What I usually do when I get a new client is, I pull up their history. That's the first thing I do. 'Cause some of them, I don't know them. Never seen them in my life. They haven't seen me in their lives. So, I like to set up a conversation in a more cordial way. Tell them what I expect from them and I'll tell 'em what they can expect from me. What I'm gonna do as their deputy... I will respect you like a human being. I'm not gonna treat you like a criminal but you're gonna act well. You're gonna be able to start doing something different, 'cause you do what you've been doing the past ten, twenty years, you're gonna get the same result... So, I'll look at their history before they come. These are all his descriptors. These are the addresses he has used in the past. These are the convictions. So, I take a look at all these things. What kind of crime has this guy been committing in the past? What kind of sentence has he received in the past? Where has he been? Prison? Probation? How did he perform while on supervision? Parole? Did he go back? Yes. On probation, was he violated? Did he go back and forth to court?

Then, Napier explained, after absorbing all this information presented in the official file, he has enough material to "study them":

> So, when I take a look at this in my mind, I start framing who I'm seeing. It starts to look like a picture. These things will tell me at least who they are on paper. Sometimes what you see may not be what you get. So, this history here will tell me who I'm dealing with... Then I ask that person the [case plan] questions based on this. 'Cause I see what his or her reaction would be. Then from there I have a plan. This person is sophisticated. This person I may be able to work with. I gotta be hard on this person. So, when that person is sitting here, I know how to approach them. That first day I set the tone. They know that this is the way Mr. Napier gonna work with me. So, if I know you are the type that's gonna come here and play games I will tell you right now, "Hey, just leave it at the door. Let's take care of business. It's all about you, not about me. It's all about your future not mine." I let them understand that.

Napier's description of how he uses a client's risk score, in combination with other information contained in the case file, to guide his initial interactions with his clients to "study them" exemplifies Smith's concept of the text-reader conversation (2005, pp. 104–105). In researching his new client before meeting him, Napier tries to answer questions posed in the case plan documents by reviewing the client's history. These questions are structured largely by the client's LS/CMI score. As Napier emphasizes, "They can manipulate you," meaning he needs to understand a client's history prior to meeting them, so that during the initial meeting, he can pose these same questions, gauge the client's response, and from there develop a sense of whether he "may be able to work with this person" or he has to "be hard on this person."

While interpreting texts in this way, Napier employs a personal touch to "set up a conversation in a more cordial way"; he recognizes that his initial meeting with a new client involves both establishing rapport and assessing the extent to which the client is being honest with him. In structuring interactions with clients in this way, Napier is carrying out the responsivity component to the risk-need-responsivity triad that structures evidence-based correctional treatment (Andrews et al., 1990).

Probation officers' increased integration of evidence-based risk assessment might be attributed to the newness of the program and the fact that everyone—both veteran and novice officers alike—have had to learn the new policies and procedures associated with PRCS.

Parole agents described a slightly different set of priorities, shaped in large part by institutional context: in addition to recent, widespread layoffs, changes in caseload composition had occurred. Whereas parole caseloads had previously been a mixture of people convicted of both more serious and non-violent crimes (e.g., drug offenses), agents were now supervising a higher proportion of people who had serious/violent criminal records. These seemingly less serious clients, who used to be, as one agent put it, "my bread and butter," or the people who were easier, less time-consuming, and less stressful to supervise, are now being supervised under the new PRCS program.

Large caseloads with a higher concentration of riskier clients contributed to agents' descriptions of constructing knowledge that was organized almost exclusively around risk and the potential for future criminality, or as several agents put it, preparing for if and when a case "blows up." Agent Cain described dealing with this dynamic by being meticulous about documenting his supervision:

> You have to show the paper trail. God forbid, say one of my guys committed a murder, they couldn't ever come to me and go, 'you made him do it.' No, I didn't. I never told him to kill somebody. What they'll do, though, is they'll audit the file and they'll find anything that you missed. If you missed a case review, then now you're dinged on it even though, had you done a case review, he still would have done it. They just basically audit the file and look for anything that they can get you on and then, knock on wood, I don't really know what the repercussions are of that 'cause I haven't had it happen.

Agent Cain's narrative reveals his thinking about risk, the high stakes involved in getting the risk assessment right (both individually/professionally and for public safety), and the resulting overall mental load that workers are carrying around with them both at home and at work.

Agents' fears were dominated not only by potential violence by supervisees but also by their absconding: leaving the local area in which parolees are required to stay, and often leaving the local parole jurisdiction, which makes coordination with law enforcement more difficult. Agent Marin recounted a similar story of someone on his caseload who absconded to another state and committed a murder. He described that he had made the required attempts to see the person within the required time period of five days, but he had not documented it fully—only in his case notes—so his supervisors had said he was not in compliance.

Having a high caseload of potentially dangerous clients means that an agent may not be able to see everyone on their caseload as frequently as the "specs" require. Marin connected the stress of the job to this dynamic:

> I have been more stressed this last year than I have in my 24 years working for California Department of Corrections whether as an officer or as a sergeant. This last year I felt my greys coming out... I'll give you a good example: the news comes out and there's breaking news in [my neighborhood]. You know what that does to my high blood pressure? It goes straight all the way... that's what I mean about blowing up, a case blowing up. It can blow up on anybody.

Marin elaborated the way that excessive caseloads and the impossibility of giving attention to all supervisees might encourage a case to "blow up":

> [For] the new parole model, we're supposed to be 53 to 1... we're not even close. I've been up to 112 to 1. And to be honest, it frightens me because I take this job serious because my job is to assist the parolee reintegrating back into the community. And when I can't see them or I only see them once, I'm held accountable. And then... the supervisors, they know that we have to meet the specs whatever the case is, two times a month, one time a month, or every other month and you don't see them, but then you see 80 but you missed these other ones that coulda blown up in your face. This person might have done a crime. Well why did you see them? Well because I prioritize seeing these 80... I feel like I'm cheating the parolee because I'm not giving 'em, – I'm giving the state 100% but I'm not giving them what they need.

Marin clearly articulates a contrast between paperwork and documentation—a necessary part of the job and one that he understands is a state priority—and "giving [parolees] what they need," which to him involves facilitating rehabilitation and reintegration.

Parole officers were not the only respondents to experience these pressures and changes in casework. Officer Perez, who had a long career as a probation officer before becoming an administrator, described similar challenges in his department:

> [The officers] do the levels of service case management inventory on them... [the] LS/CMI. And then they build a case plan and they have a series of journals. They're cognitive behavioral intervention journals – whatever their scores are, it'll tell you which ones that you could go through and then how many

times you really need to see them. Maybe per month depending on their score. And then they bring 'em in and they work through the journals and see what kind of effect they can have on some of those different risks that have been demonstrated in the LS/CMI. And that's been our model, but we haven't been able to put it in place just because of the sheer numbers that came out [because of Realignment]. Staffing, getting staff in place. I think our average is better but we're still probably about 80 [clients] to 1 [officer] and we need to be down around 40 to 1 average across the board before we can really start putting those things in place.

Similar to Marin, Officer Perez recognizes the strains placed on front-line supervision workers when caseloads are too high. This degrades the extent to which workers can implement the model evidence-based practices of case planning and journaling with each client. Although workers in both parole and probation responded to these official texts by adhering to policies about assessment and documentation, they also turned to alternative forms of knowledge in the course of their work.

Alternative Ways of Knowing

Risk assessment heavily shapes workers' expectations of their new clients, and workers did not criticize risk tools outright or report critiquing or confronting the authorities that had required them to use assessments. Yet workers routinely contradicted the logic of these tools mandated by higher authorities through their approaches to their clients. They frequently described waiting to meet a client before fully forming an opinion. Their accounts showed that it was in interacting with clients that many workers often operated outside of these official and purportedly objective forms of knowledge, using alternative ways of knowing to complement and/or resist the official forms. The way that workers recalled developing knowledge through interactions connects to ways that IE recognizes ideas as emergent through language. IE makes visible the ways in which language coordinates individuals' consciousness; in this case, workers' expressions of knowledge reflect discourses about popular psychology, femininity, masculinity, and race (Smith, 2014).

Despite the increased integration of risk assessment practices, workers still readily acknowledged the limits of these tools and spoke of risk assessment as both intuitive and ongoing. Officer Napier noted that "sometimes what you see is not what you get"—that a client's risk score, criminal history, and prison file can only tell you so much—and that he has had clients who have surprised him both positively and negatively. Officer Craig, a veteran of probation, cited clients' "attitude" as the key predictor of how successful they might be on supervision; Officer Perez, another veteran, stated: "You have to sit down with them. You have to talk with them. You have to interact at least so you can get an idea of who you're dealing with. And the continued interaction tells you more and more about this person."

A major technique that agents used as an alternative to reliance on official texts was producing knowledge through interactions and relationship-building, a process that we term *learning from clients*. As Officer Armstrong explained, "insight" and not merely what is in the case file drives his management of a case:

> Your casework, your case planning is built on the assessment. What are… the strategies you're gonna develop to work with this person and address the issues that you see? [That are] maybe causing them to continue to fall back into criminal behavior? And then I think the more difficult part is that insight. What point do you recognize something that's not on the assessment? That's not physically in front of you so it's not documented, but you're seeing or you're feeling from that interview from that contact?

As he continued, gaining these additional insights requires human interactions:

> Because again, you're not gonna get that information unless you have that interaction with a person sitting across the desk from you. And until you start doing that – until you engage that person – all you've got is a piece of paper, a bunch of data. But you don't really know how that really applies to who you're dealing with… You have to sit down with them. You have to talk with them. You have to interact at least so you can get an idea of who you're dealing with.

Officer Armstrong emphasized that it is only through "continued interaction" that he can learn increasingly more about his supervisees.

Official knowledge is decentered in such accounts. In fact, a few workers, like Agent Ramos, said that they do not look at a client's criminal history at all, to avoid bias.[13] Rather than shunning official knowledge, other workers reported using the contents of the clients' files more selectively. Officer Wilkinson recalled of one client, "He said, 'I know you already looked at my rap sheet.' And I said, 'No, I … don't wanna have a preconceived idea of you but if you do something wrong'… I said, 'Well, when we meet and what you say to me and what you do will dictate how our relationship goes from here. That's it.'"

Interpreting "demeanor" was another method through which workers learned about clients. In Agent Cain's account of interacting with clients, his reading of their non-verbal communication is especially crucial given the high stakes involved in getting the assessment right:

> So, you just you can't judge a book by its cover. You know? It's up in the air, it really is. It takes more time than [the initial interview]. You can tell a lot about a person by their demeanor. So, you know, if they speak to you in a fairly respectful manner and there doesn't seem to be animosity and all that. In general, you get the impression at that point that this might be an okay case. This might be an easy one. But sometimes the nicest-acting parolees are the ones that are getting in the most trouble too, telling you what you wanna

hear... So, it's just very difficult to judge whether they're gonna ever be on the right path.

In assessing whether someone will succeed or fail on parole, Cain readily acknowledges that it's all "up in the air," or that he can never fully predict what is going to happen. Risk is also something that is constantly assessed, as Werth's prior research noted (2011, 2012), and thus extends far beyond the initial interview to include every interaction an agent has with a parolee. Cain accepts the fact that he has "no control" over what his parolees might do as a stressful reality of his job. This is what makes the "paper trail" so important: regardless of a parolee's formal risk level, Cain needs to ensure that the case file is up to date so that if something happens, he can show that he did everything he possibly could.

It is also striking that when Cain remarked that it is "very difficult to judge whether they're gonna ever be on the right path," he was not only discussing risk; he was also expressing doubt about the efficacy of rehabilitation. In Cain's experience, although there are some key indicators he can rely on, "success" and "failure" on supervision are hard to predict. Failure is singular in nature: it is a return to criminal behavior and thus to incarceration. Success, however, is ambiguous. Success can entail the absence of criminal offending and the completion of parole, a modest definition which agents strive to achieve. Beyond this, success can also mean the completion of rehabilitative programming which will facilitate parolees' broader well-being. Agents were less likely to view themselves as influential in this sort of success. A client's failure could quickly be attributed to individual flaws and bad choices at times, as other researchers have found (Lynch, 1998, 2002; Werth, 2012, 2017). As Cain's narrative illustrates, such cases seem to reinforce agents' understanding that both risk and rehabilitation are difficult to predict—regardless of what the assessment tools indicated.

Other workers described using an array of techniques beyond what is prescribed through official case management strategies. Agent Marin, for example, described his tactics as "teamwork," while Officer Wilkinson described doing "whatever I kinda sense will get to them to make them start thinking and stop being mad at the system for not assisting you." Wilkinson described taking a read of the client and referring books to them based on what she thought would be effective, ranging from self-help books like *The Four Agreements* and *The Mastery of Love* to the Bible. In this way, Wilkinson's approach can be understood as a form of resistance to official knowledge and discourses. Moments of using this knowledge in a way that resists these discourses particularly occur around rehabilitation, which is a lower priority given the way that corrections departments are under-resourced.

Workers distinguished between how a client looks "on paper" and what the worker learns about the client through interactions. Agent James's description of a female parolee on his caseload that he deemed successful illustrates this tension. James's client had been convicted of several serious, violent offenses associated with a botched robbery, kidnapping, and murder, and she was thus classified as high-risk. Yet this classification did not match his assessment of her based on his read of salient criteria, many of which were unlikely to be factored into official risk assessments:

> So, she did her time. She's got two or three children. I don't think she's got a drug problem. I don't drug test her. She was really young when she did this. She was in her early 20s, I think. But now she gets out and she's very remorseful. She's very nice, well-spoken. A lot of these girls get loud when they wanna make a point. She's very calm. She loves her children. And she's carved her way out. She's smart enough to have used resources in her life. She has an aunt that drove buses. So, I think she's got her GED or high school diploma. Not much more than that. Now she's driving buses and she's supporting her family. She lives with her kids… She's always available. She has her own cell phone. She's got her own place to live. So, she really just handled business.

Notable in this narrative is how James describes an "ideal" parolee as "remorseful," "well-spoken," and "available." Also notable is the implied contrast between this client and other female clients he has supervised, who may be "loud when they wanna make a point"—perhaps reinforcing a stereotype of women of color as loud and/or angry. Precisely through his subjective interpretation of this client's character, James characterizes her as amiable and self-reliant.

In addition to illustrating relationship-building as a means of assessing clients, Agent James's narrative also indicates that there is very little that he has actually done to help this parolee; her success with her family and in the labor market has been achieved through a combination of her internal attributes and work that she has done on her own and with the help of her family. Even though on paper she is high-risk, she exhibits what James sees as all the "right" attributes of a "good" parolee. She already has her own cell phone and her own place to live—two hallmarks of post-incarceration success that are difficult to obtain, particularly in such a short time. James likely speaks highly of this parolee not only because of how well she has done, but also because she makes his job easier by having a cell phone through which he can reach her, and stable housing so that he knows where to find her. Thus, she has done the work of rehabilitation on her own—"she really just handled her business" and "she's smart enough to have used resources in her life"—without the assistance of parole.

James's narrative also illuminates how, given the under-resourced environment of community supervision agencies, workers must triage or engage in what Lemert (1993) called "bankloading," in which they prioritize higher-risk, often male clients over lower-risk and sometimes female clients (see also Welsh, 2019a). Bankloading has important implications for the level of fidelity through which evidence-based practices are implemented, particularly when caseloads are far higher than prescribed. Further, it has implications for when and how workers adhere to or resist these scientifically supported best practices. When workers are asked to implement and have confidence in practices such as risk assessment and case management inventories, yet they lack the time and resources to carry them out effectively, it is unsurprising that workers would then lose faith in the practices' efficacy. What does it mean when workers reject exclusive reliance on the official tools—as, in fact, nearly all workers report using some form of experiential knowledge in lieu of or in addition to the official tools? We do not propose that it is a matter of intuition being inherently opposed to science or data-driven practices. Workers have agency and discretion, and they bring an important human element into a system that is very often dehumanizing (see Smith, 1990). The use of these alternative forms of knowledge also brings us back to the design of the COMPAS and LS/CMI tools, raising questions about the intuitions and assumptions that form the basis of these algorithms. Such assumptions are often hidden within the technical design and remain unquestioned as they are disguised under the cover of authoritative and seemingly objective knowledge (Benjamin, 2019; Isard, 2017). Yet as the work reviewed above has shown, one area where we see bias integrated into the tools, then magnified with the use of the tools, is in terms of gender and race. The next section discusses what then happens when workers use a combination of official and unofficial forms of knowledge.

Hybridized Knowledge

The two forms of knowledge discussed above—knowledge derived from official accounts and assessments of criminalized people and knowledge derived through interactions and relationships—at times combine to comprise a third form of knowledge that we call *hybridized knowledge*. This hybridization may occur when, as referenced previously, workers are in triage mode and looking for shortcuts to supervising an overwhelming number of clients whom they may perceive to be high-risk and/or dangerous. This interplay of risk and experiential knowledge can produce gendered and racialized assumptions that function to replicate disparities. We observe that unofficial sources of knowledge, when they are deployed, are often used to provide help promote rehabilitation, even though there are few resources available, rather than manage riskiness or criminogenic needs. In addition to the assessment tools, workers rely on cognitive shortcuts derived from experience, stereotypes, assumptions, and gut-based interpretations of clients.

These shortcuts are evident in the ways in which workers fused elements of experience and assumption as they talked about gender and their approaches to their work with their male and female clients. Agent Mendez described women as "more emotional," explaining, "You can get to their hearts a lot faster than you would a man, to know as to what triggers them, what doesn't trigger them and stuff like that." These attributes, however, mean that "there's more hope for them." Officer Jacinto also compared traits, describing men as "more respectful" and "less emotional" and women as more likely to cry during their meetings:

> As far as female clients, they're a little bit more emotional... I never had a male come in my office and cry. Whereas the female [I was telling you about earlier] I'm trying to work with, she comes [in] and she'll start crying in my office. 'Cause she doesn't know what to do. So, she's she'll sit there and cry. As far as the male, I never had someone that emotional.

Officer Jacinto explained that these gendered tendencies impact how he approaches his clients:

> I'll try to be maybe a little bit softer with them [women]. But with the male population I think it's pretty black-and-white. Like, "This is what you need to do. If you don't, you're just gonna get violated." Then, I think, they have an understanding of that.

Agent Carrillo, meanwhile, described women as "very manipulative" yet more relatable to her as a woman, an understanding which also shapes her strategies for working with them:

> I'm not saying always use your personal experience [with women] but you kinda you just understand where they're coming from. When it comes to a man it's very different because a man doesn't wanna listen to a woman talk to him and tell him what to do... It's all about the insecurities. You know what I mean?

These narratives, from both male and female workers, demonstrate an understanding of women as having needs that the worker cannot address; women's gender was itself seen as synonymous with neediness. Based on experience and assumptions, these workers viewed women as more "emotional," potentially "manipulative," requiring separate strategies to manage on caseloads, though they also framed women as more apt to follow the rules and change.

These narratives reflect common stereotypes about gender differences. However, we also know that the assessment tools used in community supervision frequently also interpret women as less risky.[14] Because the tools already frame women in this way, the workers do not have to say that they consider women to be less risky. Workers then layer onto their interpretation of the tools their assumptions about gender that may be formed from their experiences or other unofficial sources of knowledge. This dynamic has the potential to multiply gendered bias, even though assessment tools are supposed to limit workers' biases in their unfiltered assessments.

Yet, the magnification of bias derived from *both* the tool and the judgment of the worker can be quite concerning from the vantage-point of fairness in resource allocation and surveillance. From previous research, we know this means that women can be then supervised less closely but also provided fewer resources that could be helpful (Welsh, 2019a), while men may be overly scrutinized and/or their emotional needs may not be attended to (Wyse, 2013). This observation also raises questions about whether the reverse can happen—do workers ever use knowledge from one source that could compensate for the other in a way that can neutralize bias of one source of knowledge? While we did not see this in our data, it is an important question that follows from our analysis.

Because the focus of the larger study discussed here was on gender, in interviews race was only explored indirectly. However, our data suggest similar dynamics around racialized knowledge, including the combination of racialized and gendered knowledge. Workers frequently referenced gang involvement when describing male criminality, and gang membership was often used as coded language for race. As Agent Cain explained, "I think maybe for the females… their commonality is the fact that they are females. Where with males the commonality is, you're Hispanic, I'm Hispanic. Or I'm Black and you're Black… it's race and gang affiliation." Racialized language around gang involvement was especially common among parole agents, many of whom had previously worked in adult prisons and described the racial segregation organizing prison life (see Goodman, 2008).

Conclusion

This chapter has demonstrated IE's usefulness for illuminating distinct forms of knowledge and how they are deployed in the community supervision context. Our analysis highlights how supervision workers interpret criminalized clients through languages of risk and individual responsibility as mediated by the texts they use in their daily work. Our analysis also illustrates key points at which supervision workers may choose to deviate from the prescribed, official, and text-based ways of knowing about their clients. Consistent with prior research (e.g., Cheliotis, 2006; Lynch, 1998; Werth, 2012), we find that these deviations involve workers drawing on personal and professional experience, stereotypes, assumptions, and gut-based interpretations of clients. Importantly, we also suggest that these unofficial forms of knowledge may at times work together with key texts, such as risk assessment tools, and that the use of such hybrids can produce forms of gendered and racialized bias.

We have also shown how the production of knowledge about criminalized clients often occurs in a high-stress, under-resourced environment of high caseloads and an emphasis on documentation that leads workers to prioritize some forms of knowledge over others, often at the expense of what their clients need. Indeed, there is evidence from other contexts that suggests that cognitive stressors such as high caseloads can heighten implicit racial bias (see, for example, Johnson et al. [2016] on implicit bias among emergency room physicians). Future research should examine the effects of these dynamics, not merely on adherence to evidence-based practices, but also in the generation of implicit biases that perpetuate gendered and racialized disparities that exist throughout the criminal-legal system. This line of inquiry is especially important given the push to incorporate evidence-based practices in a wider array of settings.

Lastly, this chapter raises key questions about the forms that changes to community supervision could take. What would change if administrators recognized workers' experiences as a "legitimate" form of evidence—what Foster (2015) refers to as practice-based evidence? In this way, workers' experiences and expertise could legitimately accompany or function alongside the use of top-down evidence-based measures (Foster, 2015). How would assessment tools that include this form of knowledge look? Broadening the scope and depth of data that inform workplace decisions would widen the basis for knowledge claims. Such reform could improve workplace relations by increasing worker autonomy and participation in decision-making (Slate, Wells, & Johnson, 2003), and the result could be greater effectiveness. However, we caution that this move could serve to sanction the use of greater discretion, alongside the biases that already plague the criminal-legal system. Further, this move alone would not address other dynamics that create precarity for people working on the front lines. Finally, our data suggest that some workers may deviate from—and at times outright resist—official forms of knowledge in part because they are committed to the ideal of rehabilitation, and they recognize that achieving client rehabilitation is precluded by the risk-focused model. This finding raises questions about the implications of continuing to use EBPs when workers may oppose them, and it underscores the need for a more expansive understanding of forms of knowledge.

Notes

1. The capacity of actors to rework and elaborate discourses locally, against the standardizing features of powerful extra-local discourses, is central for Dorothy Smith (1990); see especially pp. 202–208.
2. While the women's perspectives are not focal, our analysis is rooted in their standpoint and perspectives.
3. COMPAS is sold by equivant, a company with $1.67 billion in revenue (equivant, 2019). In the recidivism risk scale in COMPAS used by many corrections departments 137 attributes of the person and their criminal record are used to predict their risk of committing a felony or misdemeanor within two years (Dressel & Farid, 2018).
4. Indeed, supervision itself as an "evidence-based practice" is itself dubious, states' reliance on supervision shows no sign of slowing, and it has been suggested as a substitute for incarceration (Kleiman, 2015).
5. ProPublica's recent study of Broward County, Florida found racial bias in a comparison of predictive scores created using COMPAS to actual re-arrest rates (Angwin et al., 2016).
6. In California, frontline State parole workers are referred to as "agents," while County probation workers are referred to as "officers." For clarity, we maintain this distinction throughout. When referring to parole agents and probation officers collectively or interchangeably, we use the term "workers."

7. Assembly Bill 109, also known as the Public Safety Realignment Act of 2011, shifted supervision of people convicted of non-violent, non-serious, and non-high-risk sexual offenses from state parole to county probation (see Welsh, 2019a, 2019b).
8. This is due to multiple waves of layoffs of parole personnel as state funds were shifted to county probation departments as part of the new law. Three-quarters of these parole agents had previously had long careers as Correctional Officers (COs) in California state prisons.
9. Two-thirds of the parole agents interviewed were male, while more than two-thirds of probation officers were female. Most workers interviewed were non-white, with most identifying as either black or Hispanic/Latino.
10. Keywords are: Supervisor, Assess*, Risk, Boss*, Specs, COMPAS*, Tool*, Points [on a caseload], Evidence, Score, LS or LS-CMI, File, Trust, Experience, Gut, Relationship, Decision, Emotion*, Needs, Child*, Black, White, Gang*, Hispanic.
11. Although we do not discuss variations of social relations that impact risk assessment in this chapter, we expect that jurisdictional rules histories, and the legacy of accommodating or resisting science within agencies are all important.
12. According to promotional materials, the "Courage to Change Interactive Journaling System" is an "outcome-oriented supervision model that incorporates research-to-results and evidence-based practices for addressing the needs of participants working to successfully reintegrate into their communities" (Change Companies, 2014a). The curriculum uses a common technique in cognitive-behavioral therapy—interactive journaling—to help clients address their "individual problem areas" of criminogenic need.
13. Ramos explained that he assumes the worst about his clients. As he puts it, "basically to me, they've committed the worst crime possible and that's what I'm treating 'em as. I don't even have to look at what it is."
14. In *Loomis v. Wisconsin*, plaintiff Eric Loomis contested this issue.

References

Andrews, D., Bonta, J., & Hoge, R. (1990). Classification for effective rehabilitation. *Criminal Justice & Behavior, 17*(1), 19–52.

Angwin, J., Larson, J., Mattu, S., & Kirchner, L. (2016, May 23). Machine bias. *ProPublica*. Retrieved from https://www.propublica.org/article/machine-bias-risk-assessments-in-criminal-sentencing.

Barabas, C., Dinakar, K., & Doyle, C. (2019). Technical flaws of pretrial risk assessments raise grave concerns. *MIT Media Lab*. Retrieved from https://www.media.mit.edu/posts/algorithmic-risk-assessment/.

Benjamin, R. (2016). Catching our breath: Critical race STS and the carceral imagination. *Engaging Science, Technology, and Society, 2*, 145.

Benjamin, R. (2019). *Race after technology: Abolitionist tools for the new Jim code*. Cambridge: Polity.

Change Companies. (2014a). *The courage to change*. Retrieved from https://www.changecompanies.net/products/series.php?id=7.

Change Companies. (2014b). *The courage to change interactive journaling system brochure*. Carson City, NV: Change Companies.

Cheliotis, L. K. (2006). How iron is the iron cage of new penology? The role of human agency in the implementation of criminal justice policy. *Punishment & Society, 8*(3), 313–340.

DeMichele, M., & Payne, B. (2007). Probation and parole officers speak out: Caseload and workload allocation. *Federal Probation, 71*(3), 30–35.

Doll, A., & Walby, K. (2019). Institutional ethnography as a method of inquiry for criminal justice and socio-legal studies. *International Journal for Crime, Justice and Social Democracy, 8*(1), 147–160.

Doucet, A., & Mauthner, N. (2008). What can be known and how? Narrated subjects and the listening guide. *Qualitative Research, 8*(3), 399–409.

Dressel, J., & Farid, H. (2018). The accuracy, fairness, and limits of predicting recidivism. *Science Advances, 4*(1), eaao5580.

Electronic Privacy Information Center (EPIC). (2019). *Algorithms in the criminal justice system*. Retrieved from https://epic.org/algorithmic-transparency/crim-justice/.

equivant. (2019). *FAQ*. Retrieved from https://www.equivant.com/faq/.

Eubanks, V. (2017). *Automating inequality: How high-tech tools profile, police, and punish the poor* (1st ed.). New York, NY: St. Martin's Press.

Feeley, M., & Simon, J. (1992). The new penology: Notes on the emerging strategy of corrections and its implications. *Criminology, 30*(4), 449–474.

Flores, A. (2014, November 5). More than 60% of state parole agents' caseloads exceed policy limits. *Los Angeles Times*. Retrieved from http://www.latimes.com/local/lanow/la-me-ln-parole-agents-caseloads-20141105-story.html.

Foster, E. (2015). Rivals or roommates? The relationship between evidence-based practice and practice-based evidence in studies of Anorexia Nervosa. *Counseling Psychology Review, 30*(4), 34–42.

Garland, D. (2001). *The culture of control crime and social order in contemporary society*. Chicago: University of Chicago Press.

Gayman, M. D., & Bradley, M. S. (2013). Organizational climate, work stress, and depressive symptoms among probation and parole officers. *Criminal Justice Studies, 26*(3), 326–346.

Goodman, P. (2008). "It's just Black, White, or Hispanic": An observational study of racializing moves in California's segregated prison reception centers. *Law & Society Review, 42*(4), 735–770.

Hannah-Moffat, K. (2004). Losing ground: Gendered knowledges, parole risk, and responsibility. *Social Politics: International Studies in Gender, State & Society, 11*(3), 363–385.

Hannah-Moffat, K. (2005). Criminogenic needs and the transformative risk subject: Hybridizations of risk/need in penality. *Punishment & Society, 7*(1), 29–51.

Hannah-Moffat, K. (2006). Pandora's box: Risk/need and gender-responsive corrections. *Criminology & Public Policy, 5*(1), 183–192.

Hannah-Moffat, Kelly. (2019). Algorithmic risk governance: Big data analytics, race and information activism in criminal justice debates. *Theoretical Criminology, 23*(4), 453–470.

Harcourt, B. E. (2007). *Against prediction: Profiling, policing, and punishing in an actuarial age*. Chicago: University of Chicago Press.

Harris, D. A. (2012). *Failed evidence: Why law enforcement resists science*. New York: New York University Press.

Isard, J. (2017). Under the cloak of brain science: Risk assessments, parole, and the powerful guise of objectivity. *California Law Review, 105*(4), 1223–[vi].

Johnson, T., Hickey, R., Switzer, G., Miller, E., Winger, D., Nguyen, M., ... Hausmann, L. (2016). The impact of cognitive stressors in the emergency department on physician implicit racial bias. *Academic Emergency Medicine, 23*(3), 297–305.

Kleiman, M. (2015). Substituting effective community supervision for incarceration. *Minnesota Law Review, 99,* 1621–1629.

Lemert, E. (1993). Visions of social control: Probation considered. *Crime & Delinquency, 39,* 447–461.

Loomis v. Wisconsin. (2016). 881 N.W.2d 749.

Lynch, M. (1998). Waste managers? The new penology, crime fighting, and parole agent identity. *Law & Society Review, 32*(4), 839–870.

Lynch, M. (2000). Rehabilitation as rhetoric: The reformable individual in contemporary parole discourse and practices. *Punishment & Society, 2,* 40–65.

Lynch, M. (2002). Selling 'securityware': Transformations in prison commodities advertising, 1949–99. *Punishment & Society, 4*(3), 305–319.

Mykhalovskiy, E., Armstrong, P., Armstrong, H., Bourgeault, I., Choiniere, J., Lexchin, J.... White, J. (2008). Qualitative research and the politics of knowledge in an age of evidence: Developing a research-based practice of immanent critique. *Social Science & Medicine, 67*(1), 195–203.

Mykhalovskiy, E., & McCoy, L. (2002). Troubling ruling discourses of health: Using institutional ethnography in community-based research. *Critical Public Health, 12*(1), 17–37.

Nichols, N. (2017). Technologies of evidence: An institutional ethnography from the standpoint of "youth at risk". *Critical Social Policy, 37*(3), 1–21.

Simon, J. (1993). *Poor discipline: Parole and the social control of the underclass, 1890–1990.* Chicago: University of Chicago.

Slate, R. N., Wells, T. L., & Johnson, W. W. (2003). Opening the manager's door: State probation officer stress and perceptions of participation in workplace decision making. *Crime & Delinquency, 49*(4), 519–541.

Smith, D. (1990). *Texts, facts, and femininity: Exploring the relations of ruling.* Abingdon: Routledge.

Smith, D. (2005). *Institutional ethnography: A sociology for people.* Lanham, MD: AltaMira.

Smith, D. (2014). Discourse as social relations: Sociological theory and the dialogic of sociology. In D. Smith & S. Turner (Eds.), *Incorporating texts into institutional ethnographies* (pp. 225–252). Toronto: University of Toronto Press.

Taylor, T. (2013). Paperwork first, not work first: How caseworkers use paperwork to feel effective. *Journal of Sociology & Social Welfare, 40*(1), 9–27.

Turner, S., Hess, J., Bradstreet, C., Chapman, S., & Murphy, A. (2013). *Development of the California Static Risk Assessment (CSRA): Recidivism risk prediction in the California Department of Corrections and Rehabilitation.* Retrieved from the University of California-Irvine Center for Evidence-Based Corrections website: https://ucicorrections.seweb.uci.edu/files/2013/12/Development-of-the-CSRA-Recidivism-Risk-Prediction-in-the-CDCR.pdf.

Viglione, J., Rudes, D. S., & Taxman, F. S. (2015). Misalignment in supervision: Implementing risk/needs assessment instruments in probation. *Criminal Justice and Behavior, 42*(3), 263–285.

Walby, K. (2005). Institutional ethnography and surveillance studies: An outline for inquiry. *Surveillance & Society, 3*(2/3), 158–172.

Walby, K. (2013). Institutional ethnography and data analysis: Making sense of data dialogues. *International Journal of Social Research Methodology, 16*(2), 141–154.

Waters, N. (2015). Towards an institutional counter-cartography of nurses' wound work. *Journal of Sociology & Social Welfare, 42*(2), 127–156.

Welsh, M. (2015). Categories of exclusion: The transformation of formerly-incarcerated women into "Able-Bodied Adults Without Dependents" in welfare processing. *Journal of Sociology & Social Welfare, 42*(2), 55–77.

Welsh, M. (2019a). How formerly incarcerated women confront the limits of caring and the burdens of control amid California's carceral realignment. *Feminist Criminology, 14*(1), 89–114.

Welsh, M. (2019b). Conceptualizing the personal touch: Experiential knowledge and gendered strategies in community supervision work. *Journal of Contemporary Ethnography, 48*(3), 311–338.

Welsh, M., & Rajah, V. (2014). Rendering invisible punishments visible: Using Institutional Ethnography in feminist criminology. *Feminist Criminology, 9*(4), 323–343.

Werth, R. (2011). *Envisioning risk and constructing responsibility: Plasticity, punitive regulation, and the re-shaping of rehabilitation within California parole* (Doctoral dissertation). Retrieved from ProQuest (3457243).

Werth, R. (2012). I do what I'm told, sort of: Reformed subjects, unruly citizens, and parole. *Theoretical Criminology, 16*(3), 329–346.

Werth, R. (2017). Individualizing risk: Moral judgement, professional knowledge, and affect in parole evaluations. *British Journal of Criminology, 57*(4), 808–827.

Werth, R. (2019). Risk and punishment: The recent history and uncertain future of actuarial, algorithmic, and "evidence-based" penal techniques. *Sociology Compass, 13*(2), 1–19.

Wyse, J. (2013). Rehabilitating criminal selves: Gendered strategies in community corrections. *Gender & Society, 27*(2), 231–255.

CHAPTER 22

Public Protection as a Ruling Concept in the Management of Nurses' Substance Use

Charlotte A. Ross

People in all professions can and do have problems with substance use that affect their performance in the workplace. Although the estimated prevalence of nurses who have problems with substance use varies greatly, from 6 to 20% (Dunn, 2005; Kunyk, 2015; Monroe & Pearson, 2009; Servodidio, 2011), it is well-recognized and of particular concern that many nurses who do have such problems continue to practice and do not obtain treatment (Kunyk, 2015; Kunyk & Austin, 2011; Monroe, Kenaga, Dietrich, Carter, & Cowan, 2013). When nurses have substance use problems that negatively affect their work performance, they may compromise the safety of the public they serve (National Council of State Boards of Nursing [NCSBN], 2011).

Nurses' ongoing licensure to practice in Canada is contingent upon their adherence to designated professional practice standards (BCCNP, 2020d), of which their regulatory body adjudicates. In Canada, each province has a professional nursing *regulatory body*, which is an institution whose primary mandate is "to serve and protect the public" by regulating the licensure to practice nursing within its provincial jurisdiction (British Columbia College of Nursing Professionals [BCCNP], 2020b, para. 1). By law, an individual cannot practice as a nurse in Canada unless they hold an active registration in good standing with their provincial nursing regulatory body. Nurses' employers must also abide by any limitations or conditions that the regulatory body may impose on a nurse's license (Health Professions Act [HPA], 1996).

C. A. Ross (✉)
Coquitlam, BC, Canada
e-mail: rossc@douglascollege.ca

Nursing regulatory bodies have traditionally managed nurses' problems with substance use as an exceptional issue, such that they have addressed them with specific standardized policies and programs (NCSBN, 2011). In North America, Alternative to Discipline (ATD) programs are widely considered to be the most effective policy means by which regulatory bodies can protect the public in cases where a nurse's practice may be impaired by substance use (Monroe et al., 2011; NCSBN, 2011). In addition to their primary goal of public protection, the ATD programs also have a second function, that of supporting the nurse through a mandated treatment and monitoring regime intended to eventually return them to safe nursing practice (Monroe et al., 2011; NCSBN, 2011).

The ATD treatment regimes broadly in use throughout North America are based upon the USA's chief regulatory body's, the NCSBN's (2011), standardized guidelines for ATD programs (Darbro, 2011; Smith, Krinkle, & Barnett, 2013). Although consistently adopted as the optimal regulatory approach for health care professionals, studies have shown that the treatment aspect of this regime is very under-researched and what data do exist have found it sorely lacking (Lawson & Boyd, 2018; Ross, Jakubec, Berry, & Smye, 2019; Urbanoski, 2014). The accepted metric of the "success" of these programs has traditionally been conceptualized in the literature as the enrollment and retention rates in said programs (Ross et al., 2019). This is in itself a questionable yardstick of success for many reasons, not the least of which is that data indicate nurses avoid engaging with these programs at all (Kunyk, 2015; Kunyk & Austin, 2011; Monroe et al., 2013). The underlying causes of this low program uptake are poorly understood, as there are precious few studies in the body of nursing literature that have researched nurses' experiences within them (Astrab Fogger & McGuinness, 2009; Darbro, 2005; Horton-Deutsch, McNelis, & O'Haver Day, 2011; Ross et al., 2019; Strom-Paikin, 1996).

In considering these shortcomings of the widely implemented regime that has long been held up as the best approach to both mitigate public risk and treat nurses' substance use problems, I was left puzzled on many fronts. How had this policy arrangement come to be embraced by nurse scholars, nurses' employers, and regulators alike as the ideal way to meet these stated goals? Exactly how did a nurse come to be known and categorized as a danger to the public? What were the experiences of the nurses whose everyday lives were managed by these programs? What were the underlying discourses that organized these institutional processes and the individual nurses' experiences? Altogether, these puzzles composed the problematic that I explored by means of an Institutional Ethnography (IE). This study centered on a new ATD program in a western Canadian province that was based on the NCSBN (2011) guidelines (henceforth referred to as *The Program*). In this chapter, I begin from the nurses' experiences of The Program and explicate how the ruling discourses around public protection organized a nurse to be declared as a danger to the public and managed the activities that were intended to mitigate this said danger.

Mode of Inquiry: Institutional Ethnography

The standpoint anchoring this study was that of nurses in a western Canadian province who had participated in The Program and whose primary work responsibilities entailed direct client care provision in various hospitals throughout the province. I interviewed 12 standpoint informants, who were comprised of 11 Registered Nurses (RNs) and one Registered Psychiatric Nurse (RPN). Interviews with secondary informants were also carried out, which included: (1) two RNs who had never been enrollees in The Program but had worked with nurses who had been, (2) one physician who worked as an Independent Medical Examiner (IME) in a similar Program for other professionals, and (3) three Program Administrators, the institutional designates who managed the cases of enrollees in The Program. My Program Adminstrator interviewees were lawyers by profession, one employed with the nurses' labor union, one with a union in a comparable program for other health care profssionals, and one with the provincial regularoty body. The regulatory body's Program Administrators made recommendations that were forwarded to their Inquiry Committee[1] for adjudication of the nurses' cases. I also employed reflexive journaling from my researcher's standpoint as a practicing, dually credentialed RN and RPN with over 36 years' experience (at the time of data analysis) who has not ever been enrolled in The Program.

I analyzed the ethnographic data from the transcribed interviews with the primary and secondary informants, my reflexive journal, and the institutional texts. My aim in doing so was to uncover and trace taken-for-granted conceptual knowledge, standardized textually mediated processes, and discursive categorizations that had been taken up, authorized as official factual accounts, and activated as ruling relations in ways that managed and subsumed individuals' experiences (Lewington, 2018). I paid particular analytic attention to disjunctures between standpoint participants' experiential ways of knowing and abstracted knowledge to identify where the individuals' knowledge and experiences had been displaced.

Institutional texts are often afforded central analytic importance in IE, as they are viewed as mediators of the ruling relations that organize people's local activities (Smith, 2005). The first stage of an IE textual analysis involves locating how institutional texts occur in sequences of action at the local level (Smith, 2005). Accordingly, my textual analysis began with interrogating the standpoint informants' experiential data to reveal where and how institutional texts entered into and coordinated their activities (or *texts in use*).

In the second stage of my analysis, I employed two typical IE analytic methods, indexing and mapping (Rankin, 2017b). I did so to trace outward from these local textually mediated sequences of action, describing and mapping their links to authoritative texts in use in The Program that represented official accounts and from which institutional action followed (referred to as *boss texts* in IE) (Rankin, 2017b). I analyzed relevant Program texts to identify how they were activated as ruling relations in ways that organized the individuals' local experiences to occur as they had in *accountability circuits* (Griffith & Smith, 2014; Turner, 2006). In IE, accountability circuits refer to sequences of action whereby people's activities are converted to textual realities in order to be granted official facticity, or produce a "warrantable account," within the ruling apparatus (Rankin, 2017a, p. 6). In this second analytic stage, data from secondary informants and my reflexive experiential knowledge also identified relevant institutional texts that mediated the ruling ideologies (Campbell & Gregor, 2002). These texts included Program contracts, current and/or archived regulatory body, labor union, corporate and employer policy documents, provincial legal statutes, and professional and scholarly literature on the topic of nurses' substance use problems.

Discoveries

IE analysis of my problematic unveiled ideologically based, textually mediated institutional processes that organized, subordinated, and displaced nurses' knowledge and experiences with official accounts of public protection. These organizing features included the following: the creation and activation of a textual discourse of a dangerous nurse, the purported mitigation of this danger via accountability circuits, the emergence of disjunctures in self-regulation of nurses' "fitness to practice," practices of deputizing nurse peers, and the creation of a textual discourse of impaired nursing practice as an individual issue, all of which I explicate in what follows.

The Textual Organization of a Dangerous Nurse

The *Health Professions Act* ([HPA], 1996) is a broad, overarching provincial statute that authorizes the province's health professionals' regulatory bodies to carry out their mandates of protecting the public. It serves as a boss text that affords regulatory bodies the power and responsibility to investigate their members if a member's actions demonstrate that they could pose a danger to the public in some way (HPA, 1996, s 33(1)). Among the numerous areas of health care professionals' practices that the HPA addresses in service of this goal, it dictates that the regulatory body can conduct an investigation if it receives information indicating that a nurse may have "an addiction to alcohol or drugs *that impairs his or her ability to practise*" their profession (emphasis added, HPA, 1996, s 33.4(e)). If the subsequent investigation determines that to be the case, the HPA affords the regulatory body the right to impose limits and conditions upon, suspend, or even terminate a nurse's license to practice in order to fulfil its public protection mandate.

The substance use practices of a nurse could come to the attention of the regulatory body by one of two means: the nurse had either self-reported to their employer, regulatory body, or labor union by way of seeking help for their problems with substance use, or they were reported by another person who had concerns about their substance use. A text on the regulatory body's public website informs nurses' employers and colleagues that they are obligated to report a nurse if "there is evidence a nurse diverted narcotics" or there are "clear, witnessed signs a nurse is impaired at work" (BCCNP, 2020b, para. 2). None of the documents that I analyzed made any distinction as to whether a substance the nurse used or their substance use problem involved substances that were licit or illicit, obtained by prescription, or by other means.

If the regulatory body or employer determined that an investigation was warranted, the nurse was then assigned to a designated IME (Independent Medical Examiner) for an assessment. That physician was one of a select few who had been approved as medical "addiction specialist" assessors for The Program. If that IME then diagnosed the nurse with a "substance-use disorder" (SUD), it was so noted in the IME's report and the nurse was then entered into The Program. A *SUD* is a specific classification in the *Diagnostic and Statistical Manual of Mental Disorders* (DSM; American Psychiatric Association [APA], 2013), a symptom-based, biomedical approach to categorizing mental health problems (see also Deacon, 2013).

The IME's report activated another text, a contract between the nurse and the regulatory body, employer and labor union. This contract outlined a compulsory standardized regime that was designated as "treatment" for the duration of their involvement with The Program. Its contents were drawn from the recommendations in the IME's report that, without exception, included the same treatment activities as outlined in the NCSBN (2011) guidelines. These were the following: complete abstinence from all psychoactive substances (except nicotine and caffeine), attendance at a designated (12-Step facilitation[2]-based) in-patient treatment program and a specified number of ongoing community-based 12-Step facilitation activities (usually 2–3 meetings/week), and biological monitoring of compliance to these requirements for the length of the contract, which was generally a minimum of three years. The nurse was presented with the choice of complying with this contract or being subject to a disciplinary inquiry that potentially jeopardized their employment and licensure to practice. Even so, entrance into The Program contract was conceptually organized as "voluntary" and the treatment as a means of "public protection."

The conceptualization within these contracts of danger to the public arising from impaired nursing practice and its mitigation was organized by dominant medicalized and ideological discourses in the guiding NCSBN (2011) document. This conceptual framing was also located in literatures pertaining to the Physicians Health Program for the management of physicians' problems with substance use (DuPont, McLellan, White, Merlo, & Gold, 2009), upon which the NCSBN (2011) guidelines had been modeled. In all of these texts, substance use problems are described and defined as chronic, inevitably progressive, relapsing brain diseases that must be managed with the standardized strict abstinence/12-Step/monitoring approach in order to prevent certain worsening. However, the current norms of practice in use with the general public eschew ideological understandings such as these, which are now considered outdated, "inaccurate [and speak] ... more about values and politics" than current scientific evidence (Urbanoski, 2014, p. 11). Population and public health approaches that constitute contemporary practice are instead guided by epidemiological data. These data show that a "high degree of heterogeneity [of substance use problems exists], in terms of pattern of onset, course, intensity, functional severity...and outcome," for which individuals should be offered a variety of possible personalized treatment strategies (Chapnick, 2014, p. 9).

Current researchers also assert that for health care professionals, "a diagnosis of SUD alone is not a specific indicator of risk" (O'Neill & Cadiz, 2014, p. 17; see also Chapnick, 2014; Lenzer, 2016; MacDonald, 2016; Urbanoski, 2014). Nevertheless, the discourses that conceptualize health care professionals' substance use problems as *definitively* progressive and presenting extraordinary risk of public danger at any level of severity can also be seen in employers' position and policy texts. For example, two provincial employers' position statements assert (with exactly the same wording) that "substance abuse (sic)" that is "untreated or under-treated" (meaning, one imagines, as they do not specify their meaning, not managed in accordance with the standardized arrangements dictated in these documents) "*presents an extraordinary level of risk since these disorders are generally progressive in nature*" (emphasis added; Fraser Health Authority [FHA], 2018, p. 9; see also IHA, 2013, p. 3). Despite this confident declaration, neither of these documents provide any definition therein of what substance abuse actually means, nor do they substantiate any part of this declaration with scientific evidence. These texts are also heavily buttressed by prevailing safety-sensitive discourses that declare a job to be *safety-sensitive* when impaired job performance could cause significant risk to safety of clients, co-workers, or others in the work environment (FHA, 2018, p. 22; IHA, 2013, p. 2). One employer also takes their conceptualization of risk one step further by adding a second safety-sensitive criterion that reveals an institutional interest in this matter: the potential risk for "damage affecting the reputation of" the employer (IHA, 2013, p. 2).

By means of these discursive categorizations, the regulatory body's original criteria for their becoming involved in a nurses' substance use practices, as noted prior, a nurse's impairment at work or diverting of drugs (BCCNP, 2020b), had metamorphosed in The Program. This meant that a nurse who had been attributed a diagnosis of SUD in the assigned IME's report was thereafter categorized as part of a homogeneous group of people who were *ipso facto* dangerous to the public. Such was the case regardless of the type of substance or severity of their said SUD and whether or not they had ever been impaired in the workplace or diverted drugs. In this way, the assessment of the nurse in The Program was actually for a particular theoretical categorization, SUD, and did not specifically examine whether they were incompetent or unfit for nursing practice; rather, a diagnosis of SUD assumed this. This official accounting of nurses' substance use problems was not unlike a similar, related finding, whereby a nurse's diagnosis of a mental illness had been equated and conflated with their incompetence and unfitness for nursing practice (Chapman, Azevedo, Ballen, & Poole, 2016, p. 41).

Ethnographic data from standpoint informants showed how this ruling ideological conceptualization had organized and displaced their experiences. For instance, some participants in this study reported that they entered The Program because they had indeed practiced while impaired by substance use or had diverted drugs in their workplaces. Yet, others maintained that neither of these had been the case with them and that their substance use practices had never affected their everyday nursing work. For example, some nurses noted that they were on extended sick leave from work at the time that their substance use came to the attention of regulatory body or employer. Others stated that they had only utilized substances on their days off and were never intoxicated or impaired during their scheduled shifts. Some were never impaired at work or elsewhere but had acquired a physical dependence on a legitimately prescribed medication that they were taking for long-term health conditions and in strict accordance with their personal physicians' directives. These nurses' substance use practices had all come to the attention of their employer or regulatory body, as a consequence of their seeking help either for substance use problems or for another medical condition (more on this point to follow). Harlen, a Program Administrator, summarized how the ruling "safety-sensitive" ideologies and theoretical diagnostic categories had been activated in The Program in this way:

> So, you may have a person who has worked for ten years without incident...has demonstrated that they are not a risk in the workplace, but the physician themselves will say "substance use disorder: risk in the workplace: mandatory treatment...there's no evidence of safety issue but I'm going to find a safety issue. You can't go back to work."

Harlen continued, recommending an alternative approach grounded in the actualities of the nurses' work lives that could instead be taken up:

> It's not sufficient to just say that a nurse works in a safety-sensitive job, but ...what I would want the employer to do first is a [comprehensive] risk assessment...that might involve getting an opinion from the person's [personal physician]...,would be focused on the performance or attendance or behavioural concerns...,treat[s] people with substance use disorders in terms of sick leave, return to work, accommodation in the workplace, performance management, attendance management – all those things...in the same way that we treat people with [other potentially impairing health conditions]... [and] really to examine... the injuriousness of the work that they're engaging in, who it can harm, the severity of that harm, rather than simply focusing on 24/7 sobriety.

Mitigation of Danger to the Public by Means of Accountability Circuits

An employer's position statement that I analyzed declared that: "[the employer] will deal with employees with substance use disorders in the same manner as other diseases which can negatively affect safety, attendance, performance and behaviour" (FHA, 2018, p. 13). Harlen, a Program Administrator, refuted this statement. To illustrate his point, he informed me that unlike the assignment of a designated IME and the compulsory standardized "treatment" approach in use in The Program, nurses whose other health conditions came to the attention of regulators or employers were permitted to collaborate on the choice of their assessing and treating practitioners and treatments. Most particularly, however, he cited how nurses in The Program were uniquely singled out for management of their activities even outside of their work hours. This management occurred by way of a particular accountability circuit that involved The Program's contractual stipulation of strict *24/7* abstinence and monitoring of compliance with this requirement. This included random biological compliance monitoring of the abstinence requirement that dictated the nurse must be available 24 hours per day and 7 days per week, including vacation and days off, to produce a specimen free of psychoactive substances at the assigned laboratory within 24 hours notice of the call to do so. The monitoring contracts, of 2–3 years duration or more, typically required 24–28 random tests per year, at the IME's discretion. Failure to comply with any of these conditions was categorized as "critical non-compliance" with the contract, a designation that jeopardized the nurses' continued licensure and employment. Some of the nurse participants expressed that singling out substance use problems for monitoring outside of their work hours was unduly restrictive, intrusive and irrelevant to their safety at work. Harvey, one of the participating nurses, said:

> [I]f I can provide a drug test and prove that I'm abstinent at work, that's the only concern that my employer should have…What my personal health care choice is – whether or not I choose to seek treatment and what type of treatment that is, is my own personal health care choice and really, none of their business.

Harlen, a Program Administraor, voiced other concerns about the effectiveness this process in protecting the public:

> [If] they've tested positive, there's going to be usually a substantial time lag between their positive test and that information going to the front line employer… the person is working because your only mechanism for monitoring their performance and behaviour in the workplace is a urine test that they did three days ago… its illogical and I don't know of any research that shows it's effective in terms of reducing safety incidents at work or anything like that.

These participants' ethnographic data concurred with Chapnick's (2016) claims that setting apart substance use problems for such an extreme and intrusive level of scrutiny in this way describes an institutional process predicated upon stigma and stereotype, and not on science or the actualities of the individuals' work lives. He also articulates how such an accountability circuit is founded upon an ideological position that random testing is an effective means to ensure that nurses are free of substances during their actual work time. In reality, he asserts, it actually tests only for abstinence *at the time of testing* and not actual impairment in the workplace (Chapnick, 2016).

In the Canadian health care system, public-pay laboratories are customarily engaged for biological substance screening services; however, the monitoring services exclusively assigned to nurses in The Program were specific, designated private-pay laboratories.[3] When I asked Candace, a Program Administrator, why the nurses were assigned to these particular private labs and were not permitted to utilize the public ones, she responded:

> [We look at whether] the monitoring program is following appropriate protocols...Are they reporting back to us in a [designated] format...and doing the things that they should be doing?...We're more interested in their quality of the work being done to ensure that we know that the nurse is fit and safe to practice.

From Candace's response, it is evident that what she terms as the "quality" of the work was equated with the laboratories' ability to collect data in accordance with the stipulations in The Program's designated texts (the contracts), which had been organized as the means to ensure the nurse's "fitness and safety to practice." Yet, nurse participants brought my attention to their experiential knowledge of the laboratories' monitoring practices that begged questions of the actual quality of that work in some cases. For instance, I learned from participants and the private laboratories' protocol texts that urine specimens were not necessarily obtained from a witnessed voiding of urine. If a nurse did not wish to be observed by staff while voiding, these laboratories offered the option of using a "dry room." This is a room where there is either no water supply in the room, or if there is a commode, it contains a dyeing agent that can detect if water is substituted for or used to dilute the urine specimen. From my standpoint of a nurse who has had much experience with obtaining biological substance screening specimens, I have known the standard practice to be obtaining a *directly witnessed* specimen. This is because the main concern is not the use of water, but the surreptitious substitution of another person's biological material. I have also seen people's considerable ingenuity in their attempts to conceal and utilize others' urine for their screening tests. Because of this experiential knowledge, I questioned Fiona, a physician who had worked as an IME in a similar Program for a different profession, about the reliability of the existing practice to ensure provision of an unsubstituted specimen, and she seemed undisturbed:

> CR: Well, I'm kind of wondering, [one] could bring urine into a dry room...people get creative... nurses have access to a lot of urine...

F: Oh, there's many ways around [it]...

Jean, who identified herself as a colleague of nurses who had been in The Program, was troubled about the reliability of the urinary monitoring. She was concerned that some of her nurse colleagues in The Program were using substances at work despite their random monitoring, as they sometimes appeared to be impaired in the workplace. She also stated that several urine samples had coincidentally gone missing on their unit (more on this matter to follow). Some standpoint nurse participants also questioned their monitoring companies' quality control practices. For example, Paul, a nurse in The Program who lived in a rural area, told us that the private laboratory he was required to utilize out-sourced their services and that, "I was going to some woman's living room, peeing in her bathroom in her house."

I discovered another accountability circuit that also ostensibly managed nurses' safety to practice that, in actuality, monitored the nurses' compliance to The Program. The monitoring companies were also commissioned to provide the nurse's labor union, employer, and regulatory body with regular monthly reports that included the compiled results of their biological screening and documentation of check-ins. *Checking-in* referred to the nurses' mandated requirement to routinely (at intervals stipulated in their contract) either connect with the monitoring company's online software program, telephone a person or answering machine, or attend in-person appointments, depending upon the individual monitoring company's corporate procedures. If the checking-in activities were to be carried out with a person, these individuals were employees of their assigned monitoring companies, who were referred to as *monitors*. Their professional qualifications were determined solely by the monitoring companies. This monitoring process was not a treatment, nor was the monitor–nurse relation a therapeutic relationship. When I asked Candace, a Program Administrator, what she knew of the monitors' professional qualifications, she was not aware and made clear that such information did not concern her. She instead focused her interest on the intactness of accountability circuits:

> [I] Don't know [their qualifications]. We are in regular and open communication with them about the RNs being monitored... [and the regulatory body's] interest is in the rigor of processes and procedures. It is up to the private monitoring company to vet and hire them.

Nurse participants seemed equally in the dark about to whom they were reporting, what their actual role was, and with whom their regulatory body engaged in this "regular and open communication" about their personal information. Some nurses told me that the monitor was the physician's wife who worked at the front desk of the laboratory, others thought they were individuals who had a 12-Step participation background. In Helen's experience, "reporting to the medical monitor...[was] more commonly reporting to their receptionist." One nurse participant asked her monitor directly what their credentials were, was flatly refused this information, and told that she should not "make trouble."

Nurses told me that the monitors would ask them general questions in the manner of, "how are you doing?" "any problems?" but primarily they queried as to how the nurse was complying with the required attendance at 12-Step meetings. Molly recounted:

> Sometimes they would ask what was our favourite thing that we heard at a meeting; sometimes they'd ask us...how often you've been in contact with your [12-Step] sponsor – you know, how many meetings you're going to – just sort of questions like that.

When we asked Harvey what his monitor did, he responded: "Well, you basically go in and you'd have to give them a sheet signed off from your AA meetings that you had gone to these AA meetings... [which could easily have been] forged."

Participants reported that they had to have "a person" (whose role in the activity isn't specified) at each of their 12-Step meetings sign a designated form stating that they had attended. This was referred to as providing proof of compliance with their attendance at the stipulated number of 12-Step meetings per week in their contract. I questioned what seemed to be the rather obvious illogical basis of this requirement: As 12-Step meetings are, by definition, anonymous and really anybody could sign these forms, there was no way to confirm the authenticity of the signatures. When I voiced this concern to Fiona, an IME physician, her primary interest appeared to be the document completion, not the veracity of the document's contents. As she acknowledged, "I mean, it's entirely possible for somebody to lie on that part of it [attending 12-Step meetings], and we have no method of checking up on that because they're anonymous."

Disjunctures in Self-Regulation of Fitness to Practice

Nurses have a professional obligation to *self-regulate* their "fitness to practice" (CNA, 2017, p. 22), meaning that they self-monitor and attend to their state of health such that they are able to practice in accordance with established standards of nursing. Nurses are expected to remove themselves from practice and seek professional help when their state of health could potentially impair their provision of competent nursing care. However, I found how nurses who had been declared to have SUDs encountered unforeseen problems when they did so. These difficulties pertained to another relevant aspect of the HPA (1996, s 32.3(1)), which states that if because of admission to a hospital...for psychiatric care or treatment, or for treatment for addiction to alcohol or drugs [a nurse] is unable to practise, the chief administrative officer of the hospital, or someone acting in that capacity, and the medical practitioner who has the care of the [nurse] must promptly report the admission in writing to the [regulatory body].

Participant data revealed how nurses' personal health care providers interpreted and applied this statute inconsistently. Some participants had been admitted to hospital and had not been reported to their employer and/or regulatory body because their health care providers did not see it as necessary to do so. This was because the nurse was self-regulating and had not worked while impaired, not diverted drugs, and returned to work following treatment only when medically cleared to do so. Conversely, some other nurses' health care providers believed that it was their obligation to report them simply because they had been hospitalized and a diagnosis of SUD came to light, even though they had neither diverted drugs, nor been impaired at work, and were following medical advice.

Diane describes her experience of being hospitalized for a serious, non-substance use related health issue and was reported to authorities, per her health care provider's understanding of the HPA, because she had a diagnosis of a co-occurring SUD, despite her substance use having never affecting her nursing practice. She found this action unnecessary and heavy-handed, and her experience in The Program so intrusive and oppressive that it worsened her state of health. In the end, she seriously regretted seeking medical assistance at all

> There were never any practice concerns, no professional misconduct, no using anything while working, and I voluntarily went to a hospital, not realizing that this was the worst decision I could have made for my health.

In addition to the harms that she felt this process caused her personal health, Diane also felt that this action was counter-productive to the HPA's original aim of protecting the public from impaired nursing practice: "[this] actually puts the public at greater risk because once nurses know how this works, they may decide to hide any issues they are having to avoid getting entangled in all of this."

This ethnographic data provided by Diane and other nurses in the study concurred with findings in the nursing literature that nurses avoid seeking help for substance use problems when they perceive the help to be ultimately unsupportive to them and that such treatment avoidance is counter-productive to the goal of mitigating risk to the public (Kunyk, 2015; Kunyk & Austin, 2011; Monroe et al., 2013).

I also saw how, once categorized by their SUD diagnosis, the standardized processes within the ruling complex of The Program would focus solely on the nurse's substance use problems, overshadowing and obscuring their other co-occurring health conditions that may have indeed impaired their practices. Harvey recounted an example of this bureaucratic tunnel-vision, whereby his problems with mental health, which he identified as the primary health issue that brought him to seek treatment, was not monitored in any way during or following his time in The Program. He told me

> I never had any issues at work, I never had any attendance problems, never had any performance problems, was never intoxicated at work. The only reason that I entered the program was because I was hospitalized for a psychiatric condition, and while I was in hospital was diagnosed with a substance use disorder [and entered into The Program. Subsequently] ... I was never referred to a psychiatrist to assess my mental fitness to return to work.

This situation not only has serious implications for the nurses' well-being, but also their safety to practice, as data have also shown that nurses' ability to practice safely can be severely impaired by untreated emotional and psychological dysfunction (Smith & Hukill, 1996).

Deputizing Nurse Peers to Monitor Colleagues

To gain their experiential knowledge of how nurses reintegrated back into the workplace following treatment for substance use problems, I gathered ethnographic data from nurses who had worked closely with nurses who were enrolled in The Program and had returned to work. One such nurse, Jean, described how she and other nurse colleagues experienced considerable stress from the work of monitoring and policing their peers that fell on their shoulders, greatly adding to their already heavy workloads. She recounted how they were ultimately left feeling under-resourced, powerless, and resentful, saying

> The onus falls on the staff nurses to monitor this... you have to be aware of the stress level it puts on an existing unit... to be policing my peers for the safety of the patients...narcotic prescriptions for patients going missing, urine specimens going missing...How do I handle this? Because honestly... you usually don't know. You're so taken aback; you're like okay, now what do I do with this information? My manager would say to me "well, did you confront her?" And I said, "is that my job to be confronting her?" And [my manager] said "well, you have to"....[but] unless you actually see the person take it...and I have to be 100% sure to actually come out and say "I think you're impaired"... Do I have a right to say that to her? [both the Union and management] would say..."document, document, document and bring it to me"... [but] what am I supposed to be reporting? You can't do anything except report [and] you have to be very careful that it doesn't look like a witch hunt, right?...[and you can't document at the time], you're doing it at the end [of shift] or when you go home.

These data that Jean provided concurred with Bettinardi-Angres and Bologeorges's (2011) study that found nurse colleagues in these situations were reluctant to confront peers due to fear of reprisals, resentful of doing the additional work that policing their peers represented as they already felt too overworked with their own job demands, and hesitant to address their peers' possible impairment because of their lack of expertise and knowledge. O'Neill and Cadiz (2014) also indicated that without necessary preparation, those designated to monitor the nurse's practice may not have the knowledge and skills to identify when a nurse is impaired, or the power to take action when they do. Jean's statements echoed this finding, as she and her colleagues had neither the managerial knowledge needed to competently monitor and document these matters, nor the administrative authority to take actions necessary to remedy the issue.

Even though much of this burden fell to peers, administrators did play a role in monitoring a nurse's ability to provide competent nursing care upon return to work following assessment and treatment and did so by means of an accountability circuit. This process entailed a designate of the nurse's employer, either the nurse's manager or an individual in the human resources department, completing quarterly reports and submitting them to a regulatory body program administrator. These reports included information on a number of concerns: whether or not there had been any issues with the nurse's behavior or functioning in the workplace, attendance, ability to meet established nursing standards, and if there had been concerns identified, whether or not these had been discussed with the nurse. If the employer's designate was a human resources employee, they received this information from the nurse's manager and may not have ever met with the nurse. The nurses' managers themselves may or may not have directly observed the practice of the nurse in question. This was because in the management structure of many regional hospitals, managers generally have administrative responsibilities in several clinical areas, and have little if any direct nursing supervisory presence in the patient care areas. These actualities were of great concern, considering that O'Neill's (2015) and others' (O'Neill & Cadiz, 2014) assertions that the assignment of worksite monitors who are both qualified and have direct knowledge of the nurse's practice is a critical element of monitoring nurses' job performances following their return to work from treatment.

I was also left to wonder how the managers who did not directly observe the nurse's performance collected their data and how much in the way of the actual performance concerns were captured and registered in this accountability circuit. This was because the ethnographic data that Jean provided above revealed that many of her colleagues refused to "get involved" or report their concerns to administration. Even though they were concerned for the safety of their patients, they elected to not report colleagues' presumed impairment because they both feared retaliation and believed it was the administrators' jobs to do so. Furthermore, Jean also told me how many of these incidents happened after hours when management was not available to see the concerns for themselves, and/or the peers' documentation was completed well after the incidents of concern occurred. As a result, when administrators did follow up reports that the nurse peers did make, the situation that may have endangered patients was often long over.

The Textual Organization of Impaired Nursing Practice as an Individual Issue

In IE, identifying what is excluded from the construction of an official factual account is as important as what is included (Chapman et al., 2016). Not only did nurse participants clearly and repeatedly link their conditions of work with the development and worsening of their substance use problems, many connected improvements in their working conditions to their recoveries from substance use problems.[4] It was therefore a significant discovery that the conditions of nurses' work that may have initiated or exacerbated their substance use problems were scarcely addressed, if at all in The Program contracts. The few contractual items that did pertain to the nurses' working conditions were decontextualized, heavily individuated, and constrained to two features. One was limitations placed on their scheduled shiftwork and hours of work for a specified period of time upon their returns to work, with graduated increases back to their regular schedule patterns. These restrictions were intended to assist the nurses to cope with the demands of their work while in their early stages of their recovery.

The second feature was the restriction of the nurse's access to drugs upon their return to work. Yet, nurses in the study identified entrenched organizational arrangements that subverted the worthy intentions of these contractual restrictions. For instance, participants reported that, because of workload time-pressures, nurse colleagues would routinely "cut corners" with the institutional requirement that peers co-sign narcotic wastage in the designated texts assigned to manage handling of controlled drugs. This enabled nurses who were diverting drugs to do so more easily. Paul, a nurse in The Program, also identified how a historical, imbalanced power relation between physicians and nurses usurped the regulations for the safe handling of controlled drugs in his workplace. He noted

> The doctors that I work with continue to be lax with their handling of narcotics....the regulations are that [disposing of wasted narcotics is] witnessed by someone else and wasted down the garbage, sink, whatever...but in our facility, there is no witnessed wasting by the anesthetists... [they say] "oh I can't do it that way!"

Paul said he felt that his employer should be compelled to adhere to these established regulations. I asked him if he had considered formally reporting this matter to the provincial statutory body mandated to oversee workplace injury, but he replied that he felt too intimidated, fearful of repercussions, and ashamed to do so. He elaborated on his reluctance

> I have no plans on entertaining that idea. Things are working out well for me and if I initiated a claim, I believe things would become difficult...[the anaesthetists] would perceive it as a personal attack...[and] it would look like I was not taking personal responsibility for my actions. I do not want to rock the boat. I have humiliated myself enough.

No features of the nurses' working conditions other than these two were assessed or addressed in the nurses' contracts in The Program, although many could well have been. In this way, the dominant understandings of nurses' substance use problems in The Program had situated the problem of nurses' substance use problems within the individual nurse, while the role of the institution was erased from its conceptualization. This approach to management of nurses in The Program stood in stark contrast to the position of contemporary population and public health researchers, who regard environmental conditions as primary contributors to substance use problems (Rhodes, 2009). It is also of note that nurses have been found to face particularly overwhelming and intense working conditions that create substantial workplace obstacles to their recovery from substance use problems (Shaw, McGovern, Angres, & Rawal, 2004).

This IE analysis revealed how the ruling individuated, decontextualized discourses also displaced and rendered invisible factors other than nurses' substance use problems that could cause impaired nursing practice. Given my considerable experiential knowledge of the actualities of nurses' working conditions that could interfere with safe, competent care provision to the public, I asked Candace, a Program Administrator, about how they addressed other matters external to individual nurses that could impair nursing practice. She informed me that these issues fell outside of the regulatory body's mandate

> CR: just so I can contextualize this whole process: how are other structural impairments to nurses' safety in practice addressed?...[that have] nothing to do with substance use... if the understaffing is so bad – the lack of resources – that I can't practice safely, how is that [addressed]... is there a process?
> CANDACE: It's [between] the employer and...the union in terms of working conditions. If you're complaining about the system, we do not have jurisdiction.... You can only complain to us about another registrant...We can only respond to the complaint about a nurse.

Nurses' working conditions in the province were indeed matters addressed by contractual negotiations between the labor union and employers; however, I found it very difficult to understand how the regulatory body could have no influence or concern in institutional matters in the pursuit of their mandate for public safety. Many working conditions not addressed, let alone remediated, in The Program contracts have nevertheless been well identified in the nursing literature as causing impaired nursing practice and which therefore arguably have serious implications for public safety. These include: fatigue, understaffing, workplace bullying, and violence, among others (Bérastégui, Jaspar, Ghuysen, & Nyssen, 2018; Beletsky, Wakeman, & Fiscella, 2019; Canadian Nursing Advisory Committee, 2002; Caruso et al., 2017; Chapnick, 2016; Claire et al., 2017; D'Sa, Ploeg, Fisher, Akhtar-Danesh, & Peachey, 2018; Gantt Grace, 2016; MacDonald, 2016; MacKinnon, 2011; Shamian et al., 2001; Storch, 2005). Moreover, I would assert that the provincial regulatory body *does* involve itself with concerns pertaining to organizations and not solely those with individual nurses. As one example, it accredits the schools of nursing within its provincial jurisdiction (BCCNP, 2018), a process focused entirely on assessing how an institution meets the established nursing standards, and it is one in which I have personally been involved several times.

One might also assume that the health care institutions that employ nurses would be at the vanguard of adopting progressive measures to promote healthy work environments, but my analysis of relevant institutional texts showed that this is apparently not the case. For example, the Quality Worklife-Quality Healthcare Collaborative (TQWQHC) has established standards and guidelines for manageable workloads and the provision of sufficient resources for workers to carry out their jobs that are considered to be the best practices for healthy workplaces (Cavanaugh, 2014). Despite the encouragement of The Canadian Healthcare Association for all Canadian health care organizations to voluntarily adopt the TQWQHC standards, they have not done so to date (Cavanaugh, 2014).

In the rare instances where I did find that the texts at the health care institutional policy level had acknowledged that workplace environmental factors were contributory to substance use problems, the responsibility for the problem was nonetheless neatly redistributed back to the individual. To wit, in a guiding policy document for health care organizations on substance abuse in the workplace, the Accreditation standards and goals provided therein were entirely focused on the individual, save one, titled: "Providing a healthy work environment" (Addressing Substance Misuse in Healthcare Committee [ASMIHC], 2007, p. 2). In missing the point entirely of what might be involved in an organization's provision of a healthy workplace environment, this goal was accompanied by a lone, individually focused strategy to accomplish this objective: "educating the workforce to better manage their own health" (ASMIHC, 2007, p. 2).

In this study, I have explicated how the institutional processes in The Program ultimately subordinated the nurses' experiences therein with conceptual categorizations of nurses' substance use problems and ideological understandings of public protection. The discoveries arising from this IE analysis and implications for action are summarized and discussed in what follows.

Conclusions and Recommendations

The IE mode of inquiry is a sociology that interrogates and reveals how people are categorized, then ruled through conceptual understandings of these categories (DeVault & McCoy, 2006, p. 39). My IE analysis of The Program uncovered the regulatory power exercised in a way that organized nurses' substance use practices to conform to pre-established discursive categories around danger to the public and its mitigation that were grounded in custom and ideologies rather than evidence. These categorizations were taken up as official facts that reconstructed, displaced, and ultimately subordinated, the nurses' experiences.

Campbell (1988) asserted that "[r]uling, through documentary processes, is the production of structured appearances" (p. 34). Such structured appearances were found in The Program in the form of accountability circuits, which offered a public display of due diligence that ostensibly monitored nurses' safety to practice, but in actuality audited their compliance to a standardized regime. The Program served as an exemplar of Lewington's (2018) elucidation of the difference between good documents and good policy, in that its textually mediated policies often created obstacles instead of solving the problems they were intended to. The conceptual knowledge guiding The Program's policies was activated in ways that snared nurses who were arguably not dangerous to the public into discriminatory, largely illogical, and ineffective regimes. Nurses avoided obtaining the help they needed for substance use problems due to the unduly intrusive and restrictive standardized approach. Its singular focus on conceptual understandings of substance use problems precluded effective monitoring when the nurse did have problems with mental health and other health conditions that could have led to harm to themselves and others in their care.

Thorough individualized assessments of nurses' actual workplace activities and conditions of work need to be carried out to assess nurses' safety to practice instead of exclusive utilization of a standardized theoretical diagnosis and ideological conceptualizations of substance use problems. Evidence-supported, valid evaluative tools do exist that can assist worksite monitors to assess nurses' fitness to practice on an individualized, case-by-case basis and need to be seriously considered for use with nurses (Cadiz, Truxillo, & O'Neill, 2015).

Campbell and Gregor (2002) made the salient observation that the negative effects of institutional power may appear as individual nurses' personal problems. Nowhere have I seen such a manifestation of organizational power more clearly than in The Program. The role of the workplace has been excluded from the individuated, decontextualized construction of nurses' impaired practice, the consequent danger to the public, and its mitigation. Individual nurses have been organizationally conceptualized as instruments of danger, rather than people who are ends in themselves and who work in extremely challenging environments that can and do contribute to harm to them and the public they serve. Nurses' everyday conditions of work need to be considered in the evaluation of their practice impairment and addressed in establishing the stipulations for their returns to work.

Organizational policies that focus on the creation of healthy workplaces would certainly be a positive step toward addressing nurses' vulnerability to workplace-related health harms, including substance use problems. Unfortunately, I have not seen any indication that policy-makers or nursing scholars have embraced investigating or tending to these matters with any enthusiasm to date. The work of mitigating the risk of nurses' impaired practice has instead been redistributed to inadequately resourced peers, who have been de facto deputized to oversee their colleagues.

Because of the institutional inaction toward confronting the realities of nurses' workplaces that contribute to their impaired practice, it is very likely that this job will continue to fall to nurses. It is time, therefore, for nurses themselves to create the new ruling relations to do just that. Deveau (2009) asserted that "once the ideological connections become clear, the ideological process can be infiltrated and transformed by those who are marginalized and oppressed by it" (p. 11). This IE has revealed the ruling ideological frames in The Program, such that the information herein can be utilized in accordance with the final aim of IE research: to provide a working tool for sociopolitical change in the interests of the people involved (Smith, 2005). Nurses can use this knowledge to begin a process of building capacity within the profession to self-advocate and initiate political reforms that target the sources of harm to nurses and those for whom they provide care that are embedded in nurses' working conditions. Nurses must be empowered with the knowledge and skills they need to effectively identify and support colleagues who are struggling with substance use problems, instead of simply teaching them how to report wrongdoing. A new Program must be created that is not divorced from the reality of nurses' actual working conditions and that ultimately serves the needs of nurses and those in their care.

Notes

1. The regulatory body in the province in this study is governed by its Board, which is composed of an equal number of (a) registrants (nurses), who are voted in by registrants, and (b) members of the public, who are appointed by the provincial Ministry of Health (BCCNP, 2020a). Regulatory and Board Support Committees carry out the mandate of the regulatory body through statutory powers as outlined in its bylaws. These committees are also comprised of members of the public and registrants, all of whom are vetted volunteers. The Inquiry Committee (2020c) is the committee that adjudicates the cases of nurses in The Program, initially and on an ongoing basis. They meet in panels of three to review files. Volunteers apply and are vetted by the regulatory body's Governance Coordinator using established criteria, none of which include any knowledge or expertise in substance use problems.
2. The twelve-step facilitation approach to assisting individuals with substance use problems is based upon the tenets of Alcoholics Anonymous (AA). AA

is a community-based, peer-led group support organization that is founded on a belief system whereby problems with substance use are viewed as a medical disorder and people's uncorrected spiritual and characterological flaws (Nowinski, Baker, & Carroll, 1999). In turn, recovery is seen as the correction of these said defects.
3. Nurse and Program Administrator participants told me that several of the IMEs in The Program held financial interest in these private laboratories. The issue of potential conflicts of interest with respect to this matter has been interrogated in another work drawn from this data set (see: Ross et al., 2019).
4. See another work extracted from these data (Ross, Jakubec, Berry, & Smye, 2018) for a more extensive discussion of this finding.

REFERENCES

Addressing Substance Misuse in Healthcare Committee. (2007). *Building a framework: Taking action on alcohol and drugs in the workplace. A resource kit for healthcare organizations.*

American Psychiatric Association. (2013). *Diagnostic and statistical manual of mental disorders* (5th ed.). Arlington, VA: American Psychiatric Association.

Astrab Fogger, S., & McGuinness, T. (2009). Alabama's nurse monitoring programs: The nurse's experience of being monitored. *Journal of Addictions Nursing, 20*(3), 142–149. https://doi.org/10.1080/10884600903078928.

Beletsky, L., Wakeman, S. E., & Fiscella, K. (2019). Practicing what we preach—Ending Physician health program bans on opioid-agonist therapy. *New England Journal of Medicine, 381,* 796–798. https://doi.org/10.1056/NEJMp1907875.

Bérastégui, P., Jaspar, M., Ghuysen, A., & Nyssen, A. S. (2018). Fatigue-related management in the emergency department: A focus-group study. *Internal and Emergency Medicine, 13*(8), 1273–1281.

Bettinardi-Angres, K., & Bologeorges, S. (2011). Addressing chemically dependent colleagues. *Journal of Nursing Regulation, 2*(2), 10–17. https://doi.org/10.1016/S2155-8256(15)30281-7.

British Columbia College of Nursing Professionals. (2018). *Nursing education program & course review policies.* Retrieved from https://www.bccnp.ca/becoming_a_nurse/Documents/RN_NP_EdProgCourseReviewPolicy_490.pdf#search=accreditation.

British Columbia College of Nursing Professionals. (2020a). *BCCNP governance.* Retrieved from https://www.bccnp.ca/bccnp/governance/Pages/Default.aspx.

British Columbia College of Nursing Professionals. (2020b). *Duty to report: Narcotic diversion and substance abuse impairing practice.* Retrieved from https://www.bccnp.ca/Standards/all_nurses/resources/dutytoreport/drug_diversion/Pages/reporting_responsibilities.aspx.

British Columbia College of Nursing Professionals. (2020c). *Inquiry Committee.* Retrieved from https://www.bccnp.ca/bccnp/governance/committees/Pages/inquiry.aspx.

British Columbia College of Nursing Professionals. (2020d). *Standards.* Retrieved from https://www.bccnp.ca/Standards/RN_NP/ProfessionalStandards/Pages/Default.aspx.

Cadiz, D. M., Truxillo, D. M., & O'Neill, C. (2015). Common risky behaviours checklist: A tool to assist nurse supervisors to assess unsafe practice. *Journal of Nursing Management, 23*(6), 794–802. https://doi.org/10.1111/jonm.12214. Epub 2014 Oct 3. https://doi.org/10.1007/978-3-319-41174-3_3.

Campbell, M. (1988). Management as "ruling": A class phenomenon in nursing. *Studies in Political Economy, 27,* 29–51.

Campbell, M. L., & Gregor, F. (2002). *Mapping social relations: A primer in doing institutional ethnography.* Walnut Creek, CA: AltaMira Press.

Canadian Nurses Association. (2017). *Code of ethics for registered nurses.* Retrieved from https://www.cna-aiic.ca/~/media/cna/page-content/pdf-en/code-of-ethics-2017-edition-secure-interactive.pdf?la=en.

Canadian Nursing Advisory Committee. (2002). *Our health, our future: Creating quality workplaces for Canadian nurses.* Retrieved from https://www.canada.ca/en/health-canada/services/health-care-system/reports-publications/nursing/health-future-creating-quality-workplaces-canadian-nurses-final-report-canadian-nursing.html.

Cavanaugh, S. (2014). Improving psychological health in the workplace. *The Canadian Nurse, 110*(3), 31–33. Retrieved from http://www.cna-aiic.ca.

Chapman, C., Azevedo, J., Ballen, R., & Poole, R. (2016). A kind of collective freezing-out: How helping professionals' regulatory bodies create "incompetence" and increase distress. In B. Burstow (Ed.), *Psychiatry interrogated: An Institutional Ethnography anthology* (pp. 41–61). Cham: Palgrave Macmillan.

Chapnick, J. (2014, November). *Beyond the label: Rethinking workplace substance use policies.* Paper presented to the Human Rights Conference, Vancouver, Canada.

Chapnick, J. (2016). *Test 'em all: Drug testing law & policy.* Retrieved from https://www.academia.edu/27188393/Test_Em_All_Drug_Testing_Law_and_Policy.

Claire C. C., Baldwin, C. M., Berger, A., Chasens, E. R., Landis, C., Redeker, N. S., … Trinkoff, A. (2017). Position statement: Reducing fatigue associated with sleep deficiency and work hours in nurses. *Nursing Outlook, 65*(6), 766–768. https://doi.org/10.1016/j.outlook.2017.10.011.

Darbro, N. (2005). Alternative diversion programs for nurses with impaired practice: Completers and non-completers. *Journal of Addictions Nursing, 16*(4), 169–185. https://doi.org/10.1080/10884600500328155.

Darbro, N. (2011). Model guidelines for alternative programs and discipline monitoring programs. *Journal of Nursing Regulation, 2*(1), 42–49. https://doi.org/10.1016/S2155-8256(15)30301-X.

Deacon, B. J. (2013). The biomedical model of mental disorder: A critical analysis of its validity, utility, and effects on psychotherapy research. *Clinical Psychology Review, 33*(7), 846–861. https://doi.org/10.1016/j.cpr.2012.09.007.

Deveau, J. L. (2009). Examining the institutional ethnographer's toolkit. *Socialist Studies/Études Socialistes, 4*(2), 1–19. Retrieved from http://www.socialiststudies.com/index.php/sss/article/view/63/59.

DeVault, M. L., & McCoy, L. (2006). Institutional ethnography: Using interviews to investigate ruling relations. In D. E. Smith (Ed.), *Institutional ethnography as practice* (pp. 15–44). Lanham, MD: Rowman & Littlefield.

D'Sa, M., Ploeg, J., Fisher, A., Akhtar-Danesh, N., & Peachey, G. (2018). Potential dangers of nursing overtime in critical care. *Nursing Research, 31*(3), 48–60. https://doi.org/10.12927/cjnl.2018.25677.

Dunn, D. (2005). Substance abuse among nurses—Intercession and intervention. *AORN Journal*, *82*(5), 775–804. https://doi.org/10.1016/S0001-2092(06)60271-8.

DuPont, R. L., McLellan, A. T., White, W. L., Merlo, L. J., & Gold, M. S. (2009). Setting the standard for recovery: Physicians' health programs. *Journal of Substance Abuse Treatment*, *36*(2), 159–171. https://doi.org/10.1016/j.jsat.2008.01.004.

Fraser Health Authority. (2018). *Corporate policy, standards and procedure: Alcohol and drug use*. Retrieved from https://www.fraserhealth.ca/-/media/Project/FraserHealth/FraserHealth/About-Us/Accountability/Policies/Alcohol_and_drug_use_policy.pdf.

Gantt Grace, G. (2016). *Being bullied in the workplace and impaired professional performance: The lived experience of nurses*. Doctoral Dissertation, University of Phoenix, Arizona, USA. Available from ProQuest (document ID1880564718).

Griffith, A. I., & Smith, D. E. (2014). Introduction. In A. I. Griffith & D. E. Smith (Eds.), *Under new public management* (pp. 3–21). Toronto: University of Toronto Press.

Health Professions Act, RSBC 1996, c 183. Retrieved from http://www.bclaws.ca/civix/document/id/complete/statreg/96183_01.

Horton-Deutsch, S., McNelis, A., & O'Haver Day, P. (2011). Enhancing mutual accountability to promote quality, safety, and nurses' recovery from substance use disorders. *Archives of Psychiatric Nursing*, *25*(6), 445–455. https://doi.org/10.1016/j.apnu.2011.02.002.

Interior Health Authority. (2013). *Procedural guidelines for policy AU0200—Substance use disorder*. Retrieved from https://www.interiorhealth.ca/AboutUs/BusinessCentre/Construction/Documents/Substance%20Use%20Disorder%20Procedural%20Guidelines.pdf.

Kunyk, D. (2015). Substance use disorders among registered nurses: Prevalence, risks and perceptions in a disciplinary jurisdiction. *Journal of Nursing Management*, *23*(1), 54–64. https://doi.org/10.1111/jonm.12081.

Kunyk, D., & Austin, W. (2011). Nursing under the influence: A relational ethics perspective. *Nursing Ethics*, *19*(3), 380–389. https://doi.org/10.1177/0969733011406767.

Lawson, N. D., & Boyd, J. W. (2018). Flaws in the methods and reporting of physician health program outcome studies. *General Hospital Psychiatry*, *54*, 65–66. https://doi.org/10.1016/j.genhosppsych.2018.06.002.

Lenzer, J. (2016). Physician health programs under fire. *The BMJ*, *353*. https://doi.org/10.1136/bmj.i3568.

Lewington, S. (2018). *The power of policy: Investigating women's experiences of gender-based violence on campus*. Master's thesis, McGill University, Montreal, Quebec, Canada. Retrieved from http://digitool.library.mcgill.ca/R/-?func=dbin-jump-full&current_base=GEN01&object_id=161319.

MacDonald, S. (2016). *Expert report on Interior Health Authority and Hospital Employees' Union Policy Grievance—IH Policy AU (Substance use disorder)*. British Columbia, Canada.

MacKinnon, K. (2011). Rural nurses' safeguarding work: Reembodying patient safety. *Advances in Nursing Science*, *34*(2), 119–129. https://doi.org/10.1097/ANS.0b013e3182186b86.

Monroe, T. B., Kenaga, H., Dietrich, M. S., Carter, M. A., & Cowan, R. L. (2013). The prevalence of employed nurses identified or enrolled in substance use monitoring programs. *Nursing Research, 62*(1), 10–12. https://doi.org/10.1097/NNR.0b013e31826ba3ca.

Monroe, T. B., & Pearson, F. (2009). Treating nurses and student nurses with chemical dependency: Revising policy in the United States for the 21st century. *International Journal of Mental Health and Addiction, 7*(4), 530–540. https://doi.org/0.1007/s11469-009-9208-2.

Monroe, T. B., Vandoren, M., Smith, L., Cole, J., & Kenaga, H. (2011). Nurses recovering from substance use disorders. *Journal of Nursing Administration, 41*(10), 415–421. https://doi.org/10.1097/NNA.0b013e31822edd5f.

National Council of State Boards of Nursing. (2011). *Substance use disorder in nursing: A resource manual and guidelines for alternative and disciplinary monitoring programs.* Retrieved from https://www.ncsbn.org/SUDN_11.pdf.

Nowinski, J., Baker, S., & Carroll, K. (1999). *Twelve step facilitation therapy manual: A research guide for therapists treating individuals with alcohol abuse and dependence.* Retrieved from https://pubs.niaaa.nih.gov/publications/projectmatch/match01.pdf.

O'Neill, C. (2015). When a nurse returns to work after substance abuse treatment. *American Nurse Today, 10*(7), 8–12. Retrieved from https://www.myamericannurse.com/when-a-nurse-returns-to-work/.

O'Neill, C., & Cadiz, D. (2014). Worksite monitors protect patients from unsafe nursing practices. *Journal of Nursing Regulation, 5*(2), 16–23. https://doi.org/10.1016/S2155-8256(15)30079-X.

Rankin, J. M. (2017a). Conducting analysis in institutional ethnography: Analytical work prior to commencing data collection. *International Journal of Qualitative Methods, 16*(1), 1–9. https://doi.org/10.1177/1609406917734484.

Rankin, J. M. (2017b). Conducting analysis in institutional ethnography: Guidance and cautions. *International Journal of Qualitative Methods, 16*(1), 1–11. https://doi.org/10.1177/1609406917734472.

Rhodes, T. (2009). Risk environments and drug harms: A social science for harm reduction approach. *International Journal of Drug Policy, 20*(3), 193–201. https://doi.org/10.1016/j.drugpo.2008.10.003.

Ross, C. A., Jakubec, S. L., Berry, N. S., & Smye, V. (2018). "A two glass of wine shift": Dominant discourses and the social organization of nurses' substance use. *Global Qualitative Nursing Research Journal, 5*, 1–12. https://doi.org/10.1177/2333393618810655.

Ross, C. A., Jakubec, S. L., Berry, N. S., & Smye, V. (2019). The business of managing nurses' substance use. *Nursing Inquiry, 27*(1), e12324. https://doi.org/10.1111/nin.12324.

Servodidio, C. A. (2011). Alcohol abuse in the workplace and patient safety. *Clinical Journal of Oncology Nursing, 15*(2), 143–145. https://doi.org/10.1188/11.CJON.143-145.

Shamian, J. O'Brien-Pallas, L., Kerr, M., Koehoorn, M., Thomson, D., & Alksnis, C. (2001). *Effects of job strain, hospital organizational factors and individual characteristics on work-related disability among nurses: Final report.* Submitted to the Workplace Safety and Insurance Board (WSIB) of Ontario.

Shaw, M. F., McGovern, M. P., Angres, D. H., & Rawal, P. (2004). Physicians and nurses with substance use disorders. *Journal of Advanced Nursing, 47*(5), 561–571. https://doi.org/10.1111/j.1365-2648.2004.03133.x.

Smith, D. E. (2005). *Institutional ethnography: A sociology for people.* Lanham, MD: Altamira Press.

Smith, G. B., & Hukill, E. (1996). Nurses impaired by emotional and psychological dysfunction. *Journal of the American Psychiatric Nurses Association, 2*(60), 192–200. https://doi.org/10.1177/107839039600200603.

Smith, J., Krinkle, S., & Barnett, P. (2013). Recovery and monitoring program of New Jersey. *Journal of Addiction Nursing, 24*(1), 60–62. https://doi.org/10.1097/JAN.0b013e31828768b4.

Storch, J. L. (2005). Patient safety: Is it just another bandwagon? *Nursing Leadership, 18*(2), 39–55. https://doi.org/10.12927/cjnl.2005.17183.

Strom-Paikin, J. E. (1996). *Characteristics of American nurses and nursing which may contribute to nurses diverting drugs from patients.* Doctoral dissertation, Saybrook Institute. *Dissertation Abstracts International Section A: Humanities and Social Sciences, 56*(9-A), 3613.

Turner, S. M. (2006). Mapping institutions as work and texts. In D. E. Smith (Ed.), *Institutional ethnography as practice* (pp. 139–161). Lanham, MD: Rowman & Littlefield.

Urbanoski, K. A. (2014). *Workplace policies for employee substance misuse: An analysis of Interior Health Authority's policy.* Vancouver, Canada: Substance Use Disorder and Vancouver Coastal Health Authority's substance Use Policy.

CHAPTER 23

Producing *Functional Equivalency* in Video Relay Service

Jeremy L. Brunson

Interpreting scholars have given little attention to the work of sign language interpreting outside the moment of interpreting. Traditional analysis of interpreting has focused on the accuracy of interpretation (Cokely, 1992, Gish, 1987), settings in which interpreters work (Russell, 2002; Smith, 2013; Winston, 2004), and the effect of the interpreter on the interpretive event (Roy, 2000; Stone, 2009). Sign language interpreting has often been viewed as an event that occurs within a moment and space without regard for the socio-historical and remote processes that come to bear on the moment (Brunson, 2015; Pöchhacker, 2004; Roy, Brunson, & Stone, 2019). Two scholars have noted that there is "a dominant discourse developing that relies on the problematic assumption that 'access' for deaf people is tantamount to the availability of sign language interpreters" (De Meulder & Haualand, 2019, pp. 2–3) and have called for an examination of interpreting as a social institution. They note:

I would like to thank the participants for sharing their stories with me. I would also like to thank the editors for their insightful feedback and Cynthia B. Roy and Christopher A. Stone for their meticulous readings of different drafts of this paper.

J. L. Brunson (✉)
Independent Scholar, Phoenix, AZ, USA

© The Author(s) 2021
P. C. Luken and S. Vaughan (eds.), *The Palgrave Handbook of Institutional Ethnography*,
https://doi.org/10.1007/978-3-030-54222-1_23

> Addressing the impact of [Sign Language Interpreting Studies (SLIS)] as a social institution is crucial, especially now, since SLIS now appear to be self-sufficient, institutional services, which seem to be taken for granted by most actors involved, including deaf people. (p. 3)

Interpreting is part of the expansive "institution of access" (Brunson, 2011) whereby access denotes those relations that operate through textually mediated processes to produce, monitor, and define access. The current exploration unfolds the textual production of "functional equivalent" in video relay service as the mandated standard defined by the Federal Communications Commission (FCC).

In this chapter, I discuss how the term functional equivalency becomes defined by the agencies and companies who carry out this communicative service, and the ways in which the discourse about access becomes a discourse about numbers. Throughout this chapter I show the ways in which what gets counted as providing access—interpreting work—changes from an embodied act, to an objective numerical value and how the numerical value becomes part of textual organization of sign language interpreters' work.

Background on Interpreting Work as Access and Functionally Equivalent

In 1990 the United States passed the Americans with Disabilities Act (ADA). This Act guarantees Americans with disabilities protection from discrimination and access to services and spaces other Americans enjoy. One such service is access to telephonic communication for deaf people. Under the Federal Communications Commission, which borrowed language from the ADA, telephone services for deaf people are to be "functionally equivalent" to the phone services non-deaf people use. In 2000, the FCC expanded the definition of telecommunication relay service to include video relay service. Prior to the video relay service, deaf people communicated with non-deaf people through a telecommunication device for the deaf (TDD) whereby deaf people typed their comments and an operator read their comments verbatim to a non-deaf person. Conversely, with video relay service, deaf people use a signed language to communicate with non-signing individuals through an interpreter using video conferencing technologies. The notice from the FCC released on March 6, 2000, regarding video relay service states:

> With this Order, we amend the rules governing the delivery of telecommunications relay services to expand the kinds of relay services available to consumers and to improve the quality of relay services, based on our ten years of experience with Telecommunications Relay Service (TRS) and changes in available technologies. Title IV of the Americans with Disabilities Act of 1990 (ADA), which is codified at Sect. 225 of the Communications Act of 1934, as amended

("Communications Act"), requires the Commission to ensure that TRS is available, to the extent possible and in the most efficient manner, to individuals with hearing and speech disabilities in the United States.[1] Section 225 defines relay service to be a telephone transmission service that provides the ability for an individual with a hearing or speech disability to engage in communication by wire or radio with a hearing individual in a manner *functionally equivalent* to someone without such a disability.[2] Section 225 requires the Commission to ensure that interstate and intrastate relay services are available throughout the country and to establish regulations to ensure the quality of relay service.[3] To fulfill this mandate, the Commission first issued rules in 1991.[4] TRS has been available on a uniform, nationwide basis since July 26, 1993.[5] (emphasis added)

Significantly, in this paragraph the FCC connects the goal of "functional equivalency" within the Americans with Disability Act to this new service. With this order, the FCC changed deaf people's telephone experience for the better and created a need for interpreting work to become visible.

Although the FCC is responsible for establishing the rules that govern the provision of these communicative services and for determining the reimbursement rates for companies who provide these services, the FCC in 1983 created an agency, the National Exchange Carrier Association (NECA), to perform telephone industry tariff filings and revenue distributions following the breakup of AT&T.[6] The NECA became the funnel through which tax revenues flowed and revenue was distributed to companies providing interpreting services.

Since the U.S. Congress left the term functionally equivalency undefined, NECA was left to define it operationally and in practice. Using data from video relay service providers, NECA determined that 38% of an hour of interpreting would demonstrate that interpreters were being efficient in their call management and therefore functional equivalency was occurring.

While 38% of an hour may seem a low figure, video relay providers have a stake in keeping efficiency low at this number since it keeps the reimbursement at its current rate. This means that as call volume increases, more interpreters are needed to meet the demand. Additional interpreters lead to increased revenue for video relay service providers.

Framework and Method

Beginning in the everyday/everynight world of sign language interpreters who work in video relay service, I will show how their participation in the organization of their work is through the activation of texts. Texts are connected to other texts which are used as "facts" to receive funding in the United States from the National Exchange Carrier Association (NECA). These courses of action of interpreters, doing their work and filling out forms regarding their work activity, purport to show compliance with the Americans with Disabilities

Act of 1990, a higher order text, a text that regulates and standardizes organizational settings (Smith, 2005). Throughout this process the aim of access becomes distorted.

From 2003 to 2007 I worked as a sign language interpreter for a video relay service provider, Ease Communications, Inc.[7] This study began with a problematic in my own life. While at work one day, I heard a colleague of mine proclaim that we, through our work in the center, were "providing access." While I always believed that interpreting was about providing access, his announcement gave me pause. How were we providing access? What was the measurement of this access? Access to whom? Who endorsed our provision as access? All these questions made me want to understand how this work I was doing was organized and by whom.

Through my work as an interpreter, I met other interpreters who would later become my collaborators on the project I undertook. I collected the data discussed here through interviews with sign language interpreters, managers, supervisors/schedulers, and through participant observations. At other times, impromptu discussions would happen while I was leaving or arriving at a video relay service office. I captured these discussions using "jottings" (Emerson, Fretz, & Shaw, 1995). The interpreters worked in video relay centers in the Northeast and the Southwest of the United States. Interviews lasted, on average, one and a half hours. The interviews and informal discussions occurred in both American Sign Language and English. During the interviews we talked about their respective work in video relay service. I videotaped and transcribed all the interviews and field notes. I then examined the transcripts for institutional traces. Often these traces appeared in the form of a text.

Exploring Standardization

The project started when I attended a training for Ease Communication, Inc. There were eight other sign language interpreters in the training room, and we were in a teleconference with another site that had approximately ten more sign language interpreters. All the trainees were employed as interpreters for Ease Communication, Inc.

The training began with the trainer explaining that "it is important to have standardization in our process." I immediately began to question the feasibility of "standardizing" interpreting. Is it possible? I made a note to myself:

> What do they mean? Why should we aim for standardization? Are we making widgets or are [we] interpreting for two individuals with different aims, backgrounds, and communication needs?" (Field note 01/25/04)

Unlike mathematics or chemistry, there is no formula that consistently yields a successful interpretation. There are too many unknowns that occur in real time. Some of those unknowns are: the language preference of the deaf caller, the context of the interaction (e.g., purpose of these people talking to each other), and the limitations, based on skill and comfort with subject matter, the interpreter brings to the interaction. How comfortable is the non-signing, non-deaf person with the process of video relay service? What are the moods of all the people involved: interpreter, deaf caller, and non-deaf caller? We know that people are unique and what they bring to every situation is also unique (Smith, 2006). These factors (and many others) exist and thus make it difficult to "standardize" interpreting. Yet, the trainer told us that our work would involve standardization.

Sign language interpreters, with few exceptions, have worked autonomously. That is, they rely on skills and knowledge of situations to render interpretations. Interpreters are typically the only person in an event who understands both languages that are being used. Often interpreters must determine a correct course of action for a situation, which might include a reinterpretation to clarify, requesting time to assess the effectiveness of a given interpretation, or even a pause to inform one or both parties that an error in interpretation has been made. The trainer's comment that we now need to standardize our processes was counter to how interpreting work is often done in other contexts.

Standardization is required to allow company employers to measure that which they are attempting to manage. In video relay service this means that interpreting must be made visible. Once it is visible, it can be documented, counted, and organized within a standardization framework. However, communication is not a simple interaction. Drawing on the work of Erving Goffman, Winston and Roy (2015) suggest that

> It is sometimes helpful to think of communication as a cycle. It begins when the first utterance is made and is based on the language choices made by that person. It continues when the other person receives the utterance and uses his or her own understanding of the language choices, context, and content to construct similar meaning. It continues further when that person responds, making his or her own choices of language features to reflect the underlying meaning, and continues still further when the first interactant receives a response, continues to formulate meaning to create further understanding, and then continues with further talk, or a response (p. 97).

Every aspect of communication has an impact on how that communication is understood, and every aspect of communication occurs due to choices made by the communicators. Communication is a dynamic process in constant change depending on the people involved, topic of discussion, the participants' subject knowledge, and much more. When employers attempt to standardize the highly complex process of interpreting, they are attempting to replace this dynamic interaction with a static one.

Making Interpreting Work Visible Through Intertextuality

Part of making interpreting visible requires inscription (Smith, 1984). Inscriptions allows for events to be "known" to another as a "fact" in a document. These facts can be used to demonstrate a crime (Smith, 1988, 2014), a person's mental health (Smith, 1983), the provision of home care services (Campbell, 2008), or, as in the case of video relay service, that interpreters are providing access. Once the facts are produced, they move beyond the immediate and represent actual moments to others who then use their authority to dictate practice. It is in this way that texts concert the work of sign language interpreters in this setting.

Logs and Reports

Two key texts play an important part in the day-to-day work of sign language interpreters at the center: the Accountability Log, the Efficiency Report. These are used to compile the Minutes Generated Report. This report records the billable minutes of interpreters' work that is sent to NECA for services the company provides to deaf people. These logs and reports are automatically generated through the center's computer system.

Amber, a center manager, explained that according to the home office there are two states of being for sign language interpreters: "on call and off call." When interpreters are in their station, available to take a call, they are considered to be "on call." While they are "off call" they are unavailable to accept a call because they are working on a project or otherwise away from their station. "Each month," Amber explains, "we must submit the total number of minutes each interpreter was 'on call' and 'off call' to headquarters." These "on call" minutes add up to dollars.

Amber's point is that interpreters' time is billable to NECA and this only occurs if an interpreter is "on call." All this information Amber is discussing is captured on these logs. As she explains the process for submitting these numbers for interpreters to management, Amber also clarifies how she uses the information contained in these logs to manage and adjust the Efficiency Report for each interpreter. She reports:

> These [two reports: Efficiency Report and Accountability Log] are used within the centers. I use them to see if my people are doing what they are supposed to be doing. They aren't given to the Federal Communications Commission. Once I have adjusted an interpreter's Efficiency Report, I submit both documents to headquarters and they archive them...I think. I want to see how many times my interpreters are off the phones without a reason. I am a bit of a hard ass. I don't mind if people want to take breaks but if they are taking too many breaks then that is going to affect their coworkers and I can't have that happening. So, I use the information to help me manage my interpreters.

From Amber's comments, we see that managers use these texts to document interpreters' work as well as to manage interpreters. Amber's adjustment involves making sure that the two texts align; that is that on-call and off-call minutes match in both documents and the reasons for being off call are recorded and appropriate to allowing Ease Communications, Inc. to submit only billable minutes to NECA. She uses these logs to watch her staff, to "see if [they] are doing what they are supposed to be doing." In addition, her comments about adjusting an interpreter's efficiency report to document the mandated 38% of an hour interpreting demonstrate how, Jacob, a supervisor and scheduler, says Ease Communications is "… meeting the requirements set by the Federal Communications [since we] send NECA our monthly reports stating how many minutes we provided interpreting for." The role of texts is not just to document minutes, but to organize those minutes as well for purposes of accountability for both interpreters and the center alike.

When interpreters are at work in the video relay service centers they use the Accountability Log, a text that is used to adjust the Efficiency Report, to document when they are "off call" and thus unavailable to generate money for Ease Communication, Inc. Interpreters document the start and end time of their "off call" status and their reason for being "off call." Some of the reasons, provided by options on the form, that interpreters must choose from are Technical (issues with equipment), Handoff (switching to another interpreter), Team (helping another interpreter), Training, or Other. Not only do interpreters provide a paper trail of their time, but start time, end time, and total minutes of "off call" status is also tracked by a computer initiated by a call. The Accountability Log does not account for every possible situation. Instead, interpreters are able to use it for the most common occurrences. In addition, interpreters are asked to total the minutes in "off status."

The goal is to account for any time the interpreter is not producing billable minutes so that their efficiency (38%) can be calculated accurately. Moreover, the Accountability Log is not only used to monitor the work of interpreters. Using the Accountability Log, managers can see the number of times there are technical issues that prevent interpreters from producing minutes. They can also see how long training is taking. In this way, even though the sign language interpreters fill out these forms, they are also used to monitor the work of others (i.e., trainers, technology staff, etc.) in the organization.

These reports, although beneficial for Ease Communication, Inc., change how interpreters perform and perceive their work. Estelle, a sign language interpreter with over 30 years of experience, explains:

> One of the biggest things is this concept of our work being evaluated in numeric form, which is not…which you don't experience in the community [when interpreting]. So, things like, for example, how long you are on a call. How efficiently you end one call and pick up another call. It is sort of how they measure these little bits of a task, which is corporate because they want to see how a particular process is flowing. Is the process breaking down? And how can

we make it more efficient so we can get more "bang for our buck." I totally get that. Having that scheme imposed on us as interpreters...it's a different way of thinking about the work that we do.

Estelle's use of the term "efficiently" indicates in that she has begun to adopt the discourse of Ease Communication, Inc. She recognizes that "efficiently" implies a streamlining of processes. She knows that the goal of Ease Communication, Inc. (and other video relay service providers) is to produce an environment and employees in which every movement is money-producing so that the company attains higher profitability.

Requiring interpreters to fill out an Accountability Log makes them accountable to the organization rather than to the users. The log does not provide any space for a discussion or documentation of the practice of sign language interpreting itself (i.e., the actual work of interpreting). Schedulers and managers focus on minutes spent interpreting not whether that time resulted in effective interpretations. Management personnel within the center then analyze and determine the one change that has an impact for them, to maximize the time that sign language interpreters are on the "on call" more.

Many of the interpreters I spoke with and with whom I worked did not know where the report went after they filled it out and placed it in the scheduler's mailbox. One interpreter, Diane, told me, "It just helps them know when we are off the phones. I am not sure how helpful it is though. When I remember, I just check a box. I never really think about why I am off the phone; I just want to make note that I was off the phone." Another interpreter said, "I guess it could be used to pay us." The reality is that the Accountability Log is used to adjust another report, the Efficiency Report. This report, produced by the center manager, is the basis by which Ease Communication, Inc. is paid. While the Accountability Log is used within the particular video relay centers, the Efficiency Report is the basis for preparing a report for billable hours to NECA.

Each Efficiency Report is a sterile accounting of the interpreter's work shift. It documents the time the interpreter has logged in and logged out of the phone services within a center. Supervisor provide each interpreter with an Efficiency Report on a weekly basis. In addition to the dates and times the interpreter logged in and logged out, the report tallies the time between logging in and logging out. During a shift there can be multiple logins and logouts captured. It also provides a total number of minutes the interpreter was logged in and available to accept calls. The login times lets management at Ease Communication, Inc. know whether or not interpreters arrive on time, a time not billed to NECA. Another non-billable time is called "set up" time, a time for interpreters to get ready to accept calls. Logout times are the final times an interpreter is unavailable, but is also an indication of shift length, thus a tool for scheduling. Since interpreters are paid their hourly wage whether they are "on call" or not, management needs to make sure that interpreters are scheduled efficiently.

Jacob, a supervisor, explained that while the login and logout times are important, the Daily Total minutes, which are also shown on the Efficiency Report, are more important. During each hour, interpreters are required to be on the phones interpreting for at least twenty-four minutes. Therefore, for an eight-hour shift, minus the half-hour lunch, sign language interpreters should be available to take calls (and hopefully producing minutes) for approximately one hundred and eighty minutes (three hours). When the interpreters are not available for an average of twenty-four minutes per hour, they are considered to not be performing (i.e., not being efficient). The Daily Minutes for each interpreter for a given month is tallied and submitted to NECA in another report, the Minutes Generated report. Management adjusts the Minutes Generated using the Accountability Log. The staff at the corporate office then submit the total number of billable minutes to NECA for reimbursement.

The Efficiency Report is used in additional processes. During the hiring process, I was told by the manager of the Southwest facility that it is used to document the number of minutes per shift an interpreter is logged into the system and available to accept calls. But it is also used to monitor interpreters' attendance. And, supervisors use it to check against the weekly invoice or timecard of each interpreter to ensure the time the interpreters are billing for is the time they were on the phones.

The Efficiency Report allows management to calculate, for a given time period, the number of minutes an interpreter is logged in as well as not logged into the phones. The Accountability Log can be used to adjust the Efficiency Report so interpreters are not penalized for being away from the phones for "acceptable" reasons. Nancy, the scheduler at one of the centers, told me:

> I look at the Accountability Log and then I compare it to their Efficiency Report. If there is a time that they are off the phones [which I can see from the Efficiency Report] then they should have it documented on the Accountability Log. Most of the time they do. Sometimes they don't and I have to ask them what happened. But if it is there then I can just adjust their Efficiency Report so they don't get into trouble.

If a sign language interpreter is considered to be off the phones for an excessive amount of time, they could be approached by the manager and face sanctions; however, this is not Diane's concern. When she says "get into trouble," she means that they need to be accountable. Diane explains,

> Well it isn't like they are going to get fired. I just mean that this way numbers look ok. If I didn't adjust [the numbers] then we wouldn't know why they weren't taking calls.

Furthermore, there are other layers of accountability. That is, "the numbers" have to "look okay" to the center management who can presumably show the numbers to their superiors to demonstrate sound management over their center. In this way, management uses the Efficiency Report and Accountability Log to organize the work of sign language interpreters and the work of their supervisors.

Managers also use the Efficiency Report to determine what shift an interpreter receives. Elizabeth, a sign language interpreter who has worked for Ease Communication, Inc. since it opened a center in her hometown, told me that she was informed that the shifts are given based on efficiency. Even though Elizabeth was warned to "make her numbers," she has never heard of anyone not being allowed to work because of the numbers in their Efficiency Report:

> I know many interpreters who are never on the phone but they are still here. Also, I heard of one interpreter who got into trouble because he had really high numbers but they found out that he was really talking to his friends, not interpreting. I guess it doesn't matter because Ease Communication, Inc. still gets paid.

Here, Elizabeth is talking about a situation when someone in her center was said to have made calls from his cellular phone to video relay and then placing outgoing calls on his video phone to be billable while not actually interpreting. This interpreter was accused of tricking the system meant to ensure he was providing a functionally equivalent service.

Changing the Focus of Interpreting

The focus on functional equivalency, as measured by efficiency, and the way a company receives payment is an aspect of the work that frustrates some of the interpreters. Julia, for example, had worked for Ease Communication, Inc. for six months before she decided to stop because she felt a conflict between the field of sign language interpreting, which she sees as service driven, and Ease Communication, Inc. which is driven by the capacity "to make money." She expressed her frustration with the emphasis on numbers rather than effective interpretations:

> I hated the work. I hated it...I felt so schizophrenic. I had to be this and then be that. I was constantly being told not to do what I had been trained to do, as an interpreter. Don't deal with the language, deal with the mechanics. Don't be personable, be a robot. Don't deal with culture and language issues, just say the fucking thing and get your minutes counted so we can get paid by the FCC.

Other complaints focused on how the log and reports were used to manage interpreters. According to Elizabeth, the measurement of efficiency is a means by which Ease Communication, Inc., rewards or penalizes sign language interpreters by denying them their preferred shifts. And Julia points out, it is essential that Ease Communication, Inc. be able to tally minutes for reimbursement, and this can, at least in Julia's experience, create a stressful situation.

This accounting method examines productivity in terms of dollars and cents rather than effectiveness. The goal of access then may begin to seem secondary, or even tertiary, to making money.

What Elizabeth and Julia are talking about is what Espeland & Stevens (1998) refers to as "commensuration—the transformation of different qualities into a common metric" (p. 314). This process can "render some aspects of life invisible or irrelevant..." (p. 314). To be held accountable to the mandate of the FCC, video relay providers require interpreters' work to become numerical. Managements' aim of making interpreting visible to document access is counter to how Julia and many other interpreters value it, and this creates stress. However, management must be able to tally interpreting so they can send these numbers to funding agencies.

Minutes Generated Report

Sign language interpreters are not the only ones who must be accountable. As McCoy (1998) points out, "At the interface between organizations, accounting categories work to align one organization's work processes with those of others (funders, creditors, customers)" (p. 396). Although these reports are used internally to organize the work of sign language interpreters, they are also used to produce external reports so that the Ease Communication, Inc. can receive remuneration for their services and demonstrate that it follows the regulations established by various organizations.

Although management takes seriously the interests and needs of the interpreters to operate within these human limitations and occupational safety guidelines (Woodcock & Fischer, 2008), the video relay service providers manipulate efficiency numbers. Again, Jacob, a supervisor at Ease Communications, Inc., comments on this:

> The industry realizes the importance of keeping the efficiency low. Well, of course, we are in it to make a profit, but at the same time if the efficiency rate gets too high then there will be a demand for interpreters to produce more minutes. Which means that repetitive motion injuries, carpel tunnel syndrome, emotional trauma that occurs during calls, that interpreters do not experience out in the community, would increase. It would cause a lot of problems. In some ways efficiencies are kept artificially low to protect interpreters and to keep the reimbursement rate high.

To keep the efficiency artificially low, video relay service providers might employ more trainee interpreters so that the more experienced interpreters are spending more time providing guidance to newer interpreters than they are processing calls. That is, while these experienced interpreters are providing guidance to the newer interpreters, they are typically logged off the system and unable to take calls. These unanswered calls are used as justification for

Ease Communication, Inc. and other video relay providers to point to as a rationale for not raising NECA's efficiency percentage.

Trainee interpreters are those interpreters who do not hold a national certification. Without a national certification, trainees are typically less likely to find employment through interpreter referral agencies that supply interpreters outside of video relay. On average they are paid considerably less than a certified interpreter. While relying on non-certified interpreters to process calls, and using certified interpreters to provide guidance does help reduce burnout and protects sign language interpreters from forms of repetitive motion trauma, it also creates a pool of video relay interpreters who, once trained, will be a cheaper form of labor for video relay providers. In addition, newer interpreters who lack experience may take longer to process the same call that a seasoned interpreter could do quickly. This is because a newer interpreter may require more clarification before providing an interpretation of a message. In North Carolina, for example, the sign used for TRUCK means GRASS in Arizona due to lexical variations. Some interpreters have greater exposure to variations because they have lived in different states, others by virtue of working for a long time in the field are able to discern these regional variations with ease. During the time the newer or less experienced interpreter is getting clarification, they are still "on call" and thus these are billable minutes in accordance with NECA. Accordingly, while Jacob suggests that Ease Communication, Inc. is concerned about the well-being of sign language interpreters, their decisions are also tied to potential earnings.

A focus on billable minutes can create confusion among the interpreters since they are unsure as to the priorities of the company. Estelle blames this confusion on a lack of understanding of the "corporate culture" of Ease Communication, Inc.:

> The corporate culture...it isn't clear what [Ease Communication, Inc.] wants from me as far as the corporate culture. Do they really want me to be efficient, hitting my targets, and I do hit all my numbers so that really isn't an issue? But let's suppose two or three years from now they want to up the ante like they want to increase their efficiency to 95 percent because [Ease Communication, Inc.] wants to do better...Right now the pressure isn't on. What is the corporate culture you are trying to make? Do you want to be a company known for good customer service?

Like all the interpreters I spoke with, Estelle understands that Ease Communication, Inc. is a business. The goal of any business is to make money. However, she suggests that the potential "corporate culture" of Ease Communication, Inc. could be at odds with the work of sign language interpreters and the provision of good service. A similar perception is the reason that Julia stopped working for Ease Communication, Inc.

The interpreters I spoke with often blamed Ease Communication, Inc. for the focus on numbers. It is easy to blame the person or organization one has daily contact with for changing what counts as productive. However, Ease Communication, Inc. is merely establishing a protocol that can meet the functional equivalency requirements set by the FCC.

FUNCTIONAL EQUIVALENCY UNMASKED

Although "functional equivalency" is the desired outcome for many human services, there is no one quality definition or description for it. Depending on the service (i.e., children's education, employment, video relay, etc.) or the people doing the defining, the definition changes. There is, however, one inherent assumption in the institutional discourse across these various settings—that access can be quantified based upon measurable service units.

The goal of video relay service is to provide a telephone service for deaf people that is "functionally equivalent" to that of telephone services that non-deaf people enjoy. While interpreters are a necessary component of this service, to demonstrate to oversight agencies that access is being provided, managers within video relay service centers rely on different texts, such as the Accountability Log, the Efficiency Report, and the Minutes Generated Report. In doing so, interpreting work is made visible, measured, and tallied. This, in effect, reduces access to a numeric representation.

For service provider companies, efficiency means functional equivalency is being achieved and maintained through the activation of texts. These texts of logs and reports eventually appear in policies disseminated to workers and are embedded with the discourse of extra-local relations of ruling which begin to shape the behaviors and consciousness of sign language interpreters who engage with these texts (Smith, 1984). The words of the texts become part of the everyday vernacular of the video relay service industry. Furthermore, these texts change personalized, diversified, and sometimes messy, sign language interpreting, into a sterile "one size fits all" category that can be counted, cataloged, and understood in an objectified form. Rather than the human, communicative action that it is.

Here I have only focused on those texts that participants mentioned or took up during their work. In doing so, I have provided a glimpse into the expansive institution of access for deaf people. I have traced how video relay service centers measure access and how it gets documented and reported. There are undoubtedly other texts which are used for billing NECA, disciplining sign language interpreters, and those which demonstrate adherence to other federal regulatory bodies such as Occupational Safety and Health Administration (OSHA). The point I am attempting to make here is not the breadth of texts used but the ways in which various texts are taken up as a replacement for the actual work of people.

The work of sign language interpreters in video relay centers has transformed the notion of deaf people's access and functional equivalency into interpreter's measurable service minutes by the companies who provide services and those agencies who demand accountability. Access is not defined by the effectiveness of a sign language interpretation but by the ability of interpreters to maintain an efficiency percentage. Much like the work of social workers (see De Montigny, 1995), the documentation does not account for the actual lived experiences of the users of video relay because they are not consulted. Instead, the work is accountable to the "politico-administrative regime" (Smith, 1995) that deaf people engage when they wish to place a phone call through video relay services.

Notes

1. Pub. L. No. 101–336, § 401, 104 Stat. 327, 366–69 (1990) (adding Sect. 225 to the Communications Act of 1934, as amended, 47 U.S.C. § 225).
2. 47 U.S.C. § 225(a)(3).
3. *Id.* at § 225(b).
4. 47 C.F.R. § 64.604; Telecommunications Services for Individuals with Hearing and Speech Disabilities, and the Americans with Disabilities Act of 1990, CC Docket No. 90-571, Report and Order and Request for Comments, 6 FCC Rcd 4657 (1991) (*First Report and Order*).
5. Under section 225, common carriers providing telephone voice transmission services were required to begin providing TRS, throughout the areas they served, as of July 26, 1993. *See* 47 U.S.C. § 225(c). Prior to this time, some states offered relay services, but the services offered differed from state to state, and were subject to many limitations. *See* Strauss, Title IV – Telecommunications, in Implementing the Americans with Disabilities Act at 156–158 (Gostin & Beyer ed. 1993).
6. NECA.org http://www.neca.org/source/NECA_AboutUs_279.asp.
7. This and all names of the participants presented here are pseudonyms.

References

Brunson, J. L. (2011). *Video relay service interpreters: Intricacies of sign language access.* Washington, DC: Gallaudet University Press.

Brunson, J. L. (2015). A sociology of interpreting. In B. Nicodemus & K. Cagle (Eds.), *Sign language interpretation and translation research* (pp. 130–149). Washington, DC: Gallaudet University Press.

Campbell, M. (2008). (Dis)continuity of care: Explicating the ruling relations of home support. In M. L. DeVault (Ed.), *People at work: Life, power, and social inclusion in the new economy* (pp. 266–301). New York, NY: New York University Press.

Cokely, D. (1992). *Interpretation: A sociolinguistic model.* Burtonsville, MD: Linstok Press Inc.

De Meulder, M., & Haualand, H. (2019). Sign language interpreting services: A quick fix for inclusion? *Translation and Interpreting Studies: The Journal of the American Translation and Interpreting Studies Association.* https://www.jbe-platform.com/content/journals/10.1075/tis.18008.dem?crawler=true.

De Montigny, G. A. J. (1995). *Social working: An ethnography of front-line practice.* Toronto, ON: University of Toronto.

Emerson, R. M., Fretz, R. I., & Shaw, L. L. (1995). *Writing ethnographic fieldnotes* (2nd ed.). Chicago, IL: University of Chicago Press.

Gish, S. (1987). I understood all of the words, but I missed the point: A goal-to-detail/detail-to-goal strategy for text analysis. In M. McIntire (Ed.), *New dimensions in interpretation education: Curriculum and instruction* (pp. 125–137). Silver Spring, MD: RID Publications.

McCoy, L. (1998). Producing "what the deans know": Cost accounting and the restructuring of postsecondary education. *Human Studies, 21,* 395–418.

Pöchhacker, F. (2004). *Introducing interpreting studies.* London, UK: Routledge.

Roy, C. (2000). *Interpreting as a discourse process.* Oxford: Oxford University Press.

Roy, C. B., Brunson, J. L., & Stone, C. A. (2019). *The academic foundations of interpreting studies.* Washinton, DC: Gallaudet University Press.

Russell, D. (2002). *Interpreting in legal contexts: Consecutive and simultaneous interpretation.* Burtonsville, MD: Linstok Press Inc.

Smith, D. E. (1983). "No one commits suicide: Textual analysis of ideological practices," *Human Studies,* 6(4), 309–359.

Smith, D. E. (1984). Textually-mediated social organization. *International Social Science Journal,* 36(1), 59–74.

Smith, D. E. (2005). *Institutional ethnography: A sociology for people.* Toronto, ON: AltaMira Press.

Smith, D. E. (2006). Incorporating texts into ethnographic practice. In D. E. Smith (Ed.), *Institutional ethnography as practice* (pp. 65–88). Toronto: Rowman & Littlefield Publishers Inc.

Smith, G. W. (1988). Policing the gay community: An inquiry into textually mediated relations. *International Journal of Sociology and the Law, 16,* 163–183.

Smith, G. W. (1995). Accessing treatments: Managing the AIDS epidemic in Ontario. In M. Campbell & A. Manicom (Eds.), *Knowledge, experience, and ruling relations: Studies in the social organization of knowledge* (pp. 18–34). Toronto, ON: University of Toronto Press.

Smith, G. W. (2014). Policing the gay community: An inquiry into textually-mediated social relations. In D. E. Smith & S. M. Turner (Eds.), *Incorporating texts into institutional ethnographies* (pp. 17–40). Toronto, ON: University of Toronto Press.

Smith, M. (2013). *More than meets the eye: Revealing the complexities of an interpreted education.* Washington, DC: Gallaudet University Press.

Stone, C. (2009). *Toward a deaf translation norm.* Washington, DC: Gallaudet University Press.

Winston, E. A. (2004). Interpretability and accessibility of mainstream classrooms. In E. A. Winston (Ed.), *Educational interpreting: How can it succeed?* (pp. 132–167). Washington, DC: Gallaudet University Press.

Winston, E. A., & Roy, C. B. (2015). Discourse analysis and signed languages. In A. C. Schembri & C. Lucas (Eds.), *Sociolinguistics and deaf communities* (pp. 95–119). Cambridge, UK: Cambridge University Press.

Woodcock, K., & Fischer, S. L. (2008). *Occupational health and safety for sign language interpreters.* Toronto, ON: Ryerson University.

PART VI

Bringing Together Different Approaches and Perspectives

CHAPTER 24

Using Composites to Craft Institutional Ethnographic Accounts

Michael K. Corman

How do institutional ethnographers stay grounded in people's everyday doings—their actualities broadly conceived—while acknowledging the dialogical relationship central to data collection as they write up their research findings? (Smith, 2005) Corollary to this, how do institutional ethnographers "escape," as Dorothy Smith (2005, p. 123) puts it, from objectified forms of knowing that are inseparable from the relations of ruling and key to mainstream forms of inquiry? This chapter is about how institutional ethnographers do representation work, that is, how they represent what they have learned and how they write about their findings. Similar to all forms of representation in research, *what* is represented in any account given is selective; central to the account's production is a filtering or selection process organized by the ontological and epistemological framing of the study and the interests of the researcher.

It is in this context that all accounts may be thought of as a composite. In other words, qualitative (and quantitative) researchers always do representational or crafting work in presenting their findings, yet often this authorial

---

During the initial stages of writing this chapter, I greatly benefited from very useful feedback from Liza McCoy. Of course any limitations in this chapter are solely my own.

M. K. Corman (✉)
University of the Fraser Valley, Abbotsford, British Columbia, Canada
e-mail: michael.corman@ufv.ca

© The Author(s) 2021
P. C. Luken and S. Vaughan (eds.), *The Palgrave Handbook of Institutional Ethnography*,
https://doi.org/10.1007/978-3-030-54222-1_24

work—the work done by the author/researcher—of doing representation is displaced and subsumed by positivistic techniques that researchers use to present their findings in order to facilitate a guise of objectivity. In contrast, Mykhalovskiy (1996) argues that a reflexive social science problematizes "the abstract, disembodied voice of traditional academic discourse"; it is a "fiction, accomplished through writing and other practices which removed evidence of a text's author, as part of concealing the conditions of its production" (p. 134; see Sparkes, 1995 for a discussion of some of the strategies used in standard scientific forms of representation that negate the presence of the author). Given the work involved in crafting accounts of one's research, my focus in this chapter is on the use of composite accounts in institutional ethnography and how composite accounts can be used in conjunction with more traditional modes of representation in crafting theoretically informed analytical claims.[1]

I define composite accounts as accounts constructed by the researcher that are built from the corpus of data collected (e.g., interviews, observations, and texts). As such, these accounts are "real"[2] in as much as they are based on the accounts given by participants and/or observed by the researcher. However, whereas more conventional or mainstream modes of representation in qualitative research link actual interview talk with specific participants and observational data with specific sets of observations in order to accomplish some sort of analytical end—which can be done in conjunction with composite accounts—the accounts I refer to here as composite, and the individuals represented in them, are compiled or constructed from the entirety of the data and represented as a composite account.

The type of composite accounts discussed here occur within the context of my desire as an institutional ethnographer to provide the reader with a clear sense of work processes (broadly conceived) as they occur within and are organized by ongoing social and historical processes vis-à-vis work/institutional settings.[3] Hence, I discuss the use of composite accounts within the social ontology put forward by Dorothy Smith in her articulation of institutional ethnography (Smith, 1987, 2005). I argue that if a researcher desires to describe complex work processes as they occur within and are organized by an institutional setting or settings, composite accounts are one strategy of representation that can retain the "messiness" of social life (Law, 2004) while dually "keeping the institution in view" (McCoy, 2006). Furthermore, my use of composite accounts aims to "disrupt" mainstream ways of doing representation work[4]; it does so by not only giving a voice to participants that is grounded in their everyday lives but by also "ruptur[ing]...the monologies of institutional discourse and ideology, including the monologies of sociology" while recognizing the dialogic interplay between data collection and reporting (Smith, 2006, p. 124).

By introducing readers to an explicit discussion of composite accounts as they can be formulated within an IE framework, I aim to "stret[ch] the boundaries" of conventional representation strategies (Sandelowski, 1998, p. 375).

In addition to stretching the boundaries of representational work in institutional ethnography, this chapter is about "voice"—"a struggle to figure out how to present the author's self while simultaneously writing the respondents' accounts and representing their selves" (Hertz, 1997, p. xi). Instead of transforming embodied subjects into disembodied voices, my use of composite accounts recognizes that data collection, as Smith (2005) writes, is "always a collaborative product" (p. 125) and clearly situates my voice as the author of these accounts through my use of the first-person and presence throughout them. While some may argue that viewing such data as dialogic is problematic—because after all, "what entitles us to claim that we can describe people's doings and how they are coordinated on the basis of experiential accounts?" (p. 125)—the institutional ethnographer does not use the experience of others as a way "make statements about them" (pp. 124–125). Rather, we use people's experiences and their work processes as ways to make forays into the "*social organization* of people's activities" (p. 129). In focusing this chapter specifically on two interfacing components of voice, including the voice of the author and the voices of research participants, and how these voices are represented, I contribute to the ongoing discussion in institutional ethnography specifically and qualitative research more broadly on "how we talk about writing issues and handle them in our texts" (DeVault, 1997, p. 217).

This chapter is separated into four sections. In the first section, I situate my discussion of composite accounts within what may be thought of as the nonpositivist turn in social scientific inquiry as made visible through the crisis of representation in qualitative research. I also review how some researchers have responded to this crisis. In the second section, I discuss how my use of composite accounts differs from other nonpositivist representational strategies that have been used in the past. I do so by situating my discussion and use of composite accounts within the ontological and epistemological shift proffered by Dorothy Smith in her formulation of institutional ethnography. In the third section, I describe how I constructed and used composite accounts in an institutional ethnographic study that focused on the social organization of emergency medical services from the standpoint of paramedics (Corman, 2016, 2017). In the final section, I end with a conclusion.

THE CRISIS OF REPRESENTATION[5] IN QUALITATIVE RESEARCH

Researchers are central to the process of *how* data is collected, analyzed, and represented in research, and hence are integral to what is discovered. Furthermore, data, whether it is qualitative or quantitative, does not speak for itself. How data is interpreted and analyzed is neither neutral nor inevitable but structured by a variety of "thought collectives" (Fleck, 1979) or "paradigms" (Kuhn, 1962), which ultimately connect to the ontological framing of the study and those conducting it. The crisis of representation has brought many of these important points to the fore.

According to Denzin and Lincoln (2005), the *crisis of representation* is characterized by the struggle over how researchers locate themselves and their subjects in the written text. Much of this struggle was geared toward critiquing and moving beyond positivist "shadows" that lingered (and still do) over qualitative research (p. 11). Central to this crisis are critiques of positivist ways of knowing and representing what we know/learn; these critiques were illuminated in the linguistic/reflexive turn in sociology connected to "poststructural[ism], postmodern[ism], construction[ism] and ethnomethodology" (Holstein & Gubrium, 2002, p. 112), all of which in some way informs or connects to institutional ethnographic forms of inquiry.

With this reflexive turn in social scientific inquiry, methodological techniques of collecting data were no longer viewed as neutral avenues that could "directly capture lived experience. Such experience, it is argued, is created in the social text written by the researcher" (Denzin & Lincoln, 2005, p. 19; see also Holstein & Gubrium, 2002). In other words, rather than methods (e.g., interviews and observations) being viewed as neutral conduits for transmitting knowledge, the knowledge produced through different methodological techniques was now viewed as being social through and through; not only did this shift in thinking call into question the role of the researcher in their work of doing representation—it is the author, for example, who "decide[s] whose stories (and quotes) to display and whose to ignore" (Hertz, 1997, p. xii)—this linguistic turn also called into question the positivist epistemological status of data as factual.

The crisis of representation in qualitative research challenges us to "do representation differently" (Berbary, 2011, p. 186), a theme that is central to this chapter specifically and, more broadly, institutional ethnography's project of discovery. In light of the crisis of representation, researchers have responded with different types of nonpositivist[6] representational techniques, typically situated within the postmodern and post-structural paradigmatic turn.[7] Bochner and Ellis (1998), for example, in *Fiction and Social Research: By Ice or Fire*, dedicate an entire volume to nonpositivist forms of representation in social scientific research. The contributors exemplify how a variety of nonpositivist genres of representation—short stories, fictions, poems and plays—can be used to "bridge the gap between author and reader, between fact and truth, between cool reason and hot passion, between the personal and the collective . . ." (p. 7). Such styles of representation, the editors note, are modes of representation that "can bring the written product of social research closer to the richness and complexity of lived experience" (p. 7).

In order to illustrate this genre of writing, Sparkes (1995) provides a useful contrast between positivist forms of representation and nonpositivist genres of writing. More specifically, Sparkes (1995) discusses realist[8] and scientific tales[9] as the dominant—and positivist—forms of representation in research and contrasts them with nonpositivist genres of representation. The more positivist accounts, he argues, are characterized by the rhetorical strategy of the "style of no style" where the author is "evacuated" from the text yet is everywhere—"the author is everywhere but nowhere" (p. 161). As Sparkes (1995) explains, "although the voices of subject are certainly present in realist tales, they are usually orchestrated to serve the theoretical needs of an absent, disembodied author" (p. 164). As such, while differences exist between realist and scientific tales, they are similar in "being *author-evacuated* texts . . . a kind of textual positivism" (p. 164). Furthermore, emblematic of such realist and scientific tales is what Smith (2008) calls the "14th floor effect" whereby "the language practices of sociology [and other disciplines] . . . achieve the transition from being among people to being above them" (p. 418; see also Billig, 2013).

In response to this critique, Sparkes calls for the need for a "progressive-postmodernist rewriting" that recognizes that all knowledge is "partial, embodied, and historically and culturally situated" (Richardson, 1990b, cited in Sparkes, 1995, p. 167). He exemplifies a variety of nonpositivist representational strategies, including confessional tales, impressionist tales, narratives of the self, poetic representations, ethnographic dramas, and ethnographic fictions. In ethnographic fictions, for example, facts, identities, and events are rearranged to create fictitious characters and events "in order to draw the reader into the story in a way that enables deeper understandings of individuals, organizations, or the events themselves" (p. 313) (Tierney, 1993, cited in Sparkes, 1995, p. 180).

Other "creative analytic practices" that exemplify nonpositivist modes of representation include genres of "fiction, poetry, narrative, and performance" that "do representation differently," including the use of composite characters to represent the complex lives of those under study (Berbary, 2011, p. 187). Piper and Sikes (2010) further exemplify the benefits of using composite accounts in qualitative research. Writing in the context of pupil–teacher sex-related research, they use "composite fictions" to guard against the identification of vulnerable research participants, retain authorial presence, and describe the complexity of everyday life. More specifically, they write about combining ethnographic data with fictional accounts in order to represent the complexity of lived experiences. They do so by "creating characters, contexts, and settings – inventing dialogue and crafting plots" in the "fictionalized" accounts they give. In other words, while the accounts they describe were fictionalized, they were not fiction in the traditional sense.[10]

The genres of writing discussed in this section, and similar to the composite accounts I discuss below, not only aide in the protection of anonymity and confidentiality of research participants, but they also offer unique nonpositivist ways of representing research findings that allow the stories or data collected from participants to metaphorically "breathe" (Frank, 2010) and, as Bochner and Ellis (1998) argue, evoke "the richness and complexity of life" (p. 7, cited in Piper & Sikes, 2010, p. 568). Furthermore, these styles of representation bring to the fore the role of the researcher in the construction of an account and make more explicit the ontological positioning of the data represented.

However, characteristic of these nonpositivist modes of representation discussed above is how they are situated within (or reflective of) interpretive and constructionist traditions, which are often aimed at exploring the lived experiences of those who participated in the research. As such, characteristic of these nonpositivist genres are a "relativist ontology (there are multiple realities), a subjectivist epistemology (knower and respondent co-create understandings), and a naturalistic (in the natural world) set of methodological procedures" (Denzin & Lincoln, 2005, p. 24). In contrast, and as discussed in the section that follows, my discussion of composite accounts, while sharing many similarities, has some significant differences. More specifically, I discuss and situate my use of composite accounts within a social ontology and reflexive epistemology as constituted in Dorothy Smith's (2005) *A Sociology for People*, which is aimed at exploring the work of people as they are organized and coordinated by institutional relations central to their everyday doings. As such, embedded within the foundation from which my discussion of composite accounts is built is a complementary, albeit different, ontological shift.

Ontological and Epistemological Shifts—Institutional Ethnography

As I explain elsewhere (Corman, 2018a), institutional ethnography (IE) is a sociology that focuses on what people do—their work—and how people's everyday lives are organized by extra-local relations of ruling (Smith, 2005). In addition, while institutional ethnographers focus on exploring "what actually happens" as experienced by those who live it and breath it (Campbell & Gregor, 2002, p. 52), this is not the final analytical project. Rather, institutional ethnographers aim to move beyond description to explicating how what people do is shaped by text-mediated social organization; texts, as they are activated and used by people, are viewed by institutional ethnographers as major organizers and coordinators of people's everyday doings, and thus are viewed as "constituents of social relations" (Campbell, 2001, p. 323; for further discussion, see Smith, 1990, pp. 1–11; 1999; 2005, pp. 7–26).

IE offers a critique to positivist mainstream sociology that was, and in many ways still is, pervasively androcentric and objectifying. It does so by drawing on insights from feminism, ethnomethodology, Marx, Mead, Volosinov, and Bakhtin to put forward a social ontology that views the world as "being produced and brought into being through the social practices of people" (G. Smith, 2006, p. 34) and a reflexive epistemology that views knowledge as "being mutually produced through interaction between researchers and the people they learn from" (G. Smith, 2006, p. 31; see Corman & Barron, 2017). Hence, "truth" in the context of IE is quite different from both positivist and postmodernist notions of truth. Simply put, truth is conceptualized by positivists as being *out there* to be discovered or found through the application of scientific methods, whereas for postmodernists, truth(s) are multiple, contextual, and embodied as characterized by the notion that the only truth is that there are no (singular) truths. In contrast, Smith (1999) writes about a sociology that can "tel[l] the truth after postmodernism" by examining how truths/ways of knowing are put together or socially organized. Moving past postmodernist critiques of positivist notions of truths, IE deploys an ethnographic approach to "what counts" as real—how the what counts is put together (see Frank, Corman, Lawton, & Gish, 2010)—that orients the researcher to exploring and explicating how truths are contextually mediated by socially organized relations of coordination and control. In doing so, truth, as constituted in IE is locally situated yet extralocally and textually organized; truth is socially organized via-a-vis text mediated social organization.

Aligned with this epistemological and ontological shift, IE puts forward a conceptual framework geared toward orienting the researcher to "look here!" as McCoy (2008, p. 702) puts it, without objectifying local happenings and displacing the presence of people and their doings by a pre-determined theoretical frame (Kearney, Corman, Johnston, Hart, & Gormley, 2019; Smith, 2008). For instance, one important orienting concept particularly relevant to this chapter is Smith's generous conception of work:

> *Work* orients the researcher to what people do that involves some conscious intent and acquired skill; it includes emotional or thought work as well as physical labor or communicative action. It does not mean occupational employment in a narrow sense. An institutional ethnographer might be as interested in the work of feeding a family (DeVault, 1991) or living with HIV infection (Mykhalovskiy & McCoy, 2002) as in the work performed by teachers (Manicom, 1995) or security guards. (Walby, 2005) (McCoy, 2008, p. 705)

This concept of work "keeps the focus on what people do and what they know how to do" (McCoy, 2008, p. 705).[11] What is important for the purposes of this chapter and within the context of constructing and using composite accounts is how IE's epistemological and ontological shift orients the researcher to explore and write about what people do and how what people do is organized and coordinated by "regimes of governance" (DeVault, 2008) or "institutional relations in which people's everyday lives are embedded" (Smith, 2005, p. 38).

Based on this brief overview of IE, we can see that IE shares with other nonpositivist traditions a conception of knowledge, truth, and experience as being social through and through; experiences and how we talk about them are shaped by discursive contexts that "are given to us and in which we participate in" (McCoy, 2008, p. 705). Furthermore, as McCoy explains, experience is also shaped by our bodies and interfacing social-contextual factors. However, and differing from more interpretivist and constructionist traditions, IE's ontological framing results in a broader analytical project of discovery with a focus on social organization rather than social construction; whereas IE is concerned with how things are made visible and knowable by whom and under what circumstances—something of interest to social constructionists—it tends to be broader in scope because it casts a wider analytical lens by exploring how people fair in light of how what counts as socially organized (McCoy, 2008). Hence, while IE has some similarities with many of the genres discussed above, specifically its critical and reflexive epistemological turn, it puts forward a different, albeit complementary, project of discovery aimed at exploring how things work; IE's analytical project of discovery is geared toward exploring how what people do is socially organized by the institutional setting in which their work occurs (Corman, 2018b; Corman & Barron, 2017).

This discussion of IE has implications for how institutional ethnographers do representation. In other words, how institutional ethnographers represent their findings is informed by IE's ontological and epistemological frame that the researcher orients to and is organized by (Mantzoukas, 2004, p. 995). For example, while people's everyday doings are central to IE, their experiences are not the focus of the inquiry per se—"Experience is a starting place and a resource in institutional ethnography; it is not the final analytic object" (McCoy, 2008, p. 705). Rather, accounts are used as resources to make forays into the socially organized settings that organize and coordinate people's everyday doings; institutional ethnographers use participant accounts "in order to reveal the 'relations of ruling' that shape local experiences" (DeVault, 2008, p. 15; see also Smith, 1999). It is with this brief overview of IE in mind that I now turn to a discussion of how I went about constructing composite accounts.

An Institutional Ethtnographic Example of Constructing and Using Composite Accounts

How do researchers produce for readers a clear sense of work processes as they occur within ongoing social historical processes, are organized institutionally, and within the context of conducting institutional ethnographic research? How do I represent my data in a compelling way—"aim[ed] at a particular product" (Smith, 2005, p. 135)—while recognizing the dialogic character of data collection that is "shaped by and to the situation of talk or observation and under particular discursive conventions?" (p. 139) These were some of the questions I grappled with when deciding how to write up my research on urban paramedics. To provide some context, I was interested in exploring the following three questions:

1. What do urban paramedics actually do on the front lines of prehospital emergency medical services (EMS)?
2. How does the work of paramedics interface with other workers in EMS?
3. How is the work of paramedics organized, coordinated, and made institutionally accountable?

To provide context for my discussion of composite accounts below, as an institutional ethnographer undertaking this study, I deployed a recursive and emergent two-phase research design (see Grahame, 1998) to explore and explicate these questions. For the first phase, I began with observations of paramedics as they interfaced with their patients and their ever-changing work setting *on the streets*—nonstandard and unpredictable environments "rife with chaotic, dangerous, and often uncontrollable elements" (Nelson, 1997, cited in Campeau, 2008, p. 3). In total, I observed paramedics for around 200 hours over an 11-month period. These observations were complemented by audio-recorded interviews based on my observations. In total, I conducted 115 interviews with paramedics for phase 1, with an average length of 18 minutes (range: 2.25–81 minutes). Aligned with IE, the observations and interviews were geared toward understanding the work processes or *work knowledge* (Smith, 2005) of paramedics—"the embodied actualities of people's work" (Smith, 2006, p. 6)—and to elicit talk that "pointed to translocal processes that organized their work" (Corman, 2018b, p. 7).

The second phase of the study sought to explore and explicate how different institutional technologies—"the specific tools that workers use to accomplish their tasks and the institutionally organized procedures for accomplishing these tasks" (Pence, 2001, p. 204; see also Griffith & Andre-Bechley, 2008, p. 43)—and interfacing sites of coordination and control connect to and organize what paramedics do on and off the streets. In doing so, I aimed to expand on the complex ethnographic descriptions of work processes that was the main focus of phase 1 to explore how people's work is organized by broader text-mediated relations of coordination and control. As such, I interviewed other practitioners (e.g., emergency department physicians and nurses), administrators (e.g., EMS supervisors and administrators), and other individuals integral to the function of the emergency medical system (e.g., call-takers and dispatchers). I also did some observations at the Dispatch Centre, where I observed the work of dispatchers and call-takers. In total, I conducted 36 interviews in phase two, half of which occurred in the Dispatch Centre. The interviews lasted, on average, 53 minutes. These phase two semi-structured interviews and observations were organized around a set of topics generated from phase one and geared toward gaining a better understanding of the way EMS is organized and monitored. Key to phase two interviews and observations was investigating the role of different textual technologies (identified in phase 1) and text-mediated relations play in the social organization of EMS.[12]

From Field to Desk

Based on the theory/methodological insights and emergent phases of research discussed above, I chose to construct three composite accounts from the corpus of my data as a way to begin telling a story of the complex work paramedics do and how their work is organized in contemporary EMS. These composite accounts were geared toward painting complex pictures of the work of paramedics (see Corman, 2017) that pointed to the socially organized setting in which that work occurred, which was explicated in more detail in the latter parts of my analysis. While I mainly relied on data from phase one to construct these accounts, phase two data was central to the process of crafting these composite accounts; constructing composite accounts interweaved recursively with both phases of data in order to produce accounts that ethnographically painted a picture of the work of paramedics as it occurs within ongoing social historical process. As such, the composite accounts produced were analytically interested and strategically constructed (see Corman, 2013).

Each composite account that I constructed told the story of a unique *call* or *run* that composite paramedic characters were dispatched to. While these composite shifts represented actual calls that I observed during my field research, the episodes embedded within these composites were drawn from different sets of observations from different shifts. Furthermore, the characters embedded within these composite accounts, while based primarily on the work of specific paramedics, were also a composite, drawn from different sets of observations from different shifts, sometimes with the same paramedics and other times with different paramedics. As such, while the accounts and descriptions of work given by these characters are real, not everything that happened in the account is from one particular set of observations, interviews, or a specific set of paramedics.

In order to construct these accounts, I first organized the data into themes based on the different work practices that I had observed (e.g., *work–accountability, work–asking questions, work–getting rig [ambulance] ready*). These themes emphasized the work of paramedics and how their work connected with the work of others at different institutional sites, and the different technologies central to these interfacing sites (Corman, 2018b). Once this initial coding was complete, I began to develop scenic "chunks" or excerpts based on my institutional ethnographic orientation discussed above. In order to facilitate this process, I wrote extensively on a variety of topics, including the beginning and end of shifts, different types of calls that I observed, how paramedics interacted with their patients and different medical devices and knowledge technologies, transfers to hospital, the ambulance unit, the information provided to paramedics by personnel at the Dispatch Centre and how this information is taken up by paramedics, and the learning that occurs for paramedics on and off the streets. My goal of writing in chunks was to begin to depict complex work processes in order to help draw connections between my observations and understandings of those work processes and the institutional interface with how those work processes were organized, coordinated, and made institutionally visible.

After about five months of writing excerpts, three composite accounts began to emerge. I chose three small episodes to recount because I wanted to focus on the complexity of paramedics' work—the complex, intricate, mundane, and exhilarating work of paramedics—but as the process of analysis unfolded, it became clear to me that I could represent (though not in its entirety) this complexity in three shifts. As such, the use of composite accounts provided a way to "tell a story" about "what [I] learned" (Campbell & Gregor, 2002, p. 93) about the work processes of paramedics in order to give readers a rich understanding of what paramedics do, how their work connects to others, and to draw attention to the multiple medical devices and knowledge technologies that paramedics interface with.

For these accounts, it was necessary to create four composite characters, Jake, Julie, Hanna, and Dan (pseudonyms). These characters were based primarily on the observations of four specific paramedics I observed but were nevertheless composite characters because the description of their work and talk is supplemented or enhanced with other observations and interviews that I conducted with other paramedics. Drawing on the corpus of the data in this way allowed me to incorporate a diversity of interviews and observations to dually represent complex work processes while also pointing to "'relations of ruling' that shape local experiences" (DeVault, 2008, p. 15; see also Campbell & Gregor, 2002, pp. 89–90). Hence, a key characteristic of these composite accounts was an explicit orientation to the ways in which different institutional technologies appeared in the data with the analytical goal being to move beyond the description of local events to an explication of the socially organized setting of EMS.

To help orient me during this analytical process of crafting these composite accounts, I developed a guide for analyzing data that kept me grounded in IE. This guide relied mainly on the work of McCoy (2006), DeVault and McCoy (2006), Smith (2006), and Melon (2012). This guide was separated into two concise sections: (1) What to avoid, and (2) What to focus on. The first section emphasized the need to avoid focusing on people's opinions and speculative explanations and to avoid *analytical drift*[13] where you only focus on participants instead of the nexus between people's everyday lives as they interface with and are organized by institutional relations. The main focus of this guide was Sect. 2.

Section 2 was geared toward keeping me rooted on the ground of what paramedics do and how what they do is socially organized. Questions or analytical nudges that helped orient me included: What are people doing? What does their work feel like? How do individuals know how to do what they are doing or, as McCoy (2006) puts it, their *mental work*—what is the thinking behind the work? What does the individual think about when they do their work? McCoy (2006) succinctly summarizes orienting questions that were particularly useful for me when I was working with transcripts of interview and observational data:

> What is the work that these informants are describing or alluding to? What does it involve for them? How is their work connected with the work of other people? What particular skills or knowledge seems to be required? What does it feel like to do this work? What are the troubles or successes that arise for people doing this work? What evokes the work? (p. 111)

While focusing on the different work strategies of paramedics and other key players in EMS was an integral component of my IE analysis and crafting of my composite accounts, this guide also highlighted the importance of the need to examine the institutional processes that evoke different work strategies of individuals in the institutional setting—EMS—and how people work within such institutional process, albeit differently (McCoy, 2006, p. 115). As such, in constructing my composite accounts, and aligned with IE, I oriented to how the work of paramedics "gear" into and is shaped by different institutional processes (McCoy, 2006, p. 115), including those that dealt with accountability, the distribution of EMS resources, and the hospital and prehospital interface. Questions that oriented me included: How does the work of paramedics interconnect with others? How does their work, and talk of their work, carry social organization (remember, in IE talk is not viewed as neutral)? As McCoy (2006) puts it, "What are the institutional processes that evoke this work, these concerns?" (p. 116) How does the social context organize people's everyday doings (e.g., socioeconomic status, location, the social categories people occupy (e.g., age, race, ethnicity, gender, etc.))? How are experiences being talked about shaped by texts? Connected to this last question, how do discourses operate in "people's lives and what difference it makes for people to participate or not to participate in the discourse in various ways?" (McCoy, 2006, p. 121) Lastly, a key orienting question for me was, "how is the work [of paramedics] articulated to institutional work processes and the institutional order?" (p. 111).

My analytically interested or strategically crafted composite accounts were geared toward providing readers with accounts that not only drew attention to the work of paramedics—what do paramedics do as they know it, live it, and experience it—but also how their work gears into and is organized by institutional processes; that is, how the work of paramedics is "shaped by and oriented towards" different institutional processes (McCoy, 2006, p. 115) and the technologies central to accomplishing this link. As such, the accounts aimed to provide readers with a complex understanding of the different work processes of paramedics and the institutional processes that evoke these work processes.

In addition to my discussion above, central to how these accounts were constructed was my presence as the author. In other words, I am an analytical character throughout the composite accounts; my presence and voice as data collector and author of the representation is at the forefront. The aim of including my voice and presence throughout these accounts was twofold: (1) to reinforce the idea that data collection and representation is a dialogical and collaborative process, and (2) to ensure that my role as the author was not abstracted away from the process of representation. Hence, my presence and voice in these accounts were not only a key strategy for me to ensure reflexivity throughout the presentation of my findings, aligned with the ontological and epistemological insights offered in IE, I also wanted to emphasize the fact that I was not detached from the process of discovery; rather, by inserting myself in these accounts (and throughout all of this research) I wanted to convey my role as being active in the research and analytical process of discovery. Lastly, doing this also made my analytical thinking more visible and transparent in a way that reflected how my understanding of front-line work, and how it is socially organized, emerged, both in the field and back at my desk.

Conclusion

As I sit in our new home office (we moved recently), the irony of the name of this room given by the previous owners (one was an artist) is succinctly placed on a plaque attached to the exterior of the door—*crafts*. This crafts room, what my partner and I now call our office, is aptly named, especially as the room in which I finalize the writing of this chapter focused on the work of crafting institutional ethnographic accounts that are composite in nature. In this chapter, I oriented to the quest of institutional ethnographers to produce for readers a clear sense of work processes as they occur within ongoing social historical processes; much like my partner and I are crafting this room (and other aspects of this house) into our own, as institutional ethnographers, we are always at work (re)presenting the work of others as they are organized by text-mediated social organization. In this light, I discussed a specific use of composite accounts in the context of doing representational work in IE and exemplified the process of constructing composite accounts in the context of an institutional ethnographic study.

I also situated the use of composite accounts within the crisis of representation in qualitative inquiry and qualitative researchers' responses to this crisis, positioning composite accounts as a nonpositivist representational style and analytical technique that institutional ethnographers can use in their representational tool kit to retain some of the messiness (Law, 2004) in ethnographic inquiry while telling some form of truth after postmodernism (Smith, 1999). As exemplified by my own construction and use of composite accounts, this approach can be designed and used in a way to facilitate critical/nuanced (re)presentations of institutional ethnographic accounts without falling into positivist traps of representation. Using composite accounts such as those described here can circumvent positivist and social constructionist notions of reality/realities and truth/truth(s) while still telling some sort of truth by providing theoretically informed sociological analysis that empirically explores the complex interface between the work people do and how this work is organized and coordinated by text-mediated social organization. As such, and differing from other uses of composite accounts discussed above, the composite accounts described in this chapter are geared toward drawing attention to the complexities of people's everyday lives and how those lives are socially organized or put together by text mediated social organization.

The use of composite accounts is especially valuable when describing complex work processes that aim to retain the messiness of work processes and work settings. They are also useful in complex analyses that aim to move beyond description to explication—pointing to institutional relations that organize the everyday work of individuals in an age of technological governance. While I situated this discussion in the context of my desire to represent *the actual* in a nonpositivist manner aligned with the ontological shift proffered by Smith's IE, I suggest that this conversation has broader implications about representation and voice in qualitative research; how to do representation in qualitative inquiry is especially important since writing, or "textualization," as Marcus (1986) describes it, is at the heart of qualitative research. My hope is that this chapter will add to the complexity of how we inscribe and can inscribe the work of individuals and their socially organized work setting.

Constructing composite is an individualized process and should be done to meet the needs of the author and setting in which they are ethnographically exploring. It is in this light that I have outlined here how I crafted and used composite accounts as a way of exemplifying their potential benefits and furthering the discussion of how we do (re)presentation work in IE. Nevertheless, the use of composite accounts must be transparent and retain the presence of the author if they are to be done reflexively and in alignment with the nonpositivist modes of representation in social scientific inquiry.

NOTES

1. As discussed below, my use of composite accounts has been used in conjunction with more traditional representational styles (see Corman, 2017).
2. As Mantzoukas explains, "Far from being imposed on him [the researcher] from outside, scientific facts are, in truth, made [*faits*] by the scientist who asserts them" (Le Roy, 1901, p. 145, cited in Mantzoukas, 2004, p. 998).
3. The term *ongoing social historical processes* is used by Smith (2005) to point to how the social is happening. She explains, "each moment of action is conditioned by what is historically given and reshapes the already given in moving into the future" (p. 70).
4. Smith (2005) describes mainstream approaches to inquiry as an ideological practice of sorts, whereby "the local actualities of people's doings appear, if at all, only selectively and as instances, examples, illustrations, or expressions of institutionally constituted virtual realities" (p. 123).
5. While the Crisis of Representation is "coupled with a *crisis of legitimation* that . . . problematizes the traditional criteria used to Evaluate Qualitative Research" (Sparkes, 1995, p. 159), a discussion of the latter is outside the scope of this chapter.
6. By nonpositivist paradigms, I refer to ". . . all paradigms that do not share the positivistic thought on concepts of truth, reality, and knowledge, and, as such, are postpositivism, constructivism, critical social theory, and postmodern paradigms, to name but a few" (Mantzoukas, 2004, p. 998).
7. A comprehensive overview of these strategies is outside of the scope of this chapter.

8. These are representational strategies that predominate in qualitative and quantitative research whereby the author is absent once they are finished data collection (Sparkes, 1995). As Van Maanen (1988) explains, "Only what members of the studied culture say and do and, presumably, think are in the text" (p. 46, cited in Sparkes, p. 162).
9. A genre of writing characteristic of the "hard" or "natural" sciences.
10. In contrast to its traditional usage, the use of the term fiction here should not be viewed as false or untrue. Rather, the term fiction can be thought of as a rhetorical device that draws attention to the socially organized nature of knowledge and the nonpositivist notion that all truths are partial. As Clifford (1986) explains: "To call ethnographies fictions may raise empiricist hackles. But the word as commonly used in recent textual theory has lost its connotations of falsehood, of something merely opposed to truth. It suggests the partiality of cultural and historical truths, the ways they are systematic and exclusive. Ethnographic writings can properly be called fictions in the sense of 'something made or fashioned,' . . . Interpretive social scientists have recently come to view good ethnographies as 'true fictions,' but usually at the costs of weakening the oxymoron, reducing it to the banal claim that all truths are constructed . . . all constructed truths are made possible by powerful 'lies' of exclusion and rhetoric. Even the best ethnographic texts – serious, true fictions – are systems, or economies, of truth" (pp. 6–7).
11. While there are other important concepts relevant to an institutional ethnographic framework, an in-depth discussion of them is outside the scope of this chapter (see Smith 1987, 2005 for a comprehensive overview).
12. How texts are viewed in IE analysis provides an analytical and methodological move beyond how people talk about their experiences to explore how their experiences are hooked up with, organized, and coordinated by institutional relations.
13. Analytical drift results in a more simplistic focus on the opinion and beliefs of participants leading to more cause and effect explanations more attuned to positivist forms of qualitative and quantitative analysis. In other words, analytical drift results when researchers lose sight of people at work and fail to "keep the institutional in view" in their analysis (McCoy, 2006).

REFERENCES

Berbary, L. (2011). Poststructural writerly representations: Screenplay as creative analytic practice. *Qualitative Inquiry, 17*(2), 186–196. https://doi.org/10.1177/1077800410393887.

Billig, M. (2013). *Learn to write badly: How to succeed in the social sciences*. Cambridge: Cambridge University Press.

Bochner, A., & Ellis, C. (1998). Series editors introduction. In S. Banks & A. Banks (Eds.), *Fiction and social research: By ice or fire* (pp. 7–8). Walnut Creek, CA: AltaMira Press.

Campbell, M. (2001). Textual accounts, ruling action: The intersection of knowledge and power in the routine conduct of community nursing work. *Studies in Cultures, Organizations and Societies, 7*, 231–250. https://doi.org/10.1080/10245280108523559.

Campbell, M., & Gregor, F. (2002). *Mapping social relations: A primer in doing institutional ethnography*. Aurora, ON: Garamond Press.

Campeau, A. (2008). "Professionalism: Why paramedics require 'theories-of-practice'." *Journal of Emergency Primary Health Care, 6*(2), 1–7. https://ajp.paramedics.org/index.php/ajp/article/view/451.

Clifford, J. (1986). Introduction: Partial truths. In J. Clifford & G. Marcus (Eds.), *The poetics and politics of ethnography* (pp. 1–26). Berkeley: University of California Press.

Corman, M. K. (2013). How mothers talk about placement of their child with autism outside the home. *Qualitative Health Research, 23*(10), 1320–1332. https://doi.org/10.1177/1049732313505225.

Corman, M. K. (2016). Street medicine: Assessment work strategies of paramedics on the front lines of emergency health services. *The Journal of Contemporary Ethnography, 46*(5), 600–623. https://doi.org/10.1177/0891241615625462.

Corman, M. K. (2017). *Paramedics on and off the streets: Emergency medical services in the age of technological governance*. Toronto: University of Toronto Press.

Corman, M. K. (2018a). Titrating the rig: How paramedics work *in* and *on* their ambulance. *Qualitative Health Research, 28*(1), 47–59. https://doi.org/10.1177/1049732317739266.

Corman, M. K. (2018b). Driving to work: The front seat work of paramedics to and from the scene. *Symbolic Interaction, 41*(3), 291–310. 10.1002/symb.335.

Corman, M. K., & Barron, G. (2017). Institutional ethnography and actor-network theory: In dialogue. In J. Reid & L. Russell (Eds.), *Perspectives on and from institutional ethnography*. Studies in Qualitative Methodology, (pp. 47–68). Bingley, UK: Emerald Group Publishing.

Denzin, N. K., & Lincoln, Y. S. (2005). Introduction: The discipline and practice of qualitative research. In N. K. Denzin & Y. S. Lincoln (Eds.), *The Sage handbook of qualitative research* (pp. 1–32). Thousand Oaks: Sage.

DeVault, M. (1997). Personal writing in social research: Issues of production and interpretation. In R. Hertz (Ed.), *Reflexivity and voice* (pp. 216–228). Thousand Oaks, CA: Sage.

DeVault, M. (Ed.). (2008). *People at work: Life, power, and social inclusion in the new economy*. New York: New York University Press.

DeVault, M., & McCoy, L. (2006). Institutional ethnography: Using interviews to investigate ruling relations. In. D. E. Smith (Ed.), *Institutional ethnography as practice* (pp. 15–44). Lanham, MD: Rowman & Littlefield.

Fleck, L. (1979). *Genesis and development of a scientific fact* (T. J. Trenn & R. K. Merton, Eds.). (F. Bradley, Trans.). Chicago: University of Chicago Press.

Frank, A. W. (2010). *Letting stories breathe: A socio-narratology*. Chicago: University of Chicago Press.

Frank, A., Corman, M. K., Lawton, P., & Gish, J. (2010). Healer/patient interaction: New mediations in clinical relationships. In I. Bourgeault, R. DeVries, & R. Dingwall (Eds.), *Handbook on qualitative health research* (pp. 34–52). London: Sage.

Grahame, P. R. (1998). Ethnography, institutions, and the social organization of knowledge. *Human Studies, 21*(4), 347–360. https://www.jstor.org/stable/20011212.

Griffith, A., & Andre-Bechely, L. (2008). Institutional technologies: Coordinating families and schools, bodies and texts. In M. DeVault (Ed.), *People at work: Life, power, and social inclusion in the new economy* (pp. 40–56). New York: New York University Press.

Hertz, R. (Ed.). (1997). *Reflexivity and voice.* Thousand Oaks, CA: Sage.

Holstein, J., & Gubrium, J. (2002). Active interviewing. In D. Weinberg (Ed.), *Qualitative research methods* (pp. 112–126). Malden, MA: Blackwell.

Kearney, G., Corman, M., Johnston, J., Hart, N., & Gormley, G. (2019). Why institutional ethnography? Why now? Institutional ethnography in health professions education. *Perspectives on Medical Education, 8*(1), 17–24. https://doi.org/10.1007/s40037-019-0499-0.

Kuhn, T. S. (1962). *The structure of scientific revolutions.* Chicago: University of Chicago Press.

Law, J. (2004). *After methods: Mess in social science research.* London: Routledge.

Mantzoukas, S. (2004). Issues of representation within qualitative inquiry. *Qualitative Health Research, 14*(7), 994–1007. https://doi.org/10.1177/1049732304265959.

Marcus, G. (1986). Afterword. In J. Clifford & G. Marcus (Eds.), *The poetics and politics of ethnography* (pp. 262–266). Berkeley: University of California Press.

McCoy, L. (2006). Keeping the institution in view: Working with interview accounts of everyday experience. In D. E. Smith (Ed.), *Institutional ethnography as practice* (pp. 109–125). US: Rowman & Littlefield Publishers, Inc.

McCoy, L. (2008). Institutional ethnography and constructionism. In J. A. Holstein & J. F. Gubrium (Eds.), *Handbook of constructionist research* (pp. 701–714). New York, NY: Guilford.

Melon, K. (2012). Inside triage: The social organization of emergency nursing work. Master's thesis. ISBN: 9780494879061.

Mykhalovskiy, E. (1996). Reconsidering table talk: Critical thoughts on the relationship between sociology, autobiography and self-indulgence. *Qualitative Sociology, 19*(1), 131–151.

Pence, E. (2001). Safety for battered women in a textually mediated legal system. *Studies in Culture, Organizations, and Societies, 7,* 199–229. https://doi.org/10.1080/10245280108523558.

Piper, H., & Sikes, P. (2010). All teachers are vulnerable but especially gay teachers: Using composite fictions to protect research participants in pupil-teachers sex-related research. *Qualitative Inquiry, 16*(7), 566–574. https://doi.org/10.1177/1077800410371923.

Sandelowski, M. (1998). Writing a good read: Strategies for re-presenting qualitative data. *Research in Nursing & Health, 21,* 375–382.

Smith, D. E. (1987). *The everyday world as problematic.* Toronto: University of Toronto Press.

Smith, D. E. (1990). *Texts, facts, and femininity: Exploring the relations of ruling.* London: Routledge.

Smith, D. E. (1999). *Writing the social: Critique, theory, and investigations.* Toronto: University of Toronto Press.

Smith, D. E. (2005). *Institutional ethnography: A sociology for people.* Walnut Creek, CA: AltaMira Press.

Smith, D. E. (Ed.). (2006). *Institutional ethnography as practice.* Oxford, UK: Rowman & Littlefield.

Smith, D. E. (2008). From the 14th floor to the sidewalk: Writing sociology at ground level. *Sociological Inquiry, 78*(3), 417–422. 10.1111/j.1475-682X.2008.00248.x.

Smith, G. (2006). Political activist as ethnographer. In C. Frampton, G. Kinsman, A. K. Thompson, & K. Tilleczek (Eds.), *Sociology for changing the world: Social movements/social research* (pp. 44–70). Canada: Fernwood Publishing.

Sparkes, A. (1995). Writing people: Reflections on the dual crises of representation and legitimation in qualitative inquiry. *Quest, 47,* 158–195. 10.1080/00336297.1995.10484151.

CHAPTER 25

Attending to Messy Troubles of the Anthropocene with Institutional Ethnography and Material Semiotics: The Case for Vital Institutional Ethnography

Karly Burch

"Anthropocene" is the term used to describe our current geological epoch, a name which highlights the role of human activities in contributing to changes in Earth's biophysical processes. While debates continue regarding the exact onset of this epoch, it is clear that the transition to the Anthropocene has signified a shift from the more stable period of the Holocene, to an era marked by turbulence, uncertainty and instability; it has signified a shift from a geological epoch that was largely life-supporting, to one where the planet's ability to support human and more-than-human[1] life is under grave threat (see Tsing, 2017).

Scholars in the field of material semiotics have argued that our ability to respond to the complex, messy and interwoven troubles of the Anthropocene—climate change, global pandemics, nuclear disasters, mass extinction, and ocean acidification to name only a few—will require cultivating "response-ability" (Haraway, 2016, p. 34), that is, the ability to respond to troubles of the Anthropocene in ways that are both situated and collective. However, cultivating the ability to respond to exceedingly turbulent realities is not a straightforward process, particularly for those humans living in societies which value human exceptionalism, human exemptionalism, individualism, and other ontological framings which work to distinguish and separate humans from their wider material entanglements with plants, animals, and other elements that support life on planet Earth. This is because the widespread tendency to

---

K. Burch (✉)
University of Otago, Dunedin, New Zealand
e-mail: karly.burch@otago.ac.nz

© The Author(s) 2021
P. C. Luken and S. Vaughan (eds.), *The Palgrave Handbook of Institutional Ethnography*,
https://doi.org/10.1007/978-3-030-54222-1_25

ignore these complex relations has participated in enacting[2] troubles of the Anthropocene we are facing today (Murdoch, 2001; Tsing, Swanson, Gan, & Bubandt, 2017).

Conducting research which cultivates response-ability will, thus, require innovative, imaginative, and creative ways of noticing overlooked human and more-than-human actors[3] as well as the complex ways they relate in practice (Haraway, 2016). It will require academics to weave together fresh narratives that offer insights into unimagined opportunities for generative engagements. Here, the category of more-than-human is vast, including animals, plants, insects, bacteria, radionuclides, texts, discourses, among myriad other living creatures and nonliving things. Cultivating response-ability will, thus, require both researchers and everyday people to develop sensibilities for noticing, discussing, and acting carefully within our complex socio-material entanglements[4] with humans and more-than-humans (Tsing et al., 2017).

At the same time, however, official responses to troubles of the Anthropocene do not always encourage the development of sensibilities for noticing the entangled human and more-than-human relations involved in enacting these troubling realities. As a result, official policies may instead work to obstruct serious attempts to notice and respond to some of our most pressing challenges. To address this, I argue that scholars working to support the cultivation of response-ability in the Anthropocene could benefit greatly from adopting insights and sensibilities from both material semiotics (to seriously attend to human and more-than-human socio-material entanglements) and institutional ethnography (to trace the materially-mediated ruling relations which may be obfuscating these entanglements and, thus, obstructing the cultivation of situated response-ability to troubles of the Anthropocene).

In this chapter I introduce *vital institutional ethnography* as a method of inquiry for studying situated experiences of disorder that emerge when people are confronted with messy troubles of the Anthropocene, particularly those troubles which reveal humans' socio-material entanglements with invisible and insidious materials such as radionuclides and other "epistemologically distant objects"—those materials that are difficult to understand or identify without expertise or the use of scientific tools (Carolan, 2006, p. 234). Vital institutional ethnography materialized as I enacted my Ph.D. research exploring *konran* (disorder) related to everyday eating in the Kansai region of Japan in the aftermath of Tokyo Electric Power Company's (TEPCO's) 2011 Fukushima Daiichi Nuclear Power Plant disaster (hereafter TEPCO's nuclear disaster) (Burch, 2018). The Japanese term *konran* (混乱)—a blending of the kanji characters for "mix" (混) and "disorder" (乱)—emerged through my participants' narratives,[5] describing both the disorder they experienced in attempting to re-organize their eating habits to account for the possible presence of TEPCO's radionuclides in their everyday food, as well as the tension and disorder that arose as they tried to discuss their concerns about radionuclides with those around them—at a time when post-disaster ruling relations were pressuring people to refrain from noticing or deliberating the materiality of the disaster.

In general terms, *konran* could be understood as the disorder that erupts when multiple ways of noticing and coordinating human and more-than-human relations clash in practice—what Mol (2002, p. 142) refers to as "interference." This clash in ordering practices could result in a disjuncture between how one feels comfortable enacting these relations and how ruling texts and discourses direct their enactment. Within my particular study, *konran* refers to experiences of disorder that arose when ruling relations working to coordinate a single, "correct," homogenous way of dealing with, discussing and relating with TEPCO's radionuclides entered my life and the lives of my study participants, clashing with the ways we each wanted to address and handle the possible presence of TEPCO's radionuclides within our own particular, situated, heterogeneous material entanglements.

My study's participants—43 people who were living approximately 600 kilometers from the site of TEPCO's nuclear disaster at the time of my fieldwork in 2016, 17 of whom lived within 260 kilometers of TEPCO's damaged nuclear reactors at the onset of the disaster in 2011—were at some point concerned about and trying to respond to the possible presence of TEPCO's radionuclides in their everyday food. However, they quickly discovered that official ruling discourses such as "safety," "anxiety," and "harmful rumors" emerged along with the onset of the disaster, making it difficult to openly discuss their concerns and relate with TEPCO's radionuclides in a way that felt most appropriate to them. That is, with a focus on getting business as usual back on track as quickly as possible, post-disaster ruling relations (enacted through official food safety regulations, scientific consensus reports from powerful institutions, and ruling discourses regarding food safety which categorized people who attempted to discuss concerns about food safety as "anxious," "against recovery efforts" or propagators of "harmful rumors") were actively discouraging my participants from noticing, discussing, and carefully responding (being *response-able*) to the possible material presence of radionuclides in their everyday lives.

It was in noticing this dilemma that a vital question emerged: How could I attend to the *konran* experienced by people struggling to grapple with the possible presence of TEPCO's radionuclides in their everyday lives without allowing my research to become confined within the very ruling relations contributing to these experiences—i.e., without participating in obfuscating the possible presence of TEPCO's radionuclides and stifling any deliberation or discussion regarding these more-than-human actors? It was clear that my method of inquiry would need to seriously grapple with both the materiality of the socio-technical disaster (e.g., TEPCO's imperceptible radionuclides) as well as the textually mediated ruling relations deployed to coordinate human activities in its messy aftermath. This is where vital institutional ethnography emerged: It is a method of inquiry that allowed me to borrow sensibilities from institutional ethnography to trace textually mediated attempts to coordinate everyday activities, as well as sensibilities from the field of material semiotics to notice and attend to radionuclides and other complex socio-material entanglements that contributed to my participants' experiences of *konran*, but which were being ignored or obfuscated within the ruling relations themselves.

Therefore, in studying everyday eating in post-2011 Japan, vital institutional ethnography provided me with tools to trace the ruling texts and discourses deployed to coordinate everyday eating in the aftermath of TEPCO's nuclear disaster—which actively participated in silencing deliberation and debate related to the possible presence of radionuclides in food (see Burch, 2018; Burch, Legun, & Campbell, 2018)—without losing sight of TEPCO's radionuclides and their possible material presence in my study participants' everyday lives. The method of inquiry also allowed me to notice and highlight other heterogeneous socio-material entanglements that contributed to experiences of *konran*, but were being ignored or obfuscated within the ruling relations at play (e.g., the situated material relations that participated in enacting ruling texts and discourses related to food safety; the situated material relations that participated in enacting "safe food").

To provide a theoretical basis for this method of inquiry, I begin this chapter with a brief introduction to the field of material semiotics, followed by a discussion on how institutional ethnography's attention to socio-material relations allows for fluid dialogue across these two fields of study. I then provide an overview of how vital institutional ethnography was enacted within my Ph.D. project. Finally, I end the chapter with a short reflection on how this method of inquiry can be used to attend to questions of social justice and response-ability that arise when addressing complex, messy troubles of the Anthropocene.

Material Semiotics

Heterogeneous Socio-Materiality

Material semiotics—sometimes referred to as relational materiality—encompasses an array of methodological and analytical tools for attending to the heterogeneous socio-material relations that participate in enacting everyday realities. That is, material semiotics holds a particular analytic interest in exploring how everyday realities, entities, and situations emerge through complex, heterogenous relational entanglements among humans and more-than-humans.

While scholarship adopting material-semiotic tools and sensibilities is vast and continuously expanding—including research in science and technology studies (STS), geography, anthropology, post-colonial studies, among others (see Law, 2019)—in enacting vital institutional ethnography, I drew most of my insights from scholars working with tools and sensibilities from actor–network theory, feminist material semiotics and the assemblage approach (e.g., Haraway, 2016; Latour, 2005; Law, 2002; Mol, 2002; Tsing, 2015). That said, I follow the advice of Law (2009) who recommends speaking more broadly about material semiotics as it "better catches the openness, uncertainty, revisability, and diversity of the most interesting work" (p. 142) being enacted by scholars adopting these sensibilities.

Again, the terms *material* and *semiotic* point to an analytic interest in exploring how situated realities emerge when heterogeneous entanglements of humans and more-than-humans (materials) relate and produce realities and meanings (semiotics) in practice. To clarify, semiotics has been defined as "the dimension of meaning. It studies the structure of symbols and signs and their associated meanings" (Mazzola, Mannone, Pang, O'Brien, & Torunsky, 2016, p. 59). Material semiotics adds materials into the equation, helping to attune researchers to the heterogeneous socio-material relations that participate in enacting situated realities, entities, and situations.

Multiplicity and "Attempts at Ordering"

In asking scholars to seriously attend to the socio-material heterogeneity of everyday life, material semiotics also requires a recognition that reality is not homogenous and singular, but heterogeneous and multiple (Mol, 2002). Put differently, according to scholarship in the field of material semiotics, there is no "single reality" (Law 2002; Mol, 2002, p. 87). Instead, there are multiple realities being enacted through situated practices through complex, heterogeneous relations among humans and more-than-humans.

This realization of multiplicity, however, leads to a further question: If reality is a precarious mess of heterogeneous socio-material relations, how is it that we have come to think of anything as being organized or stable? Law (1994, p. 101, original emphasis) explains how material-semiotic attuned actor–network theory "treats the social world as a set of more or less related bits and pieces. There is no social order. Rather, there are endless attempts at order*ing*." The focus on the unfinished process of social order*ing* or social "co-ordination" (Mol, 2010, p. 264) creates an image of the social world, not as a static, steady, knowable entity, but "the recursive but incomplete performance of an unknowable number of intertwined orderings" (Law, 1994, p. 101). Material-semiotic attuned scholars see the process of translation as playing a central role in ordering projects (Law, 1994).

Similar to institutional ethnographers, material-semiotic attuned approaches illuminate how materials play an important role in attempts to coordinate and stabilize social relations. Or as Mol (2010) clearly explains: "Things are crucial to the ordering work at hand" (p. 263). According to these approaches, *things*—from discourses, to texts, to nuclear power plants—are translations. One of the main differences among more-than-human *things* rests in their durability: while a spoken word may disappear after it is enunciated, the textual representation of those words can be made into replicable copies and distributed to coordinate activities across far distances. That is, a sense of stability is achieved because "some materials last better than others. And some travel better than others" (Law, 1994, p. 102). Materials that can travel from site to site without losing their shape are what Latour (1986) has termed "immutable mobiles" (p. 8).

Law (1994) points out how it is "sociotechnical innovations that generate new forms of immutable mobiles: writing; print; paper; money; a postal system; cartography; navigation; ocean-going vessels; cannons; gunpowder; telephony" (p. 103). Immutable mobiles do not create situations of technical determinism, but are *socio-technical* in the sense that they are formed through and interact within heterogeneous socio-material relations (Law, 2009). Put differently, they represent material forms that emerge from a specific set of intentions and relations, and are deployed in an attempt to order further relations—though entanglements with other humans and more-than-humans means the results of ordering attempts are never completely predictable or controllable (e.g., Burch, 2019).

Ontological Politics

If material-semiotic attuned scholars have an interest in exploring how everyday realities emerge through complex relational entanglements among humans and more-than-humans, then how do they skillfully handle the messy heterogeneity, multiplicity, attempts at order*ing* (attempts to coordinate reality according to a singular ruling logic), and all of the other moving pieces exposed through material-semiotic sensibilities? This requires active engagement in ontological politics.

Within the field of material semiotics, ontology does not refer to an abstract concept of reality (a singular reality that exists somewhere out there beyond everyday experience), but the activities and material (or immaterial) relations that constitute situated realitie*s* (multiple realities enacted by different humans or more-than-humans within their specific socio-material entanglements). With this thinking, some ordering projects can be seen as an attempt to enact reality as singular (i.e., enact a singular ontology—a single, correct way to understand and enact one's relations with other humans and more-than-humans), which may be put in tension with other ordering projects (e.g., multiple other ways people might relate within their specific socio-material entanglements with other humans and more-than-humans).

By combining the term *ontology*—what constitutes reality—with *politics*, ontological politics encourages us to view reality not as something given, but as something that emerges from and is shaped through everyday practice. As such, it encourages scholars to explore hegemonic ontological framings attempting to label certain ways of organizing human and more-than-human relations as singular or correct, noticing who might be served by these framings, who might be harmed, and if there might be a different way of enacting these relations which causes less harm. Put by Mol (1999), "The term *politics* works to underline this active mode, this process of shaping, and the fact that its character is both open and contested" (pp. 74–75, original emphasis).

Thus, for material-semiotic attuned scholars, ontology is not given, but is something explored through empirical investigation (Law, 2019).

Law (2008) outlines what he sees as the call to action of those engaging in ontological politics: "To deal with the materialities of specific practices. To discover difference. And then to intervene in ways that might make a difference to those differences" (p. 673). Put another way, instead of trying to understand the world through master narratives, practicing ontological politics requires researchers to accept that reality is neither singular nor given. Instead it must be understood as heterogeneous, multiple and produced through situated, everyday practices—some which are coordinated by extra-local forces. It requires taking to heart the idea that the present does not dictate the future. Or, as Law (1991) puts it, practicing ontological politics requires scholars to maintain a "sense that what is seemingly so 'natural' *could have been otherwise*" (p. 6, original emphasis). Thus, it is through everyday activities that situated realities—situated entanglements with humans and more-than-humans—are put in tension with attempts at ordering—attempts to press the multiplicity of everyday experiences into alignment with a singular ruling logic.

Dialoguing Institutional Ethnography and Material Semiotics

In the past decade, some scholars have found value in combining insights from both institutional ethnography and material semiotics in enacting their research (e.g., Tummons, 2010). One reason is because institutional ethnography provides well-defined methodological tools and sensibilities for seriously attending to and materially tracing the coordination of various forms of social organization—methodological tools and accompanying commitments to study participants which are not as clearly defined within field of material semiotics. While I am aware of cautions against blending institutional ethnography with actor–network theory and other material-semiotic attuned approaches (e.g., Rankin, 2017), I discovered many productive opportunities for exchange between these fields of study, particularly when it comes to addressing troubles of the Anthropocene: in my case, exploring everyday eating in the aftermath of TEPCO's nuclear disaster. In this section I will outline how I came to enact my Ph.D. research as a vital institutional ethnography, as well as the generative engagements that emerged as I worked within these two fields of scholarship.

The Choice to Blend

When first attempting to explore everyday eating in the aftermath of TEPCO's nuclear disaster, I was initially drawn to institutional ethnography for two reasons: first, because it offered a clear method for explicating materially mediated ruling relations which begins and ends with the realities of everyday people experiencing disjuncture; and second, because it is a method of inquiry that explicitly attempts to produce knowledge that is useful in assisting study participants to better understand how these troubling experiences emerged—thus, providing hints on useful ways to respond (i.e., to become *response-able*) in trying times. However, it became clear that when dealing with radionuclides—insidious, yet imperceptible materials which everyday people were being encouraged to ignore or forget in the aftermath of TEPCO's nuclear disaster—that I would need further sensibilities for ensuring both the socio-materiality of ruling relations and the possible material presence of TEPCO's radionuclides remained vitally present within my study. It was at this point that I recognized the contribution material semiotics could bring to my institutional ethnographic explorations: through borrowing sensibilities from both fields of study, I could begin with experiences of *konran* faced by my participants, using sensibilities from institutional ethnography to explicate the post-disaster ruling relations attempting to coordinate their everyday eating, and sensibilities from material semiotics to ensure the materiality of radionuclides and other human and more-than-human actors contributing to experiences of *konran* remained vitally present in my analysis.

In short, blending sensibilities from both fields of study was invaluable to my Ph.D. project. It allowed me to creatively engage with the complex, heterogeneous socio-materiality unleashed in the aftermath of TEPCO's nuclear disaster (a strength of material semiotics), while also providing me with well-defined tools for noticing and tracing the ruling relations contributing to my participants' experiences of *konran* (a strength of institutional ethnography). As a result, I was able to notice materially-mediated post-disaster ruling relations as well as the human and more-than-human socio-material entanglements (i.e., people's attempts to relate with TEPCO's imperceptible radionuclides; historical cases of human–pollutant or human–radionuclide relationality which participated in enacting post-disaster ruling texts and discourses; among others) that were obfuscated or ignored within and through the activation of ruling texts and discourses.

Points of Dialogue and Difference

While there are a number of differences between institutional ethnography and material semiotics, their shared interest in noticing and tracing socio-material relations provided a unique opportunity for a productive dialogue between the two fields of scholarship. In this section I will describe some essential points of dialogue and difference I discovered as I worked with scholarship across these fields and how I handled them in enacting a vital institutional ethnography.

To begin, institutional ethnography is similar to material-semiotic attuned methods in its rejection of grand narrative theory (D. E. Smith, 2005). Additionally, as with material-semiotic attuned methods, institutional ethnography is not considered a methodology with a prescribed way of conducting research. Instead, it is referred to as a *method of inquiry* which directs researchers on how to go about uncovering the ways in which people participate in the enactment of ruling relations—how their everyday activities are coordinated by material texts and discourses produced in extra-local settings and established through trans-local material relations (McCoy, 1999).

Very similar to Latour's concept of immutable mobiles, institutional ethnography's ruling texts do not only refer to printed or digital documents, reports, and forms, but also photographs, sound recordings, videos, drawings and other formulations. In both cases, it is their ability to be mass-produced and widely distributed across distance and time that allows these materials and discourses to participate in organizing social relations (DeVault & McCoy, 2002). What institutional ethnography valuably offers to those thinking about the socio-materiality of ruling relations is a well-defined method for investigating institutions and other forms of social organization, not as taken-for-granted or abstract entities, but as a "complex of textually-coordinated work processes" (D. E. Smith, 2001, p. 177)—a complex of ruling relations that are accomplished through the *activation* of ruling texts in local settings (D. E. Smith, 1990, 1999).

Given institutional ethnography's focus on explicating the material coordination of social organization, the method of inquiry finds most common ground with studies and conversations in the field of material semiotics focusing on processes of coordination across difference (e.g., Tsing, 2015) and the ways in which ceaseless attempts at order*ing* are actualized—or not— through situated practices (e.g., Law, 1986). This shared focus on the material coordination of situated, embodied activities reflects institutional ethnography's own form of ontological politics: its grounding in the "ontology of the social" (D. E. Smith, 2005, pp. 51–54).

The ontology of the social is intended to guide researchers to view the social, not as an entity in itself, but as an enactment of a number of locally situated, extra-locally coordinated activities. Thus, within institutional ethnographies the lived, embodied experiences of participants do not disappear into abstract categories used to explain the social, nor is the social considered to be located entirely within discourse as in many postmodern conceptualizations (see DeVault, 1999). Instead, the social, or various forms of social organization and social order, are enacted through the activities of situated people whose experiences and realities are necessarily diverse. Institutional ethnography's conceptualization aligns well with Latour's (2005) decision to "define the social not as a special domain, a specific realm, or a particular sort of thing, but only as a very peculiar movement of re-association and reassembling" (p. 7). Law (1994) similarly describes the social as a hybrid enactment: "what we call the social is *materially heterogeneous:* talk, bodies, texts, machines, architectures, all of these and many more are implicated in and perform 'the social'" (p. 2, original emphasis) Thus, it seems that scholars in both fields are in general agreement that simplified, abstract categorizations of the social conceal the real messiness, contingency and heterogeneous human and more-than-human socio-material entanglements involved in its enactment.

Borrowing Marx's method of historical materialism, institutional ethnographers also share with the field of material semiotics an understanding of the contingency and indeterminacy of history and the material relations that participate in enacting social order. However, institutional ethnography is notably explicit in the need to recognize the agency of study participants in enacting ruling relations, as well as participants' abilities to comprehend their own embeddedness within these relations. Thus, the method is referred to as a "reflexive-materialist methodology" (G. W. Smith, 1995, p. 24). That is, its goal is not only to serve as an academic exercise of tracing or mapping ruling relations, but to produce knowledge *for* study participants about their own embeddedness within these relations, giving them the opportunity to use this information to enhance their own understandings of their experiences of disjuncture (D. E. Smith, 2005). This particular commitment to social justice is not explicitly articulated as an essential aspect of material-semiotic explorations—which are sometimes critiqued as being apolitical in nature (e.g., Bessire & Bond, 2014). Therefore, I argue that this commitment to produce knowledge *for* study participants could greatly support material-semiotic attuned scholars interested in seriously attending to questions of ontological politics *and* how to best cultivate response-ability to troubles of the Anthropocene.

An additional point of difference between the two fields of scholarship requiring further exploration is the topic of ontology. As mentioned, in the field of institutional ethnography, the *ontology of the social* is used to discuss the nature of the social or various forms of social order, highlighting that these are not macro systems existing somewhere *out there*, but emerge through the situated activities of people coordinated across space and time. Similarly, in the field of material semiotics, the social and social ordering projects are viewed as specific ways of organizing human and more-than-human relations in alignment with a singular ruling logic (with materials such as immutable mobiles participating in attempts to coordinate human activities). As such, they can be understood as attempts to organize human activities (how humans notice and relate with other humans and more-than-humans) in alignment with a *single reality* or singular ontological framing. Here we see how these understandings of a single or ruling ontology are somewhat compatible, however the particular analytic interests of each field of scholarship adds nuance to how each attends to questions of multiplicity and multiple ontologies which I will discuss below.

To begin, institutional ethnographers have an analytic interest in tracing the ruling texts and discourses that participate in enacting the social or forms of social order. They refer to this work as *explicating* ruling relations. On the other hand, analytic explorations in the field of material semiotics aim to open up seemingly singular ontological framings, exposing the complex socio-materiality that enacts and is imbued within them—many of which are ignored or obfuscated within these framing projects (i.e., exposing reality as situated, materially heterogeneous and multiple as opposed to abstract and singular). Thus, there is an analytic interest in exploring the multiple, situated socio-material entanglements (e.g., the situated activities and material relations that participate in enacting safe food according to government standards) that participate in enacting a seemingly singular reality (e.g., "the nuclear disaster is under control" or "all food sold in supermarkets is safe") or seemingly singular objects (e.g., safe food), but which might be obfuscated or ignored within these ontological framing projects themselves (see Law, 2002; Mol, 2002). This analytic work could be understood as *re-entangling*—a process which might involve tracing ruling texts and discourses, but also noticing complex relations among myriad other humans and more-than-humans that participate in enacting peoples' everyday realities, the ruling texts themselves, among other situations and objects.

In an attempt to handle these differences, in enacting vital institutional ethnography, I drew on sensibilities from the field of material semiotics to conceptualize my analytic work as an active engagement in ontological politics. As a result, I decided to use the well-defined methodological tools and sensibilities from institutional ethnography to *explicate* the material relations that participated in enacting post-disaster ruling relations (what I viewed as a *single reality*). At the same time, I would use sensibilities from material semiotics to *re-entangle* my study participants within complex socio-material relations to highlight the socio-material multiplicity (multiple ways of organizing human and more-than-human relations which I viewed as *multiple realities*) that can be ignored or obfuscated when coordinating people's activities in alignment with a dominant, singular ontology.

Ultimately, while important differences do exist between these two fields of scholarship, a shared commitment to noticing and tracing socio-material relations in a way that recognizes the participation of human and more-than-human actors in enacting everyday realities is where I found the real potential for institutional ethnography and material semiotics to link up. Both methods are grounded in strong ethical commitments: institutional ethnography offers a robust, well-defined method of tracing trans-local ruling relations and attending to the agency of participants in the research process; and material-semiotic sensibilities provide guidance on directly engaging with ontological politics and noticing other heterogeneous human and more-than-human relationality—as well as the tensions permeating these relations—that contribute to everyday, situated experiences of disorder and disjuncture, but which may be obfuscated or ignored within ruling relations themselves.

In my Ph.D. thesis, I was guided by insights from both the fields of institutional ethnography and material semiotics, a collaboration which emerged as a vital institutional ethnography—a relational-materialist-reflexive method of inquiry for explicating ruling relations while remaining attentive to the reflexive capacity and subjectivity of study participants, as well as other socio-material entanglements being obfuscated or ignored within Japan's post-2011 ruling relations.

Piecing Together a Vital Institutional Ethnography

Similar to other studies in institutional ethnography, I structured my Ph.D. thesis to engage in two different levels of investigation: an entry level, ethnographic investigation beginning with the everyday activities and lived experiences of human actors experiencing *konran* related to everyday eating; and a secondary level analytic investigation tracing how these experiences have emerged through situated entanglements with textually-mediated ruling relations. However, the analysis did not end with attention to explicating ruling relations. Instead, I expanded my analysis, adopting sensibilities from the field of material semiotics to notice other socio-material entanglements that contributed to experiences of *konran* shared by my participants, but which were being obfuscated or ignored within the ruling relations at play. Thus, my analysis not only traced ruling texts and discourses contributing to these experiences but, following Mol (2002), worked to "unravel" these experiences in ways that attended to "[a]n endless list of heterogeneous elements that can either be highlighted or left in the background, depending on the character and purpose of the description" (p. 26). By welcoming this wider heterogeneous socio-materiality into the analysis, I was able to engage in ontological politics so that my analysis could guide my participants to notice their own embeddedness within a complex and precarious "established disorder" (Haraway, 1994)—a conceptual space where the singular (e.g., ruling relations) and the multiple (e.g., people's everyday embodied experiences and entanglements with humans and more-than-humans; the messy socio-material relations that participate in enacting ruling texts and discourses; among others), as well as the tensions, coherences, and incoherences among them, coexist and are accessible for reflection and analysis.

Expanding my analysis to explicate how ruling relations were enacted within the established disorder, I adopted the "logic of oscillation" presented by Law (2002, p. 9) as a way of attuning to the wavering between the singular (e.g., ruling relations) and the multiple (e.g., situated, entangled experiences of my participants). I additionally borrowed the concept of *single reality*—as discussed by both Mol (2002) and Law (2002)—to illustrate how ruling texts and discourses attempted to coordinate the activities of my study participants to align with a single, correct, established way of doing or being. This focus allowed me to explore how single realities, translated into ruling texts and discourses, participated in the process of social coordination. At the same time, I was able to explore how behind the *presence* of a seemingly coherent object (e.g., safe food) were myriad heterogeneous relations left *absent*, what Law and Singleton (2005, pp. 343–344) refer to as "absent presence."

Law and Singleton's absent presence is similar to the figures of *ghosts* and *monsters* that appear in the book *Arts of Living on a Damaged Planet* (Tsing et al., 2017). The book's editors describe how they use ghosts as a figure to help in thinking through various historical events—and their human and more-than-human participants—that have been brushed aside or ignored in the linear, forward-moving industrial progress projects of modernity, as well as how their enduring existence haunts humans and more-than-humans who inhabit the Anthropocene—e.g., radionuclides from the Chernobyl nuclear disaster which take hundreds or thousands of years to decay. They additionally use monsters as a figure to describe the frightening, monstrous qualities of some socio-material entanglements—e.g., latest biological explorations which view humans as *holobionts*: "an organism plus its persistent communities of symbionts" (Gilbert, 2017, p. M73)—and the need to attune to these messy material-semiotic relations through careful, and oftentimes uncomfortable, "arts of noticing" (Tsing, 2015, p. 17).

Throughout my Ph.D. thesis, I attuned to the absent presence of both ghosts and monsters of TEPCO's nuclear disaster by attending to the oscillation between the "multiple absence" of heterogeneous relationality lying behind the "singular presence" of ruling texts and discourses (Law, 2002, p. 9), while at the same time noticing how relations among these heterogeneous elements played out in my participants' everyday experiences. I also explored how the single realities being deployed through ruling relations worked to "mute" (Latour, 2005, p. 40) and marginalize various human and more-than-human actors and activities at the expense of others. In the following sections I will provide further details into how both the entry level and secondary level investigations were actualized within my Ph.D. project.

Entry-Level Ethnographic Investigation

As with other institutional ethnographic studies, in conducting a vital institutional ethnography, ethnographic observation and immersion into a specific local setting served as an entry point for discovering and exploring my study's problematic (discussed below). In the case of my Ph.D. research, this stage involved exploring people's experiences of eating in the aftermath of TEPCO's nuclear disaster and searching for clues into how people's experiences of *konran* were embedded within, and emerged from, trans-local textually mediated ruling relations. Borrowing sensibilities from material semiotics, I also used the entry-level investigation as a chance to notice other human and more-than-human actors involved in enacting experiences of *konran* shared by my study's participants. The following sections will address some aspects of this entry-level ethnographic investigation.

Entering the Material-Semiotic Field

Guided by insights from institutional ethnography, fieldwork involved in-depth interviews and focus group discussions with 43 participants in conjunction with participant observation, casual conversations, and auto-ethnographic reflections (Campbell & Gregor, 2004). The interviews and focus groups were of great importance as they were opportunities to collect very rich descriptions and detailed accounts of people's experiences of *konran* following TEPCO's nuclear disaster. While my fieldwork was designed according to the principles of institutional ethnography—i.e., designed to notice textually mediated ruling relations—the attentiveness to "events-in-practice" (Mol, 2002, p. 21) produced process-narratives that were also useful for an analysis using material-semiotic sensibilities. What resulted were thick descriptions where experiences, objects and practices emerged as "both material and active" (Mol, 2002, p. 20), making them accessible for analysis using sensibilities from both fields of scholarship.

Attuning to Ruling Relations

Following institutional ethnographers, in my Ph.D. thesis my focus was not on ruling texts and discourses as mere material entities, but on how "people *participate* in discursive activity" (Campbell & Gregor, 2004, p. 41, original emphasis). During my fieldwork, I had to learn to see my participants', as well as my own, everyday activities as being embedded within textually mediated ruling relations, while at the same time being fully aware that such relations were often not visible to most people in their everyday lives. While conducting my interviews, I was aware that my analytic task would not involve *making* connections between the local and extra-local institution, but *explicating*—making visible—*how* ruling relations were being enacted through everyday practices (DeVault & McCoy, 2002). Thus, during my interviews I attentively listened for traces of discourses or texts in people's narratives, as these would make up the material clues necessary for later explicating ruling relations.

Analysis

Like other material-semiotic attuned approaches, institutional ethnography is not fixed in its form, but can be realized in a variety of ways. DeVault and McCoy (2002) describe how investigations in institutional ethnography are not easily planned out in advance, but are reminiscent of a ball of string, where a thread is discovered and an unraveling begins. Similar metaphors have been used to discuss analytical processes in the field of material semiotics (e.g., Haraway, 2016). The difference I see between these practices is that while institutional ethnographers are trained to follow threads of materially-mediated ruling relations, material-semiotic sensibilities allow for following other messier and somewhat wilder knotted and tangled threads (e.g., threads leading to the ghostly materiality of historical pollution incidents and the ruling relations deployed to manage them which continued to influence post-disaster ruling relations in 2011; threads leading to the historical evolution of the scientific data, methods and metrics activated within ruling texts and discourses; among others).

Following the principals of institutional ethnography, I designed my Ph.D. analysis so that it both began and ended with the experiences of my study participants (Campbell, 1998), providing insights into how they came to experience *konran* related to everyday eating in the aftermath of TEPCO's nuclear disaster. As mentioned, while part of this explication involved tracing textually-mediated ruling relations, it also included an exploration of other human and more-than-human entanglements, including how attempts to coordinate everyday eating followed a *logic of oscillation* between singular ruling logics and the multiplicity of everyday experiences. Thus, throughout my analysis, I attended to the vacillation between the singular (e.g., ruling relations; ruling texts and discourses) and the multiple (e.g., people's everyday realities enacted within their situated socio-material entanglements; the heterogeneous socio-materiality that participated in enacting ruling texts and discourses) in a way that attuned to myriad heterogeneous relations contributing to my participants' experiences of *konran*. The following sections will provide a brief overview of some of the concepts and sensibilities from both fields of study that guided my vital institutional ethnographic analysis.

The Research Problematic and Guiding Questions

A major step in my analysis was to clarify my study's problematic. According to the principles of institutional ethnography, identifying the study's problematic involves discovering troubling experiences which point to clues of a disjuncture existing between what people are experiencing in their everyday lives and the official explanations of how things are happening (Campbell & Gregor, 2004). Thus, disjunctures provide fertile opportunities for discovering how people's everyday lives are embedded within textually mediated ruling relations, and how people themselves participate in those relations.

Smith (1987, pp. 49–50) refers to a disjuncture as a "point of rupture" which directs researchers to focus on understanding how an experience or activity is organized and the social relations involved in its enactment. I believe the concepts of "breakdowns" (Latour, 2005, p. 81) and "interferences" (Mol, 2002, pp. 142–149) discussed in the field of material semiotics both complement and enhance the concept of disjuncture. In my Ph.D. thesis, it was in exploring my own and my participants' experiences of *konran* that pointed me to experiences of disjuncture and to my research problematic.

However, the concepts of disorder and interference were also helpful in attuning me to myriad other human and more-than-human actors that participated in enacting these troubling experiences. Thus, focusing on experiences of *konran* offered an opportunity to notice experiences of disjuncture while also uncovering traces of humans and more-than-humans that were silenced, ignored or muted through the development and activation of ruling texts and discourses. Therefore, a blending of sensibilities and insights from both institutional ethnography and material semiotics provided a space to analyze the tensions and incompatibilities that emerged when standardized, single-reality wielding attempts to control and direct activities (translated into ruling texts and discourses) entered the everyday lives of my study participants, where specific, local, messy and multiple realities were being enacted within heterogeneous socio-material entanglements of humans and more-than-humans.

As mentioned, my study's problematic originally arose from my own experience of *konran* related to everyday eating while living in Japan following TEPCO's nuclear disaster. Though I myself was living in the Kansai region—approximately 600 kilometers from the nuclear disaster—I found myself as an active participant in a complex food system, compelled to understand my new relationship with historically reemerging more-than-human actors: anthropogenic radionuclides. My awareness that I was embedded within complex socio-material relations was accompanied with a burning curiosity to understand how my own experiences were "hooked up" (D. E. Smith, 2005, p. 41) within greater post-disaster ruling relations. However, as a foreigner living with my Japanese partner, I wanted to include the experiences of other locally situated people in my study—people whose own particular experiences of *konran* related to everyday eating in the aftermath of TEPCO's nuclear disaster could enrich my analysis.

In order to address the multiple experiences of *konran* felt by myself and my study participants, the institutional ethnographic problematic guiding my analysis developed as: *How is everyday eating being coordinated in the aftermath of TEPCO's nuclear disaster?* This question was designed to open up the institutional complex of post-disaster ruling relations to allow me to explore and trace materially mediated ruling relations that appeared within my participants', and my own, everyday experiences. However, this problematic also paved the way for using sensibilities from material semiotics for exploring two further questions pertinent to eating in the aftermath of TEPCO's nuclear disaster: First, *how do multiple "safe foods" emerge and relate to each other in practice?* Second, *how do experiences of konran emerge through the enactment of post-disaster ruling relations, and how do processes of highlighting or muting relations among actors—human and more-than-human—contribute to people's suffering?* These guiding questions, paired with sensibilities from both fields of scholarship, provided me with a clear objective, yet an unrestricted pathway for exploring the heterogeneous socio-material relationality contributing to my participants', and my own, experiences of *konran* following TEPCO's nuclear disaster.

Structuring the Analysis

As previously mentioned, vital institutional ethnography provided me with an opportunity to creatively explore my study's problematic, something I found to be invaluable when dealing with a complex, ever-evolving socio-technical disaster. I consider my Ph.D. to be a co-constructed text as the experiences, knowledges and thick descriptions offered by my participants inspired my writing, directing me toward the strings that needed to be followed to explicate ruling relations as well as other ghostly and monstrous socio-material entanglements that needed to be attended to. The analytic work of *explicating* my study's problematic and *re-entangling* my participants within ghostly and monstrous socio-material relations took place within four chapters: one analytic background chapter and three analysis chapters.

In Chapter 4 of my Ph.D. thesis, I situated my participants' experiences living in the aftermath of TEPCO's nuclear disaster within Japan's long history of industrial pollution. In retelling entangled stories that highlighted the ghostly and monstrous socio-material entanglements and the roles of ruling texts in muting humans and more-than-humans living within industrial ruins (Tsing, 2015), I produced a number of insights into the coordination of human activities in the aftermath of socio-technical disasters which guided the analytic projects of explication and re-entanglement I undertook in Chapters 5, 6, and 7.

My interviews and focus group sessions revealed that all of my study participants were concerned in some way about the origins and scientific validity of the 100 Bq/kg reference limit for radionuclides in food, a metric they all interacted with which was used to ensure the safety of the food lining supermarket shelves they visited. Thus, in Chapter 5, I followed a string from their situated experiences of *konran* into the vast institutional complex of radiation protection standards. Through the process of explicating how ruling texts and discourses relating to radiation protection evolved, were enacted and activated in practice, I also highlighted many of the ghostly and monstrous entanglements they obfuscated or ignored.

In Chapter 6, I followed another string from my participants' experiences, this time explicating how TEPCO's radionuclides and my participants' concerns about food safety were muted through the activation of ruling texts and discourses. Here, telling entangled stories that highlighted the human and more-than-human actors that participated in enacting multiple versions of safe food allowed me to illustrate the complex ways ruling texts and discourses attempted to coordinate my participants' everyday eating following the nuclear disaster and silence their attempts to discuss their concerns about the possible presence of TEPCO's radionuclides in their everyday food.

Finally, in Chapter 7, I focused exclusively on the experiences of my study participants, telling entangled stories of how they carefully enacted their lives and attended to the materiality of TEPCO's radionuclides within the constrictive ruling relations explicated in Chapters 5 and 6.

Findings and Feedback

Ultimately, the combined analytic work of explication and re-entanglement in enacting a vital institutional ethnography resulted in a number of insights that could support myself and my study participants in better understanding our experiences of *konran* related to everyday eating in the aftermath of TEPCO's nuclear disaster. One of the most important findings was my ability to clearly depict how post-disaster ruling discourses (e.g., the ruling discourses of "safety," "anxiety," and "harmful rumors") pressured people to ignore the possible material presence of TEPCO's radionuclides in their everyday lives, as the activation of ruling discourses participated in categorizing those people attempting to discuss or carefully relate with TEPCO's radionuclides as being "unscientific," "anxious," "against disaster recovery efforts," or "causing economic damage through spreading harmful rumors." Additionally, through focusing on both explication and re-entanglement, feedback to my study participants could not only provide insights into the role of ruling texts and discourses in contributing to their experiences of *konran*, but how focusing on socio-materiality offered opportunities for more openly deliberating the nuclear disaster and, as a result, discovering concrete ways for responding to the situated troubles they faced. Thus, in cases like mine where ruling texts and discourses were working to silence deliberation in the aftermath of a complex socio-technical disaster, focusing on the materiality of ruling texts, ruling discourses and radionuclides provided an important language for deliberation—a language that could support myself and my study participants in possibly challenging the efficacy of ruling discourses in muting such discussions.

CONCLUSION

My goal in writing this chapter has been to introduce readers to the possibility of enacting a vital institutional ethnography, particularly when studying messy troubles of the Anthropocene that involve imperceptible pollutants, radionuclides and other epistemologically distant materials. For those adopting material-semiotic sensibilities, providing thick ethnographic accounts which allow for noticing human and more-than-human socio-material entanglements has been one way to address troubles of the Anthropocene, enriching debates among scholars concerned with cultivating response-ability and curbing the "tide of ruination" threatening livelihoods and lifeways throughout the globe (e.g., Haraway, 2016; Tsing et al., 2017, p. G1). In borrowing sensibilities from both material semiotics and institutional ethnography, vital institutional ethnography aims to further enrich scholarly attempts to cultivate response-ability to troubles of the Anthropocene, providing tools for attending to the socio-materiality of ruling relations and the ways textually mediated ruling relations participate in constraining or supporting people's abilities to notice and discuss their material realities—and thus their abilities to respond in ways beyond those endorsed by the ruling relations themselves.

In particular, I strongly believe that institutional ethnography's explicit commitment to social justice—its commitment to producing research *for* study participants, providing them with insights so they might better understand their own embeddedness within ruling relations and act accordingly—can greatly serve those scholars seriously working to cultivate response-ability in the Anthropocene. That is, the method of inquiry provides a clear framework for and, in fact, requires the sharing of research findings with study participants. When studying troubles of the Anthropocene, adopting this particular sensibility from institutional ethnography would ensure that research findings would be produced *for* and shared *with* those people on the frontlines attempting to respond to some of the most pressing troubles we face—many of which threaten livability on planet Earth.

Overall, while blending sensibilities from both institutional ethnography and material semiotics does not result in a pure institutional ethnographic study, I found sensibilities and tools from both of these fields of scholarship to be vital to the exploration of everyday eating in the aftermath of TEPCO's nuclear disaster—where grappling with the materiality of ruling relations and other human and more-than-human socio-material entanglements became necessary to prevent my own research from becoming confined by post-disaster ruling relations deployed to manage and contain people's responses to the disaster. My ultimate hope is that other scholars will find my insights useful, if not essential (vital) to their own study topics, particularly those projects addressing troubles of the Anthropocene and working to ensure livability (vitality) on planet Earth.

Notes

1. I follow Whatmore (2002) and others in using the term *more-than-human* as it opens up the category of nonhuman in a way which strives to prevent a potentially constrictive binary and hierarchy from emerging.
2. The term "enact" comes from Mol (2002, p. vii) who uses it to illustrate how realities, entities and situations do not appear from nowhere, but are enacted through situated actions or practices taking place within complex socio-material relational entanglements.
3. Material semiotics views reality as emerging from within complex relational entanglements among actors, human and more-than-human. Thus, in this paper *actor* does not of refer to an autonomous individual entity with complete agency over their actions. Instead it is used as a term to recognize the relationally entangled entities—human and more-than-human—that participate in enacting situated realities and objects (see Law & Mol, 2008).
4. Again, material semiotics has an analytic interest in exploring heterogeneous human–more-than-human relations (or *socio-material relations*). The term *socio-material* works to highlight the complex relationality among humans and more-than-humans which participate in enacting realities and objects (see MacLeod, Cameron, Ajjawi, Kits, & Tummons, 2019).
5. As a general introduction to the theoretical and methodological characteristics of vital institutional ethnography, this chapter will not include any direct quotations or detailed empirical examples from my Ph.D. research. Please refer to my thesis (Burch, 2018) for these empirical details.

References

Bessire, L., & Bond, D. (2014). Ontological anthropology and the deferral of critique. *American Ethnologist, 41*(3), 440–456.

Burch, K. A. (2018). *Eating a nuclear disaster: A vital institutional ethnography of everyday eating in the aftermath of Tokyo Electric Power Company's Fukushima Daiichi Nuclear Power Plant disaster* (Doctoral dissertation). University of Otago.

Burch, K. A. (2019). When overflow is the rule: The evolution of the transnational nuclear assemblage and its technopolitical tools for framing human–radionuclide relationality. *Geoforum, 107,* 66–76.

Burch, K. A., Legun, K., & Campbell, H. (2018). Not defined by the numbers: Distinction, dissent and democratic possibilities in debating the data. *Agri-environmental governance as an assemblage: Multiplicity, power, and transformation* (pp. 127–144). New York: Routledge.

Campbell, M. L. (1998). Institutional ethnography and experience as data. *Qualitative Sociology, 21*(1), 55–73.

Campbell, M. L., & Gregor, F. M. (2004). *Mapping social relations: A primer in institutional ethnography.* Lanham, MD: AltaMira Press.

Carolan, M. S. (2006). Do you see what I see? Examining the epistemic barriers to sustainable agriculture. *Rural Sociology, 71*(2), 232–260.

DeVault, M. L. (1999). *Liberating method: Feminism and social research.* Philadelphia: Temple University Press.

DeVault, M. L., & McCoy, L. (2002). Institutional ethnography: Using interviews to investigate ruling relations. In J. Gubrium & J. Holstein (Eds.), *Handbook of interview research* (pp. 751–776). Thousand Oaks, CA: Sage.

Gilbert, S. F. (2017). Holobiont by birth: Multilineage individuals as the concretion of cooperative processes. In A. L. Tsing, H. A. Swanson, E. Gan, & N. Bubandt (Eds.), *Arts of living on a damaged planet: Ghosts and monsters of the Anthropocene* (pp. M73–M89). Minneapolis: University of Minnesota Press.

Haraway, D. J. (1994). A game of cat's cradle: Science studies, feminist theory, cultural studies. *Configurations, 2*(1), 59–71.

Haraway, D. J. (2016). *Staying with the trouble: Making kin in the Chthulucene.* Durham: Duke University Press.

Latour, B. (1986). Visualisation and cognition: Drawing things together. In E. Long & H. Kuklick (Eds.), *Knowledge and society: Studies in the sociology of culture past and present* (Vol. 6, pp. 1–40). Greenwich, CT: JAI Press.

Latour, B. (2005). *Reassembling the social: An introduction to actor-network-theory.* Oxford: Oxford University Press.

Law, J. (1986). On the methods of long-distance control: Vessels, navigation and the Portuguese route to India. In J. Law (Ed.), *Power, action, and belief: A new sociology of knowledge?* (pp. 234–263). Boston: Routledge and Kegan Paul.

Law, J. (1991). Introduction. *A sociology of monsters: Essays on power, technology, and domination* (pp. 1–23). London: Routledge.

Law, J. (1994). *Organizing modernity.* Oxford and Cambridge, MA: Blackwell.

Law, J. (2002). *Aircraft stories: Decentering the object in technoscience.* Durham: Duke University Press.

Law, J. (2008). On sociology and STS. *Sociological Review, 56*(4), 623–649.

Law, J. (2009). Actor network theory and material semiotics. *The new Blackwell companion to social theory* (pp. 141–158). Oxford: Wiley-Blackwell.

Law, J. (2019, January 30). *Material semiotics*. Retrieved June 12, 2019, from www.heterogeneities.net/publications/Law2019MaterialSemiotics.pdf.

Law, J., & Mol, A. (2008). The actor-enacted: Cumbrian sheep in 2001. *Politica Y Sociedad, 45*(3), 75–92.

Law, J., & Singleton, V. (2005). Object lessons. *Organization, 12*(3), 331–355.

MacLeod, A., Cameron, P., Ajjawi, R., Kits, O., & Tummons, J. (2019). Actor-network theory and ethnography: Sociomaterial approaches to researching medical education. *Perspectives on Medical Education, 8*(3), 177–186. https://doi.org/10.1007/s40037-019-0513-6.

Mazzola, G. G., Mannone, M., Pang, Y., O'Brien, M., & Torunsky, N. (2016). *All about music: The complete ontology—Realities, semiotics, communication, and embodiment*. Cham: Springer International Publishing.

McCoy, L. (1999). *Accounting discourse and textual practices of ruling, a study of institutional transformation and restructuring in higher education* (Doctoral dissertation). University of Toronto.

Mol, A. (1999). Ontological politics: A word and some questions. *Sociological Review, 47*(S1), 74–89. http://doi.org/10.1111/j.1467-954X.1999.tb03483.x.

Mol, A. (2002). *The body multiple: Ontology in medical practice*. Durham: Duke University Press.

Mol, A. (2010). Actor-network theory: Sensitive terms and enduring tensions. *Kolner Zeitschrift Fur Soziologie Und Sozialpsychologie, Sonderheft, 50*, 253–269.

Murdoch, J. (2001). Ecologising sociology: Actor-network theory, co-construction and the problem of human exemptionalism. *Sociology, 35*(1), 111–133.

Rankin, J. (2017). Conducting analysis in institutional ethnography: Guidance and cautions. *International Journal of Qualitative Methods, 16*(1), 160940691773447–11. https://doi.org/10.1177/1609406917734472.

Smith, D. E. (1987). *The everyday world as problematic: A feminist sociology*. Toronto: University of Toronto Press.

Smith, D. E. (1990). *Texts, facts, and femininity: Exploring the relations of ruling*. New York: Routledge.

Smith, D. E. (1999). *Writing the social: Critique, theory, and investigations*. Toronto: University of Toronto Press.

Smith, D. E. (2001). Texts and the ontology of organizations and institutions. *Studies in Cultures, Organizations and Societies, 7*(2), 159–198. https://doi.org/10.1080/10245280108523557.

Smith, D. E. (2005). *Institutional ethnography: A sociology for people*. Lanham, MD: AltaMira Press.

Smith, G. W. (1995). Accessing treatments: Managing the AIDS epidemic in Ontario. In M. Campbell & A. Manicom (Eds.), *Knowledge, experience, and ruling relations: Studies in the social organization of knowledge* (pp. 18–34). Toronto: University of Toronto Press.

Tsing, A. L. (2015). *The mushroom at the end of the world: On the possibility of life in capitalist ruins*. Princeton: Princeton University Press.

Tsing, A. L. (2017). A threat to Holocene resurgence is a threat to livability. In M. Brightman & J. Lewis (Eds.), *The anthropology of sustainability* (pp. 51–65). New York: Palgrave Macmillan.

Tsing, A. L., Swanson, H. A., Gan, E., & Bubandt, N. (Eds.). (2017). *Arts of living on a damaged planet: Ghosts and monsters of the Anthropocene*. Minneapolis: University of Minnesota Press.

Tummons, J. (2010). Institutional ethnography and actor–network theory: A framework for researching the assessment of trainee teachers. *Ethnography and Education, 5*(3), 345–357. https://doi.org/10.1080/17457823.2010.511444.

Whatmore, S. (2002). *Hybrid geographies: Natures cultures spaces.* London: Sage.

CHAPTER 26

Institutional Ethnography for Social Work

Gerald de Montigny

INTERVIEW #1

SW: So thanks for participating.
C: haa ok [nervous laughter]
SW: eh'ok [inhale laugh], um maybe you can just ahh tell me how it. waas that youu. um came about with being involved with CAS
C: hggm [cough] woo last year, like (year), I got/ like I didn't get along with my family I was like really suicidal I wasss. my parents said I was crazy like . I didn't do anything they said, I was always threatening them, pushing my mom around . I was physically violeent, I was like . I'd would do anything, say anything to get my way and if I didn't get my way I'd be all like . I'd flip out on them and make it seem like it was all their fault and they jist couldn' handle it anymore so.
SW: So ha/ how did that process come about?
C: Um well I'd been in the' hospital on the psychiatric ward . for a couple of months
SW: At [hospital name]?
C: Ya, aand ahh my pssychiatrist or . whatever you wanna call her toold my parents that maybe they should look into group homes cuz .. they though that, well my psychiatrist thought that I was being too hard on my parents and my parents were going through like .. uhm, I don't know what you'd call it, but my mom was having like, a crazy

---

G. de Montigny (✉)
Ottawa, ON, Canada
e-mail: Gerald.demontigny@carleton.ca

© The Author(s) 2021
P. C. Luken and S. Vaughan (eds.), *The Palgrave Handbook of Institutional Ethnography*,
https://doi.org/10.1007/978-3-030-54222-1_26

thing you know like . she was losing it, so the psychiatrist said it'd be best to get me outta the house.

SW: Okay .. so when you say your mom was having sortah a crazy thing, is that a breakdown=

C: =A break down ya

SW: is that sort of a history in her, her life, or just sortah what was happening for her at the time?

C: Uhm, they said like I caused it on her .. cuz . I was always saying I'm gonna kill myself, I'm gonna run away, I'm gonna do this I was, I was, like self mutilatiing an . . I haven't done any of that for a long time but then I was <u>really</u> crazy but I took potato peelers to my arms and just totally tore all the skin off . and my mom she went crazy cause you know like I'm her kid an, it jist, I guess it really hurt her to see me doing that .she couldn't handle it.

SW: ◦Ok◦, do you remember the day that, sortof yoou, that you, got connected with CAS?

C: Like when they first brought me to my first group home?

SW: Yah.

C: Yahhhe [nervous laughter]. It was uuhmm last April and I had jist gotten out of the hospital annd, I was over at my boyfriend at the time's house and I didn't want to go home like and his mom was driving me home and I flipped out in the car I'm like no you're not taking me there and I was crying and so she's like ok. So she took me back to their house, I spent the night there, and the next day my parents called and they told her that they called the cops.. and so they called the cops . annd, me I was flipping out there I was crying me and my friend, well my boyfriend and his twin sister, she was like my best friend. We locked the cops out and the ambulance had came t' get me . I don't know why there was an ambulance but - we locked them out we were flipping out, annd eventually they got in and the ambulance took me down too (hospital name) for some reason, and I sat in one of their little rooms and waited for ah CAS person to come, like my Dad was there too but I was so mad like I wouldn't talk to him, I wouldn't see him. Soo uhm the social worker came and brought me to my first group home. It was like, I got there at like twelve o'clock at night.

SW: Did you know this was planned?

C: mm hrrhr [cough] no

SW: So when you were at your boyfriend's the reason you didn't want to go home wasn't because you knew you were [ah]

C: [na] it was just I didn't want to like see my parents, I didn't want to be around them I was pissed off at them it was just I didn't want to go home.

SW: Ok. So uhm, so a social worker came, took you to your first group home Do you remember what you were feeling that day?

Preliminary Groundings

At the top of this chapter, and below are transcriptions of turns-at-talk between social workers (SW) and C and M (two youth in care) which have been transcribed as according nominally to notation conventions from conversation analysis.[1] In what follows, the development of institutional ethnography is informed by both ethnomethodology and conversation analysis. Ethnomethodology, with its focus on everyday and mundane practices, along with conversation analysis with its focus on investigations into the details of everyday talk-as-interaction, combine effectively with institutional ethnography (IE) with its focus on members' socially organized practices of collaboratively and interactively co-accomplishing forms and orders of occasions, both as locally realized and as articulated to extra-local and institutional orders. The insights and tools derived from conversation analysis and ethnomethodology are not only compatible with and useful for doing IE, they also allow us to focus on and explicate the local accomplishment of socially identifiable occasions. Indeed, a focus on members' practices allow us to explicate or show in the details of mundane and everyday interactions just how people quite practically go about accomplishing textually mediated orders and connect here-and-now activities to extra-local and textually mediated orders. The attentions of ethnomethodology, conversation analysis, and institutional ethnography are particularly useful for social workers who seek to understand just how it is that they practically go about performing social work itself, whether as interviews, therapy, counselling, and so on (de Montigny, 2017, 2018a, 2018b; Fitzgerald, 2013).

Harold Garfinkel (1917–2011), the originator of ethnomethodology, along with Harvey Sacks (1935–1975) who developed conversation analysis, focused on the ways that people, through their everyday interactions produced recognizable and ubiquitous socially ordered occasions, such as chats, interviews, courtroom adjudications, surgeries, biomedical laboratories, and so on. Garfinkel and Sacks (1970) observed that attention to doing makes visible the ways that "accountable-conversation-as-a-practical-accomplishment consists only and entirely in and of its work" adding that a focus on doing underscores that "this work of accountable conversation is members' work" (p. 352). In ethnomethodology and conversation analysis the imperative is to examine just how it is that people produce, as a practical matter, ordinary, and quite familiar social scenes. How do people accomplish or do queuing for groceries, chatting with a friend in a café, or a social work interview? Through an attention to the details of talk-in-interaction, conversation analysis provides us with a window into understanding the minutia of embodied interactions, through which people constitute turn-by-turn and moment after moment ordinary forms of social interaction. Although ethnomethodology and conversation analysis provide tools for identifying and analyzing the ways that everyday coherence and orders are practically accomplished, IE simultaneously expands our attention to an appreciation of the ways that people here-and-now quite practically work to tie and to make accountable local and situated interactions and occasions to extra-local and textually mediated instructions, forms, and directions.

By applying ethnomethodology and conversation analysis to IE, we can explore in detail the mundane, ordinary, and largely taken-for-granted ways that people in interaction accomplish recognizable local social scenes and orders. In turn, this allows us to understand just how people, through their quite practical and at-hand practices knit their local activities to extra-local institutional structures. Through detailed attention to local interactions, such as those social workers use to conduct a child-protection investigation, we can begin to empirically document just how it is that practitioners knit home visits, studied observation, selection of specific details and relevancies, as at-hand and focused professional attentions to thereby create records, documents, and case files. Supplemental to ethnomethodology and conversation analysis, IE directs our attention to the practicalities for effecting textually mediated practices, thereby linking empirically everyday practices to extended and extra-local institutionally mandated orders.

Importantly, the attention in IE to extended courses of action (Smith, 2005, p. 160) connects people's day-to-day documentary and textually mediated work in local sites to webs of institutional control and regulation. It is through participation in extended courses of action that we move from our homes, commute along city streets and navigate traffic signs and signals, to arrive at and enter our offices, meet with and interview clients, produce documentary records of those meetings, and enter case notes into file systems. It is in lived courses of action that we bridge seemingly individual, isolated, and particular attentions and actions to extra-local institutional structures. IE directs our attention to examine just how it is that we, as practitioners of everyday worlds, quite practically go about connecting our local and mundane experiences, work, and realities to extra-local and documentary organizational forms. IE provides us direction for explicating the feminist insight that the personal is political.

An appreciation of courses of action allows us to examine just how social workers on these occasions interacted with youth in care. We can study just how, turn-by-turn, social workers endeavored to conduct themselves as professional, and just how that which they said, purposefully anticipated not just my review of the audiotapes of their interviews, but their internalization and realization of multiple enfolded institutionally organized relations. Through attention to courses of action we glimpse just how that which was left unsaid and silent is as important for professional practice as that which was said (de Montigny, 2018a). For instance, if a youth had disclosed an untoward occurrence—e.g., sexual abuse, suicidal ideation, threats against others—such disclosures would have demanded intervention, e.g., documenting, investigating, or reporting the matter to the police. Clearly, whatever might have occurred here-and-now in an interview was ultimately accountable to the orders of professional responsibility and mandated authority.

Taking "the everyday world as problematic" (Smith, 1987) allows us to begin inquiry into intersections between people's experiences and everyday practices for rendering their accounts and their lives into the taken-for-granted form of professional social work. Smith's (2005) call, "To write a sociology from people's standpoint as contrasted with a standpoint in a theory-governed discourse" (p. 1), turns our attention to the moments of work, participation, and play, realized by SW, C, and M. Although the stories that emerge in these segments are putatively and ostensibly C's and M's, conversation analysis allows us to see the ways that the narrative details from their lives emerge in interaction with SWs. C and M interact with SWs who encourage them to speak about and to provide coherent formulations and understandings about personal experiences of coming into care. The putative coherence and orders of C and M's stories emerges turn-by-turn interactively, although not just through talk, but through the embodied presence and interaction.[2]

Beyond words and talk is the plenitude of forms of embodied sensory being and situated action. C, M, and the social workers met in specific spaces, likely a room in a child protection office or at a group home. As occupants of these spaces, they oriented and performed themselves and the appropriate actions within that space. Beyond their talk was a plenitude of interactive signals and exchanges, e.g., smiles, nods, hand gestures, facial expressions, twitches, stutters, communicating the embodied, situated, and temporal dimensions of performance. Simply, we recognize through conversation analysis that doing or accomplishing talk is more than an exchange of words, representations, or meanings. Talk is an interactive corporeal exchange with its own orders, boundaries, and possibilities. Jefferson's (2004) transcription conventions articulate this insight, as she sought to indicate through transcriptions the multiple ways that talk is embodied performance, marked by speed and pace, rising and falling tone and pitch, pauses, inhalations of breath, etc.

Institutional Analysis of Interview #1

C outlines the complex intersections between her life experience and the sanctioned and mandated work processes of institutional workers, e.g., psychiatrists, ambulance drivers, police, and social workers. C's actions, and those of her family members, provide warranted grounds or material for response and the deployment of institutional mandates. Actions and interactions between C and others, notably her mother and family, become accountable and remarkable material to be worked up by various institutionally situated actors into organizationally relevant categories. Details from her talk—e.g., "I was crazy like. I didn't do anything they said, I was always threatening them, pushing my mom around. I was physically violent"—can be assembled to mobilize institutional forms of action, e.g., calling "the cops," being taken to the hospital, being admitted to a psychiatric ward, being discharged from the hospital, and being placed in the care of the Children's Aid Society (CAS).[3]

C's experience emerges in the interactions of an interview which was an element in a social work and university research process. As such her story as it emerges articulates an intersection of personal concerns with the institutionalized relevancies of the interviewer, the research project, and social work. As such this segment from her talk-in-interaction comes to be presented in this chapter, as taken-up and out of the multiple contexts of C's life. C's narrative presented in this chapter, comes to be recast and situated in an intellectual space far removed from C's purposes, intentions, and imaginings. C's story, like that of M below, and the other youth interviewed for this research project, came to be produced in interaction with social workers, whose job was to produce an interview which accorded with an interview schedule which I, as the research organizer, had provided. Youth and social workers knew that whatever they said would be audio-recorded, and while they generally acted as if being recorded was of little consequence, almost invariably youth or social workers would acknowledge that what had been said, or what was about to be said, would be recorded. Additionally, social workers would reference the interview schedule and say something like, "I have turned on the recorder," speak of "checking the recording levels," or ask aloud, "is it working" (de Montigny, 2018a).

For social workers and other professional staff even a cursory review of C's narrative reveals grounds for warranting and legitimatizing institutionalized forms of action, e.g., arrest by police, detention in a psychiatric hospital, court hearings, and being found (by a judge) to be a "child in need of protection" (CFSA, 1990a). C, once found by a judge to be "in need of protection," could be placed in care in an approved and authorized group home and given mental health counselling. As various institutional workers (police, psychiatrists, child protection workers) come to review, assess, categorize, and classify C's actions, she becomes both the subject and the object of institutional work. For police who might investigate C's assault on her mother, she might be the "accused." For the psychiatrist who encountered C's narrative and admission of self-harm, and who likely examined her scars, this evidence would warrant application of the mental health act. C would warrantably be found to be a person who "has attempted or is attempting to cause bodily harm to himself or herself" (Ontario, Form 1, 2012). For a child protection worker C's unmanageable and out of control behavior might mean that she is a "child in need of protection." C's actions, narratives, and life experiences provide a locus of action by police, social workers, psychiatrists, nurses, and other staff. C's situation, interactions, and actions are taken-up, absorbed, and accounted for in ways that are outside, and likely alien to, C's understandings or intentions.

When considering this segment, we must also recognize the differentiation of moments of conducting and recording an interview, delivering the recording to the researcher, gathering multiple recordings of interviews with "youth in care," playback and transcribing interviews into text, and then, for the purposes of this chapter, selecting a segment of text to provide an analysis which accords with IE. Each moment in this work process emerges from out of, relies on, and presumes the social organization of membership in shared institutionalized work, whether those of social workers, sociologists, ethics review staff, research funding bodies, book editors, and so on. The production of the segment at the top of this chapter, and the one that follows, need to be approached and explicated as indexical artifacts of work processes produced across multiple institutional sites.

Whether or not I desire or claim that my work and this chapter is on the side of youth in care, the institutional contexts of this work shapes the production of these materials. They are embedded incorrigibly in and articulated to social locations in a university, my work as a faculty employee, and imperatives of career development. Additionally, the conduct of these interviews was shaped by and accountable to a university ethics review board, and its processes for approving, sanctioning, and legitimizing university research. My own work, albeit infused by a desire to be on the side of youth, is undermined by what Smith calls the "macro-foundations of a microsociology" (2005, p. 35). Regardless of intentions, and political projects, the work of interviewing, recording, and transcribing irreversibly alters, shifts, and distorts the existential realities of situated interactions. Further absorption of talk-in-interaction into transcriptions, conversation analysis and sociological and methodological arguments displaces the relevancies of youth and social workers.

The presentation of this segment and this chapter in a text on institutional ethnography relies on a referencing of a community of mutual interests and identities, i.e., those interested in, wanting to learn about, and doing IE. The subject of this chapter, the flow of the argument, and even choice of vocabulary and syntax combine to reference and rely on specific forms of academic author-text-reader relationships and membership. Membership directs us to ask just who has interest in reading this text, and how are such interests shaped by education, mentorship, credentialing, university careers, tenure (job security), promotion, and economic, class, and social status? IE demands that we recognize the tensions or puzzles we face working in ways that are critical, feminist, and Marxist while also working inside the epistemic, ideological, and textual orders of our increasingly corporatized institutional locations.

Commonly researchers engaged in ethnographic studies treat peoples' stories, such as that presented above, as claims about an interviewee's experiences, realities, and life. Such putative claims can be subsumed and reordered according to generalized sociological and professional schemata and formulations. As artfully assembled such narratives provide materials informing generalized formulations about life in marginalized families, poverty, mental illness, conflict, addictions, and so on. The presentation of narratives purports to allow readers to grasp or understand those social and life elements that lead to youth coming into care. Indeed, I have taken such direction in my own research (de Montigny, 2018a).

The Institutional Organization of the Interview

Campbell and Gregor (2002) observe that "Knowing involves a relation between the researcher and what is known." Accordingly, they ask, "How does this happen as it does? How are these relations organized?" (p. 7). Campbell and Gregor push us to take a reflexive turn, which explicates just how it is that researchers go about accomplishing the taken-for-granted everyday orders of their work as elements within their work lives. IE, as with ethnomethodology, conversation analysis, and Husserl's phenomenology, demands bracketing the everyday, the taken-for-granted, that is, a "natural attitude" (Husserl, 1983). A bracket leads to a reflexive turn and explication of that which is palpably encountered as obvious. Further, with the insights of IE we articulate the obviousness of any present and here-and-now to extra-local forms of organization, texts, and discourses. A phenomenological turn allows us to pull apart largely taken-for-granted forms of being and forms of life as socially organized and effected by and within extended and extra-local institutional relations. The taken-for-granted forms of our everyday being becomes a terrain for examination as practically accomplished and emergent day-after-day, congregationally, through our participation with nexus of others.

Readers encounter a transcribed segment, as this bit of text, which in its format purports to represent a moment of talk between a social worker and a youth in care. What is invisible in this at-hand presentation of text is the work process which led to its production. In IE, as with Marx and Engels' materialist method as set out in the *German Ideology*, what matters are peoples' actual processes of work effected over time. It is in and through at-hand and given presentation of things that we begin to trace back to interconnected work processes coordinated across diverse work-sites, involving complex cadres of people, who as work and play congregationally bring omnipresent institutional orders into being. Smith's development of IE was explicitly informed by Marx and Engels' materialism which requires examining situated knowing, as work effected both in immediate social relationships, as well as in evolving, historical transformations of broad social and economic relations (1999).

The social worker interviewers who participated in this research project performed through reference to professional membership and employment as child protection workers. Although participants to interaction may seem to disattend, or not make remarkable the institutionalized contexts of their interaction, their employment, organizational position, and professional membership is tacitly referenced turn-by-turn in and through details of interaction. For instance, unfolding interactions between youth in care and social workers are, and become accountable as, ethical, proper, and oriented to professional purposes and regulations, whether as subject to provincial colleges of social work, e.g., Ontario College of Social Workers and Social Service Workers "Code of Ethics and Standards of Practice" (2008), the national "Code of Ethics" (2005) of the Canadian Association of Social Workers Code of Ethics,[4] or CAS regulations, policies, and procedures for protecting the "best interests of a child" (CFSA, 1990a, p. 28), client confidentiality, proper exercise of authority, and so on. Indeed, the marked asymmetry of the talk between youth in care and social workers, evidenced by social workers posing questions and youth responding, reveals not only the fundamental design of an interview, but the structured effectuation of authority. Youth in care, although allowed to hold the floor and to narrate their life experiences, become the focus, and the source for information, as their stories, as shaped, molded, and cultivated are the expression of a social worker's competent production. Absent from these segments and interviews are any extended narrations by social workers of their own life stories and experiences, as these are simply not relevant for the work at-hand. Such lack of self-narration or self-disclosure for social workers is unremarkable. Indeed, while sharing personal stories would in itself become remarkable, and may be judged to be untoward, improper, or unprofessional as inappropriate self-disclosure.

A social worker's self-disclosure must be demonstrably in the interests of the client.[5] As such self-disclosure demands justification through reference to clinical objectives, e.g., building trust, forming alliance, and reducing stigma. Self-disclosure can be deemed inappropriate when it consists of sharing personal material which might compromise therapeutic objectives, harm a client, or put a social worker's interests or needs before the clients. Simply, self-disclosure, by a social worker, or other clinician, needs to be examined, and absorbed into the institutionalized orders as an element of therapeutic discourse. At worst, self-disclosure can be treated as a manifestation of a therapist's potentially problematic countertransference[6] (Farber, 2016; Raines, 1996). For example, Danzer and Andresen (2019) note:

> Contemporary analysts and psychodynamic practitioners usually concede that perfect neutrality is virtually impossible, though continue to err on the side of discouraging disclosure based on concern about contaminating the transference, countertransference, and inappropriate gratification of client curiosities. (p. 17)

The problem of self-disclosure allows us to recognize that if a social worker were to have had an open and friendly dialogue with a youth in care, or any other client, anything which might have been construed to have been sharing of personal rather than a professional information, or the formulation of a personal commitment or relationship, could be subject to professional review. Personal rather than professional relationships with clients require justification, and such justification almost inevitably results in differing assessments, appraisals, and judgements.

A feature of social worker/client and social worker/youth in care interactions is that they are, in the main, to be treated as confidential and oriented to a series of organizationally mandated forms of work-at-hand. So just how was it that I was able to not only get social workers to use time at work to conduct interviews with youth in care for this research project, to be allowed to record interviews, and then to submit these audio-recordings to me? My access to these materials was rooted in my organizational identification as a university faculty member, a social worker, and as a bona fide researcher in a school of social work. My ability to enlist social workers as research participants relied on our mutual acknowledgments of personal, professional, and organizational locations, identifications, and affiliations. This mutuality provided for understandings about proper handling and management of confidential materials, contacts with youth in care, anonymization of youth identities, protection of youth and the agency interests, and so on.

Beyond "the details of the talk or other conduct in the materials" (Schegloff, 1992, p. 110), institutional ethnography directs us to consider and to disclose the ways that any social worker's here-and-now interactive performance of an interview articulates extra-local, extended, and textually mediated relevancies. Social workers in the mundane performance as work shape that which they do through reference to the supervision and accountability to child protection managers and administrators. As such social workers must attend to the need to safeguard the confidentiality, privacy and personal information about youth in care. The obligation to safeguard information required submission of various documents, including the original research proposal, Research Ethics Board (REB) approval, confidentiality forms, and an interview schedule. Such documents provide evidence for proper review, and attest that my intentions, purposes, and actions were properly authorized by a bona fide university. The documents worked to protect managers, who could claim that they exercised due diligence to protect confidentiality and privacy, ensure safe and proper storage, handling of materials, and recourse to legally binding confidentiality agreements, etc. It should also be noted that the web of research regulation extended beyond the university REB as it was governed in turn by Tri-Council Guidelines for Ethical conduct for research involving humans (2014). Finally, conducting this research relied on Social Sciences and Humanities Research Council research funding to pay research assistants, honoraria for youth in care, travel expenses, recording equipment, transcription machines, office supplies, and so on.

By deploying a reflexive turn, IE allows us to examine people's actual practices for accomplishing textual and institutional forms of governance, including the mundane production of these audio-recorded interviews. Just as commodities express the alienated relations between capital and labor so too do the products of state workers, whether interviews, reports, running records, and various documents, express the foundational alienation of textually regulated forms of institutional action. Indeed, child protection work, as with other forms of state, bureaucratic, and organization labor, is accomplished as mandated and accountable to textually organized laws, policies, and procedures. As referencing and as organized by the relevancies of texts and documents social workers' situated moments of practice simultaneously reproduce the state sanctioned authority and the realities of child protection itself.

The Institutional Substance

Now, having set out institutional preliminaries, I want to return to a more detailed analysis of the substance of the first interview presented above. I begin by noting that, after listing a series of troubles C summarizes by noting, "they jist couldn' handle it anymore so." The social worker responds, "So ha/how did that process come about?" Initially, reading SW's response it may seem curious, as she references "that process" without specifying just what or which process is intended. However, once we understand the context— a social worker interviewing a youth in care about the experience of coming into care—the question about process references just how C became "involved with CAS." Note, however, that the social worker's naming of a process reveals the expectation that just how this youth, and indeed all youth, come into care is systematic, regulated, and iterative. C responds to the social worker's question, "I'd been in the' hospital on the psychiatric ward for a couple of months." C does not set out a clear chronology of when she came to be on a psychiatric ward, nor does she provide details about when she left the hospital to go into CAS care. Instead, C relies on her narration of troubles at home as sufficient grounds for being brought into care. Later in the segment, she discloses what will be heard by the social worker as serious self-harming[7] actions and follows by saying that she was placed in a psychiatric hospital for several months. C understands that for mental health professionals her behaviors and actions warranted psychiatric treatment and extended hospitalization along with the professional attention of hospital staff, nurses, psychiatrists, and social workers.

C also recognizes that SW tries to redirect her away from the litany of troubles at home, to talk instead about just how she became "involved with CAS." C responds by listing behaviors which she identifies as leading to her hospitalization, i.e.: "I was physically violent," "I'd flip out on them," "I was always saying I'm gonna kill myself," "I was, like self mutilatiing," and disturbingly, "I took potato peelers to my arms and just totally tore all the skin off." C has come to understand that for her parents, mental health professionals, and child protection workers these behaviors would have been sufficient to warrant professional intervention.

Mental health professionals, and likely C's social worker, would have interpreted her troubles through reference to knowledge about mental illness and health, and more broadly to their professional obligations under the provincial mental health act. They would have focused on the question of whether or not C was at risk or danger of harming herself or others. Once they deemed that she was at risk of harm to self or others they would have contacted a doctor or psychiatrist to recommend that they proceed with authorizing an involuntary psychiatric hospitalization. As a result C's actions and behaviors, the physical evidence that she had self-harmed, and the accounts of her parents, would have provided grounds for seeing C and treating C as needing involuntary psychiatric care. Whatever C's actions might have been, they would be taken-up and out of the contexts of their performance by professionals to become assembled as multiple indicators of risk. These risks would be deemed to warrant hospitalization and apprehension. C's narrative of troubles clearly provides sufficient grounds for social workers to recognize that psychiatric hospitalization was likely required. For instance, most social workers in Ontario are familiar with the provincial Ministry of Health Form 1 (Mental Health Act, 1990b), an application to be completed by a physician for psychiatric assessment. It sets out the following:

> I have reasonable cause to believe that the person:
> [ ] has threatened or is threatening to cause bodily harm to himself or herself
> [ ] has attempted or is attempting to cause bodily harm to himself or herself
> [ ] has behaved or is behaving violently toward another person
> [ ] has caused or is causing another person to fear bodily harm from him or her; or
> [ ] has shown or is showing a lack of competence to care for himself or herself. (Ontario, 2012)

Indeed, it is a relatively easy matter to recognize the correspondence between C's narrative of self-harm and violence directed to her parents and the criteria set out in the Form 1. The Form 1, along with policies, guidelines, and forms, shape and direct professional accounts as assessments and affirmations as legally binding and actionable. Documents and textual directives provide essential and necessary reference for organizational action by social workers, nurses, doctors, and so on, who are expected to reference documents on file to inform their actions. Cadres of professional workers study legislation and policy, as guidelines for their practice. In turn they treat documents and records as veridical representation not only of a history of organizational service, but as indicating and attesting to professional judgements about individuals' pathology, disturbance, and problems requiring intervention.

As we leave C, we recognize the complex ways that her narration of details from her life articulate complex institutional intersections. The readily at-hand nature of her narrative becomes sensible and understandable only through an understanding and awareness of how an extended cadre of workers in diverse organizations come to produce the warranted forms of their practice. We see in this brief segment of C's talk the ways that her, and indeed our own everyday talk, is informed by the intersection and organization of our lives with complex institutions, whether we talk about school, a visit to a doctor or hospital, or psychiatric hospitalization.

INTERVIEW #2

SW: <u>Anyways</u>, okay, uhm, how do you find .. its affected all oof/the, do you find the worrying and all that kind of stuff has affected your relationships with other people?
M: No.
SW: No. So how do you get along with group home staff.
M: I hate them.
SW: Why do you hate them.
M: Because they are a bunch of pricks.
SW: Why are they a bunch of pricks.
M: They just are.
SW: Well why?
M: they try to make my life miserable, and their doing a damn good job.
SW: Why do they try to make your life miserable.
M: It's their job.
SW: Ahhrr, and how are they making your life miserable?
M: Everything.
SW: Why
M: Just everything .
SW: Well, in general, like do they go out of their way to make meals you hate?
M: Yah.
SW: Are there any meals you like?
M: No.
SW: hehhehhehhehhehhehheh except .. pizza, once in a while right? hehe uhm, and the odd ice cream as long as it's healthy
M: Yah
SW: yah, okay, uhm,
M: well if you ever see me maybe we can have an ice cream together. You never come to see me unless its something like this.
SW: Ah, hahhohoho. Actually, you know its funny cause I was doing the base, in card hospital, and I think you are right.
M: °me too° (softly)
SW: uh:hm:m, I ah, I mean I see you probably more than I see a lot of other kids.
M: Yah about, once every two months.
SW: No, I thin/I saw you four times since you left. .
M: Yah all in one month, heh, heh
SW: Heh, heh, heh, no, no, actually I saw in you in November. I saw you in December, and I saw you in January. an twice actually in February. So you'd like it to be a bit more than that.
M: Yah.
SW: How often would you like to see me.
M: every day

SW: nhhe, that's not really realistic though is it.
M: adopt me.
SW: Adopt you! . . And then you'd live at my house.
M: yah
SW: and not eat my food and complain about it.
M: yah
SW: Yah, he, heh . .
M: Just think of all the ºlonely times in your lifeº
SW: I don't think it works out like that, heh, heh, heh. You'd still ultimately like to end up in somebody's home, right?
M: Yah.
SW: yah, so uhm, you find, like would you miss the other kids and stuff? out there
M: would I miss them?
SW: yah.

INSTITUTIONAL ANALYSIS OF INTERVIEW #2

This second segment has been selected for this chapter, as it reveals a youth in care (M) who contests and opposes her social worker's rhetoric or care and concern. Turn-by-turn M blocks SW's attempt to reference and to deploy their relationship to elicit information. Despite SW's invocation and reliance on referencing their relationship, M decisively opposes SW's strategy. M challenges SW's presupposition of care and concern when she sets out the challenge, "adopt me." In what follows I want to examine the ways that M practically resists the social worker's seductions. Her resistance exposes the structured limits of professional care and concern, the existential problems posed by professional boundaries, and an instrumentality and alienation at the heart of social work.

The segment begins as SW explores the effects of coming in care and M's worrying—social anxiety—about relations with others. SW explores this relation by asking "So how do you get along with group home staff? M aggressively replies, "I hate them," and adds, "they are a bunch of pricks." When pressed to explain what makes them "pricks," M demurs initially, but adds, "they try to make my life miserable." M's complaint, though expressed passionately, is presented without substantive details or examples. SW recognizes M's anger; however, what is missing is substance and examples fueling the emotion. She attempts to move M to provide details by asking, "How are they making your life miserable?" Again, M refuses to be specific. Instead she provides a general response, "everything."

M's recourse to generalized and totalizing accusations and her refusal to provide examples signals a reluctance to cooperate with SW's project. This leads SW to push M, by referencing background knowledge about M's dietary habits, which she conjoins with stereotypic understandings about teenage food choices. She asks, "do they go out of their way to make meals you hate?" M responds, "Yah," which leads SW, perhaps in an expression of frustration to comment, "pizza, once in a while right? hehe uhm, and the odd ice cream as long as it's healthy." SW reliance on incongruence and sarcasm is recognized by M, as she responds aggressively, "You never come to see me unless it's something like this." This is a withering attack, which not only refutes SW's bonhomie, but acts to counter the pretense that SW cares and is concerned about M's welfare.

When M's refers to "something like this," she indicates that their meetings and their relationship is founded and rooted in SW's work, and in so doing articulates her recognition that this relationship with SW is one of obligation, duty, and employment. M knows that SW is required to conduct regular visits with youth in care on her caseload. However, SW refuses, or perhaps even fails, to recognize the depth of M's existential challenge. She responds initially by seeming to agree with M and conceding, "Ah, hahhohoho. Actually, you know its funny cause I was doing the base, in card hospital, and I think you are right." SW's concession that M might be right, also tacitly recognizes that M is indeed just another case, and a number in a caseload, or base count. M's less aggressive and quieter response "ome tooo" communicates deflation and sadness, likely evoked by SW's dismal admission that indeed she is just another youth in care on a caseload.

Sadly, and unfortunately, SW misses the opportunity to reach out to M's feelings of abandonment and inconsequentiality. She fails to focus on M's challenge to instead return to self-justification, responding, "I mean I see you probably more than I see a lot of other kids." SW's defensive offer leads M to return to opposition, countering, "Yah about, once every two months." SW disputes M's claim, by arguing, "No, I thin/I saw you four times since you left." Although M does not deny this claim, she points out that it occurred, "…all in one month, heh, heh." SW relies on her memory of the documentary record, to counter, "Heh, heh, heh, no, no, actually I saw in you in November. I saw you in December, and I saw you in January. an twice actually in February." Then SW, finally, moving away from a defensive and self-justifying position, asks, "How often would you like to see me?" This leads M to respond, "every day," evoking the worker's challenge, "is that realistic?" Of course, that which is realistic is conditioned by the fact that SW's and M's relationship is mandated and a function of SW's work. The worker's invocation of that which is realistic creates yet another opening for challenge, as M demands, "adopt me."

Along with M, we too need to challenge SW's invocation of the "realistic." That which is realistic is structured by the social worker's relation with M as a youth in care on her caseload. It is structured by her employment and her position as a professional social worker, and the ways that these structural obligations shape the form of her relations with clients. SW's relationship with M must be shaped, and must be accountable as professional, and as ordered and organized by her function as a child protection social worker. In the nexus of this obligatory functional instrumentality M is a client, a youth in care, a record of work, and a quantum on her caseload. M is entered into a nexus of exchange as an institutionalized object and as a case, which must be managed and processed according to policies, laws, and professional ethics and obligations as are other cases. SW's successful management of M, expressed as outcomes, successful placement, and treatment, works to build her reputation as a social worker, and her career. To manage M, SW must ensure that her interactions accord with her job description, legislated authority, legal responsibilities, and professional obligations. Employment, and her employment as a social worker does not include being a care provider or a parent to M or to other children and youth in care.

In this relationship with SW, M is just another youth in care on a caseload, and as such contacts are entered into a count, a tally, and through such numerical calculations an indication of having discharged statutory and professional responsibilities. Against M's demand for an unconditional commitment we recognize a systematic reproduction of relationships marked by distance, alienation, and loss at the center of institutional orders. Warranted forms of professional relationship are not genuinely reciprocal, unconditional, nor most importantly embedded in a durée or form of life in which "we grow older together" (Schutz, 1970, p. 198). Instead, under the guise and rhetoric of professional care genuine emotional commitments, solidarities, and unconditional love are banned, in favor of distance, objectivity, and dispassionate intervention. That which the social worker can allow herself to become in interaction is a professional self as ordered, controlled, regulated, and perhaps most importantly, organizationally accountable.

M's response "Adopt me" is deeply transgressive and challenges the objectivist core of a professional relationship. In an instant M exposes the emotional hollow at the rhetorical claims of institutional and professional care and commitment. M reveals the boundaries and limits of an institutional care founded on the social organization of employment and professional relations. Professional relationships are regulated relationships, marked by fear of negative evaluation and even punishment should a worker become over-involved, over-identified with a client. The danger of violating professional boundaries acts a powerful limit to investment and commitment to those who are clients. The implicit tension and dark dynamic of engagement with clients is marked by fear of review, wariness, and distance.

Every day social workers meet people. They listen to the sounds of their breathing, the tone, pitch, volume, and speeds of their voices. They absorb their scents, smells, and see their movements through the spaces of daily life. Yet, the challenge is to render these encounters into talk, and into documents as instances of work, such that people become institutional objects, as clients. People become visible as the discursive and textually mediated objects of work. In the nexus and lived flows of professional practice, social workers and their clients become transformed into identifiable institutionally relevant objective forms. As such that which emerges and comes to be counted as proper social work inherently articulates a dialectic, and a praxis where the inchoate particularities of lived worlds are subsumed under the orders of legal, professional, and organizational discourses. Organic ineffability and existential indeterminacy are bracketed through imposition of institutionalized orders.

To be a social worker, intentionally effectuates forms of order that shape not only our being in the world and relationships with others but warranted accounts of professional self in relationships and presence with others. Social work practice in its regulated, iterative and discursively accomplished forms, emerges, turn-by-turn, and moment by moment, as a living practice for regulating engagement with others. As we do social work, we accomplish the orders of self, profession, and practice as institutionally regulated, controlled, and answerable.

Conclusion

To draw out and make explicit the institutional grounding which informs these two interview segments let us return to the identification of that which is being performed as an interview and to the naming of participants as social worker and youth in care. Such seemingly obvious identifiers point to regulated and accountable forms of social interaction in which participants interactively perform their talk as interviews. We have seen how those in the position of social workers talk to others as youth in care or clients, turn-by-turn in ways that intentionally and accountably produce this occasion as an interview. In the turn-by-turn movement of talk we recognize the ways that participants mutually shape sense and order including performance of their specific identity in interaction.

The extension, depth, and multi-dimensionality of institutional relations, and the iterative forms of practice required and engaged in by institutional actors produces the durability of organizational structures. Iterative forms of practice are in turn subject to iterative accountabilities. IE allows us to examine just how such seemingly simple things as an interview comes to emerge through peoples' practices, that is, as actual socially organized activities imbricated in complex, extended, and textually mediated institutional processes and projects.

To proceed as sociologists, social workers, and activists without recognizing our own interpellation into these structures necessarily means acting as discursive and textually absorbed subjects of institutional structures. Failure to develop a reflexive analysis of our socially organized practices reproduces the hegemonic normalcy of institutionalized social relations. Against conformity and compliance our task must be rooted in an opposition not only to external institutional forms, but the internalization of subjective forms and orders of accountability.

A reflexive turn in IE leads to self-consciously locating our work, our practice, so that we can question, resist, and develop alternatives to an adoption of the ideological forms of textually mediated institutional knowledge. As institutionalized subjects we actively engage in and become enmeshed in discursive and textual webs which extend from the most intimate and seemingly private moments of our daily lives to public and visible dimensions of our practice at work. Organizational apparatuses, whether a Children's Aid Society, a government ministry, or a university are not merely objective structures.

Institutions, texts, and documents are not the subject that does x, y, or z. Rather they emerge, day-after-day, and are realized through the lives of a congregational nexus of people at work. A CAS does not protect children. Rather a cadre or cohort of people, working in congregation across diverse work-sites, including CAS offices, court rooms, police stations, hospitals, and so on work to protect children, as they go about articulating this and that case to a hermeneutic and discursive interpretation of legislation and policy.

We who live in this new millennium are caught in a tsunami of expanding global capitalism, which brings an accelerating advance of technologies for surveillance, monitoring, and management of people in their everyday lives (Zuboff, 2018). The ordinary and taken-for-granted substance of our lives, including everyday and mundane interactive performances, casual encounters with others, and even thoughts and dreams, come to articulate dialectical intersections between our embodied and living self and extra-locally coordinated institutional orders. While the institutional emerges from what Garfinkel calls the immortal everyday practices of people who in concert work to bring about the forms of institutions day-after-day, with no time out (Garfinkel, 2002), just how our here-and-now comes to reproduce the penetrating order and forms and institutional reality is the problematic of IE. To be a member of our society is to have our lives taken-up and managed by institutionalized actors, whether teachers in schools, faculty in universities, doctors in hospitals, and so on. In segments of talk-in-interaction we begin to glimpse just how the relevancies of organizational location shape not just the activity, as work, of the social worker, but of youth in care. Youth find themselves engaged with social workers, not just as this person, but as someone who is also a mandated and authoritative actor. These segments in their detail, as talk-in-interaction, provide insight into the taken-for-granted and ubiquitous existential paradoxes of everyday institutionalized work.

Despite whatever good or progressive intentions I might have had to present the voices of youth in care and to conduct "a sociology for people" (Smith, 2005), the puzzle has been to find a way to bridge a critical examination of the institutionalized processes which governed my actions, and those of participants, with a plan and a politics of resistance and change. How can we resist institutional alienation, objectification, and ideological distortion? What are limits of resistance and opposition as we give voice to the reflexive orderings of our practice? IE can help us to recognize our personal and collective participation and responsibility for reproducing institutionalized systems of oppression. Armed with such insights we can begin to create and to experiment with forms of work which move forward in opposition and solidarity.

Notes

1. The two segments of talk-in-interaction presented in this paper were originally transcribed to conform with Jefferson's (2004) conventions for conversation analysis. Jefferson set out transcription conventions to record morphological features of talk-in-interaction. These included speakers' use of sound stretches, rising and falling pitch, increasing and decreasing speed of talk, increases and diminutions of volume, as well as interactive features, including latched or closely proximate turns at talk, interruptions, timed intervals between turns, and overlapping talk. While these conventions are vital to the analysis of in vivo enactment of talk-in-interaction, because of the focus in this paper on the contribution of conversation analysis to institutional ethnography, this attention to the morphology of talk has in large part been ignored. Yet, some morphological features of talk have been preserved for no other reason than that they work to represent and present the enacted, in vivo, and embodied performance of talk-in-interaction. The recognition that talk is not simply an exchange of words, but is an embodied interactive and social exchange is critically important for an understanding of socially organized practices, both intimate and institutional. In general I have represented speaker's talk using proper spellings of words, however, when speakers quite clearly employed local dialects and unique sound forms I have tried to render these using phonetic spellings. In a similar vein I have presented sound stretches, although represented with repeating vowels or consonants rather than in the conventional form of conversation analysis through colons, i.e., ha::a. Self and other interruptions have been retained, i.e., / or //, latched turns at talk, i.e., = , as well as overlapping talk [yah] [yah]. I have not included rising or falling pitch (a↑h or a↓h), increased speed of talk (<whatever<), though I have retained particularly soft or quieter talk, i.e., °yes°. The morphological features of talk not only reveal the different roles and positions of participants' to institutional talk—youth in care and social worker, youth and adult—but provide recourse to determinations of gender, nationality, and race as manifested through accents, tone of voice, and so on. Morphological features of talk are used to assemble understandings about ourselves and others?
2. Similarly, Smith recalls watching a video sequence in which a receptionist approaches a patient waiting in a doctor's office, and the ways that "the bodily movements of the two, one approaching, the other recognizing and orienting, coordinate with one another...like a dance" (2005, p. 60).
3. Children's Aid Society (CAS) in Ontario are mandated by the Child and Family Services Act (1990a)—repealed and replaced by the Child, Youth and Family Services Act (2017).
4. The provincial College of social workers and social service workers is the regulatory body established under provincial legislation to regulate social workers and to ensure competent and ethical practice. The CASW is the national body responsible for developing the Code of Ethics which social workers are expected to adhere to.

5. Raines identified five dimensions in a therapeutic relationship governing use of self-disclosure, "my theoretical understanding of the therapeutic relationship, the timing of the statement within the treatment frame, the type of disclosure, my working model of the client...and my sense of whether the client was justified in her observation of my physical state" (1996, p. 358). Raines' permissive approach to self-disclosure elicited a critical response from Herbert Strean, who urged redirecting client requests that the therapist share personal information, back onto the client, by examining what the client's questions mean for the client (1997).
6. Farber in an edited text focused on self-disclosure notes, "In my training the notion that the analysts' own transferences and countertransferences might be used to impact the treatment positively was never considered" (2016, p. 7).
7. Self-harming incidents by a child in care require serious and deliberate response, which usually includes an expectation that a "Serious Occurrence Report" (SOR) will be filed, to ensure that the youth's behavior becomes a matter of record (Snow, 2017).

References

Campbell, M., & Gregor, F. (2002). *Mapping social relations: A primer in doing institutional ethnography.* Toronto, ON: University of Toronto Press.

Canadian Association of Social Workers (CASW). (2005). *Code of ethics.* Ottawa, ON: Author.

Canadian Institutes of Health Research, Natural Sciences and Engineering Research Council of Canada, & Social Sciences and Humanities Research Council of Canada. (2014). *Tri-Council policy statement: Ethical conduct for research involving humans.* Ottawa, ON: Author.

Danzer, G. S., & Andresen, K. (2019). Theoretical and clinical perspectives. In G. Danzer (Ed.), *Therapist self-disclosure: An evidence based guide for practitioners* (pp. 16–23). London, UK: Routledge.

de Montigny, G. (2017). Ethnomethodological indifference: Just a passing phase? *Human Studies, 40,* 331–364.

de Montigny, G. (2018a). *Conversation analysis for social work: Talking with youth in care.* London, UK: Routledge.

de Montigny, G. (2018b, September 3). Engaging ethnomethodology for social work. *Journal of Social Work,* Online first.

Farber, S. K. (2016). Introduction nothing to hide, plenty to celebrate. In S. K. Farber (Ed.), *Celebrating the wounded healer psychotherapist: Pain, post-traumatic growth and self-disclosure* (pp. 3–16). London, UK: Routledge.

Fitzgerald, P. (2013). *Therapy talk: Conversation analysis in practice.* New York, NY: Palgrave.

Garfinkel, H. (2002). *Ethnomethodology's program: Working out Durkheim's aphorism* (A. W. Rawls, Ed.). Lanham, MD: Rowman & Littlefield.

Garfinkel, H., & Sacks, H. (1970). On formal structures of practical action. In J. C. McKinney & E. A. Tiryakian (Eds.), *Theoretical sociology: Perspectives and developments* (pp. 338–366). New York, NY: Appleton-Century-Crofts.

Husserl, E. (1983). *Ideas pertaining to a pure phenomenology and to a phenomenological philosophy: First book: General introduction to a pure phenomenology* (F. Kersten, Trans.). The Hague: Martinus Nejhoff.

Jefferson, G. (2004). Glossary of transcript symbols with an introduction. In G. H. Lerner (Ed.), *Conversation analysis: Studies from the first generation* (pp. 13–31). Amsterdam: John Benjamins.

Ontario. (1990a). Child and Family Services Act (CFSA), R.S.O. 1990. c. C. 11. Toronto, ON.

Ontario. (1990b). Mental Health Act, R.S.O. 1990, C. M. 7. Toronto, ON.

Ontario. (2012). Ministry of Health. Form 1. Mental Health Act: Application by physician for Psychiatric Assessment. Toronto, ON.

Ontario. (2017). Child, Youth and Family Services Act (CYFSA) S.O. 2017, c. 14, Sched. 1. Toronto, ON.

Ontario College of Social Workers and Social Service Workers. (2008). *Code of ethics and standards of practice handbook* (2nd ed.). Toronto, ON: Author.

Raines, J. C. (1996). Self-disclosure in clinical social work. *Clinical Social Work Journal, 24*(4), 357–375.

Schegloff, E. (1992). On talk and its institutional occasions. In P. Drew & J. Heritage (Eds.), *Talk at work: Interaction in institutional settings* (pp. 101–135). New York, NY: Cambridge University Press.

Schutz, A. (1970). *Collected papers: Studies in phenomenological philosophy* (Vol. 3). The Hague, Netherlands: Martinus Nijhott.

Smith, D. E. (1987). *The everyday work as problematic: A feminist sociology*. Toronto, ON: University of Toronto Press.

Smith, D. E. (1999). *Writing the social: Critique, theory, and investigations*. Toronto, ON: University of Toronto Press.

Smith, D. E. (2005). *Institutional ethnography: A sociology for people*. Lanham, MD: AltaMira.

Snow, K. (2017). *Serious occurrences report follow up to SOR preliminary report*. Toronto, ON: Office of the Provincial Advocate for Children and Youth.

Zuboff, S. (2018). *The age of surveillance capitalism: The fight for a human future at the new frontier of power*. New York, NY: Public Affairs.

CHAPTER 27

Institutional Ethnography and Youth Participatory Action Research: A Praxis Approach

Naomi Nichols and Jessica Ruglis

When Smith conceived of institutional ethnography (IE) as an alternative sociological approach, she was, in part, seeking a sociological orientation that would enable academic researchers to use their sociological training to serve activist and community organizing aims. Like other progressive or alternative social science approaches that eschewed the promise of a Cartesian or universal standpoint, Smith sought to create a sociology that began in and remained accountable to actual people's lives. As much as this reflected Smith's empirical and ontological commitments, the move also reflects Smith's pragmatic commitments, that is, IE was designed to be useful.

Indeed, Smith has described IE as emerging out of her experiences within the women's movement and in particular, community organizing work with women in rural British Columbia, Canada. In these spaces, women found there were limited words available to them to name the problems they were experiencing (Smith, 2006). Terms and tools afforded by traditional sociology served to turn people into the objects of sociological discourse, obscuring the possibility of generating knowledge that would enable them to name and transform the relations of subjugation that they experienced (Smith, 2005). They started by naming their experiences, in other words, because there was

---

N. Nichols (✉)
Department of Sociology, Trent University, Peterborough, ON, Canada
e-mail: naominichols@trentu.ca

J. Ruglis
Faculty of Education, McGill University, Montreal, QC, Canada
e-mail: Jessica.ruglis@mcgill.ca

© The Author(s) 2021
P. C. Luken and S. Vaughan (eds.), *The Palgrave Handbook of Institutional Ethnography*,
https://doi.org/10.1007/978-3-030-54222-1_27

no other place to start. If the goal was to solve problems together, like getting the city to build sidewalks so that they could safely push baby carriages up and down winding mountain roads (Direct communication, Smith, 2016), then they needed to generate a knowledge-base that brought into view the politico-institutional processes through which municipal planning decisions are made and road safety is legislated. This is knowledge that is useful to their organizing efforts. While other progressive social science traditions have sought to "give voice" to people who have not traditionally held court in institutional spaces, Smith was looking for a research and analytic process that would bring into view and make accessible the institutional and political-economic processes through which people's everyday lives and the problems they encounter are organized. In this chapter, we have shown how IE, designed to enable organizing efforts, also enables opportunities for learning and development for all those involved in a project together, particularly when researchers incorporate participatory and educative strategies from other action-oriented social science research approaches.

Smith's insistence that IE is a sociology and not a methodology encourages researchers not to be methodologically dogmatic, static or protective. Within IE's sociological frame, one can use a range of research methods that allows us to learn how the grounds of experience are organized, socially and institutionally, as long as the research methods reflect the particular ontological and epistemological commitments of IE. That is, that (1) Rather than conceiving of social relations as abstract theoretical entities, we understand them to be actual material relations among people; and (2) We can trace ethnographically from these social relations (that is, what people know, think and do together), in order to discover how particular social practices are coordinated by language, institutionalized modes of action, and texts (broadly conceived to include any media—electronic or not—which serves a communicative purpose, connecting people across time and space). Methodologically, institutional ethnographers use a range of approaches to uphold these commitments. This chapter highlights our use of IE as a mode of inquiry and organizing within a Youth Participatory Action Research (YPAR) project we co-led in Montreal, Canada. We intend for this chapter to be useful to institutional ethnographers interested in co-conducting a project with youth co-researchers.

In a chapter in *Perspectives on and from Institutional Ethnography*, Nichols, Griffith, and McLarnon (2018) describe how community-based and participatory action research methodologies can be employed within IE's distinctive sociological frame. Our contribution to this handbook is an extension of this earlier conversation. Here, we seek to bring our own research activities under ethnographic scrutiny, as we describe our use of a YPAR methodology within IE. As such, we do not offer readers an IE analysis; rather, we offer up accounts of our own work—our methodological and educative strategies as well as the outcomes of this work in terms of young people's own critical analytic, communicative, and creative organizing efforts. By offering descriptive accounts of our use of participatory and action-oriented research strategies, we illuminate how IE's particular ontological and epistemological orientation can fruitfully intersect with a YPAR methodology. Specifically, we highlight our use of participatory strategies to build an IE project design that reflects young people's actual concerns and experiences and our use of institutional ethnographic modes of thought and analysis to build young people's critical social analytic capacities over two and a half years of collective work. Although the project also enabled several youth-led actions (e.g., a podcast series), this work is not the focus of this chapter.

The project we describe, "Sampling Youth Development," was a participatory exploration of the institutional contexts of young people's lives. It was informed by Jessica's experience as a social determinants of health researcher and Naomi's experience as an institutional ethnographer along with both our experience using community-based and participatory research methods. In this chapter, we are doing three things: first, we describe the methodological principles associated with YPAR and its utility within an institutional ethnographic sociological frame; second, we describe what we actually did to design "Sampling Youth Development" and the importance of youth participation throughout all stages of the project; and finally, we suggest that YPAR methodologies within an IE project can enable praxis—that is, an opportunity to collectively improve our capacities for critical social analysis and co-produce a plan for action. To make this final claim, we draw on excerpts of interview data, interviews we conducted with our youth team as well as those they conducted with one another, in order to show how a participatory and pedagogical approach to IE improves its accessibility and utility outside of academic settings.

Practicing Methodological Dexterity and Reflexivity: Youth Participatory Research Strategies Within IE

Participant Action Research (PAR is an umbrella methodology that can draw on a range of approaches to inquiry as long as they are participative, grounded in experience, and oriented to action. PAR traces its roots to Marxism, sociology of knowledge, adult education, social psychology, community and international development, popular education, and pragmatist philosophy (Fals-Borda, 2001; Jacobs, 2016; Khanlou & Peter, 2005; Maguire, 1987; Reason & Bradbury, 2001; Teram, Schacter, & Stalker, 2005). YPAR is a specific branch of PAR research, which explicitly facilitates the active involvement of young people as researchers in processes of inquiry and action (Fox et al., 2010). The degree of participation in a research project varies from the involvement of young people in a consultative or advisory capacity (e.g., through the use of youth advisory boards) to their fulsome involvement in and leadership of all aspects of project design and implementation. For a youth research project to be viewed as participatory, youth co-researchers must be able to meaningfully influence the research process, outcomes, and actions that emerge (Checkoway & Richards-Schuster, 2003). There is also a considerable body of literature about the potential effects of participation for young people in terms of their development (Checkoway & Richards-Schuster, 2001) and political self-efficacy (Fox et al., 2010; Wang & Burris, 1997).

In so far as PAR approaches stress the importance of peoples' critical analysis and transformation of their own lives and experiences of oppression, the methodology is inspired by the work and ideas of critical social theorists and educators like Paulo Freire and Orlando Fals-Borda and social-psychologist Kurt Lewin (Brown & Rodriguez, 2009), as well as the critical and revolutionary work of W.E.B. Dubois, Gloria Anzaldùa, and Maxine Green (Fine & Torre, 2004). PAR approaches strive to be methodologically rigorous, practical, and pedagogical. Research is usually conducted by teams of traditionally trained academic researchers and co-researchers with direct-experience of the topic under investigation and who may have little formal research training. Both groups are valued as knowledge-producers and social change agents, and much time and energy are dedicated to knowledge-sharing within a team. One critique of PAR scholarship is a lack of transparency in terms of the specificities of research training and knowledge-sharing among participants (Brown & Rodriguez, 2009). Our chapter responds to this critique by bringing attention to the actual things we did as researchers leading a YPAR project within a larger institutional ethnographic frame.

Many scholars whose work is inspired by Dorothy Smith's scholarship, also conduct their research as part of an action-oriented or activist process (see, e.g., Frampton, Kinsman, Thompson, & Tilleczek, 2006; Nichols, 2014, 2016; Pence, 2002; Smith, 1990; Wilson & Pence, 2006). Aligned with PAR's insistence that people's experiences are critical resources in cycles of inquiry and action, an institutional ethnographic process of discovery always begins with people's "actual situations and with our [their] own good knowledge of the practicalities and organization of our [their] everyday and every night worlds" (Smith, 1999, p. 30). Participatory methods can be usefully employed throughout an IE to unearth what people know about their lives and experiences, ensure critical social inquiry and analysis skills are accessible and useful to people in their everyday lives, and ensure findings have a direct benefit to people's lives. Participatory approaches allow institutional ethnographers to share the investigative and sense-making practices associated with IE as a sociological frame and generate insights that advance people's collective efforts to resolve a problem that they have identified from the relevancies of their own lives.

WHAT WE DID: SYNTHESIZING METHODOLOGICAL EXPERIENCE IN "SAMPLING YOUTH DEVELOPMENT"

In this section, we engage descriptively with our own research process. Our intention is to grant the work ethnographic visibility, bringing transparency and clarity to the actual things we did to cultivate a youth research team, distill a project focus, and conduct a project that was accountable to the institutional relevancies of youth and adult team-members.

When we (Jessica and Naomi) met in the fall of 2015, the first thing we did together was to write a Notice of Intent (NOI) to apply for provincial funding through a call for research on school climate, intercultural relations and academic perseverance. We co-created an NOI to conduct a YPAR study to learn: (1) how school climate is influenced by intercultural relations between communities and schools and (2) how schools and communities might collectively foster democratic and inclusive school cultures that promote academic perseverance and success for all students. In the NOI, we wrote that our research would "reveal and redress inter-institutional processes of exclusion that shape disparities in retention and academic success among diverse youth in Montreal." Ultimately, our NOI was deemed "non-pertinent" by the government, and we were not asked to prepare a full application. But in the process of pulling together this proposal, we were introduced to the Executive Director (ED) of a small youth-serving organization in one of Montreal's most racially and linguistically diverse neighborhoods, for whom our proposal turned out to be entirely pertinent. He invited us to come to the organization and meet a group of young musicians he had been working within the hopes that we might carry out a participatory research project with them. Specifically, he was hoping our project might respond to concerns young people brought forward to him about experiences of overt and implicit racial discrimination at school.

When we started, Naomi had recently joined the Board of Directors at the youth center while Jessica joined the following year. We were still relatively new in Montreal, and we did not live in the neighborhood where the youth center is located. We are white English-speaking academics coming into a neighborhood, composed largely of people who are economically, ethnically, racially, and linguistically not like us. It was thus important that we were invited to be involved in the center by the then Executive Director, a Black Haitian Montreal musician, who was interested in collaborating with us because we had both done research on racism and education and because he was keenly aware of the economic pressures experienced by most youth at the center and the difficulties they faced finding part-time work. Despite not getting the provincial grant, we had made it clear to the Executive Director that we had the economic and human resources to support people's meaningful involvement. We combined our own research funds to hire and train young people to participate in all aspects of the project including team-building, training, research, analysis, and dissemination.

Beginning with Experience

The study design for "Sampling Youth Development" thus emerged out of a series of conversations with two different groups of young people who participate in the organization's studio arts program. The conversations began with an invitation to talk about people's experiences going to school in Montreal. Within a couple of months, we had solidified a working relationship with single group of hip-hop artists, attending one of Montreal's public English high schools and the scope of the project grew to incorporate their experiences with other public institutions (e.g., policing and public transit). Talking with people about the actual conditions of their lives, that is, the things that they have experienced and which concern and/or inspire them, is central to community organizing efforts (Warren & Mapp, 2011) and it is the backbone of institutional ethnographic ways of working (Smith, 2005). People's actual lives and experiences, not theorizations of youth development, always constitute the starting place for a project. Often institutional ethnographers describe themselves as beginning their inquiry from a particular standpoint. References to standpoint in IE serve as a reminder to begin one's investigation on the ground, learning about and through embodied action and experiences, rather than a predefined social category (e.g., youth at-risk) or the concealed (white, straight masculine) standpoint of traditional universal theory-building. Experience is the anchorage point for inquiry.

In our case, we began with months of bi-weekly and then weekly Wednesday night meetings in a youth center with five young people (Eva, Destry, Jarem, Alon, and Khaled[1]), a doctoral student research assistant and often two artistic mentors and youth workers at the center.[2] The regular meetings served a number of purposes. They offered us a chance to get to know the youth and each other better, learn about one another's lives, and brainstorm possibilities for a collaborative project. These informal team-building and knowledge-sharing activities are key to a YPAR process; they are also useful to institutional ethnographers seeking to identify a research problematic that resonates strongly for the people one is working with.

During early team-building meetings, we took notes using notebooks and chart paper, which were accessible to anyone who was sitting at the table. The notes served as an important reflexive guide, focusing our engagements with one another each week and serving as a record of our collective work to date. Jessica, Naomi and a doctoral researcher shared a big black notebook which anyone was invited to write in, and the youth also each had their own notebooks. Two musician mentors and youth workers also often participated in these weekly sessions, as part of their work to coordinate the studio arts program at the youth organization. Each week when we met, we would summarize the main points of the discussion from the week before in order to check that we had accurately captured what we had discussed. Sometimes the young people shared insights and song lyrics recorded in their personal journals in between meetings. From here, we would ask people to reflect and move the conversations forward using prompts like, "What has happened (in the world and in our lives) since our last meeting that we should all know about/consider?" and "Where does the conversation/work need to go next?" Talking with people in the ways that we describe here does not represent formal data collection. Rather, these grounding conversations ultimately comprised the foundation for research we would go on do together (Smith, 2005).

Building and sustaining reciprocal relations of learning and care is fundamental to the feminist praxis at the root of our use of a YPAR methodology. These relational activities, sharing stories, making art, and dreaming up a project together, also have the potential to usefully serve an institutional ethnographers' efforts to anchor inquiry in the lives and relevancies of those to whom their research is meant to accountable. Certainly, we do not think YPAR strategies represent the only tenable avenue for ensuring IE scholarship is relevant to those outside academy; rather, we humbly offer up our experiences using participatory and arts-based approaches as potential tools to improve the accessibility and relevance of our work to those to whom we are most accountable.

Learning Critical Social Analysis

The weekly workshops and conversations with our youth team also provided important opportunities to engage in critical conversations about the social relations which condition our lives and experiences. Specifically, for those members of our team who had experienced or witnessed discriminatory treatment, or had experiences that promoted a feeling of discomfort or disquiet, these conversations were important opportunities to see personal experiences as connected to and reflecting social and institutional relations shaping the provision and management of public institutions more broadly. That is, in conversation with adult allies (e.g., community youth workers, artists, and researchers), as well as in conversation with one another, young people develop and experiment with new vocabularies and practical insights for identifying and interpreting the reflexive social relations within which an individual's experiences unfold.

To provide an engaging framework for thinking and dialogue, we facilitated artful approaches to critical social analysis. For example, we developed opportunities for our inter-generational team to work with and analyze the issues we had been discussing as a team by making found poetry using words and phrases from various print media sources (e.g., McGill student newspapers, fashion magazines, the Montreal Gazette, old conference program listings, etc.). In an attempt to relay what found poetry is to the group, Khaled drew a comparison to music-making practices: "it's like sampling" the practice of taking small clips of songs, vocals, beats or instrumentals and using these samples to create a new song or recording. Khaled's observation about sampling in music-making, served as an opportunity for us to introduce the team to the concept of sampling in research. In addition to formal (i.e., planned, structured) research training sessions, we also actively sought to capitalize on opportunities for knowledge exchange or informal (i.e., non-structured, unplanned) learning as these arose within the project's ordinary rhythms.

In a subsequent week, we invited young people to read through blinded interview transcripts from another similar research project, which Naomi conducted with colleagues Alison Griffith and Uzo Anucha in Toronto, Ontario (The project was Nichols, Griffith and Anucha, 2013–2018). People were invited to talk about what stood out for them in the transcripts as they read. We read silently, pausing from time to time to read a passage out loud to the group for people to think about and discuss. These became opportunities for Naomi to talk about the findings from this other project (on community and school safety) and for Jessica to make connections to similar or divergent findings from projects she had been part of in Baltimore and New York City and for the youth to draw comparisons to their own lives. In this way, young people began to identify social processes that are suggestive of systemic rather than personal failures, and Jessica and Naomi were able to introduce key research terms, principles, and techniques (e.g., what is an interview and why does one do it) without having to lecture or engage in decontextualized research training exercises. Demystifying institutional and discipline-specific language and ideas, as well as building research and communicative skills are important dimensions of a PAR approach, enabling each person on the team to fully and confidently engage in all aspects of the research process. In a reciprocal learning process, the exchange of information is multi-directional, as academically trained researchers explicate esoteric terms and practices and co-researchers elucidate the experiential knowledge and practices that researchers may otherwise misinterpret. Our own project was unique, perhaps, in so far as team-members also sought to share and clarify the artistic and technical knowledges associated with music production as well as later in the project, a range of media and communicative practices meant to engage the public with the project findings (e.g., photography, social media, web-based publishing, and pod-casting).

At subsequent meetings, Naomi brought more transcripts, pieces of analyzed data, glue and scissors and young people were invited to cut these up and experiment with creating lyrical poetry out of the data. These activities served as enabling processes for team-building and knowledge-sharing. As the weeks progressed, encouraged by one of their adult artist-mentors from the studio program, the young people also performed the poetry and songs they'd been working on, and we would talk about these as a group as well. People brought music and videos to share with the group, and we explored other interesting arts and research-informed projects happening in the world. One evening, as we sat quietly reading transcripts, one of the youth workers jumped up and asked whether people wanted to listen to music. The transcript he was reading was reminding him of a new album, and he thought we should listen. He promptly put on the song he was thinking about and we discussed the musician's critical social and artistic project, while the two youth workers educated us all about Hip Hop's roots in social justice organizing. Against this backdrop of informal knowledge exchange, we talked about what it was we wanted to do together. One night someone asked, "Is this a project?" and another person responded, "Let's call it a mixed tape." In this case, the "project" to which the speaker referred in his question ("Is this a project?") is a musical project, as in, are we producing an album out of this work we are doing? The answer ("Let's call it a mix tape") was suggested to enable us to carve out a number of distinct, but connected, smaller projects that we could work on as a collective. Each week we met, we spent part of our time together engaged in ideational work: brainstorming possibilities for collective projects. Many of these brainstorms, and the early stages of research ideation were captured on scraps of paper, notebooks, and chart paper. After a few months of these meetings, we began coalescing these early project ideas into a single participatory research design and research ethics submission.

Designing a Project

We began the more focused aspects of research training and project design by looking at other research tools (e.g., large-scale survey instruments) that had been developed and are commonly used in research about youth development. As a group we reviewed these tools, discussed how surveys are typically used in a research process, and our experiences taking and administering them. Young people candidly revealed that they did not honestly answer surveys that are distributed in school, fearing these answers would be shared with educators. They and their friends would not, for example, accurately fill out surveys about their substance-use, sexual, mental, or physical health despite researcher assurances that survey data would not be linked to individuals. The fact that the surveys were produced from the standpoints of those who govern and were administered in schools, by school administration and teachers who youth did not trust, undermined their faith in the instruments and the data collection processes themselves. This review and discussion about survey tools led to a discussion of the utility and validity of youth survey research, conducted in schools, and through which many policies related to youth health and development are constructed. As a result of these discussions, our team decided that youth-to-youth anonymous interviews would be central to our methodology. We talked about how to ask research questions and began working on developing these ourselves.

Not all of our work on the project design occurred collaboratively. Just like the young people on our team worked on music, writing, and video projects on their own and in small groups, bringing their work into the larger groups to share and discuss, on many occasions, we (Jessica and Naomi) would take the chart papers and scraps back to our offices in order to transform the emerging ideas, questions, and concerns of the group into the beginnings of a research design that corresponded with the relevancies of further fund-seeking work and the research ethics review board process. During the formalizing research design phase, we would bring draft research questions and instruments back to the group for feedback, returning later to our computers to continue to try to stitch all the pieces together. Our work in this respect is similar to most projects that happen in, or in relation to, institutionally organized processes through which the work must be read as accountable. Our actual work together was periodically transposed into the specified accounting fields of a funding report in the community organization where the work occurred or our annual faculty merit reports that distinguished us a researchers and university professors. Similarly, the young people on our team transposed conversations about critical issues influencing young people's lives and experiences in the registers and discursive genres that distinguished them as hip-hop artists, as they wrote about key issues arising from our meetings into the songs of their first album—a key outcome of the first summer youth research institute we hosted.

Summer Institutes as Sites of Informal Learning

Each summer during 2016 and 2017 of this project, the youth research team participated in a paid (five days/week for seven weeks) summer institute, focusing on research, community development and mixed media. The first institute combined training and skills development in research, mixed media (e.g., video, photography) production, writing and music production with community-building opportunities within the team and within the city more broadly (e.g., developing a community garden with a doctoral student; cooking; and engaging in play-writing with a local dramaturge). The institute also included a full day each week for studio work, so that the youth could finish their first hip-hop album. In addition to Jessica and Naomi, two graduate students and a community artist provided weekly workshops on research, writing, mixed media, production, and community development. Although research training began before the internship with the production of research questions, discussion and review of research approaches, instruments, and methods, in the summer, the training became more deliberate and focused. The institutes, funded by a government of Canada employment grant, provided a structure to our work as we had to ensure all members of the youth research team had a meaningful and educative full-time employment experience.

We began the first summer institute learning about research ethics. We investigated a number of cases of ethical misconduct, such as the Tuskegee Trials, where syphilis was left untreated in poor Black men to allow white scientists to track the untreated progression of the disease. Like he had done at other occasions, one of the studio youth workers deepened the discussion by introducing us to a powerful song, written by Jazz clarinetist, Don Byron. An abstract discussion of the racist and objectifying tendencies in research took a profoundly more affective turn as we listened, stunned, to the cacophonic sounds of Byron's jazz composition, the Tuskegee Experiments. We also watched pop-cultural representations of research in "marginalized" urban communities (e.g., from the television show, "The Wire") as we learned about subjectivity, objectivity, insider/outside issues, and the politics of evidence and representation. In this way, our research training began with an exploration of the historical and present-day relationship between knowledge-production, race and processes of racialization and epistemic violence.

Over the next couple of weeks, young people also worked together to complete Canada's Tri-Council Panel on Research Ethics Course on Research Ethics (CORE) together in McGill's computer lab enabling young people to link the informal discussions of research ethics in the youth center to formal processes for demonstrating accountability and ethical compliance that are coordinated federally. By working through the course together, young people could help one another, and we could as a group pause as we made our way through each module to discuss what we were learning. As we wrapped up the course, we moved into developing expertise with particular methods we had identified that allowed us to generate insights into our project's central methods. In our case these methods were one-on-one short (street) or in-depth interviews, focus groups and observations.

For example, young people were provided with opportunities to practice listening, observing, and asking questions. Sometimes they were asked to close their eyes and listen. At other times, they were invited to go out in the world and pay attention with all of their senses. They walked along busy streets full of shoppers and stood in line at fast-food restaurants, soaking in the experiences, jotting notes in their books and returning to the university to produce and share their field notes and the experience of producing them. They talked about what it felt like in their bodies to be completely still, mindful, and observant in the context of so much movement and, as they noted, so much consumerism. Thus we circled back to a conversation we would return to over and over again: how to balance one's artistic ambitions with the need to make money, how to be present in our lives by identifying and seeking to resist the forces that turn us into "clones" and "zombies" (words used by the young people to describe the pressures of a consumeristic culture). The themes that emerged in these writing sessions ran through the research training components and young people's music production, while allowing us to pick up on and respond to the things young people really cared about as the project progressed.

The second year of the project, the summer institute focused less on preparation for data collection, which happened in the intervening winter and fall and more on training in coding, analysis and podcast production vis a vis the research we had done during the school year. In the Spring, the team spent one intensive week together, reading through interview data and developing a working analytic framework and a codebook. Both were developed inductively from our data. Pragmatically, we used sticky notes and a big wall to collect and organize our codes as these emerged in the context of reading and discussing our data. The development of an analytic framework at this point in a project may appear idiosyncratic to institutional ethnographers; however, this was not a framework which we would subsequently apply to our data and test deductively or propose as a key outcome of our research. The analytic resource we developed served more as a heuristic to guide how we might come to engage with the data during the coding process and thus comprised the frontpage of our team's codebook (see Fig. 27.1).

Figure 27.1 reflects our efforts to co-produce an analytic resource with young people that attends to and connects various themes and contexts identified by them in our data. It does not represent a map of a particular institutional process (as would be a typical way to present one's IE findings). The figure here conveys the things young people do in their lives to survive and/or be well, the experiences they have, the ways these phenomena are mediated by key institutions (e.g., family, school, police) and the policies and laws that intersect and connect them. This diagram is also a means of giving

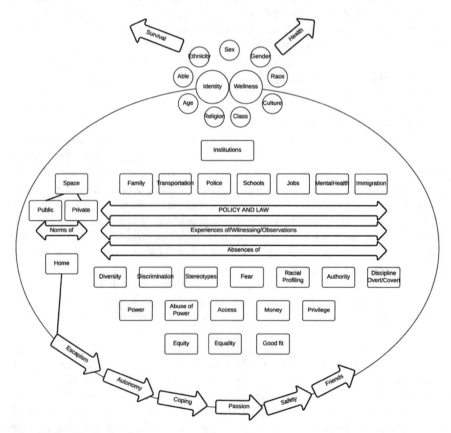

Fig. 27.1 Youth development as social practice

precedent to the words and conceptual frames offered up by our youth co-researchers, even as some of these might be at-odds with how institutional ethnographers traditionally talk. An important ethical dimension of participatory work is that the process not contribute to forms of epistemic injustice, that is, social processes whereby young people's discursive repertoires, insights, or interests are diminished. As such, the diagram speaks to the team's specific interest in the capacity for particular social relations to promote feeling good (i.e., health) or simply survival (i.e., coping). We sought to develop a heuristic devise that captured, rather than subdued the complexity and variation in experience young people described, as well as the social processes and objectified categories of social organization to which their stories pointed.

After pilot-testing and refining our codebook as a group, the youth research team proceeded to develop and implement a coding protocol and went on to code the interviews. In addition to coding, in the second summer, a McGill doctoral student was hired to train the youth in podcast production. Their first podcast introduced listeners to our project. The second took up an issue that they had identified in the data as an important to how young people in Montreal grow up (i.e., experiences of racial profiling). For their second podcast, the youth created a show about young people's experiences of profiling and discrimination as well the work of local activists and academics who are seeking to combat systemic racism through research, community mobilizing, and music. They shared their podcasts at a block party organized by the youth center later that fall.

Conducting Research

Data collection began in the fall, after our first summer institute and continued throughout the academic year until the end of the second Summer Institute. As well as conducting more than 70 anonymous youth-to-youth street interviews all over the city of Montreal, graduate student and youth research assistants produced field notes, recorded sound samples of the public spaces where these interviews took place, drew and photographed the visual contexts for each interview location. We also used a co-interviewing approach (adult and youth co-conducting research interviews) to conduct in-depth interviews and focus groups with youth participants, until youth researchers were ready to conduct in-depth interviews with other young people themselves. The interviews ($n = 27$) and focus groups ($n = 2$) did not focus on young people, but on the public and institutional contexts that shape how young people grow up—e.g., schools, public transportation, housing, policing, and health services. Street interviews focused on a single institutional context of a young person's life (e.g., education), while the in-depth interviews focused on all the intersecting institutional contexts shaping young people's lives and development: education, health, safety, housing, and transit.

We also conducted five pilot interview and a focus group debrief with our team at the end of the first Summer Institute and interviewed the two new youth researchers (Tasha and Marianne) who joined our team for the second Summer Institute. Indeed, in the final sections of this chapter we draw on these interviews as we highlight the ways YPAR and IE serve as important frameworks for learning with young people.

The Pedagogical Potential of YPAR and IE with Youth

By the end of the first seven-week summer institute, youth researchers reported a deepened awareness and analysis of institutionally organized inequalities. They had sharpened their writing skills and developed strategies to effectively navigate powerful mainstream institutions (for example, with Jessica's support, Alon acquired all of the citizenship documentation he needed to participate in the formal economy). They also clearly developed strategies for inviting other young people to connect the dots between their personal experiences (e.g., of safety, learning, taking care of their health, getting around the city) and the larger matrix of social and institutional relations that mediate how young people experience these things. In this final section, we re-articulate our central argument that YPAR strategies—that is, the development of inclusive and equitable structures for people to learn how to do IE and participate in a study as a co-researcher—may allow for the pedagogical and political potential of IE to be more fully realized. We make this argument by focusing on the shifts in thought and action young people experienced as co-researchers on this project.

In what follows, we illuminate some of the changes experienced by members of our team, as they come into view during interviews, conducted across the lifespan of the project. In this part of the chapter, we are interested in the how young people's participation in, and questions about, a range of popular and institutional discourses contour and are contoured by their everyday experiences. We include interview excerpts where they are actively grappling with academic and popular discourses about institutionalized racism, bringing them into the interviews they conduct with one another and the debriefing conversations they have with Jessica and Naomi. Much like Smith's (1990) discussions of femininity as discourse, we are interested in illuminating how young people's thinking work (i.e., their engagement with and questions about popular and academic discourse), shapes and is shaped by their participation in various intersecting institutional relations.

In this project, we looked at growing up (what other scholars would describe as development) as something young people actively do. The research was organized around the idea that part of this work is about coming to know yourself in relation to others and the institutions that permeate young people's lives. Here we share excerpts from interview conversations, where young people discuss all of the things they do to figure out who they are and how they should be in particular spaces of their lives (school, streets, parties, homes), where and how to move in the city, who to call for help (if anyone), and how to make sense of these experiences. We begin with an interview between Naomi and Destry, showing how a line of inquiry, which emerged in this first interview was carried forward into subsequent interviews. Engaging in this collective process of inquiry allowed Destry (and others on the team) to bring into view a diversity of experiences and sense-making practices that reflect their participation in particular discursive practices and institutional relations. When Naomi invited Destry to tell her where he feels, "most comfortable or at ease, safest in the city," a whole world of institutional and social activity opened up for the two of them to look at together. In the passage that follows, we learn about Destry's movements through the city, his experiences of safety and unsafety, as well as the forms of knowledge (e.g., about Blackness and the city), which condition these things:

DH: Like, from my house to downtown. That's the only spot I would be at.
NN: Kind of cutting across Sherbrooke [street] or something?
DH: Yeah.
NN: What is it about that track that you [like]?
DH: Well, because I grew up around there, and I never really visited or spent too much time in, for example, Montmorency, up there … Yeah. I don't know. I've just never been there a lot, so I don't feel comfortable hanging around there. I'll go if I need to do something, but I can't chill there.
NN: What would make you feel un-at-ease in a place where you haven't been very much or in one of those places?
DH: Mm, because I don't know the area like the back of my hand. But around here, I know everything.
NN: And what do you need to know to be safe?
DH: Police activity. [laughs]

At first, this passage appears to be about Destry's experiential geographic knowledge of the city, based on the routes he travels and spaces where he and his friends can hang around and chill: "I don't know the [other] area like the back of my hand. But around here, I know everything." But it quickly becomes clear that the knowledge he needs to feel safe is not simply cartographic. Montreal is divided into boroughs. The places where Destry is comfortable are in or adjacent to the large borough (Notre Dame de Grace) where he grew up. These are also parts of the city, where Destry is likely to find someone who speaks his first language (English) in a provincial context where French is the official majority language. But as Destry is prompted to explain "what he needs to know to be safe," his response makes it clear that he is not simply talking about his geographic familiarity with the west side of the city. Indeed, Destry goes on to note that some of the things he needs to know are the patterns of police activity in a neighborhood, particularly in those neighborhoods that are notorious in popular consciousness, as (a) racialized and (b) criminally engaged. In what follows, Destry tells Naomi about his work to be safe. Part of Destry's work to navigate the city safely involves grappling with how objectified forms of knowing (or popular consciousness) about the city, shape the institution of policing, as well as his own movements and experiences of (un)safety as a young Black man

NN: Yeah, tell me about that. What do you need to know about the police activity?
DH: Because you hear rumors about up there – like, the North and the East where there's gang-related activities. And you don't want to go into that. You just want to be safe, so you kind of stay in your little part of town. But, yeah, it's like the police look for a specific group of people—like, Black people—and if you go over there and you're not meant to be over there, they'll still think you're a part of them [gangs].
NN: Because of the color of your skin and the way you dress?
DH: Exactly. And then it's downhill from there ... you know in the States it's Black people getting killed by police. It's coming to here too. It's crazy. So, if you try to stay alive, you should stay where you're safe and not go out of your way to accidentally get shot, "accidentally." [chuckles]

Where Destry talks about rumors, we might use the term discourse or racist ideology, but we are referencing a similar phenomenon, that is, those objectified forms of knowledge, which appear authorless, and which we feel as though we have inherited or somehow always just known. While Smith (1999, 2004) has shown us that these bodies of thought have discoverable origins in actual people's thoughts, actions, and textual representation, their widespread adoption and use across a range of sources, locations, and historical moments, makes them appear to exist in an objectified form independent of us, and even in some cases acting on and through us. We see Destry working in this domain here in the interview with Naomi, as he talks about parts of the city he would avoid and how he knows that these spaces would be unsafe for him. Destry suggests he would not want to be in particular Black neighborhoods he associates with gang activity because he is more likely to encounter police there who will read his skin and the ways he dresses as an indication of criminality. This association between policing practice and anti-Black racism is less grounded in Destry's direct-experience (he had not actually had many encounters with the police yet when we did this interview) than in his engagement with media documentation of police violence and a growing public consciousness about anti-Black racism in the United States and Canada. Nevertheless, Destry's engagement with popular media and participation in activist discourses about systemic anti-Black racism, contours his direct-experiences, as he moves through the city and makes decisions about how to keep himself safe. This interview took place in the summer of 2016, when a number of high-profile police shootings of unarmed Black men were recorded via cell phone and uploaded to Youtube (https://www.nytimes.com/interactive/2017/08/19/us/police-videos-race.html). In Montreal that summer, people demonstrated their solidarity with Black Lives Matters activists across North America and voiced their concerns about anti-Black racism and racist police violence in Montreal. Destry's understanding of where and how he will experience safety in the city intersects in multiple ways with popular representations of the predominately Black neighborhood as gang-associated[3] and policing as an anti-Black institution. Objectified forms of knowledge (e.g., representations of anti-Black racism) condition Destry's movements through the city and his interactions with the institutions that ostensibly operate to promote public safety, in this case, the police. At the end of this passage, Destry tells Naomi that the police are unlikely to "care that much" about his safety because he does not believe "Black people are the priority:"

> NN: So, if you were feeling threatened in any way, what would you do? Who would you ask for help?
> DH: That's the thing; I can't ask anybody for help if I felt threatened ... I could [ask the police for help], but the police wouldn't do anything. They'd listen to me, but they're not going to care that much.
> NN: Why?
> DH: They have priorities too, and I don't think Black people are the priority.

Later on in the project, police profiling practices became a central line of inquiry for our team, contoured by their experiences talking to other Black youth and each other, their engagement with the research data from Naomi's early work in Toronto and with various media outlets documenting and discussing the disproportionate numbers of Black people shot by the police in North American cities, their engagement in Hip Hop, as well as their increasing knowledge of emerging and historical forms of resistance to this violence. Thus, when Destry interviewed, Tasha—who is a young Black women—he invited her to engage in an investigation of this topic with him. It is here, where we see the critical analytic and pedagogical potential of an IE mode of interviewing come into view.

Destry interviewed Tasha before she joined the project, and within the first lines of the interview transcript, we see evidence of his relational approach to interviewing in his invitation to Tasha to share "any stories about your room that makes you feel like, 'Ooh, yeah, this is my spot.'" This part of the interview was similarly focused on the social and institutional relations comprising public and personal safety, and thus began with an invitation for Tasha to talk about the places where she experiences (un)safety. Destry's prompt, aligned with the generous notions of safety we were working with and oriented to anchoring the interview in Tasha's embodied experiences, served as a playful invitation for Tasha to elaborate on her initial answer in greater descriptive detail.

After introducing the topic of safety and asking Tasha where she feels safest, Destry tells Tasha he's going to move on to "a serious problem" that "gets me triggered," asking her what she "thought of the police in Montreal ... Or where you live in general?" Tasha responded that she hasn't had "any issues with police personally" but that she had "seen and heard of, you know, a lot of—not a lot, but just certain negative things that the police have done." Destry and Tasha are knowledgeable participants in activist discourses about anti-Black racism and policing; but, Destry is not seeking to draw Tasha into an ideological account of police activity in this interview. His interest is in how processes of racialization operate in and through the institutions young people interact with every day. When Tasha explains experienced "any issues with police personally" he pivots and asks Tasha to reflect on her experiences in school—specifically to consider the racial—ethnic make-up of her school. The move comes across as an effort on Destry's part to bring a race-analysis into their shared conversation without relying on conceptual explanations that obscure the ways race is produced in reflexively organized relations among people, which are mediated by seemingly ordinary institutional processes. His invitation is for Tasha to build her response to his question from her own embodied experiences, rather than rely only on conceptual explanations with which they are both familiar. To his more pointed question about race and education, Tasha revealed that she was one of only two Black youth in the population of "mainly white people" comprising the enriched Math and Science program she attended. In this way, Tasha begins to question how ordinary practices in education—practices she had previously considered to be neutral and fair—actually sort students such that enrichment opportunities are not as accessible to Black students like her and Destry. This move to get Tasha thinking about race, culture and schooling reflects Destry's attentiveness to the subtle ways that social processes of racialization contour young lives and his desire to engage Tasha in a conversation about these processes. Destry is not using leading questions; on the contrary, he uses open-ended prompts to learn about Tasha's experiences and invite her to connect the dots across the different themes of the interview (i.e., policing, education, neighborhoods/housing, health, and others).

Institutional ethnographic interviewing can be experienced as a series of analytic moves, as the interviewer and interviewee examine a particular institutional process, policy, or body of knowledge from the standpoint of the interviewee. There is an effort to engage relationally in conversation—not as a unidirectional data collection mechanism, but as a means of bringing the institutional relations backgrounding people's experiences into view for both parties. When Destry invited Tasha to think about the institutions that were shaping her own life, she was initially hesitant to consider how her experiences may have shaped and been shaped by objectified forms of consciousness[4] and the material social relations of race, class, gender, ability, sexuality, and so forth. But a few months into the project herself, when Tasha and Naomi interviewed a young white woman (Marianne) who joined the team, Tasha took up the line of inquiry that emerged in her conversation with Destry and offered it to Marianne, inviting her to reflect on her own interactions with the police. Destry's sense that interactions with the police are likely to cause him harm, particularly in some parts of the city, stands in stark contrast to Marianne's sense that "nothing bad is really going to happen" given her observation that policing practices in her largely white suburban US neighborhood tend to lead to minor charges coupled with community sanctions, e.g., participating in drug-testing and taking a class. Marianne and Destry's participation in relations of ruling (in this case, objectified forms of knowing) produce their divergent sentiments that the police are dangerous/harmless. Because of our interest in how institutional and social processes shape young people's thoughts, explanations, and sense-making practices, we paid attention to the ways that young people came to know what they know. In tracing through these accounts in sequence, the ways in which young people are participating in and refiguring the social relations of identity as they participate in this project come into view:

MS: …there's also kind of a knowledge that nothing bad is really gonna happen to us. Through other friends, there's been interaction with the police. Several of my friends in high school actually, lots of my friends in high school [laughs] were caught with possession charges. But, really, what happens when you get a possession charge in the suburbs is basically, you get drug tested for a certain period of time, and you have to take a class.
…
TM: That's interesting. It was also interesting when you said the cops would bust the parties that you were at. You guys all knew that they weren't really going to do anything. Why is that? Why do you think that you guys felt that safety or comfort or whatever it was?

MS: Money. Not myself, personally. I think that also plays a lot into my identity. Like I said, my suburb, where I'm from, there's a lot of money. But my family is not, I mean, I'm very financially privileged. My parents are helping me with this [school], and they help me with my rent. But I was never as rich as anyone around me … But there's a lot of rich people at my school whose parents are lawyers or who can hire really good lawyers. Police know that and the parents know that and the kids know that, so it's about money, yeah … Also, when you have money, there's more—your future is at stake and stuff like that. No one wants to give a kid who's going to go to an Ivy League a record and stuff like that.

In response to Tasha's question about how Marianne knew the police would not cause her and her friends harm, Marianne provides an ideological explanation: class. At the end of the interview, Tasha, Marianne, and Naomi discussed this part of the interview again and the ways Marianne's experiences and interpretations of her experiences differed from Tasha's. We talked about the institutional relations we can see through Marianne's explanation of her experience with the police (e.g., the operations of criminal-legal system and socially organized relations between policing and the courts). We also observed that Marianne was quick to interpret her experiences with police as a function of her wealthy suburban upbringing, whereas Tasha immediately questioned whether these experiences were actually the result of the racial composition of the neighborhood (i.e., white) and racist policing practices. By paying attention to the ideological explanations that are close at hand for youth, and to which they turn when making sense of their experiences growing up, identity development comes into view as a social process that is shaped as much by young people's direct-experiences as the discursive tools that they draw on to make sense of and interpret these experiences. These interviews and the line of inquiry they trace for those doing the interviewing and those being interviewed—have the potential to engender critical social analytic capacities and participatory institutional ethnographies with young people, thus have the potential to be more educative and transformative for youth than other more formal educational opportunities.

Indeed, during the interviews and focus group discussion we held with our team at the end of the first Summer Institute, the youth were asked to reflect on whether/how their thinking about any of the interview topics had shifted over the course of the summer. Alon's response to the question in relation to schooling was representative of the group's sentiment, particularly shifts in how they understood the social relations of access to secondary and post-secondary education in the city:

> With me, honestly, being at McGill and stuff—I always told myself I'm never going to go to university. Now this makes me want to go to university because this is a privilege place ... Whenever I think of this kind of work and school right now, [I think] this is the best thing ever because I'm learning. I'm actually learning because I'm interested. Even though it's a topic maybe not interesting, there's a way to make it interesting because you guys find a way to make it interesting ... But I never had any experiences like that at school, never in my life.

The young people we have worked with illuminate a potential in youth participatory research that is not being, and perhaps cannot be, realized in formal educational settings. Large class sizes, standardized curricula, and an emphasis on testing and ranking (Nichols & Griffith, 2009) undermine opportunities for shared inquiry, particularly inquiries grounded in young people's experiences and illuminating how these experiences have been socially organized to unfold as they do.

Conclusion

This chapter highlights the synergy between YPAR's methodological and ethical commitments to learning and/or consciousness raising and action and the pragmatic, ontological, and epistemological commitments, which underpin IE's sociological project, that is, (1) that an IE project should be useful to people outside of the academy; (2) that social relations are actual material relations among people; and (3) that researchers can trace from these social relations (that is, what people know, think and do together) in order to discover how particular social practice are coordinated by language, institutionalized modes of action, and texts. We have aimed to reveal precisely how we employed particular YPAR strategies and methodological principles to ensure our research was grounded in, and accountable to, the lives and experiences of young people. We also endeavored to demonstrate using our own project as the object of our analysis that the experience of participating in a study like this has the potential to be pedagogically transformative for young people, who have opportunities to develop and implement new strategies for making sense of their lives and experiences.

At the end of the first Summer Research Institute, we conducted a focus group with everyone on our team and in-depth interviews with each of the youth researchers. In part, these interviews and the focus group were used to pilot test our interview protocol, but they also as a means of enabling systematic reflexivity in our process. In the interviews and the focus group, young people contrasted their experiences in school with their experiences on this project. There were clear affinities between their critiques of schooling and the critiques of objectifying modes of research at the heart of IE's development as an alternative sociology. The young men, in particular, felt surveilled, punished, and trapped in mainstream educational environments. All of our youth co-researchers felt they were not truly known, heard, challenged, or inspired in school. Nor did many of them put much effort into the work that was expected of them there. They contrasted these experiences with their engagement on this project, noting that their experiences help them reidentify a capacity for, and excitement about learning. When prompted for specific suggestions about what was missing in their formal schooling experience, one of our co-researchers, Alon, suggested he simply needed a place to begin, and it could not be a beginning structured from within the relevancies of the provincial curriculum: "NN: And what parts did you need help with? AB: Just finding my interest...Getting started." Participatory youth research, particularly where it is organized to begin in and emerge from the relevancies of young people's own lives, experiences and passions, is a means for getting started and for engaging in a process of unfolding inquiry and action together.

Notes

1. We have used pseudonyms for our youth research team members in this chapter. To write this chapter, we drew on data from interviews and focus groups with them, conducted as part of an evaluation of the first year of the project and a pilot test of our interview guide.
2. Just like we conduct research as part of our salaried jobs, the doctoral student, the youth workers, and the youth were also paid to attend these meetings. Payment is important in participatory research with youth because it removes barriers for young people who would otherwise be prevented from participating; economic precarity makes volunteering difficult. Indeed, our capacity to offer paid research positions to youth has been an important dimension to this project.
3. For example, a quick search of mainstream French media reveals considerable media coverage of street gang activity in Montreal Nord, such as the following https://www.lapresse.ca/actualites/justice-et-faits-divers/201903/23/01-521 9348-gangs-de-rue-des-funerailles-sous-surveillance.php. Indeed, even as one types Montreal Nord into a google search engine, gang is the seventh algorithmically generated item included in the dropdown list which one is prompted to use to finish their search.
4. As objectified forms of consciousness and organization, socio-political categories are key coordinators of relations of ruling. Indeed, in the age of data- or evidence-led service delivery and governance, institutional decision-making increasingly pivots on the use of data, interrelated systems of classification and measurement have an even greater influence on how political decisions are made and how public services are delivered. As such, their use also produces clear material effects in terms of people's lives and opportunities, even though it is true that the categories themselves have no agency. Indeed, the fact that these categories are produced and used by people to serve a particular (typically institutional or political) function is not obvious in their everyday use. This is part of their function in relations of ruling.

References

Anucha, U., & Griffith, A. (2013). *Schools, safety and the urban neighbourhood*. Social Science and Humanities Research Council Insight Grant (435-2013-1518).

Brown, T. M., & Rodriguez, L. F. (2009). *Issue editors' notes: New directions for youth development, youth in participatory action research, No. 123*. Wiley Online Library. https://doi.org/10.1002/yd.309.

Checkoway, B., & Richards-Schuster, K. (2001). *Second year evaluation of Lifting New Voices*. Ann Arbor: Lifting New Voices, School of Social Work, University of Michigan.

Checkoway, B., & Richards-Schuster, K. (2003). Youth participation in community evaluation research. *American Journal of Evaluation, 24,* 21–33. https://doi.org/10.1177/109821400302400103.

Fals-Borda, O. (2001). Participatory (action) research in social theory: Origins and challenges. In P. Reason & H. Bradbury (Eds.), *Handbook of action research* (pp. 27–37). Thousand Oaks, CA: Sage.

Fine, M., & Torre, M. E. (2004). Re-membering exclusions: Participatory action research in public institutions. *Qualitative Research in Psychology, 1,* 15–37.

Fox, M., Mediratta, K., Ruglis, J., Stoudt, B., Shah, S., & Fine, M. (2010). Critical youth engagement: Participatory action research and organizing. In L. R. Sherrod, J. Torney-Purta, & C. A. Flanagan (Eds.), *Handbook of research and policy on civic engagement in youth* (pp. 621–649). Hoboken, NJ: Wiley.

Frampton, C., Kinsman, G., Thompson, A. K., & Tilleczek, K. (Eds.). (2006). *Sociology for changing the world: Social movements/social research.* Halifax, NS: Fernwood.

Jacobs, S. (2016). The use of participatory action research within education-benefits to stakeholders. *World Journal of Education, 6*(3), 48–55.

Khanlou, N., & Peter, E. (2005). Participatory action research: Considerations for ethical review. *Social Science and Medicine, 60,* 2333–2340.

Maguire, P. (1987). *Doing participatory research: A feminist approach.* Amherst, MA: The Centre for International Education, University of Massachusetts.

Nichols, N. (2014). *Youth work: An institutional ethnography of youth homelessness.* Toronto, ON: The University of Toronto Press.

Nichols, N. (2016). Investigating the social relations of human service provision: Institutional ethnography and activism. *Journal of Comparative Social Work,* Special Edition on Institutional Ethnography, *11*(1). Available at http://journal.uia.no/index.php/JCSW/article/view/360.

Nichols, N., & Griffith, A. I. (2009). Talk, texts and educational action: An institutional ethnography of policy in practice. *Cambridge Journal of Education, 39*(2), 241–255.

Nichols, N., Griffith, A. I., & McLarnon, M. (2018). Community-based and participatory approaches in institutional ethnography. In J. Reid & L. Russell (Eds.), *Perspectives on and from institutional ethnography* (pp. 107–124). Bingley, UK: Emerald Books.

Pence, E. (2002). Safety for battered women in a textually mediated legal system. *Studies in Cultures, Organizations and Societies, 7,* 199–229.

Reason, P., & Bradbury, H. (2001). Introduction: Inquiry and participation in search of a world worthy of human aspiration. In P. Reason & H. Bradbury (Eds.), *Handbook of action research: Participative inquiry and practice* (pp. 1–14). Thousand Oaks, CA: Sage.

Smith, D. E. (1999). *Writing the social: Critique, theory, and investigations.* Toronto, ON: University of Toronto Press.

Smith, D. E. (2004). Ideology, science, and social relations: A reinterpretation of Marx's epistemology. In S. Carpenter & S. Mojab (Eds.), *Educating from Marx: Race, gender, and learning* (pp. 19–40). New York, NY: Palgrave Macmillan US. https://doi.org/10.1057/9780230370371_2.

Smith, D. E. (2005). *Institutional ethnography: A sociology for people.* Lanham, MD: Altamira Press.

Smith, D. E. (2006). *Institutional ethnography as practice*. Lanham, MD: Rowman and Littlefield.

Smith, G. W. (1990). Political activist ethnographer. *Social Problems, 37*(4), 629–648.

Teram, E., Schacter, C. L., & Stalker, C. A. (2005). The case for integrating grounded theory and participatory action research: Empowering clients to inform professional practice. *Qualitative Health Research, 15*(8), 1129–1140.

Wang, C., & Burris, M. A. (1997). Photovoice: Concept, methodology, and use for participatory needs assessment. *Health Education and Behavior, 24,* 369–387.

Warren, M. R., & Mapp, K. L. (2011). *A match on dry grass: Community organizing as a catalyst for school reform*. New York, NY: Oxford University Press.

Wilson, A., & Pence, E. (2006). U.S. legal interventions in the lives of battered women: An indigenous assessment. In D. E. Smith (Ed.), *Institutional ethnography as practice* (pp. 199–225). Toronto: Rowman and Littlefield.

Index

A

Academia, 125, 162, 168
Academic, 13, 21, 23, 122, 125, 128, 146, 152, 153, 157, 158, 161–164, 167–171, 175, 176, 178, 185, 248, 259–262, 265–277, 310, 324, 349, 361, 362, 364, 370, 376–378, 389, 400, 466, 511, 527, 531, 539, 540
Accommodations, 375–393, 429
Accomplish/accomplishment, 170, 262, 275, 276, 293, 347, 352, 439, 466, 473, 507, 508, 521
Accountability, 128, 129, 132, 133, 241, 245, 249, 260, 267, 269, 270, 276, 277, 293, 313, 342, 347, 360, 361, 366, 371, 375, 381, 390, 391, 405, 452–456, 459, 476, 514, 521, 537
Accountability circuit, 244, 365, 369, 426, 430–432, 436, 440
Accounts, 111, 112
Activating text, 216, 250
Activist research, 324
Actor network studies, 42
Act-text-act sequence, 145, 146, 151
Affective responses, 162
Aging in place, 82, 83, 90, 91
Alienation, 514, 518, 520, 522
Alternate sociology, 176, 181, 186, 239
Alternative forms of knowledge, 410, 414

Alternative sociology, 1, 3, 4, 7, 36, 48, 50, 60, 61, 102, 398
American Sign Language (ASL), 182, 450
Americans with Disabilities Act (ADA), 376, 377, 379–383, 390–393, 448, 450
Analysis of visual materials, 122
Anthropocene, 6, 483, 484, 486, 489, 492, 495, 500, 501
Arts-based methods, 85
Assessment, 105, 128, 184, 227, 229, 238, 240–242, 244–246, 248, 249, 251, 262, 264, 266, 267, 295, 296, 302, 303, 332, 334, 335, 338, 341, 342, 347, 361, 367, 369, 381, 397–402, 404–406, 408, 410, 412–417, 427–429, 436, 440, 513, 516
Attention Deficit Hyperactivity Disorder (ADHD), 309, 377–380, 382, 383, 388, 390–393
Audit, 237, 238, 244, 254, 262, 266, 267
Australia, 237–241, 245–248, 251, 254
Autophotography, 122

B

Bauman, Z., 361
Ethics, 361

morality, 361
Best practices, 288, 290, 298, 301, 414, 439

C

California Realignment or the Public Safety Realignment Act of 2011 (Assembly Bill 109), 403, 418
  notorious cases of crimes by parolees, 403
Campbell, M., 3, 12, 16, 19, 24, 26, 53, 61, 90, 104, 108, 115, 135, 144, 158, 324, 426, 440, 512
Care and commitment, 520
Care responsibility, 267, 268, 273, 274, 277
Care work, 41, 42, 84, 88–90, 92, 261, 270, 273–275
Caseload, 401, 404, 408–410, 413, 415, 416, 519, 520
Case management, 341, 397, 404, 412, 414
Case processing, 22, 332, 334, 335, 342, 347, 348, 350, 353
Children's Aid Society (CAS), 505, 506, 509, 513, 515, 522, 523
Chile, 213–221, 223–227, 229–233
  Constitution, 215
Climate Negotiations, Copenhagen (2009), 198
Closed-circuit television (CCTV), 126, 127, 129, 398
College, 178, 266, 291, 295, 376–378, 380, 385, 386, 389, 392, 423, 512, 523
Colonial cultures of planning, 232
Colonialism, 232
Community Foundations, 320, 321
Community supervision, 397–399, 413, 415–417
  parole, 400, 402, 404
  post-release community supervision (PRCS), 403, 405, 408
  probation, 402, 404
Composite accounts, 6, 466, 467, 469–478

Congregation/congregational/congregationally, 512, 522
Constitution, 219–221, 223–225, 231
Constitutional Tribunal (TC), 220, 221
Consultation, 112, 214–219, 221, 223–233, 350
Convention 169, 214–216, 219, 221, 223–225, 227, 229, 231
Convention on Biological Diversity (CBD), 194, 201, 202, 204–209
Conversation analysis, 6, 507–509, 511, 512, 523
Coordination, 25–27, 29, 35, 38–44, 67, 81, 90, 99, 105, 126, 143, 145, 158, 162, 171, 200, 253, 317, 376, 378, 379, 390, 409, 471, 489, 491, 494, 499
Copyright, 4, 141–148, 150–153
Corman, Michael, 6, 42, 55
Correctional Offender Management Profiling for Alternative Sanctions (COMPAS), 400, 402, 405, 406, 414, 417
Courses of action, 70, 74, 77, 145, 146, 151, 215, 217, 219, 226, 300, 379, 449, 508
COVID-19 discourse, 2
Criminal-legal system, 397–399, 417, 546
Crisis of representation, 467, 468, 477
Critical social analysis, 529, 533
Culture-aware practices, 304
Culture-based practices, 291

D

Data analysis, 180, 268, 425
Data collection, 84, 86, 123, 195, 243, 249, 342, 345, 349, 352, 368, 381, 466, 467, 476, 479, 533, 535, 537, 539, 545
  dialogic character, 472
Data elicitation, 82, 85, 86
Deaf, 182, 184, 187, 447–452, 459, 460
Debates, 121, 159, 164, 180, 194, 198, 208, 225, 227, 324, 483, 486, 500
  Juridical debates, 217

de Montigny, G., 6, 15, 69–74, 77, 367, 507, 508, 510, 511
DeVault, M., 4, 12, 20, 23, 24, 43, 48, 53, 81, 84, 93, 115, 135, 159, 160, 179, 197, 262, 273, 276, 364, 440
Deveau, J.L., 40, 90, 441
Diamond, Timothy, 3, 19, 20, 26, 41, 42, 177, 186
Digital technologies text/visual reactivation, 27, 123, 150
Disability, 5, 176–181, 183–187, 242, 243, 245, 375–377, 379–387, 391–393, 448, 449
Disability education, 175, 243, 379, 392
Disability services, 375, 376, 378–380, 382–384, 387, 390
Disability Studies, 175, 176, 178, 186
Discourse, ideology, 15, 20, 24, 108, 364, 427, 542, 544
Discourse (of), 14, 16, 20, 25, 27, 70, 72, 125, 146, 151, 171, 266, 269, 334, 361, 370, 426, 454, 459
  Academic, 365
  early language stimulation, 370
  Ease Communication, Inc., 454
  femininity, 25
  food safety, 485
  impaired nursing practice, 426
  mothering discourse, 25
  play, 370
  safety, 428, 430
Discovery, 7, 71, 102, 103, 141, 158, 171, 180, 186, 197, 251, 286, 292, 300, 313, 437, 439, 468, 471, 472, 476, 477, 530
Disjuncture, 14, 17, 106, 108, 132, 152, 242, 245, 253, 260, 274, 311, 313, 366, 368, 399, 425, 426, 485, 489, 492, 493, 497
Dispossession, 214
Division on Institutional Ethnography, 6
Dos Passos, John, 1, 2
Duty to consult, 214–217, 219, 221, 223–225, 228–233

E
Early Childhood Education and Care, 241

Eastwood, L., 17, 216, 218, 219, 226–228
Efficiency, 24, 115, 260, 276, 277, 320, 375, 385, 390, 391, 449, 452–460
Eight methods of Institutional Analysis, 338, 352
Epistemic inequality(ies), 157, 161, 167, 171
Equity, 17, 244, 245, 248
Ethics, 42, 49, 55, 83, 90, 112, 181, 185, 255, 275, 361, 511, 512, 520, 523, 535–537
Ethics/confidentiality, 94, 116, 385, 469, 513, 514
EthnoAlly, 138
Ethnography, 52, 58, 77, 112, 122, 136, 137, 176, 180, 187, 196, 199, 200, 210, 325
  auto-ethnography, 128
Ethnomethodology, 14, 17, 40, 52, 468, 507, 508, 512
Evidence, 72–74, 132, 181, 186, 241–243, 247, 250, 292, 295, 297, 299, 301, 361, 365, 366, 371, 388, 398, 399, 416, 417, 427, 428, 440, 466, 510, 514, 515, 543, 548
Evidence-based practices (EBP), 5, 115, 397–402, 410, 413, 416, 417
Exclusion, 16, 39, 101, 158, 163, 171, 223, 224, 531
Exclusion narratives, 164, 170

F
Fair use, 142, 144, 147, 150, 152, 153
Family caregiving, 82
Family photos, 122
Family violence, 17
Federal Communications Commission (FCC), 448, 449, 452, 457, 459
Federal government, 82, 244, 309, 312, 325, 391
Feminist/feminism, 1, 7, 13, 14, 17–21, 28, 52, 71, 100, 101, 103, 114–116, 157–164, 166, 167, 169, 171, 176–179, 186, 486, 508, 511, 533
Finland, 157, 158, 161, 162, 164, 171, 204

554   INDEX

Fitness to practice, 426, 433, 440
Focus groups, 127–130, 132–134, 137, 343, 345, 350, 495, 499, 539, 547
Foucault, M., 20, 52
Frontline work, 248
Frontline workers (supervision as work), 298, 304, 376, 378, 390, 401–403
Functional equivalency, 5, 448, 449, 456, 459

G
Ganohkwasra, 284, 286, 287
Gap(s), 15, 101, 113, 182, 238, 239, 296, 321, 331–333, 335, 343, 350, 379, 403, 468
  implementation gaps, 217
Gay bathhouse, 74
Gender, 20, 39, 114, 162–164, 171, 247, 260, 274, 276, 330, 402, 403, 414–416, 523
Gender-based violence, 5, 329, 332, 341
Gender studies, 157, 158, 161–167, 169–171
Gender system, 272
Gestures, 66, 509
Governing text, 25, 215–217, 219, 223, 226, 227, 231, 233, 244, 376
Graduate education, 49
Griffith, A., 5, 14, 15, 18, 20, 23, 24, 28, 69, 83, 85, 240, 246–248, 250, 253, 254, 426

H
Harding, Sandra, 17, 159, 160
Harmful outcomes, 333, 355
Harper, Richard, 201
Haudenosaunee, 284
Health Professional Act (HPA), 423, 426, 433, 434
Hegemonic, 158, 163, 260, 488, 521
Hegemonic feminism, 163, 167
Hegemony, 163, 164, 171, 215
Hekman, Susan, 159
Hierarchical text, 145
Higher education, 253, 259, 260, 275–277, 379, 381, 392
HIV, 21, 58, 100–102, 104–111, 113–117, 177, 471

Women living with HIV, 100, 102
Hussey, I., 323
Hybrid use of visuals, 125

I
Identity, 59, 72, 105, 157, 171, 175, 187, 215, 226, 363, 511, 514, 521, 545, 546
Ideological code, 16, 91, 125, 126, 169, 237, 240, 243, 245, 250–252, 254, 261, 276, 362, 364, 366
Ideology/ideological, 12, 13, 15, 18, 20, 24, 27, 108, 226, 248, 251, 254, 260, 270, 276, 341, 349, 364, 379, 427, 429, 431, 439–441, 466, 511, 522, 542, 544, 546
Ideology/ideological practices, 11, 13
Images, 39, 122–126, 128–130, 132, 133, 137, 143, 144, 146, 148–151, 153, 179, 180, 365
Imagocentrism, 123
Indecency, 75
Indigenous dispossession, 214, 216, 219, 230, 232, 233
Indigenous peoples, 28, 194, 196, 198, 204, 207–209, 214–219, 223, 224, 226–233, 305
Indigenous rights, 214–217, 219, 223–225, 227–232
Individualized Educational Plans (IEP), 377, 381, 383, 386
Individuals with Disabilities Education Act (IDEA), 377, 383, 391
Information, 22, 40, 82–91, 93, 94, 105–107, 109, 110, 112, 116, 117, 137, 150, 193, 201, 218, 228, 261, 262, 292, 295, 302, 335, 336, 339, 340, 342–348, 381, 382, 384, 385, 387, 388, 390–393, 398, 399, 405–407, 426, 432, 435, 436, 452, 474, 492, 513, 514, 524, 534
Information activities, needs, world, 82–86, 89–93
Infringement, 141, 142, 146, 148, 150–152
Institutional activity, 24
Institutional Analysis (IA), 5, 329, 330, 333, 353

Institutional as in institutional processes, 36, 41, 105, 145, 197, 200, 240, 329, 333, 345, 349, 362, 371, 424, 426, 439, 476, 521, 544
Institutional capture, 4, 71, 91, 93, 158, 171, 227, 262, 362, 363, 366, 371
Institutional circuit, 360, 371, 388
Institutional complex of work processes, 300
Institutional concepts, 71, 72
Institutional contexts, 48, 49, 99, 107, 276, 408, 511, 529, 539
Institutional courses/sequences of action, 67, 69, 70, 72–77, 145, 167, 184, 233, 347, 425, 426
Institutional discourse, 70, 74, 91, 125–127, 145, 260, 262, 266–268, 270, 275–277, 346, 359, 362, 364, 365, 368–371, 459, 540
Institutional discrimination, 215
Institutional ethnography (IE), 2, 4, 6, 7, 12, 16–20, 22, 23, 26, 27, 35, 36, 39–45, 47–50, 52–59, 61, 81, 92, 93, 121–124, 128, 133–138, 157, 177, 179, 214, 216, 233, 237, 238, 240–243, 245, 248, 250–254, 285, 286, 288, 305, 310, 312, 313, 316, 320, 322–325, 331, 333, 335, 342, 359, 364, 398, 404, 410, 416, 424–426, 437–441, 470–472, 475, 477, 478, 489, 507, 508, 510–512, 514, 521–523, 527–529, 532, 538, 540, 547
Institutional language, 4, 68, 70, 71, 74, 76, 77, 91, 105, 261
Institutional modes of action, 547
Institutional terms, 73
Institution of access, 448, 459
Institutions, 5, 18, 19, 21, 23, 25, 65, 70, 77, 90, 105, 106, 111, 113, 116, 132, 133, 159, 161, 179, 200, 201, 214, 215, 217, 224, 226, 228, 254, 261, 262, 265, 266, 276, 277, 312, 320, 323, 329, 330, 333–338, 342, 343, 345, 346, 348–353, 360–362, 364, 379, 388, 390, 423, 438, 439, 448, 485, 496, 516, 522, 533, 538, 542, 545. *See also* Institutional activity;

Institutional as in institutional processes; institutional contexts; Institutional modes of action
Institutions of social management, 338, 355
Institution talk, 69
Intellectual property, 142, 147, 148
International Labour Organization (ILO), 214–216, 233
International law, 214, 217, 219, 224, 231
interpretation, 86, 91, 111, 126–129, 133, 135–137, 146, 148, 180, 247, 376, 383, 388, 390, 414–416, 447, 450, 451, 454, 456, 458, 460, 522
Interpreter, 5, 182, 186, 447–459
Intersectionality, 59, 136, 164
Intertextual, 126, 145, 215, 223
Intertextuality, 223, 228, 232
Intertextual relations, 219, 224–226
Interviews, 21, 26, 52, 53, 56, 70, 76, 83, 84, 86, 89–93, 109–113, 126–130, 132–134, 137, 161, 162, 164, 165, 167–171, 179, 218, 230, 233, 253, 261, 268, 271, 274, 275, 289, 290, 292, 294, 296, 298, 300, 312, 324, 333, 336, 339, 343–345, 348–351, 356, 363–371, 378–380, 382–384, 392, 393, 399, 403, 404, 406, 407, 416, 425, 450, 466, 468, 473–475, 495, 496, 499, 507, 508, 510, 511, 513–515, 521, 529, 534, 535, 537, 539–544, 546–548
life-story, 162
Interviews with video or photography, 122
Investment, 19, 166, 167, 169–171, 197, 214, 218, 219, 226, 227, 229, 320, 321, 369, 520
Invisible work, 93, 182, 262, 389
Iterative practice, 521

J
Japan, 484
Junior scholars, 54

K
Knot of trouble, 181

Knowledge industries, 141, 142
konran, 484

L
Language, 39
  Academic, 363
Lead poisoning, 309, 311, 312, 314, 315, 317, 320, 322
  lead paint, 310
Learning, 25, 37, 48–50, 60, 65, 68, 101, 109, 161, 176–178, 180, 183, 186, 241, 242, 244, 246, 261–263, 286, 288, 292, 294, 295, 324, 342, 345, 349, 380, 386, 388, 399, 474, 528, 532–534, 540, 547
Level of Service/Case Management Inventory (LS/CMI), scores, 400, 402, 405–407, 409, 410, 414
Life story interview, 162
Lived experiences, 41, 123, 176, 186, 260, 262, 277, 311–313, 315, 322, 324, 378, 382, 392, 393, 460, 468–470, 494
Local and extra-local, 240, 496
Logocentrism, 123
Luken, P., 16, 43, 125, 126, 135, 137, 141, 144, 177, 186, 366

M
Making Gray Gold, 3, 19, 177
Managerialism, 178, 371
Map-building, 286, 293
Mapping, map, maps, 4, 5, 7, 26, 41, 81, 82, 84–86, 88–93, 101, 113, 134, 136, 158, 199, 214, 238, 240, 253, 260, 286, 290, 292, 293, 295, 298–301, 303, 305, 310, 312–314, 316, 317, 319, 320, 322–324, 334, 342, 350–353, 365, 425, 492, 538
  GIS mapping, 122
  grounded theory mapping, 122
  IE mapping, 319
  mental or cognitive mapping, 122
Marx, Karl, 12, 14, 36, 37, 44, 52, 491, 512
Masking or visual masking, 129, 137
Material culture, 85, 122
Materialism, 42, 187, 491, 512
Materialist method, 36, 512
Material objects, 68, 123, 180
Material semiotics, 6, 483, 484, 486–498, 500, 501
Maternity, 100, 104, 116, 251
McCoy, L., 4, 14, 20, 21, 25, 26, 43, 48, 52, 53, 81, 85, 91, 101, 108, 109, 111, 127–129, 135, 177, 179, 262, 364, 440, 457, 476
Mead, George Herbert, 14, 37, 52, 66, 470
  mind, 37
Measurement, 117, 248, 260, 262, 268, 275–277, 450, 456, 548
Mental health/psychiatry, 176, 183, 187, 339, 340, 427, 435, 440, 452, 510, 515, 516
Merleau-Ponty, 159
More-than-human, 6, 483–495, 497–501
Mothering, 18
Mykhalovskiy, E., 4, 21, 27, 43, 48, 52, 53, 55, 57–59, 61, 101, 111, 175–177, 179, 310, 324, 466

N
Narrative writing, 180
National Assessment Program—Literacy and Numeracy (NAPLAN), 242, 246–249
National Exchange Carrier Association (NECA), 449, 452–455, 458
Neoliberal ideology, 28, 260
New materialism, 42
New penology, 400
New Public Management (NPM), 23, 24, 238, 248, 360, 375, 390
Northwestern University, 17
Nuclear disaster, 484–486, 489, 490, 493, 495–501
Nurses, 5, 14, 19, 24, 26, 105, 177, 423–442, 510, 515, 516

O
Objectified forms of consciousness, 542, 545, 548. *See also* Discourse, ideology

Observations, 20, 41, 42, 49, 52, 66, 67, 69, 72, 74, 76, 127, 185, 266, 267, 312, 333, 343–345, 347–351, 365, 367, 371, 382, 416, 440, 468, 473–475, 495, 508, 524
Observing, 106, 179, 194, 199, 208, 210, 342, 344, 349, 537
Office of Disability Services (ODS), 376, 378–385, 387–393
Officers (community corrections), 21, 22, 75, 149, 286, 290–297, 299, 300, 334, 338–340, 344, 398, 399, 401–406, 408, 417, 434
Official forms of knowledge, 399, 400, 403, 417
  criminal history as, 411
  files as, 405, 411
Ontario Institute for Studies in Education (OISE), 17
Ontological politics, 488, 489, 491–494
Ontological shift, 40, 102, 106, 176, 187, 471, 478
Ontology, 14, 27, 28, 35–40, 42–45, 50, 52, 55, 92, 104, 123, 159, 179, 186, 195, 197, 205, 210, 217, 470, 488, 489, 491–493
Opposition, 366, 367, 369–371, 398, 519, 521–523
Oral collaborative mapping process, 292
Organizing and coordinating workers, 352
Orthodoxy, 5, 48, 53–56, 60, 176

P
Paramedics, 42, 467, 472–476
Participant observation, 42, 133, 134, 162, 495
Participant selection procedures, 162
Participatory research, 21, 100, 134, 531, 535, 546
Patients, 105
Pence, E., 5, 21, 22, 55, 228, 229, 252, 332, 349
Performance, 24, 26, 69, 166–170, 247, 249, 253, 262, 267, 268, 270, 274–277, 341, 360, 378, 382, 423, 428–430, 435, 436, 469, 509, 514, 516, 522, 523

Performativity, 260, 265–267, 269, 270, 276, 277
Perinatal, 101, 104, 107–109, 113, 116
Phenomenology, 52, 512
Philanthropic action, 320–322
Philanthropy, 316, 319, 324
Phone call, 265, 268
Photo-elicitation, 122, 124, 127, 128, 132, 133, 135, 137
Photography, photographs, 43, 45, 121, 122, 125, 127, 134, 136, 144, 148–150
Photovoice, 85, 93, 122, 133, 134, 137
Planning, 26, 81, 143, 162, 183, 214–219, 227, 231–233, 263, 271, 274, 293, 302, 351, 377, 405, 410, 411
  land-use, 26
Point of departure, 158, 159, 206, 214, 310, 317, 322, 324
  subject position, 159
Policy, 16, 17, 19, 20, 22–25, 29, 82, 85, 93, 100, 101, 106, 116, 136, 141, 145, 147, 176, 178, 181, 184, 193, 195–197, 199–201, 203, 205–207, 209, 210, 213, 216–218, 228, 233, 238–244, 246, 249, 251–254, 259–261, 276, 283, 291, 296, 298, 310, 314, 316, 320–325, 336, 347, 349, 361, 375, 377–379, 382, 385, 392, 393, 398, 401, 408, 410, 424, 426, 428, 439–441, 459, 484, 513, 514, 516, 520, 522, 535, 538
Policy change, 239, 241, 253, 254, 317–320
Power inequalities in research, 135
Practice-based evidence, 398, 417
Practitioners, 60, 181, 195, 197, 200, 201, 210, 214, 218, 219, 227–229, 237, 248, 252, 302, 310, 329, 331, 334–338, 340, 343–349, 352, 353, 434, 508, 513
Praxis, 521, 529, 533
Praxis International, 5, 22, 329, 332
Problematic, 4, 27, 52, 55, 57, 81, 83, 101, 103, 104, 113, 144, 160, 161, 273, 311, 313, 315, 323, 330, 339, 343, 344, 346, 347, 353, 366, 399,

424, 426, 450, 495, 497–499, 509, 513, 522, 532
Problematic practices, 343, 348, 349, 352
Proceduralization, 225, 232
Professional discourse, 18, 70, 73, 143, 147, 367, 368
Professional practice, 43, 129, 130, 137, 241, 247, 252, 361, 362, 364, 367, 423, 508, 520
Professional process, 70, 133, 244, 520
Professional relationship, 513, 520
Professional standards, 242
Professional talk, 367, 371, 372
Publication agreements, 143, 144, 146, 151
Public ethnography, 136
Publishing, 114, 143, 145–147, 149, 151–153, 168, 169, 267, 272

Q

Qualitative analysis, research, 99–101, 122, 179, 271, 393, 466, 468, 469, 478

R

Race (disparities, bias), 400, 401, 414, 416, 417
Rankin, J., 24, 26, 48, 53, 57, 92, 110, 111, 115, 313, 425, 426
Reducing Emissions from Deforestation and Forest Degradation (REDD), 206, 207
Reflexivity, 103, 104
  reflected, 110
  reflexive, 115
  reflexive practice, 104
  reflexive writing, 104
Regulation, 16, 20, 25, 58, 92, 121, 143, 145, 152, 181–183, 215, 217–219, 228, 229, 231, 232, 239, 259, 261, 262, 266, 267, 276, 295, 300, 319, 334, 335, 338, 340, 347, 361, 375, 392, 426, 437, 449, 457, 508, 512–514
Regulatory body, 423, 424, 426, 427, 429, 432, 434, 436, 438, 439, 441, 459, 523

Rehabilitation, 375, 400, 412–414, 417
Rehabilitation Act of 1973, 375, 380, 381, 391
Replicability of a text, 123, 137
Reports, 26, 71, 74, 75, 83, 121, 126, 129, 132, 162, 167, 182, 184, 218, 227, 243, 266, 269, 276, 292–295, 301, 302, 333–335, 339, 340, 345–348, 381, 382, 392, 402, 405, 410, 427, 428, 432, 434, 436, 437, 441, 452–457, 459, 514, 524, 536
Research, 4, 16, 21, 23, 24, 26, 36, 40–45, 48, 49, 53, 56–59, 66, 70, 81, 83, 85, 93, 99–106, 110–116, 121, 123, 124, 128, 130, 133–137, 141, 143, 147, 151, 158, 161, 162, 166, 167, 169, 171, 176–178, 180, 185, 187, 195–197, 199, 200, 213, 233, 239, 240, 242, 246–248, 250, 252, 253, 264, 266–268, 271, 276, 290, 305, 312, 322, 324, 325, 362, 378, 416, 478, 479
Research and Independent Non-Governmental Organizations (RINGOs), 193, 194, 198
Research training, 534, 535, 537
risk tools, 402, 405, 410
  algorithmic basis of, 399
  assessments, 398, 399, 402, 410
  purported objectivity of, 401, 402
Ruling, 3–5, 7, 15, 19, 21, 23, 24, 28, 29, 40, 48, 55, 57, 58, 66, 77, 81, 99, 101, 103, 107, 109, 111, 115, 121, 126, 127, 135, 144, 160, 163, 167, 170, 186, 197, 210, 215, 220, 221, 223, 225, 231, 238, 240, 243–245, 249–251, 254, 260, 270, 305, 312, 360, 366, 376, 379, 424, 426, 429, 434, 438, 441, 459, 470, 475, 485, 486, 488–497, 499, 500, 545, 548
Ruling/ruling practices, 11
Ruling relations, 4, 6, 19, 26, 28, 43, 50, 55, 57, 65, 69, 71, 81–83, 85, 93, 103, 108, 111, 112, 124, 144, 145, 153, 160, 161, 179, 200, 201, 215, 224, 232, 233, 237, 242, 244, 245, 250–254, 266, 364, 366, 371,

392, 425, 441, 484–486, 489–496, 498, 500, 501

S

Safety-sensitive, 428, 429
School education, 18, 237, 238, 240, 241, 243, 248, 249, 251, 377
Self-disclosure, 513, 524
Semi-fictional method, 138
Service work, 261, 266, 268, 276
Sisterhood, 114, 115
Six Nations of the Grand River Reserve, 284
Smith, Dorothy E., 1, 4, 7, 11, 13, 17, 23, 28, 36, 43, 101–104, 107, 112, 114, 116, 159, 161, 176, 177, 186, 240, 246, 248, 260, 285, 298, 304, 305, 312, 313, 332, 341, 379, 399
Smith, G.W., 3, 21, 22, 58, 59, 74, 101, 102, 176, 179, 187, 323
Social justice, 43, 106, 114, 115, 175, 187, 245, 492, 500, 535
Social organization, 16, 17, 24, 26, 28, 39, 42, 43, 50–52, 58, 61, 77, 92, 104, 148, 165, 167, 170, 171, 179, 200, 219, 231, 232, 260, 269, 362, 379, 470, 471, 473, 476, 477, 489, 491, 511, 520, 539
Social organization of knowledge, 15, 27, 43
Social relations, 3, 5, 7, 14, 16, 29, 36, 39, 43, 53, 75, 77, 82, 89, 91, 101, 104, 109, 125, 135, 143, 145, 146, 150, 151, 159, 160, 162, 165, 176, 197, 199, 200, 239–241, 243, 245, 246, 250, 251, 254, 260, 324, 364, 368, 371, 376, 378, 470, 487, 491, 497, 521, 528, 533, 539, 545, 547
Social theory, 14, 17, 51, 52, 60
Social work, 15, 23, 48, 60, 70, 72, 109, 245, 507, 509, 510, 512, 514, 518, 521
Society for the Study of Social Problems (SSSP), 6, 177
Sociology of knowledge, 3, 176, 529
Sonnenwald, D.H., 86
Stakeholders, 136

Standardization, 74, 76, 125, 246–248, 341, 371, 388, 450, 451
Standardized testing, 69, 242, 246, 250, 254
Standpoint, 4, 18, 23, 24, 47, 102, 103, 113–116, 124, 128, 134, 135, 143, 144, 157–161, 197, 201, 241, 251–253, 283, 285, 301, 305, 311, 312, 323, 343, 346, 378, 399, 403, 417, 425, 431, 432, 467, 509, 532, 535, 544
  embodied subject, 102
Standpoint feminism, 159
Street-level bureaucrats, 362
Struggle, 16–18, 58, 71, 114, 157, 159, 164, 171, 186, 217, 238, 253, 259, 267, 268, 274, 365, 370, 467, 468
Student, 4, 5, 14, 16, 18, 41, 43, 48–52, 54–61, 114, 116, 175–187, 237–239, 241–251, 254, 259, 262–265, 269–271, 375–393, 531, 532, 536, 539, 544, 548
  Attention Deficit Hyperactivity Disorder (ADHD), 378, 387
Subject-at-work, 370
Subject-in-discourse, 366
Summer institutes, 536, 537, 539, 540, 546
Syllabus, 181, 262, 263

T

Taken-for-granted, 70, 84, 85, 159, 179, 239, 342, 347, 364, 368, 372, 425, 508, 509, 512, 522
Talk-in-interaction, 507, 510, 511, 522, 523
Teachers' work, 18, 238, 242, 243, 246, 249, 250, 370
Teaching, 4, 18, 23, 48–52, 54, 55, 57–61, 69, 169, 175, 177, 178, 186, 238, 241–243, 246, 248, 249, 254, 261–264, 266, 268, 271, 276, 288, 304, 441
Team-building, 531, 532
Telecommunication, 448
Telecommunication Device for the Deaf (TDD), 448
Text-based work process mapping, 293

Text-mediated relations, 48
Text-reader conversation (textual mediation), 19, 25, 27, 109, 127, 215, 219, 399, 404, 407
Texts, 7, 11, 15, 19, 20, 24–27, 40, 41, 43, 48, 49, 56, 65, 66, 69, 70, 72, 74, 76, 81, 90, 105, 107–109, 113, 121, 123, 126–129, 135, 137, 143, 145–147, 149–152, 176, 179, 184, 185, 193–204, 208–210, 217–219, 223–227, 238, 240–242, 244–246, 249, 253, 254, 261, 271, 288, 289, 291, 292, 295–297, 300–302, 316, 333–336, 338, 344–347, 349, 351, 362, 364, 366, 368, 371, 376–379, 388, 390, 392, 398–400, 404, 408, 410, 411, 425–428, 431, 439, 449, 450, 453, 468, 471, 477, 485, 486, 490, 491, 493–497, 499, 510–512, 514, 522, 524, 547
Textual analysis, 425
Textual realities, 74, 76, 262, 347, 388, 426
Textual trails, 185
Transcription, 6, 194, 268, 507, 509, 511, 514, 523
Turner, S., 5, 23, 26, 48, 53, 81, 85, 123, 137, 143, 184, 214, 253, 285, 293, 302, 426

U
Undergraduate, 4, 175, 181, 185, 186
United Nations, 209
United Nations Conference on Environment and Development (UNCED), 194, 195, 201, 205, 206, 208
United Nations Declaration on the Rights of Indigenous Peoples (UNDRIP), 209
United Nations Framework Convention on Climate Change (UNFCCC), 193, 194, 196, 198, 206
United Nations Permanent Forum on Indigenous Issues (UNPFII), 195, 209
United Nations (UN), 17, 194, 195, 199–202, 209, 214, 215, 218, 224

University/Universities, 14, 23, 48, 49, 69, 70, 83, 99, 113, 138, 143, 144, 147, 148, 151–153, 157, 162, 167, 168, 170, 175–179, 181, 186, 213, 238, 244, 245, 248, 253–255, 259–262, 264–268, 270, 271, 273, 275, 276, 304, 333, 375–377, 381, 383, 390, 510, 511, 514, 522, 536, 537, 546
  McMaster University, 99
  Padua, 138
  Ryerson University, 175
  Universiteit Antwerpen, 138
  University of California Berkeley, 50
  York, 48
University administration, 185, 260, 262–267, 269, 270, 276, 277
U.S.A., 125, 141, 175, 184, 309, 310, 381, 424
U.S. Digital Millennium Copyright Act in 1998, 141

V
Vaughan, S., 16, 23, 43, 48, 125, 126, 135, 137, 144, 177, 186, 366
Verbal generalizing, 68
Verbs, use of, 186
Video conferencing, 448
Videorecording, 126, 129, 132, 133, 137
Video relay service, 448–454, 457, 459, 460
Virtual environment, 178
Visual dissemination, methods, 121, 136
Visual methods, 82, 84, 85, 91–93, 121–124, 128, 134–138
Visuals, 4, 43, 85, 86, 89–91, 121–128, 132–137, 180, 198, 250, 539
  visuals as data, 128, 135, 137
  visuals as texts, 121, 123–128, 135, 137
  visuals as tools, 122
Vital institutional ethnography, 6, 484–486, 489, 490, 493, 495, 498–500
Vocal gestures, 66
Vocational Education and Training (VET), 244

W

Walby, K., 44, 103, 126, 127, 398
Warren, Leanne, 26, 43
Women, 12–14, 17–20, 22, 28, 55, 71, 72, 84, 100–106, 109–117, 125, 143, 144, 159, 160, 163, 178, 186, 261, 272–274, 276, 277, 285, 303, 306, 332, 337, 399, 402, 403, 413, 415, 417, 527, 543
  battered women, 333
  violence against, 71
  Women in Peru, 14
  Women of color, 19
  Women's activism, 13
  Women's consciousness, 17
  Women's experiences, 18
  Women's household work, 24
  Women's movement, 13
  Women's positioning, 20
Women's studies, 18
Women (sociology for women), 3, 17, 19, 48, 176
Words as practices, 65–67, 70, 73
Work, 1–7, 11–29, 37, 38, 41, 42, 44, 45, 48, 49, 51–60, 65, 66, 69–74, 76, 77, 81–86, 88–94, 99, 101, 102, 104–116, 123–129, 133, 136–138, 141–153, 157–171, 176–182, 185, 186, 194–197, 199–203, 205–210, 215–218, 226, 228, 238–255, 259–277, 283–305, 311, 312, 316, 323–325, 329, 330, 333–338, 341–355, 360–364, 366–371, 375–379, 382, 383, 386, 388–393, 397–401, 403–411, 413–416, 423, 425, 427–432, 434–437, 439–442, 447–454, 456–460, 465–468, 470–479, 483–484, 487, 491–493, 499, 507–514, 519–523, 527–533, 535, 536, 539, 540, 542, 543, 546, 547
Working standpoint, 286
Work knowledge, 84, 90–93, 158, 161, 171, 194, 210, 262, 366, 370, 378, 386

Y

You are here, 179, 313, 314
Young people, 243, 244, 248, 250, 251, 398, 528, 529, 531, 533–539, 541, 547
Youth, 23, 85, 134–136, 185, 339, 398, 508, 510, 511, 513–515, 522–524, 528, 529, 533, 534, 536, 538, 539, 543
Youth in care/state care, 507, 508, 510–515, 518–523
Youth Participatory Action Research (YPAR), 6, 528, 529, 531–533, 540, 547. *See also* Participatory research

Printed in the United States
by Baker & Taylor Publisher Services